Microsoft®

OLE DB 2.0 Programmer's Reference and Data Access SDK

Microsoft® Press

PUBLISHED BY
Microsoft Press
A Division of Microsoft Corporation
One Microsoft Way
Redmond, Washington 98052-6399

Library of Congress Cataloging-in-Publication Data
Microsoft OLE DB 2.0 Programmer's Reference and Data Access SDK /
Microsoft Corporation.
p. cm.
Includes index.
ISBN 0-7356-0590-4
1. Computer software--Development. 2. Database management.
3. OLE (Computer file) I. Microsoft Corporation.
QA76.76.D47M524 1998
005.7--dc21 98-39268
CIP

Printed and bound in the United States of America.

1 2 3 4 5 6 7 8 9 WCWC 3 2 1 0 9 8

Distributed in Canada by ITP Nelson, a division of Thomson Canada Limited.

A CIP catalogue record for this book is available from the British Library.

Microsoft Press books are available through booksellers and distributors worldwide. For further information about international editions, contact your local Microsoft Corporation office or contact Microsoft Press International directly at fax (425) 936-7329. Visit our Web site at mspress.microsoft.com.

Acquisitions Editor: Eric Stroo
Project Editor: Alice Turner

Contents

About the OLE DB Documentation

This documentation assumes the following:

- A working knowledge of the C or C++ programming language
- Knowledge of COM

In addition, a general knowledge of databases and SQL is helpful.

The code examples in this documentation are designed for illustration purposes only. Because they are written primarily to demonstrate OLE DB principles, efficiency has sometimes been set aside in the interest of clarity. In addition, whole sections of code have sometimes been omitted for clarity. These include the definitions of non–OLE DB functions and most error handling.

The following typographic conventions are used.

Format	Used for
DBPROPFLAGS	Uppercase letters indicate certain values, SQL statements, and macro names.
`#include <oledb.h>`	Monospace font is used for sample command lines and program code.
argument	Italicized words indicate programmatic arguments, information that the user or the application must provide, or word emphasis.
IRowset	Bold type indicates that syntax must be typed exactly as shown, including method names.

PART 1

Introduction to OLE DB

CHAPTER 1

Overview of OLE DB

Today, a vast amount of critical information necessary to conduct day-to-day business is found outside of traditional, corporate production databases. Instead, this information is found in file systems, in indexed-sequential files such as Btrieve, and in personal databases such as Microsoft® Access and Microsoft® Visual FoxPro®; in productivity tools such as spreadsheets, project management planners, and electronic mail; and on the World Wide Web. To take advantage of the benefits of database technology, such as declarative queries, transactions, and security, businesses have traditionally had to move the data from its original containing system into a database management system (DBMS).

This process is expensive and redundant. Furthermore, businesses need to be able to exploit the advantages of database technology not only when accessing data within a DBMS but also when accessing data from any other information container. To address this need, Microsoft created OLE DB.

OLE DB is a set of Component Object Model (COM) interfaces that provide applications with uniform access to data stored in diverse information sources and that also provide the ability to implement additional database services. These interfaces support the amount of DBMS functionality appropriate to the data store, enabling it to share its data.

Access to Diverse Sources

OLE DB enables the development of applications that access diverse data stores. For example, consider a sales representative who wants to find all e-mail messages received within the last two days from Seattle customers, including these customers' addresses, to which no one has yet replied. This query involves searching the mailbox file containing the sales representative's e-mail, as well as a Customers table stored in a Microsoft Access DBMS to identify customers. The query can be formulated in an extended SQL syntax as follows. (This query is designed for illustration only. It is not implemented in any product known to Microsoft.)

```
SELECT  m1.*, c.Address FROM
   MakeTable(Mail, d:\mail\smith.mmf) m1,
   MakeTable(Access, d:\access\Enterprise.mdb, Customers) c
   WHERE m1.Date >= date(today(), -2)
      AND m1.From = c.Emailaddr
      AND c.City = "Seattle"
      AND NOT EXISTS
         (SELECT * FROM MakeTable(Mail, d:\mail\smith.mmf) m2
         WHERE m1.MsgId = m2.InReplyTo);
```

Assume that **MakeTable** is a function that makes the mail file D:\Mail\Smith.mmf into a table. It also exposes the Customers table from a Microsoft Access database (D:\Access\Enterprise.mdb). The function **date** takes a date and a number of days as arguments and produces a date.

OLE DB makes it easy for applications to access data stored in diverse DBMS and non-DBMS information sources. DBMS sources may include mainframe databases such as IMS and DB2, server databases such as Oracle and Microsoft® SQL Server™, and desktop databases such as Microsoft Access and Microsoft Visual FoxPro. Non-DBMS sources might include information stored in file systems such as Microsoft Windows NT® and UNIX, indexed-sequential access method (ISAM) files, e-mail, spreadsheets, project management tools, and the World Wide Web.

Component Database Management Systems

OLE DB uses the Component Object Model (COM) infrastructure, which reduces unnecessary duplication of services and provides a higher degree of interoperability, not only among diverse information sources but also among existing programming environments and tools. Indeed, OLE DB is the way to access data in a COM environment. OLE DB defines an open, extensible collection of COM interfaces that encapsulate reusable portions of DBMS functionality. These interfaces define the boundaries of DBMS components, such as row containers, query processors, and transaction coordinators, that provide uniform transactional access to diverse information sources. Such components factor a DBMS into a set of cooperating components that consume and produce data through a uniform set of interfaces.

The OLE DB functional areas include data access and updates (rowsets), query processing, catalog information, notifications, transactions, security, and remote data access. By defining a uniform set of interfaces to access data, OLE DB components not only contribute to uniform data access among diverse information sources but also help to reduce the application's complexity by enabling developers to use only the DBMS functionality they need. The following illustration shows how an application can employ OLE DB interfaces to initiate actions by a query processor to access different data structures.

A component DBMS architecture using OLE DB interfaces

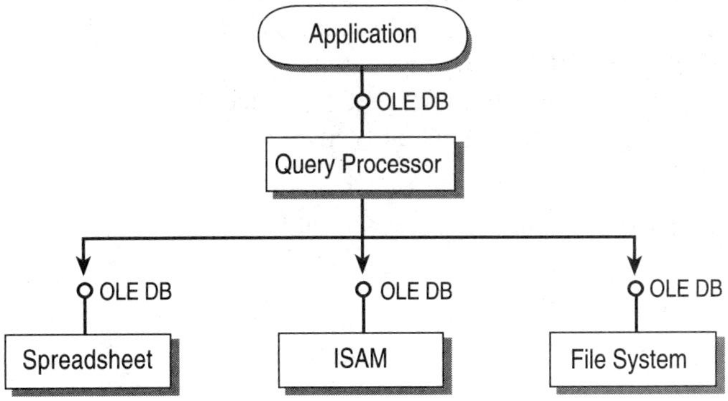

Consumers and Providers

Described in COM terms, an OLE DB *consumer* is any piece of system or application code that consumes an OLE DB interface. This includes OLE DB components themselves. An OLE DB *provider* is any software component that exposes an OLE DB interface.

OLE DB interfaces may be directly exposed by a data store or exposed by a separate piece of code that communicates at a lower level with an interface on the data store. In both cases, the code that exposes the OLE DB interfaces is referred to as the *data provider*. In some cases, a data provider won't own data at all but will use another OLE DB data provider as its store, exposing custom behavior on top of that data provider. Such providers are often called *custom providers*. Examples of data providers include relational DBMSs, storage managers, spreadsheets, ISAMs, and e-mail.

A *service component* is an OLE DB component that implements a common set of OLE DB functionality, for example, **IRowsetFind**, on top of any provider. Service components, where available, are automatically invoked by the Service Component Manager, included as a core component of the OLE DB SDK, when a consumer requests some OLE DB functionality that is not supported by the data provider.

Component DBMSs offer the potential for greater efficiency than traditional DBMSs because consumers generally require only a portion of the database management functionality offered, thereby reducing resource overhead. OLE DB allows simple tabular data providers to implement functionality native to their data store. At a minimum, they can use only the interfaces that expose data as tables. This opens the opportunity for the development of query processor components, such as SQL or geographical query processors, which can consume tabular information from any provider that exposes its data through OLE DB. In addition, SQL DBMSs can expose their functionality in a more layered manner by using the OLE DB interfaces.

The following section describes the architecture and main interface areas of OLE DB.

OLE DB Objects

OLE DB defines the following COM objects:

- Enumerator objects
- Data source objects
- Session objects
- Transaction objects
- Command objects
- Rowset objects
- View objects
- Error objects

For example, a consumer might use the objects shown in the following illustration.

Typical use of OLE DB objects by a consumer

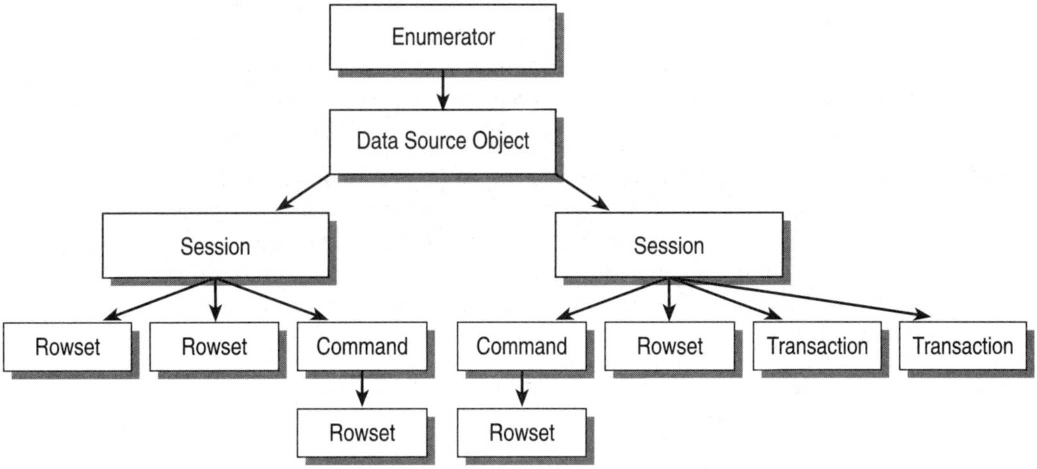

For each of these COM objects, OLE DB defines a cotype. A *cotype* is a way to define a group of COM objects, such as rowsets or commands, that have similar characteristics. All COM objects that belong to a particular cotype must expose the mandatory interfaces in that cotype. In addition, they can expose the optional interfaces in the cotype and any interfaces not in the cotype.

Enumerator Objects

Enumerators are COM objects that search for available data source objects and other enumerators. Consumers that are not customized for a particular provider can use enumerators to search for an appropriate data source object to use.

An enumerator object exposes the **ISourcesRowset** interface, which returns a rowset describing all data source objects and enumerators that are known to the enumerator. A root enumerator, shipped in the Microsoft Data Access Software Development Kit (SDK), traverses the registry looking for data source objects and other enumerators. For more information about the root enumerator object, see "Root Enumerator Object" in the OLE DB Core Components documentation. Other enumerators traverse the registry or search in a provider-specific manner. For example, an enumerator over the file system might search for subdirectories.

Data Source Objects, Session Objects, and Transaction Objects

In OLE DB, a data source object (DSO) is a COM object through which a consumer connects to a provider's underlying data store, such as a file or a DBMS. Each OLE DB provider defines its own data source object class. To connect to the provider, a consumer must create and initialize an instance of this class. For more information about creating instances of data source objects, see Chapter 2, "Data Source and Session Objects." Data source objects are factories for session objects.

Session objects provide a context for transactions and can be implicitly or explicitly transacted. A single data source object may be able to create multiple sessions. (This is provider-specific.) Session objects are a factory for command and rowset objects, which provide methods for creating command objects and rowsets and for creating and modifying tables and indexes. Session objects can also act as factories for transaction objects, which are used to control nested transactions.

Transaction objects are used when committing or aborting nested transactions at any level other than the lowest level.

Command Objects

A command object is a container for a text command. In OLE DB, a *text command* is a string to be passed from a consumer to a provider's data source object for execution by the provider's underlying data store. Most commonly, the text command is an SQL **SELECT** statement. If the text command is an SQL **SELECT** statement, the command object becomes a factory for a rowset. (A single session object may be able to create multiple commands.) A command object holds a text command and any command properties to be requested from the provider. *Command properties* are properties that either control execution of the command or, if executing the command causes a rowset to be created, affect the behavior of the resulting rowset.

Command objects expose various interfaces representing different areas of functionality of a query processor, including query formulation, preparation, and execution. For example, if a command object exposes the **ICommandWithParameters** interface, the command object can support dynamic parameters in addition to a text command and command properties.

Accessors

Accessors are groups of binding structures that enable consumers to define simultaneous access to multiple columns or parameters and enable providers to optimize access to these multiple columns or parameters.

Binding structures describe relationships between elements in a consumer structure and columns in a rowset or parameters in a text command. Consumers use binding structures to communicate to providers how they expect data to be transferred from the provider to the consumer's buffer, and vice versa. Binding structures include information such as the column or parameter being accessed, the data type in the consumer's buffer, the offset to the data in the consumer's data structure, the amount of space available for the data value, and the precision and scale for numeric values. For columns containing COM objects, the consumer can also request the interface that must be returned to the consumer when the object is fetched.

Rowset Objects

A rowset is the central object that enables all OLE DB data providers to expose data in tabular form. Conceptually, a rowset is a set of rows in which each row has columns of data. Data providers present their data in the form of rowsets. Service components (such as query processors) also present data (such as the result of queries) in the form of rowsets. This makes it possible to efficiently aggregate components that consume or produce data through the same object.

The most basic rowset object exposes the interfaces described in the following table.

Interface	Purpose
IAccessor	Permits the definition of groups of column bindings describing the way tabular data is bound to consumer program variables.
IColumnsInfo	Provides information about the columns of the rowset.
IConvertType	Provides information about the availability of type conversions on the rowset.
IRowset	Contains methods for fetching rows in the rowset sequentially.
IRowsetInfo	Provides information about the rowset itself.

By using **IRowset**, a consumer can traverse the rows in the rowset, including traversing backward if the rowset supports it. The following illustration shows the data structures a generic rowset object might support.

Data structures supported by a generic rowset object

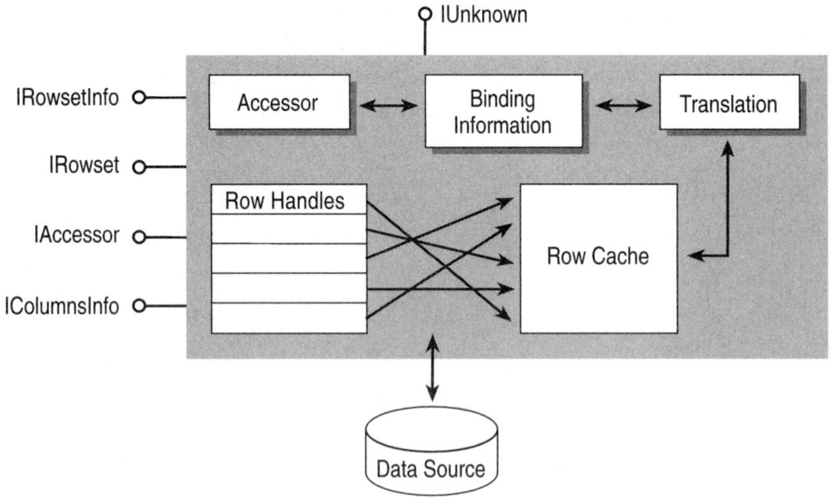

Other rowset interfaces expose additional rowset capabilities. For example, there is an interface to insert, delete, and update rows and interfaces that expose richer row navigation models, such as direct access and approximate positioning.

Rowsets can be created over base data in one of two ways. First, they can be created as the result of a query. Second, they can be created directly as the result of calling **IOpenRowset::OpenRowset**. All providers support creation by calling **IOpenRowset::OpenRowset**. However, simple providers—such as those built over a base table, index, file, or in-memory structure rather than a relational DBMS—usually do not support creation by query.

Schema Rowsets

Schemas are DBMS objects that contain structural information, or *metadata*, about a database. Some OLE DB providers for DBMSs support schema rowset objects. *Schema rowsets* are rowsets that contain schema information. For more information about schema rowsets, see Appendix B, "Schema Rowsets."

Index Rowsets

An *index* is a DBMS object that provides access to data in the rows of a table, based on key values. Providers over ISAM data typically support index rowset objects. Index rowsets are rowsets containing index information. For more information about index rowsets, see Chapter 8, "Index Rowsets."

View Objects

In OLE DB, a *view object* defines a subset of the rows and columns from a rowset. A view object contains no data of its own. OLE DB view objects cannot be used to combine data from multiple rowsets.

Error Objects

In addition to the return codes and status information returned by each method in OLE DB, providers can expose OLE DB error objects containing extended error information, such as a description of the error or the appropriate SQLSTATE. Error objects can be created by any interface on any OLE DB object. Providers can also choose to define custom error objects.

Transaction Management

OLE DB defines a basic set of interfaces for transaction management. A transaction enables consumers to define units of work within a provider. These units of work have the atomicity, concurrency, isolation, and durability (ACID) properties. Transactions allow the specification of various isolation levels to enable more flexible access to data among concurrent consumers.

Local Transactions

Local transactions refer to transactions running in the context of a resource manager. A provider that supports transactions exposes **ITransactionLocal** on the session. A call to **ITransactionLocal::StartTransaction** begins a transaction on the session. A session can be inside or outside of a transaction at any time. When created, a session is outside of a transaction and all the work done under the scope of the session is immediately committed on each OLE DB method call. When a session enters a local or coordinated transaction, all the work done under the session—between the **ITransactionLocal::StartTransaction** and **ITransaction::Commit** or **ITransaction::Abort** method calls and including other objects created underneath it (commands or rowsets)—is part of the transaction.

StartTransaction supports various isolation levels that consumers can request when creating a transaction. OLE DB providers do not need to support all possible transaction options defined. A consumer can interrogate the transaction capabilities of a provider through **IDBProperties**.

For providers that support nested transactions, calling **StartTransaction** within an existing transaction begins a new nested transaction below the current transaction. Calling **ITransaction::Commit** or **ITransaction::Abort** on the session commits or aborts, respectively, the transaction at the lowest level.

Distributed Transactions

OLE DB defines an interface, **ITransactionJoin**, for consumers to request that providers enlist in a coordinated transaction among multiple (possibly distributed) data providers and other types of resource managers. The details of how providers enlist themselves as resource managers with the transaction coordinator are described in the Microsoft Transaction Server documentation.

Event Notifications

OLE DB uses an ActiveX® controls notification model to implement notifications among OLE DB providers and consumers. Notifications are used by groups of cooperating consumers sharing a rowset. All consumers and rowset-generating actions are assumed to be working within the same transaction. Local notifications enable cooperating consumers sharing a rowset to be informed about actions on the rowset performed by their peers.

For example, consider a form containing two data controls, one displaying data in a grid and the other displaying data as a two-dimensional histogram. Both controls receive their data from the same rowset and operate individually as consumers of the rowset. An end user can send an update to the rowset through the grid control. Notifications enable the other control to be informed of this change as it occurs, giving it the opportunity to update the histogram as appropriate and ultimately providing a consistent view of the data within the form.

For more information about notifications, see Chapter 9, "OLE DB Object Notifications."

CHAPTER 2

Data Source and Session Objects

Two types of COM objects are necessary for consumers to connect to providers: data source objects and session objects.

To connect to an OLE DB provider, a consumer must first create and initialize an instance of the provider's data source object. This data source object can then be used to create a session object, which in turn acts as a factory for transactions, commands, and rowsets. The primary function of a session is to define a transaction. A transaction is a mechanism used to define persistent units of work within a provider and to define how the different units relate to each other in a system with parallel activities.

For more information on	Go to
Data providers and service components	"Consumers and Providers" in Chapter 1, "Overview of OLE DB"
Transactions	Chapter 12, "Transactions"
Consumers and providers	"Consumers and Providers" in Chapter 1, "Overview of OLE DB"
OLE DB connection model	"Data Source Objects, Session Objects, and Transaction Objects" in Chapter 1, "Overview of OLE DB"
Data source object	"Data Source Objects" in this chapter
Session	"Session Objects" in this chapter
Rowsets	Chapter 4, "Rowsets"

Data Source Objects

In OLE DB, a data source object is a COM object through which a consumer connects to a provider's underlying data store.

It is important to distinguish a provider's data source object, which provides data from the data store to a consumer, from the data store itself, which contains the data but interacts with the consumer only through the data source object. For example, a data store might be a comma-separated-value (CSV) text file, an SQL DBMS, or an in-memory array in an application.

The data source object cotype is defined as follows. For more information about cotypes, see "OLE DB Objects" in Chapter 1, "Overview of OLE DB."

```
CoType TDataSource {
   [mandatory] interface IDBCreateSession;
   [mandatory] interface IDBInitialize;
   [mandatory] interface IDBProperties;
   [mandatory] interface IPersist;
   [optional]  interface IConnectionPointContainer;
   [optional]  interface IDBAsynchStatus;
   [optional]  interface IDBDataSourceAdmin;
   [optional]  interface IDBInfo;
   [optional]  interface IPersistFile;
   [optional]  interface ISupportErrorInfo;
}
```

For information about the registry entries used by providers to register classes of data source objects, see "Provider Registry Entries" in Chapter 14, "Programming Considerations."

Creating Data Source Objects

The OLE DB connection model defines how OLE DB consumers locate and activate OLE DB data providers. Two objects are the basis for the OLE DB connection model: the data source object and the session object. To access an OLE DB provider, a consumer must first create an instance of the provider's data source object. Each provider is identified by a unique class identifier (CLSID) in the registry.

Prior to OLE DB 2.0, consumers created a provider's data source object through the root enumerator or by passing the provider's CLSID to **CoCreateInstance**, such as in the following code:

```
// Create an instance of CLSID_MSDASQL
CoCreateInstance(CLSID_MSDASQL, NULL, CLSCTX_INPROC_SERVER,
IID_IDBInitialize,(void**)pIDBInitialize);
```

This model requires applications to hard-code provider CLSIDs or to obtain the CLSID at run time through application-specific mechanisms. OLE DB 2.0 provides common services that consumers can leverage by calling **IDataInitialize** or **IDBPromptInitialize** methods. The **IDataInitialize** interface is exposed by the Service Component Manager, which can be instantiated by using CLSID_MSDAINITIALIZE. The **IDBPromptInitialize** interface is exposed by the Data Links component, which can be instantiated by using CLSID_DataLinks. For more information about these interfaces, see "**IDataInitialize**" and "**IDBPromptInitialize**" in the OLE DB Core Components documentation, which is included in the Microsoft Data Access SDK.

For example, to create an instance of a provider that can take advantage of OLE DB 2.0 services, based on the provider's CLSID, the preceding code would look like the following:

```
// Create an instance of the OLE DB Initialization Component
CoCreateInstance(CLSID_MSDAINITIALIZE, NULL, CLSCTX_INPROC_SERVER,
IID_IDataInitialize,(void**)pIDataInitialize);

// Create an instance of CLSID_MSDASQL with supported Services
pIDataInitialize->CreateDBInstance(CLSID_MSDASQL, NULL, CLSCTX_INPROC_SERVER, NULL,
IID_IDBInitialize,(IUnknown**)pIDBInitialize);
```

Alternatively, the consumer could use the Data Links component of OLE DB to prompt the user to indicate the provider to use, as well as other properties to be used to initialize the data source object:

```
// Create an intstance of the Data Links component
CoCreateInstance(CLSID_DataLinks, NULL, CLSCTX_INPROC_SERVER,
IID_IDBPromptInitialize, (void **)&pIDBPromptInitialize);

// Initialize output pointer
*pIDataInitialize = NULL;

// Prompt the user for the provider and initialization properties
pIDBPromptInitialize->PromptDataSource(NULL, hWndParent,
DBPROMPTOPTIONS_WIZARDSHEET, 0, NULL, NULL, IID_IDataInitialize,
(IUnknown **)&pIDataInitialize);

//Initialize the data source object
pIDataInitialize->Initialize();
```

The data source object exposes **IDBProperties**, which the consumer uses to provide basic authentication information such as user ID and password (for cases when the data source object does not exist in an authenticated environment) as well as the name of the data store (file or database) containing the data to be accessed. It also exposes **IDBInitialize**, which the consumer uses to connect to the provider by initializing the data source object.

After a data source object has been successfully initialized, the consumer can call **IDBProperties::GetPropertyInfo** on the data source object to get information about the capabilities of the provider. These capabilities include the interfaces, rowset properties such as approximate positioning, transaction properties such as supported isolation levels, and the SQL dialects (if any) a provider supports. The consumer can then call **IDBCreateSession::CreateSession** to create a session object.

The session acts as a rowset, command, and transaction object factory. Not all OLE DB providers support command objects. However, all data providers, whether or not they support commands, must expose the **IOpenRowset** interface, which enables providers to expose their data directly as rowsets without the use of commands.

Data Source Object States

When a data source object is created, it is in an uninitialized state. For example, if the underlying data store is a file, the data source object has not yet opened the file; if the data store is an SQL database, the data source object has not yet connected to the database.

In the uninitialized state, the consumer can do only the following with the data source object:

- Call **QueryInterface** for **IUnknown**, **IConnectionPointContainer**, **IDBAsynchStatus**, **IDBDataSourceAdmin**, **IDBInitialize**, **IDBProperties**, **IPersist**, **IPersistFile**, or **ISupportErrorInfo**.
- Call **AddRef** or **Release** on any interface obtained from **QueryInterface**.
- Call methods on **IConnectionPointContainer**, **IDBDataSourceAdmin**, **IDBInitialize**, **IDBAsynchStatus**, **IPersist**, **IPersistFile**, or **ISupportErrorInfo**.
- Call methods on **IDBProperties** for properties in the Initialization property group.

If the consumer calls any other OLE DB method, the provider returns E_UNEXPECTED. The provider may also return E_NOINTERFACE if the consumer calls **QueryInterface** for an interface other than those listed.

To initialize the data source object, usually the consumer first calls **IDBProperties::SetProperties** to set the value of properties in the Initialization property group. For example, if the data store is a text file, the consumer might specify the name and location of the file. If the data store is a database in a DBMS, the consumer might specify the name of the server on which the database resides, along with the user ID and password to use.

Certain properties in the Initialization property group are required by the data source object for initialization. To determine which properties these are, the consumer calls **IDBProperties::GetPropertyInfo** for properties in the Initialization property group. For required properties, the DBPROPFLAGS_REQUIRED bit is set in the *dwFlags* element of the returned DBPROPINFO structure.

After the consumer has finished setting properties, it calls **IDBInitialize::Initialize**. **Initialize** can prompt for additional information, especially if the consumer has not set values for all required properties. The consumer can set properties to control how much **Initialize** prompts, including suppressing prompting altogether. After **Initialize** returns successfully, the data source object is in an initialized state. The consumer can also create and initialize a new data source object by calling **IDBDataSourceAdmin::CreateDataSource**.

Data Source Object Example

The code in this example shows how to create and initialize a data source object.

```
/////////////////////////////////////////////////////////////////
// myCreateDataSource
//
// This function creates an OLE DB data source object for a
// provider selected by the user, sets initialization properties
// for the data source, and initializes the data source. The
// function returns a pointer to the data source object's
// IUnknown in *ppUnkDataSource.
//
/////////////////////////////////////////////////////////////////
HRESULT myCreateDataSource
   (
   IUnknown **          ppUnkDataSource
   )
{
   HRESULT              hr;
   IDataInitialize *    pIDataInitialize        = NULL;
   IDBPromptInitialize *pIDBPromptInitialize    = NULL;
   IDBInitialize *      pIDBInitialize          = NULL;
   CLSID                clsid                   = CLSID_MSDASQL;

   // Use the Microsoft Data Links UI to create the data source
   // object; this will allow the user to select the provider
   // to connect to and to set the initialization properties
   // for the data source object, which will be created by the
   // Data Links UI.
   if( g_dwFlags & USE_PROMPTDATASOURCE )
   {
      // Create the Data Links UI object and obtain the
      // IDBPromptInitialize interface from it
      XCHECK_HR(hr = CoCreateInstance(
               CLSID_DataLinks,                //clsid -- Data Links UI
               NULL,                           //pUnkOuter
               CLSCTX_INPROC_SERVER,           //dwClsContext
               IID_IDBPromptInitialize,        //riid
               (void**)&pIDBPromptInitialize   //ppvObj
               ));
```

```
    // Invoke the Data Links UI to allow the user to select
    // the provider and set initialization properties for
    // the data source object that this will create
    XCHECK_HR(hr = pIDBPromptInitialize->PromptDataSource(
            NULL,                               //pUnkOuter
            GetDesktopWindow(),                 //hWndParent
            DBPROMPTOPTIONS_PROPERTYSHEET,      //dwPromptOptions
            0,                                  //cSourceTypeFilter
            NULL,                               //rgSourceTypeFilter
            NULL,                               //pwszszzProviderFilter
            IID_IDBInitialize,                  //riid
            (IUnknown**)&pIDBInitialize         //ppDataSource
            ));

    // We've obtained a data source object from the Data Links UI. This
    // object has had its initialization properties set, so all we
    // need to do is Initialize it.
    XCHECK_HR(hr = pIDBInitialize->Initialize());
}
// We are not using the Data Links UI to create the data source object.
// Instead, we will enumerate the providers installed on this system
// through the OLE DB Enumerator and will allow the user to select
// the ProgID of the provider for which we will create a sata source
// object.
else
{
    // Use the OLE DB Enumerator to obtain a rowset of installed providers,
    // and then allow the user to select a provider from this rowset
    CHECK_HR(hr = myCreateEnumerator(CLSID_OLEDB_ENUMERATOR, &clsid));

    // We will create the data source object through the OLE DB service
    // component IDataInitialize interface, so we need to create an
    // instance of the data initialization object
    XCHECK_HR(hr = CoCreateInstance(
            CLSID_MSDAINITIALIZE,           //clsid -- data initialize
            NULL,                           //pUnkOuter
            CLSCTX_INPROC_SERVER,           //dwClsContext
            IID_IDataInitialize,            //riid
            (void**)&pIDataInitialize       //ppvObj
            ));
```

```
      // Use IDataInitialize::CreateDBInstance to create an uninitialized
      // data source object for the chosen provider. By using this service
      // component method, the service component manager can provide
      // additional functionality beyond what is natively supported by the
      // provider if the consumer requests that functionality.
      XCHECK_HR(hr = pIDataInitialize->CreateDBInstance(
               clsid,                        //clsid -- provider
               NULL,                         //pUnkOuter
               CLSCTX_INPROC_SERVER,         //dwClsContext
               NULL,                         //pwszReserved
               IID_IDBInitialize,            //riid
               (IUnknown**)&pIDBInitialize   //ppDataSource
               ));

      // Initialize the data source object by setting any required
      // initialization properties and calling IDBInitialize::Initialize
      CHECK_HR(hr = myDoInitialization(pIDBInitialize));
   }

CLEANUP:
   *ppUnkDataSource = pIDBInitialize;
   if( pIDataInitialize )
      pIDataInitialize->Release();
   if( pIDBPromptInitialize )
      pIDBPromptInitialize->Release();
   return hr;
}


/////////////////////////////////////////////////////////////////
// myDoInitialization
//
// This function sets initialization properties that tell the
// provider to prompt the user for any information required to
// initialize the provider and then calls the provider's
// initialization function
//
/////////////////////////////////////////////////////////////////
HRESULT myDoInitialization
   (
   IUnknown *          pIUnknown
   )
```

```
{
   HRESULT              hr;
   IDBInitialize *      pIDBInitialize              = NULL;
   IDBProperties *      pIDBProperties              = NULL;
   HWND                 hWnd                        = GetDesktopWindow();

   const ULONG          cProperties                 = 2;
   DBPROP               rgProperties[cProperties];
   DBPROPSET            rgPropSets[1];

   // In order to initialize the data source object, most providers require
   // some initialization properties to be set by the consumer. For example,
   // these might include the data source to connect to and the user ID and
   // password to use to establish identity. We will ask the provider to
   // prompt the user for this required information by setting the following
   // properties:
   myAddProperty(&rgProperties[0],DBPROP_INIT_PROMPT,VT_I2,DBPROMPT_COMPLETE);
   myAddProperty(&rgProperties[1],DBPROP_INIT_HWND,  VT_I4,(LONG)hWnd);

   rgPropSets[0].rgProperties     = rgProperties;
   rgPropSets[0].cProperties      = cProperties;
   rgPropSets[0].guidPropertySet  = DBPROPSET_DBINIT;

   // Obtain the needed interfaces
   XCHECK_HR(hr = pIUnknown->QueryInterface(IID_IDBProperties,
            (void**)&pIDBProperties));
   XCHECK_HR(hr = pIUnknown->QueryInterface(IID_IDBInitialize,
            (void**)&pIDBInitialize));

   // If a provider requires initialization properties, it must support the
   // properties that we are setting (_PROMPT and _HWND). However, some
   // providers do not need initialization properties and may therefore
   // not support the _PROMPT and _HWND properties. Because of this, we will
   // not check the return value from SetProperties.
   hr = pIDBProperties->SetProperties(1, rgPropSets);

   // Now that we've set our properties, initialize the provider
   XCHECK_HR(hr = pIDBInitialize->Initialize());

CLEANUP:
   if( pIDBProperties )
      pIDBProperties->Release();
   if( pIDBInitialize )
      pIDBInitialize->Release();
   return hr;
}
```

Enumerators

An enumerator is an object that lists available data source objects and other enumerators.

The enumerator object cotype is defined as follows. For more information about cotypes, see "OLE DB Objects" in Chapter 1, "Overview of OLE DB."

```
CoType TEnumerator {
   [mandatory] IParseDisplayName;
   [mandatory] ISourcesRowset;
   [optional]  IDBInitialize;
   [optional]  IDBProperties;
   [optional]  ISupportErrorInfo;
}
```

Enumerating Data Source Objects and Enumerators

Generic consumers that do not want to use the OLE DB Data Links component to select a data source and set initialization properties can use enumerators to search for data source objects and other enumerators. By using enumerators, rather than searching the registry directly, consumers will continue to work if the registry information changes or if new root enumerators with additional functionality, such as the ability to enumerate data source objects on other machines, become available later. To create an instance of an enumerator, the consumer calls **CoCreateInstance** with the class ID of the enumerator.

To list the data source objects and enumerators visible to the current enumerator, the consumer calls **ISourcesRowset::GetSourcesRowset**. This method returns a rowset containing information about the currently visible data source objects and enumerators. To create an instance of a data source object or enumerator listed in this rowset, the consumer first calls **IParseDisplayName::ParseDisplayName** for the returned display name. This method returns a moniker that the consumer can then use to instantiate the data source object or enumerator.

Each row in the rowset returned by **ISourcesRowset** contains a SOURCES_ISPARENT column. If the row describes an enumerator, this column contains the value VARIANT_TRUE if the enumerator is the same one that can enumerate the current one. For example, if the enumerator lists files and directories in the file system, this is the parent directory. The SOURCES_ISPARENT column thus allows the consumer to traverse backward through a hierarchy of enumerators, such as might be found over a file system. If the row describes a data source object, the SOURCES_ISPARENT column should be ignored by the consumer.

A root enumerator is shipped in the Microsoft® Data Access Software Development Kit (SDK). This enumerator traverses the registry searching for providers and enumerators. For more information about it, see "Root Enumerator Object" in the OLE DB Core Components documentation.

Providers can choose to support their own enumerators, in addition to the root enumerator, although they are not required to do so. Provider-specific enumerators search for data source objects and enumerators known to the provider. For example, suppose a provider exposes data in an SQL DBMS that supports multiple, separate databases in a single installation where the DBMS treats each database as a separate data store. The enumerator for this provider might search the DBMS for databases, which the provider could then expose as separate data source objects, one for each database. The rowset returned by the enumerator would include one row for each database it finds, marking that database as a data source object.

Or suppose a provider exposes data that is stored in text files and treats each directory as a separate data store and each text file in that directory as a table. The enumerator for this provider might traverse the file system for text files, which the provider could then expose as separate data source objects, one for each text file. For each directory it finds, the rowset returned by the enumerator would include one row as an enumerator and one or more rows as data source objects. To access the files in a directory, the consumer would create an instance of a data source object over the directory, using the display name from the row marked as a data source object. To search for subdirectories, the consumer would create an instance of an enumerator over the directory, using the display name from the row marked as an enumerator.

For information about the registry entries used by enumerators, see "Enumerator Registry Entries" in Chapter 14, "Programming Considerations."

Enumerator States

If an enumerator does not require initialization, it is created in an initialized state and remains in that state. For example, an enumerator that searches the registry does not require initialization.

If an enumerator requires initialization, it is created in an uninitialized state. For example, if it enumerates directories, the enumerator does not yet know the starting directory. If it enumerates databases in an SQL DBMS, the enumerator has not yet connected to the DBMS.

To determine whether an enumerator requires initialization, the consumer calls **QueryInterface** for **IDBInitialize**. If this interface is exposed, the enumerator requires initialization and must also expose **IDBProperties**. If it is not exposed, the enumerator does not require initialization. The remainder of this section discusses enumerators that require initialization.

In the uninitialized state, the consumer can do only the following with the enumerator:

- Call **IUnknown::QueryInterface** for **IUnknown**, **IDBInitialize**, **IDBProperties**, or **ISupportErrorInfo**.
- Call **AddRef** or **Release** on any interface obtained from **QueryInterface**.
- Call methods on **IDBProperties** for properties in the Initialization property group.
- Call methods on **IDBInitialize** or **ISupportErrorInfo**.

If the consumer calls any other OLE DB method, the provider returns E_UNEXPECTED. The provider may also return E_NOINTERFACE if the consumer calls **QueryInterface** for an interface other than those listed.

To initialize the enumerator, the consumer first calls **IDBProperties::SetProperties** to set the value of properties in the Initialization property group. For example, if the enumerator enumerates directories, the consumer might specify the server and directory the enumerator should start with. If the enumerator enumerates databases in an SQL DBMS, the consumer might specify the name of the server on which the DBMS resides, along with the user ID and password to use.

Certain properties in the Initialization property group are required by the enumerator for initialization. To determine which properties these are, the consumer calls **IDBProperties::GetPropertyInfo** for properties in the Initialization property group. For required properties, the DBPROPFLAGS_REQUIRED bit is set in the *dwFlags* element of the returned DBPROPINFO structure.

After the consumer has finished setting properties, it calls **IDBInitialize::Initialize**. **Initialize** can prompt for additional information, especially if the consumer has not set values for all required properties. The consumer can set properties to control how much **Initialize** prompts, including suppressing prompting altogether. After **Initialize** returns successfully, the enumerator is in an initialized state.

If the consumer needs to reinitialize the enumerator after it has been initialized, it must first uninitialize it. For example, if the enumerator enumerates directories and the consumer needs to enumerate directories on a different server, the consumer must disconnect from the first server before connecting to the second. If the enumerator enumerates databases in an SQL DBMS and the consumer needs to enumerate databases in a different installation of that DBMS, the consumer must disconnect from the first DBMS before connecting to the second. To uninitialize the enumerator, the consumer calls **IDBInitialize::Uninitialize**.

The following illustration shows the enumerator states and the methods that change them.

Enumerator states

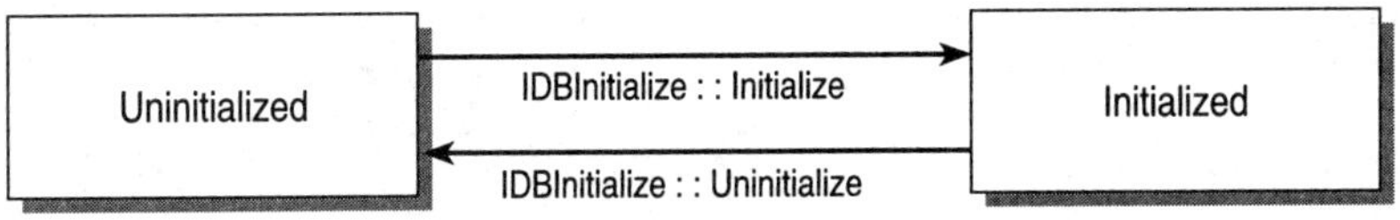

Enumerator Example

The code in this example shows how to create and use an enumerator object.

```
////////////////////////////////////////////////////////////////////////
// myCreateEnumerator
//
// This function creates an enumerator, obtains a sources rowset
// from it, displays the rowset to the user, and allows the user
// to specify the ProgID of a provider. The CLSID that matches
// this ProgID is retuned to the caller in *pCLSID.
//
////////////////////////////////////////////////////////////////////////
HRESULT myCreateEnumerator
   (
   REFCLSID             clsidEnumerator,
   CLSID *              pCLSID
   )
{
   HRESULT              hr;
   IUnknown *           pIUnkEnumerator            = NULL;
   ISourcesRowset *     pISourcesRowset            = NULL;
   IRowset *            pIRowset                   = NULL;
   IDBInitialize *      pIDBInitialize             = NULL;
   WCHAR                wszProgID[MAX_NAME_LEN + 1] = {0};

   const ULONG          cProperties                = 2;
   DBPROP               rgProperties[cProperties];
   DBPROPSET            rgPropSets[1];
```

```
// Create the enumerator object. We ask for IUnknown when creating
// the enumerator because some enumerators may require initialization
// before we can obtain a sources rowset from the enumerator. This is
// indicated by whether the enumerator object exposes IDBInitialize
// or not. (We don't want to ask for IDBInitialize, since enumerators
// that don't require initialization will cause the CoCreateInstance
// to fail.)
XCHECK_HR(hr = CoCreateInstance(
         clsidEnumerator,          //clsid -- enumerator
         NULL,                     //pUnkOuter
         CLSCTX_INPROC_SERVER,     //dwClsContext
         IID_IUnknown,             //riid
         (void**)&pIUnkEnumerator  //ppvObj
         ));

// If the enumerator exposes IDBInitialize, we need to initialize it
if( SUCCEEDED(hr = pIUnkEnumerator->QueryInterface(IID_IDBInitialize,
             (void**)&pIDBInitialize)) )
{
   CHECK_HR(hr = myDoInitialization(pIUnkEnumerator));
}

// Set properties on the rowset, to request additional functionality
myAddRowsetProperties(rgPropSets, cProperties, rgProperties);

// Obtain a sources rowset from the enumerator. This rowset contains
// all of the OLE DB providers that this enumerator is able to list.
XCHECK_HR(hr = pIUnkEnumerator->QueryInterface(IID_ISourcesRowset,
         (void**)&pISourcesRowset));
XCHECK_HR(hr = pISourcesRowset->GetSourcesRowset(
         NULL,                     //pUnkOuter
         IID_IRowset,              //riid
         1,                        //cPropSets
         rgPropSets,               //rgPropSets
         (IUnknown**)&pIRowset     //ppRowset
         ));

// Display the rowset to the user. This will allow the user to
// perform basic navigation of the rowset and will allow the user
// to select a row containing a desired provider.
CHECK_HR(hr = myDisplayRowset(pIRowset,
         L"SOURCES_NAME", MAX_NAME_LEN, wszProgID));

// Obtain the ProgID for the provider to use from the user.
// The default value for this is the value of the SOURCES_NAME
// column in the row selected by the user previously.
myGetInputFromUser(wszProgID, L"\nType the ProgID of a provider"
                   L" to use [Enter = `%s`]: ", wszProgID);
XCHECK_HR(hr = CLSIDFromProgID(wszProgID, pCLSID));
```

```
CLEANUP:
   if( pIUnkEnumerator )
      pIUnkEnumerator->Release();
   if( pISourcesRowset )
      pISourcesRowset->Release();
   if( pIRowset )
      pIRowset->Release();
   if( pIDBInitialize )
      pIDBInitialize->Release();
   return hr;
}
```

Session Objects

Session objects provide methods for creating commands and rowsets and for creating and modifying tables and indexes. They also define transaction scope and can be used to create transaction objects, which are used to control nested transactions.

The session object cotype is defined as follows. For more information about cotypes, see "OLE DB Objects" in Chapter 1, "Overview of OLE DB."

```
CoType TSession {
   [mandatory  interface IGetDataSource;
   [mandatory] interface IOpenRowset;
   [mandatory] interface ISessionProperties;
   [optional]  interface IAlterIndex;
   [optional]  interface IAlterTable;
   [optional]  interface IDBCreateCommand;
   [optional]  interface IDBSchemaRowset;
   [optional]  interface IIndexDefinition;
   [optional]  interface ISupportErrorInfo;
   [optional]  interface ITableDefinition;
   [optional]  interface ITransaction;
   [optional]  interface ITransactionJoin;
   [optional]  interface ITransactionLocal;
   [optional]  interface ITransactionObject;
}
```

If the session supports **ITransactionLocal**, the consumer can call **ITransactionLocal::StartTransaction** to start an explicit transaction. The session is then said to be in *manual-commit mode,* and any work done in the session must be explicitly committed or aborted. If **ITransactionLocal** is not supported or if the consumer does not call **StartTransaction**, the session is said to be in *auto-commit mode,* and any work done in the session is automatically committed. It cannot be aborted. For more information about transactions, see Chapter 12, "Transactions."

To create a session, a consumer calls **IDBCreateSession::CreateSession** on the data source object. A single data source object can support multiple sessions and, therefore, multiple transactions. From a session, the consumer can do the following:

- Create a command object by calling **IDBCreateCommand::CreateCommand**. A single session can support multiple commands. Some providers do not support commands.
- Create a rowset by calling **IOpenRowset::OpenRowset**. This is equivalent to creating a rowset over a single table and is supported by all providers.
- Create or modify tables and indexes with **ITableDefinition** and **IIndexDefinition**. Although providers are not required to support these interfaces, any provider built over a data store that supports creating and modifying tables and indexes should support them. For simple providers, such as a provider built over an array of data, **ITableDefinition** might be the only way to create or modify table definitions.
- Create a schema rowset by calling **IDBSchemaRowset::GetRowset**, if the provider supports schema rowsets. For more information about schema rowsets, see Appendix B, "Schema Rowsets."

Session Object Example

The code in this example shows how to create a session object.

```
/////////////////////////////////////////////////////////////////
// myCreateSession
//
// Create an OLE DB session object from the given data source
// object. The IDBCreateSession interface is mandatory, so this
// is a simple operation.
//
/////////////////////////////////////////////////////////////////
HRESULT  myCreateSession
   (
   IUnknown *           pUnkDataSource,
   IUnknown **          ppUnkSession
   )
{
   HRESULT              hr;
   IDBCreateSession *   pIDBCreateSession = NULL;
```

```
    // Create a session object from a data source object
    XCHECK_HR(hr = pUnkDataSource->QueryInterface(
             IID_IDBCreateSession, (void**)&pIDBCreateSession));
    XCHECK_HR(hr = pIDBCreateSession->CreateSession(
             NULL,                 //pUnkOuter
             IID_IOpenRowset,      //riid
             ppUnkSession          //ppSession
             ));

CLEANUP:
    if( pIDBCreateSession )
        pIDBCreateSession->Release();
    return hr;
}
```

CHAPTER 3

Commands

This chapter discusses the use and states of command objects, processing multiple result sets, binding input parameters and using output parameters, and the use of rowset properties in command objects Commands can be in one of four states: Initial, Unprepared, Prepared, or Executed. Parameters can be used with commands to bind to consumer variables at execution time. When executed, a command returns either a single result, which can be either a rowset object or a row count, or multiple results, which must be returned in a multiple results object.

For more information on	Go to
Using commands	"Using Commands" in this chapter
Command states	"Command States" in this chapter
Input and output parameters	"Using Parameters" in this chapter
Multiple results	"Multiple Results" in this chapter

A command object is used to execute a provider-specific text command, such as an SQL statement. Text commands are expressed in a provider-specific language—usually SQL92—and are usually used for creating a rowset—for example, executing an SQL **SELECT** statement.

Providers are not required to support commands. In general, providers built on top of a DBMS, such as an SQL DBMS, support commands, and providers built on top of a simple data structure, such as a file or an array of data in an application, do not support commands.

The command object cotype is defined as follows. For more information about cotypes, see "OLE DB Objects" in Chapter 1, "Overview of OLE DB."

```
CoType TCommand {
   [mandatory] interface IAccessor;
   [mandatory] interface IColumnsInfo;
   [mandatory] interface ICommand;
   [mandatory] interface ICommandProperties;
   [mandatory] interface ICommandText;
   [mandatory] interface IConvertType;
   [optional]  interface IColumnsRowset;
   [optional]  interface ICommandPersist;
   [optional]  interface ICommandPrepare;
   [optional]  interface ICommandWithParameters;
   [optional]  interface ISupportErrorInfo;
}
```

Using Commands

Before a consumer can use a command, it must determine whether commands are supported by the session. To do this, the consumer calls **QueryInterface** for **IDBCreateCommand** on the session object. If this interface is exposed, the provider supports commands. To create a command, the consumer then calls **IDBCreateCommand::CreateCommand** on the session. A consumer can use a single session to create multiple commands.

When the command is first created, it does not contain command text. The consumer sets the command text with **ICommandText::SetCommandText**. Because the text command syntax is provider-specific, the consumer passes the GUID of the syntax to use. This can be one of the following dialect values, or it can be a provider-specific value specifying some provider specific syntax.

Dialect value	Meaning
DBGUID_DEFAULT	The command text is to be interpreted according to the provider's default grammar. If the command text is an SQL statement and the provider supports SQL, the provider must recognize and process the command text as an SQL statement, even if the provider's default grammar is not SQL. This is required for maximum interoperability.
DBGUID_SQL	The command text is to be interpreted according to a superset of SQL syntax rules. To determine the level of SQL syntax supported by a provider, a consumer calls **IDBProperties::GetProperties** for the DBPROP_SQLSUPPORT property. Providers reporting this syntax are free to use extensions to SQL, or any subset of SQL according to their reported level of support, but must comply with the rules defined in SQL for any supported syntax defined in that specification. **Note** DBGUID_SQL was added in OLE DB version 1.5 and is not supported in earlier providers. Consumers should use DBGUID_SQL only when calling a version 1.5 or greater provider that supports DBPROP_SQLSUPPORT. In most cases, unless the provider is trying to distinguish between different dialects, the consumer can just pass DBGUID_DEFAULT. (See above for DBGUID_DEFAULT.)

To execute the command, the consumer calls **ICommand::Execute**. If the command text specifies a rowset, such as an SQL **SELECT** statement, **Execute** creates an instance of the rowset and returns an interface pointer to it.

By calling **ICommandProperties::SetProperties** before executing a command that creates a rowset, the consumer can request properties that control execution of the command and affect the behavior of the resulting rowset (such as the interfaces to expose). For more information, see "Setting Rowset Properties" in Chapter 4, "Rowsets." The consumer can also get information about the columns of the rowset by calling **IColumnsInfo::GetColumnInfo**, which all providers must support, or **IColumnsRowset::GetColumnsRowset**, which providers may support, on the command.

Before calling **GetColumnInfo** or **GetColumnsRowset**, the consumer must set the command text and, if the provider supports command preparation, prepare the command object.

If a command is to be executed multiple times with the same text command or if the consumer needs information about the rowset it will create, the consumer can *prepare* the command by calling **ICommandPrepare::Prepare**. This is equivalent to compiling the command.

Prepared commands can be used with *parameters,* which are variables in the text command. For example, if the provider supports SQL, the consumer might prepare and repeatedly execute the following parameterized SQL statement to update the salaries of a number of employees:

```
UPDATE Employees SET (Salary = ?) WHERE EmployeeID = ?
```

Support for parameterized commands is optional. Providers that support them must expose **ICommandWithParameters** on command objects. To use parameters, the consumer first describes the parameters to the provider by calling **ICommandWithParameters::SetParameterInfo**. Some providers themselves can describe parameters and do not need consumers to call **SetParameterInfo**. The consumer then creates an accessor that specifies the structure of a buffer and places parameter values in this buffer. Finally, it passes the handle of the accessor and a pointer to the buffer to **Execute**. On later calls to **Execute**, the consumer simply places new parameter values in the buffer and calls **Execute** with the accessor handle and buffer pointer. For more information, see Chapter 6, "Getting and Setting Data."

Command States

Commands can be in one of four states:

- **Initial**—No command text is set. A command is in this state after **IDBCreateCommand::CreateCommand** is called.
- **Unprepared**—The command text is set but the command is not prepared. A command is in this state after **ICommandText::SetCommandText** is called.
- **Prepared**—The command text is set and the command is prepared. A command is in this state after **ICommandPrepare::Prepare** is called.
- **Executed**—The command text is executed. A command is in this state after **ICommand::Execute** is called.

The following table lists each state and shows the value returned by each method in a command interface when it is called in that state. This table uses the following abbreviations:

OK = S_OK
NC = DB_E_NOCOMMAND
NP = DB_E_NOTPREPARED
OO = DB_E_OPENOBJECT

Method	Initial	Unprepared	Prepared	Executed
IColumnsInfo::GetColumnInfo	NC	OK (**ICommandPrepare** is not supported) - or - NP (**ICommandPrepare** is supported)	OK	OK (**ICommandPrepare** is not supported) - or - NP (**ICommandPrepare** is supported)
IColumnsInfo::MapColumnIDs	NC	OK (**ICommandPrepare** is not supported) - or - NP (**ICommandPrepare** is supported)	OK	OK (**ICommandPrepare** is not supported) - or - NP (**ICommandPrepare** is supported)
IColumnsRowset::-GetAvailableColumns	NC	OK (**ICommandPrepare** is not supported) - or - NP (**ICommandPrepare** is supported)	OK	OK (**ICommandPrepare** is not supported) - or - NP (**ICommandPrepare** is supported)
IColumnsRowset::-GetColumnsRowset	NC	OK (**ICommandPrepare** is not supported) - or - NP (**ICommandPrepare** is supported)	OK	OK (**ICommandPrepare** is not supported) - or - NP (**ICommandPrepare** is supported)
ICommand::Cancel	OK	OK	OK	OK
ICommand::Execute	NC	OK	OK	OK
ICommand::GetDBSession	OK	OK	OK	OK

Method	Initial	Unprepared	Prepared	Executed
ICommandPrepare::-Prepare	NC	OK	OK	OK (**Execute** did not create a rowset) - or - OO (**Execute** created a rowset, and the rowset is still open)
ICommandPrepare::-Unprepare	OK	OK	OK	OK (**Execute** did not create a rowset) - or - OO (**Execute** created a rowset, and the rowset is still open)
ICommandProp-erties::GetProperties	OK	OK	OK	OK
ICommandProp-erties::SetProperties	OK	OK	OK	OK (**Execute** did not create a rowset) - or - OO (**Execute** created a rowset, and the rowset is still open)
ICommandText::Get-CommandText	NC	OK	OK	OK
ICommandText::Set-CommandText	OK	OK	OK	OK (**Execute** did not create a rowset) - or - OO (**Execute** created a rowset, and the rowset is still open)

Method	Initial	Unprepared	Prepared	Executed
ICommandWith-Parameters::Get-ParameterInfo	OK (**SetParameterInfo** has been called) - or - NC (**SetParameterInfo** has not been called)	OK (**SetParameter-Info** has been called) - or - NP (**ICommand-Prepare** is supported, and **SetParameterInfo** has not been called)	OK	OK
ICommandWith-Parameters::Map-ParameterNames	OK (**SetParameterInfo** has been called) - or - NC (**SetParameterInfo** has not been called)	OK (**SetParameter-Info** has been called) - or - NP (**ICommand-Prepare** is supported, and **SetParameterInfo** has not been called)	OK	OK
ICommandWith-Parameters::Set-ParameterInfo	OK	OK	OK	OK (**Execute** did not create a rowset) - or - OO (**Execute** created a rowset, and the rowset is still open)

The following figures illustrate the state transitions for a command. The first shows the command text set to an empty string; the second shows the command text set to a nonempty string.

Command text set to an empty string and to a nonempty string

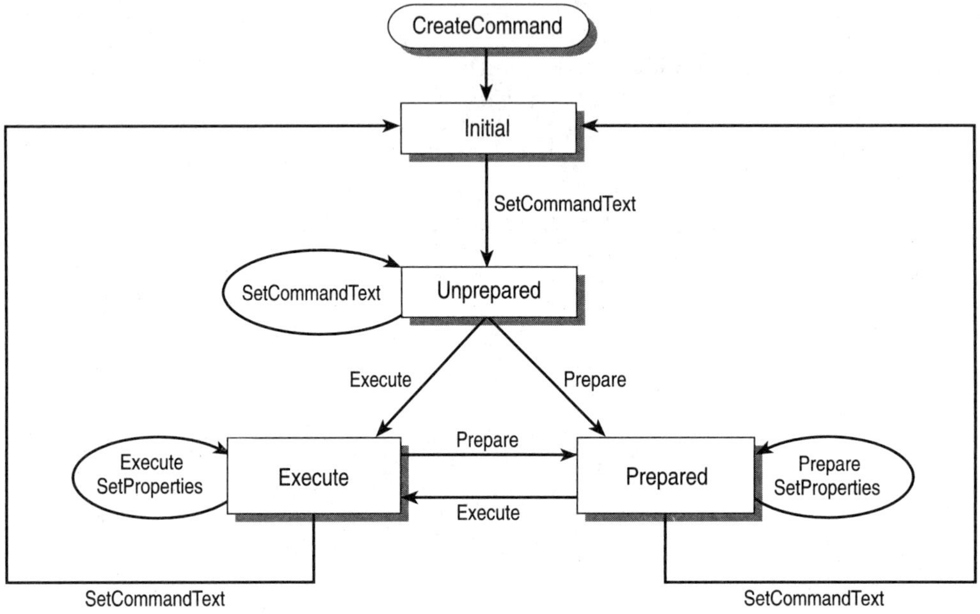

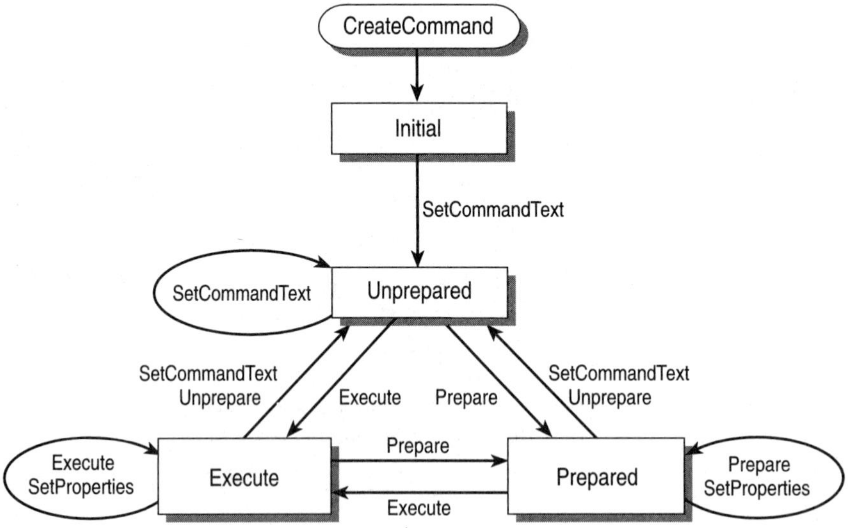

Command Object Example

The code in this example shows how to create and execute a command object.

```
/////////////////////////////////////////////////////////////////
// myCreateCommand
//
// This function takes an IUnknown pointer on a session object
// and attempts to create a command object using the session's
// IDBCreateCommand interface. Since this interface is optional,
// this may fail.
//
/////////////////////////////////////////////////////////////////
HRESULT  myCreateCommand
   (
   IUnknown *           pUnkSession,
   IUnknown **          ppUnkCommand
   )
{
   HRESULT              hr;
   IDBCreateCommand *   pIDBCreateCommand = NULL;

   // Attempt to create a Command object from the session object
   XCHECK_HR(hr = pUnkSession->QueryInterface(
            IID_IDBCreateCommand, (void**)&pIDBCreateCommand));
   XCHECK_HR(hr = pIDBCreateCommand->CreateCommand(
            NULL,            // pUnkOuter
            IID_ICommand,    // riid
            ppUnkCommand     // ppCommand
            ));

CLEANUP:
   if( pIDBCreateCommand )
      pIDBCreateCommand->Release();
   return hr;
}
```

```
//////////////////////////////////////////////////////////////////////
// myExecuteCommand
//
// This function takes an IUnknown pointer on a Command object
// and performs the following steps to create a new Rowset
// object:
//   - Sets the given properties on the command object; these
//     properties will be applied by the provider to any Rowset
//     created by this Command.
//   - Sets the given command text for the command.
//   - Executes the command to create a new rowset object.
//
//////////////////////////////////////////////////////////////////////
HRESULT  myExecuteCommand
   (
   IUnknown *             pUnkCommand,
   WCHAR *                pwszCommandText,
   ULONG                  cPropSets,
   DBPROPSET*             rgPropSets,
   IUnknown **            ppUnkRowset
   )
{
   HRESULT                hr;
   ICommandText *         pICommandText         = NULL;
   ICommandProperties * pICommandProperties  = NULL;

   // Set the properties on the command object
   XCHECK_HR(hr = pUnkCommand->QueryInterface(
            IID_ICommandProperties, (void**)&pICommandProperties));
   XCHECK_HR(hr = pICommandProperties->SetProperties(cPropSets, rgPropSets));

   // Set the text for this command, using the default command text
   // dialect. All providers that support commands must support this
   // dialect, and providers that support SQL must be able to recognize
   // an SQL command as SQL when this dialect is specified.
   XCHECK_HR(hr = pUnkCommand->QueryInterface(
            IID_ICommandText, (void**)&pICommandText));
   XCHECK_HR(hr = pICommandText->SetCommandText(
            DBGUID_DEFAULT,      // guidDialect
            pwszCommandText      // pwszCommandText
            ));
```

```
    // And execute the command. Note that the user could have
    // entered a non-row returning command, so we will check for
    // that and return failure to prevent the display of the
    // nonexistent rowset by the caller.
    XCHECK_HR(hr = pICommandText->Execute(
                NULL,                   // pUnkOuter
                IID_IRowset,            // riid
                NULL,                   // pParams
                NULL,                   // pcRowsAffected
                ppUnkRowset             // ppRowset
                ));

    if( !*ppUnkRowset )
    {
        printf("\nThe command executed successfully, but did not " \
                "return a rowset.\nNo rowset will be displayed.\n");
        hr = E_FAIL;
    }


CLEANUP:
    if( pICommandText )
        pICommandText->Release();
    if( pICommandProperties )
        pICommandProperties->Release();
    return hr;
}
```

Multiple Results

When executed, commands return results. A *result* can be either a rowset or a row count, which is the number of rows affected by a command that updates, deletes, or inserts rows. Commands can return multiple results if the command text comprises multiple, separate text commands—such as a batch of SQL statements—or if more than one set of parameters is passed to a command.

The multiple results object cotype is defined as follows. For more information about cotypes, see "OLE DB Objects" in Chapter 1, "Overview of OLE DB."

```
CoType TMultipleResults {
   [mandatory] interface IMultipleResults;
   [optional]  interface ISupportErrorInfo;
}
```

To retrieve multiple results, consumers use multiple results objects. Providers are not required to support these, however. The DBPROP_MULTIPLERESULTS property in the Data Source Information property group specifies whether a provider supports multiple results objects.

To create a multiple results object, the consumer sets the DBPROP_IMultipleResults property on the command and requests the **IMultipleResults** interface when it calls **ICommand::Execute**. **Execute** returns an interface pointer on the multiple results object to the consumer.

To retrieve each rowset or row count created by the command, the consumer calls **IMultipleResults::GetResult**. **GetResult** returns results in the order they were specified in the command text. If the current result is a rowset, some providers require the consumer to release the rowset before **GetResult** returns the next result. The DBPROP_MULTIPLERESULTS property specifies whether this is required.

Using Parameters

Parameters are placeholders that can be inserted into a command object. These placeholders are bound to consumer variables at execution time. By using input parameters, consumers can specify a command once and execute it multiple times, each with a different set of values. Parameters are also useful for inserting nonstring values into a command. By using parameters, consumers can execute a command, such as a stored procedure, that contains output arguments.

The provider determines how parameters are specified within a command. SQL providers that report at least a DBPROP_SQLSUPPORT value of DBPROPVAL_SQL_ODBC_MINIMUM or DBPROPVAL_SQL_ANSI92_INTERMEDIATE must support parameters in conjunction with the DBGUID_SQL dialect. SQL providers represent parameter markers within a command as question marks (?). In most cases, parameter markers can legally appear only in certain positions within an SQL statement. They cannot take the place of an identifier, such as a column name in the SELECT list or a table name in the FROM clause, and are not allowed in data definition language (DDL) statements.

Not all SQL providers support the ability to describe the parameters embedded within a command. For providers that do support describing parameters, consumers can obtain parameter information by calling **ICommandWithParameters::GetParameterInfo**. Consumers that know the number and types of the parameters can specify this information by calling **ICommandWithParameters::SetParameterInfo**. The provider uses this information to determine how to convert parameter data from the type supplied by the consumer to the native type used by the data store. This is particularly useful for providers that cannot describe the parameters embedded within a command. It can also lead to more efficient code because the provider does not have to go through the potentially expensive operation of describing the command.

The consumer variables from which input parameter values are taken and to which output parameter values are written are passed at run time to **ICommand::Execute** in the DBPARAMS structure. Multiple sets of parameter values can be passed in a single call to **Execute**, which has the effect of executing the statement multiple times, once with each set of parameter values. The consumer describes the layout of parameter information within the buffer passed in the DBPARAMS structure by creating a parameter accessor and passing a handle to the parameter accessor in its call to **Execute**. For more information about parameter accessors, see "Using Accessors" in Chapter 6, "Getting and Setting Data."

Parameters may be named or unnamed but are always identified within the parameter accessor according to ordinal, using the *iOrdinal* member of the DBBINDING structure. In most cases, the ordinal of a parameter within a textual command is its one-based position within the command.

To bind parameters, the consumer does one of the following:

- If the consumer knows the ordinals and server types of the parameters to be bound, it calls **SetParameterInfo**, supplying the ordinals of the parameters and specifying the name, if known, along with the data type of each parameter in the DBPARAMBINDINFO structure. The *iOrdinal* members of the DBBINDING structure correspond to the ordinal values specified in **SetParameterInfo**.
- If the consumer knows the names but not the ordinals of the parameters, it can obtain a list of ordinals corresponding to a set of named parameters by calling **ICommandWithParameters::MapParameterNames**. The consumer then calls **SetParameterInfo** using these ordinal values with the names. The *iOrdinal* members of the DBBINDING structure correspond to the ordinal values specified in **SetParameterInfo**. The ordinals returned by **MapParameterNames** do not necessarily indicate the position of the parameters in the command but represent how the provider associates the parameter name to the ordinal specified in the accessor.
- If the consumer does not know the ordinals of the parameters to be bound, and the provider supports describing parameters, the consumer can call **GetParameterInfo** to determine the parameter name, if applicable, along with the type of each parameter ordinal. The *iOrdinal* members of the DBBINDING structure correspond to the ordinal values returned in **GetParameterInfo**.
- If the consumer does not know the ordinals of the parameters, and the provider does not support describing the parameters, the consumer must try to determine the number and order of parameters. It must either obtain parameter information from the user or "guess" at the data types to bind each parameter. If the consumer does not need to convert between the bound type and the type of data on the server and does not need to use named parameters, it can simply create an accessor using the ordinals of the parameters and execute the statement without calling any method from **ICommandWithParameters**.

Output parameters are filled in when the provider has completely finished processing the execution. For some providers, this does not occur until the rowset is released, and the memory specified for the output parameters must remain valid until the rowset is released. To determine when output parameters are populated and memory can be released, the consumer should check the DBPROP_OUTPUTPARAMETERAVAILABILITY data source information property.

Rowset Properties in Command Objects

When creating a command that returns a rowset, the consumer can specify properties from the rowset property group that must be supported by the rowset. For example, all providers are required to expose the **IRowset** interface on rowset objects. **IRowset** enables consumers to, at minimum, navigate forward in the rowset. By requesting the DBPROP_CANSCROLLBACKWARDS rowset property, a consumer can specify that the rowset must enable the consumer to navigate through the rowset in both directions.

Other rowset properties specify interfaces that the rowset must support in addition to the mandatory ones. For example, a consumer might require interfaces to enable direct positioning within a rowset with bookmarks (DBPROP_IROWSETLOCATE), approximate positioning (DBPROP_IROWSETSCROLL), updatability of rows (DBPROP_IROWSETCHANGE), and deferred updatability (DBPROP_IROWSETUPDATE). Consumers can also specify additional properties that specialize the behavior of certain interfaces—for example, to make some columns of the rowset updatable and the rest read-only.

CHAPTER 4

Rowsets

This chapter explains how to create and release rowsets, as well as how to set their properties, such as supported interfaces. Rowsets are the central objects that enable OLE DB components to expose and manipulate data in tabular form. A *rowset object* is a set of rows in which each row has columns of data. For example, providers present data, as well as metadata, to consumers in the form of rowsets. Query processors present query results in the form of rowsets. The use of rowsets throughout OLE DB makes it possible to aggregate components that consume or produce data through the same object.

Also presented in this chapter are ways to manage the activity of individual rows or rowsets: fetching, reference counting of row handles, and column access and reference. Rowset reference and fetching are discussed in the use of bookmarks, views, and chapters. The consumer uses *bookmarks* to return quickly to a row. *Views* can expose simple operations such as sorting or filtering a rowset. *Chapters* define groups of rows within a rowset. This chapter also discusses *hierarchical rowsets*, which are rowsets that are linked together by using chapters.

For more information on	Go to
Creating rowsets	"Creating Rowsets" in this chapter
Column access	"Deferred Columns" and "Column IDs" in this chapter
Rows	"Rows and Row Handles" in this chapter
Fetching rows	"Fetching Rows" in this chapter
Bookmarks	"Bookmarks" in this chapter
Chapters	"Chapters" in this chapter
Views	"Views" in this chapter
Hierarchical rowsets	"Hierarchical Rowsets" in this chapter
Navigation of hierarchical rowsets	"Navigating Hierarchical Rowsets" in this chapter
Lifetime of row handles and chapters	"Lifetime of Row Handles Within Chapters" in this chapter

The rowset object cotype is defined as follows. For more information about cotypes, see "OLE DB Objects" in Chapter 1, "Overview of OLE DB."

```
CoType TRowset {
   [mandatory] interface IAccessor;
   [mandatory] interface IColumnsInfo;
   [mandatory] interface IConvertType;
   [mandatory] interface IRowset;
   [mandatory] interface IRowsetInfo;
   [optional]  interface IChapteredRowset;
   [optional]  interface IColumnsRowset;
   [optional]  interface IConnectionPointContainer;
   [optional]  interface IDBAsynchStatus;
   [optional]  interface IRowsetChange;
   [optional]  interface IRowsetChapterMember;
   [optional]  interface IRowsetFind;
   [optional]  interface IRowsetIdentity;
   [optional]  interface IRowsetIndex;
   [optional]  interface IRowsetLocate;
   [optional]  interface IRowsetRefresh;
   [optional]  interface IRowsetScroll;
   [optional]  interface IRowsetUpdate;
   [optional]  interface IRowsetView;
   [optional]  interface ISupportErrorInfo;
}
```

All rowsets must expose the interfaces described in the following table.

Interface	Use
IRowset	Contains methods for fetching rows, getting row data, and maintaining reference counts on row handles.
IAccessor	Permits the definition of groups of column bindings describing the way tabular data is bound to consumer program variables.
IColumnsInfo	Provides information about the columns of the rowset.
IRowsetInfo	Provides information about the rowset itself.
IConvertType	Provides information about the data type conversions supported by the rowset.

Creating Rowsets

A consumer obtains a rowset object in one of the following ways:

- The consumer calls **IOpenRowset::OpenRowset** on the current session object to create a rowset directly. All providers must support **IOpenRowset**.
- The consumer calls **IDBCreateCommand::CreateCommand** on the session object to obtain a command object. The consumer then calls **ICommand::Execute** on the command object. If the command is one that returns rows, such as an SQL **SELECT** statement, **ICommand::Execute** returns either a rowset or, if the consumer has requested **IMultipleResults**, a multiple results object.
- The consumer invokes a method that returns a rowset or schema rowset, such as **IColumnsRowset::GetColumnsRowset**, **IDBSchemaRowset::GetRowset**, **IViewRowset::OpenViewRowset**, or **ISourcesRowset::GetSourcesRowset**.
- The consumer calls some other method that returns tabular results as a rowset.

Creating a Rowset with IOpenRowset

Some providers need to expose very simple rowsets to their consumers. Conceptually, these rowsets represent the result of the simple query **SELECT * FROM** *Tablename*. To allow providers to interpret this simple query without the overhead of supporting a complete query language, OLE DB provides a simple rowset interface, **IOpenRowset**. **IOpenRowset** effectively exposes a rowset in the absence of a command. **IOpenRowset** is implemented on the session as shown in the following illustration.

Creating a rowset directly with IOpenRowset

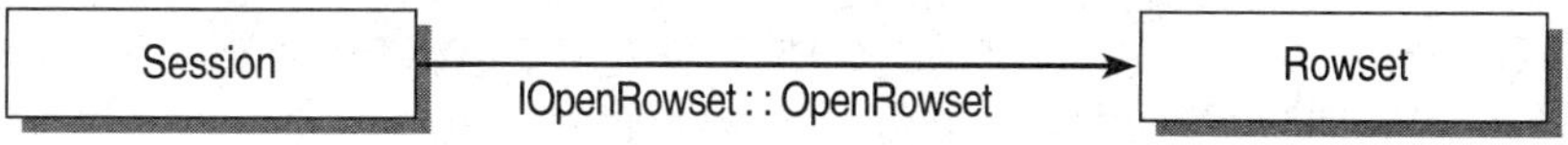

Fully Qualified Names

A consumer may need to construct a fully qualified table name incorporating the names of the associated schema and catalog.

To construct a fully qualified name if DBPROP_CATALOGLOCATION is DBPROPVAL_CL_START or the provider does not support the DBPROP_CATALOGLOCATION property, a consumer follows these steps:

1. If DBLITERAL_CATALOG_NAME is not NULL (*fSupported* is TRUE in DBLITERALINFO), get the appropriate catalog name for the table (for example, from the TABLES schema rowset) and append the value of DBLITERAL_CATALOG_SEPARATOR (*pwszLiteralValue* in DBLITERALINFO).
2. If DBLITERAL_SCHEMA_NAME is not NULL (*fSupported* is TRUE in DBLITERALINFO), get the appropriate schema name for the table (for example, from the TABLES schema rowset) and append the value of DBLITERAL_SCHEMA_SEPARATOR (*pwszLiteralValue* in DBLITERALINFO). Append this to the catalog information from the previous step.
3. Append the object (table) name.

To construct a fully qualified name if DBPROP_CATALOGLOCATION is DBPROPVAL_CL_END, a consumer follows these steps:

1. If DBLITERAL_SCHEMA_NAME is not NULL (*fSupported* is TRUE in DBLITERALINFO), get the appropriate schema name for the table (for example, from the TABLES schema rowset) and append the value of DBLITERAL_SCHEMA_SEPARATOR (*pwszLiteralValue* in DBLITERALINFO).
2. Append the object (table) name.
3. If DBLITERAL_CATALOG_NAME is not NULL (*fSupported* is TRUE in DBLITERALINFO), append the value of DBLITERAL_CATALOG_SEPARATOR (*pwszLiteralValue* in DBLITERALINFO) and the appropriate catalog name for the table (for example, from the TABLES schema rowset).

Note Consumers should provide qualified table names only to reference tables in other schemas or catalogs. Further, consumers should not quote table names unless such quoting is required to make table names unambiguous (such as, to enforce case sensitivity). Providers for which quoting a simple table name has no meaning may not support quoting tables in **IOpenRowset::OpenRowset** while they do support quoting tables as part of a command text for parsing reasons. Providers should not require table names to be quoted and should guarantee that unquoted table names correctly open the specified table, even if the table name contains special characters, as long as the table can be unambiguously identified without quoting.

Creating a Rowset with a Command

Providers that implement their own query or data definition language (DDL) can offer their consumers additional functionality by using a command.

To implement a query or DDL by using a command, a consumer should follow these steps:

1. Create a session. (For more information, see "Session Objects" in Chapter 2, "Data Source and Session Objects.")
2. Call **IDBCreateCommand::CreateCommand** on the session to obtain a command object. When the command is first created, it does not contain command text. Set the command text by calling **ICommandText::SetCommandText**.

   The text command can be expressed in SQL or some other provider-specific language. For more information about creating command objects, see "Using Commands" in Chapter 3, "Commands."
3. Call **ICommandProperties::SetProperties** to request properties that control execution of the command and affect the behavior of the resulting rowset (such as the interfaces to expose).
4. Call **ICommand::Execute** on the command.

   If the command is one that returns rows, such as an SQL **SELECT** statement, **ICommand::Execute** returns either a rowset or, if the consumer has requested **IMultipleResults**, a multiple results object. See the following illustration.

Creating a rowset through a command

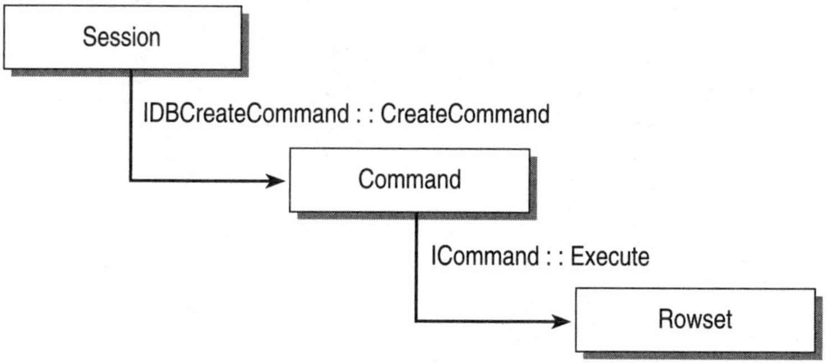

The consumer calls **ICommandProperties::SetProperties** on the command object to request properties that control execution of the command and affect the behavior of the rowsets returned by **ICommand::Execute**. The most commonly requested properties are the interfaces the rowset must support.

All rowsets must support **IRowset**, **IAccessor**, **IColumnsInfo**, **IRowsetInfo**, and **IConvertType**. Providers can choose to return rowsets exposing additional interfaces if doing so does not break consumer code that is not expecting them. For example, **IRowsetLocate** can be exposed on the rowset even if the consumer does not request it, because this interface does not change the rowset's behavior. In contrast, **IRowsetUpdate** cannot safely be exposed if the consumer does not request it, because exposing **IRowsetUpdate** on the rowset changes the behavior of the rowset's **IRowsetChange** interface. In most cases, the *riid* parameter passed to **ICommand::Execute** is the IID for one of the interfaces listed in the **TRowset** cotype.

For a complete description of how consumers use properties, see Chapter 11, "Properties."

Rowset Creation Example

The code in this example shows how to create a rowset.

```
/////////////////////////////////////////////////////////////////
// myCreateRowset
//
// This function creates an OLE DB rowset object from the given
// provider's session object. It first obtains a default table
// name from the user through the tables schema rowset, if
// supported, and then creates a rowset object by one of two methods:
//
// - If the user requested that the rowset object be created
//   from a command object, it creates a command object and then
//   obtains command text from the user, sets properties and
//   the command text, and finally executes the command to
//   create the rowset object.
// - Otherwise, the function obtains a table name from the user
//   and calls IOpenRowset::OpenRowset to create a rowset object
//   over that table that supports the requested properties.
//
/////////////////////////////////////////////////////////////////
HRESULT  myCreateRowset
   (
   IUnknown *          pUnkSession,
   IUnknown **         ppUnkRowset
   )
{
   HRESULT             hr;
   IUnknown *          pUnkCommand                   = NULL;
   IOpenRowset *       pIOpenRowset                  = NULL;
   WCHAR               wszTableName[MAX_NAME_LEN + 1]  = {0};

   const ULONG         cProperties                   = 2;
   DBPROP              rgProperties[cProperties];
   DBPROPSET           rgPropSets[1];
```

```
// Obtain a default table name from the user by displaying the
// tables schema rowset if schema rowsets are supported
CHECK_HR(hr = myCreateSchemaRowset(DBSCHEMA_TABLES, pUnkSession,
   MAX_NAME_LEN, wszTableName));

// Set properties on the rowset, to request additional functionality
myAddRowsetProperties(rgPropSets, cProperties, rgProperties);

// If the user requested that the rowset be created from a
// command object, create a command, set its properties and
// text, and execute it to create the rowset object
if( g_dwFlags & USE_COMMAND )
{
   WCHAR    wszCommandText[MAX_NAME_LEN + 1];

   // Attempt to create the command object from the provider's
   // session object. Note that commands are not supported by
   // all providers, and this will fail in that case.
   CHECK_HR(hr = myCreateCommand(pUnkSession, &pUnkCommand));

   // Get the command text that we will execute from the user
   if( !myGetInputFromUser(wszCommandText, L"\nType the command "
      L"to execute [Enter = `select * from %s`]: ", wszTableName) )
   {
      swprintf(wszCommandText, L"select * from %s", wszTableName);
   }

   // And execute the command the user entered
   CHECK_HR(hr = myExecuteCommand(pUnkCommand, wszCommandText,
         1, rgPropSets, ppUnkRowset));
}
// Otherwise, the user gets the default behavior, which is to use
// IOpenRowset to create the rowset object from the session object.
// IOpenRowset is supported by all providers; it takes a TableID
// and creates a rowset containing all rows in that table. It is
// similar to using SQL command text of "SELECT * FROM TableID"
else
{
   DBID                    TableID;

   // Create the TableID
   TableID.eKind           = DBKIND_NAME;
   TableID.uName.pwszName  = wszTableName;

   // Obtain the table name from the user
   myGetInputFromUser(wszTableName, L"\nType the name of the table "
      L"to use [Enter = `%s`]: ", wszTableName);
```

```
      // Get the IOpenRowset interface, and create a rowset object
      // over the requested table through OpenRowset
      XCHECK_HR(hr = pUnkSession->QueryInterface(
                IID_IOpenRowset, (void**)&pIOpenRowset));
      XCHECK_HR(hr = pIOpenRowset->OpenRowset(
                NULL,          // pUnkOuter
                &TableID,      // pTableID
                NULL,          // pIndexID
                IID_IRowset,   // riid
                1,             // cPropSets
                rgPropSets,    // rgPropSets
                ppUnkRowset    // ppRowset
                ));
   }

CLEANUP:
   if( pIOpenRowset )
      pIOpenRowset->Release();
   if( pUnkCommand )
      pUnkCommand->Release();
   return hr;
}
```

Rows and Row Handles

Conceptually, a rowset is a set of rows. A *row* is a set of related data items, or *columns,* that are treated as a unit. In OLE DB, each row in a rowset object is stored in a separately allocated data buffer that the provider maintains on behalf of the consumer. Thus a rowset's row data, stored in these row buffers, is external to the rowset object, which contains a set of handles to the row buffers. These handles are called *row handles.*

Row handles are of type HROW, which is defined as follows:

```
typedef ULONG HROW;
```

The consumer can use row handles to manage the activity of individual rows or sets of rows in a rowset. A rowset may have a limit on the number of open row handles it can hold. This limit is imposed by the rowset's DBPROP_MAXOPENROWS property.

When a consumer fetches a row, the data for the row appears to be cached in the provider and left there until the row is released. The consumer accesses the data in the row through the functions **IRowset::GetData** and **IRowsetChange::SetData**, which use accessor objects to define how the data is to be transferred. For more information, see "Accessors" in Chapter 6, "Getting and Setting Data."

By having a local copy of the row, multiple consumers can get data from the row without making additional trips to the data store, which might reside on a separate server.

Consumers can also coordinate changes to the row without transmitting them to the data store until all consumers are ready.

However, caching rows in the provider means that it is costly to keep materialized row handles—those defined by creating an instance. Although a particular provider might not enforce a preset limit on the number of active row handles, keeping even a few hundred row handles deteriorates provider performance. Some providers might be expected to handle rowsets with millions of rows, but no provider is expected to materialize many rows simultaneously. Consumers are therefore encouraged to release row handles whenever possible and keep bookmarks to these rows if it is necessary to refetch them. Consumers can keep a small number of frequently accessed row handles in materialized form.

Fetching Rows

Methods such as **IRowsetFind::FindNextRow**, **IRowset::GetNextRows**, **IRowsetLocate::GetRowsAt**, **IRowsetLocate::GetRowsByBookmark**, and **IRowsetScroll::GetRowsAtRatio** are used to fetch rows from a rowset. The consumer can use these methods to get multiple row handles with a single call.

The provider manages its row buffers on behalf of the consumer. When a row is fetched, the provider stores the row data in a buffer local to the provider. The row is usually stored in a native format, although how this is done is provider-specific. The consumer does not have direct access to the provider's data. Instead, the consumer calls **IRowset::GetData** to fetch row data into its own buffer and **IRowsetChange::SetData** to make changes to it. For more information, see Chapter 6, "Getting and Setting Data."

The rowset's DBPROP_CANHOLDROWS property specifies whether row handles previously obtained from earlier calls to methods such as **GetNextRows** must be released before the consumer can call **GetNextRows** to retrieve new row handles.

Reference Counting of Row Handles

Row handles are of type HROW and are not COM objects. Nevertheless, each row handle has its own associated reference count. These reference counts are incremented by calling **IRowset::AddRefRows** and decremented by calling **IRowset::ReleaseRows**. All methods that fetch rows are required to increment the reference counts on the returned row handles. The provider holds the rows until the consumer releases them with **IRowset::ReleaseRows**. The consumer must call **ReleaseRows** on a row once for each time it was fetched and each time **AddRefRows** was called on it.

Rows held by the provider are freed after the rowset's final reference has been released or after all references on the row handle have been freed. Deleting a row does not release the row handle. It does not matter whether the row is deleted by calling **IRowsetUpdate::Update** on a row with a pending deletion, calling **IRowsetUpdate::Undo** on a row with a pending insert, or calling **IRowsetChange::DeleteRows**: The consumer must call **ReleaseRows** to release the row.

Next Fetch Position

The OLE DB provider keeps track of the next fetch position so that a sequence of calls to **GetNextRows** (with no skips, changes of direction, or intervening calls to **FindNextRow**, **Seek**, or **RestartPosition**) reads the entire rowset without skipping or repeating any row. The next fetch position is changed either by calling **IRowset::GetNextRows**, **IRowset::RestartPosition**, or **IRowsetIndex::Seek**, or by calling **FindNextRow** with a NULL *pBookmark* value. Calling **FindNextRow** with a non-NULL *pBookmark* value has no effect on the next fetch position.

If the rowset supports reversible fetch direction and the fetch direction is reversed from the previous call to **GetNextRows** (or **FindNextRow** with a NULL *pBookmark* value), the next fetch position for **GetNextRows** or **FindNextRow** in the new direction is the last row that was fetched in the previous direction. Otherwise, the next fetch position is the row following the last row fetched by **GetNextRows** (or **FindNextRow** with a NULL *pBookmark* value).

Fetch Direction

Methods that return row handles can take a negative count of requested rows. This means that the absolute count of rows is returned, beginning with the first specified row and then moving backward (that is, in decreasing order of row number). For example, the next fetch row in **GetNextRows** or the bookmarked row in **IRowsetLocate::GetRowsAt** is the specified row, so those preceding it up to the absolute count are returned. This behavior is independent of skip (offset) counts, which also can be negative.

Uniqueness of Rows in the Rowset

If a row is fetched more than once without any intervening calls to release it, the DBPROP_LITERALIDENTITY property determines whether the rowset contains one or multiple copies of the row.

Providers that can detect whether a newly fetched row is already represented by a currently held row handle should simply return the existing row handle with an incremented reference count. For such providers, the DBPROP_LITERALIDENTITY property is set to VARIANT_TRUE.

If DBPROP_LITERALIDENTITY is set to VARIANT_FALSE, multiple different concurrently held row handles can represent the same row in the underlying data store. To the rowset, these generally appear as separate rows. Therefore, changes made through one row handle are not reflected when reading the row through a second row handle. Calling **RefreshVisibleData**, **Undo**, or **Update** affects only changes made through the specified row handle.

The consumer can call **IRowsetIdentity::IsSameRow** to determine whether two row handles represent the same row. Such comparisons are necessary, for example, when the consumer receives a row handle through one of the methods in **IRowsetNotify** and needs to know if it is the handle of a row that the consumer already holds. Whether the handles of newly inserted rows—that is, rows inserted during the lifetime of the rowset—can be compared at all depends on the value of the DBPROP_STRONGIDENTITY property.

Deferred Columns

For a *deferred column,* the provider is not required to retrieve data from the data store until **IRowset::GetData** is called for that column. If the column contains a COM object, the provider need not retrieve data until a method used to access that object is called. It is provider-specific when the data in a deferred column is actually retrieved. For example, it might be retrieved when the command is executed, when the row handle is fetched, lazily in the background, or when **GetData** or a method on another interface is called for the column. If a column is deferred, the DBCOLUMNFLAGS_MAYDEFER enumerated type flag returned by **IColumnsInfo::GetColumnsInfo** is set for the column.

Whether the provider caches the data for a deferred column depends on the setting of the DBCOLUMNFLAGS_CACHEDEFERRED property returned by **GetColumnsInfo**. If this property is set to VARIANT_TRUE, the column value is cached when first read. The cached value is returned whenever the column is read. It can be changed by calling **IRowsetChange::SetData** or **IRowsetRefresh::RefreshVisibleData**. In that case, it is released only when the row handle is released. If the DBCOLUMNFLAGS_CACHEDEFERRED flag is not set, multiple calls to **GetData** can return different values. Otherwise, such calls are not guaranteed to reflect a change to the underlying column unless **RefreshVisibleData** has been called.

Whether or not a column is deferred by default is provider-specific and may vary depending on the column. To retrieve a column as deferred or cache deferred, the consumer sets the DBPROP_DEFERRED or DBPROP_CACHEDEFERRED column property on the column, respectively. To determine whether or not a column is deferred, the consumer checks the DBCOLUMNFLAGS_CACHEDEFERRED and DBCOLUMNFLAGS_MAYDEFER bits in the *dwFlags* element of the DBCOLUMNINFO structure returned by **IColumnsInfo::GetColumnsInfo** or the DBCOLUMN_FLAGS column returned in **IColumnsRowset::GetColumnsRowset**.

Note The value of DBPROP_DEFERRED is automatically set to VARIANT_TRUE if DBPROP_CACHEDEFERRED is set to VARIANT_TRUE.

Using deferred columns increases isolation risk for consumers because deferred data might be read at a different time than nondeferred data. If the consumer is not using repeatable-read transaction isolation or a higher isolation level, it might encounter discrepancies between the original and the deferred access to a row. In particular, the consumer might find that the column is missing because the row has been deleted, or the column might not match the rest of the row. However, under some circumstances, a row version column in conjunction with both original and deferred access can be used to warn a consumer about a situation where a concurrent error has occurred. A consumer can determine whether a column contains a row version by examining the DBCOLUMNFLAGS_ISROWVER flag in **GetColumnInfo**.

Column IDs

Consumers use column IDs primarily when executing commands on data stores for which there are no stable column ordinals. Because column IDs are relatively slow to use on a repeated basis, consumers use column ordinals to identify columns in DBBINDING structures. (For more information about DBBINDING structures, see "DBBINDING Structures" in Chapter 6, "Getting and Setting Data.") A consumer calls **IColumnsInfo::MapColumnIDs** to retrieve a column ordinal from a column ID:

```
typedef struct tagDBID {
   union {
      GUID guid;
      GUID * pguid;
      } uGuid;
      DBKIND eKind;
   union {
      LPOLESTR pwszName;
      ULONG ulPropid;
      } uName;
} DBID;
```

The values of DBKIND are described in the following table.

Value	Meaning
DBKIND_GUID_NAME	Use the *guid* and *pwszName* elements.
DBKIND_GUID_PROPID	Use the *guid* and *ulPropid* elements.
DBKIND_NAME	Use only the *pwszName* element; ignore the *uGuid* element.
DBKIND_PGUID_NAME	Use the *pGuid* and *pwszName* elements.
DBKIND_PGUID_PROPID	Use the *pGuid* and *ulPropid* elements.
DBKIND_PROPID	Use only the *ulPropid* element; ignore the *uGuid* element.
DBKIND_GUID	Use only the *guid* element; ignore the *uName* element.

The members of a DBID are represented in schema rowset columns as follows.

DBID *eKind*	**Schema columns**
DBKIND_GUID_NAME	_GUID and _NAME column values must be provided.
DBKIND_GUID_PROPID	_GUID and _PROPID column values must be provided.
DBKIND_NAME	_NAME column value must be provided.
DBKIND_PGUID_NAME	_GUID and _NAME column values must be provided.
DBKIND_PGUID_PROPID	_GUID and _PROPID column values must be provided.
DBKIND_PROPID	_PROPID column value must be provided.
DBKIND_GUID	_GUID column value must be provided.

Consumers should treat table and column names within DBID structures as case-sensitive.

OLE DB providers never return *pGuid*-style bindings (for example, when the consumer inquires about the bindings for an accessor). They are provided as a convenient shortcut for consumers supplying bindings all covered by the same GUID, which is expected to be common.

The value DB_NULLID is defined as the DBID structure containing all zeroes. Because *pwszName* is a NULL pointer for DB_NULLID, you should not attempt to free this string.

When constructing DBIDs to identify tables, indexes, or columns, consumers use the non-NULL columns in the appropriate schema rowset to determine the DBKIND value of the DBID. For example, when specifying a table ID, a consumer would call **IDBSchemaRowset::GetRowset** and examine the TABLES schema rowset. On discovering that TABLE_NAME has a value and TABLE_GUID is NULL, the consumer specifies DBKIND_NAME for the table ID. In methods that take column DBIDs as parameters, the validation of the DBID should include a check on the validity of the DBID's *eKind*.

Bookmarks

Bookmarks are placeholders that enable the consumer to return quickly to a row. Consumers that use bookmarks to identify rows to a provider should treat bookmarks as opaque binary values. Consumers should not try to interpret these values. Bookmarks are returned in columns in the rowset. An application retrieves them in the same manner as it retrieves data from any other column in the rowset. That is, it creates an accessor that binds to the bookmark column and calls **IRowset::GetData** using this accessor.

Bookmarks are valid only during the lifetime of the rowset to which they refer. For indexes that use bookmarks to reference rows in a base table, the bookmark returned as the pointer column in the index rowset is a valid bookmark in the rowset built over the base table; therefore, the bookmark is valid for the table rowset.

Bookmark columns have DBCOLUMNFLAGS_ISBOOKMARK set in their column information. A bookmark can be of a fixed scalar type such as DBTYPE_I4, or it can be a character sequence that appears, for example, as a DBTYPE_STR column. There is no specialized bookmark data type. Providers can return any valid type indicator in **IColumnsInfo::GetColumnInfo** for a bookmark column.

Bookmarks can always be read and passed as binary values. When using a bookmark to identify a row to a provider, consumers can always bind bookmark values as DBTYPE_BYTES. Alternatively, if the consumer knows the actual DBTYPE of the bookmark, it can bind to that specific type. For more information about data types, see Appendix A, "Data Types."

Bookmarks are not the same thing as primary keys or row IDs (see "Bookmark Types," later in this chapter). They can be related, and it is possible to use a primary key or row ID to implement a bookmark, but often there are more compact or swifter bookmark schemes that work only for the current contents of the rowset. It is important to take advantage of those optimizations in places such as command optimization or result set navigation. Furthermore, bookmarks are not necessarily the same as row handles, because they may have ordering semantics or might be used to track nonresident members of very large rowsets.

A rowset implements only one kind of bookmark. The provider may have incompatible solutions for implementing primary key or row ID semantics on bookmarks, so it cannot support both simultaneously.

Bookmarks operate as logical pointers. The encapsulation allows transient, rowset-level bookmarks to be implemented as pointers, although this would likely be used only for rowsets small enough to be efficiently instantiated.

If **IRowsetLocate** or one of its direct descendants is present on a rowset, column 0 is the bookmark for the rows. Column 0 is present in a rowset only if the rowset has the property DBPROP_BOOKMARKS set to VARIANT_TRUE. Reading this column yields a bookmark value that can be used to position itself again to the same row. This is called the *self bookmark*. Other bookmark columns referring to the same rowset, such as a Spouse column in a query about people, are not self bookmarks.

Bookmark columns can be returned on any rowset, regardless of its source (for example, **ICommand::Execute**, **IOpenRowset::OpenRowset**, **IColumnsRowset::GetColumnsRowset**, or **IDBSchemaRowset::GetRowset**) or whether bookmarks were requested.

The DBIDs of the bookmark columns in a rowset are based on a property set identified by the GUID DBCOL_SPECIALCOL. These DBIDs are constructed as follows:

- The *eKind* element is DBKIND_GUID_PROPID or DBKIND_PGUID_PROPID.
- The *guid* (or *pGuid*) element is, or points to, DBCOL_SPECIALCOL.
- The *ulPropid* element is 2 for the self bookmark. It is greater than 2 for bookmarks other than the self bookmark. The *ulPropid* element must not be the same as the *ulPropid* element in the DBID of another bookmark in the same rowset.
- If bookmark column A appears before bookmark column B in the specification of the rowset, the *ulPropid* element in the DBID of bookmark column A is less than the *ulPropid* element in the DBID of bookmark column B.

The DBIDs of bookmark columns can be passed to **IColumnsInfo::MapColumnIDs** to determine the ordinals of those columns. There is no need to pass the DBID of the self bookmark column to **MapColumnIDs**, because the ordinal of this column is always zero.

Bookmark Types

OLE DB supports two kinds of bookmarks: numeric and key value. The DBPROP_BOOKMARKTYPE property indicates the bookmarks that a provider supports.

Numeric Bookmarks

Numeric bookmarks are based on a position or index into the rows selected for a rowset. In most cases, the rowset builds a set of information about the rows, which enables the same row to be retrieved easily. It does not guarantee the existence or consistency of those rows throughout the transaction; that still depends on the transaction isolation level. It returns the same row entity if it can.

The numeric value can be of any size. A small rowset might use a 16-bit index, whereas a rowset against an Oracle table might use Oracle ROWIDs, which are around 6 bytes each. There is no significance to the ordering of numeric values, either logical or physical. The implementation should simply be fast.

If the primary key value of a row is changed while working with a row for which the consumer has a numeric bookmark, the bookmark still points to the same row instance. This is required for a numeric bookmark. The row also has a nonoverlapping candidate key; the primary key may change entirely, but the same value remains in the candidate key column.

Key Value Bookmarks

When a rowset is ordered and there is some combination of columns (not necessarily the primary keys of the base tables) that form a unique key for each row, it becomes useful to use these values as a bookmark. At first it might seem redundant, because one could expect an interface such as **IRowsetIndex** to take key values and rapidly return a numeric bookmark. However, the numeric bookmark itself may be costly and unwanted. In some cases, the key values enable the provider to access the underlying tables without storing any kind of temporary table.

With a key value bookmark, a consumer could, in theory, synthesize a set of values that could occur but do not. The result of doing this is undefined; that is, providers are not required to detect forgeries.

If the key value columns of a row are changed while working with a row for which the consumer has a key value bookmark, the bookmark can become disassociated or point to a new row that usurps the old values.

Comparing Bookmarks

Bookmarks can be compared only if they belong to the same rowset and are used within the lifetime of that rowset. The results of comparing bookmarks from different rowsets, or outside the lifetime of the rowset to which they belong, are undefined.

The optimal way to compare bookmarks is by a direct memory comparison. However, some rowsets may include hints within the bookmark that depend on time or rowset generation. This might cause binary comparisons between two bookmarks for the same row to fail. If the provider does put hints in the bookmarks, they must expose **IRowsetLocate**, which has methods to compare two bookmarks and to return a stable hash value for a bookmark.

If the DBPROP_LITERALBOOKMARKS property is VARIANT_TRUE, consumers can do the comparison themselves. The method used depends on the scalar type of the bookmark. For example, if the bookmark was defined as a sequence of DBTYPE_BYTES values, the comparison is of unsigned bytes, with the most significant byte in position 0.

A consumer does not need an ordered query to have ordered bookmarks. In particular, it does not need an SQL **ORDER BY** clause. If a consumer requests **SELECT * FROM** *Table-name* and the smart query processor delivers the scan in the least-cost physical seek order (meaningless ordering in terms of content), the consumer can still be given a rowset with ordered bookmarks. To guarantee ordered bookmarks, the consumer specifies the DBPROP_ORDEREDBOOKMARKS property as VARIANT_TRUE in **ICommandProperties::SetProperties**. For some providers, bookmarks are always ordered.

If DBPROP_ORDEREDBOOKMARKS is VARIANT_TRUE, the order of the bookmarks reflects the order of delivery. That is, if the consumer has bookmark $i < j$, it calls **IRowsetLocate::GetRowsAt** for bookmark *i* and keeps scanning. It is guaranteed to find *j* unless it is deleted. If it is deleted, the consumer can see the gap in order as it passes by. Conversely, if the consumer starts at *j* and scans forward, it never sees *i*. It just reaches the end of the rowset.

Standard Bookmarks

Three standard bookmark values are provided: DBBMK_INVALID, DBBMK_FIRST, and DBBMK_LAST. All single-byte (length 1) bookmark values of type DBTYPE_BYTES are reserved for standard bookmarks. Ordinary bookmarks of type DBTYPE_BYTES must be at least length 2. The following constant is defined in Oledb.h as the standard bookmark length:

```
#define STD_BOOKMARKLENGTH 1
```

The values of the standard bookmarks listed in the following table are guaranteed to be the same for all providers.

Value	Meaning
DBBMK_INVALID	DBBMK_INVALID can be used by applications to initialize and subsequently check bookmark validity.
DBBMK_FIRST	The first row of the rowset. A consumer can fetch forward from this point. For example, if *cRows* is greater than zero and *lRowsOffset* is zero, **IRowsetLocate::GetRowsAt** returns the first *cRows* rows of the rowset. A consumer cannot fetch backward before this point. For example, if *cRows* is -1 and *lRowsOffset* is zero, **GetRowsAt** returns this row. If *cRows* is less than –1, it then returns DB_S_ENDOFROWSET.
DBBMK_LAST	The last row of the rowset. If the rowset is being populated asynchronously, this is the last row identified so far. A consumer can fetch backward from this point. For example, if *cRows* is less than zero and *lRowsOffset* is zero, **GetRowsAt** returns the last *cRows* rows of the rowset. A consumer cannot fetch forward past this point. For example, if *cRows* is one and *lRowsOffset* is zero, **GetRowsAt** returns this row. If *cRows* is greater than one, it then returns DB_S_ENDOFROWSET.

The consumer can begin a sequential scan at either the first or last row.

Invalid Bookmarks

A bookmark can become invalid for any of the following reasons:

- The row it points to is deleted.
- It is based on a primary key, and some of those key values were changed.
- The row it points to is no longer in the rowset. This occurs only in rowsets that support DBPROP_OWNUPDATEDELETE when a row is changed in such a way that it no longer meets the search criteria of the rowset, is released, and then is refetched by **IRowset::GetNextRows**. For example, if the rowset contains only those rows with a job title of Assistant Manager, changing the job title in a row to Manager would remove that row from the rowset. From the point of view of that rowset, the row was deleted.

Bookmarks that have been returned by the provider are guaranteed to have predictable behavior, even if they have become invalid. If the DBPROP_BOOKMARKSKIPPED property is VARIANT_TRUE, the provider skips the bookmarked row and proceeds to the next row. If the DBPROP_BOOKMARKSKIPPED property is not VARIANT_TRUE, the provider usually returns an error. The provider must never terminate abnormally for a bookmark that it has returned to the user.

However, it is a programming error to pass a random bookmark value that has not been obtained from the provider. The effect of specifying an unknown, random bookmark value is undefined and might include abnormal termination.

Views

By creating a view object, providers that do not support full command syntax can still expose simple operations such as sorting or filtering a rowset. Views can be applied when opening a rowset, or they can be applied to an existing rowset to return either a new chapter on that rowset or a completely new rowset with the additional functionality. OLE DB view objects are not equivalent to SQL92 views and cannot be used to combine multiple results.

Views are similar to commands, with the following restrictions:

- The source of the view is a single rowset, fixed at the time the view is created.
- Views support only simple operations such as filtering and sorting. They do not support complex semantics such as subqueries, joins, or dynamic parameters.

View operations are expressed through method calls as opposed to textual statements.

- The view object cotype is defined as follows. For more information about cotypes, see "OLE DB Objects" in Chapter 1, "Overview of OLE DB."

```
CoType TView {
   [mandatory] interface IColumnsInfo;
   [optional]  interface IAccessor;
   [optional]  interface ISupportErrorInfo;
   [optional]  interface IViewChapter;
   [optional]  interface IViewFilter;
   [optional]  interface IViewRowset;
   [optional]  interface IViewSort;
};
```

Views are created either by applying a view when opening a rowset or by applying a view to an existing rowset. A view object may be returned in place of a rowset when executing any rowset-returning method.

- To apply a view when opening a rowset, the following steps occur:

  1. The consumer requests one of the following properties from the View property group (either directly or by requesting the associated IID) when opening the rowset:

     DBPROP_IVIEWCHAPTER

     DBPROP_IVIEWFILTER

     DBPROP_IVIEWROWSET

     DBPROP_IVIEWSORT

     When one or more of these properties are set, the consumer must request an interface supported by a view object or the provider will return E_NOINTERFACE. Requesting any other interface when opening the rowset, and not explicitly requesting an interface from the View property group, returns the rowset object, regardless of other properties specified on the rowset.

  2. The consumer applies operations such as filtering and sorting to the view object through interfaces such as **IViewFilter** and **IViewSort**.

  3. The consumer calls **IViewRowset::OpenViewRowset** on the view object to return the actual rowset with the view applied.

- To apply a view to an existing rowset, the following steps occur:
  1. The consumer calls **IRowsetView::CreateView** on the rowset.
  2. The consumer applies operations such as filtering and sorting to the view object through interfaces such as **IViewFilter** and **IViewSort**.
  3. The consumer calls **IViewChapter::OpenViewChapter** on the view to return a new chapter on the original rowset that reflects the view operations.
     - or -
     The consumer calls **IViewRowset::OpenViewRowset** on the view to return a new rowset with the view operations applied.

Chapters

Chapters are used to identify a group of rows within a rowset. The group of rows may have a common characteristic, such as satisfying a filter condition or having a common parent in a hierarchical rowset, and may have an imposed order. Chapter handles are defined as follows:

```
typedef ULONG HCHAPTER;
```

Because chapters have significant overhead, they must be managed. This is done automatically according to the following rules:

- The rules for sequential rowsets take precedence, so a grouped sequential rowset's chapters can be opened only in the proper sequence and cannot be revisited after they have been scanned. It might be necessary to close a prior chapter before the next can be opened.
- A chapter is opened upon use, if it is not already in an active state.

When the reference count on a chapter is released to zero, the resources needed to manage the chapter can be discarded or marked as eligible for discard. However, if the reference count on a chapter falls to zero and the chapter contains rows with pending changes, the chapter's resources might not be freed until the pending change status on the rows is cleared through a call to either **IRowsetUpdate::Update** or **IRowsetUpdate::Undo**.

Hierarchical Rowsets

A *rowset hierarchy* is a collection of rowsets linked together by using chapters. Hierarchies model 1:*n* relationships between tables, such as a master-detail relationship between Customers, Orders, and Items. A rowset hierarchy can be stored persistently in a data source object or computed by a command. This section discusses only computed hierarchies.

Chapters are identifiers of groups of details within a rowset. Chapters work as distinct collections with a beginning and an end but also share the facilities, such as accessors and notifications, of the rowset to which they belong.

The following example illustrates how a computed hierarchy is generated. The database schema contains the following three tables:

```
CREATE TABLE customer_table
        ( cust_no    INTEGER,
        cust_name    VARCHAR(20),
        city         VARCHAR(20),
        PRIMARY KEY (cust_no) )

CREATE TABLE order_table
        ( cust_no    INTEGER,
        ord_no       INTEGER,
        ord_date     DATE,
        total        DECIMAL(9,2),
        PRIMARY KEY (ord_no),
        FOREIGN KEY (cust_no) REFERENCES customer_table )

CREATE TABLE order_item_table
        ( ord_no        INTEGER,
        item_no         INTEGER,
        description     VARCHAR(30),
        quantity        SMALLINT,
        unit_price      DECIMAL(6,2),
        PRIMARY KEY (ord_no, item_no),
        FOREIGN KEY (ord_no, REFERENCES order_table )
```

The following extended SQL command generates a rowset hierarchy. The syntax of this query is used only for illustration. Providers may use other syntaxes to generate hierarchy.

```
SELECT (cust_no,
         cust_name,
         city,
         SELECT (ord_no,
               ord_date,
               total,
               SELECT (item_no,
                        description,
                        quantity,
                        unit_price,
                        (quantity * unit_price) AS ext_price
                        )
                  FROM order_item_table
                  WHERE order_item_table.ord_no = order_table.ord_no
                  AS item_rows
                  )
            FROM order_table
            WHERE order_table.cust_no = customer_table.cust_no
            AS order_rows
         )
   FROM customer_table
```

One Rowset for Each Hierarchy Level

The result of the preceding command contains three rowsets. Each rowset represents a complete hierarchy level in the result. The root rowset—the rowset returned from **ICommand::Execute**, which we call the Customer rowset—contains columns cust_no, cust_name, and city, as well as a chaptered column named order_rows. The second rowset, which we call the Orders rowset, contains columns ord_no, ord_date, and total, as well as a chaptered column named item_rows. Finally, the third rowset, which we call the Items rowset, contains columns item_no, description, quantity, unit_price, and ext_price.

A single rowset may apply to more than one level of a recursive set of objects, but the specification also uses recursion so that the rowset is defined only once in the specification, and all bookmarks or chapters refer to that. Hence there is only one rowset at execution time.

Navigating Hierarchical Rowsets

When the consumer executes a hierarchical query, the method returns the requested interface on the root rowset. This root rowset contains one or more chapter columns.

Before using a chapter, the consumer must obtain a pointer to the child rowset by passing the ordinal of the chapter-valued column to either **IParentRowset::GetChildRowset** or **IRowsetInfo::GetReferencedRowset**. Consumers use **GetChildRowset** to obtain an aggregated instance of the child rowset. They use **GetReferencedRowset** to obtain a reference on a previously retrieved rowset or to create an instance of a nonaggregated rowset if the child rowset does not already exist.

Calling **GetReferencedRowset** for a child rowset that has already been obtained takes an additional reference count on that rowset. Calling **GetReferencedRowset** for a child rowset that has not previously been obtained returns the requested interface on a nonaggregated instance of the rowset.

GetChildRowset can be called only once for each child rowset and, if called, must be called before any calls to **GetReferencedRowset** for that child. The *pUnkOuter* argument specified in **GetChildRowset** defines the controlling unknown for all references to that child rowset for the lifetime of the parent. The parent rowset must call **AddRef** on this controlling unknown to guarantee that it doesn't go away before the parent. Even though the controlling unknown is constant for the lifetime of the parent, the consumer must not assume that rowset state information, such as accessors and row position, is held when all references to the rowset are released. Furthermore, providers must ensure that the next fetch position within the child rowset is reset once all references to that child rowset have been released. Calling **GetChildRowset** for a child rowset that has already been obtained returns DB_E_OBJECTOPEN.

For example, after executing the above command and calling **IParentRowset::GetChildRowset** with the ordinal of the order_rows column, the consumer can get an additional reference on the Orders rowset by calling **GetReferencedRowset** on the Customer rowset with the ordinal of the order_rows column.

The consumer navigates rows inside a chapter by using methods such as **IRowset::GetNextRows**, **IRowsetLocate::GetRowsAt**, and **IRowsetLocate::GetRowsByBookmark**, passing the chapter handle obtained from a parent rowset as an input argument to the method. For example, suppose the Customer rowset has a row for Jones containing a chapter *chJonesOrders*. Jones's orders are fetched by calling **GetNextRows** on the Customer rowset and passing *chJonesOrders* as an input argument to the method.

Chapter Columns

The consumer obtains chapter handles by calling **IRowset::GetData** with an appropriate accessor. For example, the rowset Customer has a chapter-valued column order_rows containing chapter handles referring to rows in the Orders rowset. The order_rows column in Customer has DBCOLUMNFLAGS_ISCHAPTER set in its column information. Chapter handles are DWORD values of type DBTYPE_HCHAPTER. The chapter values obtained from Customer are used to navigate rows in the Orders rowset, and the chapter values from Customer work as long as the Orders rowset remains active.

Chapters and Detail Groupings

Each grouping of a detail set, such as the orders for a particular customer, is treated as a subset with a particular beginning and end. A chapter identifies this detail group. A chapter is usually a partial key to the details. Because it is partial, it might lead to a set rather than a single row. The functions that take a chapter as a parameter, such as **GetRowsAt**, use the beginning, membership, and end specified by the chapter to limit the rows that the request may return.

Chapters are opened as they are used, with usage tracked by reference counts. This is done transparently and allows the provider to minimize overhead dedicated to chapters. A reference count is taken on the chapter handle each time it is retrieved through **GetRowsAt** on the parent rowset, or by calling **IChapteredRowset::AddRefChapter**. The reference counts must be explicitly released by using **IChapteredRowset::ReleaseChapter** on the child rowset (that is, the rowset on which the chapter handle is used).

Although a chapter value may be held in a column of a table, that value is not the same thing as the physical instantiation of the chapter. The chapter may be instantiated when a command is executed or on demand when the chapter value is used. In any case, the actual chapter belongs not to the rowset that had the value column but to the rowset within which the chapter is defined. In the hierarchy example shown earlier in the section "Hierarchical Rowsets," the chapter handles for the Customer-Orders portion of the hierarchy above are in the order_rows column in Customer but the members of the chapter are in the Orders rowset. Hence, the release of a chapter is an action on the rowset owning the content. (In the example above, the consumer would use **pOrders->ReleaseChapter(...)**).

When chapters and bookmarks are used together, the chapter does not qualify the bookmark. But methods that take bookmarks also take a chapter, and if several bookmarks (**IRowsetLocate::GetRowsByBookmark**) are used, they must all be in the same chapter. This is a consequence of managing the overheads of chapters. Because multiple chapters may contain a reference to the same row, the consumer needs to choose which chapter to use. The chapter acts to restrict the domain of rows, which can be retrieved. Bookmarks are unique within the chapter from which they are returned.

Lifetime of Row Handles Within Chapters

The lifetime of row handles and the lifetime of their containing chapters are handled independently. Releasing a row handle containing a chapter does not imply that the row handles contained in the chapter are released or that the chapter contained in the row handle being released becomes invalid. To invalidate a chapter, the consumer must explicitly release it. Also, chapters may be used when navigating a child rowset, even after their containing row handle in the parent rowset has been released.

However, some providers keep an implicit reference on the parent row handle until the chapter handle obtained from that row is released. Therefore, if the DBPROP_CANHOLDROWS property is VARIANT_FALSE for the rowset, the consumer cannot obtain additional rows from the parent rowset until all chapters are released for the current set of held row handles. As a standard practice, consumers wanting to work with any provider should release all references on chapter handles before attempting to retrieve additional rows.

Providers may impose additional restrictions, such as supporting only one active chapter at a time on a rowset. For such providers, the consumer must call **ReleaseChapter** for any retrieved chapters before calling **GetData** in order to retrieve (and thus implicitly take a reference on) another chapter handle. In this case, attempting to call **GetData** on a column containing a chapter handle returns DB_E_CHAPTERNOTRELEASED.

Releasing Rowsets

When the consumer is done with the rowset, it must release it as follows:

- If the consumer has created any accessors on the rowset, it must release them by calling **IAccessor::ReleaseAccessor** on each accessor individually.
- To release the rowset object itself, the consumer must call **IUnknown::Release** on each interface pointer retrieved on the rowset. When the rowset is released, it forces the release of any remaining row handles the consumer holds. Such handle objects are subordinate to the rowset and cannot cause it to linger beyond the point where all the interfaces for the rowset have been released. The rowset is responsible for cleaning up all such subordinate objects.

  Note If the consumer obtained the rowset by executing a command containing output parameters and the provider populates output parameters when the rowset is released (that is, the value of DBPROP_OUTPUTPARAMETERAVAILABILITY is DBPROP_OA_ATROWRELEASE), the consumer must ensure that memory allocated for the output parameters that were bound at **Execute** time must still be valid when the rowset is released. Not doing so is a serious programming error that can cause abnormal termination.

CHAPTER 5

Updating Data in Rowsets

Consumers can change row data either through commands, such as the **UPDATE**, **DELETE**, and **INSERT** commands in SQL, or through rowsets. This chapter discusses how consumers, by calling methods in **IRowsetChange**, change row data through rowsets. Two update modes are presented: immediate and deferred. The visibility of changes is discussed, both as it relates to the state of the row and as it relates to other changes affecting the row. Inserting rows in the desired position, resynchronizing rows, and refreshing row values are also discussed.

For more information on	Go to
Consumers	"Consumers and Providers" in Chapter 1, "Overview of OLE DB"
Commands	Chapter 3, "Commands"
Rowsets	Chapter 4, "Rowsets"
Changing data by calling **SetData**, **DeleteRows**, and **InsertRow** in **IRowsetChange**	"Changing Data" in this chapter
Immediate vs. deferred update mode	"Immediate vs. Deferred Update Mode" in this chapter
The state of the row in deferred update mode	"Row States in Deferred Update Mode" in this chapter
Visibility of changes	"Visibility of Changes" in this chapter
Other changes affecting the row	"Visibility of Other Changes" in this chapter
Inserting rows in the desired position	"Position of Inserted Rows" in this chapter
Refreshing row values	"Refreshing Row Data" in this chapter

Changing Data

Providers that allow consumers to change rowset data do so by exposing **IRowsetChange** on the rowset object. Consumers use the methods in **IRowsetChange** to update the values of columns in existing rows, delete existing rows, or insert new rows. These methods operate on the rows in the rowset. Whether these changes are immediately transmitted to the underlying data store depends on whether the rowset exposes **IRowsetUpdate**.

If the rowset does not expose **IRowsetUpdate**, it is said to be in *immediate update mode*. In immediate update mode, the methods in **IRowsetChange** transmit changes from the rowset to the underlying data store, where they become visible to other transactions running at the Read Uncommitted transaction isolation level. Such changes are called *transmitted changes*.

If the rowset does expose **IRowsetUpdate**, it is said to be in *deferred update mode*. In deferred update mode, the methods in **IRowsetChange** do not transmit changes to the data store. Instead, they buffer the changes in the rowset. Such changes are *pending changes*. While changes are pending, they are wholly local to the rowset and therefore not visible to other transactions, even those running at the Read Uncommitted isolation level.

To transmit pending changes to the underlying data store, the consumer calls **IRowsetUpdate::Update**. As in immediate update mode, such changes then become visible to other transactions running at the Read Uncommitted transaction isolation level and are transmitted changes.

If the rowset was created in the context of a transaction, the consumer can commit or abort transmitted changes by calling **ITransaction::Commit** or **ITransaction::Abort**. Committed changes become visible to other transactions running at the Read Committed transaction isolation level. If the consumer commits or aborts transmitted changes and there are still pending changes, what happens to those pending changes depends on the DBPROP_COMMITPRESERVE and DBPROP_ABORTPRESERVE properties. For more information, see Commit and Abort Behavior in Chapter 12, "Transactions."

The following illustration shows how the methods in **IRowsetChange**, **IRowsetUpdate**, and **ITransaction** update data.

IRowsetChange, IRowsetUpdate, and ITransaction methods updating data

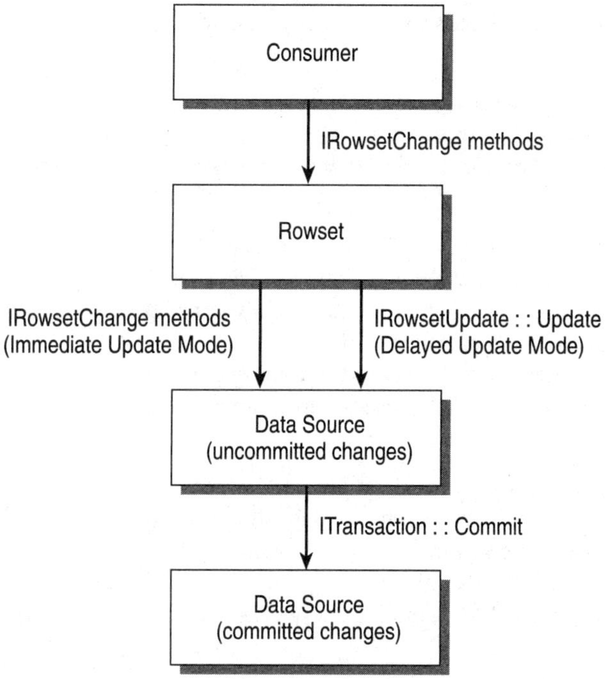

To get a read-only rowset, the consumer does not request **IRowsetChange** or **IRowsetUpdate** as a property of the rowset.

Immediate vs. Deferred Update Mode

Whether the consumer uses immediate or deferred update mode depends on how many consumers share the rowset and how they use the rowset. In most cases, the primary user of immediate update mode is a single consumer that wants to transmit changes immediately to the data store. Consumers use deferred update mode for many reasons, including the following:

- **Shared rowsets**—If multiple consumers share a rowset, they often use notifications to coordinate multiple changes. By using deferred update mode, consumers can coordinate their changes locally in the rowset before transmitting them to the data store.
- **Multiple changes to the same row**—If a consumer makes multiple changes to the same row, such as when multiple accessors are used or when users input changes at different times, the row might be left in an invalid state. For example, if a key consists of several columns and each column is changed in a separate call to **IRowsetChange::SetData**, the intermediate states might be invalid. By using deferred update mode, the consumer can buffer these changes in the rowset before transmitting them to the data store.
- **Network traffic**—If a rowset resides on one node in a network and the data store resides on another node, transmitting changes from the rowset to the data store requires a network call. By using deferred update mode, the consumer can batch changes to multiple rows and send them across the network with a single call to **IRowsetUpdate::Update**. This is particularly critical for wide area networks such as the Internet, on which network calls are very expensive.
- **Undoing changes—IRowsetUpdate::Undo** enables the consumer to undo pending changes. By using deferred update mode, consumers can expose an undo capability to users without having to implement it.

Row States in Deferred Update Mode

A row has a state that depends on whether it has been changed and whether that change is pending or transmitted. Consumers call **IRowsetUpdate::GetRowStatus** to determine the state of a row. They call **IRowsetUpdate::GetPendingRows** to get all rows in a pending change state. The state is indicated by the DBPENDINGSTATUS enumerated type. The values in this type and their meanings are listed in the following table.

Status value	Row state	Description
DBPENDINGSTATUS_ NEW	Pending Insert	The row has a pending insert.
DBPENDINGSTATUS_ CHANGED	Pending Update	The row has a deferred change.
DBPENDINGSTATUS_ DELETED	Pending Delete	The row has a pending delete. This state is sometimes called *soft delete*.
DBPENDINGSTATUS_ UNCHANGED	Unchanged	No changes have been made to the row, or changes that were made to the row have been transmitted or undone.
DBPENDINGSTATUS_ INVALIDROW	Invalid	The row has been deleted and that deletion has been transmitted to the data store. This status is also used when a row handle passed to **GetRowStatus** was invalid. This state is sometimes called *hard delete*.

The Unchanged and Invalid states are the *nonpending change states*. The Pending Insert, Pending Update, and Pending Delete states are the *pending change states*. The following illustration shows these states, how methods affect them, and the corresponding DBPENDINGSTATUS values.

Pending change states

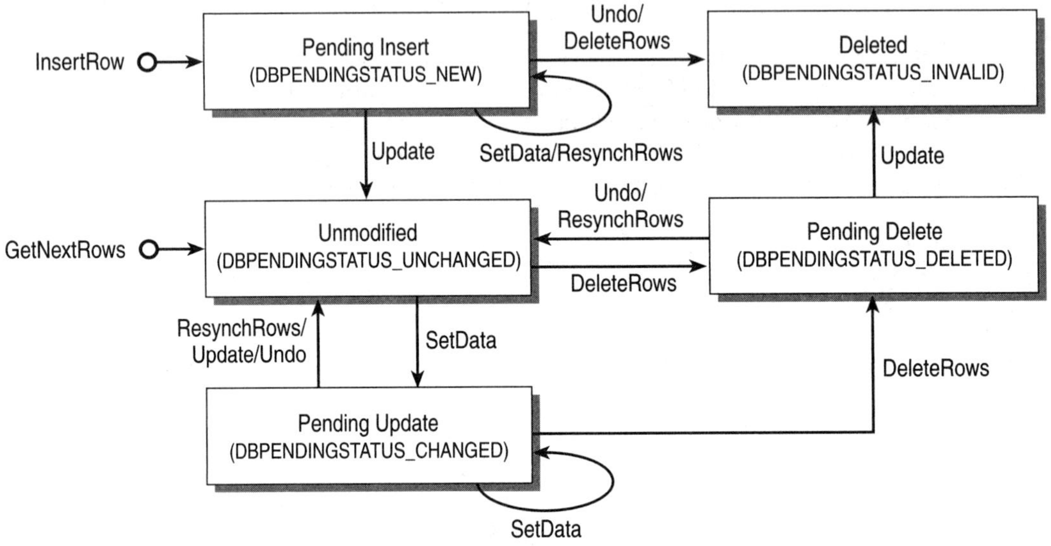

If the consumer calls **IRowset::ReleaseRows** for a row and the reference count for that row falls to zero, release of the row and its resources depends on the row's state. In the nonpending change states, the row and its resources are usually released when the reference count falls to zero, although the actual point of release is provider-specific.

In the pending change states, the row and its resources are not released when the reference count falls to zero, nor are the pending changes lost. The row remains valid until the changes are transmitted or *undone* (the row moves to a nonpending change state), and then the row and its resources are released. Rows in a pending change state that have a reference count of zero are still considered active when, for example, calculating row limits such as those returned by the DBPROP_MAXOPENROWS and DBPROP_MAXPENDINGROWS properties. Although the row handle might remain valid for such rows, consumers should not rely on this.

Visibility of Changes

If a consumer makes a change to a row in a rowset, releases the row handle for that row, refetches the same row from the data store into the rowset, and calls **IRowset::GetData** on the row, does the consumer see the change it made? If so, then the change is said to be *visible* to the rowset. If other rowsets also make changes to the same row, those changes may or may not be visible to the first rowset.

Whether a change to a row is visible, and to whom, depends on many factors, such as whether the change is pending or transmitted, whether it affects the row's position in the rowset, and whether it was made inside a transaction. It also depends on the values of various rowset properties. The following sections discuss these properties and their effects on visibility of changes.

Visibility of Pending Changes

If the consumer completely releases and then refetches a row that has a pending update or delete, the visibility of that pending update or delete depends on whether DBPROP_LITERALIDENTITY is set to VARIANT_TRUE. If DBPROP_LITERALIDENTITY is set to VARIANT_TRUE, the rowset contains only one copy of any given row. Therefore, the rowset recognizes that the newly fetched row matches the existing row, which contains the pending update or delete, and returns a handle through which the pending update or delete is visible. If DBPROP_LITERALIDENTITY is not set to VARIANT_TRUE, the rowset can contain multiple copies of the same row and might return a handle through which the pending update or delete is not visible. For more information, see "Uniqueness of Rows in the Rowset" in Chapter 4, "Rowsets."

Whether methods that fetch rows can retrieve pending insert rows (that is, rows that have been inserted in deferred update mode but for which **IRowsetUpdate::Update** has not been called) depends on the DBPROP_RETURNPENDINGINSERTS property.

> **Note** Many providers cannot return pending inserts because they use the row-returning mechanisms of the data store. Because pending inserts have not yet been transmitted to the data store, the mechanisms there cannot return them.

Visibility of Transmitted Changes

If a consumer completely releases and then refetches a row for which changes have been transmitted to the data store, the visibility of those changes depends on the values of the DBPROP_OWNUPDATEDELETE, DBPROP_OWNINSERT, and DBPROP_REMOVEDELETED properties. When multiple consumers share the same rowset, these properties apply to all changes transmitted by any consumer of the rowset. For more information, see "Rowset Properties" in Appendix C, "Property Tables."

Position of Inserted Rows

The DBPROP_IMMOBILEROWS property specifies the position of inserted rows, both pending and transmitted, in the rowset. If this property is VARIANT_TRUE, inserted rows always appear at the end of the rowset. If this property is VARIANT_FALSE, inserted rows appear in the rowset's proper order if the rowset is ordered, or in indeterminate order if the rowset is not ordered.

For information about whether inserted rows are visible, see "Visibility of Pending Changes" and "Visibility of Transmitted Changes" earlier in this chapter.

Visibility of Other Changes

If a consumer completely releases and then refetches a row handle on a row that has been changed by another rowset or consumer, whether the consumer can see these changes depends on the DBPROP_OTHERUPDATEDELETE and DBPROP_OTHERINSERT properties.

The visibility of changes made by other rowsets in the same transaction depends only on these properties. It does not depend on the transaction isolation level because the changes are in the same transaction.

The visibility of changes made by applications outside the current transaction depends on the values of these properties as well as on the transaction isolation level, as shown in the following table.

Property value	Read uncommitted	Read committed	Repeatable read	Serializable
DBPROP_OTHERUPDATE-DELETE:				
VARIANT_TRUE	Yes	Yes	No	No
VARIANT_FALSE	No	No	No	No
DBPROP_OTHERINSERT:				
VARIANT_TRUE	Yes	Yes	Yes	No
VARIANT_FALSE	No	No	No	No

Refreshing Row Data

A consumer can refresh the row data in its data buffer by completely releasing its row handles, refetching the rows into the rowset, and retrieving the data from the rowset's copies of the refetched rows. However, this process is somewhat cumbersome, particularly for applications in which multiple consumers are making changes to the same rows in the data store. To address the needs of such consumers, providers can support the **IRowsetRefresh** interface.

The methods in **IRowsetRefresh** enable the consumer to refetch rows from the data store into the rowset and to refresh row data in its own data buffer. To update rows in the rowset with data that is currently visible to the rowset in the data store, the consumer calls **IRowsetRefresh::RefreshVisibleData**. If *fOverwrite* is set to TRUE in the call to **RefreshVisibleData**, the provider discards any pending changes to a given row and accepts the visible values from the data store as the current values. If *fOverwrite* is set to FALSE, pending changes are not discarded. After calling **RefreshVisibleData**, the consumer calls **IRowsetRefresh::GetLastVisibleData** to retrieve the new row data into its data buffer.

> **Note** For deferred columns and for providers that do not cache visible data in the rowset, calling **RefreshVisibleData** with *fOverwrite* set to FALSE has no effect. However, consumers that need to work with general providers should always call **RefreshVisibleData** before calling **GetLastVisibleData** for any nondeferred columns; thus, they can be sure they get the latest data values from the data store.

GetLastVisibleData also allows the consumer to fetch row data directly from the data store, bypassing the rowset, when necessary to diagnose and repair collisions that occur under optimistic concurrency control. For more information, see "IRowsetRefresh::GetLastVisibleData" in the reference section.

Although the ability to obtain visible data is influenced by the DBPROP_OWNUPDATEDELETE, DBPROP_OWNINSERT, DBPROP_OTHERUPDATEDELETE, and DBPROP_OTHERINSERT properties, it is independent of them. In other words, the value of these properties can be VARIANT_FALSE and the rowset can still expose **IRowsetRefresh**. However, because this is often difficult for providers to implement, many rowsets do not expose **IRowsetRefresh** unless the values of the DBPROP_OWNUPDATEDELETE and DBPROP_OTHERUPDATEDELETE properties are VARIANT_TRUE.

CHAPTER 6

Getting and Setting Data

This chapter discusses how data is transferred between OLE DB consumers and providers and introduces the three parts of data—*value, length* of the value, and *status* of the value. An *accessor* is a collection of information that describes how data is stored in the consumer's buffer. A special type, the reference accessor, is also discussed in this chapter. Defined another way, an accessor is a collection of *bindings*, and each binding associates a single column or parameter to the consumer's buffer. DBBINDING structures, memory management, and data transfer complete this chapter's discussion of getting and setting data.

For more information on	Go to
Consumers and providers	"Consumers and Providers" in Chapter 1, "Overview of OLE DB"
OLE DB objects	"OLE DB Objects" in Chapter 1, "Overview of OLE DB"
Length of a data value	"Length" in this chapter
Status of a data value	"Status" in this chapter
Accessors	"Accessors" in this chapter
Optimized accessors	"Optimized Accessors" in this chapter
Reference accessors	"Reference Accessors" in this chapter
DBBINDING structures	"Bindings" in this chapter
Memory management in data transfer	"Responsibility for Freeing Memory" in this chapter
Data transfer procedures	"Data Transfer Procedures" in this chapter

Data refers collectively to parameter data and rowset data. *Parameter data* is the data used for parameters in commands. For example, in the text command **SELECT * FROM MyTable WHERE Name = ?**, the question mark represents a parameter and the consumer sends data for this parameter to the provider when the consumer executes the command. *Rowset data* is the data returned in a rowset, for example, the rowset generated by executing the command (such as the **SELECT *** statement in this paragraph) and the key column values passed to an *index rowset* when setting the index range or searching for a key value. (For more information on index rowsets, see Chapter 8, "Index Rowsets.")

Data is stored in both the consumer and the provider. The consumer stores data in a buffer. A *binding* associates, or *binds*, a single column or parameter in the data store to a column in the consumer's buffer. A group of bindings is gathered together in an *accessor*. When transferring data, the consumer passes the provider a handle to the accessor and a pointer to the consumer's data buffer. In the provider, how a rowset's row data is handled is provider-specific. For example, row data can be cached in a set of row buffers belonging to the rowset. Or it may be passed directly to and from the data store.

The provider transfers the data from consumer to provider and provider to consumer. *Getting* data is defined as transferring data from the provider to the consumer, as when getting rowset data with **IRowset::GetData** or getting output parameter data with **ICommand::Execute**. *Setting* data is defined as transferring data from the consumer to the provider, as when setting rowset data with **IRowsetChange::SetData**, key values with **IRowsetIndex::SetRange**, or input parameter data with **Execute**.

Binding Data Values

In OLE DB, a data value has three parts: *value*, *length* (for variable-length data types), and *status*. The consumer can bind one, two, or all three of these parts. Usually the consumer binds all three.

If the consumer is getting data and does not bind a part, the provider does not return that part. Although this is not an error, the result is generally of little or no use. For example, if the consumer binds the status but not the value and calls **SetData** with a status of DBSTATUS_S_ISNULL, the provider writes a null value to the column. If the provider attempts to call **SetData** with this binding and a status of DBSTATUS_S_OK, the provider returns an error.

If the consumer is setting data and does not bind a part, the provider sends the data if it has sufficient information; otherwise, it returns an error. For example, if the consumer binds the status but not the value, the provider sets the value to NULL and the status to DBSTATUS_S_ISNULL. If the consumer had already set the status to DBSTATUS_S_OK, the provider sets the value to NULL, sets the status to DBSTATUS_S_ISNULL, and returns an error.

The following table explains the behavior of the consumer and provider for each combination of bound parts.

Value	Length	Status	Use when getting data	Use when setting data
Y	Y	Y	Most commonly used combination when getting variable-length data.	Most commonly used combination when setting variable-length data.
Y	Y	N	Not generally used. If the method returns DB_S_ERRORSOCCURRED or DB_E_ERRORSOCCURRED, the consumer must assume that the method did not successfully get or set the value for the column. If the column is nullable, the consumer cannot determine the validity of the returned value or length because it does not know whether the column value is NULL.	Not generally used. If the method returns DB_S_ERRORSOCCURRED or DB_E_ERRORSOCCURRED, the consumer must assume that the method did not successfully get or set the value for the column. The provider assumes the status is DBSTATUS_S_OK.
Y	N	Y	Most commonly used combination when getting fixed-length data.[1]	Most commonly used combination when setting fixed-length data. The provider assumes that string data is null-terminated.[2]
Y	N	N	Not generally used. If the method returns DB_S_ERRORSOCCURRED or DB_E_ERRORSOCCURRED, the consumer must assume that it did not successfully get or set the value for the column. If the column is nullable, the consumer cannot determine the validity of the returned value or length because it does not know whether the column value is NULL.	Not generally used. If the method returns DB_S_ERRORSOCCURRED or DB_E_ERRORSOCCURRED, the consumer must assume that it did not successfully get or set the value for the column. The provider assumes the status is DBSTATUS_S_OK. The provider assumes that string data is null-terminated.

Value	Length	Status	Use when getting data	Use when setting data
N	Y	Y	Used to get the length and status of the value (for example, to allocate memory for variable-length data) without actually refreshing the value.	Used to specify the length of a long variable-length column prior to passing any data. This is required by providers that must know the number of bytes of BLOB data that will be sent before any data is sent. If **IColumnsInfo::GetColumnInfo** does not return DBCOLUMNFLAGS_ISLONG for the column, the provider returns DB_S_ERRORSOCCURRED or DB_E_ERRORSOCCURRED.
N	Y	N	Not generally used. If the method returns DB_S_ERRORSOCCURRED or DB_E_ERRORSOCCURRED, the consumer must assume that the method did not successfully get or set the length for the column. If the column is nullable, the consumer cannot determine the validity of the returned value or length because it does not know whether the column value is NULL.	Not generally used. If the method returns DB_S_ERRORSOCCURRED or DB_E_ERRORSOCCURRED, the consumer must assume that the method did not successfully get or set the value for the column. The provider assumes the status is DBSTATUS_S_OK.

Value	Length	Status	Use when getting data	Use when setting data
N	N	Y	Not generally used.	Can be used to set the value of a column or parameter to NULL or to specify that the provider is to use the default value for an input or input/output parameter in a procedure. If the status is DBSTATUS_S_OK, the provider returns a status of DBSTATUS_E_UNAVAILABLE.
N	N	N	**IAccessor::CreateAccessor** returns DBBINDSTATUS_ BADBINDINFO for the binding.	**IAccessor::CreateAccessor** returns DBBINDSTATUS_ BADBINDINFO for the binding.

[1] Consumers should always include the length data part when retrieving variable-length, non-null-terminated data. If the length is not bound, the provider populates the value and status with the correct values but the consumer must rely on some intimate knowledge of the data to derive its length.

[2] Consumers should always include the length data part when specifying non-null values of type DBTYPE_BYTES. If *wType* in the DBBINDING structure is DBTYPE_BYTES and the status, if bound, is DBSTATUS_S_OK, providers should use the value of *cbMaxLen* in the DBBINDING structure as the number of bytes to read. However, consumers should not rely on this behavior, because many providers return an error for this case.

Value

The *value* is the actual value of the data. For example, the value of a column containing last names might be "Smith." Unless the type indicator of the data is DBTYPE_BSTR or is combined with DBTYPE_BYREF, DBTYPE_ARRAY, or DBTYPE_VECTOR, the data is stored directly at the offset specified in the binding. Sufficient space must be allocated for the data.

For example, if the type indicator is DBTYPE_I2, a two-byte integer is stored at the specified offset and two bytes must be available for write at that offset. If the type indicator is DBTYPE_STR, an ANSI string is stored at the specified offset. If the length of the string in bytes is longer than the number of bytes specified in the *cbMaxLen* element of the DBBINDING structure, the string is truncated.

If the type indicator is DBTYPE_BSTR or is combined with DBTYPE_BYREF, DBTYPE_ARRAY, or DBTYPE_VECTOR, a pointer to the data is stored at the offset specified in the binding and the data is stored in separately allocated memory. For example, if the type indicator is DBTYPE_STR | DBTYPE_BYREF, a pointer to an ANSI string is stored at the specified offset and **sizeof(char *)** bytes must be allocated at that offset. The string itself is stored in separately allocated memory. For more information, see "Type Indicators" in Appendix A, "Data Types."

The only exception to these rules is when a reference accessor is used, in which case the value is a pointer to the provider's buffer for rowset data or a pointer to the consumer's buffer for input parameter data. For more information, see "Reference Accessors" later in this chapter.

Length

The *length* of a data value is its size in bytes as it is stored in the consumer's data buffer. When the consumer gets data, length is the size of the data after it is converted from the provider type to the consumer type. When the consumer sets data, length is the size of the data before it is converted from the consumer type to the provider type.

The consumer specifies the buffer length with the *cbMaxLen* element of the DBBINDING structure. For information about how the provider uses the buffer length in conjunction with the data length, see *cbMaxLen* in "DBBINDING Structures," later in this chapter.

Length Values

The length value itself is a ULONG. The value stored in this ULONG depends on the data type as follows:

- **Variable-length data types**—The length of variable-length data types is the actual length of the untruncated data value in bytes. For string data, the length does not include the length of the null-termination character. If the length is bound, the string can include embedded null characters; that is, the length, rather than the null-termination character, is used in determining the end of the string. Consumers are encouraged not to use embedded null characters. Nevertheless, providers must support them. If the length is not bound, the string is assumed to be null-terminated.
- **Fixed-length data types**—When the consumer gets data, the returned length of a fixed-length data value is the size of its data type. When the consumer sets data, the provider ignores the length of fixed-length data types.
- **DBTYPE_IUNKNOWN, DBTYPE_IDISPATCH**—When setting or getting data through **ISequentialStream**, the length is used to specify the total number of bytes (which does not include space for a null because data returned through **ISequentialStream** is not null-terminated) that will be sent or returned through **ISequentialStream**. When binding to any other object as DBTYPE_IUNKNOWN or DBTYPE_IDISPATCH, the returned length is **sizeof(IUnknown*)**, not the size of the object itself. If there is a way to determine the length of the object, it is through a method on the object itself. The provider ignores the length field when binding as DBTYPE_IUNKNOWN or DBTYPE_IDISPATCH to an object other than **ISequentialStream**.

- **DBTYPE_BYREF**—The length is the same as if DBTYPE_BYREF is not used. That is, it is the length of the data being pointed to. For example, if the type indicator is DBTYPE_STR | DBTYPE_BYREF, the length is the length of the string in bytes, not the length of the pointer.
- **DBTYPE_VECTOR, DBTYPE_ARRAY**—The returned length is ignored when getting data, because while only a single length is returned, a vector or array can contain multiple values, each of which has a different length. When setting data, the provider ignores the length.

Status

The status indicates whether the data value or some other value, such as a NULL, is to be used as the value of the column or parameter. If the data value is to be used, the consumer sets the status to DBSTATUS_S_OK on input. On output, the provider returns information about whether the consumer was able to set or get the value.

Status Values Used When Getting Data

To get rowset or output parameter data, use **ICommand::Execute**, **IMultipleResults::GetResults**, **IRowset::GetData**, **IRowsetRefresh::GetLastVisibleData**, and **IRowsetUpdate::GetOriginalData**. As the provider returns the data, it sets the status of each column or output parameter so that the consumer can determine which data values it got successfully. It produces the return codes as follows:

- **Success return code (S_OK)**—No errors occurred while getting data for any columns or parameters. Warning conditions may have occurred for any columns or parameters.

  Note Truncation of variable length data is a warning condition when getting data. The corresponding status is set to DBSTATUS_S_TRUNCATED.

- **DB_S_ERRORSOCCURRED**—Errors occurred while getting data for one or more columns or parameters, but data was successfully returned for at least one column or parameter. Warning conditions may have occurred for any nonerror columns or parameters. If status is bound, the consumer can check the status value to learn why the column failed.
- **DB_E_ERRORSOCCURRED**—Errors occurred while getting data for all columns or parameters. Warning conditions did not occur for any columns or parameters.

If the provider returns a fatal error other than DB_E_ERRORSOCCURRED, such as E_FAIL, the returned status values are undefined.

The following table explains the meaning of each returned status value, whether it is a success, error, or warning condition, and whether data was successfully returned.

Status value	Success, warning, or error	Data returned	Description
DBSTATUS_S_OK	Success	Y	The provider returned a non-null value.
DBSTATUS_S_ISNULL	Success	Y	The provider returned a null value.
DBSTATUS_S_ TRUNCATED	Warning	Y	Variable-length data was truncated.
DBSTATUS_E_ BADACCESSOR	Error	N	Accessor validation was deferred and was performed while the method returned data. The binding was invalid for this column or parameter. For a description of the cases that might cause deferred accessor validation to fail, see the description of the DBBINDSTATUS values listed under the *rgStatus* argument in **IAccessor::CreateAccessor** in Part 2, "OLE DB Reference."
DBSTATUS_E_ CANTCONVERTVALUE	Error	N	The data value could not be converted for reasons other than sign mismatch or data overflow. For example, the data was corrupted in the data store, but the row was still retrievable.
DBSTATUS_E_ CANTCREATE	Error	N	One of the following conditions: The provider could not allocate memory in which to return data. The type indicator for the column was DBTYPE_IUNKNOWN, the provider supports only one open storage object at a time (DBPROP_ MULTIPLESTORAGEOBJECTS was VARIANT_FALSE), and a storage object was already open on the rowset.
DBSTATUS_E_ DATAOVERFLOW	Error	N	Conversion failed because the data value overflowed the type specified for the value part in the consumer's buffer.

Status value	Success, warning, or error	Data returned	Description
DBSTATUS_E_ SIGNMISMATCH	Error	N	Conversion failed because the data value was signed and the type specified for the value part in the consumer's buffer was unsigned.
DBSTATUS_E_ UNAVAILABLE	Error	N	The provider could not determine the value. For example, the row was just created, the default for the column was not available, and the consumer had not yet set a new value.

Status Values Used When Setting Data

To set rowset data or to set input parameter data, use **ICommand::Execute**, **IRowsetChange::SetData**, **IRowsetChange::InsertRow**, **IRowsetIndex::Seek**, and **IRowsetIndex::SetRange**. When calling these methods, the consumer must set the status to one of the values in the following table.

Status value	Description
DBSTATUS_S_OK	The value sent to the provider is not NULL and is passed in the consumer's buffer at the offset specified by *obValue* in the binding.
DBSTATUS_S_ISNULL	The value sent to the provider is NULL. The provider ignores the contents of the value and length parts of the consumer's buffer.
DBSTATUS_S_ DEFAULT	The provider is to use the default value in **SetData** or **InsertRow** or as the input value for an input or input/output parameter in a procedure. The provider ignores the contents of the value and the length parts of the consumer's buffer on input, although it sets them on output for input/output parameters. This status value is never returned when getting data. If the provider can determine the default value, that value is returned along with a status of DBSTATUS_S_OK if the default is not NULL, or DBSTATUS_S_ISNULL if the default is NULL. If the provider cannot determine the default value, it returns DBSTATUS_E_UNAVAILABLE when calling **GetData** for columns set as DBSTATUS_S_DEFAULT. Consumers should be prepared for OLE DB 1.0 or 1.1 providers to return DBSTATUS_E_BADSTATUS when attempting to specify DBSTATUS_S_DEFAULT in **SetData** or **InsertRow**.

Status value	Description
DBSTATUS_S_IGNORE	The provider is to skip this column when setting data. The provider ignores the contents of the value and the length parts of the consumer's buffer for this column and does not change the underlying column value. DBSTATUS_S_IGNORE is not valid for parameters and returns DBSTATUS_E_BADSTATUS. Consumers should use DBSTATUS_S_DEFAULT to pass default parameter values. Consumers should be prepared for OLE DB 1.*x* providers to return DBSTATUS_E_BADSTATUS when attempting to specify DBSTATUS_S_IGNORE in **SetData** or **InsertRow**.

As the provider transfers data from the consumer to the provider, it sets the status of each column or input parameter so that the consumer can determine which data values were successfully set. The provider produces return codes as follows:

- **Success return code (S_OK)**—No errors occurred while setting data for any columns or parameters.
- **DB_S_ERRORSOCCURRED**—Errors occurred while setting data for one or more columns or parameters, but data was successfully set for at least one column or parameter.

  Note Truncation of variable-length data is an error condition when setting data. The corresponding status is set to DBSTATUS_E_CANTCONVERTVALUE.

- **DB_E_ERRORSOCCURRED**—Errors occurred while setting data for all columns or parameters.

If the provider returns a fatal error other than DB_E_ERRORSOCCURRED, such as E_FAIL, the returned status values are undefined. If the consumer did not bind the status for a column or input parameter and the method returns DB_S_ERRORSOCCURRED or DB_E_ERRORSOCCURRED, the consumer must assume that the value for that column or input parameter was not successfully set.

The following table explains the meaning of each returned status value, whether it is a success or error condition, and whether data was successfully sent.

Status value	Success, warning, or error	Data sent	Description
DBSTATUS_S_OK	Success	Y	A non-null value was sent to the provider.
DBSTATUS_S_ISNULL	Success	Y	A null value was sent to the provider.
DBSTATUS_S_DEFAULT	Success	Y	The provider used the default value for an input parameter in a procedure. If the provider used the default value on input for an input/output parameter, the status is set to the status of the output value on output.
DBSTATUS_S_IGNORE	Success	N	• The consumer specified DBSTATUS_S_IGNORE when setting data, and the provider ignored the column.
DBSTATUS_E_BADACCESSOR	Error	N	Accessor validation was deferred and was performed while the method sent data. The binding was invalid for this column or parameter. For a description of the cases that may cause deferred accessor validation to fail, see the description of the DBBINDSTATUS values listed under the *rgStatus* argument of in the reference entry for "IAccessor::CreateAccessor
DBSTATUS_E_BADSTATUS	Error	N	One of the following conditions: • The status value sent to the provider was not DBSTATUS_S_OK, DBSTATUS_S_ISNULL, DBSTATUS_S_IGNORE, or DBSTATUS_S_DEFAULT. • The status value was DBSTATUS_S_DEFAULT, the binding was used in a method other than **SetData** or **InsertData**, and the binding was not passed as an input or input/output parameter in a procedure.

Status value	Success, warning, or error	Data sent	Description
			• The status value was DBSTATUS_S_DEFAULT, the binding was not for an input or input/output parameter in a procedure, and the provider was a 1.0 or 1.1 provider. • The binding used in **SetData** contained only the status part, and the status value was not DBSTATUS_S_ISNULL. • The status value sent to the provider was DBSTATUS_S_IGNORE, and the binding was for a parameter in a procedure. • The status value sent to a provider was DBSTATUS_S_IGNORE, and the provider was a 1.*x* provider.
DBSTATUS_E_ CANTCONVERTVALUE	Error	N	The data value could not be converted for reasons other than sign mismatch or data overflow. For example, converting the data would have truncated it, including truncating nonsignificant digits in numeric data.
DBSTATUS_E_ CANTCREATE	Error	N	The type indicator for the column was DBTYPE_IUNKNOWN, the provider supports only one open storage object at a time (DBPROP_ MULTIPLESTORAGEOBJECTS was VARIANT_FALSE), and a storage object was already open on the rowset.
DBSTATUS_E_ DATAOVERFLOW	Error	N	Conversion failed because the data value overflowed the type used by the provider.
DBSTATUS_E_ INTEGRITYVIOLATION	Error	N	The data value violated the integrity constraints for the column.
DBSTATUS_E_ PERMISSIONDENIED	Error	N	The DBPROP_COLUMNRESTRICT property was VARIANT_TRUE, and the user did not have permission to write to the column.
DBSTATUS_E_ SCHEMAVIOLATION	Error	N	The data value violated the schema's constraint for the column.

Status value	Success, warning, or error	Data sent	Description
DBSTATUS_E_ SIGNMISMATCH	Error	N	Conversion failed because the data value was signed and the type used by the provider was unsigned.
DBSTATUS_E_ UNAVAILABLE	Error	N	• One of the following conditions: • The consumer did not bind the value part of the data, and the status was DBSTATUS_S_OK. • The consumer did not bind the length part of the data, the status was DBSTATUS_S_OK, and *wType* in the DBBINDING structure was DBTYPE_BYTES. • The value was not sent for an undetermined reason. For example, the provider encountered an error while sending a column or parameter value and stopped processing. If the provider backs out changes it made before the error, it also sets the status of the columns from which it backs data out to DBSTATUS_E_UNAVAILABLE.

Accessors

An *accessor* is a data structure created by the consumer that describes how row or parameter data from the data store is to be laid out in the consumer's data buffer. For each column in a row (or parameter in a set of parameters), the accessor contains a binding. A *binding* is a data structure that holds information about a column or parameter value, such as its ordinal value, data type, and destination in the consumer's buffer. When calling a method that transfers data, such as **IRowset::GetData**, **IRowsetChange::SetData**, or **ICommand::Execute**, the consumer passes as parameters to the method an accessor handle (or, when transferring parameter data, a DBPARAMS structure containing an accessor handle) and a pointer into the consumer's data buffer. The provider uses the accessor to determine how to transfer the data to or from the consumer's buffer.

An accessor is identified by its handle, as follows:

```
typedef ULONG HACCESSOR;
```

Using Accessors

Accessors are created by calling **IAccessor::CreateAccessor**, reference-counted by calling **IAccessor::AddRefAccessor**, and released by calling **IAccessor::ReleaseAccessor**. They can be created or released at any time. An accessor can be a *parameter accessor* (used for accessing parameter data), a *row accessor* (used for accessing rowset data), or both. Parameter accessors can be created and used only on command objects. Row accessors can be created on command and rowset objects, but they can be used only on rowset objects. (All row accessors created on a command object are inherited by any rowsets created by that command object.) Row accessors created on a rowset after a row is fetched from that rowset can still be used against that row.

Consumers can create and use more than one accessor at a time on any row. Therefore, the consumer can get or set multiple copies of the same data. For example, suppose a rowset contains employee data including a picture of the employee. The consumer might create two accessors: one for all of the columns except the picture column and another for the picture column. The consumer might then pass the handle of the first accessor to **IRowset::GetData** to get all of the data except the picture. When the user requests the picture, the consumer would then pass the handle to the second accessor to **GetData** to get the picture.

When **ICommand::Execute** creates a rowset, the rowset inherits all row accessors that have been created on that command. To the consumer, it appears as if each accessor has been copied from the command to the rowset: the bindings, flags, and handle of each accessor are the same on both the rowset and the command. After the rowset is opened, it gets its own independent copy of the accessors. Calling **IAccessor** methods on the command object has no effect on the accessors available on any existing rowsets, and calling **IAccessor** methods on the rowset has no effect on the accessors available on any existing commands.

For example, suppose the text command that creates a rowset contains parameters. The consumer might create multiple rowsets by repeatedly executing this text command with different parameters. Because the rowsets are created from the same text command, all can use the same row accessors. To create a row accessor on a command, the consumer must know the column ordinals.

Optimized Accessors

Row accessors can be optimized. How this is done is provider-specific. It is usually faster to use an optimized accessor than an unoptimized accessor. For example, the provider might structure its internal row buffers to match the types used in the accessor. Optimized row accessors must be created before any rows are fetched.

Flagging accessors as optimized affects only providers that support optimized accessors. In general, providers are not required to recognize optimized accessors, nor are they required to enforce any of the restrictions associated with optimized accessors.

Clients written to consume data from general OLE DB providers should never include the same column in more than one optimized accessor, and for all bindings to a particular column, clients should use a data type coercible from the type specified in any optimized accessor for that column.

Reference Accessors

A *reference accessor* enables consumers to get rowset data directly from the provider's buffer and enables providers to get input parameter data directly from the consumer's buffer. Consumers cannot use these accessors with output parameters or when setting row data.

Reference accessors require the consumer to have prior knowledge of the provider's buffer layout. The consumer cannot discover this information through OLE DB interfaces at run time. Because of this, reference accessors are designed for use by tightly coupled consumer/provider pairs. Because they allow direct access to the provider's buffers, providers are not required to support them.

To use reference accessors, the layout of the consumer's bindings must exactly match the layout of the provider's buffer. If the provider's buffer does not contain length or status parts, the consumer cannot bind these parts and, in the same manner as the provider, must determine length and whether the data value is NULL.

To use a reference accessor, the consumer passes the handle of the accessor and a pointer to a buffer to the provider. For rowset data, the provider returns a pointer to its internal buffer in the buffer supplied by the consumer. The consumer then dereferences this pointer and reads directly from the provider's buffer. For input parameter data, the consumer's buffer contains a pointer to the buffer that actually contains the data. The provider dereferences this pointer and reads directly from the consumer's other buffer.

The consumer (for rowset data) or provider (for input parameter data) must not write to this buffer, nor can it free this buffer.

For rowset data, the pointer returned by the provider is guaranteed to remain valid until the consumer calls **IRowsetChange::SetData**, **IRowsetChange::DeleteRows**, **IRowsetRefresh::RefreshVisibleData**, **IRowsetUpdate::Undo**, or **IRowsetUpdate::Update** for the row, calls **IRowset::ReleaseRows** for the row and the reference count falls to zero, or releases the rowset. For input parameter data, the pointer is guaranteed to remain valid only until **ICommand::Execute** returns.

Bindings

An accessor is a collection of *bindings*. Each binding contains information about the consumer's buffer. The most notable information is the ordinal of the column or parameter to which the binding applies, what is bound (the data value, its length, and its status), the offsets in the buffer to each of these parts, and the length and type of the data value as it exists in the consumer's buffer. For more information, see "Binding Data Values," earlier in this chapter, and "DBBINDING Structures," later in this chapter.

Each binding associates, or *binds,* a single column or parameter to the consumer's buffer. The consumer can bind columns and output parameters more than once in a single accessor but can bind input parameters only once in a single accessor. It is usually a consumer programming error to bind a column more than once in a single accessor and then use that accessor to set the value of the column, such as with **IRowsetChange::SetData**, because the result of doing so is unpredictable.

For example, the following illustration shows a consumer's buffer containing 10 bytes for a string, two unused bytes to properly align the string's status and length values, four bytes for the string's status, four bytes for the string's length, two unused bytes to properly align the integer's status value, two bytes for a two-byte integer, and four bytes for the integer's status. It also shows the main binding information used to bind the string to column 1 and the integer to column 2. The table following the figure summarizes the bindings in this example.

Main binding information as shown in a consumer's buffer

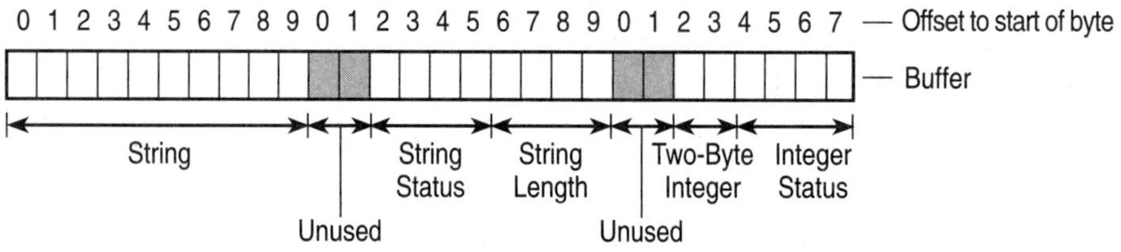

Element	String binding	Integer binding
Ordinal	1	2
Bound parts	DBPART_VALUE | DBPART_LENGTH | DBPART_STATUS	DBPART_VALUE | DBPART_STATUS
Offset to data value	0	22
Offset to status	12	24
Offset to length	16	N/A
Data type	DBTYPE_STR	DBTYPE_I2
Buffer length	10	2

When the consumer gets data, the provider uses the information in each binding to determine where and how to return data in the consumer's buffer. When the consumer sets data, the provider uses the information in each binding to determine where and how to retrieve data from the consumer's buffer.

DBBINDING Structures

A binding associates a single column or parameter to the consumer's buffer and contains information about the buffer.

The DBBINDING structure describes a single binding:

```
typedef struct tagDBBINDING {
   ULONG         iOrdinal;
   ULONG         obValue;
   ULONG         obLength;
   ULONG         obStatus;
   ITypeInfo *   pTypeInfo;
   DBOBJECT *    pObject;
   DBBINDEXT *   pBindExt;
   DBPART        dwPart;
   DBMEMOWNER    dwMemOwner;
   DBPARAMIO     eParamIO;
   ULONG         cbMaxLen;
   DWORD         dwFlags;
   DBTYPE        wType;
   BYTE          bPrecision;
   BYTE          bScale;
} DBBINDING;
```

The elements of this structure are used as described in the following table.

Element	Description
iOrdinal	The ordinal of the column or parameter to which the binding applies. Column ordinals are fixed for the lifetime of the rowset. The self bookmark column is column 0, and other columns have values greater than 1. To retrieve column ordinals, consumers call **IColumnsInfo::GetColumnInfo**, **IColumnsRowset::GetColumnsRowset**, or **IColumnsInfo::MapColumnIDs**. If the rowset is generated from a command, the column ordinals returned by **GetColumnInfo** or **GetColumnsRowset** on the rowset must match the column ordinals returned by the same methods on the command. To retrieve parameter ordinals, consumers call **ICommandWithParameters::GetParameterInfo** on the command object.
obValue	The offset in bytes in the consumer's buffer to the value part. The value of *obValue* is ignored unless the DBPART_VALUE bit is set in *dwPart*. For more information about the value part, see "Value" earlier in this chapter. This offset must be properly aligned for the processor architecture of the consumer's machine. If data is improperly aligned, consumers can expect alignment faults to occur when getting and setting data values. Consumers should use addresses that are multiples of the size of the data type. For example, if *wType* is DBTYPE_I4, the value part should be LONG aligned.
obLength	The offset in bytes in the consumer's buffer to the length part. The value of *obLength* is ignored unless the DBPART_LENGTH bit is set in *dwPart*. For more information about the length part, see "Length" earlier in this chapter. The length itself is a ULONG. This offset must be properly aligned for the processor architecture of the consumer's machine. That is, it should be a multiple of **sizeof(ULONG)**. If it is improperly aligned, consumers can expect alignment faults when getting and setting length values.
obStatus	The offset in bytes in the consumer's buffer to the status part. The value of *obStatus* is ignored unless the DBPART_STATUS bit is set in *dwPart*. For more information about the status part, see "Status" earlier in this chapter. The status part itself is a DBSTATUS value, which is a DWORD. This offset must be properly aligned for the processor architecture of the consumer's machine. That is, it should be a multiple of **sizeof(DWORD)**. If it is improperly aligned, consumers can expect alignment faults when getting and setting status values.
pTypeInfo	Reserved for future use. Consumers should set *pTypeInfo* to a null pointer.

Element	Description
pObject	Pointer to a DBOBJECT structure. For columns or parameters that can hold BLOBs or COM objects, this structure gives information needed to access the object:

```
typedef struct tagDBOBJECT {
   DWORD dwFlags;
   IID iid;
} DBOBJECT;
```

The elements of this structure are used as follows:

- *dwFlags*—The combined storage mode flags to use when creating an instance of the COM object.
- *iid*—The interface to be exposed on the COM object.

The storage mode flags are defined by the Structured Storage model in OLE. These are:

- STGM_READ = OF_READ
- STGM_WRITE = OF_WRITE
- STGM_READWRITE = OF_READWRITE
- STGM_SHARE_DENY_NONE = OF_SHARE_DENY_NONE
- STGM_SHARE_DENY_READ = OF_SHARE_DENY_READ
- STGM_SHARE_DENY_WRITE = OF_SHARE_DENY_WRITE
- STGM_SHARE_EXCLUSIVE = OF_SHARE_EXCLUSIVE
- STGM_DIRECT
- STGM_TRANSACTED
- STGM_CREATE = OF_CREATE
- STGM_CONVERT
- STGM_FAILIFTHERE
- STGM_PRIORITY
- STGM_DELETEONRELEASE

Element	Description
	The value of *pObject* is ignored unless the DBPART_VALUE bit is set in *dwPart* and *wType* is DBTYPE_IUNKNOWN. If neither of these conditions is true, it should be set to a null pointer. **Note** Consumers should not set ***wType*** to DBTYPE_IUNKNOWN and the DBPART_VALUE bit in ***dwPart*** without specifying a non-null value for ***pObject***. However, providers can assume in this case that the interface to be bound is IID_IUnknown.

pBindExt	The DBBINDEXT structure can be used for future extensions to the binding structure. The *pBindExt* value is reserved for future use, and consumers should set it to a null pointer:
	
	`typedef struct tagDBBINDEXT{`
	`   BYTE * pExtension;`
	`   ULONG  ulExtension;`
	`} DBBINDEXT;`

dwPart	Specifies which buffer parts are to be bound to the column or parameter. It is one or more DBPARTENUM values combined. These values have the following meaning: • DBPART_VALUE—The binding includes a value part. • DBPART_LENGTH—The binding includes a length part. • DBPART_STATUS—The binding includes a status part.
dwMemOwner	For bindings in row accessors, specifies memory allocated by the provider for a column and for which a pointer is returned to the consumer. For example, when *wType* is DBTYPE_BYREF | DBTYPE_STR, the provider allocates memory for the string and returns a pointer to the string to the consumer. The *dwMemOwner* value specifies whether the consumer or provider is responsible for freeing this memory. The provider ignores this when the consumer sets rowset data. The following is a description of each of these values: • DBMEMOWNER_CLIENTOWNED—The consumer owns the memory and is responsible for freeing it. • DBMEMOWNER_PROVIDEROWNED—The provider owns the memory and is responsible for freeing it. When getting data, the provider returns a pointer into its copy of the row. When using provider-owned memory, the consumer's type must exactly match the provider's type, except that if *wType* is X | DBTYPE_BYREF, the provider's type can be X or X | DBTYPE_BYREF. If a column is NULL, the provider returns a null pointer for the data value.

Element	Description
	The consumer must not write to or free the memory to which the pointer points. The lifetime of the pointer is provider-specific. However, pointers to row data are guaranteed to be valid until **IRowset::ReleaseRows** is called for the row and its reference count falls to zero, the rowset is freed, or a method is called for the row that might invalidate the pointer. The methods that might invalidate the pointer depend on the method that returned it, as follows:

Pointer returned by	Might be invalidated by
GetData	**DeleteRows** [1] **RefreshVisibleData** **SetData** **Update** **Undo**
GetLastVisibleData	**GetLastVisibleData**
GetOriginalData	**RefreshVisibleData** **SetData** **Update**

Although the consumer must not write to provider-owned memory, it can pass pointers to provider-owned memory when setting data. For example, suppose that the consumer wants to copy data efficiently from row A to row B. The consumer creates an accessor to the columns in row A in which *wType* is X | DBTYPE_BYREF and sets *dwMemOwner* to DBMEMOWNER_PROVIDEROWNED. When the consumer calls **IRowset::GetData**, the provider returns pointers to its copy of row A. The consumer then calls **IRowsetChange::SetData** for row B with the same accessor and a pointer to the memory passed to **GetData**. The provider dereferences the pointers and copies the data from the rowset's copy of row A to the rowset's copy of row B.

[1] Immediate update mode.

Element	Description
	For bindings in row accessors, consumer-owned memory must be used unless *wType* is DBTYPE_BSTR, X | DBTYPE_BYREF, X | DBTYPE_ARRAY, or X | DBTYPE_VECTOR, in which case either consumer-owned or provider-owned memory can be used. However, the provider might not support using provider-owned memory to retrieve columns for which **IColumnsInfo::GetColumnInfo** returns DBCOLUMNFLAGS_ISLONG for the column. Consumers can mix bindings for provider-owned and consumer-owned memory in the same accessor. For bindings in parameter accessors, consumer-owned memory must always be used. The value of *dwMemOwner* is ignored in reference accessors. **All providers must support binding to client-owned memory. Providers support provider-owned memory only if they can efficiently return a pointer to a cached value. Providers are not required to support binding deferred columns to provider-owned memory.**
eParamIO	For parameter accessors, *eParamIO* specifies whether the parameter with which the binding is associated is an input, input/output, or output parameter. Providers support only those parameter I/O types that are supported by their underlying data store. The value of *eParamIO* is one or more DBPARAMIOENUM values combined. These values have the following meaning: • DBPARAMIO_NOTPARAM—The accessor is not used for parameters. In most cases, *eParamIO* is set to this value in row accessors to remind the programmer that it is ignored. • DBPARAMIO_INPUT—The parameter is an input parameter. • DBPARAMIO_OUTPUT—The parameter is an output parameter. • DBPARAMIO_INPUT | DBPARAMIO_OUTPUT—The parameter is both an input and an output parameter. For row accessors, the value of *eParamIO* is ignored.

Element	Description
cbMaxLen	The length in bytes of the consumer's data structure allocated for the data value. That is, it is the number of bytes allocated at offset *obValue* for the data value. The value of *cbMaxLen* is ignored unless the DBPART_VALUE bit is set in *dwPart* and the data value stored at that location is of variable length. For information about variable-length data types, see "Fixed-Length and Variable-Length Data Types" in Chapter 10, "Data Types in OLE DB." The value of *cbMaxLen* is used as follows: • **Variable-length data types**—The provider checks the length in bytes of variable-length data types against *cbMaxLen*. If the length is greater than *cbMaxLen*, the provider truncates the data to *cbMaxLen* bytes. When getting string data, this is a warning and the provider sets the status to DBSTATUS_S_TRUNCATED and sets the length to the actual number of bytes of data available after conversion and before truncation. Thus, the consumer can determine the actual number of bytes of data available. When setting data, this is an error and the provider sets the status to DBSTATUS_E_CANTCONVERTVALUE. In most cases, this is a consumer programming error. • **Fixed-length data types**—The provider ignores *cbMaxLen* for fixed-length data types and assumes that the number of bytes available in the consumer's buffer for the data is the size of the data type. • **DBTYPE_BYREF, DBTYPE_VECTOR, DBTYPE_ARRAY**—The provider ignores *cbMaxLen* and assumes that the number of bytes available in the consumer's buffer is the size dictated by DBTYPE_BYREF, DBTYPE_VECTOR, or DBTYPE_ARRAY. For DBTYPE_BYREF and DBTYPE_ARRAY, this is **sizeof(void *)**. For DBTYPE_VECTOR, this is **sizeof(DBVECTOR)**. **Important** If DBTYPE_BYREF is combined with the type indicator for a variable-length data type, the data is not truncated to *cbMaxLen* bytes. This is because the data is in separately allocated memory, not the consumer's buffer, and *cbMaxLen* does not apply to this memory. The provider allocates this memory based on the length of the data, as bound at the offset *obLength*, so consumers can guarantee that variable-length data is not truncated if it is retrieved in this manner.

Element	Description
dwFlags	The consumer can set *dwFlags* to specify information about how returned data is to be formatted. The following flag is recognized: DBBINDFLAG_HTML The provider should format the returned data in HTML. If the provider does not support HTML formatting, the bit is ignored and regular text is returned. Providers that do not support HTML formatting cannot use accessors created with the HTML flag to set data.
wType	The indicator of the data type of the value part of the buffer. For more information about type indicators, see "Type Indicators" in Appendix A, "Data Types." This type forms an implied conversion between the buffer type and the type of the column or parameter. For information about conversions that providers are required to support, see "Data Type Conversion" in Chapter 10, "Data Types in OLE DB."
bPrecision	The maximum precision to use when getting data and *wType* is DBTYPE_NUMERIC or DBTYPE_VARNUMERIC. This is ignored in three cases: when setting data; when *wType* is not DBTYPE_NUMERIC or DBTYPE_VARNUMERIC; and when the DBPART_VALUE bit is not set in *dwPart*. For more information, see "Conversions Involving DBTYPE_NUMERIC or DBTYPE_DECIMAL" in Appendix A, "Data Types."
bScale	The scale to use when getting data and *wType* is DBTYPE_NUMERIC, DBTYPE_VARNUMERIC, or DBTYPE_DECIMAL. This is ignored in three cases: when setting data; when *wType* is not DBTYPE_NUMERIC, DBTYPE_VARNUMERIC, or DBTYPE_DECIMAL; and when the DBPART_VALUE bit is not set in *dwPart*. For more information, see "Conversions Involving DBTYPE_NUMERIC or DBTYPE_DECIMAL" in Appendix A, "Data Types."

Note The offsets specified in *obValue*, *obLength*, and *obStatus* must not point to overlapping areas of memory. The provider is not required to check for the occurrence of this condition. Consumers must be careful to avoid this condition when constructing bindings.

Binding and Accessor Example

The code in this example shows how to set up bindings and use them to create an accessor.

```
/////////////////////////////////////////////////////////////////
// mySetupBindings
//
// This function takes an IUnknown pointer from a rowset object
// and creates a bindings array that describes how we want the
// data we fetch from the rowset to be laid out in memory. It
// also calculates the total size of a row so that we can use
// this to allocate memory for the rows that we will fetch
// later.
//
// For each column in the rowset, there will be a corresponding
// element in the bindings array that describes how the
// provider should transfer the data, including length and
// status, for that column. This element also specifies the data
// type that the provider should return the column as. We will
// bind all columns as DBTYPE_WSTR, with a few exceptions
// detailed below, as providers are required to support the
// conversion of their column data to this type in the vast
// majority of cases. The exception to our binding as
// DBTYPE_WSTR is if the native column data type is
// DBTYPE_IUNKNOWN or if the user has requested that BLOB
// columns be bound as ISequentialStream objects, in which case
// we will bind those columns as ISequentialStream objects.
//
/////////////////////////////////////////////////////////////////
HRESULT mySetupBindings
   (
   IUnknown *          pUnkRowset,
   ULONG *             pcBindings,
   DBBINDING **        prgBindings,
   ULONG *             pcbRowSize
   )
```

```
{
   HRESULT              hr;
   ULONG                cColumns;
   DBCOLUMNINFO *       rgColumnInfo      = NULL;
   LPWSTR               pStringBuffer     = NULL;
   IColumnsInfo *       pIColumnsInfo     = NULL;

   ULONG                iCol;
   ULONG                dwOffset          = 0;
   DBBINDING *          rgBindings        = NULL;

   ULONG                cStorageObjs      = 0;
   BOOL                 fMultipleObjs     = FALSE;

   // Obtain the column information for the rowset; from this, we can find
   // out the following information that we need to construct the bindings
   // array:
   //   - the number of columns
   //   - the ordinal of each column
   //   - the precision and scale of numeric columns
   //   - the OLE DB data type of the column
   XCHECK_HR(hr = pUnkRowset->QueryInterface(
            IID_IColumnsInfo, (void**)&pIColumnsInfo));
   XCHECK_HR(hr = pIColumnsInfo->GetColumnInfo(
            &cColumns,       // pcColumns
            &rgColumnInfo,   // prgColumnInfo
            &pStringBuffer   // ppStringBuffer
            ));

   // Allocate memory for the bindings array. There is a one-to-one
   // mapping between the columns returned from GetColumnInfo and our
   // bindings.
   rgBindings = (DBBINDING*)CoTaskMemAlloc(cColumns * sizeof(DBBINDING));
   CHECK_MEMORY(hr, rgBindings);
   memset(rgBindings, 0, cColumns * sizeof(DBBINDING));

   // Determine if the rowset supports multiple storage object bindings.
   // If it does not, we will bind only the first BLOB column or IUnknown
   // column as an ISequentialStream object, and will bind the rest as
   // DBTYPE_WSTR.
   myGetProperty(pUnkRowset, IID_IRowset, DBPROP_MULTIPLESTORAGEOBJECTS,
      DBPROPSET_ROWSET, &fMultipleObjs);

   // Construct the binding array element for each column
   for( iCol = 0; iCol < cColumns; iCol++ )
   {
      // This binding applies to the ordinal of this column
      rgBindings[iCol].iOrdinal   = rgColumnInfo[iCol].iOrdinal;
```

```
// We are asking the provider to give us the data for this column
// (DBPART_VALUE), the length of that data (DBPART_LENGTH), and
// the status of the column (DBPART_STATUS)
rgBindings[iCol].dwPart = DBPART_VALUE|DBPART_LENGTH|DBPART_STATUS;

// The following values are the offsets to the status, length, and
// data value that the provider will fill with the appropriate values
// when we fetch data later. When we fetch data, we will pass a
// pointer to a buffer that the provider will copy column data to,
// in accordance with the binding we have provided for that column.
// These are offsets into that future buffer.
rgBindings[iCol].obStatus   = dwOffset;
rgBindings[iCol].obLength   = dwOffset + sizeof(DBSTATUS);
rgBindings[iCol].obValue    = dwOffset + sizeof(DBSTATUS) + sizeof(ULONG);

// Any memory allocated for the data value will be owned by us, the
// client. Note that no data will be allocated in this case, as the
// DBTYPE_WSTR bindings we are using will tell the provider to simply
// copy data directly into our provided buffer.
rgBindings[iCol].dwMemOwner = DBMEMOWNER_CLIENTOWNED;

// This is not a parameter binding
rgBindings[iCol].eParamIO   = DBPARAMIO_NOTPARAM;

// We want to use the precision and scale of the column
rgBindings[iCol].bPrecision = rgColumnInfo[iCol].bPrecision;
rgBindings[iCol].bScale     = rgColumnInfo[iCol].bScale;

// Bind this column as DBTYPE_WSTR, which tells the provider to
// copy a Unicode string representation of the data into our buffer,
// converting from the native type if necessary
rgBindings[iCol].wType      = DBTYPE_WSTR;

// Initially, we set the length for this data in our buffer to 0.
// The correct value for this will be calculated directly below.
rgBindings[iCol].cbMaxLen   = 0;

// Determine the maximum number of bytes required in our buffer to
// contain the Unicode string representation of the provider's native
// data type, including room for the NULL-termination character
switch( rgColumnInfo[iCol].wType )
```

```
{
   case DBTYPE_NULL:
   case DBTYPE_EMPTY:
   case DBTYPE_I1:
   case DBTYPE_I2:
   case DBTYPE_I4:
   case DBTYPE_UI1:
   case DBTYPE_UI2:
   case DBTYPE_UI4:
   case DBTYPE_R4:
   case DBTYPE_BOOL:
   case DBTYPE_I8:
   case DBTYPE_UI8:
   case DBTYPE_R8:
   case DBTYPE_CY:
   case DBTYPE_ERROR:
      // When the above types are converted to a string, they
      // will all fit into 25 characters, so use that plus space
      // for the NULL-terminator
      rgBindings[iCol].cbMaxLen = (25 + 1) * sizeof(WCHAR);
      break;

   case DBTYPE_DECIMAL:
   case DBTYPE_NUMERIC:
   case DBTYPE_DATE:
   case DBTYPE_DBDATE:
   case DBTYPE_DBTIMESTAMP:
   case DBTYPE_GUID:
      // Converted to a string, the above types will all fit into
      // 50 characters, so use that plus space for the terminator
      rgBindings[iCol].cbMaxLen = (50 + 1) * sizeof(WCHAR);
      break;

   case DBTYPE_BYTES:
      // In converting DBTYPE_BYTES to a string, each byte
      // becomes two characters (e.g., 0xFF -> "FF"), so we
      // will use double the maximum size of the column plus
      // include space for the NULL-terminator
      rgBindings[iCol].cbMaxLen =
         (rgColumnInfo[iCol].ulColumnSize * 2 + 1) * sizeof(WCHAR);
      break;

   case DBTYPE_STR:
   case DBTYPE_WSTR:
   case DBTYPE_BSTR:
```

```
            // Going from a string to our string representation,
            // we can just take the maximum size of the column,
            // a count of characters, and include space for the
            // terminator, which is not included in the column size
            rgBindings[iCol].cbMaxLen =
               (rgColumnInfo[iCol].ulColumnSize + 1) * sizeof(WCHAR);
            break;

        default:
            // For any other type, we will simply use our maximum
            // column buffer size, since the display size of these
            // columns may be variable (e.g. DBTYPE_VARIANT) or
            // unknown (e.g. provider-specific types)
            rgBindings[iCol].cbMaxLen = MAX_COL_SIZE;
            break;
    };

    // If the provider's native data type for this column is
    // DBTYPE_IUNKNOWN or this is a BLOB column and the user
    // has requested that we bind BLOB columns as ISequentialStream
    // objects, bind this column as an ISequentialStream object if
    // the provider supports our creating another ISequentialStream
    // binding
    if( (rgColumnInfo[iCol].wType == DBTYPE_IUNKNOWN ||
         ((rgColumnInfo[iCol].dwFlags & DBCOLUMNFLAGS_ISLONG) &&
          (g_dwFlags & USE_ISEQSTREAM))) &&
        (fMultipleObjs || !cStorageObjs) )
    {
        // To create an ISequentialStream object, we will
        // bind this column as DBTYPE_IUNKNOWN to indicate
        // that we are requesting this column as an object
        rgBindings[iCol].wType = DBTYPE_IUNKNOWN;

        // We want to allocate enough space in our buffer for
        // the ISequentialStream pointer we will obtain from
        // the provider
        rgBindings[iCol].cbMaxLen = sizeof(ISequentialStream *);

        // To specify the type of object that we want from the
        // provider, we need to create a DBOBJECT structure and
        // place it in our binding for this column
         rgBindings[iCol].pObject          =
                      (DBOBJECT *)CoTaskMemAlloc(sizeof(DBOBJECT));
        CHECK_MEMORY(hr, rgBindings[iCol].pObject);

        // Direct the provider to create an ISequentialStream
        // object over the data for this column
        rgBindings[iCol].pObject->iid = IID_ISequentialStream;
```

```
            // We want read access on the ISequentialStream
            // object that the provider will create for us
            rgBindings[iCol].pObject->dwFlags = STGM_READ;

            // Keep track of the number of storage objects (ISequentialStream
            // is a storage interface) that we have requested, so that we
            // can avoid requesting multiple storage objects from a provider
            // that supports only a single storage object in our bindings
            cStorageObjs++;
        }

        // Ensure that the bound maximum length is no more than the
        // maximum column size in bytes that we've defined
        rgBindings[iCol].cbMaxLen
            = min(rgBindings[iCol].cbMaxLen, MAX_COL_SIZE);

        // Update the offset past the end of this column's data so
        // that the next column will begin in the correct place in
        // the buffer
        dwOffset = rgBindings[iCol].cbMaxLen + rgBindings[iCol].obValue;

        // Ensure that the data for the next column will be correctly
        // aligned for all platforms or, if we're done with columns,
        // that if we allocate space for multiple rows that the data
        // for every row is correctly aligned
        dwOffset = ROUNDUP(dwOffset);
    }

    // Return the row size (the current dwOffset is the size of the row),
    // the count of bindings, and the bindings array to the caller
    *pcbRowSize     = dwOffset;
    *pcBindings     = cColumns;
    *prgBindings    = rgBindings;

CLEANUP:
    CoTaskMemFree(rgColumnInfo);
    CoTaskMemFree(pStringBuffer);
    if( pIColumnsInfo )
        pIColumnsInfo->Release();
    return hr;
}
```

```
/////////////////////////////////////////////////////////////////
// myCreateAccessor
//
// This function takes an IUnknown pointer for a rowset object
// and creates an accessor that describes the layout of the
// buffer we will use when we fetch data. The provider will fill
// this buffer according to the description contained in the
// accessor that we will create here.
//
/////////////////////////////////////////////////////////////////
HRESULT myCreateAccessor
   (
   IUnknown *            pUnkRowset,
   HACCESSOR *           phAccessor,
   ULONG *               pcBindings,
   DBBINDING **          prgBindings,
   ULONG *               pcbRowSize
   )
{
   HRESULT               hr;
   IAccessor *           pIAccessor = NULL;

   // An accessor is basically a handle to a collection of bindings.
   // To create the accessor, we need to first create an array of
   // bindings for the columns in the rowset.
   CHECK_HR(hr = mySetupBindings(pUnkRowset, pcBindings, prgBindings,
      pcbRowSize));

   // Now that we have an array of bindings, tell the provider to
   // create the accessor for those bindings. We get back a handle
   // to this accessor, which we will use when fetching data.
   XCHECK_HR(hr = pUnkRowset->QueryInterface(
            IID_IAccessor, (void**)&pIAccessor));
   XCHECK_HR(hr = pIAccessor->CreateAccessor(
            DBACCESSOR_ROWDATA,     // dwAccessorFlags
            *pcBindings,            // cBindings
            *prgBindings,           // rgBindings
            0,                      // cbRowSize
            phAccessor,             // phAccessor
            NULL                    // rgStatus
            ));

CLEANUP:
   if( pIAccessor )
      pIAccessor->Release();
   return hr;
}
```

Responsibility for Freeing Memory

When the consumer calls a method that gets or sets data, such as **IRowset::GetData**, **IRowsetChange::SetData**, or **ICommand::Execute**, it passes a pointer to a consumer-owned data buffer. The consumer is responsible for allocating and freeing memory for this buffer. The provider can only read this memory. It must not free this memory nor should it assume that this memory exists after the method returns.

If the type indicator is DBTYPE_BSTR or is combined with DBTYPE_BYREF, DBTYPE_ARRAY, or DBTYPE_VECTOR, the consumer's memory contains a pointer to a separately allocated data buffer. This separate data buffer actually contains the data value, as distinct from the length and status, for the column or parameter. For example, if the type indicator is DBTYPE_BYREF | DBTYPE_STR, the data value in the consumer's memory is a pointer to an ANSI string. If the type indicator is DBTYPE_BSTR, the data value is a BSTR, which is a pointer to a length-prefixed, null-terminated string of Unicode characters. The remainder of this section discusses how this separate data buffer is managed.

> **Note** A consumer can bind an input/output parameter with a type indicator of DBTYPE_BSTR or with a type indicator that is combined with DBTYPE_BYREF, DBTYPE_ARRAY, or DBTYPE_VECTOR. If the consumer does this, and when the provider returns the output value for the parameter, the provider overwrites the pointer in the consumer's buffer that points to the input value. To ensure access to the input value after the provider returns the output value—for example, to free it—the consumer should keep a separate copy of the pointer to the input value.

When getting data, the provider is responsible for allocating the separate data buffer. The method by which the provider allocates this memory and the responsibility for freeing it is determined by the *dwMemOwner* element of the applicable binding.

If *dwMemOwner* is DBMEMOWNER_PROVIDEROWNED, the provider allocates the memory and frees it by whatever method it chooses. The consumer can only read the memory and must not free it or write to it. The memory is part of the rowset's copy of the row, which saves the provider from separately allocating it and the consumer from freeing it. Consumers usually use provider-owned memory when they need fast, read-only access to the data. For more information about provider-owned memory, see *dwMemOwner* in "DBBINDING Structures" earlier in this chapter.

If *dwMemOwner* is DBMEMOWNER_CLIENTOWNED, the provider allocates and the consumer frees the memory as noted in the following list. Although the provider must not access this memory after the method returns, the consumer can access it at any time until it is freed. Consumers use consumer-owned memory when they need their own copy of the data and when they send data to the provider.

- **DBTYPE_BSTR**—BSTRs are allocated and freed by calling COM string manipulation functions such as **SysAllocString** and **SysFreeString**. For more information, see Appendix A, "Data Types."
- **DBTYPE_BYREF**—Memory is allocated and freed by calling the COM task allocator's **IMalloc** methods.
- **DBTYPE_ARRAY**—SAFEARRAY structures are allocated and freed by calling COM array manipulation functions such as **SafeArrayCreate** and **SafeArrayDestroy**. For more information, see Appendix A, "Data Types."
- **DBTYPE_VECTOR**—Memory is allocated and freed by calling the COM task allocator's **IMalloc** methods.

The consumer can mix bindings in which pointers to the data and the data itself are returned. For example, suppose a rowset has two columns containing ANSI strings, one of which has a maximum length of 10 characters and the other of which has a maximum length of 32,000 characters. The consumer might choose to get the first string directly in its buffer (*wType* is DBTYPE_STR, *cbMaxLen* is 11, and *dwMemOwner* is DBMEMOWNER_CLIENTOWNED) and get a pointer to the provider's data cache for the second string (*wType* is DBTYPE_STR | DBTYPE_BYREF, and *dwMemOwner* is DBMEMOWNER_PROVIDEROWNED).

The consumer can also mix bindings in which the consumer and provider own the memory. For example, suppose a rowset includes two columns that contain ANSI strings with a maximum length of 32,000 characters but only one column is updatable. The consumer might choose to get pointers to both strings (*wType* is DBTYPE_STR | DBTYPE_BYREF) but to use consumer-owned memory (*dwMemOwner* is DBMEMOWNER_CLIENTOWNED) for the updatable string and provider-owned memory (*dwMemOwner* is DBMEMOWNER_PROVIDEROWNED) for the read-only string.

Data Transfer Procedures

The following sections discuss what the consumer and provider do to transfer data:

Getting Data

Setting Data

Getting Data

To get data—such as by using **IRowset::GetData** for rowset data or **ICommand::Execute** for output parameter data—the consumer must perform the following actions:

1. Create an accessor to bind the columns or output parameters.
2. Allocate a buffer to hold the data returned by the provider.
3. Call a method that gets data and passes the handle to the accessor and a pointer to the buffer.

For each column or output parameter specified in the accessor, the provider performs the actions in the following procedure. This procedure assumes that the consumer has bound the value, length, and status for each column or output parameter. If any of these are not bound, the procedure is the same except that the provider does not return the unbound part.

> **Note** If the accessor is a reference accessor, the provider does not follow this procedure but returns a pointer to the provider's memory that contains the data. For more information, see "Reference Accessors," earlier in this chapter.

4. Validate the accessor against the metadata if it has not already done so.

   The provider can validate the entire accessor before returning any data or on a binding-by-binding basis while returning data. If validation fails in the former case, the provider produces the appropriate return code and does not return any data. If it fails in the latter case, the provider sets the status of the column or output parameter to DBSTATUS_E_BADACCESSOR and proceeds to the next column or output parameter.

5. Check whether the data is NULL.

   If it is, either the provider sets the status to DBSTATUS_S_ISNULL and ignores the value and length or the provider sets the status to DBSTATUS_S_OK and sets the value to VT_EMPTY. The provider then proceeds to the next column or output parameter. The address where the status value is placed is calculated from the buffer address passed to the method and the *obStatus* element of the binding. A variant whose type is VT_NULL is different from a column status of DBSTATUS_S_ISNULL. Providers supporting variants, as well as consumers binding to variants, must be prepared to handle either type of NULL. However, if DBSTATUS_S_ISNULL is specified in the status binding, the contents of the value binding, regardless of type, are undefined.

6. Convert the data to the type specified by the *wType* element of the binding.

   If an error occurs while converting the data, the provider sets the status accordingly and proceeds to the next column or output parameter.

   For a list of status values that describe conversion errors, see "Status Values Used When Getting Data" in "Status," earlier in this chapter. For more information about converting data, see "Data Type Conversion Rules" in Appendix A, "Data Types."

7. Set the length.

   The address where the length value is placed is calculated from the buffer address passed to the method and the *obLength* element of the binding as follows:

   - **Variable-length data types**—The length of the untruncated data in bytes, not counting the null-termination character for strings.
   - **Fixed-length data types**—The size of the data type. If *wType* is DBTYPE_IUNKNOWN or DBTYPE_IDISPATCH, the length is **sizeof(IUnknown*)**, not the size of the object to which the interface pointer points. If *wType* is DBTYPE_BSTR, the length is **sizeof(BSTR)**, not the length of the string itself.
   - **DBTYPE_BYREF**—Does not affect the length value. For example, if *wType* is DBTYPE_BYREF | DBTYPE_STR, the length is the length in bytes of the string, not the length of the pointer.
   - **DBTYPE_VECTOR, DBTYPE_ARRAY**—If the type indicator is joined in a logical OR with DBTYPE_ARRAY or DBTYPE_VECTOR, the length is zero.

8. Set the data value to the converted data.

   The address where the data value is stored is calculated from the buffer address passed to the method and the *obValue* element of the binding as follows:

   - **Variable-length data types**—If the length in bytes of the converted, variable-length data is greater than *cbMaxLen* bytes, the provider truncates the data to *cbMaxLen* bytes before placing it in the consumer buffer and sets the status to DBSTATUS_S_TRUNCATED. Otherwise, the provider places the data in the consumer buffer without truncating it. For more information, see "String Data" in Chapter 10, "Data Types in OLE DB."
   - **Fixed-length data types**—The provider places the converted, fixed-length data in the consumer's buffer. The provider ignores *cbMaxLen*. It does not truncate the data before placing it in the consumer's buffer.

     If the type indicator is DBTYPE_IUNKNOWN or DBTYPE_IDISPATCH, the data value is a pointer to an interface on the COM object, not the object itself. For more information, see Chapter 7, "BLOBs and COM Objects."

     If the type indicator is DBTYPE_BSTR, the provider places the converted data in a BSTR and places the BSTR in the consumer's buffer. The provider ignores *cbMaxLen*. It does not truncate the data before placing it in the consumer's buffer. For information about how the BSTR is allocated and freed, see "Responsibility for Freeing Memory," earlier in this chapter.
   - **DBTYPE_BYREF, DBTYPE_VECTOR, DBTYPE_ARRAY**—For DBTYPE_BYREF, the provider places the converted data in separately allocated memory and places a pointer to this memory in the consumer's buffer. For DBTYPE_VECTOR, the provider places the converted data in an array and places the count of array elements and a pointer to the array in a DBVECTOR structure in the consumer's buffer. For DBTYPE_ARRAY, the provider places the converted data in a SAFEARRAY structure and places a pointer to the SAFEARRAY in the consumer's buffer. In each case, the provider ignores *cbMaxLen*. That is, it does not truncate the data before placing it in the separate memory, array, or SAFEARRAY. For information about how the separate memory, array, or SAFEARRAY is allocated and freed, see "Responsibility for Freeing Memory," earlier in this chapter.

9. Set the status to DBSTATUS_S_OK if it hasn't already been set to another value.

   If the provider encounters an error while returning a column or output parameter value, it sets the status value of that column or output parameter. The provider then continues to process the remaining columns or output parameters. After it has processed all columns or output parameters, if one or more errors have occurred, the provider produces one of the following return codes:

   DB_S_ERRORSOCCURRED—The method successfully returned data for at least one column or output parameter.

DB_E_ERRORSOCCURRED—The method did not successfully return data for any columns or output parameters.

The consumer checks the status values to determine the columns or output parameters for which data was successfully returned. If the consumer did not bind a status value for a column or output parameter, and a method returns DB_S_ERRORSOCCURRED or DB_E_ERRORSOCCURRED, the consumer must assume that all column or output parameter values were not successfully returned.

The provider frees any memory it allocated for return to the consumer but did not return to the consumer due to an error. If the method fails completely, the contents of the consumer's buffer are undefined.

Setting Data

To set data, such as with **IRowsetChange::SetData** for rowset data or **ICommand::Execute** for input parameter data, the consumer will perform the following actions:

1. Create an accessor to bind the columns or input parameters.
2. Allocate a buffer to hold the data to pass to the provider.
3. Place data in this buffer. (For more information, see the next procedure.)
4. Call a method that sets data and passes the handle to the accessor and a pointer to the buffer.

For each column or input parameter specified in the accessor, the consumer performs the following actions. When passing key values to an index rowset, the consumer performs these actions only for the number of key columns specified in the *cKeyValues* argument in **IRowsetIndex::Seek** or in the *cStartKeyValues* or *cEndKeyValues* arguments in **IRowsetIndex::SetRange**.

> **Note** This procedure assumes that the consumer has bound the value, length, and status for each column or input parameter. If any of these are not bound, the actions to be performed are the same except that the consumer does not set the unbound part.

5. proceeds to the next column or input parameter.

   If the provider is to use the default as the input value for an input or input/output parameter in a procedure, or if the provider updates the column, the consumer sets the status to DBSTATUS_S_DEFAULT and proceeds to the next column or input parameter.

   If the provider is to ignore this column in performing an insert or update, the consumer sets the status to DBSTATUS_S_IGNORE.

   Otherwise, the consumer sets the status to DBSTATUS_S_OK.

   The address where the status value is stored is calculated from the buffer address passed to the method and the **obStatus** element of the binding.

6. If *wType* is a variable-length data type, the consumer sets the length to the length of the data in bytes, not counting the null-termination character for strings.

   For all other data types, the provider ignores the length, so the consumer does not need to set it.

7. The consumer sets the data value.

   The address where the data value is stored is calculated from the buffer address passed to the method and the *obValue* element of the binding. If *wType* is DBTYPE_BSTR or is combined with DBTYPE_BYREF, DBTYPE_VECTOR, or DBTYPE_ARRAY, the consumer stores the data in separately allocated memory and stores in its buffer a pointer to the data. For information about how this memory is allocated and freed, see "Responsibility for Freeing Memory," earlier in this chapter.

For each column or input parameter specified in the accessor, the provider performs the following actions. When passing key values to an index rowset, the provider performs this procedure only for the number of key columns specified in the *cKeyValues* argument in **Seek** or in the *cStartKeyValues* or *cEndKeyValues* arguments in **SetRange**. This procedure assumes that the consumer has bound the value, length, and status for each column or input parameter. If any of these are not bound, the procedure is the same except that the provider does not attempt to retrieve the unbound part from the consumer's buffer. For more information, see "Binding Data Values," earlier in this chapter.

8. If it has not already done so, the provider validates the accessor against the metadata.

   The provider can validate the entire accessor before setting any data or on a binding-by-binding basis while setting data. If validation fails before the provider sets data, the provider produces the appropriate return code and does not set any data. If it fails when the provider is setting data, the provider sets the status to DBSTATUS_E_BADACCESSOR and proceeds to the next column or output parameter.

9. The provider retrieves the status value from the consumer's buffer, depending on the status setting, as follows:

   - **DBSTATUS_S_ISNULL**—The provider uses a null value and proceeds to the next column or input parameter.
   - **DBSTATUS_S_DEFAULT**—The provider uses the default value and proceeds to the next column or input parameter.
   - **DBSTATUS_S_IGNORE**—The provider skips the column and proceeds to the next column to be inserted or updated.
   - **DBSTATUS_S_OK**—The provider proceeds to the next step.

   If the status is any other value, the provider sets the status to DBSTATUS_E_BADSTATUS and proceeds to the next column or input parameter.

   The address from which the status value is retrieved is calculated from the buffer address passed to the method and the *obStatus* element of the binding.

10. If *wType* is a variable-length data type, the provider retrieves the length from the consumer's buffer.

    For all other data types, the provider ignores the length. The address from which the length value is retrieved is calculated from the buffer address passed to the method and the *obLength* element of the binding.

11. The provider retrieves the data value from the consumer's buffer. The address from which the data value is retrieved is calculated from the buffer address passed to the method and the *obValue* element of the binding.

    - **Variable-length data types**—The provider retrieves the number of bytes of variable-length data as specified by the length, up to *cbMaxLen* bytes. It is usually a consumer programming error if the length is greater than *cbMaxLen*. If no length is bound, the provider retrieves strings up to the first null-termination character.
    - **Fixed-length data types**—The provider retrieves the number of bytes of fixed-length data from the consumer's buffer based on the size of the data type. It ignores *cbMaxLen,* as well as the bound length pointed to at the offset indicated by *obLength.*

      If the type indicator is DBTYPE_IUNKNOWN or DBTYPE_IDISPATCH, the provider retrieves a pointer to an interface on the object from the consumer's buffer. For information about how the provider retrieves the object itself, see Chapter 7, "BLOBs and COM Objects."

      If the type indicator is DBTYPE_BSTR, the provider retrieves the pointer to the BSTR from the consumer's buffer and the BSTR itself from the memory to which this pointer points. The provider ignores *cbMaxLen*. That is, it does not truncate the BSTR to *cbMaxLen* bytes.

- **DBTYPE_BYREF**—The provider retrieves a pointer to the data from the consumer's buffer and the data from the memory to which this pointer points. The provider retrieves the data from this memory as if it were retrieving it directly from the consumer's buffer, except that it always ignores *cbMaxLen*, even when DBTYPE_BYREF is combined with DBTYPE_STR, DBTYPE_WSTR, DBTYPE_VARNUMERIC, or DBTYPE_BYTES.

  Note It is an error to combine DBTYPE_BYREF and DBTYPE_BYTES with no bound length.

- **DBTYPE_VECTOR**—The provider retrieves a pointer to an array of data and a count of the number of elements in the array from a DBVECTOR structure in the consumer's buffer. It retrieves the data itself from the array to which this pointer points. The provider retrieves the data from this memory as if it were retrieving it directly from the consumer's buffer.

- **DBTYPE_ARRAY**—The provider retrieves a pointer to a SAFEARRAY structure from the consumer's buffer. It retrieves the data from the SAFEARRAY to which this pointer points.

12. The provider converts the data from the type that is stored in the consumer's buffer, as specified by the *wType* element of the binding, to the type of the column or input parameter.

    If an error occurs while converting the data, the provider sets the status accordingly and proceeds to the next column or output parameter. For a list of status values that describe conversion errors, see "Status Values Used When Setting Data" in " Status," earlier in this chapter. For more information about converting data, see "Data Type Conversion Rules" in Appendix A, "Data Types."

If the provider encounters an error while retrieving a column or input parameter value, it sets the status value of that column or input parameter. Depending on the provider, it also does one of the following:

- Stops processing and backs out any changes already made
- Stops processing and leaves any changes already made
- Continues processing the remaining columns or input parameters

If the provider stops processing, it must set the status value to DBSTATUS_E_UNAVAILABLE for any column or input parameter that was not in error and was not successfully set. Thus, the consumer can determine which column or input parameter values were valid, which were invalid, and which were not validated.

When setting column data, except when searching for a key value or setting the index range, the provider then produces one of the following return codes:

- **DB_S_ERRORSOCCURRED**—The method successfully set data for at least one column.
- **DB_E_ERRORSOCCURRED**—The method did not successfully set data for any columns.

When setting input parameter data, searching for a key value, or setting the index range, the provider then returns DB_E_ERRORSOCCURRED.

CHAPTER 7

BLOBs and COM Objects

Some providers support the storage and retrieval of *binary large objects* (*BLOBs*) in rowsets. To the provider (and thus the rowset), a BLOB is a sequence of uninterpreted bytes. The consumer is responsible for interpreting the contents of the BLOB. The provider is responsible only for providing the mechanism or mechanisms with which the consumer stores and retrieves BLOBs and COM objects. Whether a provider supports BLOBs and COM objects is provider-specific.

This chapter discusses ways to access BLOB data as in-memory data, storage objects, and columns. In-memory data is treated as a sequence of bytes sent or retrieved in one piece. A storage object—that is, a COM object that exposes a storage interface such as **ISequentialStream**, **IStream**, **IStorage**, or **ILockBytes**—can be retrieved or sent in pieces. The rows in the rowset act as *containers* for the storage objects. This chapter also discusses limitations and lifetimes of storage objects. COM objects—for example, objects that support **IPersist*** interfaces—can also be stored in columns in a rowset. The manipulation, update semantics, and transaction considerations of **IPersist*** objects are explained in this chapter.

For more information on	Go to
Accessing BLOB data	"Accessing BLOB Data" in this chapter
In-memory data	"BLOBs as In-Memory Data" in this chapter
Storage object	"BLOBs as Storage Objects" in this chapter
Rowsets	Chapter 4, "Rowsets"
Limitations and lifetimes of storage objects	"Limitations of Storage Objects" in this chapter
	"Lifetime of Storage Objects" in this chapter
IPersist* objects	"**IPersist*** Objects" in this chapter

OLE DB defines handling of the following kinds of objects:

- **BLOB**—An uninterpreted sequence of bytes or characters. There is no behavior encapsulated in a BLOB. All the logic for interpreting a BLOB is in the consumer. The type indicator of a BLOB column is DBTYPE_BYTES, DBTYPE_STR, or DBTYPE_WSTR.
- **IPersist* object**—A COM object that exposes **IPersistStream**, **IPersistStreamInit**, or **IPersistStorage**. The type indicator of an **IPersist*** column is DBTYPE_IUNKNOWN.

The consumer can determine what types of BLOBs and COM objects a provider supports by calling **IDBProperties::GetProperties**, passing the DBPROP_OLEOBJECTS property as a parameter.

Accessing BLOB Data

BLOBs can be accessed as in-memory data—a sequence of bytes sent or retrieved as a single unit—or as storage objects, through **ISequentialStream**, **IStream**, **IStorage**, or **ILockBytes**.

The provider can set the DBCOLUMNFLAGS_ISLONG flag to inform the consumer that the provider supports treating BLOBs as storage objects. Although the consumer can still choose to access the BLOB as in-memory data, there might be provider-specific problems in doing so. For example, the BLOB might be truncated due to machine limits on memory. Also, limitations on BLOB columns might apply to binding BLOBs as in-memory data. For example, **IRowset::GetData** might fail if called more than once for the BLOB. For more information on possible limitations when accessing BLOB columns, see "Limitations of Storage Objects" in this chapter.

If the DBCOLUMNFLAGS_ISLONG flag is not set, the consumer can access the BLOB as in-memory data. It is provider-specific whether the provider supports reading such data through a storage interface. Most consumers allocate sufficient memory to hold such columns in their entirety and treat them as in-memory data.

BLOBs as In-Memory Data

When a BLOB is treated as in-memory data, it is sent or retrieved in a single piece of memory. If the consumer allocates the memory for the BLOB, it usually binds the column with a type indicator of DBTYPE_BYTES, DBTYPE_STR, or DBTYPE_WSTR, depending on the data contained in the BLOB. When getting data, if the consumer wants the provider to allocate the memory for the BLOB, it usually binds the column with one of the preceding type indicators combined with DBTYPE_BYREF.

To get the BLOB data, the consumer calls a method such as **IRowset::GetData** with an accessor containing this binding, and the provider returns the entire contents of the BLOB to the consumer. To set the BLOB data, the consumer calls a method such as **IRowsetChange::SetData** with an accessor containing this binding and sends the entire contents of the BLOB to the provider. This is no different from binding and getting or setting data in other columns, such as getting or setting data in an integer column. If consumers get or set character data in this manner, the data is null-terminated.

BLOBs as Storage Objects

A COM object that exposes one or more *storage interfaces* such as **ISequentialStream**, **IStream**, **IStorage**, or **ILockBytes** is known as a *storage object*. In OLE DB, BLOBs can be bound as storage objects. When a BLOB is stored in a column as a storage object, the provider indicates this by setting the DBCOLUMNFLAGS_ISLONG bit in the *dwFlags* element of the column's DBCOLUMNINFO structure. The consumer can get or set the BLOB by calling methods on one of its storage interfaces.

The rows in the rowset act as *containers* for the storage objects. The relationship between a storage object and the row that contains it is the same as the relationship between an **IStream** or **IStorage** object and its parent **IStorage** object.

This relationship dictates the behavior of the storage object with respect to its containing row in many circumstances. For example, COM requires that, when a parent **IStorage** object is released, all child objects are invalidated. If **IRowset::ReleaseRows** frees a row handle and no other references to the row remain, any storage objects open in that row enter a zombie state. In this case, releasing the object usually is the only valid consumer action.

The following table shows the rowset methods and interfaces that are analogous to **IStorage** methods and modes.

IStorage method or mode	Rowset method, interface, or mode
Transacted mode	Deferred update mode
Direct mode	Immediate update mode
IStorage::Commit	**IRowsetUpdate::Update**
IStorage::Revert	**IRowsetUpdate::Undo**
IStorage::CreateStream, **IStorage::OpenStream**, **IStorage::CreateStorage**, **IStorage::OpenStorage**	**IRowset::GetData** In most cases, BLOB data is not fetched and storage objects are not created until **GetData** is called. Methods that fetch rows, such as **IRowset::GetNextRows**, do not usually return data for BLOB columns in the rowset's copy of the row. For more information, see "Getting and Setting BLOB Data with Storage Objects," later in this chapter and "Deferred Columns" in Chapter 4, "Rowsets."
IStorage::DestroyElement	**IRowsetChange::SetData** For more information, see "Getting and Setting BLOB Data with Storage Objects," later in this chapter.

Limitations of Storage Objects

Storage objects are subject to the following limitations. Whether these limitations always exist is provider-specific.

- **Number of storage objects**—Some providers can support only one open storage object at a time, while others can support multiple open storage objects. If the provider supports only one open storage object at a time, any method that attempts to open a second storage object returns a status of DBSTATUS_E_CANTCREATE for the column or parameter, whether or not the objects are constructed over the same column, different columns in the same row, or different rows. A consumer determines whether a provider supports one or many storage objects by calling **IDBProperties::GetProperties** for the DBPROP_MULTIPLESTORAGEOBJECTS property.

- **Exclusionary behavior of storage objects**—Because of the way storage objects are implemented by some providers, using a storage object might prevent the use of other methods on the rowset. That is, after a storage object is created and before it is released, methods other than those on the storage object might return E_UNEXPECTED. By calling **IDBProperties::GetProperties** in the DBPROP_BLOCKINGSTORAGEOBJECTS property, a consumer determines whether storage objects might prevent the use of other methods.
- **Length of storage object must be known**—Some providers need to know the number of bytes of BLOB data that will be sent before any of the data is sent. This is usually related to a similar requirement in the underlying DBMS. For more information, see "Getting and Setting BLOB Data with Storage Objects," later in this chapter.

Lifetime of Storage Objects

Storage objects are freed in the same manner as other COM objects. Thus, when a consumer no longer needs a storage object created by a provider, it calls **Release** on that object. If the provider supports a VT_FALSE value for DBPROP_MULTIPLESTORAGEOBJECTS, the consumer must always call **Release** on the storage object before it can open a new storage object on any row. Releasing a reference to a storage object does not free the storage object. Doing so only causes the reference count on the storage object to be decremented. When the object's reference count reaches zero, the object is freed automatically.

In addition, a storage object might enter a zombie state if one of the following events occurs:

- The rowset containing the storage object is destroyed.
- The rowset's copy of the row containing the storage object is destroyed.
- The consumer calls **ITransaction::Commit** or **ITransaction::Abort**, and the retaining flag is set so that the rowset enters a zombie state.
- The consumer deletes the row containing the storage object and transmits the deletion to the underlying data store.

When a storage object enters a zombie state, it is not automatically released. Instead, if the consumer calls any method on the storage object except **Release**, that method returns E_UNEXPECTED. It is the consumer's responsibility to release the storage object, even if it is in a zombie state.

Getting and Setting BLOB Data with Storage Objects

The following sections discuss how to bind, get, and set BLOB data using storage objects.

Binding BLOB Data as a Storage Object

To bind BLOB data as a storage object, a consumer creates an accessor that includes a binding to the BLOB column. The consumer will perform the following actions:

1. Set the *wType* element of the DBBINDING structure for the BLOB column to DBTYPE_IUNKNOWN.
2. Set the *iid* element of the DBOBJECT structure in the binding to IID_ISEQUENTIALSTREAM, IID_ISTREAM, IID_ISTORAGE, or IID_ILOCKBYTES.

   If the consumer specifies an interface that is not supported by the provider, the provider returns E_NOINTERFACE when it validates the accessor. This can occur in **IAccessor::CreateAccessor** or in a method that uses the accessor, such as **IRowset::GetData**. To determine which interfaces are supported by the provider, the consumer calls **IDBProperties::GetProperties** with the DBPROP_STRUCTUREDSTORAGE property.
3. Set the *dwFlags* element of the DBOBJECT structure in the binding.

   If the consumer specifies any invalid or unsupported flags, the provider returns DB_E_BADSTORAGEFLAG when it validates the accessor. This can occur in **CreateAccessor** or in a method that uses the accessor, such as **GetData**.

Getting BLOB Data with Storage Objects

To get BLOB data by using a storage object, a consumer will perform the following actions:

1. Create an accessor that includes a binding for the column. (For more information, see "Binding BLOB Data as a Storage Object," earlier in this section.)
2. Call **IRowset::GetData**, **IRowsetRefresh::GetLastVisibleData**, or **IRowsetUpdate::GetOriginalData** with this accessor.

   The provider creates a storage object over the BLOB's data and returns a pointer to the requested storage interface (**ISequentialStream**, **IStream**, **IStorage**, or **ILockBytes**) on this object. If the provider supports only a single open storage object at a time and another storage object is open, the method returns a status of DBSTATUS_E_CANTCREATE for the column.

3. Call methods on the storage interface to get the BLOB's data, such as **ISequentialStream::Read**, **IStream::Read**, **ILockBytes::ReadAt**, or **IStorage::OpenStream**. If these methods are used to get character data, the data is not null-terminated.

If the consumer calls **GetData**, **GetLastVisibleData**, or **GetOriginalData** multiple times for the BLOB column, the provider returns distinct pointers to storage interfaces on each call. This is similar to opening a file multiple times and returning a different file handle each time. It is the consumer's responsibility to call **Release** on each of these storage interfaces separately.

For example, the following code binds a BLOB column and uses **ISequentialStream::Read** to get the data:

```
#include<oledb.h>

IRowset*       pIRowset;
IAccessor*     pIAccessor;
IMalloc*       pIMalloc;

int main() {
   // Assume the consumer has a pointer (pIRowset) that
   // points to the rowset. Create an accessor for the
   // BLOB column. Assume it is column 1.

   HACCESSOR      hAccessor;
   DBBINDSTATUS   rgStatus[1];
   DBOBJECT       ObjectStruct;
   DBBINDING      rgBinding[1] = {
      1,                             // Column 1
      0,                             // Offset to data
      0,                             // Ignore length field
      sizeof(IUnknown *),            // Offset to status field
      NULL,                          // No type info
      &ObjectStruct,                 // Object structure
      NULL,                          // Ignore binding extensions
      DBPART_VALUE|DBPART_STATUS,    // Bind value and status
      DBMEMOWNER_CLIENTOWNED,        // Consumer owned memory
      DBPARAMIO_NOTPARAM,            // Not a parameter
      0,                             // Ignore size of data
      0,                             // Reserved
      DBTYPE_IUNKNOWN,               // Type DBTYPE_IUNKNOWN
      0,                             // Precision not applicable
      0                              // Scale not applicable
   } ;
```

```
    // Set the elements in the object structure so that the
    // provider creates a readable ISequentialStream object over
    // the column. The consumer will read data from this object.
    ObjectStruct.dwFlags = STGM_READ;
    ObjectStruct.iid = IID_ISequentialStream;

    pIRowset->QueryInterface(IID_IAccessor, (void**) &pIAccessor);
    pIAccessor->CreateAccessor(DBACCESSOR_ROWDATA, 1, rgBinding,
                sizeof(IUnknown *) + sizeof(ULONG), &hAccessor, rgStatus);
  pIAccessor->Release();

    // Allocate memory for the returned pointer and the
    // status field. The first sizeof(IUnknown*) bytes are
    // for the pointer to the object, and the next sizeof(ULONG)
    // bytes are for the status.

    void * pData = pIMalloc->Alloc(sizeof(IUnknown *) + sizeof(ULONG));

    // Get the next row, and get the pointer to ISequentialStream
    HROW  *  rghRows = NULL;
    ULONG    cRows;

    pIRowset->GetNextRows(NULL, 0, 1, &cRows, &rghRows);
    pIRowset->GetData(rghRows[0], hAccessor, pData);

    // Read and process 5000 bytes at a time
    BYTE     gBuffer[5000];
    ULONG    cb;

    if ((ULONG)((BYTE*)pData)[rgBinding[0].obStatus] == DBSTATUS_S_ISNULL) {
    // Process NULL data
    } else if ((ULONG)((BYTE *)pData)[rgBinding[0].obStatus] == DBSTATUS_S_OK) {
       do {
          (*((ISequentialStream **)pData))->Read(rgBuffer, sizeof(rgBuffer), &cb);
          if (cb > 0)
             ; // Process data

       } while (cb >= sizeof(rgBuffer));
    };

    pIMalloc->Free(rghRows);
}
```

Setting BLOB Data with Storage Objects

There are two ways a consumer can set BLOB data by using a storage object:

- **By writing data directly to the provider's storage object**—The provider creates a storage object over the BLOB column and returns a pointer to this storage object to the consumer. The consumer writes data directly to this storage object.
- **By passing a pointer to a consumer's storage object**—The consumer creates a storage object containing the data and passes a pointer to this storage object to the provider. The provider then reads data from the consumer storage object and writes it to the BLOB column.

Writing Data Directly to the Provider's Storage Object

To write data directly to the provider's storage object, the consumer performs the following actions:

1. Creates an accessor that binds the value of the BLOB column.

   The consumer must specify that it needs to have write access to the storage object. For more information, see "Binding BLOB Data as a Storage Object," earlier in this section.

2. Calls **IRowset::GetData** with the accessor that binds the value of the BLOB column.

   The provider creates a storage object over the BLOB's data and returns a pointer to the requested storage interface (**ISequentialStream**, **IStream**, **IStorage**, or **ILockBytes**) on this object. If the provider supports only a single open storage object at a time and another storage object is open, the method returns a status of DBSTATUS_E_CANTCREATE for the column.

3. Calls a method on the storage interface to set data, such as **ISequentialStream::Write**, **IStream::Write**, or **ILockBytes::WriteAt**.

   Character data set with these methods is not null-terminated.

For a similar code example, see "Getting BLOB Data with Storage Objects," earlier in this section. The code for setting BLOB data is essentially the same, except that the consumer must set the *dwFlags* element of the *ObjectStruct* structure so that it can write to the storage object. Also, the consumer calls **ISequentialStream::Write** instead of **ISequentialStream::Read**.

Passing a Pointer to a Consumer's Storage Object

To pass a pointer to its own storage object, the consumer must perform the following actions:

1. Create an accessor that binds the value of the BLOB column. For more information, see "Binding BLOB Data as a Storage Object," earlier in this section.
2. If the consumer's storage object exposes **ISequentialStream** and the provider needs to know the number of bytes of BLOB data that will be sent before any of the data is sent, this accessor must also bind the length of the BLOB column. For more information, see "Limitations of Storage Objects" earlier in this chapter.Call **IRowsetChange::SetData** or **IRowsetChange::InsertRow** with the accessor that binds the BLOB column, passing a pointer to a storage interface on the consumer's storage object.

If the consumer's storage object exposes **ISequentialStream** and the provider needs to know the number of bytes of BLOB data that will be sent before any of the data is sent, this accessor must also bind the length of the BLOB column. For more information, see "Limitations of Storage Objects" earlier in this chapter.Call **IRowsetChange::SetData** or **IRowsetChange::InsertRow** with the accessor that binds the BLOB column, passing a pointer to a storage interface on the consumer's storage object.

If the provider already has a storage object open over the BLOB's data, the method might return a status of DBSTATUS_E_CANTCREATE for the column. Otherwise, the provider copies the data from the consumer's storage object to the BLOB column. This is equivalent to the provider destroying the existing data, creating a new (empty) storage object over the BLOB column, repeatedly calling methods to read data from the consumer's storage object and write data to the storage object over the BLOB column, and, if the storage mode is transacted, committing the changes on the storage object over the BLOB column. Character data set in this manner is not null-terminated.

If the provider needs to know the number of bytes of BLOB data that will be sent before any of the data is sent, it uses the **Stat** method on the consumer's storage object if the consumer's storage object exposes **IStream**, **IStorage**, or **ILockBytes**, or retrieves this number from the length part of the binding if the consumer's storage object exposes **ISequentialStream**. If the consumer binds the length and the provider does not need to know this information, or if the consumer's storage object exposes **IStream**, **IStorage**, or **ILockBytes**, the provider ignores the bound length value.

When the provider has finished using the consumer's storage object, it calls **Release** to release the pointer. After **SetData** or **InsertRow** returns, the provider must not hold any pointers or reference counts on the consumer's storage object. If the consumer wants to ensure access to its storage object after **SetData** returns, it must call **AddRef** on the pointer before calling **SetData**.

To set the BLOB column to a zero-length value, the consumer sets the status flag to DBSTATUS_S_OK. It then either passes a null pointer (instead of a pointer to its own storage object) or passes a pointer to a storage object that contains no data. The provider sets the column to a zero-length value. This is different from setting the status value for the column to DBSTATUS_S_ISNULL. If the consumer sets the column value to NULL and then calls **GetData**, the **GetData** method returns a status value of DBSTATUS_S_ISNULL. If the consumer sets the column to a zero-length value and then calls **GetData**, the **GetData** method returns a pointer to a storage object that contains no data.

> **Note** Not all providers support setting a BLOB column to a zero-length value.

For example, the following code passes a pointer to a different **ISequentialStream** object to **SetData** to overwrite the existing value:

```
#include<oledb.h>

IRowsetChange *      pIRowsetChange;
IAccessor *          pIAccessor;
ISequentialStream *  pISeqStr;
HROW                 hrow;

int main() {

   // Assume the consumer has a pointer (pIRowsetChange)
   // that points to the rowset's IRowsetChange interface
   // and a pointer (pISeqStr) that points to an
   // ISequentialStream object not in the rowset. Create an
   // accessor for the BLOB column. Assume it is column 1.

   HACCESSOR          hAccessor;
   DBBINDSTATUS       rgStatus[1];
   DBOBJECT           &ObjectStruct;
   DBBINDING          rgBinding[1] = {
      1,                             // Column 1
      0,                             // Offset to data
sizeof(IUnknown*),                   // obLength length field

      0,                             // Ignore status field
      NULL,                          // No type info
      ObjectStruct,                  // Object structure
      NULL,                          // Ignore binding extension
      DBPART_VALUE|DBPART_LENGTH,    // Bind value and length
      DBMEMOWNER_CLIENTOWNED,        // Consumer owned memory
      DBPARAMIO_NOTPARAM,            // Not a parameter binding
      0,                             // Ignore maxlength
      0,                             // Reserved
      DBTYPE_IUNKNOWN,               // Type DBTYPE_IUNKNOWN
      0,                             // Precision not applicable
```

```
      0,                              // Scale not applicable
   };

   // Set the elements in the object structure so that the
   // provider creates a writable ISequentialStream object
   // over the column. The provider will read data from the
   // ISequentialStream object passed to SetData and will
   // write it to this object.
   ObjectStruct.dwFlags = STGM_READ ;
   ObjectStruct.iid     = IID_ISequentialStream;

   pIRowsetChange->QueryInterface(IID_IAccessor, (void**) &pIAccessor);
   pIAccessor->CreateAccessor(DBACCESSOR_ROWDATA, 1, rgBinding, sizeof(IUnknown *),
pIAccessor->Release();

   // Assume you already have a row handle (HROW). Call
   // SetData and pass it the address of the pointer to the
   // object ISequentialStream not in the rowset. The rowset
   // will copy the data from the ISequentialStream object to
   // the rowset. Set up pData row buffer.
BYTE* pData=(BYTE*)CoTaskMemAlloc(sizeof(IUnknown*)+sizeof(ULONG));

// Value - pass ISequentialStream pointer to the provider
*(ISequentialStream**)(pData+rgBinding[0].obValue)=pISeqStr;
// LENGTH - Some providers need to know the length of the
// stream ahead of time....
*(ULONG*)(pData+rgBinding[0].oblength)=5000;

// SetData - The provider will then do an ISequentialStream::Read
// on the pISeqStr pointer passed in....
   pIRowsetChange->SetData(hrow, hAccessor, pData);
   CoTaskMemFree(pData);
return 0;
} ;
```

Getting and Setting BLOB Data with Storage Objects with Parameters

Consumers get and set BLOBs and COM objects in command parameters in a manner similar to accessing BLOB columns.

Storage Objects and Rowset Update Semantics

When does the data that is set in a storage object become visible to other transactions operating at the Read Uncommitted transaction isolation level? For providers built over database servers, this question can also be phrased as, "When does data that is set in a storage object become visible in the data store?"

The rules for storage objects are similar to the rules for data in other columns. That is, if the rowset is in immediate update mode, data made available to the rowset is immediately made available to Read Uncommitted transactions. If the rowset is in deferred update mode, data made available to the rowset is not made available to Read Uncommitted transactions until the consumer calls **IRowsetUpdate::Update**.

However, storage objects differ in two ways from other, nonstorage columns in the rowset:

Storage mode—Storage objects can have another layer of buffering based on the storage mode in which they operate. If the storage object operates in transacted mode, data is not available to the rowset until the consumer calls **Commit** on the storage interface. If the storage object operates in direct mode, data is immediately available to the rowset when the consumer sets it in the storage object.

Ignore deferred update mode—Storage objects can be large. Therefore, using them in deferred update mode can be expensive because the provider may locally cache any changes to them until **Update** is called. Consumers need to control this expense, so the DBPROP_DELAYSTORAGEOBJECTS property controls whether storage objects are always in immediate update mode, whether or not the rowset is in immediate or deferred update mode. For some providers, this is a read-only property. See the following illustration.

Storage object update visibility

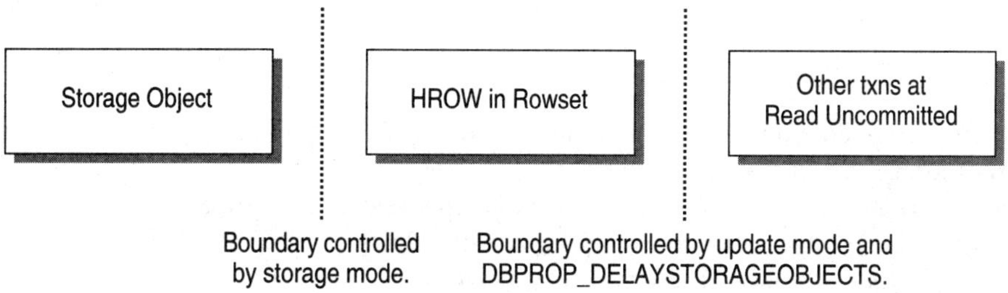

The following table shows the sequence of calls needed to make data that is set in a storage object visible to other transactions operating at the Read Uncommitted isolation level. In this table, **Write** refers collectively to any method on a storage interface that sets data, such as **ISequentialStream::Write**, **IStream::Write**, or **ILockBytes::WriteAt**, and **SetData** refers collectively to **IRowsetChange::SetData** and **IRowsetChange::InsertRow**. **ILockBytes** storage objects are always in Direct mode.

Storage mode	Update mode	DBPROP_DELAY-STORAGEOBJECTS	Calls needed to expose data to other transactions running at Read Uncommitted
Direct	Immediate	Not applicable	**Write** – or – **SetData**
Direct	Deferred	VARIANT_FALSE	**Write** – or – **SetData**
Direct	Deferred	VARIANT_TRUE	**Write** **Update** – or – **SetData** **Update**
Transacted	Immediate	Not applicable	**Write** **Commit** on storage interface – or – **SetData**
Transacted	Deferred	VARIANT_FALSE	**Write** **Commit** on storage interface – or – **SetData**
Transacted	Deferred	VARIANT_TRUE	**Write** **Commit** on storage interface **Update** – or – **SetData** **Update**

When the rowset is in deferred update mode, the consumer cannot undo any pending changes made through a storage object that is still open. That is, if the provider creates a storage object over the BLOB and returns a pointer to it through **IRowset::GetData**, the consumer must release this storage object before calling **IRowsetUpdate::Undo**. If the consumer fails to release the storage object, **Undo** returns a status of DBROWSTATUS_E_OBJECTOPEN for the row.

Storage Objects and Transactions

Whether storage objects are transacted depends on the DBPROP_TRANSACTEDOBJECT property, which can be set on a per-column basis. If the value of this property is VARIANT_TRUE, any storage object created on the column is transacted. That is, when a consumer calls **ITransaction::Commit** and the provider commits all data visible to the rowset, this includes data made visible to the rowset through storage objects. When a consumer calls **ITransaction::Abort** and the provider rolls back all data visible to the rowset, this includes data made visible to the rowset through storage objects. For information about what data in storage objects is visible to the rowset, see "Storage Objects and Rowset Update Semantics" earlier in this chapter.

Whether uncommitted data in transacted storage objects remains valid and whether the storage objects themselves remain valid when the transaction is committed or aborted depend on the retaining flag (*fRetaining*) used in the call to **ITransaction::Commit** or **ITransaction::Abort**. The retaining flag set to TRUE implicitly begins a new unit of work. If a commit is retaining, the storage objects and any uncommitted data in them remain valid. If an abort is retaining, the storage objects remain valid but any uncommitted data in them is lost; furthermore, the provider must synchronize the object with its state in the data store after the transaction was aborted there. If the rowset is not preserved after a commit or abort, the storage objects enter zombie states and any uncommitted data in them is lost. The consumer can only call **Release** on such objects. All other methods return E_UNEXPECTED. Whether the rowset is preserved depends on the DBPROP_COMMITPRESERVE and DBPROP_ABORTPRESERVE properties. For more information on committing and aborting a transaction, see Chapter 12, "Transactions."

If the value of DBPROP_TRANSACTEDOBJECT is VARIANT_FALSE, any storage object created on the column is not transacted. That is, all changes to the storage object are permanent once they are made visible in the data store. Calling **Commit** or **Abort** on a session containing a rowset with nontransacted storage objects should not affect the state of the storage object.

IPersist* Objects

COM objects can be stored in columns in a rowset. Such objects are required to expose **IPersistStream**, **IPersistStreamInit**, or **IPersistStorage**. The rowset has to know how to create instances of these objects, so it must store the objects' class IDs. How this is done is provider-specific.

Getting and Setting IPersist* Objects

The following sections explain how consumers get and set **IPersist*** objects and how these objects are stored by providers.

Getting IPersist* Objects

To get an **IPersist*** object from a column, a consumer performs the following actions:

1. Creates an accessor that includes a binding to the column. It sets the *wType* element of the DBBINDING structure to DBTYPE_IUNKNOWN and sets the *iid* element of the DBOBJECT structure in the binding to the needed interface.
2. Calls **IRowset::GetData**, **IRowsetRefresh::GetLastVisibleData**, or **IRowsetUpdate::GetOriginalData**.

If the object is not currently loaded, the provider will perform the following actions:

1. Create an instance of the **IPersist*** object and obtain an **IPersistStorage**, **IPersistStreamInit**, or **IPersistStream** pointer on it.

   For example, the provider might call **CoCreateInstance** with *rclsid* set to the class ID of the object and *riid* set to IID_IPERSISTSTORAGE. How the provider determines the class ID of the object is provider-specific.

2. Create an **IStream** or **IStorage** instance over the data in the column. If there is no data in the column, as is the case for a newly created row, the provider then calls **InitNew** on either **IPersistStorage** or **IPersistStreamInit**.

   If the provider supports only a single open storage object at a time and another storage object is open, the method returns a status of DBSTATUS_E_CANTCREATE for the column.

3. Load the **IPersist*** object: that is, call **Load** on the **IPersist*** interface on the object and pass the interface pointer obtained in step 2.

4. Perform the operations required to enable future calls to the method to detect that the object has already been loaded (for example, using a moniker to the object) and to return a pointer on the loaded object.
5. Return a pointer to the requested interface to the consumer.

   If the object does not support the requested interface, the method returns E_NOINTERFACE. After the method returns, the rowset does not hold any reference counts on the object.

If the object is currently loaded—which the provider can determine by virtue of the operations performed in step 4 in the preceding procedure—the provider will return a pointer to the requested interface to the consumer.

If the object does not support this interface, the method returns E_NOINTERFACE.

If any errors occur during these procedures, the provider ensures that no objects remain instantiated when **GetData**, **GetLastVisibleData**, or **GetOriginalData** returns.

Setting IPersist* Objects

To set an **IPersist*** object in a column, a consumer uses one of two procedures. The first procedure should be used only by consumers that know what kind of **IPersist*** objects should be stored in a column. Because the storage object, which is implemented by the rowset, does not have a pointer to the **IPersist*** object, the rowset cannot determine whether the **IPersist*** object uses a class ID that matches the class ID used by the objects in the column. The possibility therefore arises that the consumer could store an object in the column of a type that the rowset will not be able to later create an instance of.

In this first procedure, the consumer will perform the following actions:

1. Call **IRowset::GetData** to retrieve an **IStorage** or **IStream** pointer over the object's data.

   It does this in the same way it retrieves an **IStorage** or **IStream** pointer over BLOB data. The provider does not load the object, as is the case when the consumer calls **GetData** and requests a different interface, such as **IPersistStorage**. If the provider supports only one open storage object at a time and another storage object is open, the method returns a status of DBSTATUS_E_CANTCREATE for the column.
2. Call **Save** on the **IPersist*** interface of the **IPersist*** object and pass it the storage interface pointer retrieved in step 1.
3. Call **IPersistStorage::SaveCompleted** on the **IPersist*** object if **IPersistStorage** is used.

   The consumer should be careful if it sets the *pStgNew* parameter to a non-null pointer, because the provider does not dissociate the column's storage object from the **IPersist*** object.

The second procedure can be used by any consumer. It should be used by consumers that do not know what kind of **IPersist*** objects can be stored in the column because the provider can check the class ID of the object before storing it. In this second procedure, the consumer will call **IRowsetChange::SetData** or **IRowsetChange::InsertRow** and pass a pointer to an interface on the **IPersist*** object.

In turn, the provider will perform the following actions:

1. Create a new storage object for the column and retrieve a storage interface pointer on that object.

   If there is an existing storage object on the column that the provider cannot release, **SetData** or **InsertRow** returns a status of DBSTATUS_E_CANTCREATE for the column. For example, this occurs if there is an **IPersist*** object loaded on the column. If the provider supports only one open storage object at a time and a storage object is open over another column or row, the method might return a status of DBSTATUS_E_CANTCREATE for the column.

2. (Optional) Call **IPersist::GetClassID** on the **IPersist*** object to verify that the specified **IPersist*** object is of a type that can be stored in the column.

3. Call **Save** on the **IPersist*** interface of the **IPersist*** object and pass it the storage interface pointer retrieved in step 1.

   If the provider calls **IPersistStorage::Save**, it sets the *fSameAsLoad* argument to FALSE. If the provider calls **IPersistStream::Save** or **IPersistStreamInit::Save**, it sets the *fClearDirty* flag to TRUE.

4. Call **IPersistStorage::SaveCompleted** on the **IPersist*** object if **IPersistStorage** is used. The provider sets the *pStgNew* argument to a null pointer.

5. Perform the operations required to enable future calls to **GetData**, **GetLastVisibleData**, or **GetOriginalData** to detect whether the object is loaded and to return a pointer on the loaded object.

   After **SetData** or **InsertRow** returns, the rowset does not hold any reference counts on the **IPersist*** object.

Lifetime of IPersist* Objects

An ***IPersist**** *object* is a COM object that supports an **IPersist** interface. An **IPersist*** object instance created by the provider remains valid until it is released. However, if the row associated with the **IPersist*** object is released, the storage object associated with the **IPersist*** object enters a zombie state and the **IPersist*** object will no longer be able to use it.

IPersist* Objects, Rowset Update Semantics, and ITransaction

IPersist* objects provide yet another layer between the object and the data in the data store. Data stored in an **IPersist*** object is not exposed to its underlying storage object—and hence, to other transactions—until it is persisted by using **IPersist***. After the data is persisted, the storage object to which it was persisted controls when it is available to the rowset and to other transactions. For more information, see "Storage Objects and Rowset Update Semantics" and "Storage Objects and Transactions," earlier in this chapter.

The methods on **ITransaction** can indirectly affect **IPersist*** objects. For example, committing or aborting a transaction might send into a zombie state the storage object associated with the **IPersist*** object. For more information, see "Storage Objects and Transactions," earlier in this chapter.

CHAPTER 8

Index Rowsets

This chapter discusses the interfaces, use, and structure of an index rowset. An OLE DB *index,* also known as an *index rowset,* is a rowset built over an index in a data store. It is generally used in conjunction with a rowset built over a base table in the same data store. Each row of the index rowset contains a bookmark that points to a row in the base table rowset. Thus, the consumer can traverse the index rowset and use it to access rows in the base table rowset. Index structures can be either of two types: one or more columns that form a key value, or a column containing a bookmark. This chapter also includes an index example.

For more information on	Go to
Rowset	Chapter 4, "Rowsets"
Bookmark	"Bookmarks" in Chapter 4, "Rowsets"
Structure	"Structure of Index Rowsets" in this chapter
Use of indexes	"Using Index Rowsets" in this chapter
Index example	"Index Example" in this chapter

The index object cotype is defined as follows. For more information about cotypes, see "OLE DB Objects" in Chapter 1, "Overview of OLE DB."

```
CoType TIndex {
   [mandatory] interface IAccessor;
   [mandatory] interface IColumnsInfo;
   [mandatory] interface IConvertType;
   [mandatory] interface IRowset;
   [mandatory] interface IRowsetIndex;
   [mandatory] interface IRowsetInfo;
   [optional]  interface IRowsetChange;
   [optional]  interface IRowsetFind;
   [optional]  interface IRowsetIdentity;
   [optional]  interface IRowsetLocate;
   [optional]  interface IRowsetRefresh;
   [optional]  interface IRowsetScroll;
   [optional]  interface IRowsetUpdate;
   [optional]  interface IRowsetView;
   [optional]  interface ISupportErrorInfo;
};
```

The primary consumer for the **IRowsetIndex** interface is a query processor component that uses it during query execution. Although an SQL provider can expose **IRowsetIndex** by translating **IRowsetIndex** methods into SQL statements, this is not efficient. Instead, typical consumers of SQL providers should use the **ICommand** interface as the primary data access mechanism and rely on the query processor in the SQL provider to optimize access to data.

The primary index interface, **IRowsetIndex**, exposes the functionality required by file access methods based on ISAM and B+-trees. It does not support functionality such as the following: hashing, required by unordered indexes; R+-trees, required by access methods for spatial data; or signature files, required by access methods for text.

Index rowsets can be used in the following situations:

- Reading records efficiently by means of a *key,* which is one or more columns whose values, taken together, uniquely identify a row. The following are examples of SQL queries whose execution plans can exploit the capabilities of the **IRowsetIndex** interface:
  - Retrieving rows ordered by some column. For example where *x* is indexed:

    ```
    SELECT * FROM Table ORDER BY Table.x
    ```

  - Scanning records having a column value within a continuous range. For example:

    ```
    SELECT * FROM Table WHERE Table.x BETWEEN 4 AND 20
    ```

  - Computing joins. For example:

    ```
    SELECT * FROM R INNER JOIN S ON R.x = S.x
    ```

  - Retrieving distinct rows. For example, where R.x is indexed:

    ```
    SELECT DISTINCT R.x FROM R
    ```

  - Positioning at a particular index entry, such as skipping over key entries within a range.
- Supporting indexes with multicolumn keys. The values in each column can be in ascending or descending order.
- Traversing indexes in ascending or descending order to support **ORDER BY** clauses.

Structure of Index Rowsets

A row in an index rowset consists of at least two types of information: one or more columns that form a key value used to search in the index rowset, and a column containing a bookmark. The bookmark points to the row in the corresponding base table rowset that contains the key value. The provider must guarantee that these bookmarks consistently identify a row in the base table rowset.

The key columns must occur in the order of most significant key column to least significant key column. The consumer can determine this order from the *iOrdinal* values returned by **IColumnsInfo::GetColumnInfo**. The consumer can determine which columns are key columns from the DBINDEXCOLUMNDESC structure returned by **IRowsetIndex::GetIndexInfo**.

The bookmark that points to the base table rowset is not the *self* bookmark. That is, it is not the bookmark in column 0 that points to the row in the index rowset. Instead, it is a column with an ordinal greater than zero for which the DBCOLUMNFLAGS_ISBOOKMARK flag returned by **GetColumnInfo** is set.

The index rowset can contain other columns in addition to the key value columns and bookmark column. For example, it might contain a time stamp column. Such columns should be discussed in the documentation that describes the index provider. Although such columns are not barred from containing bookmarks, additional bookmark columns preclude the ability of generic query processors to use the index rowset. That is, such query processors are unable to determine which column contains the bookmark pointing to the base table rowset and which column contains a bookmark pointing elsewhere.

Using Index Rowsets

Index implementations vary in their support of certain capabilities. Before an index rowset is created, consumers can determine the capabilities of the underlying index by calling **IDBSchemaRowset::GetRowset** for the INDEXES schema rowset. They can determine the capabilities of an index rowset to which they already have an interface pointer by calling **IRowsetIndex::GetIndexInfo**.

To use an index rowset, a consumer must perform the following actions:

1. Create an instance of a rowset over a base table and create an index rowset over an index on the same base table.
2. Call **IColumnsInfo::GetColumnInfo** on the index rowset to determine which column contains the bookmarks that point to rows in the base table column.

   The ordinal of this column is greater than zero, and the DBCOLUMNFLAGS_ISBOOKMARK flag is set on it. **GetColumnInfo** also returns the key columns in the order of most significant column to least significant column. The consumer can determine which columns are the key columns by inspecting the DBINDEXCOLUMNDESC structure returned by **GetIndexInfo**.
3. (Optional) Call **IRowsetIndex::SetRange** on the index rowset to set the range in which to search for key values in the index. If the consumer does not call **SetRange**, the index rowset will search the entire index.
4. Call **IRowsetIndex::Seek** on the index rowset to set the next fetch position to a specified key value. This key value must be in the range set in step 3, which is optional. If the consumer did not perform step 3, **Seek** will search the entire index.
5. Call **IRowset::GetNextRows** on the index rowset to get the row or rows from the index starting with the key value specified in step 4. **GetNextRows** is limited to the range set in step 3, which is optional. If the consumer did not perform step 3, **GetNextRows** can traverse the entire index.
6. Call **IRowset::GetData** on the index rowset for each fetched row to get the bookmarks pointing to the base table rowset.
7. Call **IRowsetLocate::GetRowsByBookmark** on the base table rowset to retrieve the rows in that rowset that correspond to the index rows fetched in step 5.

Because an index is a rowset, the consumer can treat it like any other rowset. Therefore, the consumer can update the index by calling **IRowsetChange** methods. However, the provider is not required to validate the consumer's updates to the index.

Index Example

The code in this example accesses the Employees table through the Emp_LastName_Index index, using **IRowsetIndex** for the index and **IRowsetLocate** for the table.

The index has two columns. The first column, Emp_LastName, is of type DBTYPE_WSTR with a length of 30 characters and is the key column. The second column is of type DBTYPE_BYTES with a length of 4 bytes and contains the bookmark for the Employees table. In the information returned by **IColumnsInfo::GetColumnInfo** for this column, the DBCOLUMNFLAGS_ISBOOKMARK is set.

The code sample will perform the following actions:

1. Initialize the database and create a session (not shown).
2. Obtain interfaces for the table and index. (Only the latter is shown.)
3. Get information about the column types of the index rowset (not shown).
4. Establish bindings for the table and index columns. (Only the latter is shown.)
5. Create accessors for the table and index rowsets. (Only the latter is shown.)
6. Read the index rowset and retrieve the corresponding row from the table rowset.

```
#include<oledb.h>
#include<stddef.h>

GetTableRowsetLocate(IOpenRowset* , BSTR, IRowsetLocate**);
PrintData(OLECHAR*, ULONG, HROW*);
IMalloc *         pMalloc;           // pMalloc is the default memory allocator
HRESULT           hr;

int main() {
   IOpenRowset*    pIOpenRowset    = NULL;
   DBID            IndxId;
   IRowsetIndex*   pIndex          = NULL;
   IRowset*        pIndexRows      = NULL;
   IRowsetLocate*  pIRSLocate      = NULL;
   ULONG*          pColumns        = NULL;
   DBCOLUMNINFO**  prgInfo;
   OLECHAR**       ppStringsBuffer;
   IColumnsInfo*   pIndxColsInfo   = NULL;
   IAccessor*      pIndxAccsr      = NULL;
   HACCESSOR       hIndexAccBmk    = DB_INVALID_HACCESSOR;

   // Code not shown. Initialize the database, create a session, and obtain, from the
   // session object, a pointer pIOpenRowset to an IOpenRowset interface.

   // Use IOpenRowset::OpenRowset to obtain a pointer to IRowsetIndex.
   // Set the Index's DBID.
   IndxId.eKind = DBKIND_NAME;
   IndxId.uName.pwszName = OLESTR("Emp_LastName_Index");

   // Open the index with default properties and default interfaces (IRowsetIndex,
   // IAccessor, IRowset, IColumnsInfo, IRowsetInfo)
   pIOpenRowset->OpenRowset(NULL, NULL, &IndxId, IID_IRowsetIndex, 0, NULL,
                        (IUnknown**) &pIndex);

   // Get a rowset for the table using a helper function.
   GetTableRowsetLocate(pIOpenRowset, OLESTR("Employees"), &pIRSLocate);
```

```
// Get an accessor for the index
pIndex->QueryInterface(IID_IAccessor, (void**) &pIndxAccsr);

// Get a rowset for index traversal
pIndex->QueryInterface(IID_IRowset, (void**) &pIndexRows);

// Get a pointer to IColumnsInfo on the index, and get information about the columns
// of the index
pIndex->QueryInterface(IID_IColumnsInfo, (void**) &pIndxColsInfo);
pIndxColsInfo->GetColumnInfo(pColumns, prgInfo, ppStringsBuffer);

// Code not shown. Explore the DBCOLUMNINFO structures. The structure not corresponding
// to column 0 and with a flag DBCOLUMNFLAGS_ISBOOKMARK set is the bookmark to the base
// table. Suppose that the IColumnsInfo says that there are two columns, that
// column 1 (which corresponds to the key) contains a string, and that the base
// table bookmark is in column 2 and that it needs 4 bytes.
// Code shown: Create index and table bindings and corresponding accessors.
typedef struct tagBmk{
   OLECHAR*     Name;
   ULONG        cBookmark;
   BYTE         vBookmark[4];
} Bmk;

DBBINDSTATUS rgStatus[2];
static DBBINDING IndxBinds[2]= {
   {
   1,                              // Ordinal of key column
   0,                              // obValue
   0,                              // No length
   0,                              // No status
   NULL,                           // No TypeInfo
   NULL,                           // No object
   NULL,                           // No binding extensions
   DBPART_VALUE,                   // Bind value
   DBMEMOWNER_CLIENTOWNED,         // Client-owned memory
   DBPARAMIO_NOTPARAM,
   0,                              // cbMaxLen ignored
   0,
   DBTYPE_WSTR | DBTYPE_BYREF,     // DBTYPE
   0,                              // No Scale
   0                               // No Precision
   },
   {
   2,                              // Ordinal of base table bookmark
   offsetof(Bmk, vBookmark),       // Offset to value
   offsetof(Bmk,cBookmark),        // Offset to length
   0,                              // No status
   NULL,                           // No Type Info
   NULL,                           // No object
```

```
    NULL,                           // No binding extensions
    DBPART_VALUE | DBPART_LENGTH,   // Bind value and length
    DBMEMOWNER_CLIENTOWNED,         // Client-owned memory
    DBPARAMIO_NOTPARAM,
    4,                              // max length
    0,
    DBTYPE_BYTES,                   // DBTYPE
    0,                              // No Scale
    0                               // No Precision
    }
};

pIndxAccsr->CreateAccessor(DBACCESSOR_ROWDATA, 2, IndxBinds, 0, &hIndexAccBmk,
                           rgStatus);
//

// Set a range Emp_LastName LIKE "Smith*". Notice that only the Name element of the
// Bmk structure is used.
Bmk Bookmark;
Bookmark.Name = OLESTR("Smith");
pIndex->SetRange(hIndexAccBmk, 1, &Bookmark, 0, NULL, DBRANGE_PREFIX);
pIndex->Seek(hIndexAccBmk, 1, &Bookmark, DBSEEK_GE);

// Traverse index within the range. For each matching index entry, retrieve the
// corresponding record in the Employees table.
ULONG          cIdxRows = 0, cTabRows = 0;
HROW           *phIdxRows = NULL, *phTabRows = NULL;
DBROWSTATUS    rgRowStatus[1];

while(SUCCEEDED(hr = pIndexRows->GetNextRows(0, 0, 1, &cIdxRows, &phIdxRows)) &&
                cIdxRows > 0) {
   // Extract the bookmark from the index and read the table directly
   pIndexRows->GetData(*phIdxRows, hIndexAccBmk, &Bookmark);
   pIRSLocate->GetRowsAt(0, NULL, Bookmark.cBookmark, &(Bookmark.vBookmark[0]), 0,
                         1, &cTabRows, &phTabRows);
   PrintData(Bookmark.Name, cTabRows, phTabRows);

   // Release memory
   pMalloc->Free(Bookmark.Name);

   // Release the index and table rows
   pIndexRows->ReleaseRows(cIdxRows, phIdxRows, NULL, rgRowStatus, rgRowOptions);
   pIRSLocate->ReleaseRows(cTabRows, phTabRows, NULL, rgRowStatus, rgRowOptions);
};
```

```
    //Release the accessor
pIndxAccsr->ReleaseAccessor(hIndexAccBmk);

    //
};
```

CHAPTER 9

OLE DB Object Notifications

Notifications permit consumers to be informed of changes to objects, such as data source objects and rowsets, when these objects are shared with other consumers. When significant changes occur to the state of a shared object, the provider notifies all consumers that currently share access to the object. Support for notifications is provider-specific.

This chapter explains when notifications are sent, as well as how to nest and group them. It also discusses ways for consumers to screen out notifications of unwanted events or phases. To illustrate ways of issuing notifications, diagrams of states and state transitions in providers and consumers are provided.

For more information on	Go to
When notifications are sent	"When Notifications Are Sent" in this chapter
Nested notifications	"When Notifications Are Sent" in this chapter
Grouped notifications	"When Notifications Are Sent" in this chapter
States and state transitions in providers	"States and State Transitions in Providers" in this chapter
States and state transitions in consumers	"States and State Transitions in Consumers" in this chapter
Threading and notifications	"Threading and Notifications" in Chapter 14, "Programming Considerations"

When Notifications Are Sent

Providers send notifications when changes occur to provider objects, such as rowsets, that are shared by two or more consumers. For example, when several consumers share a rowset, and one of them changes the rowset by calling an **IRowsetChange** method, the provider can notify the other consumers in case they need to refresh their local copies of row data. To receive these notifications, consumers must implement **IRowsetNotify** and register it on a connection point with the provider, which calls **IRowsetNotify** methods to send notifications to consumers.

Notifications also can be used to coordinate sets of changes performed by multiple consumers. Often such changes occur in phases, during which participating consumers make changes based on changes made by other consumers in previous phases.

Note Providers do not send notifications when changes are attempted but fail.

Notifications can be nested. That is, sending one notification can cause a consumer to take actions that cause another notification to be sent.

Notifications can also be grouped. For example, providers that support notifications can be instructed to send only two notifications for an operation on multiple rowsets: one for all rows that succeeded and one for all rows that failed. If a provider supports grouping of notifications, it reports a value of DBPROPVAL_NT_MULTIPLEROWS for the property DBPROP_NOTIFICATIONGRANULARITY.

If an action causes the provider to send multiple notifications, all of those notifications must be approved by the consumer before the provider performs the action. If a consumer cancels a single notification, the provider does not perform the action and returns DB_E_CANCELED. For example, if a call to **IRowsetChange::SetData** changes multiple columns, the consumer must approve the changes to all of the columns before the provider changes any of the columns. If the consumer does not allow a change to any of the columns, no columns are updated. For more information, see the entry for **IRowsetChange::SetData** in the reference section.

Consumers can screen out unwanted events or phases of an event by returning DB_S_UNWANTEDREASON or DB_S_UNWANTEDPHASE when the provider calls the consumer's **IRowsetNotify** methods to report the unwanted events. Providers are not required to stop notifying consumers of the unwanted events or phases. However, for performance reasons, providers can choose not to send notifications of unwanted events. Screening out a phase applies only to that particular event. Other events will still send out notifications for all phases unless they are also screened.

States and State Transitions in Providers

The following diagram shows the events that take place within a rowset method, such as **IRowsetChange::SetData**, when it is implemented in a provider that supports notifications.

Provider state/state transition diagram

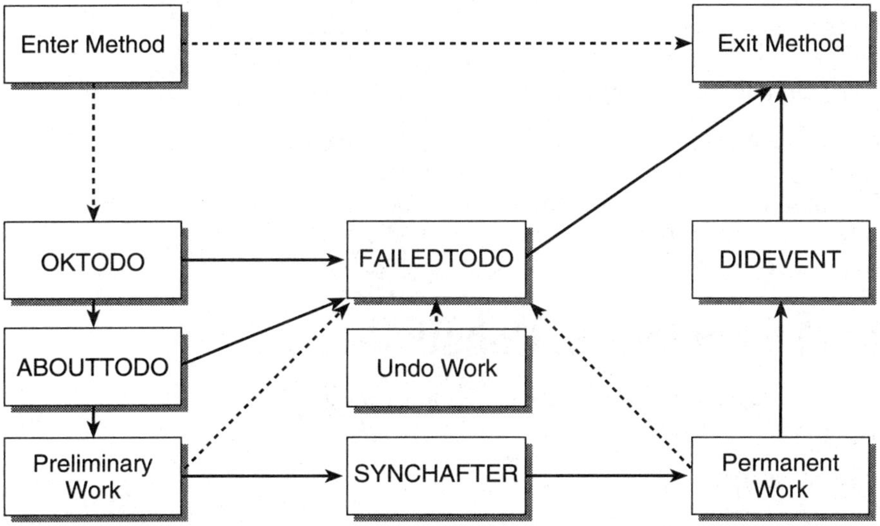

States

- Enter Method and Exit Method are conceptual states representing the initial and final states of a method issuing notifications.
- OKTODO, ABOUTTODO, SYNCHAFTER, DIDEVENT, and FAILEDTODO are states representing notifications sent by the method to consumers.
- Preliminary Work, Permanent Work, and Undo Work are internal states representing work done by the provider between notification phases.

Transitions

- Arrows with a heavy continuous line represent transitions within states when all consumers return S_OK as a result of the notification sent by the state at the start of the arrow. In general, a transition through a heavy continuous line represents an acceptance path by the consumer on the notification.
- Arrows with a light continuous line represent transitions within states when at least one consumer returns S_FALSE as a result of the notification sent by the state at the start of the arrow. In general, a transition through a light continuous line represents a cancellation path by the consumer on the notification.
- Arrows with a dashed line represent internal transitions within the method. The transitions from Preliminary Work or Permanent Work to FAILEDTODO are transitions that result from some error in the execution of the method. A transition from Enter Method to Exit Method represents a path where the method detects some error condition that implies no notification work.

States and State Transitions in Consumers

The following diagram shows the actions that can take place within a consumer that supports notifications through **IRowsetNotify**.

Consumer state/state transition diagram

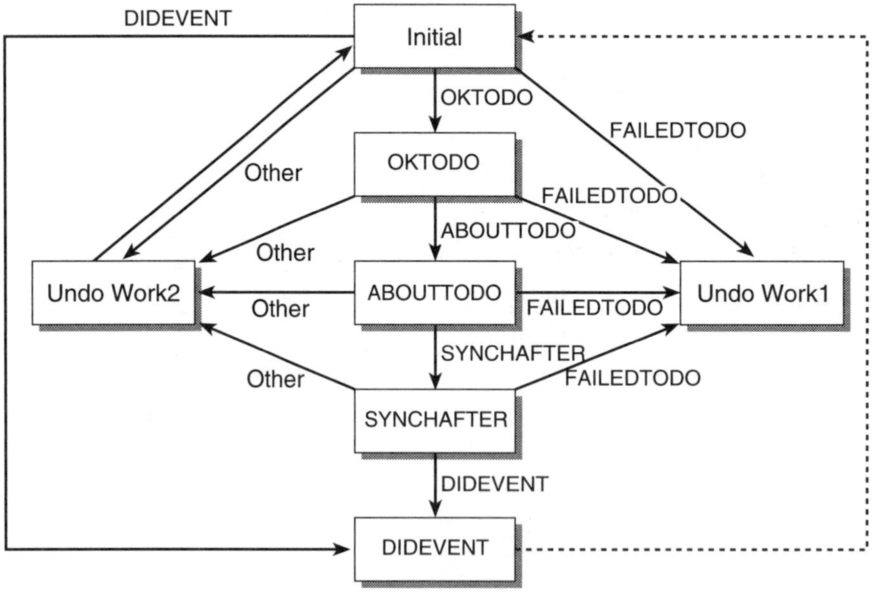

States

- Initial is a conceptual state denoting the initial state of any **IRowsetNotify** method before any phase starts. At this point, full phased events such as DBREASON_COLUMN_SET can receive an OKTODO or FAILEDTODO phase. Any other phase at this point is unexpected, causing the method to undergo a transition to the Undo Work2 state that returns S_FALSE.
- OKTODO, ABOUTTODO, SYNCHAFTER, and DIDEVENT are states to which the method undergoes a transition when the method receives the phase having the same name as the respective state. All these states can involve some internal work by the consumer. All states, except DIDEVENT, can receive a FAILEDTODO notification, which causes the method to undergo a transition to the Undo Work1 state.
- Undo Work1 is an internal state to which the listener undergoes a transition from any state (except DIDEVENT) on reception of a FAILEDTODO phase. In this state, any work done by the consumer is undone. After the work is undone, the method reverts back to the Initial state and returns S_OK.
- Undo Work2 is an internal state that captures any unexpected phase. In this state, any work done by the consumer is undone. Once the work is undone, the method reverts back to the Initial state and returns S_FALSE.

Transitions

- Arrows with a continuous heavy line represent transitions within states upon reception of some expected phase.
- Arrows with a continuous light line represent transitions resulting from receiving an unexpected phase.
- Arrows with a dashed line represent an internal transition by the consumer.

CHAPTER 10

Data Types in OLE DB

This chapter introduces OLE DB data type indicators. Providers use these type indicators to tell consumers what data types they support. Consumers use them when creating tables and when getting and setting data. Example mappings from native data types to OLE DB data type indicators are given for an ANSI SQL provider, a Microsoft Access provider, and a Microsoft SQL Server provider. The treatment of string values and provider support for data type conversions are also discussed.

For more information on	Go to
Consumers and providers	"Consumers and Providers" in Chapter 1, "Overview of OLE DB"
Using type indicators in providers	"Using Type Indicators in Providers" in this chapter
Type indicators in an ANSI SQL Provider	"Type Indicators in an ANSI SQL Provider" in this chapter
Type indicators in a Microsoft Access provider	"Type Indicators in a Microsoft Access Provider" in this chapter
Type indicators in a Microsoft SQL Server provider	"Type Indicators in a Microsoft SQL Server Provider" in this chapter
Using type indicators in consumers	"Using Type Indicators in Consumers" in this chapter
Using type indicators when creating tables in consumers	"Using Type Indicators When Creating Tables" in this chapter
Using type indicators when getting and setting data in consumers	"Using Type Indicators When Getting and Setting Data" in this chapter
Determining the type of data from a string	"String Data" in this chapter
Fixed-length and variable-length data	"Fixed-Length and Variable-Length Data Types" in this chapter
Provider support for data type conversions	"Data Type Conversion" in this chapter

OLE DB uses standard OLE and Windows data types. To describe a data type, a *type indicator* is used. This is a variable of the enumerated type DBTYPE that is passed as metadata. Although it is easy to confuse the two, type indicators are not data types. For example, DBTYPE_GUID is an integer with a value of 72, not a GUID. It is used to indicate that a piece of memory contains a GUID. For more information on how data types map to type indicators, see "Type Indicators" in Appendix A, "Data Types."

Places where type indicators are used include the following:

- **Metadata.** Type indicators are used to specify the data type of a column or parameter.
- **DBBINDING structures.** The *wType* element of the DBBINDING structure describes the type of the bound data value. When getting data, this is the type to which the provider converts the data before returning it to the consumer. When setting data, this is the type from which the provider converts the data after retrieving it from the consumer.
- **VARIANT structures.** The *vt* element, a short integer, of the VARIANT structure indicates the type of the data that is stored in the structure. The remainder of the structure is 14 bytes, which are structured according to the *vt* tag. The DBTYPE enumerated type is a superset of the VARENUM enumerated type, so some DBTYPE values cannot be used in VARIANT structures.

For a complete list of type indicators, see "Type Indicators" in Appendix A, "Data Types."

Using Type Indicators in Providers

OLE DB defines a standard set of data type indicators for the most commonly used data types. Providers use these data type indicators to tell consumers what data types they support. Each provider maps its own underlying data types to these data type indicators and advertises its support for them through the PROVIDER_TYPES schema rowset. The underlying data types used by the provider are unimportant to the consumer. What is important is that the provider guarantees that it can always safely transfer data in the type represented by the indicator it advertises for a column or parameter. For examples of how various providers might map underlying data types to OLE DB data types, see the following sections.

Providers are not required to support all of the OLE DB data types listed in "Type Indicators" in Appendix A, "Data Types," nor are they required to support all possible conversions among them. For information about what conversions all providers are required to support, see "Data Type Conversion," later in this chapter.

Although OLE DB attempts to provide a unified type system, it is subject to the following limitations:

- It does not standardize type names as used in text commands. The TYPE_NAME column in the PROVIDER_TYPES schema rowset contains the type name consumers should use when executing Data Definition Language (DDL) commands. This saves providers from having to parse such commands before passing them to the data source.
- It exposes data store–specific type names for parameters in text commands. For more information, see ICommandWithParameters::SetParameterInfointhereferencesection.

Type Indicators in an ANSI SQL Provider

This table shows how an ANSI SQL provider might map its data types to OLE DB data types.

SQL data type	OLE DB type indicator
CHAR (n)	DBTYPE_STR
VARCHAR (n)	DBTYPE_STR
CLOB	DBTYPE_STR
DECIMAL (p, s)	DBTYPE_NUMERIC
NUMERIC (p, s)	DBTYPE_NUMERIC
BIT	DBTYPE_BOOL
TINYINT	DBTYPE_I1
SMALLINT	DBTYPE_I2
INTEGER	DBTYPE_I4
BIGINT	DBTYPE_I8
REAL	DBTYPE_R4
FLOAT	DBTYPE_R8
DOUBLE PRECISION	DBTYPE_R8
BINARY (n)	DBTYPE_BYTES
VARBINARY (n)	DBTYPE_BYTES
BLOB	DBTYPE_BYTES
DATE	DBTYPE_DBDATE
TIME	DBTYPE_DBTIME
TIMESTAMP	DBTYPE_DBTIMESTAMP

Type Indicators in a Microsoft Access Provider

This table shows how a Microsoft Access provider might map its data types to OLE DB data types.

Microsoft Access data type	OLE DB type indicator
BINARY (< 255 bytes)	DBTYPE_BYTES
BIT	DBTYPE_BOOL
BYTE	DBTYPE_UI1
COUNTER	DBTYPE_I4
CURRENCY	DBTYPE_CY
DATETIME	DBTYPE_DATE
DOUBLE	DBTYPE_R8
GUID	DBTYPE_GUID
LONG	DBTYPE_I4
LONGBINARY	DBTYPE_BYTES
LONGTEXT	DBTYPE_STR
SHORT	DBTYPE_I2
SINGLE	DBTYPE_R4
TEXT (< 255 bytes)	DBTYPE_STR

Type Indicators in a Microsoft SQL Server Provider

This table shows how a Microsoft SQL Server provider might map its data types to OLE DB data types.

Microsoft SQL Server data type	OLE DB type indicator
char [(n)] ($1 \leq n \leq 255$)	DBTYPE_STR
varchar [(n)] ($1 \leq n \leq 255$)	DBTYPE_STR
binary [(n)] ($1 \leq n \leq 255$)	DBTYPE_BYTES
varbinary [(n)] ($1 \leq n \leq 255$)	DBTYPE_BYTES
numeric [(p[,s])]	DBTYPE_NUMERIC
decimal [(p[,s])]	DBTYPE_NUMERIC

Microsoft SQL Server data type	OLE DB type indicator
tinyint	DBTYPE_UI1
smallint	DBTYPE_I2
int	DBTYPE_I4
real	DBTYPE_R4
float [(n)]	DBTYPE_R8
smalldatetime	DBTYPE_DATE, DBTYPE_DBTIMESTAMP
datetime	DBTYPE_DATE, DBTYPE_DBTIMESTAMP
timestamp	DBTYPE_BYTES (DBCOLUMNFLAGS_ISROWVER is set)
text	DBTYPE_STR
image	DBTYPE_BYTES
smallmoney	DBTYPE_CY
money	DBTYPE_CY
user-defined-type	DBTYPE_UDT

Using Type Indicators in Consumers

Consumers use type indicators when creating and altering tables and when getting and setting data. To determine which data types are supported by the provider, the consumer calls **IDBSchemaRowset::GetRowset**, passing DBSCHEMA_PROVIDER_TYPES as a parameter. This method returns the provider's predefined PROVIDER_TYPES schema rowset, which contains detailed information about the data types that are supported by the provider. For more information about the PROVIDER_TYPES schema rowset, see "PROVIDER_TYPES Rowset" in Appendix B, "Schema Rowsets."

Using Type Indicators When Creating Tables

Consumers can create tables in two ways. One is to call **ICommand::Execute** on a command object containing an SQL **CREATE TABLE** statement as its command text. (For more information, see Chapter 3, "Commands.") The other is to call either **ITableDefinition::CreateTable** or **ITableDefinitionWithConstraints::CreateTableWithConstraints**. When creating a table by calling **ITableDefinition** or **ITableDefinitionWithConstraints** methods, the consumer creates a DBCOLUMNDESC structure whose elements specify the columns of the table. The *wType* and *pwszTypeName* elements of this structure correspond to the DATA_TYPE and TYPE_NAME column values from the PROVIDER_TYPES schema rowset. A consumer is guaranteed to always get a safe conversion when getting or setting values of the column by using the type indicator specified in *wType*.

For example, a provider built on top of an SQL92-compliant DBMS might contain the following rows in the PROVIDER_TYPES schema rowset.

TYPE_NAME	DATA_TYPE	COLUMN_ SIZE	MINIMUM_ SCALE	MAXIMUM_ SCALE
"CHAR"	DBTYPE_STR	32000	NULL	NULL
"VARCHAR"	DBTYPE_STR	32000	NULL	NULL

For the CHAR type, COLUMN_SIZE indicates the maximum length in characters of a value of that type supported by this provider. When defining a column of this type, the consumer is free to assign any value between 1 and 32000 to the *ulColumnSize* element of the DBCOLUMNDESC structure associated with the column. Internally, the provider may choose any representation for values of the type, provided that it always returns data to the consumer as a null-terminated string.

For more information about the DBCOLUMNDESC structure, see "ITableDefinition::CreateTable" in the reference section.

Using Type Indicators When Getting and Setting Data

Most consumers, when they allocate memory in which to get or set data, use the type corresponding to the indicator returned by **IColumnsInfo::GetColumnInfo** for the column. When a consumer gets or sets data according to the type returned by **GetColumnInfo**, the provider guarantees it can always transfer the data safely. The consumer specifies this indicator in the *wType* element of the DBBINDING structure used to bind the memory.

The consumer can allocate and bind memory of a different type only if the provider supports conversion between that type and the type returned by **GetColumnInfo**. For more information, see "Data Type Conversion" later in this chapter.

String Data

The term *string* is used collectively to refer to ANSI strings, Unicode strings, and BSTRs. When used as metadata—for example, in a schema rowset, a metadata interface such as **IColumnsInfo**, or a data definition interface such as **ITableDefinition**—string lengths are always measured in characters. When passing data, such as with **IRowset::GetData**, string lengths are always measured in bytes.

When a consumer gets string data from a provider as an in-memory string rather than through a storage object, the provider always returns a null-terminated string to the consumer. If the consumer's buffer is smaller than the sum of the length of the character data plus the length of the null-termination character, the provider truncates the data and adds a null-termination character to the truncated data. String data retrieved through a storage object is not null-terminated.

> **Note** Consumers cannot assume that multibyte character set (MBCS) string data was truncated at a character boundary.

To ensure that strings returned by the provider are not truncated, consumers should allocate space for a null-termination character. The following examples illustrate three cases where the buffer size determines whether all significant data is copied into the consumer's buffer:

- When the size of the buffer is less than the size in bytes of the string (that is, *cbMaxLen* is less than the length in bytes), the string is truncated and a null-termination character is added. For example, the ANSI string ABCDEF\0 is stored in a 5-byte buffer as ABCD\0.
- When the size of the buffer is equal to the size in bytes of the character data but no allowance has been made for the null-termination character (that is, *cbMaxLen* equals the length in bytes), the string is truncated and a null-termination character is added. One character of data is lost, even though the size of the buffer is equal to the size in bytes of the character data. For example, the ANSI string ABCDEF\0 is stored in a 6-byte buffer as ABCDE\0.
- When the size of the buffer is greater than or equal to the size in bytes of the character data plus space for the null-termination character, the complete string is copied into the consumer's buffer. For example, the ANSI string ABCDEF\0 is stored in a 7-byte buffer as ABCDEF\0.

> **Note** It is an error to set *cbMaxLen* to less than the size of the null-termination character.

Whether character data is stored in the provider with a null-termination character is specific to each provider. If the consumer binds the character as another type, such as binary, the character data is returned without a null-termination character.

For ANSI strings and Unicode strings, the length returned in the length part of the binding is the actual length of the data in bytes. The null-termination character is not counted. For BSTRs, the length returned in the length part of the binding is **sizeof(BSTR)**, not the length of the actual string. The length of the actual string can be obtained by calling **SysStringLength**. For more information, see "Type Indicators" in Appendix A, "Data Types."

Fixed-Length and Variable-Length Data Types

The provider determines how much memory to allocate for each data value based on its data type indicator. For fixed-length data types, such as Booleans and integers, the provider simply allocates enough space to hold one item of that type. For variable-length data types, the provider must rely on the consumer to specify how much memory must be allocated for the data. The consumer does this by setting the value of *cbMaxLen* appropriately.

When the length part of a binding is applied to a column, the length includes all bytes of the value. It should be the same as the length passed to **IMalloc** to allocate a buffer big enough to hold the data value. For strings, this length must include space for a null-termination character. If the value is to be converted, the length should be the length in bytes that the value has after it is converted into the type specified by the consumer.

If a variable-length string value is copied into a buffer that is too small to hold it, the string is truncated abruptly to fit the buffer. No attempt is made to trailing-align or trim the value, although strings are null-terminated. The returned length is the length in bytes of the untruncated value, which the consumer can compare to *cbMaxLen* to determine how many bytes were lost when the string was truncated.

> **Note** Variable-length numeric data values are not truncated. Attempting to copy a variable-length numeric value into a buffer that is too small to hold the entire value is a programming error.

DBTYPE_BYREF, DBTYPE_ARRAY, and DBTYPE_VECTOR are modifiers of data types and do not affect whether a data type is fixed-length or variable-length. However, these modifiers do affect how data is stored and how *cbMaxLen* is used in the DBBINDING structure.

For a complete list of fixed-length and variable-length data types, see "Fixed-Length Data Types" and "Variable-Length Data Types" in Appendix A, "Data Types."

Data Type Conversion

Providers must be able to convert bound data values as follows:

- To the native type used by the provider for the column or parameter, as returned by **IColumnsInfo::GetColumnInfo** or **ICommandWithParameters::GetParameterInfo**. Such transfers must be performed without loss of data.
- To and from DBTYPE_WSTR if such a conversion is defined by OLE DB. For more information, see "Conversion Tables" in Appendix A, "Data Types." Conversions to and from DBTYPE_WSTR are defined for virtually all types.

Support for additional conversions is optional and might result in truncation of data or a conversion error. The consumer can determine what conversions a provider supports by calling **IConvertType::CanConvert** with the indicators for the "to" and "from" types. If a provider offers additional functions that the consumer can call to convert data types, these functions are described in a type library pointed to by the PROVIDER_TYPES schema rowset.

For more information about how data is converted, see "Data Type Conversion Rules" in Appendix A, "Data Types."

CHAPTER 11

Properties

This chapter defines and discusses properties, property sets, and property groups. Consumers can expose and set object properties as well as retrieve information about properties. Property structures and enumerated types are used to pass property values and information about properties. This chapter explains how this is accomplished and provides a detailed description of these structures and types.

Properties are attributes of an object. For example, a rowset has properties that describe the maximum number of rows that can be open at one time and whether or not the rowset exposes bookmarks.

Consumers set property values to request specific object behavior. For example, consumers use properties to specify which interfaces they want a rowset to expose.

Consumers get property values to determine the capabilities of an object. For example, consumers use properties to determine what transaction isolation levels a data source object can support.

Each property has a value, a type, a description, a read/write attribute, and, for rowset properties, an indicator of whether it can be applied on a column-by-column basis.

For more information on	Go to
Rowsets	Chapter 4, "Rowsets"
Data source object	"Data Source Objects" in Chapter 2, "Data Source and Session Objects"
Property sets and groups	"Property Sets and Property Groups" in this chapter
How a consumer sets property values	"Setting Property Values" in this chapter
How a consumer gets property values	"Getting Property Values" in this chapter
How a consumer gets property information	"Getting Information About Properties" in this chapter
Property structures and enumerated types	"Property Structures and Enumerated Types" in this chapter

Property Sets and Property Groups

A property can be associated with an OLE DB object, such as a data source object, or with an entity that is not directly represented as an OLE DB object, such as a table or column. Every OLE DB property belongs to a *property set*. Each property is identified by its property set's GUID and an integer property ID that is unique within the property set. Taken together, the property set's GUID and the property ID uniquely identify the property. OLE DB predefines a number of property sets and the properties in them. Providers also can define provider-specific property sets containing their own properties.

Each property belongs to a *property group*. A property group is a set of logically related properties that could apply to an OLE DB object, such as a rowset or a data source object. Property groups are identified by a DBPROPFLAGS value that is returned in the DBPROPINFO structure. OLE DB defines property groups. Providers cannot define provider-specific property groups.

Property sets and property groups overlap. That is, a property group can contain properties from more than one property set

Property Sets

The following table shows property sets that are defined by OLE DB. Providers also can define their own property sets.

Property set GUID	Description
DBPROPSET_COLUMN	All OLE DB–defined properties in the Column property group.
DBPROPSET_DATASOURCE	All OLE DB–defined properties in the Data Source property group.
DBPROPSET_ DATASOURCEINFO	All OLE DB–defined properties in the Data Source Information property group.
DBPROPSET_DBINIT	All OLE DB–defined properties in the Initialization property group.
DBPROPSET_INDEX	All OLE DB–defined properties in the Index property group.
DBPROPSET_ROWSET	All OLE DB–defined properties in the Rowset property group.
DBPROPSET_SESSION	All OLE DB–defined properties in the Session property group.
DBPROPSET_TABLE	All OLE DB–defined properties in the Table property group.

Property set GUID	Description
DBPROPSET_ PROPERTIESINERROR	If **ICommand::Execute**, **ICommandPrepare::Prepare**, or **IDBInitialize::Initialize** returns DB_S_ERRORSOCCURRED or DB_E_ERRORSOCCURRED, the consumer can immediately call **ICommandProperties::GetProperties** or **IDBProperties::GetProperties** with a single DBPROPIDSET structure to return all the properties that were in error. This property set is not returned by **GetPropertyInfo**. In the DBPROPIDSET structure, the consumer sets *guidPropertySet* to DBPROPSET_PROPERTIESINERROR, *cPropertyIDs* to 0, and *rgPropertyIDs* to a null pointer. If the consumer fails to set any of these correctly, **GetProperties** returns E_INVALIDARG. It is an error to pass this property set to any method that sets properties. The method returns the same error it would for any other unsupported property set. Methods that return information about properties do not return information about this property set. If any other property sets are passed to **GetProperties** with this property set, **GetProperties** returns E_INVALIDARG. Calling **GetProperties** with DBPROPSET_PROPERTIESINERROR at a time other than immediately after the call that returns DB_S_ERRORSOCCURRED or DB_E_ERRORSOCCURRED might yield inconsistent results, because the consumer's actions might have caused the provider to clear or alter the list of properties in error.

Property Groups

The following table shows the property groups that are defined by OLE DB. Providers cannot define their own property groups. Each property group is a set of logically related properties that could apply to an OLE DB object, to an operation on an OLE DB object, or to an object that is not directly represented as an OLE DB object.

Property group	Description
Column	Properties used to create columns.
Data Source	Properties that apply to data source objects. These properties can be set for some providers.
Data Source Creation	Properties used to create data source objects.
Data Source Information	Properties that describe data source objects. These properties are read-only for all providers and constitute a set of static information about the provider and its data source object.
Initialization	Properties used to initialize the data source object or enumerator.
Index	Properties used to create and describe indexes.
Rowset	Properties that apply to rowsets.
Session	Properties that apply to sessions.
Table	Properties used to create tables.

For information about how a consumer determines which group a property is in, see "Getting Information about Properties" later in this chapter.

Setting Property Values

To set property values, a consumer must perform the following actions:

1. Determine the properties for which to set values. To set the value of a property to a different value, the property must be settable. However, consumers can set the value of a read-only property to its default value. For information about how to determine if a property is settable, see "Getting Information about Properties" later in this chapter.
2. Determine the property sets that contain the identified properties.
3. Allocate an array of DBPROPSET structures, one for each identified property set.
4. Allocate an array of DBPROP structures for each property set. The number of elements in each array is the number of properties, identified in step 1, that belong to that property set.
5. Store the property's value in that property's DBPROP structure, along with a flag showing whether it is required or optional.

   If the provider cannot satisfy a required property, it fails to create the object to which the property applies, and the object-creation method returns DB_E_ERRORSOCCURRED. If the provider cannot set the value of an optional property, it creates the object to which the property applies, and the method returns DB_S_ERRORSOCCURRED.

If the property belongs to the Rowset property group and applies to a single column, the consumer sets the *colid* element of the DBPROP structure to the ID of the column. Otherwise, the consumer sets the value of *colid* to DB_NULLID.

Note In cases where the *colid* element in the DBPROP structure for specified properties is ignored, the consumer must nevertheless set the value of *colid* to DB_NULLID. Not to do so is a programming error.

6. For each property set, place the property set GUID in the DBPROPSET structure. It then places in the DBPROPSET structure the count of elements in, as well as the pointer to, the corresponding DBPROP array.
7. Call a method that sets properties and pass it the count and array of DBPROPSET structures. The provider returns the status of each property in the *dwStatus* element of the DBPROP structure for that property—that is, whether the property was set and, if not, why it was not set.

For example, assume that the consumer wants to set values for five properties, where properties 1, 2, and 3 are in property set A and properties 4 and 5 are in property set B. The consumer uses the structures shown in the following illustration.

An example of setting property values

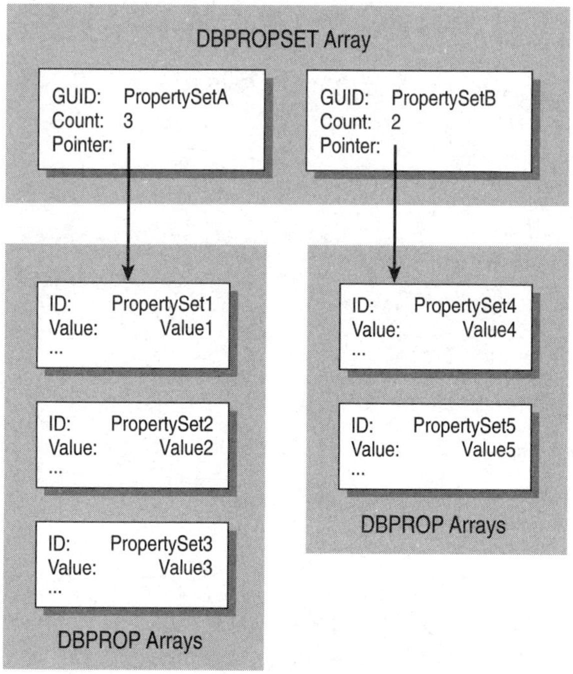

The following table lists methods consumers can call to set property values.

Property group	Methods used to set property values
Column	ITableDefinition::CreateTable
Data Source	IDBProperties::SetProperties
Data Source Creation	IDBDataSourceAdmin::CreateDataSource
Data Source Information	IDBProperties::SetProperties
Initialization	IDBProperties::SetProperties
Index	IIndexDefinition::CreateIndex
Rowset	IColumnsRowset::GetColumnsRowset, ICommandProperties::SetProperties, IDBSchemaRowset::GetRowset, IOpenRowset::OpenRowset, ISourcesRowset::GetSourcesRowset, ITableDefinition::CreateTable
Session	ISessionProperties::SetProperties
Table	ITableDefinition::CreateTableIAlterTable::AlterTable

Read-only properties can always be set to their default values or to VT_EMPTY. Setting read-only properties to any other values will cause an error.

Getting Property Values

To get property values, a consumer must perform the following actions:

1. Determine the properties for which to get values.
2. Determine the property sets that contain the identified properties.
3. Allocate an array of DBPROPIDSET structures, one for each identified property set.
4. Allocate an array of DBPROPIDs for each property set.

   The number of elements in the array is determined by the number of properties identified in step 1 that belong to that property set.
5. Store the ID of each property in the appropriate DBPROPID array.
6. Store the GUID for each property set in the appropriate DBPROPIDSET structure. The consumer then stores a pointer to the corresponding DBPROPID array, along with the number of elements in the array, in the same DBPROPIDSET structure.
7. Call a method that gets properties and pass it the count and array of DBPROPIDSET structures.

To return property values, the provider must perform the following actions:

1. Allocate an array of DBPROPSET structures.

   The elements of this array correspond to the elements of the DBPROPIDSET array.

2. For each element of the DBPROPIDSET array, allocate an array of DBPROP structures.

   The elements of the DBPROP array correspond to the elements of the DBPROPID array.

3. Store the value, column ID, whether the property is required or optional, and status of each property in the DBPROP structure that corresponds to the DBPROPID value for that property.

4. Store the GUID for each property set in the appropriate DBPROPSET structure. The provider then stores a pointer to the corresponding DBPROP array, along with the number of elements in the array, in the same DBPROPSET structure.

5. Return the number of DBPROPSET structures, along with the array of DBPROPSET structures itself, to the consumer.

For example, assume that the consumer wants to get values for five properties, where properties 1, 2, and 3 are in property set A and properties 4 and 5 are in property set B. The consumer uses the structures shown in the following illustration.

An example of how a consumer gets property values

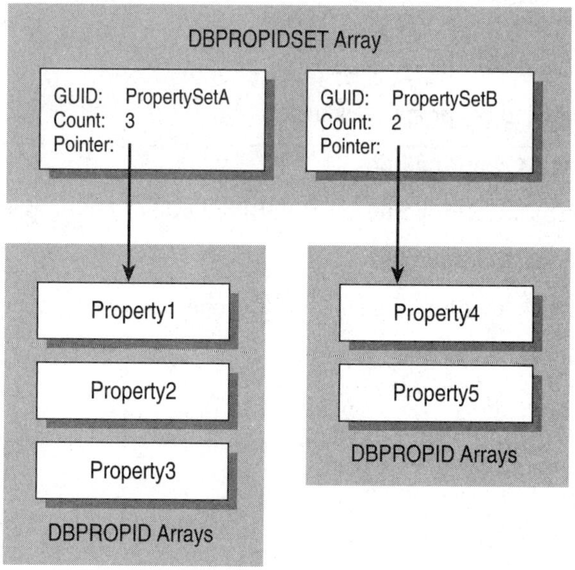

The provider returns the structures shown in the following illustration.

An example of what property values a provider returns

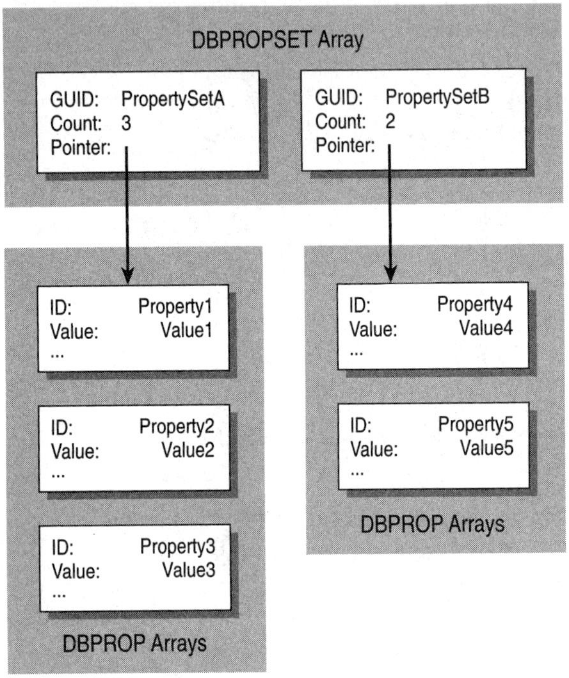

The following table lists methods consumers can call to get property values.

Property group	Methods used to get property values
Data Source	IDBProperties::GetPropertie
Data Source Information	IDBProperties::GetPropertiesoledbIDBProperties__GetProperties
Index	IRowsetIndex::GetIndexInfo
Initialization	IDBProperties::GetPropertiesoledbIDBProperties__GetProperties
Rowset	ICommandProperties::GetProperties, IRowsetInfo::GetProperties
Session	ISessionProperties::GetProperties

Getting Information About Properties

To get information about properties, a consumer can perform the following actions:

1. Determine the properties for which to get information.
2. Determine the property sets that contain the identified properties.
3. Allocate an array of DBPROPIDSET structures, one for each identified property set.
4. Allocate an array of DBPROPIDs for each property set.

   The number of elements in the array is determined by the number of properties identified in step 1 that belong to that property set.
5. Store the ID of each property in the appropriate DBPROPID array.
6. Store the GUID for each property set in the appropriate DBPROPIDSET structure. The consumer then stores a pointer to the corresponding DBPROPID array, along with the number of elements in the array, in the same DBPROPIDSET structure.
7. Call a method that gets properties and pass it the count and array of DBPROPIDSET structures.

To return property values, the provider can perform the following actions:

1. Allocate an array of DBPROPINFOSET structures.

   The elements of this array correspond to the elements of the DBPROPIDSET array.
2. For each element of the DBPROPIDSET array, allocate an array of DBPROPINFO structures. The elements of the DBPROPINFO array correspond to the elements of the DBPROPID array.
3. Store the ID, description, type, property group, whether the property can be read from or written to, and list of valid values of each property in the DBPROPINFO structure that correspond to the DBPROPID value for that property. For properties that do not apply to columns, the provider sets the column ID to NULL_ID.
4. Store the GUID for each property set in the appropriate DBPROPINFOSET structure. The provider then stores a pointer to the corresponding DBPROPINFO array, along with the number of elements in the array, in the same DBPROPINFOSET structure.
5. Return the number of DBPROPINFOSET structures, along with the array of DBPROPINFOSET structures itself, to the consumer.

For example, assume that the consumer wants to get information about five properties, where properties 1, 2, and 3 are in property set A and properties 4 and 5 are in property set B. The consumer uses the structures shown in the following illustration.

An example of how a consumer gets information about properties

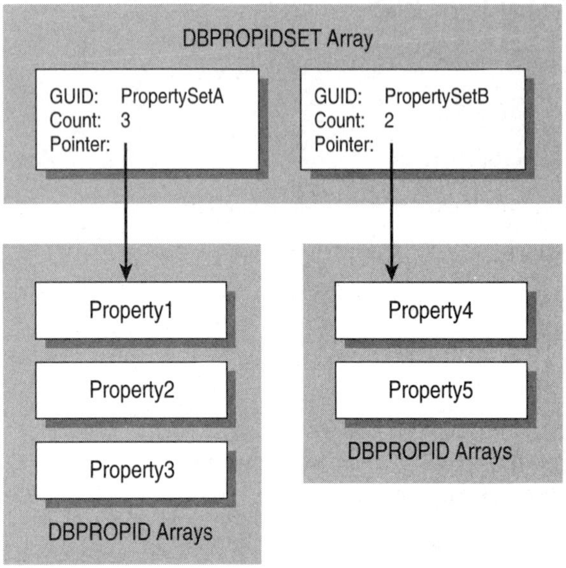

The provider returns the structures shown in the following illustration.

An example of what property information a provider returns

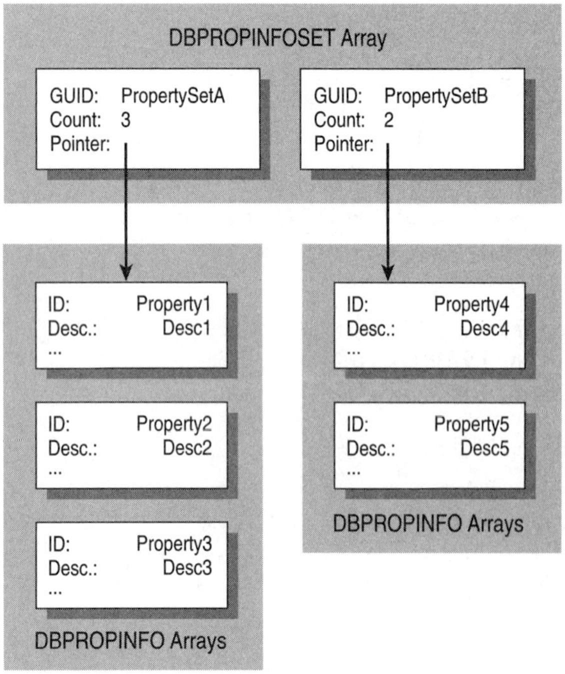

The following table lists methods consumers can call to get information about properties.

Property group	Methods used to get information about properties
All property groups	IDBProperties::GetPropertyInfo
Data Source Creation	IDBDataSourceAdmin::GetCreationProperties
Initialization	IDBDataSourceAdmin::GetCreationProperties
Session	IDBDataSourceAdmin::GetCreationProperties

Property Structures and Enumerated Types

The following structures and types are used to pass property values and information about properties. They are described in other sections in this chapter.

Structure or enumerated type	Description
DBPROP	A structure used by the consumer or provider to pass a value for a single property.
DBPROPFLAGS	A value used by the provider in a DBPROPINFO structure to describe a single property.
DBPROPID	A value used by the consumer or provider to identify a property. This value is used in conjunction with a property set GUID.
DBPROPIDSET	A structure used by the consumer to pass an array of DBPROPID values that identify properties for which the consumer wants to get values or information.
DBPROPINFO	A structure used by the provider to return information about a single property.
DBPROPINFOSET	A structure used by the provider to return an array of DBPROPINFO structures.
DBPROPOPTIONS	A value used in a DBPROP structure by the consumer or provider to specify whether a property value is required or optional.
DBPROPSET	A structure used by the consumer or provider to pass an array of DBPROP structures.
DBPROPSTATUS	A value used in a DBPROP structure by the provider to specify whether it was able to set a property value.

DBPROP Structure

Consumers and providers use DBPROP structures to pass property values. An array of DBPROP structures, one for each property in the property set, is passed in a DBPROPSET structure. Each DBPROPSET structure represents one property set.

The DBPROP structure is defined as:

```
typedef struct tagDBPROP {
   DBPROPID       dwPropertyID;
   DBPROPOPTIONS  dwOptions;
   DBPROPSTATUS   dwStatus;
   DBID           colid;
   VARIANT        vValue;
} DBPROP;
```

The elements of this structure are described in the following table.

Element	Description
dwPropertyID	The ID of the property.
dwOptions	The options for this property. For example, when setting a property, the consumer can specify that the property is optional; therefore the provider should continue even if it cannot satisfy the property. Alternatively, the consumer can specify that a property is required; therefore the provider should fail if it cannot satisfy the property.
dwStatus	The status returned by the provider to indicate success or failure in setting or getting the property value. This value is ignored on input and need not be set by the consumer. For properties the provider does not support, the provider returns DBPROPSTATUS_NOTSUPPORTED in this element and the values of *dwOptions*, *colid*, and *vValue* are undefined.
colid	An optional ID for a column to which the property applies. To specify that a particular property applies to all columns, the consumer sets *colid* to DB_NULLID. This is ignored unless the property can be applied to a column—that is, unless the DBPROPFLAGS_COLUMNOK flag is returned for the property in the *dwFlags* element of the DBPROPINFO structure. **Note** The consumer is required to set *colid* to a valid DBID value or to DB_NULLID, even if the actual value of *colid* is ignored by the provider. Not setting *colid* to a valid value or to DB_NULLID is a programming error.

Element	Description
vValue	The value of the property. When getting property values, if the consumer requests the value of a property that has not been set and has no default, VT_EMPTY is returned. When setting property values, specifying VT_EMPTY returns the property to its default value. **Note** The consumer is required to set *vValue* to a valid VARIANT value or to VT_EMPTY, even if the actual value of *vValue* is ignored by the provider. Not setting *vValue* to a valid value or to VT_EMPTY is a programming error.

DBPROPFLAGS Enumerated Type

Providers use DBPROPFLAGS values to describe the property, such as the group to which a property belongs and whether the property can be read from or written to. DBPROPFLAGS is used in the DBPROPINFO structure.

The DBPROPFLAGS enumerated type is described in the following table. These flags can be combined except as noted.

Value	Description
DBPROPFLAGS_NOTSUPPORTED	The property is not supported, or the consumer has requested information about properties not in the Initialization property group and the data source object is uninitialized. If this value is returned, it cannot be combined with any of the other DBPROPFLAGS values.
DBPROPFLAGS_COLUMN	The property belongs to the Column property group. The flags DBPROPFLAGS_COLUMN, DBPROPFLAGS_DATASOURCE, DBPROPFLAGS_DATASOURCECREATE, DBPROPFLAGS_DATASOURCEINFO, DBPROPFLAGS_DBINIT, DBPROPFLAGS_INDEX, DBPROPFLAGS_ROWSET, DBPROPFLAGS_SESSION, and DBPROPFLAGS_TABLE are mutually exclusive. For a description of property groups, see "Property Groups" earlier in this chapter.

Value	Description
DBPROPFLAGS_DATASOURCE	The property belongs to the Data Source property group.
DBPROPFLAGS_DATASOURCECREATE	The property belongs to the Data Source Creation property group.
DBPROPFLAGS_DATASOURCEINFO	The property belongs to the Data Source Information property group.
DBPROPFLAGS_DBINIT	The property belongs to the Initialization property group.
DBPROPFLAGS_INDEX	The property belongs to the Index property group.
DBPROPFLAGS_ROWSET	The property belongs to the Rowset property group.
DBPROPFLAGS_SESSION	The property belongs to the Session property group.
DBPROPFLAGS_TABLE	The property belongs to the Table property group.
DBPROPFLAGS_COLUMNOK	This flag applies only to properties in the Rowset property group and can be set only when DBPROPFLAGS_ROWSET is set. If it is set, the property can be applied to all columns in the rowset or to a specific column in the rowset. Whether the property applies to a specific column or to all columns depends on the value of *colid* in the DBPROP structures used to set or get the property value. If it is not set, the property applies to all columns in the rowset. Setting this flag means the provider supports the property on a per-column basis.
DBPROPFLAGS_READ	A method can get the property's value. For a list of methods that get properties, see "Getting Property Values" earlier in this chapter.
DBPROPFLAGS_WRITE	A method can set the property's value. For a list of methods that set properties, see "Setting Property Values" earlier in this chapter.

Value	Description
DBPROPFLAGS_REQUIRED	The property must be set. When returned by **IDBProperties::GetPropertyInfo**, this flag applies only to properties in the Initialization property group and can be set only when DBPROPFLAGS_DBINIT is set. If this flag is set, the consumer must specify a value for the property before calling **IDBInitialize::Initialize** to initialize the data source or enumerator. Whether or not a property is required for a particular provider can vary depending on other properties specified (for example, DBPROP_DATASOURCE) or on other provider-specific factors. Providers should mark as required only those properties that are always required for that instance of the data source object. Consumers should be aware that, depending on other factors, such as the combination of initialization properties specified, additional properties not marked as required may need to be specified. When returned by **IDBDataSourceAdmin::GetCreationProperties**, this flag applies to properties in the Data Source Creation and Session property groups and properties in the Initialization property group that can be used in data source object creation. If it is set, the consumer must specify a value for the property when calling **IDBDataSourceAdmin::CreateDataSource**. If it is not set, the data source object can be created even if the consumer does not specify a value for the property.

DBPROPID Type

Consumers and providers use DBPROPID values, in conjunction with property set GUIDs, to identify properties. An array of DBPROPID values is passed in a DBPROPIDSET structure.

Within a property set, each property has a unique ID. All property IDs must be greater than or equal to 2. (Property IDs 0 and 1 are reserved.)

The DBPROPID type is defined as follows:

```
typedef DWORD DBPROPID;
```

DBPROPIDSET Structure

Consumers use DBPROPIDSET structures to pass an array of property IDs for which the consumer wants to get values or information. The properties identified in a single DBPROPIDSET structure all belong to the same property set.

The DBPROPIDSET structure is defined as:

```
typedef struct tagDBPROPIDSET {
   DBPROPID *  rgPropertyIDs;
   ULONG       cPropertyIDs
   GUID        guidPropertySet;
} DBPROPIDSET;
```

The elements of this structure are described in the following table.

Element	Description
rgPropertyIDs	A pointer to an array of property IDs for which to return values or information. If *cPropertyIDs* is zero, this is ignored.
cPropertyIDs	The number of properties from the property set for which to return values or information. If *cPropertyIDs* is zero, the method ignores *rgPropertyIDs* and returns values for or information about all of the properties in the property set.
guidPropertySet	A GUID that identifies the property set to which the properties belong. If the provider does not support this property set, the method to which this is passed returns DB_S_ERRORSOCCURRED or DB_E_ERRORSOCCURRED. If *cPropertyIDs* is zero, the method sets *cProperties* and *rgProperties* in the corresponding DBPROPSET structure or *cPropertyInfos* and *rgPropertyInfos* in the corresponding DBPROPINFOSET structure to zero and a null pointer, respectively. If *cPropertyIDs* is not zero, then for each property specified in *rgPropertyIDs*, the method sets *dwStatus* in the corresponding DBPROP structure to DBPROPSTATUS_NOTSUPPORTED or *dwFlags* in the corresponding DBPROPINFO structure to DBPROPFLAGS_NOTSUPPORTED.

DBPROPINFO Structure

Providers use DBPROPINFO structures to return information about properties. An array of DBPROPINFO values is passed in a DBPROPINFOSET structure.

The DBPROPINFO structure is defined as follows:

```
typedef struct tagDBPROPINFO {
   LPOLESTR       pwszDescription;
   DBPROPID       dwPropertyID;
   DBPROPFLAGS    dwFlags;
   VARTYPE        vtType;
   VARIANT        vValues;
} DBPROPINFO;
```

The elements of this structure are described in the following table.

Element	Description
pwszDescription	A text description of the property. For properties defined by OLE DB, this must be the description listed for the property in Appendix C, "Property Tables." This property description is used to construct connection strings and is required to be kept unlocalized.
dwPropertyID	The ID of the property.
dwFlags	A bitmask that describes the property, such as the group it belongs to and whether it can be read from or written to. For more information, see "DBPROPFLAGS Enumerated Type" earlier in this chapter. If the property is not supported, this is DBPROPFLAGS_NOTSUPPORTED. In this case, *pwszDescription* is set to NULL, and *vtType* and *vValues* are set to indicate VT_EMPTY.
vtType	The type indicator of the property. This is used in the *vt* element of the VARIANT structure passed in the DBPROP structure.

Value	Description
vValues	A list of the supported values for the property. Normally this list is returned only if the property can be set and either: • The property type is an integer and the possible values of the property are an enumerated type. • The property type is an integer whose bits are to be read as a bitmask and all supported bits are set. • The property type is a string and the possible values form a small, well-defined set. The definition of a small, well-defined set is provider-specific. For example, the provider might return the list of possible authentication services (DBINIT_OPT_AUTH_INTEGRATED property) but not the list of possible user IDs (DBINIT_OPT_AUTH_USERID property). If this list is returned, the *vt* element in *vValues* is VT_ARRAY combined with the type indicator returned in *vtType*. If this list is not returned, the *vt* element is VT_EMPTY. The consumer must free any memory pointed to by elements of *vValues* by calling the COM function **VariantClear**.

DBPROPINFOSET Structure

Providers use DBPROPINFOSET structures to return an array of DBPROPINFO structures. The properties identified in a single DBPROPINFOSET structure all belong to the same property set.

The DBPROPINFOSET structure is defined as follows:

```
typedef struct tagDBPROPINFOSET {
   DBPROPINFO*    rgPropertyInfos;
   ULONG          cPropertyInfos;
   GUID           guidPropertySet;
} DBPROPINFOSET;
```

The elements of this structure are described in the following table.

Element	Description
rgPropertyInfos	A pointer to an array of DBPROPINFO structures in which information is being returned.
cPropertyInfos	The number of properties from the property set for which information is being returned.
GuidPropertySet	A GUID that identifies the property set to which the properties belong.

DBPROPOPTIONS Enumerated Type

Consumers use DBPROPOPTIONS values to specify whether a property value is required or optional. The values of DBPROPOPTIONS are mutually exclusive. DBPROPOPTIONS is used in the DBPROP structure.

The values of DBPROPOPTIONS have the following meanings.

Value	Description
DBPROPOPTIONS_ REQUIRED	The specified property value is required. If the provider does not support the specified property, it sets the *dwStatus* element of the DBPROP structure to DBPROPSTATUS_NOTSUPPORTED and returns DB_E_ERRORSOCCURRED. Whatever action the method was to take, such as initializing a data source object or creating a rowset, fails. If the provider supports the specified property, all methods except **ICommandProperties::SetProperties** or **IDBProperties::SetProperties** can determine whether the provider supports setting the property to the requested value. For these methods, if the provider does not support setting the property to the requested value, it sets *dwStatus* to DBPROPSTATUS_NOTSUPPORTED and returns DB_E_ERRORSOCCURRED. Whatever action the method was to take, such as initializing a data source or creating a rowset, fails. For **ICommandProperties::SetProperties** or **IDBProperties::SetProperties**, if the provider supports the specified property, and **SetProperties** determines that the provider does not support setting the property to the requested value, it sets *dwStatus* to DBPROPSTATUS_NOTSUPPORTED and returns DB_S_ERRORSOCCURRED if one or more properties passed to **SetProperties** were successfully set, or DB_E_ERRORSOCCURRED if none of the properties could be set. If the provider supports the specified property, but **SetProperties** cannot determine whether the provider supports the requested value, it sets *dwStatus* to DBPROPSTATUS_OK. When **ICommand::Execute** or **IDBInitialize::Initialize** is called, the provider determines whether it can support the requested value. If the provider cannot support the requested value, **ICommand::Execute** or **IDBInitialize::Initialize** returns DB_E_ERRORSOCCURRED.

Value	Description
DBPROPOPTIONS_ OPTIONAL	The specified property value is optional. If the provider does not support the specified property, it sets the *dwStatus* element of the DBPROP structure to DBPROPSTATUS_NOTSUPPORTED and returns DB_S_ERRORSOCCURRED. Whatever action the method was to take, such as initializing a data source object or creating a rowset, succeeds. If the provider supports the specified property, all methods except **ICommandProperties::SetProperties** or **IDBProperties::SetProperties** can determine whether the provider supports setting the property to the requested value. For these methods, if the provider cannot support the specified value, it sets *dwStatus* to DBPROPSTATUS_NOTSET and returns DB_S_ERRORSOCCURRED. Whatever action the method was to take, such as initializing a data source object or creating a rowset, succeeds. For **ICommandProperties::SetProperties** or **IDBProperties::SetProperties**, if the provider supports the specified property and **SetProperties** cannot determine whether the provider supports setting the property to the requested value, it sets *dwStatus* to DBPROPSTATUS_OK. **ICommandProperties::GetProperties** or **IDBProperties::GetProperties** returns the specified value in *vValue* and DBPROPOPTIONS_OPTIONAL in *dwOptions*. When **ICommand::Execute** or **IDataInitialize::Initialize** is called, the provider determines whether it can support the specified value. If the provider does not support setting the property to the requested value, **ICommand::Execute** or **IDataInitialize::Initialize** returns DB_S_ERRORSOCCURRED but successfully executes the command or initializes the data source object.

DBPROPSET Structure

Consumers and providers use DBPROPSET structures to pass an array of DBPROP structures. The properties identified in a single DBPROPSET structure all belong to the same property set.

The DBPROPSET structure is defined as follows:

```
typedef struct tagDBPROPSET {
   DBPROP * rgProperties;
   ULONG    cProperties;
   GUID     guidPropertySet;
} DBPROPSET;
```

The elements of this structure are described in the following table.

Element	Description
rgProperties	A pointer to an array of DBPROP structures. These structures contain property values. If *cProperties* is zero, this is ignored.
cProperties	The number of properties from the property set for which to set or get values. If *cProperties* is zero, the provider ignores *rgProperties* and does not set or get values for any properties in the set.
guidPropertySet	A GUID that identifies the property set to which the properties belong.

DBPROPSTATUS Enumerated Type

Providers use DBPROPSTATUS values to return information about whether property values could be set. DBPROPSTATUS is used in the DBPROP structure.

The values of DBPROPSTATUS have the following meanings.

Value	Description
DBPROPSTATUS_OK	The property's value was successfully set. This includes the case where the value of a read-only property was set to its current value.
DBPROPSTATUS_BADCOLUMN	The *colid* element of the DBPROP structure was invalid.
DBPROPSTATUS_BADOPTION	The value of *dwOptions* was invalid.
DBPROPSTATUS_BADVALUE	The data type in *vValue* was not the data type of the property or was not VT_EMPTY. For example, the property was DBPROP_MEMORYUSAGE, which has a data type of VT_I4, and the data type was VT_I8. The value in *vValue* was not a valid value. For example, the property was DBPROP_MEMORYUSAGE and the value was negative. The value in *vValue* was a valid value for the property, and the provider supports the property as a settable property, but the provider does not support the value specified by *vValue*.
DBPROPSTATUS_CONFLICTING	The property's value was not set because doing so would have conflicted with an existing property.

Value	Description
DBPROPSTATUS_NOTALLSETTABLE	A property was specified to be applied to all columns but could not be applied to one or more of them.
DBPROPSTATUS_NOTSET	The property's value was not set to the specified value because *dwOptions* was DBPROPOPTIONS_OPTIONAL and setting the property to the specified value was not possible.
DBPROPSTATUS_NOTSETTABLE	The property was read-only, or the consumer attempted to set values of properties in the Initialization property group after the data source object was initialized. Consumers can set the value of a read-only property to its current value.
DBPROPSTATUS_NOTSUPPORTED	The property's value was not set because the provider did not support the property, the provider did not support the property set, or the consumer attempted to get or set values of properties not in the Initialization property group and the data source object is uninitialized. The provider can return DBPROPSTATUS_NOTSUPPORTED for properties that do not apply to the provider. For example, a read-only provider might always return DBPROPSTATUS_NOTSUPPORTED if the consumer called **IDBProperties::GetPropertyInfo** for DBPROP_UPDATABILITY.

Property Example

The code in this example shows how to get the value of a property and how to add properties to a rowset.

```
/////////////////////////////////////////////////////////////////
// myGetProperty
//
// This function gets the BOOL value for the specified property
// and returns the result in *pbValue
//
/////////////////////////////////////////////////////////////////
HRESULT myGetProperty
    (
    IUnknown *              pIUnknown,
    REFIID                  riid,
    DBPROPID                dwPropertyID,
    REFGUID                 guidPropertySet,
    BOOL *                  pbValue
    )
{
    HRESULT                 hr;
    DBPROPID                rgPropertyIDs[1];
    DBPROPIDSET             rgPropertyIDSets[1];

    ULONG                   cPropSets       = 0
    DBPROPSET *             rgPropSets      = NULL;

    IDBProperties *         pIDBProperties  = NULL;
    ISessionProperties *    pISesProps      = NULL;
    ICommandProperties *    pICmdProps      = NULL;
    IRowsetInfo *           pIRowsetInfo    = NULL;

    // Initialize the output value
    *pbValue = FALSE;

    // Set up the property ID array
    rgPropertyIDs[0] = dwPropertyID;

    // Set up the Property ID Set
    rgPropertyIDSets[0].rgPropertyIDs      = rgPropertyIDs;
    rgPropertyIDSets[0].cPropertyIDs       = 1;
    rgPropertyIDSets[0].guidPropertySet    = guidPropertySet;

    // Get the property value for this property from the provider, but
    // don't try to display extended error information, since this may
    // not be a supported property. A failure is, in fact, expected if
    // the property is not supported.
```

```
if( riid == IID_IDBProperties )
{
   XCHECK_HR(hr = pIUnknown->QueryInterface(IID_IDBProperties,
            (void**)&pIDBProperties));
   CHECK_HR(hr = pIDBProperties->GetProperties(
            1,                          // cPropertyIDSets
            rgPropertyIDSets,           // rgPropertyIDSets
            &cPropSets,                 // pcPropSets
            &rgPropSets                 // prgPropSets
            ));
}
else if( riid == IID_ISessionProperties )
{
   XCHECK_HR(hr = pIUnknown->QueryInterface(IID_ISessionProperties,
            (void**)&pISesProps));
   CHECK_HR(hr = pISesProps->GetProperties(
            1,                          // cPropertyIDSets
            rgPropertyIDSets,           // rgPropertyIDSets
            &cPropSets,                 // pcPropSets
            &rgPropSets                 // prgPropSets
            ));
}
else if( riid == IID_ICommandProperties )
{
   XCHECK_HR(hr = pIUnknown->QueryInterface(IID_ICommandProperties,
            (void**)&pICmdProps));
   CHECK_HR(hr = pICmdProps->GetProperties(
            1,                          // cPropertyIDSets
            rgPropertyIDSets,           // rgPropertyIDSets
            &cPropSets,                 // pcPropSets
            &rgPropSets                 // prgPropSets
            ));
}
else
{
   XCHECK_HR(hr = pIUnknown->QueryInterface(IID_IRowsetInfo,
            (void**)&pIRowsetInfo));
   CHECK_HR(hr = pIRowsetInfo->GetProperties(
            1,                          // cPropertyIDSets
            rgPropertyIDSets,           // rgPropertyIDSets
            &cPropSets,                 // pcPropSets
            &rgPropSets                 // prgPropSets
            ));
}

// Return the value for this property to the caller if
// it's a VT_BOOL type value, as expected
if( V_VT(&rgPropSets[0].rgProperties[0].vValue) == VT_BOOL )
   *pbValue = V_BOOL(&rgPropSets[0].rgProperties[0].vValue);
```

```
CLEANUP:
   if( rgPropSets )
   {
      CoTaskMemFree(rgPropSets[0].rgProperties);
      CoTaskMemFree(rgPropSets);
   }
   if( pIDBProperties )
      pIDBProperties->Release();
   if( pISesProps )
      pISesProps->Release();
   if( pICmdProps )
      pICmdProps->Release();
   if( pIRowsetInfo )
      pIRowsetInfo->Release();
   return hr;
}



/////////////////////////////////////////////////////////////////////
// myAddProperty
//
// This function initializes the property structure pProp
//
/////////////////////////////////////////////////////////////////////
void myAddProperty
   (
   DBPROP *           pProp,
   DBPROPID           dwPropertyID,
   VARTYPE            vtType,
   LONG               lValue,
   DBPROPOPTIONS      dwOptions
   )
{
   // Set up the property structure
   pProp->dwPropertyID      = dwPropertyID;
   pProp->dwOptions         = dwOptions;
   pProp->dwStatus          = DBPROPSTATUS_OK;
   pProp->colid             = DB_NULLID;
   V_VT(&pProp->vValue)     = vtType;

   // Since VARIANT data is a union, we can place the value in any
   // member (except for VT_DECIMAL, which is a union with the whole
   // VARIANT structure--but we know we're not passing VT_DECIMAL)
   V_I4(&pProp->vValue) = lValue;
}
```

```
//////////////////////////////////////////////////////////////////////
// myAddRowsetProperties
//
// This function sets up the given DBPROPSET and DBPROP
// structures, adding two optional properties that describe
// features that we would like to use on the rowset created
// with these properties applied:
//   - DBPROP_CANFETCHBACKWARDS--The rowset should support
//     fetching rows backwards from our current cursor position.
//   - DBPROP_IRowsetLocate--The rowset should support
//     the IRowsetLocate interface and its semantics.
//
//////////////////////////////////////////////////////////////////////
void myAddRowsetProperties(DBPROPSET* pPropSet, ULONG cProperties, DBPROP* rgProperties)
{
   // Initialize the property set array
   pPropSet->rgProperties     = rgProperties;
   pPropSet->cProperties      = cProperties;
   pPropSet->guidPropertySet  = DBPROPSET_ROWSET;

   // Add the following two properties (as OPTIONAL) to the property
   // array contained in the property set array in order to request
   // that they be supported by the rowset we will create. Because
   // these are optional, the rowset we obtain may or may not support
   // this functionality. We will check for the functionality that
   // we need once the rowset is created and will modify our behavior
   // appropriately.
   myAddProperty(&rgProperties[0], DBPROP_CANFETCHBACKWARDS);
   myAddProperty(&rgProperties[1], DBPROP_IRowsetLocate);
}
```

CHAPTER 12

Transactions

In this chapter, simple transactions, nested transactions, distributed transactions, and transaction isolation are discussed.

A *transaction* enables a consumer to specify that a sequence of operations within a session must be performed as a single unit. Whether providers support transactions is provider-specific. If the provider supports transactions, a session object that supports **ITransactionLocal** can enter a simple (that is, non-nested) transaction.

A *nested transaction* occurs when a transaction is begun within the scope of another transaction. This inner transaction is represented by a *transaction object*. Providers that support nested transactions can choose to commit or abort a transaction at the outermost level or to commit or abort one of the inner transactions. **ITransactionOutcomeEvents** is implemented by the consumer to discover the outcome of transaction events.

For more information on	Go to
Simple transactions	"Simple Transactions" in this chapter
Transaction retention	"Transaction Retention" in this chapter
Rowset preservation	"Rowset Preservation" in this chapter
Nested transactions	"Nested Transactions" in this chapter
Discovering the outcome of transaction events	"Event Notifications" in this chapter
Methods to perform distributed transactions	"Distributed Transactions" in this chapter
Transaction isolation levels	"Isolation Levels" in this chapter
Locking resources to regulate sharing and isolation	"Transaction Locks" in this chapter

The transaction object and transaction options object cotypes are defined as follows. For more information about cotypes, see "OLE DB Objects" in Chapter 1, "Overview of OLE DB."

```
CoType TTransaction {
   [mandatory] interface IConnectionPointContainer;
   [mandatory] interface ITransaction;
   [optional]  interface ISupportErrorInfo;
};

CoType TTransactionOptions {
   [mandatory] interface ITransactionOptions;
   [optional]  interface ISupportErrorInfo;
};
```

Simple Transactions

At any point in its lifetime, a session can be inside or outside a transaction. When created, a session is outside a transaction, and all work done within the scope of that session and that is visible to the data store is immediately committed on each method call. (This is sometimes referred to as *auto-commit mode* or *implicit mode*.) When a session enters a transaction, all work done within the scope of that session and that is visible to the data store is part of that transaction and is committed or aborted as a single unit. (This is sometimes referred to as *manual-commit mode*.)

When the consumer calls **ITransactionLocal::StartTransaction**, a new local transaction is started. If there is already an active transaction on the session, the new transaction is started as a nested transaction below the current transaction. If the provider does not support nested transactions, calling **StartTransaction** when there is already an active transaction on the session returns XACT_E_XTIONEXISTS.

The transaction ends when the consumer calls **ITransaction::Commit** or **ITransaction::Abort**, at which time all changes to the rowset that have been transmitted to the data store are committed or aborted.

A single data source object can create multiple session objects, each of which can be inside or outside the scope of a transaction at any time.

Committing and Aborting Simple Transactions

When a transaction is committed or aborted, two behaviors are of interest:

- Retention—whether the session object enters a new transaction.
- Preservation—whether the rowset can still be used after the transaction has ended.

Transaction Retention

Committing or aborting the transaction with the *fRetaining* flag in **ITransaction::Commit** or **ITransaction::Abort** set to TRUE (also called a *retaining* commit or abort) causes a new transaction to be started immediately after the current one ends. If the *fRetaining* flag is set to FALSE, the transaction is committed or aborted and no new transaction is created. Any new work done on the session is outside the scope of a transaction. Attempting to explicitly commit or abort a transaction when there is no outstanding transaction returns an error.

A command object created within the scope of a transaction remains fully functional after the transaction is ended by a retaining commit or abort. The command also remains active in the case of a nonretaining commit or abort, but its prepared state may be lost.

Rowset Preservation

After a transaction ends, one of the following states is possible: The full functionality of the relevant rowset is preserved, or the rowset enters a zombie state. A preserved rowset retains all of its capabilities. A rowset that enters a *zombie state* is an object whose functionality is virtually lost. Specifically, zombie rowsets support only **IUnknown** operations and incrementing and decrementing reference counts on outstanding row and accessor handles. In general, all other operations on the zombie rowset produce the error E_UNEXPECTED.

The behavior of a rowset after a commit is determined by the property DBPROP_COMMITPRESERVE. If the value of this property is VARIANT_FALSE, the rowset enters a zombie state after the commit. However, if the value of the property is VARIANT_TRUE, the rowset remains fully functional after the commit, with all of its rows, bookmarks, pending changes, and so on still valid.

Similarly, the behavior of a rowset on an abort is determined by the property DBPROP_ABORTPRESERVE. If the value of the property is VARIANT_FALSE, rowsets created within the scope of the aborted transaction enter a zombie state after the abort. If the value of the property is VARIANT_TRUE, the rowsets remain fully functional, with all of their rows, bookmarks, pending changes, and so on still valid.

Preserved rowsets are not automatically refreshed from the underlying data store. For example, if the transaction is aborted and the value of DBPROP_ABORTPRESERVE is VARIANT_TRUE, any pending changes are not undone in the rowset. The consumer must call **IRowsetRefresh::RefreshVisibleData** to synchronize the rowset with the data store.

Even if a rowset is created with preserving properties, it can enter a zombie state if other objects on which it depends are destroyed as a side effect of an abort. For example, a rowset can enter a zombie state if a table on which it was built was created as part of the same transaction that was aborted.

Nested Transactions

A nested transaction occurs when a new transaction is started on a session that is already inside the scope of an existing transaction. The new, *nested transaction* is said to be nested within (or below the level of) the existing transaction. Changes made within the nested transaction are invisible to the top-level transaction until the nested transaction is committed. Even then, the changes are not visible outside the top-level transaction until that transaction is committed. Providers that expose **ITransactionLocal** and support nested transactions can choose to support only a limited number of nested transactions, including zero.

For providers that support nested transactions, calling **ITransactionLocal::StartTransaction** on a session with an existing transaction begins a new transaction nested below the current transaction. The return level indicates the level of nesting: a return value of 1 indicates a top-level transaction (that is, a transaction that is not nested within another transaction); 2 indicates a second-level transaction (a transaction nested within a top-level transaction); and so on.

Each nested transaction is represented by a *transaction object*.

Calling **ITransaction::Commit** or **ITransaction::Abort** on the session object commits or aborts the transaction at the current (lowest) nesting level. Calling **Commit** or **Abort** on a transaction object nested at a given level commits or aborts the transaction at that nesting level. Committing or aborting a transaction commits or aborts all transactions nested below it as well.

Calling **Commit** or **Abort** on a transaction object with the *fRetaining* flag set to TRUE implicitly begins a new unit of work and the transaction object remains valid. Calling **Commit** or **Abort** with *fRetaining* set to FALSE terminates the transaction, and the transaction object enters a zombie state. At this point, the only valid action that can be performed on the transaction object is to release it.

Before the resources used by a transaction object can be freed by the provider, the transaction object and all transaction objects nested below it must be released. Releasing a transaction object aborts any uncommitted work performed in that transaction.

ITransactionObject

Providers can support extended transaction functionality by exposing **ITransactionObject** on session objects. The consumer can call **ITransactionObject::GetTransactionObject** to get an **ITransaction** interface pointer on the transaction object associated with a particular transaction nesting level. This transaction object can be used to commit or abort a nested transaction at a particular level or to enlist in transaction outcome events for any level.

Distributed Transactions

A *distributed transaction* is a transaction that updates data on two or more networked computer systems. If the provider supports distributed transactions, it exposes **ITransactionJoin** on the session. To determine whether the provider supports distributed transactions, the consumer calls **QueryInterface** to request an **ITransactionJoin** interface pointer on the session object. The consumer calls **JoinTransaction** on this interface pointer to enlist the session in a distributed transaction. After the consumer has joined a distributed transaction, it uses the **ITransaction** interface of the transaction coordinator to commit or abort the transaction. Consumers must set *fRetaining* to FALSE when committing or aborting a coordinated transaction. Following the commit or abort, **ITransaction** becomes invalid and the session is no longer part of a coordinated transaction.

It is an error to call **ITransactionJoin::JoinTransaction** if the session is already enlisted in a local transaction. In addition, the provider might require that any existing distributed transactions be committed or aborted before enlisting in a new distributed transaction. To unenlist from the transaction, the consumer calls **ITransactionJoin::JoinTransaction** on the session with *pUnkTransactionCoord* set to NULL.

If the consumer calls **ITransactionLocal::StartTransaction** to begin a local transaction while in a distributed transaction, that new transaction acts as a nested transaction within the distributed transaction. This is not supported by most providers.

Isolation Levels

Transaction isolation levels are a measure of the extent to which changes made outside a transaction are visible to that transaction. In particular, transaction isolation levels are defined by the presence or absence of the following phenomena:

- **Dirty read**—A dirty read occurs when a transaction reads data that has not yet been committed. For example, suppose transaction 1 changes a row. Transaction 2 reads the changed row before transaction 1 commits the change. If transaction 1 aborts the change, transaction 2 will have read data that is considered to have never existed.

- **Nonrepeatable read**—A nonrepeatable read occurs when a transaction reads the same row twice but gets different data each time. For example, suppose transaction 1 reads a row. Transaction 2 changes or deletes that row and commits this change or deletion. If transaction 1 attempts to reread the row, it retrieves different row values or discovers that the row has been deleted.

- **Phantom**—A phantom is a row that matches the search criteria but is not initially seen. For example, suppose transaction 1 reads a set of rows that satisfy some search criteria. Transaction 2 inserts a new row that matches the search criteria for transaction 1. If transaction 1 reexecutes the statement that read the rows, it gets a different set of rows.

According to these phenomena, the isolation levels defined by OLE DB are as follows:

- **Read Uncommitted** (also called **Browse)**—A transaction operating at the Read Uncommitted level can see uncommitted changes made by other transactions. At this level of isolation, dirty reads, nonrepeatable reads, and phantoms are all possible.
- **Read Committed** (also called **Cursor Stability)**—A transaction operating at the Read Committed level cannot see changes made by other transactions until those transactions are committed. At this level of isolation, dirty reads are not possible but nonrepeatable reads and phantoms are possible.
- **Repeatable Read**—A transaction operating at the Repeatable Read level is guaranteed not to see any changes made by other transactions in values it has already read. At this level of isolation, dirty reads and nonrepeatable reads are not possible but phantoms are possible.
- **Serializable** (also called **Isolated)**—A transaction operating at the Serializable level guarantees that all concurrent transactions interact only in ways that produce the same effect as if each transaction were entirely executed one after the other. At this isolation level, dirty reads, nonrepeatable reads, and phantoms are not possible.

Transaction Locks

Locking is the process by which a DBMS restricts access to a row in a multiuser environment. Transactions lock rows to regulate their sharing and isolation.

Locking can occur with any of the methods that interact with rows on the data source. These include **IRowsetLocate::GetRowsAt**, **IRowsetLocate::GetRowsByBookmark**, **IRowsetUpdate::Update**, and others. These operations take locks and can wait for locks to be released by other transactions. A lock held by another transaction usually does not invalidate an operation, but the lock delays the operation until the other transaction has finished and released the lock. Therefore, the default behavior on encountering a lock is to queue until it is released. There is a time limit on how long to queue before returning with a time-out failure, and the time-out can be set to zero for infinite time-out. Various time-out settings can be chosen by setting transaction properties.

The data source object implements transaction locking by using a strategy that corresponds to the transaction isolation level. These strategies are specific to the data source object.

Event Notifications

The provider can support transaction outcome event notification by exposing **IConnectionPointContainer** on the session object. The consumer can expose the **ITransactionOutcomeEvents** interface to receive notification from the provider when a transaction is committed or aborted.

To receive event notifications, the consumer must implement the methods in **ITransactionOutcomeEvents** and register the interface with the provider's connection point mechanism. To do this, the consumer calls **QueryInterface** to request an **IConnectionPointContainer** interface pointer on the session, obtains the **IConnectionPoint** interface for IID_ITRANSACTIONOUTCOMEEVENT, and passes its **ITransactionOutcomeEvents** interface to that connection point. When a transaction is committed or aborted, the provider notifies each registered **ITransactionOutcomeEvents** interface of the outcome of the transaction.

For more information about **ITransactionOutcomeEvents** interface and its methods, see the *Microsoft Distributed Transaction Coordinator Programmer's Reference*. For more information about **IConnectionPoint** and **IConnectionPointContainer**, see the COM reference documentation.

CHAPTER 13

Errors

This chapter addresses the ability of OLE DB to process errors by using methods that either return a code or create an error object. Error objects can return detailed error information. Handling of multiple error items is discussed in the section "Arrays of Errors," later in this chapter.

The mechanics of how an Automation component returns and/or retrieves an error object, as well as its use of threads, is presented here. OLE DB extends Automation error objects by adding the ability for an error object to contain multiple error records. Provider-specific error lookup services are also discussed.

For more information on	Go to
Return codes	"Return Codes" in this chapter
Arrays of errors	"Arrays of Errors" in this chapter
How an Automation component returns an error object	"How an Automation Component Returns an Error Object" in this chapter
How an Automation consumer retrieves an error object	"How an Automation Consumer Retrieves an Error Object" in this chapter
OLE DB error objects	"OLE DB Error Objects" in this chapter
Error object example	"Error Object Example" in this chapter
Error records	"Error Records" in this chapter
Error record example	"Error Record Example" in this chapter
Interfaces used by OLE DB error objects	"Interfaces Used by OLE DB Error Objects" in this chapter
How a provider returns an error object	"How a Provider Returns an OLE DB Error Object" in this chapter
How a consumer retrieves an error object	"How a Consumer Retrieves an OLE DB Error Object" in this chapter

For more information on	Go to
Use of threads	"OLE DB Error Objects and Threads" in this chapter
	"Threading and Error Objects" in Chapter 14, "Programming Considerations"
Provider-specific error lookup services	"Error Lookup Services" in this chapter
	"Error Lookup Service Registry Entries" in Chapter 14, "Programming Considerations"

Methods return error information in two ways. The code returned by a method indicates the overall success or failure of the method. *Error objects* provide detailed information about the error, such as text describing the error, the Help file containing information about the error, a text description of the program that was the source of the error, and any provider-specific error information. Error objects in OLE DB are an extension of the error objects in Automation, use many of the same mechanisms, and can be used as Automation error objects.

The error object, custom error object, and error record object cotypes are defined as follows. For more information about cotypes, see "OLE DB Objects" in Chapter 1, "Overview of OLE DB."

```
CoType TErrorObject {
   [mandatory] interface IErrorRecords;
}


CoType TCustomErrorObject {
   [optional]  interface ISQLErrorInfo
   [optional]  interface IErrorLookup;
}


CoType TErrorRecord {
   [mandatory] interface IErrorInfo;
}
```

Return Codes

Each method returns a *return code,* which indicates the overall success or failure of the method. These return codes are of type HRESULT. There are two classes of return codes: *success and warning* codes, and *error* codes.

Success and warning codes begin with S_ or DB_S_ (for example, S_OK) and indicate that the method successfully completed. If the return code is other than S_OK or S_FALSE, it is likely that an error occurred from which the method was able to recover. For example, **IRowset::GetNextRows** returns DB_S_ENDOFROWSET when it is unable to return the requested number of rows due to reaching the end of the rowset or chapter. If a single warning condition occurs, the method returns the code for that condition; if multiple warning conditions occur, the method describes the hierarchy of warning return codes—that is, which warning code should be returned when given a choice between multiple warning return codes.

Error codes begin with E_ or DB_E_ (for example, DB_E_BADACCESSORHANDLE) and indicate that the method failed and was unable to do any useful work. For example, **GetNextRows** returns E_INVALIDARG when the pointer in which it is to return a pointer to an array of row handles (*prghRows*) is null. One exception is that some of the methods that return DB_E_ERRORSOCCURRED allocate memory in which to return additional information about these errors. Consumers must free this memory. Although error codes can indicate run-time errors such as running out of memory, they usually indicate programming errors. If multiple errors occur, which code is returned is provider-specific. If both errors and warnings occur, the method fails and returns an error code.

All methods can return S_OK, E_FAIL, and E_OUTOFMEMORY. The reference section entries in Part 2, "OLE DB Reference," list S_OK and E_FAIL for all methods. In most cases, E_OUTOFMEMORY is listed only for those methods that allocate memory that is returned to the consumer. The reason for listing E_OUTOFMEMORY in these sections is to remind consumers that they might be able to call the method successfully by requesting fewer returned values, such as fewer rows from **GetNextRows**.

In addition to the return codes for errors listed in the *OLE DB Programmer's Reference,* providers can return provider-specific error codes. However, providers must not return success codes other than those listed in the *Programmer's Reference*.

> **Note** Methods that can return DB_S_ERRORSOCCURRED do so only when one or more errors occur. Methods that fail entirely (that is, encounter nothing but errors) can return DB_E_ERRORSOCCURRED. Some providers incorrectly return DB_S_ERRORSOCCURRED (instead of S_OK) when no errors but one or more warnings occur.

Arrays of Errors

A number of methods operate on multiple items or arrays of items. For example, **IRowsetLocate::GetRowsByBookmark** accepts an array of bookmarks and retrieves the rows associated with those bookmarks. When methods that operate on multiple items encounter an item-level error, such as when the row associated with a bookmark has been deleted, they flag that error and continue processing.

If the consumer requests it, these methods also return an array of status values, which detail the specific errors and warnings that occurred. The array is returned if the method returns a success code (such as S_OK), a warning code (such as DB_S_ERRORSOCCURRED), or the error code DB_E_ERRORSOCCURRED; it is not returned if the method returns any other error (E_ or DB_E_) code. DB_S_ERRORSOCCURRED is returned only if an error occurred. If only successes or warnings occurred, the method returns a success code or a warning code other than DB_S_ERRORSOCCURRED.

Automation Error Objects

The following sections provide a brief description of Automation error objects as background information. They are followed by a discussion of OLE DB error objects, which use many of the same mechanisms.

- How an Automation Component Returns an Error Object
- How an Automation Consumer Retrieves an Error Object

How an Automation Component Returns an Error Object

When a component using Automation causes an error, it can return an object to describe that error. To do this, the component must do the following:

1. Call **CreateErrorInfo** in the Automation DLL. This function creates an Automation error object that exposes **ICreateErrorInfo** and **IErrorInfo**.
2. Call the methods in **ICreateErrorInfo** to store information in the error object, such as the string describing the error and the GUID of the interface that caused the error.
3. Call **QueryInterface** to retrieve the **IErrorInfo** interface pointer on the error object. This interface pointer identifies the error object to all Automation components.

4. Call **SetErrorInfo** in the Automation DLL and pass it the **IErrorInfo** interface pointer. This function replaces its current error object, if any, with the new error object and adds a reference count to the new error object.

5. Call **Release** to release the **ICreateErrorInfo** and **IErrorInfo** interface pointers. This effectively transfers ownership of the error object from the component that caused the error to the Automation DLL.

How an Automation Consumer Retrieves an Error Object

When an Automation consumer retrieves an error object in response to a return code it received, the consumer performs the following actions:

1. If it does not already have an **ISupportErrorInfo** interface pointer on the component, the consumer can request one by calling **QueryInterface** on the component.

   ISupportErrorInfo must be supported by all components that create error objects.

2. If it has not already determined whether the interface that returned the code supports error objects, the consumer calls **ISupportErrorInfo::InterfaceSupportsErrorInfo** and passes it the IID of the interface containing the method that returned the code.

   ISupportErrorInfo::InterfaceSupportsErrorInfo returns S_OK if the interface supports error objects (meaning the consumer should retrieve the current error object, if one exists) and returns S_FALSE if the interface does not support error objects (meaning the consumer should not retrieve the current error object because it applies to another interface and method).

3. Call **GetErrorInfo** in the Automation DLL. This function returns an **IErrorInfo** interface pointer on the current error object and releases its reference count on the error object, transferring ownership of the error object to the consumer.

4. Call the methods in the **IErrorInfo** interface to retrieve information from the error object.

5. Call **Release** on the error object to release it.

OLE DB Error Objects

Automation error objects do not support two capabilities required by OLE DB:

- The ability to return multiple error records from a single call
- The ability to return provider-specific error information

For example, each service component in the stack of service components might want to add its own error information to the existing error information, and a provider might want to expose error information that is unique to it.

To solve this problem, OLE DB extends Automation error objects. In particular, it adds the ability for an error object to contain multiple error records. That is, an Automation error object effectively contains a single error record and looks like the example shown in the following illustration.

Automation error object

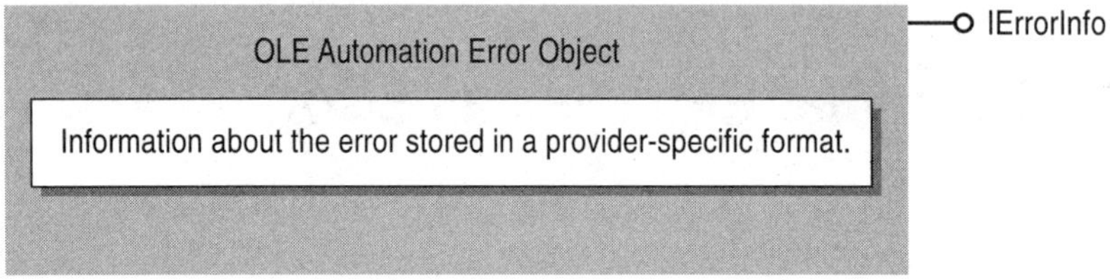

An OLE DB error object contains multiple error records and looks like the example shown in the following illustration.

OLE DB error object

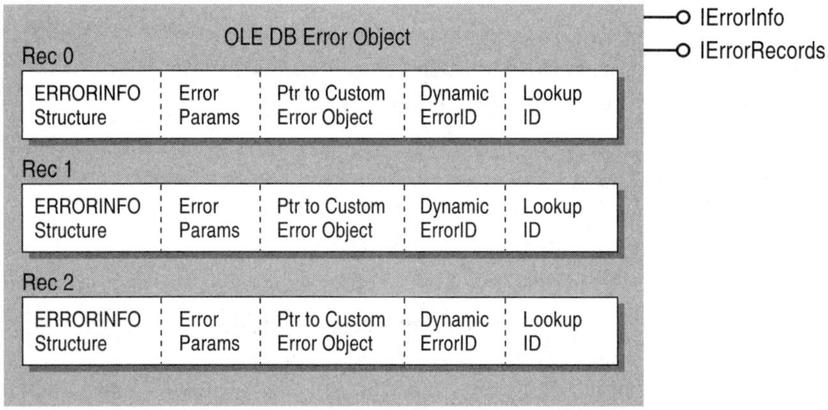

Support for OLE DB error objects is provider-specific. Providers can choose to generate them from all, none, or a subset of their interfaces. Consumers can call **ISupportErrorInfo::InterfaceSupportsErrorInfo** for each interface to determine whether the interface supports error objects.

OLE DB error objects can be created by any method call. Although they are most commonly created when the method returns an error or warning, such as the DB_E_ERRORSINCOMMAND code returned by **ICommand::Execute** or the DB_S_ERRORSOCCURRED code returned by **IRowsetUpdate::Update**, they can also be returned when the method succeeds and returns S_OK.

OLE DB providers are not required to generate error objects, even if a method on an interface that supports error objects returns an error. In this case, even though **ISupportErrorInfo** returns S_OK, calling **GetErrorInfo** returns a null value. However, the provider is required to clear any existing error objects when any method on an interface that supports error objects is called, whether or not that method returns an error. Therefore, the consumer can be assured that if an error object does exist after calling a method on an interface that supports error objects, the error object describes the outcome of that method.

Error Object Example

The code in this example illustrates the use of error objects in OLE DB error handling.

```
/////////////////////////////////////////////////////////////////////////////
// myHandleResult
//
// This function is called as part of the XCHECK_HR macro. It takes an
// HRESULT, which is returned by the method called in the XCHECK_HR
// macro, and the file and line number where the method call was made.
// If the method call failed, this function attempts to get and display
// the extended error information for the call from the IErrorInfo,
// IErrorRecords, and ISQLErrorInfo interfaces.
//
/////////////////////////////////////////////////////////////////////////////
HRESULT myHandleResult
   (
   HRESULT                hrReturned,
   LPCWSTR                pwszFile,
   ULONG                  ulLine
   )
{
   HRESULT                hr;
   IErrorInfo *           pIErrorInfo       = NULL;
   IErrorRecords *        pIErrorRecords    = NULL;
   ULONG                  cRecords;
   ULONG                  iErr;

   // If the method called as part of the XCHECK_HR macro failed,
   // we will attempt to get extended error information for the call
   if( FAILED(hrReturned) )
   {
      // Obtain the current error object, if any, by using the
      // OLE Automation GetErrorInfo function, which will give
      // us back an IErrorInfo interface pointer if successful
      hr = GetErrorInfo(0, &pIErrorInfo);
```

```
        // We've got the IErrorInfo interface pointer on the error object
        if( SUCCEEDED(hr) && pIErrorInfo )
        {
           // OLE DB extends the OLE Automation error model by allowing
           // error objects to support the IErrorRecords interface. This
           // interface can expose information on multiple errors.
           hr = pIErrorInfo->QueryInterface(IID_IErrorRecords,
                                      (void**)&pIErrorRecords);
           if( SUCCEEDED(hr) )
           {
              // Get the count of error records from the object
              CHECK_HR(hr = pIErrorRecords->GetRecordCount(&cRecords));

              // Loop through the set of error records and
              // display the error information for each one
              for( iErr = 0; iErr < cRecords; iErr++ )
              {
                 myDisplayErrorRecord(hrReturned, iErr, pIErrorRecords,
                    pwszFile, ulLine);
              }
           }
           // The object didn't support IErrorRecords; display
           // the error information for this single error
           else
           {
              myDisplayErrorInfo(hrReturned, pIErrorInfo, pwszFile, ulLine);
           }
        }
        // There was no Error object, so just display the HRESULT to the user
        else
        {
           wprintf(L"\nNo Error Info posted; HResult: 0x%08x\n"
              L"File: %s, Line: %d\n", hrReturned, pwszFile, ulLine);
        }
     }

  CLEANUP:
     if( pIErrorInfo )
        pIErrorInfo->Release();
     if( pIErrorRecords )
        pIErrorRecords->Release();
     return hrReturned;
  }
```

Error Records

OLE DB error objects store error information in *error records*. Each error record is composed of the following parts: an ERRORINFO structure, error parameters, a pointer to a custom error object, a dynamic error ID, and a lookup ID. Each of these parts is described more fully in this section.

Records in OLE DB error objects are numbered starting from zero. By using the methods in **IErrorRecords**, consumers can specify the record from which to retrieve error information. As error records are added, they are added to the top of the list. (That is, the number of the existing error records is increased by 1 and a new record 0 is added.) Thus, consumers can start with the highest level of error information and then retrieve increasingly more detailed information.

ERRORINFO Structure

The ERRORINFO structure returns most of the basic information associated with an error:

```
typedef struct tagERRORINFO {
   HRESULT  hrError;
   DWORD    dwMinor;
   CLSID    clsid;
   IID      iid;
   DISPID   dispid;
} ERRORINFO;
```

The elements of this structure are used as described in the following table.

Element	Description
hrError	The code returned by the method. This might be different in different records in the error object. For example, suppose a query processor service component opens rowsets provided by base table data providers. If **ICommand::Execute** in the query processor calls **IOpenRowset::OpenRowset** in a base table data provider and **OpenRowset** fails with DB_E_NOTABLE, **Execute** might return DB_E_ERRORSINCOMMAND.
dwMinor	A provider-specific error code.
clsid	The class ID of the object that returned the error.

Element	Description
iid	The interface ID of the interface that generated the error. The value of *iid* can be different from the ID of the interface that defines the method the consumer called. For example, if a consumer calls **Execute** in a query processor and if the query processor then calls **OpenRowset** in a base table data provider and **OpenRowset** fails, *iid* is IID_IOPENROWSET, not IID_ICOMMAND. If the method that generates an error belongs to more than one interface because of inheritance, this value is the ID of the first interface in which the method is defined. For example, suppose **IRowsetLocate::GetRowsAt** is called through a pointer to **IRowsetScroll**, which inherits from **IRowsetLocate**. If **GetRowsAt** fails, *iid* is IID_IROWSETLOCATE, not IID_IROWSETSCROLL.
dispid	Optional and provider-specific. Could be used, for example, to indicate the method that returned the error.

Error Parameters

Error parameters are provider-specific values that are incorporated into error messages. For example, the provider might associate the error message "Cannot open table <*param1*>" with a *dwMinor* value of 10.

In the example, the error parameters would be used to supply the name of the table (<*param1*>) that could not be opened. Error parameters are inserted into error messages by a provider-specific error lookup service. Therefore, the format of error parameters and how they are substituted into error messages are completely provider-specific. The code in **IErrorInfo** calls the error lookup service. For more information, see "Error Lookup Services" later in this chapter.

Custom Error Objects

A custom error object can be associated with each error record. An interface pointer to the object is stored in the record. If no custom error object exists, this pointer is null. The custom error object is the mechanism by which OLE DB error objects are extensible.

When an error record is added, the error object calls **AddRef** to add a reference to the custom error object. The provider that created the custom error object calls **Release** to release its hold on the custom error object. In this way, ownership of the custom error object is effectively transferred from the provider to the error object. The error object releases all custom error objects when it is released.

For example, ODBC-related providers can expose **ISQLErrorInfo** on a custom error object to return the SQLSTATE value. For more information, see **ISQLErrorInfo** in Part 2, "OLE DB Reference."

Dynamic Error ID

The dynamic error ID is the ID of an error message created at run time by the error lookup service, as opposed to an error message hard-coded in the lookup service. The error object uses the dynamic error ID to release the dynamic error message when the error object is released. In most cases, all error messages associated with a single error object have the same dynamic error ID. For more information, see "Error Lookup Services" later in this chapter.

Lookup ID

The error lookup service uses the lookup ID in conjunction with the return code to identify the error description, Help file, and context ID for a specific error. The lookup ID also can be a special value, IDENTIFIER_SDK_ERROR, that tells the implementation of **IErrorInfo** that is shipped with the Microsoft Data Access SDK to ignore the provider's lookup service and use the description supplied in the error resource DLL shipped with the Data Access SDK. For more information, see "Error Lookup Services" later in this chapter.

Error Record Example

The code in this example shows how to process the contents of an error record.

```
/////////////////////////////////////////////////////////////////////////////////
// myDisplayErrorRecord
//
// This function displays the error information for a single error
// record, including information from ISQLErrorInfo, if supported
//
/////////////////////////////////////////////////////////////////////////////////
HRESULT myDisplayErrorRecord
   (
   HRESULT              hrReturned,
   ULONG                iRecord,
   IErrorRecords *      pIErrorRecords,
   LPCWSTR              pwszFile,
   ULONG                ulLine
   )
{
   HRESULT              hr;
   IErrorInfo *         pIErrorInfo       = NULL;
   BSTR                 bstrDescription   = NULL;
   BSTR                 bstrSource        = NULL;
   BSTR                 bstrSQLInfo       = NULL;

   static LCID          lcid              = GetUserDefaultLCID();

   LONG                 lNativeError      = 0;
   ERRORINFO            ErrorInfo;
```

```
   // Get the IErrorInfo interface pointer for this error record
   CHECK_HR(hr = pIErrorRecords->GetErrorInfo(iRecord, lcid, &pIErrorInfo));

   // Get the description of this error
   CHECK_HR(hr = pIErrorInfo->GetDescription(&bstrDescription));

   // Get the source of this error
   CHECK_HR(hr = pIErrorInfo->GetSource(&bstrSource));

   // Get the basic error information for this record
   CHECK_HR(hr = pIErrorRecords->GetBasicErrorInfo(iRecord, &ErrorInfo));

   // If the error object supports ISQLErrorInfo, get this information
   myGetSqlErrorInfo(iRecord, pIErrorRecords, &bstrSQLInfo, &lNativeError);

   // Display the error information to the user
   if( bstrSQLInfo )
   {
      wprintf(L"\nErrorRecord:  HResult: 0x%08x\nDescription: %s\n"
         L"SQLErrorInfo: %s\nSource: %s\nFile: %s, Line: %d\n",
         ErrorInfo.hrError,
         bstrDescription,
         bstrSQLInfo,
         bstrSource,
         pwszFile,
         ulLine);
   }
   else
   {
      wprintf(L"\nErrorRecord:  HResult: 0x%08x\nDescription: %s\n"
         L"Source: %s\nFile: %s, Line: %d\n",
         ErrorInfo.hrError,
         bstrDescription,
         bstrSource,
         pwszFile,
         ulLine);
   }

CLEANUP:
   if( pIErrorInfo )
      pIErrorInfo->Release();
   SysFreeString(bstrDescription);
   SysFreeString(bstrSource);
   SysFreeString(bstrSQLInfo);
   return hr;
}
```

```
/////////////////////////////////////////////////////////////////////////
// myDisplayErrorInfo
//
// This function displays basic error information for an error object
// that doesn't support the IErrorRecords interface
//
/////////////////////////////////////////////////////////////////////////
HRESULT myDisplayErrorInfo
   (
   HRESULT              hrReturned,
   IErrorInfo *         pIErrorInfo,
   LPCWSTR              pwszFile,
   ULONG                lLine
   )
{
   HRESULT              hr;
   BSTR                 bstrDescription  = NULL;
   BSTR                 bstrSource       = NULL;

   // Get the description of the error
   CHECK_HR(hr = pIErrorInfo->GetDescription(&bstrDescription));

   // Get the source of the error--this will be the window title
   CHECK_HR(hr = pIErrorInfo->GetSource(&bstrSource));

   // Display this error information
   wprintf(L"\nErrorInfo:  HResult: 0x%08x, Description: %s\nSource: %s\n"
            L"File: %s, Line: %d\n",
            hrReturned,
            bstrDescription,
            bstrSource,
            pwszFile,
            ulLine);

CLEANUP:
   SysFreeString(bstrDescription);
   SysFreeString(bstrSource);
   return hr;
}
```

```
/////////////////////////////////////////////////////////////////////
// myGetSqlErrorInfo
//
// If the error object supports ISQLErrorInfo, get the SQL error
// string and native error code for this error
//
/////////////////////////////////////////////////////////////////////
HRESULT myGetSqlErrorInfo
   (
   ULONG                 iRecord,
   IErrorRecords *       pIErrorRecords,
   BSTR *                pBstr,
   LONG *                plNativeError
   )
{
   HRESULT               hr;
   ISQLErrorInfo *       pISQLErrorInfo    = NULL;
   LONG                  lNativeError      = 0;

   // Attempt to get the ISQLErrorInfo interface for this error
   // record through GetCustomErrorObject. Note that ISQLErrorInfo
   // is not mandatory, so failure is acceptable here.
   CHECK_HR(hr = pIErrorRecords->GetCustomErrorObject(
            iRecord,                               // iRecord
            IID_ISQLErrorInfo,                     // riid
            (IUnknown**)&pISQLErrorInfo            // ppISQLErrorInfo
            ));

   // If we obtained the ISQLErrorInfo interface, get the SQL
   // error string and native error code for this error
   if( pISQLErrorInfo )
      hr = pISQLErrorInfo->GetSQLInfo(pBstr, &lNativeError);

CLEANUP:
   if( plNativeError )
      *plNativeError = lNativeError;
   if( pISQLErrorInfo )
      pISQLErrorInfo->Release();
   return hr;
}
```

Interfaces Used by OLE DB Error Objects

The following table describes which interfaces providers must implement to support OLE DB error objects, which interfaces are implemented in the Microsoft Data Access SDK, and which functions are implemented by the OLE DB error object.

Interface or function	Comments
ISupportErrorInfo	**Defined by:** Automation **Implemented by:** Provider **Implemented on:** OLE DB object (for example, rowset or command) The consumer uses this interface to determine whether an object can return OLE DB error objects and, if so, which interfaces on that object can return OLE DB error objects.
IErrorLookup	**Defined by:** OLE DB **Implemented by:** Provider **Implemented on:** Error lookup service The error lookup service is required by the OLE DB error object and is used by that code to implement **IErrorRecords** and **IErrorInfo**. For more information, see "Error Lookup Services" later in this chapter.
IErrorInfo	**Defined by:** Automation **Implemented by:** Data Access SDK **Implemented on:** OLE DB error object OLE DB error objects expose **IErrorInfo** so that they can be treated by the Automation DLL and by Automation consumers as Automation error objects. If the methods on this interface are called, they will retrieve the information from record 0 using the default locale ID. To retrieve error information from a record, the consumer can call **IErrorRecords::GetErrorInfo** and pass the record number and locale ID. The OLE DB error object returns a pointer to an **IErrorInfo** interface, which will return error information from the specified error record by using the specified locale ID.
IErrorRecords	**Defined by:** OLE DB **Implemented by:** Data Access SDK **Implemented on:** OLE DB error object This is the main interface through which OLE DB error objects are accessed.

Interface or function	Comments
IClassFactory	**Defined by:** Automation **Implemented by:** Data Access SDK **Implemented on:** OLE DB error object class factory OLE DB error objects are created by a class factory exposed by the error object code in the Data Access SDK. You can create them by calling **CoCreateInstance** with the CLSID_EXTENDEDERRORINFO class ID or by calling **IClassFactory::CreateInstance** on a class factory object retrieved by using **DllGetClassObject**. If the provider frequently creates error objects, the latter method is faster and therefore preferred. OLE DB error objects cannot be created by the **CreateErrorInfo** function in the Automation DLL because the function can create only Automation error objects.
GetErrorInfo	**Defined by:** Automation **Implemented by:** Automation DLL **Implemented on:** N/A **GetErrorInfo** transfers ownership of the OLE DB error object on the current thread from the Automation DLL to the consumer. It identifies error objects by their **IErrorInfo** interface pointer, which is one reason OLE DB error objects directly expose **IErrorInfo**.
SetErrorInfo	**Defined by:** Automation **Implemented by:** Automation DLL **Implemented on:** N/A **SetErrorInfo** transfers ownership of the OLE DB error object on the current thread from the provider to the Automation DLL. It identifies error objects by their **IErrorInfo** interface pointer, which is one reason OLE DB error objects directly expose **IErrorInfo**.

How a Provider Returns an OLE DB Error Object

When an error occurs in a provider, the provider can return an OLE DB error object to describe that error. To do this, it should perform the following actions:

1. Call **GetErrorInfo** in the Automation DLL to obtain ownership of the error object on the current thread and request an **IErrorInfo** interface pointer on it. (The error object is not required to support **IErrorInfo**.)

   Such an error object will exist only if added by a lower-level provider. Therefore, a provider at the bottom of a chain of providers will not find an error object. A provider in the middle (a service component) might find such an object. In the latter case, the service component is merely gaining temporary ownership of the error object before returning it to the Automation DLL.

2. Create an OLE DB error object if none was retrieved in step 1. To do this, the provider calls **CoCreateInstance** with the CLSID_EXTENDEDERRORINFO class ID or **IClassFactory::CreateInstance** on a class factory object created earlier for this class.

   The latter method is faster and therefore preferred if the provider frequently creates error objects.

3. Call **IErrorRecords::AddErrorRecord** to add one or more error records to the error object. To add by using **AddErrorRecord**, the provider passes an ERRORINFO structure, the lookup ID, the error parameters (if any), an interface pointer on the custom error object that further describes the error, and a dynamic error ID.

4. Call **QueryInterface** to retrieve an **IErrorInfo** interface pointer on the error object.

   This interface pointer identifies the error object to all Automation components.

5. Call the function **SetErrorInfo** in the Automation DLL and pass it the **IErrorInfo** interface pointer. **SetErrorInfo** replaces the current error object (if any) on the thread with the new error object and adds a reference count to hold the new error object.

6. Call **Release** to release all of its references to the error object. This transfers ownership of the error object from the provider to the Automation DLL.

The following code shows an example of how a provider that is unable to open a table might respond by creating an OLE DB error object and transferring ownership of the object to the Automation DLL:

```
#include <oledb.h>

IClassFactory *       m_pErrorObjectFactory;
IParseDisplayName *   pppwow;
DWORD                 errCantOpenTable;
IOpenRowset *         pSimpleProvider;
IRowset *             pRowset;
DBID                  TableID;
extern GUID           CLSID_THISISAM;
extern DISPID         DISPID_OpenRowset;
BSTR                  bstrTableName;

int main() {
   ERRORINFO          ErrorInfo;
   HRESULT            hr, hrErr;
   IErrorInfo *       pErrorInfo;
   IErrorRecord *     pErrorRecords;

   // Clear the current error object
   SetErrorInfo(0, NULL);
```

```
// Try to open the table or call another provider to do it
   hrErr = pSimpleProvider->OpenRowset(NULL, &TableID, NULL, IID_IRowset, 0,
                                       NULL, (IUnknown**) &pRowset);

   if (!FAILED(hrErr))
      return hrErr;

   // An error or warning occurred while opening the table.
   // Get the current error object. If one does not exist,
   // create a new one.

   GetErrorInfo(0, &pErrorInfo);

   CoGetClassObject(CLSID_EXTENDEDERRORINFO,
      CLSCTX_INPROC_SERVER,
      NULL,                                 // reserved, must be NULL
      IID_IClassFactory,
      (LPVOID *)&m_pErrorObjectFactory));

   if (!pErrorInfo)
   hr = m_pErrorObjectFactory->CreateInstance(NULL, IID_IErrorInfo,
      (void**) &pErrorInfo);

   // Get an IErrorRecords interface pointer on the error object
   hr = pErrorInfo->QueryInterface(IID_IErrorRecords, (void**) &pErrorRecords);

   // Set up a parameter to pass to the object
   VARIANTARG  varg;
   VariantInit (&varg);
   DISPPARAMS  dispparams = {&varg, NULL, 1, 0};

   varg.vt = VT_BSTR;
   varg.bstrVal = SysAllocString(bstrTableName);

   // Fill in the ERRORINFO structure and add the error record

   ErrorInfo.hrError = hrErr;
   ErrorInfo.dwMinor = errCantOpenTable;
   ErrorInfo.clsid   = CLSID_THISISAM;
   ErrorInfo.iid     = IID_IOpenRowset;
   ErrorInfo.dispid  = DISPID_OpenRowset;
   hr = pErrorRecords->AddErrorRecord(&ErrorInfo,ErrorInfo.dwMinor,&dispparams,NULL,0);

   VariantClear(&varg);

   // Call SetErrorInfo to pass the error object to the Automation DLL
   hr = SetErrorInfo(0, pErrorInfo);
```

```
// Release the interface pointers on the object to finish transferring
   // ownership ofthe object to the Automation DLL

   pErrorRecords->Release();
   pErrorInfo->Release();
   return hr;
};
```

The following code example shows how a provider adds a record to an OLE DB error object that includes a pointer to a custom error object:

```
#include <oledb.h>

class CSQLStateObject:public ISQLErrorInfo {
   public:
      CSQLStateObject(OLECHAR );
      CSQLStateObject();
      HRESULT __stdcall QueryInterface(REFIID, void** );
      ULONG __stdcall AddRef(void);
      ULONG __stdcall Release(void);
      HRESULT __stdcall GetSQLInfo(
         /* [out] */ BSTR __RPC_FAR *pbstrSQLState,
         /* [out] */ LONG __RPC_FAR *plNativeError);
};

IClassFactory *g_pErrorObjectFactory ;
extern DISPID  DISPID_GetData;
extern GUID    CLSID_THISISAM;
DWORD          errGeneralError;

int main() {
   ERRORINFO      ErrorInfo;
   HRESULT        hr, hrErr;
   IErrorInfo *   pErrorInfo;
   IErrorRecords *pErrorRecords;

   // Clear the current error object
   SetErrorInfo(0, NULL);

   // (Not shown.) Do something that causes an error to occur.

   if (!FAILED(hrErr))
      return hrErr;
```

```
// An error or warning occurred. Get the current error object.
   // If one does not exist, create one.

   GetErrorInfo(0, &pErrorInfo);

   CoGetClassObject(CLSID_EXTENDEDERRORINFO,
      CLSCTX_INPROC_SERVER,
      NULL,                                // reserved, must be NULL
      IID_IClassFactory,
      (LPVOID *)&m_pErrorObjectFactory));

   if (!pErrorInfo)
   hr = g_pErrorObjectFactory->CreateInstance(NULL, IID_IErrorInfo,
                                            (void**) &pErrorInfo);

   // Get an IErrorRecords interface pointer on the error object
   hr = pErrorInfo->QueryInterface(IID_IErrorRecords, (void**) &pErrorRecords);

   // Create a custom error object
   CSQLStateObject* pMyErrObj = new CSQLStateObject(OLESTR("HY000"));

   // Fill in the ERRORINFO structure and add the error record
   ErrorInfo.hrError = hrErr;
   ErrorInfo.dwMinor = errGeneralError;
   ErrorInfo.clsid   = CLSID_THISISAM;
   ErrorInfo.iid     = IID_IRowset;
   ErrorInfo.dispid  = DISPID_GetData;
   hr = pErrorRecords->AddErrorRecord(&ErrorInfo, ErrorInfo.dwMinor, NULL,
                                    (void**) pMyErrObj, 0);

   // Release the interface pointer on the custom error object
   // to finish transferring ownership of it to the error object
   pMyErrObj->Release();

   // Call SetErrorInfo to pass the error object to the Automation DLL
   hr = SetErrorInfo(0, pErrorInfo);

   // Release the interface pointers on the object to finish
   // transferring ownership of the object to the Automation DLL
   pErrorRecords->Release();
   pErrorInfo->Release();
   return hr;
};
```

How a Consumer Retrieves an OLE DB Error Object

When a consumer wants to retrieve an error object in response to a return code it received, it must perform the following actions:

1. If it does not already have an **ISupportErrorInfo** interface pointer on the component, the consumer can request one by calling **QueryInterface** on the component.

   ISupportErrorInfo must be supported by all components that create error objects.

2. If it has not already determined whether the interface that returned the code supports error objects, the consumer can call **ISupportErrorInfo::InterfaceSupportsErrorInfo** and pass it the IID of the interface containing the method that returned the code.

   ISupportErrorInfo::InterfaceSupportsErrorInfo returns S_OK if the interface supports error objects (meaning the consumer should retrieve the current error object, if one exists) and returns S_FALSE if the interface does not support error objects (meaning the consumer should not retrieve the current error object because it applies to another interface and method).

3. Call the **GetErrorInfo** function in the Automation DLL. This function returns an **IErrorInfo** interface pointer on the current error object (or NULL, if there is no current error object) and releases its reference count on the error object, transferring ownership of the error object to the consumer.

4. Call **QueryInterface** to return an **IErrorRecords** interface pointer on the error object.

5. Call the methods in **IErrorRecords** to retrieve information from the error object. To retrieve the error message, source, Help file, or Help context ID from a particular record, the consumer first calls **IErrorRecords::GetErrorInfo** to retrieve an **IErrorInfo** interface pointer for that record. (This interface pointer is different from the one retrieved in step 3, because it applies to a specific record.) The consumer then calls methods using this pointer.

6. Call **Release** on the error object to release all references to it.

The following code shows how a consumer might retrieve and use an OLE DB error object:

```
#include <oledb.h>
#include <stdio.h>
IUnknown *pMyObject;
ExternGUID IID_IMyInterface;
DWORD    MYLOCALEID;
BSTR     bstrSourceOfError, bstrDescriptionOfError;

int main() {
   IErrorInfo *         pErrorInfo;
   IErrorInfo *         pErrorInfoRec;
   IErrorRecords *      pErrorRecords;
   ISupportErrorInfo *  pSupportErrorInfo;
   HRESULT              hr, hrErr;
   ULONG                i, ulNumErrorRecs;
   ERRORINFO            ErrorInfo;

   // (Not shown.) Error or warning occurs when calling method.
   if (!FAILED(hrErr))
      return (hrErr);

   // Check that the current interface supports error objects
   hr = pMyObject->QueryInterface(IID_ISupportErrorInfo,
                                  (void**) &pSupportErrorInfo);

   if (SUCCEEDED(hr)) {
      hr = pSupportErrorInfo->InterfaceSupportsErrorInfo(IID_IMyInterface);
      if (hr == S_OK) {
         // Get the current error object. Return if no
         // error object exists.
         GetErrorInfo(0,&pErrorInfo);
         if (!pErrorInfo) return (hrErr);

         // Get the IErrorRecord interface and get the count
         // of error recs
         pErrorInfo->QueryInterface(IID_IErrorRecords, (void**) &pErrorRecords);
         pErrorRecords->GetRecordCount(&ulNumErrorRecs);

         // Read through error records and display them
         for (i = 0; i < ulNumErrorRecs; i++) {
            // Get basic error information
            pErrorRecords->GetBasicErrorInfo(i, &ErrorInfo);
```

```
            // Get error description and source through the
            // IErrorInfo interface pointer on a particular record
            pErrorRecords->GetErrorInfo(i, MYLOCALEID, &pErrorInfoRec);
            BSTR bstrDescriptionOfError = NULL;
            BSTR bstrSourceOfError = NULL;

            pErrorInfoRec->GetDescription(&bstrDescriptionOfError);
            pErrorInfoRec->GetSource(&bstrSourceOfError);

            // At this point, you could call GetCustomErrorObject
            // and query for additional interfaces to determine
            // what else happened

            wprintf(
               OLESTR("HRESULT: %lx, Minor Code: %lu, Source: %s, Description: %s"),
               ErrorInfo.hrError,
               ErrorInfo.dwMinor,
               bstrSourceOfError,
               bstrDescriptionOfError);

            // Free the resources
            SysFreeString(bstrDescriptionOfError);
            SysFreeString(bstrSourceOfError);
            pErrorInfoRec->Release();
         }

         // Release the error object
         pErrorInfo->Release();
         pErrorRecords->Release();
      }
   }
   return (hrErr);
};
```

OLE DB Error Objects and Threads

Like Automation error objects, OLE DB error objects use the Automation DLL to maintain one error object per thread. Because the consumer is not required to retrieve the error object, the Automation DLL might be holding the error object generated by the previous method when a new method is called. Therefore, providers that return error objects must call the **SetErrorInfo** function with a null pointer at the start of each method in an interface that can generate error objects. This clears the current error object on the thread and ensures that any error object available after the method returns applies to the current method.

Because providers at each level must clear the current error object, providers should be careful not to transfer ownership of an error object to the Automation DLL and then call a method in a lower-level provider. Doing so might result in the lower-level provider clearing the just-created error object from the thread and losing the information it contains. To prevent this problem, the provider should first call local methods and then post its error object.

Error Lookup Services

The ERRORINFO structure does not contain the error messages and help file information that **IErrorInfo** can return. Instead, this information is stored in a provider-specific lookup service. There are three important reasons for this: First, it allows the information to be easily localized. Second, it means that memory need not be allocated to store the information until the information is requested. Third, it provides an easy mechanism by which the provider can parameterize error messages.

The information in this lookup service can be created when the lookup service is written or it can be created at run time. The former case, which creates what are called *static errors,* is common when the lookup service is tied to a single database and the programmer knows ahead of time what the error messages are. For example, a provider built directly over an Oracle database might use static errors. The run-time case, which creates *dynamic errors,* is common when the lookup service is not tied to any particular database and the programmer cannot predict the error messages. For example, a provider built on top of any ODBC driver might use dynamic errors. The lookup service creates dynamic errors at run time and releases them when the error object with which they are associated calls **IErrorLookup::ReleaseErrors** as part of its release code. Dynamic errors are identified by a *dynamic error ID.* In most cases, all dynamic errors associated with a single error object have the same ID. This is not required, but it is more efficient when releasing error objects.

An error lookup service must be created by each provider that supports OLE DB error objects. The lookup service exposes the **IErrorLookup** interface. For information about the registry entries used by error lookup services, see "Error Lookup Service Registry Entries" in Chapter 14, "Programming Considerations."

When a consumer calls **IErrorInfo::GetDescription** or **IErrorInfo::GetSource** for a particular record in an OLE DB error object, the error object creates an instance of the error lookup service. The error object then calls **IErrorLookup::GetErrorDescription** and passes the *hrError* element of the record's ERRORINFO structure, along with the lookup ID, the locale ID, and the parameters. **GetErrorDescription** uses the information provided to retrieve the error description and inserts the parameters into this description. However, if the lookup ID is set to IDENTIFIER_SDK_ERROR, the error object bypasses the error lookup service and retrieves the error description from the error resource DLL shipped with the Data Access SDK. Finally, the error object returns the completed, localized error message and source to the error object, which returns error messages to the consumer.

A similar process occurs when the consumer calls **IErrorInfo::GetHelpFile** or **IErrorInfo::GetHelpContext**, although no parameters are passed. If the lookup ID is set to IDENTIFIER_SDK_ERROR, the error object uses the error lookup service to get the Help file and Help context ID.

CHAPTER 14

Programming Considerations

This chapter discusses various OLE DB programming considerations.

For more information on	Go to
OLE DB support for aggregation	"Aggregation" in this chapter
Registering OLE DB components	"Registry Entries" in this chapter
Identifying enumerators in the registry	"Enumerator Registry Entries" in this chapter
Identifying provider registry entries	"Provider Registry Entries" in this chapter
Identifying error lookup registry entries	"Error Lookup Service Registry Entries" in this chapter
Provider support for single, apartment, and free-threaded OLE DB objects	"Provider Threading Models" in this chapter
Provider threading responsibilities	"Provider Threading Responsibilities" in this chapter
Free-threaded consumer responsibilities	"Consumer Threading Responsibilities" in this chapter
Preventing interruptions from the wrong thread	"Threading and Notifications" in this chapter
Error objects and thread types	"Threading and Error Objects" in this chapter
Threading and transaction assumptions	"Threading and Transactions" in this chapter
Storage objects and **IPersist*** objects threading types	"Threading and COM Objects" in this chapter
Freeing memory by the consumer	"Argument Memory" in this chapter

Aggregation

OLE DB objects, like other COM objects, support aggregation. To facilitate this, all methods that create a new object accept an **IUnknown** interface pointer to the controlling unknown. If a method, such as **IRowsetInfo::GetSpecification**, returns an interface pointer to an existing object, it should use the controlling unknown of the object to return the interface pointer, as opposed to using the object itself.

OLE DB providers are required to support aggregation of all objects.

Registry Entries

OLE DB defines registry entries for providers, enumerators, and error lookup services. These entries contain the class ID of the component and its associated DLL, description, display name, and so on. Following are several reasons for registering these OLE DB components:

- Registration is required as part of being an OLE COM component and provides a way to create an instance of an COM object.
- Registration provides the mechanism for the Data Links UI component and the root enumerator shipped with the OLE DB component of the Data Access SDK to obtain a list of providers on the machine.
- Registration provides the mechanism for the root enumerator to obtain a list of other enumerators. An enumerator is an OLE COM server that implements **ISourcesRowset**.
- Registration provides the mechanism for the standard OLE DB error object to invoke the provider's custom error lookup service.
- Data may be available in different formats. Registration provides a way to obtain a list of data formats and the providers that support those data formats. Data formats are created by providers and might be provider-specific. Each provider might consider itself capable of supporting many data formats. A usage example would be to group providers together and help consumers interactively decide which provider might work for them.

Enumerator Registry Entries

Enumerators are identified in the registry by the **OLE DB Enumerator** subkey under the class ID of the enumerator. Under **HKEY_CLASSES_ROOT**, enumerators must have the following subkeys and values for the programmatic identifier (ProgID).

Keys and subkeys	Name	Values
HKEY_CLASSES_ROOT		
CLSID		
EnumeratorCLSID	**(Default)**	*FriendlyDisplayName*
InprocServer32	**(Default)**	*EnumeratorDLLFilename*
	ThreadingModel	**Apartment|Free|Both**
OLE DB Enumerator	**(Default)**	*Description*
ProgID	**(Default)**	*EnumeratorProgID*
VersionIndependentProgID	**(Default)**	*VersionIndependentProgID*

For more information about enumerators, see "Enumerators" in Chapter 2, "Data Source and Session Objects."

Provider Registry Entries

Providers are identified in the registry by the **OLE DB Provider** subkey under the class ID of the provider. Under **HKEY_CLASSES_ROOT**, providers must have the following subkeys and values for the extension of persisted data source object files and for the programmatic identifier.

Keys and subkeys	Name	Value
HKEY_CLASSES_ROOT		
CLSID		
ProviderCLSID	**(Default)**	*ProviderProgID*
	OLEDB_SERVICES	*SupportedServices* [1]
ExtendedErrors [2]	**(Default)**	**Extended Error Service**
ErrorLookupCLSID [2]	**(Default)**	*FriendlyDisplayName*
InprocServer32	**(Default)**	*ProviderDLLFilename*
	ThreadingModel	**Apartment|Free|Both**
OLE DB Provider	**(Default)**	*Description*

Keys and subkeys	Name	Value
ProgID	**(Default)**	*ProviderProgID*
VersionIndependentProgID	**(Default)**	*VersionIndependentProgID*
ProviderProgID	**(Default)**	*Description*
Clsid	**(Default)**	*ProviderCLSID*

[1] Generally *0xffffffff*.

[2] If Error Lookup Service is supported.

When an instance of the object is first created, providers return an interface pointer on a data source object. For more information about data source objects, see "Data Source Objects" in Chapter 2, "Data Source and Session Objects."

Error Lookup Service Registry Entries

Error lookup services are identified in the registry by the **ExtendedErrors** subkey under the class ID of the error lookup service. Under **HKEY_CLASSES_ROOT**, error lookup services must have the following subkeys and values for programmatic identifier (ProgID).

Keys and subkeys	Name	Value
HKEY_CLASSES_ROOT		
CLSID		
ErrorLookupCLSID	**(Default)**	*FriendlyDisplayName*
InprocServer32	**(Default)**	*ErrorLookupDLLFilename*
	ThreadingModel	**Apartment|Free|Both**
ProgID	**(Default)**	*ErrorLookupProgID*
VersionIndependentProgID	**(Default)**	*VersionIndependentErrorLookupProgID*

Note that the first two class ID entries are entered under the class ID of the provider to identify the error lookup service for that provider. For more information about error lookup services, see "Error Lookup Services" in Chapter 13, "Errors."

Provider Threading Models

Providers can support single, apartment, or free-threaded OLE DB objects as long as they advertise which models are supported. It is recommended that providers build free-threaded implementations, which provide the best combination of speed and safety.

The threading model of a provider is described by a combination of the threading model registered for its Class ID in the registry, the DBPROP_DSOTHREADMODEL property, and the DBPROP_ROWTHREADMODEL property. The threading model for all nonrowset objects supported by the provider is described by the property DBPROP_DSOTHREADMODEL, and the threading model for rowsets is described by the property DBPROP_ROWTHREADMODEL. The threading model returned in DBPROP_DSOTHREADMODEL and DBPROP_ROWTHREADMODEL might be stricter than the thread model registered under the provider's CLSID in the case where additional threading limitations are imposed by underlying components, or where different services are invoked to support different objects. For more information, see "Rowset Properties" in Appendix C, " Property Tables."

Single-Threaded Providers and Consumers

Single-threaded providers work reliably only with single-threaded consumers. Single-threaded consumers can work with all types of objects.

Provider Threading Responsibilities

Free-threaded in-process OLE DB objects have the following threading responsibilities:

- To implement the guarding mechanisms necessary to guarantee safe operation of the OLE DB objects when objects are called from different threads. The choice of these mechanisms is provider-specific.
- To guarantee an operation free of deadlocks and of starvation.
- In the case of rowset objects, to shield other threads executing concurrently from the effects of methods like **IRowsetUpdate::Update** or **IRowsetRefresh::RefreshVisibleData** that may change the state of the rowset's copies of the rows. **Update** should be an atomic operation. While working in immediate update mode, all methods that modify the rowset's copies of the rows (**IRowsetChange::SetData**, **IRowsetChange::DeleteRows**, and so on) should also be atomic operations.

- In the case of rowset objects, to guarantee that all other provider-implemented objects for which the rowset is a factory (such as other rowsets or storage objects) are also free-threaded.
- To guarantee a minimum of marshaling support for their use by apartment-model consumers; for example, by aggregating to them an **IMarshal** object obtained from **CoCreateFreeThreadedMarshaler**. The provider can perform this aggregation lazily—that is, defer it until **QueryInterface** requests **IMarshal**.

Apartment model in-process OLE DB objects have the following threading responsibilities:

- The provider must assume that the OLE DB object will always receive direct calls on the same thread (apartment) on which it was created. Objects, however, can be created on different threads. Apartment objects belong to the same thread for all their existence.
- Apartment objects must use a proxy-stub mechanism to accept calls from other apartments. For this, **CoMarshalInterface** accepts a flag (MSHCTX_INPROC) to describe an interapartment communication. In the apartment model, calls using these proxy-stubs are synchronized in the same manner as Windows messages synchronize calls.

Apartment model in-process OLE DB objects

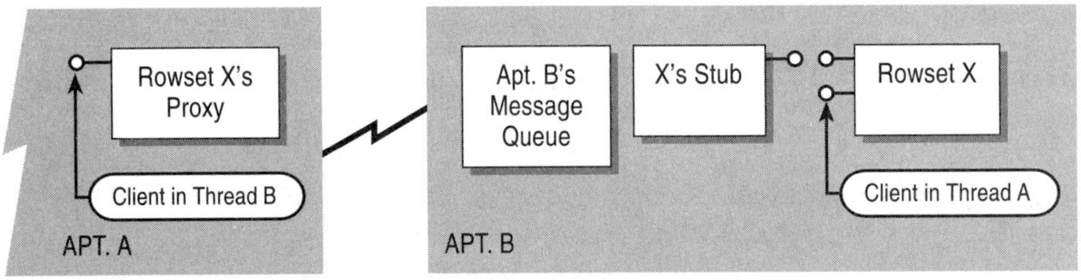

- In the case of rowset objects, the provider should guarantee that all other objects created by the rowset and returned by it, such as other rowsets or storage objects, are also apartment model and belong to the same thread as their ancestor rowset.
- Apartment OLE DB objects should not share state with other OLE DB objects because these objects may reside in different threads. The exception to this rule is OLE DB objects that have an ancestor/descendant relationship, such as those created by **IColumnsRowset::GetColumnsRowset**. Because these objects belong to the same apartment, they are guaranteed to execute serially and may share state safely, if needed.
- The provider should furnish marshaling support (proxy/stub) for all the object's interfaces.

Consumer Threading Responsibilities

Free-threaded consumers have the following threading responsibilities:

- To call **CoInitializeEx** on each thread, with a null pointer as the first parameter and COINIT_MULTITHREADED as the second parameter, to initialize it as free-threaded.
- When passing interfaces to other threads, to transfer pointers directly only when the other thread is free-threaded and when the pointers correspond to free-threaded objects.

  The set of threads initialized as free-threaded acts similarly to single big apartment, so pointers can be freely passed between these threads. To transfer a free-threaded object to a real apartment, it is recommended, although not required, to marshal the pointer at the source and unmarshal it at the destination. To transfer an apartment-threaded object to any free-threaded thread, it is necessary to marshal the pointer at the source and unmarshal it at the destination.

Apartment-threaded consumers have the following threading responsibilities:

- To implement a message queue.
- To call **CoInitialize** or **OLEInitialize** on the thread.
- To always marshal pointers of OLE DB and other COM objects to other apartments by using **CoMarshalInterface** and **CoUnmarshalInterface** calls. Calls to these methods trigger the deployment of proxies and stubs by the COM infrastructure. Well-behaved apartment-model consumers may interact efficiently with free-threaded servers if the free-threaded server aggregates with a generic free-threaded marshaler that COM supplies by using **CoCreateFreeThreadedMarshaler**.

Threading and Notifications

In the case of free-threaded rowset objects, **IConnectionPoint** should be enabled to handle apartment-model or single-thread listeners. Single-threaded listeners should always be called on their thread so that the listeners are not unduly interrupted from the wrong thread.

The creator of a rowset must use **CoMarshalInterface** when making the object's interfaces available to other threads. Because these are free-threaded rowsets, COM will stay out of the way. If **IConnectionPoint** receives an interface from **IRowsetNotify** and it wants to use that interface on another thread, it must also use **CoMarshalInterface** to move the interface to another thread. Whatever moves the interface to another thread must call **CoMarshalInterface**. The receiving thread doesn't just get the pointer but becomes involved by extracting the pointer through **CoUnmarshalInterface**.

This entails a rowset that is written internally to use multiple threads, not just to run on multiple threads. Consequently, a rowset should keep track of the threads on which a listener is connected to it.

Multiple threads

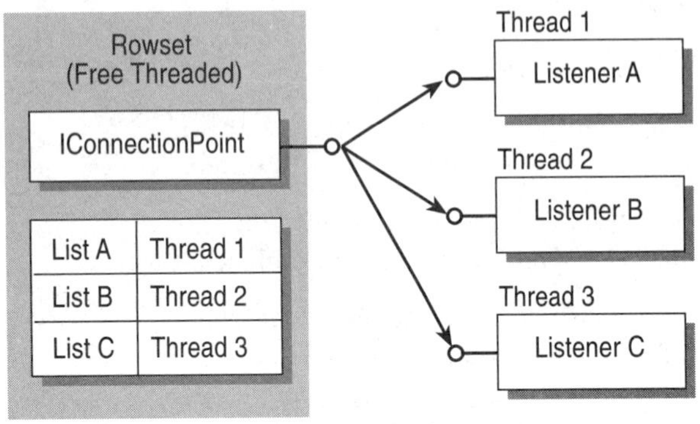

Threading and Error Objects

Free-threaded OLE DB objects should produce free-threaded error objects. Apartment-threaded OLE DB objects should produce apartment-model error objects, which will be associated to the same thread.

Because Automation maintains an error object for each thread, a provider that implements free-threaded rowsets must take care of calling **SetErrorInfo** by using the same thread that invoked the offending method.

Threading and Transactions

All consumers accessing a shared object such as a rowset through different threads are assumed to be within the same transaction.

Threading and COM Objects

OLE DB supports two kinds of COM objects in columns and parameters: storage objects and **IPersist*** objects.

Rowsets are factories of storage objects and determine the threading model of these objects. While accessing a storage object through **IRowset::GetData**, free-threaded rowsets return free-threaded objects, and apartment rowsets return apartment objects that will belong to the same thread.

IPersist* objects are implemented by the other parties. Their threading model is dictated by threading marking of their class factory. This marking may be absent, and if present, it can be either "Apartment" or "Both." Consumers need mechanisms to obtain information about the **IPersist*** object's threading marking when **GetData** returns the object.

For more information about storage objects and **IPersist*** objects, see Chapter 7, "BLOBs and COM Objects."

Argument Memory

The consumer can safely free memory at any time after a method return. It does not matter if this memory was allocated by the consumer and passed to the provider or allocated by the provider and returned to the consumer. From the provider's point of view, this means that the provider must not access any memory used by a method except while that method is executing.

Argument Validation

With few exceptions as noted, OLE DB defines specific error conditions for invalid arguments passed to various methods. Compliant providers are required to provide this argument validation. Providers are allowed, however, to expose provider-specific mechanisms, such as provider-specific properties or registry entries, for disabling such argument validation.

CHAPTER 15

Asynchronous Processing

Asynchronous processing enables methods to return immediately without blocking on the calling thread. Consumers request asynchronous processing when initializing a data source object or when opening or populating a rowset. The consumer must explicitly request asynchronous processing. Otherwise, the provider can perform asynchronous operations in the background but must behave synchronously, blocking if necessary, until the underlying asynchronous operation completes.

Data Source Initialization properties are used when consumers initialize a data source object asynchronously. Consumers wishing to asynchronously open a rowset use the Command Execution and Rowset Generation properties. Consumers wishing to asynchronously populate a rowset use properties of Rowset Population.

For more information on	Go to
Calling thread	"Provider Threading Models" in Chapter 14, "Programming Considerations"
Consumers	"Consumers and Providers" in Chapter 1, "Overview of OLE DB"
Data source objects	"Data Source Objects" in Chapter 2, "Data Source and Session Objects"
Rowset	Chapter 4, "Rowsets"
Asynchronously initialize a data source	"Asynchronous Data Source Initialization" in this chapter
Asynchronously open a rowset	"Asynchronous Command Execution and Rowset Generation" in this chapter
Asynchronously populate a rowset	"Asynchronous Rowset Population" in this chapter

Consumers can poll for the status of an asynchronous operation by calling **IDBAsynchStatus::GetStatus** on the object being asynchronously processed, or can register for progress notifications by passing the consumer's **IDBAsynchNotify** interface to the connection point of the object being asynchronously processed.

Asynchronous processing can occur in phases. If the object is asynchronously initialized, the initialization phase occurs first. While the object is in the initialization phase, it is in an uninitialized state. Attempting to call other interfaces may fail, and attempting to call **QueryInterface** for interfaces other than **IConnectionPointContainer** or **IDBAsynchStatus** may return E_NOINTERFACE.

Once all asynchronous processing has completed for an operation, the provider calls **IDBAsynchNotify::OnProgress** with *ulAsynchPhase* set to DBASYNCHPHASE_COMPLETE for that operation, followed by **IDBAsynchNotify::OnStop** to notify listeners that asynchronous processing has completed. Any calls to **IDBAsynchStatus::GetStatus** for that operation return an HRESULT indicating the outcome of the operation, with *ulAsynchPhase* set to DBASYNCHPHASE_COMPLETE, *pulProgress* equal to *pulProgressMax*, and *ppwszStatusString* set to a provider-specific value indicating completion, or NULL.

Asynchronous Data Source Initialization

Consumers wishing to initialize a data source asynchronously set the DBPROPVAL_ASYNCH_INITIALIZE bit in the DBPROP_INIT_ASYNCH property prior to calling **IDBInitialize::Initialize**. When this property is set, the provider returns immediately from the call to **Initialize** with either S_OK, if the operation has completed immediately, or DB_S_ASYNCHRONOUS, if the initialization will continue asynchronously. Consumers can call **IDBAsynchStatus::GetStatus** to get the status of the initialization or can register for progress notifications by passing the consumer's **IDBAsynchNotify** interface to the data source object's connection point. The consumer must explicitly request Asynchronous Data Source Initialization. Otherwise, **IDBInitialize::Initialize** does not return until the data source object is completely initialized.

Asynchronous Command Execution and Rowset Generation

Consumers that want to asynchronously open a rowset set the DBPROPVAL_ASYNCH_INITIALIZE bit in the DBPROP_ROWSET_ASYNCH property. When setting this bit prior to calling **Execute**, **OpenRowset**, **GetRowset**, **GetColumnsRowset**, **GetResult**, **GetSourcesRowset**, or any other method that returns a rowset, *riid* must be set to IID_IDBAsynchStatus, IID_IConnectionPointContainer, or IID_IUnknown.

The method returns immediately with S_OK if the rowset initialization completes immediately, or with DB_S_ASYNCHRONOUS if the rowset will continue initializing asynchronously, with *ppRowset* set to the requested interface on the rowset. Until the rowset is fully initialized, it behaves as if it is in a zombie state, and calling **QueryInterface** for interfaces other than IID_IConnectionPointContainer or IID_IDBAsynchStatus may return E_NOINTERFACE. Unless the consumer explicitly requests asynchronous processing, the rowset is initialized synchronously. All requested interfaces are available when the method requesting the rowset returns. This does not necessarily mean that the rowset is fully populated, but it must be complete and fully functional.

If the executed command does not return a rowset, it still returns immediately with an object that supports **IDBAsynchStatus**.

If output parameters are specified on the command, they usually are not available until the rowset is completely initialized, and might not be available until all of the data has been read from the rowset.

To obtain multiple results, the consumer sets the DBPROPVAL_ASYNCH_INITIALIZE bit of the DBPROP_ROWSET_ASYNCH property prior to executing the command and then calls **ICommand::Execute** with DBPROP_IMultipleResults set to VARIANT_TRUE and *riid* set to IID_IMultipleResults; and finally, the consumer calls **IMultipleResults::GetResult** with *riid* set to IID_IDBAsynchStatus or IID_IConnectionPointContainer to retrieve individual results asynchronously. When consumers request a multiple-results object from **Execute**, providers should return immediately with the multiple-results object and save processing until the consumer calls **GetResult**.

To cancel creation of the rowset, the consumer can call **IDBAsynchStatus::Abort** or can simply release all interfaces on the rowset. Once the rowset's reference count goes to zero, any asynchronous processing is canceled and the rowset is released. Calling **IDBAsynchStatus::Abort** still requires releasing the interface.

Asynchronous Rowset Population

Consumers wishing to asynchronously populate a rowset set the DBPROPVAL_ASYNCH_SEQUENTIAL or DBPROPVAL_ASYNCH_RANDOM bits of the DBPROP_ROWSET_ASYNCH property prior to opening the rowset.

During the DBASYNCHPHASE_POPULATION phase, even though the rows are not fully *populated,* the rowset itself is fully *initialized*; that is, all interfaces supported by the rowset are available and fully functional (although the set of rows returned may be restricted).

An *asynchronously populated* rowset is distinct from a *lazily populated* rowset. A lazily populated rowset may return a rowset prior to completely populating the rows, but methods that return rows wait, if necessary, in order to return the requested rows. Therefore, a lazily populated rowset appears as a synchronously populated rowset to the consumer. In contrast, an asynchronously populated rowset returns from a request to retrieve rows immediately with as many of the requested rows as are available at the moment. If fewer than the requested number of rows are available at the time of the call, the method returns DB_S_ENDOFROWSET even though additional rows may appear later. The consumer must request notifications or call **IDBAsynchStatus** to determine when population is complete. Unless the consumer explicitly requests asynchronous population, the provider must behave as if the rowset is fully populated upon creation. The method used to request rows waits to return until the requested number of hRows are obtained or the end of the rowset is reached.

Asynchronously populated rowsets may be *sequentially asynchronously populated,* if rows are always appended to the end of the rowset, or *randomly asynchronously populated,* if new rows can be inserted randomly within the rowset.

Sequentially asynchronously populated rowsets call **IDBAsynchNotify::OnProgress** to signal the addition of new rows to the end of the rowset as a result of asynchronous population. Randomly asynchronously populated rowsets call **IRowsetNotify::OnRowChange** with DBREASON_ROW_ASYNCHINSERT to signal the addition of new rows as a result of asynchronous population.

CHAPTER 16

Integrated Indexes

OLE DB indexes are designed for use with base tables (tables opened by **IOpenRowset::OpenRowset**). Providers built over command processors, such as SQL query processors, are expected to use indexes internally but not expose them through OLE DB. The primary consumers of OLE DB indexes are:

- Query processors accessing data in OLE DB providers, such as DBMS storage engines and ISAMs, which do not support commands.
- Service components or providers that implement **IViewRowset**, **IViewFilter**, or **IViewSort**.

OLE DB provides the ability to open separate rowsets over base tables and indexes, allowing the consumer to traverse each separately. However, certain providers can support indexes and base table data on the same rowset (also known as a *clustered index*). Providers can expose this as an integrated index by exposing **IRowsetIndex** directly on the base table rowset. This allows the consumer to set index ranges and seek index values directly on the base table rowset, without having a separate (and in this case redundant) index rowset. Such rowsets are said to have integrated index behavior. Providers can support separate indexes, integrated indexes, or both.

This chapter discusses requesting, using, and the structure of integrated indexes. The structure is more loosely defined than a nonintegrated index rowset. A useful element of integrated indexes, of course, is the ability to fetch data. The topic of row fetching includes rowset order, next fetch position, range, updating index rows, visibility of index changes, and the effect of changes on the next fetch position and index range. *Accessors,* the collection of information that describes how data is stored in the consumer's buffer, are discussed in light of methods and restrictions. Restrictions on integrated indexes and executing commands are discussed also. An integrated index code example is provided.

For more information on	Go to
Nonintegrated indexes	Chapter 8, "Index Rowsets"
Requesting integrated indexes	"Requesting Integrated Indexes" in this chapter
Using integrated indexes	"Using Integrated Indexes" in this chapter
Structure of integrated indexes	"Structure of Integrated Indexes" in this chapter
Fetching rows	"Fetching Rows" in this chapter

For more information on	Go to
Accessor methods and restrictions	"Accessors" in this chapter
	"Accessors" in Chapter 6, "Getting and Setting Data"
Restrictions on integrated indexes and commands	"Integrated Indexes and Commands" in this chapter
	Chapter 3, "Commands"
Calling threads	"Provider Threading Models" in Chapter 14, "Programming Considerations"

Requesting Integrated Indexes

Whether an index on a base table is integrated or not is reported in the INTEGRATED column of the INDEXES schema rowset. (See Appendix B, "Schema Rowsets.")

You can obtain integrated index behavior by opening a rowset on an integrated index—that is, passing valid table and index IDs to **OpenRowset**. In this case, the consumer deals with a single rowset to read the data in index order, to have access to all base table columns, and to update both the base table and associated index based on calls to **IRowsetChange** on the rowset.

Using Integrated Indexes

To fetch base table rows using two separate rowsets, one over the base table and another over the index, the consumer should do the following:

1. Call **IRowsetIndex::SetRange** on the index rowset to set the range.
2. (Optional) Call **IRowsetIndex::Seek** on the index rowset to seek a particular index value. This sets the next fetch position on the index rowset to the first row in the index rowset that matches the specified value.
3. Call **IRowset::GetNextRows** on the index rowset to fetch the index entry.
4. Extract a bookmark from the index row that points to the corresponding row in the base table rowset.
5. Call **IRowsetLocate::GetRowsAt** on the base table rowset with the extracted bookmark to get the base table row.

To fetch base table rows using an integrated index, the consumer should do the following:

1. Call **IRowsetIndex::SetRange** on the base table rowset to set the range.
2. (Optional) Call **IRowsetIndex::Seek** on the base table rowset to seek a particular index value. This sets the next fetch position on the base table rowset to the first row in the index that matches the specified value.
3. Call **IRowset::GetNextRows** on the base table rowset to fetch the base table row.

When using an integrated index rowset, there are three important differences from using separate index and base table rowsets:

- The consumer sets index ranges and seeks for index values on the base table rowset itself.
- No bookmarks are used in the process. This means that the base table rowset does not need to expose bookmarks, nor does it need to expose **IRowsetLocate**.
- Updates applied on this rowset are simultaneously applied to the base table and index.

Structure of Integrated Indexes

The structure of a nonintegrated index rowset is rigidly defined: The key columns of the index occur in order, and there is a separate column—not column 0—that contains the bookmarks that point to the base table rowset.

These restrictions do not apply to rowsets with integrated indexes. Forcing the key columns to occur in order could force the rowset to reorder the rowset columns each time the consumer changes the current index—an unacceptable result. The separate column of bookmarks pointing to base tables is not needed, as was explained in the preceding section, "Using Integrated Indexes."

To determine which columns are key columns and the order in which they occur, the consumer calls **IRowsetIndex::GetIndexInfo**. The provider returns an array of DBINDEXCOLUMNDESC structures with the DBIDs of the key columns and the key types (ascending or descending) of each column. The arrays are returned in order from most significant to least significant. To determine the ordinals of the key columns, the consumer calls **IColumnsInfo::MapColumnIDs** with the returned DBIDs.

Fetching Rows

Three areas of fetching rows are affected by integrating indexes and rowsets: rowset order, next fetch position, and range.

Rowset Order

An index implies an order in which a base table is to be traversed. With nonintegrated indexes, this order is entirely contained in the index rowset. The consumer imposes this order on the base table rowset by reading the index rowset sequentially and fetching rows in the base table rowset by bookmark.

With integrated indexes, this order is imposed directly on the base table rowset. The methods that require a rowset order (**IRowset::GetNextRows**, **IRowsetLocate::GetRowsAt**, and **IRowsetScroll::GetRowsAtRatio**) fetch rows in the order specified by the current index. For **GetNextRows**, this means that repeated calls will traverse the entire rowset in index order. For **GetRowsAt** and **GetRowsAtRatio**, this means that the method will start at the specified row and, if more than one row is requested, it will fetch rows in index order. **IRowsetLocate::GetRowsByBookmark** is not affected because it fetches only single, isolated rows.

If there is no current index (the base table rowset was opened without an index), these methods traverse the rowset in an undefined order, typically in the order that data is stored in the base table.

Next Fetch Position

With nonintegrated indexes, the next fetch position on the base table rowset was affected only by **GetNextRows** and **RestartPosition**. In a rowset with an integrated index, this can also be changed by **IRowsetIndex::Seek**. This is the same as the **Seek** functionality on separate index rowsets.

Range

With nonintegrated indexes, the range on the base table rowset used by **GetNextRows**, **GetRowsAt**, and **GetRowsAtRatio** was always the entire rowset. In a rowset with an integrated index, this can be changed by **IRowsetIndex::SetRange**. This is the same as the **SetRange** functionality on nonintegrated index rowsets.

Updating Index Rows

When the consumer updates, deletes, or inserts a base table row with **IRowsetChange**, the provider automatically updates, deletes, or inserts the corresponding entries in all integrated indexes associated with the base table. In other words, for integrated indexes, DBPROP_INDEX_AUTOUPDATE is always VARIANT_TRUE.

Visibility of Changes in the Index

The visibility of pending changes in the index is governed by the same mechanisms that govern the visibility of pending changes in the base table, with one important difference: If an index column in a row is updated, this is considered to be the same as deleting that row from the index and inserting a new row with the new value. Therefore, the visibility of pending deletes for completely released and refetched rows depends on whether the rowset exposes **IRowsetIdentity**. The visibility in the index of pending inserts depends on DBPROP_RETURNPENDINGINSERTS. Pending updates to key columns might not appear in the correct position in the index until the update is transmitted to the data store.

The visibility in the index of transmitted changes is governed by the same mechanisms that govern the visibility of transmitted changes in the base table. In other words, it depends on the DBPROP_OWNUPDATEDELETE, DBPROP_OWNINSERT, and DBPROP_REMOVEDELETED properties.

Effect of Changes on the Next Fetch Position

The next fetch position is unaffected by updates, deletes, and inserts. However, the definition of *unaffected* is provider specific due to the complexity of implementation strategies.

For example, suppose the current index applies to column 1, which has values in succeeding rows of "A", "B", "C", "D", "E", and "F". If the last row fetched contains the value "C" and the consumer changes this value to "EE", in most cases the next row fetched will contain the value "D", not "F". Assuming changes are visible, they will be fetched in the expected order. For example, if the last row fetched contains the value "C" and the consumer changes this value to "CC", the next row fetched might contain the value "CC" or "D".

Effect of Changes on the Index Range

The current index range is unaffected by updates, deletes, and inserts.

Whether and where changed rows are visible within the current range depends on the rules governing visibility of changes in the index. For example, suppose the range on an index column is "A" to "L" and the last row fetched had a value in this column of "H". If the value of that column in a currently held row is changed from "B" to "K", the change is transmitted to the data store, and if transmitted updates are visible in the index, then the row will be fetched if the consumer completes the scan to the end of the range. If the value of the column is changed instead to "M" and transmitted, the row will not be fetched.

Accessors

Accessors used with **IRowsetIndex::SetRange** and **IRowsetIndex::Seek** for an integrated index follow the same restrictions as accessors used with these methods for a separate index:

- For each key column bound in the accessor, all more-significant key columns must also be bound.
- Key columns must be bound in order from most significant to least significant.
- If the accessor binds any non-key columns, key columns must be bound first.

Accessors used with **SetRange** and **Seek** for an integrated index can also be used with other methods, such as **IRowset::GetData**, and vice versa.

Because the order of significance of columns can change for each index, it is usually necessary to define a different accessor to be used on **SetRange** or **Seek** calls for each index.

Integrated Indexes and Commands

Integrated indexes usually cannot be exposed by rowsets generated by executing a command. Therefore, if the consumer attempts to set DBPROP_IRowsetIndex to VARIANT_TRUE, **ICommandProperties::SetProperties** returns DBPROPSTATUS_NOTSUPPORTED in the DBPROP structures for this property.

The primary reason for this restriction is that commands can impose an order on a rowset, such as the ORDER BY clause in SQL, and this would conflict with the order imposed by the index.

Integrated Index Example

The following code performs the same function as the code example in "Index Example" in Chapter 8, "Index Rowsets," except that the index is integrated, not separate. It gains access to the Employees table through the Emp_LastName_Index index, using **IRowsetIndex** to specify and seek that range. The index has a single key column, Emp_LastName, of type DBTYPE_WSTR with a length of 30 characters.

The code sample performs the following actions:

1. (Not shown.) Initializes the database and creates a session.
2. Sets properties to request **IRowsetIndex**, which tells the rowset to use integrated indexes.
3. Opens the Employees table with the Emp_LastName_Index index and obtains interfaces for the rowset.
4. Gets information about the key columns in the Emp_LastName_Index.
5. Establishes bindings for the index columns and creates an accessor for the key column.
6. Sets a range on the rowset.
7. Reads rows from the rowset in the specified range.

```
#include <oledb.h>
#include <stddef.h>

PrintData(OLECHAR*, DWORD);

int main() {
   IOpenRowset *          pIOpenRowset     = NULL;
   DBID                   IndexId, TableId;
   IRowsetIndex *         pIRowsetIndex    = NULL;
   IRowset *              pIRowset = NULL;
   IColumnsInfo *         pIColumnsInfo    = NULL;
   IAccessor *            pIAccessor       = NULL;
   ULONG                  cColumns, cKeyCols, cProperties;
   DBCOLUMNINFO *         rgInfo;
   OLECHAR *              pStringsBuffer;
   DBINDEXCOLUMNDESC *    rgIndexColDesc;
   DBPROPSET *            rgProperties;
   HACCESSOR              hIndexAccessor   = DB_NULL_HACCESSOR;
   HRESULT                hr;

   // Code not shown. Initialize the database, create a session,
   // and obtain, from the session object, a pointer pIOpenRowset
   // to an IOpenRowset interface.
```

```
// Set the DBIDs for the table and the index
TableId.eKind            = DBKIND_NAME;
TableId.uName.pwszName   = OLESTR("Employees");
IndexId.eKind            = DBKIND_NAME;
IndexId.uName.pwszName   = OLESTR("Emp_LastName_Index");

// Set properties to request IRowsetIndex
DBPROPSET   rgPropSet[1];
DBPROP      rgProp[1];

rgPropSet[0].rgProperties      = rgProp;
rgPropSet[0].cProperties       = 1;
rgPropSet[0].guidPropertySet   = DBPROPSET_ROWSET;

rgProp[0].dwPropertyID         = DBPROP_IRowsetIndex;
rgProp[0].dwOptions            = DBPROPOPTIONS_REQUIRED;
rgProp[0].dwStatus             = DBPROPSTATUS_OK;
rgProp[0].colid                = DB_NULLID;
V_VT(&(rgProp[0].vValue))      = VT_BOOL;
V_BOOL(&(rgProp[0].vValue))    = VARIANT_TRUE;


// Use IOpenRowset::OpenRowset to open the table with the
// Emp_LastName_Index index and get a pointer to IRowsetIndex.
// Call QueryInterface to get pointers to IRowset, IAccessor,
// and IColumnsInfo. Note that all of these interfaces are on
// the base table rowset.
pIOpenRowset->OpenRowset(NULL, &TableId, &IndexId, IID_IRowsetIndex, 1, rgPropSet,
                        (IUnknown**) &pIRowsetIndex);
pIRowsetIndex->QueryInterface(IID_IRowset, (LPVOID FAR*) &pIRowset);
pIRowsetIndex->QueryInterface(IID_IAccessor, (LPVOID FAR*) &pIAccessor);
pIRowsetIndex->QueryInterface(IID_IColumnsInfo, (LPVOID FAR*) &pIColumnsInfo);

// Get information about the rowset columns and information
// about the index.
pIColumnsInfo->GetColumnInfo(&cColumns, &rgInfo, &pStringsBuffer);
pIRowsetIndex->GetIndexInfo(&cKeyCols, &rgIndexColDesc, &cProperties, rgProperties);

// Code not shown. Explore the DBINDEXCOLUMNDESC and DBCOLUMNINFO
// structures to determine which columns are key columns and
// what their metadata is. For each key column, call
// IColumnsInfo::MapColumnIds to determine the ordinal of
// the column. Suppose that these structures show that there
// is a single key column (column 1) that contains a 30-byte
// string. Free the structures allocated by the methods.
```

```
// Create an accessor to use when setting the index range
// and seeking for values.
typedef struct tagNameStruct {
   DWORD          dwStatus;
   OLECHAR        szLastName[30];
} NameStruct;
DBBINDSTATUS      rgStatus[1];
static DBBINDING  rgIndexBinding[1] = {
   {
      1,                                     // Ordinal of key column
      offsetof(NameStruct, szLastName),      // Offset to value
      0,                                     // No length--assume null-
                                             //  termination
      offsetof(NameStruct, dwStatus),        // Offset to status
      NULL,                                  // No TypeInfo
      NULL,                                  // No object
      NULL,                                  // No binding extensions
      DBPART_VALUE | DBPART_STATUS,          // Bind value and status
      DBMEMOWNER_CLIENTOWNED,                // Client-owned memory
      DBPARAMIO_NOTPARAM,                    // Not a parameter
      30,                                    // cbMaxLen
      0,                                     // Flags ignored
      DBTYPE_WSTR,                           // Bind as fixed-length
                                             //  string
      0,                                     // No scale
      0                                      // No precision
   }
};

pIAccessor->CreateAccessor(DBACCESSOR_ROWDATA, 1, rgIndexBinding, 0,
                           &hIndexAccessor, rgStatus);

// Set the range LastName LIKE "Smith*", and position the
// next fetch position to the start of this range
NameStruct nsNameStruct;
nsNameStruct.szLastName = OLESTR("Smith");
nsNameStruct.dwStatus   = DBSTATUS_S_OK;
pIRowsetIndex->SetRange(hIndexAccessor, 1, &nsNameStruct, 0, NULL, DBRANGE_PREFIX);
```

```
    // Traverse the Employees table within the range and print
    // each name found
    ULONG          cRows = 0;
    HROW *         rghRows = NULL;
    DBROWSTATUS    rgRowStatus[1];

    while(SUCCEEDED(hr=pIRowset->GetNextRows(0, 0, 1, &cRows, &rghRows)) && cRows > 0) {
       // Reuse the same accessor to get the name from the row
       // and print it
       pIRowset->GetData(rghRows[0], hIndexAccessor, &nsNameStruct);
       PrintData(nsNameStruct.szLastName, nsNameStruct.dwStatus);

       // Release the row
       pIRowset->ReleaseRows(cRows, rghRows, NULL, NULL, rgRowStatus);
    };

    // Release the accessor
    pIAccessor->ReleaseAccessor(hIndexAccessor);

    // Release the rowset
    pIRowsetIndex->Release();
    pIColumnsInfo->Release();
    pIAccessor->Release();
    pIRowset->Release();
};
```

PART 2

OLE DB Reference

IAccessor

IAccessor provides methods for accessor management. For information about accessors, see "Accessors" in Chapter 6, "Getting and Setting Data."

When to Implement

All rowsets and commands must implement **IAccessor**.

Accessors can be used for rowset data, parameter data, or both. Row and parameter accessors can be created on a command. The consumer must verify that row accessors created on the command are still valid following a change to the command. Accessors created on a command are not persisted with that command. Accessors created on a command are inherited by the rowsets it creates. To the consumer, it appears as if each accessor has been copied from the command to the rowset: the bindings, flags, and handle of each accessor are the same on both the rowset and the command.

Accessors created on a rowset are available only to that rowset. They are not available to the command that created the rowset or other rowsets created by the command.

When an accessor is created on a rowset or command, it has a reference count of 1. If a rowset inherits an accessor from a command, the accessor has a reference count of 1 on the rowset, regardless of the reference count of the same accessor on the command. Calls to **AddRefAccessor** increment the reference count of the accessor, and calls to **ReleaseAccessor** decrement the reference count of the accessor. When the reference count of an accessor reaches zero, the accessor and all resources used by that accessor are released. If the accessor is created on a command and inherited by the rowset, releasing the accessor on the command does not affect the "copy" of the accessor on the rowset and vice versa.

When the reference count of a rowset reaches zero, all accessors created on that rowset or inherited from the command that created it are released completely. If any accessors were inherited from the command, the "copies" of these parent accessors on the command are not affected.

When the reference count of a command reaches zero, all accessors created on the command are released completely. If any rowsets inherited accessors from the command, the "copies" of these accessors on the rowsets are not affected.

When to Call

To create an accessor, a consumer calls **CreateAccessor**. The consumer may create and release accessors at any time while the rowset or command remains in existence. When one thread of a consumer shares an accessor with another thread, it calls **AddRefAccessor** to increment the reference count of that accessor.

When the consumer is done with a rowset, it calls **ReleaseAccessor** to release any accessors on the rowset, including accessors inherited from the command. When the consumer is done with a command, it calls **ReleaseAccessor** to release any accessors created on the command. In either case, the consumer must call **ReleaseAccessor** once for each reference count on the accessor.

Method	Description
AddRefAccessor	Adds a reference count to an existing accessor.
CreateAccessor	Creates an accessor from a set of bindings.
GetBindings	Returns the bindings in an accessor.
ReleaseAccessor	Releases an accessor.

IAccessor::AddRefAccessor

Adds a reference count to an existing accessor.

```
HRESULT AddRefAccessor (
   HACCESSORhAccessor,
   ULONG *       pcRefCount);
```

Parameters

hAccessor
[in]
The handle of the accessor for which to increment the reference count.

pcRefCount
[out]
A pointer to memory in which to return the reference count of the accessor handle. If *pcRefCount* is a null pointer, no reference count is returned.

Return Code

S_OK
The method succeeded.

E_FAIL
A provider-specific error occurred.

E_UNEXPECTED
ITransaction::Commit or **ITransaction::Abort** was called, and the object is in a zombie state. This error can be returned only when the method is called on a rowset.

DB_E_BADACCESSORHANDLE
hAccessor was invalid.

Comments

The consumer must increment the reference count on an accessor by calling **AddRefAccessor** before passing it to another thread.

See Also

IAccessor::CreateAccessor, **IAccessor::ReleaseAccessor**

IAccessor::CreateAccessor

CreateAccessor creates an accessor from a set of bindings.

```
HRESULT CreateAccessor (
   DBACCESSORFLAGS        dwAccessorFlags,
   ULONG                  cBindings,
   const DBBINDING        rgBindings[],
   ULONG                  cbRowSize,
   HACCESSOR *            phAccessor,
   DBBINDSTATUS           rgStatus[]);
```

Parameters

dwAccessorFlags

[in]

A bitmask that describes the properties of the accessor and how it is to be used. These flags have the following meanings.

Value	Description
DBACCESSOR_ INVALID	This flag is used by **GetBindings** to indicate that the method failed.
DBACCESSOR_ PASSBYREF	The accessor is a reference accessor. The value passed in the consumer buffer is a pointer to the passer's internal buffer. This pointer need not point to the start of the internal buffer as long as the relative offsets of all elements of the buffer align with the offsets specified in the accessor. The passee must know the internal structure of the passer's buffer in order to read information from it. The passee must not free the buffer at the pointer, nor may it write to this buffer. For row accessors, this buffer is the rowset's copy of the row. The consumer reads information directly from this copy of the row at a later point in time, so the provider must guarantee that the pointer remains valid. For parameter accessors, this buffer is the consumer's buffer. The provider reads data from this buffer only when **ICommand::Execute** is called, so the pointer is not required to remain valid after **Execute** returns. Support for this flag is optional. A consumer determines whether a provider supports this bit by calling **IDBProperties::GetProperties** for the DBPROP_BYREFACCESSORS property. When this flag is used, the *dwMemOwner* in the DBBINDING structure is ignored. If the accessor is used for row data, the accessor refers to the provider's memory; the consumer must not write to or free this memory. If the accessor is used for input parameters, the provider copies the row of data without assuming ownership. It is an error to specify an output or input/output parameter in a reference accessor. For more information, see "Reference Accessors" in Chapter 6, "Getting and Setting Data."
DBACCESSOR_ ROWDATA	The accessor is a row accessor and describes bindings to columns in the rowset. An accessor may be a row accessor, a parameter accessor, or both.
DBACCESSOR_ PARAMETERDATA	The accessor is a parameter accessor and describes bindings to parameters in the command text. In a parameter accessor, it is an error to bind an input or an input/output parameter more than once.

Value	Description
DBACCESSOR_OPTIMIZED	The row accessor is to be optimized. This hint may affect how a provider structures its internal buffers. A particular column can be bound by only one optimized accessor. The column can also be bound by other, nonoptimized accessors, but the types specified in the nonoptimized accessors must be convertible from the type in the optimized accessor. All optimized accessors must be created before the first row is fetched with **IRowset::GetNextRows**, **IRowsetLocate::GetRowsAt**, **IRowsetLocate::GetRowsByBookmark**, or **IRowsetScroll::GetRowsAtRatio**. This flag is ignored for parameter accessors.

cBindings
[in]
The number of bindings in the accessor.

If *cBindings* is zero, **CreateAccessor** creates a null accessor. Null accessors are used only by **IRowsetChange::InsertRow** to create a new row in which each column is set to its default value, NULL, or a status of DBSTATUS_E_UNAVAILABLE. Providers that support **InsertRow** must support the creation of null accessors. For more information, see **InsertRow**.

rgBindings
[in]
An array of DBBINDING structures. For more information, see "DBBINDING Structures" in Chapter 6, "Getting and Setting Data."

cbRowSize
[in]
The numer of bytes allocated for a single set of parameters or criteria values in the consumer's buffer.

cbRowSize is used by **ICommand::Execute** to process multiple sets of parameters and by **IViewFilter::GetFilter** and **IViewFilter::SetFilter** to get and set multiple OR' conditions in criteria. In either case, a single accessor may describe multiple sets of values. *cbRowSize* is generally the size of the structure that contains a single set of parameter or critieria values and is used as the offset to the start of the next set of values within the array of structures. For example, if *cParamSets* is greater than 1 in the DBPARAMS structure passed to **Execute**, the provider assumes that the *pData* element of this structure points to an array of structures containing parameter values, each *cbRowSize* bytes in size. Similarly, if *cRows* is greater than 1 in **SetFilter**, the provider assumes that the *pCriteriaData* argument points to an array of structures containing criteria values, each *cbRowSize* bytes in size.

cbRowSize must be large enough to contain the structure defined by the bindings in *rgBindings*. The provider is not required to verify this, although it may.

cbRowSize is not used when fetching rowset data.

phAccessor
[out]
A pointer to memory in which to return the handle of the created accessor. If **CreateAccessor** fails, it must attempt to set **phAccessor* to a null handle.

rgStatus
[out]
An array of *cBindings* DBBINDSTATUS values in which **CreateAccessor** returns the status of each binding; that is, whether or not it was successfully validated. If *rgStatus* is a null pointer, no bind status values are returned. The consumer allocates and owns the memory for this array. The bind status values are returned for the following reasons.

Value	Description
DBBINDSTATUS_OK	No errors were found in the binding. Because accessor validation can be deferred, a status of DBBINDSTATUS_OK does not necessarily mean that the binding was successfully validated.
DBBINDSTATUS_ BADORDINAL	A parameter ordinal was zero in a parameter accessor. If the accessor is validated against the metadata when **CreateAccessor** is called, DBBINDSTATUS_BADORDINAL can be returned for the following reasons: • In a row accessor, a column ordinal in a binding was outside the range of available columns on the rowset. • In a parameter accessor, a parameter ordinal was greater than the number of parameters in the command text. These reasons cause a status value of DBSTATUS_E_BADACCESSOR to be returned if the accessor is validated when used. Some providers may support binding more parameters than the number of parameters in the command text, and such providers do not return DBBINDSTATUS_BADORDINAL in this case.

Value	Description
DBBINDSTATUS_ UNSUPPORTED CONVERSION	If the accessor is validated against the metadata when **CreateAccessor** is called, DBBINDSTATUS_UNSUPPORTEDCONVERSION can be returned for the following reasons: • The specified conversion was not supported by the provider. For a list of conversions the accessor must support, see "Data Type Conversion" in Chapter 10, "Data Types in OLE DB." • The consumer attempted to convert a column to a storage object (**ISequentialStream**, **IStorage**, **IStream**, **ILockBytes**) and the particular conversion is not supported by the provider. These reasons cause a status value of DBSTATUS_E_BADACCESSOR to be returned if the accessor is validated when used.
DBBINDSTATUS_ BADBINDINFO	*dwPart* in a binding was not one of the following: DBPART_VALUE DBPART_LENGTH DBPART_STATUS *eParamIO* in a binding in a parameter accessor was not one of the following: DBPARAMIO_INPUT DBPARAMIO_OUTPUT DBPARAMIO_INPUT | DBPARAMIO_OUTPUT A row accessor was optimized and a column ordinal in a binding was already used in another optimized accessor. In a parameter accessor, two or more bindings contained the same ordinal for an input or input/output parameter. *wType* in a binding was DBTYPE_EMPTY or DBTYPE_NULL. *wType* in a binding was one of the following: DBTYPE_BYREF | DBTYPE _EMPTY, DBTYPE_BYREF | DBTYPE_NULL, or DBTYPE_BYREF | DBTYPE_RESERVED. *wType* in a binding was used with more than one of the following mutually exclusive type indicators: DBTYPE_BYREF, DBTYPE_ARRAY, or DBTYPE_VECTOR. *wType* in a binding was DBTYPE_IUNKNOWN, and *pObject* in the same binding was a null pointer.

Value	Description
	Provider-owned memory was specified for a nonpointer type in a nonreference row accessor. Provider-owned memory was specified for a column and the provider does not support binding to provider-owned memory for this column. Provider-owned memory was specified for a column for which **IColumnsInfo::GetColumnInfo** returned DBCOLUMNFLAGS_ISLONG. In a nonreference parameter accessor, a binding specified provider-owned memory. An output or input/output parameter was specified in a parameter reference accessor. *dwFlags* in a binding was set to DBBINDFLAG_HTML, and *wType* for the same binding was not a string value. If the accessor is validated against the metadata when **CreateAccessor** is called, DBBINDSTATUS_BADBINDINFO can be returned for the following reasons: • A row accessor was not optimized, a column number in a binding specified a column that was already used in an optimized accessor, and the provider did not support a conversion from the type specified in the optimized accessor for the column to the type specified in *wType*. • In a parameter accessor, *eParamIO* in a binding specified the incorrect I/O type for the parameter. Some providers cannot determine parameter I/O types and never return DBBINDSTATUS_BADBINDINFO in this case. • In a reference accessor, the value specified for *dwPart*, *obValue*, *cbMaxLen*, or *wType* in a binding did not match the format of the corresponding element in the rowset's copy of the row. • In a nonreference accessor, a binding specified provider-owned memory, *wType* was X | DBTYPE_BYREF, and the data type of the corresponding element of the rowset's copy of the row was not X or X | DBTYPE_BYREF.

Value	Description
	• In a nonreference accessor, a binding specified provider-owned memory, *wType* was DBTYPE_BSTR, and the data type of the corresponding element of the rowset's copy of the row was not DBTYPE_BSTR.The accessor was used for passing key column values in **IRowsetIndex::Seek** or **IRowsetIndex::SetRange**, and the order in which the key columns were bound did not match the order in which they were returned in **IColumnsInfo::GetColumnInfo**. • The accessor was used for passing key column values in **Seek** or **SetRange**, and a less-significant key column was bound without binding all more-significant key columns. • The accessor was used for passing key column values in **Seek** or **SetRange**, and a non-key column was bound before the last bound key column. These reasons cause a status value of DBSTATUS_E_BADACCESSOR to be returned if the accessor is validated when used.
DBBINDSTATUS_ BADSTORAGE FLAGS	*dwFlags*, in the DBOBJECT structure pointed to by a binding, specified invalid storage flags. • If the accessor is validated against the metadata when **CreateAccessor** is called, DBBINDSTATUS_BADSTORAGEFLAGS can be returned if *dwFlags*, in the DBOBJECT structure pointed to by a binding, specified a valid storage flag that was not supported by the object. This causes a status value of DBSTATUS_E_BADACCESSOR to be returned if the accessor is validated when used.
DBBINDSTATUS_ NOINTERFACE	If the accessor is validated against the metadata when **CreateAccessor** is called, DBBINDSTATUS_NOINTERFACE can be returned for the following reasons: • The provider did not support the storage interface specified in *iid* in the DBOBJECT structure pointed to by a binding in the accessor. • The COM object in a column or parameter did not support the interface specified in *iid* in the DBOBJECT structure pointed to by the corresponding binding in the accessor.

Value	Description
	• The provider supports only one open storage object at a time—that is, DBPROP_MULTIPLESTORAGEOBJECTS is VARIANT_FALSE—and *wType* in more than one binding was DBTYPE_IUNKNOWN. These reasons cause a status value of DBSTATUS_E_BADACCESSOR to be returned if the accessor is validated when used.

Return Code

S_OK
: The method succeeded. If *rgStatus* is not a null pointer, each element is set to DBBINDSTATUS_OK.

E_FAIL
: A provider-specific error occurred.

E_INVALIDARG
: *phAccessor* was a null pointer.

cBindings was not zero and *rgBindings* was a null pointer.

E_UNEXPECTED
: **ITransaction::Commit** or **ITransaction::Abort** was called, and the object is in a zombie state. This error can be returned only when the method is called on a rowset.

DB_E_BADACCESSORFLAGS
: *dwAccessorFlags* was invalid.

The DBACCESSOR_PARAMETERDATA bit was set in *dwAccessorFlags*, and the provider does not support parameters.

Neither the DBACCESSOR_PARAMETERDATA bit nor the DBACCESSOR_ROWDATA bit was set in *dwAccessorFlags*.

A method that fetches rows (**IRowset::GetNextRows**, **IRowsetLocate::GetRowsAt**, **IRowsetLocate::GetRowsByBookmark**, or **IRowsetScroll::GetRowsAtRatio**) had already been called, and the DBACCESSOR_OPTIMIZED bit in *dwAccessorFlags* was set.

The DBACCESSOR_ PARAMETERDATA bit was set, and **CreateAccessor** was called on a rowset.

DB_E_BYREFACCESSORNOTSUPPORTED
: *dwAccessorFlags* was DBACCESSOR_PASSBYREF, and the value of the DBPROP_BYREFACCESSORS property is VARIANT_FALSE.

DB_E_ERRORSOCCURRED
Accessor validation failed. To determine which bindings failed, the consumer checks the values returned in *rgStatus*, at least one of which is not DBBINDSTATUS_OK.

DB_E_NOTREENTRANT
The provider called a method from **IRowsetNofity** in the consumer that had not yet returned, and the provider does not support reentrancy in this method.

DB_E_NULLACCESSORNOTSUPPORTED
cBindings was zero and the rowset does not support **IRowsetChange::InsertRow**, or **CreateAccessor** was called on a command.

Comments

For general information about accessors, see "Accessors" in Chapter 6, "Getting and Setting Data."

CreateAccessor always checks all error conditions that do not require it to validate the accessor against the metadata. As a general rule, this means it checks the error conditions for all of the return codes except those that return DB_E_ERRORSOCCURRED. **CreateAccessor** may validate the accessor against the metadata for row accessors created on the rowset; it never validates the accessor against the metadata for row or parameter accessors created on the command. When **CreateAccessor** validates the accessor against the metadata, it validates each binding in the accessor, setting the appropriate DBBINDSTATUS values as it goes. If **CreateAccessor** fails in any way, it does not create the accessor and sets **phAccessor* to a null handle.

If **CreateAccessor** does not validate the accessor against the metadata, the validation is said to be *delayed*. **CreateAccessor** simply creates the accessor, and validation is done by the first method that uses the accessor. If the accessor is found to be invalid, it remains in existence and can be used again.

If accessor validation is delayed, the provider determines whether the method validating the accessor validates it against the metadata before or during data transfer. If the method validates the accessor before transferring any data, it can return any of the return codes listed below for this purpose. If the method validates the accessor while transferring the data, it sets the status value of any column or parameter for which the accessor is invalid (within the context of the method) to DBSTATUS_E_BADACCESSOR and returns DB_S_ERRORSOCCURRED or DB_E_ERRORSOCCURRED. Whether the method continues processing other columns or parameters depends on both the method and the provider.

The following return codes are returned by methods that perform delayed accessor validation before transferring any data. The DBBINDSTATUS value to which each corresponds is also listed.

Return code	DBBINDSTATUS value
E_NOINTERFACE	DBBINDSTATUS_NOINTERFACE
DB_E_BADBINDINFO	DBBINDSTATUS_BADBINDINFO
DB_E_BADORDINAL	DBBINDSTATUS_BADORDINAL
DB_E_BADSTORAGEFLAGS	DBBINDSTATUS_ BADSTORAGEFLAGS
DB_E_UNSUPPORTEDCONVERSION	DBBINDSTATUS_ UNSUPPORTEDCONVERSION

Providers that do not support conversion of BLOB or non-BLOB data to a data structured storage interface should fail the accessor creation method with DB_E_ERRORSOCCURED and report DBBINDSTATUS_UNSUPPORTEDCONVERSION on the column specifying the incorrect binding.

See Also

IAccessor::GetBindings, **IAccessor::ReleaseAccessor**, **IConvertType::CanConvert**, **IRowset::GetData**, **IRowsetChange::SetData**

IAccessor::GetBindings

Returns the bindings in an accessor.

```
HRESULT GetBindings (
   HACCESSOR              hAccessor,
   DBACCESSORFLAGS *      pdwAccessorFlags,
   ULONG *                pcBindings,
   DBBINDING **           prgBindings);
```

Parameters

hAccessor
[in]
The handle of the accessor for which to return the bindings.

pdwAccessorFlags
[out]
A pointer to memory in which to return a bitmask that describes the properties of the accessor and how it is intended to be used. For more information, see *dwAccessorFlags* in CreateAccessor. If this method fails, **pdwAccessorFlags* is set to DBACCESSOR_INVALID.

pcBindings
[out]
A pointer to memory in which to return the number of bindings in the accessor. If this method fails, **pcBindings* is set to zero.

prgBindings
[out]
A pointer to memory in which to return an array of DBBINDING structures. One DBBINDING structure is returned for each binding in the accessor. The provider allocates memory for these structures and any structures pointed to by elements of these structures; for example, if *pObject* in a binding structure is not a null pointer, the provider allocates a DBOBJECT structure for return to the consumer. The provider returns the address to the memory for these structures; the consumer releases the memory for these structures with **IMalloc::Free** when it no longer needs the bindings. If **pcBindings* is zero on output or the method fails, the provider does not allocate any memory and ensures that **prgBindings* is a null pointer on output. For information about bindings, see "DBBINDING Structures" in Chapter 6, "Getting and Setting Data."

Return Code

S_OK
The method succeeded.

E_FAIL
A provider-specific error occurred.

E_INVALIDARG
pdwAccessorFlags, *pcBindings*, or *prgBindings* was a null pointer.

E_OUTOFMEMORY
The provider was unable to allocate sufficient memory in which to return the binding structures.

E_UNEXPECTED
ITransaction::Commit or **ITransaction::Abort** was called, and the object is in a zombie state. This error can be returned only when the method is called on a rowset.

DB_E_BADACCESSORHANDLE
hAccessor was invalid.

DB_E_NOTREENTRANT
The provider called a method from **IRowsetNofity** in the consumer that had not yet returned, and the provider does not support reentrancy in this method.

Comments

This method makes no logical change to the state of the object.

If the accessor is a null accessor, the method sets **pcBindings* to zero and **prgBindings* to a null pointer.

See Also

IAccessor::CreateAccessor

IAccessor::ReleaseAccessor

Releases an accessor.

```
HRESULT ReleaseAccessor (
   HACCESSOR      hAccessor,
   ULONG *        pcRefCount);
```

Parameters

hAccessor
[in]
The handle of the accessor to release.

pcRefCount
[out]
A pointer to memory in which to return the remaining reference count of the accessor handle. If *pcRefCount* is a null pointer, no reference count is returned.

Return Code

S_OK
The method succeeded.

E_FAIL
A provider-specific error occurred.

DB_E_BADACCESSORHANDLE
hAccessor was invalid.

DB_E_NOTREENTRANT
The provider called a method from **IRowsetNofity** in the consumer that had not yet returned, and the provider does not support reentrancy in this method.

Comments

ReleaseAccessor decrements the reference count of the accessor. If the reference count reaches zero, it releases the accessor and all resources used by the accessor. After an accessor is released, methods called with the handle to that accessor return DB_E_BADACCESSORHANDLE.

On rowsets, accessors are read-only and can be shared among threads in a free-threaded style without synchronization. The consumer must call **ReleaseAccessor** to decrement the reference count on an accessor that has been passed to a thread and is no longer needed by that thread.

This method can be called while the rowset is in a zombie state to enable the consumer to clean up after a transaction has been committed or aborted.

See Also

IAccessor::AddRefAccessor, **IAccessor::CreateAccessor**

IAlterIndex

The **IAlterIndex** interface exposes methods to alter tables, indexes, and columns.

Method	Description
AlterIndex	Alters the index ID and/or properties associated with an index.

IAlterIndex::AlterIndex

AlterIndex alters the ID and/or properties associated with an index.

```
HRESULT AlterIndex(
   DBID *        pTableID,
   DBID *        pIndexID,
   DBID *        pNewIndexID,
   ULONG         cPropertySets,
   DBPROPSET     rgPropertySet[]);
```

Parameters

pTableID
[in]
The DBID of the indexed base table.

pIndexID
[in]
The DBID of the existing index to alter.

pNewIndexID
[in]
The new DBID of the index. If this is the same as *pIndexID*, or a null pointer, then the ID of the index is unchanged.

cPropertySets
[in]
The number of DBPROPSET structures in *rgPropertySets*. If this is zero, the provider ignores *rgPropertySets*.

rgPropertySets
[in/out]
An array of DBPROPSET structures containing properties and values to be set. The properties specified in these structures must belong to the index property set.

Return Code

S_OK
The method succeeded.

DB_S_ERRORSOCCURRED
The index was altered but one or more properties—for which the *dwOptions* element of the DBPROP structure was DBPROPOPTIONS_OPTIONAL—were not set. The consumer checks *dwStatus* in the DBPROP structures to determine which properties were not set. The method can fail to set properties for a number of reasons, including:

- The property was not supported by the provider.
- The property was not in the Index property group.
- The property set was not supported by the provider.
- It was not possible to set the property.
- The *colid* in the DBPROP structure was not DB_NULLID.
- The data type in *vValue* in the DBPROP structure was not the data type of the property or was not VT_EMPTY.
- The value in *vValue* in the DBPROP structure was invalid.
- The property's value conflicted with an existing property.

E_FAIL
A provider-specific error occurred.

E_INVALIDARG
pTableID was a null pointer.

pIndexID was a null pointer.

DB_E_NOTABLE
The table specified in **pTableID* does not exist in the data store.

DB_E_NOINDEX
The index specified in **pIndexID* does not exist in the data store or does not apply to the specified table.

DB_DUPLICATEINDEXID
The index specified in **pNewIndexID* already exists in the data store.

DB_SEC_E_PERMISSIONDENIED
The consumer did not have sufficient permission to alter the index.

DB_E_BADINDEXID
**pNewIndexID* was an invalid index ID.

DB_E_ERRORSOCCURRED
The index was not altered because one or more properties—for which the *dwOptions* element of the DBPROP structure was DBPROPOPTIONS_REQUIRED or an invalid value—were not set. The consumer checks *dwStatus* in the DBPROP structures to determine which properties were not set. None of the satisfiable properties are remembered. The method can fail to set properties for any of the reasons specified in DB_S_ERRORSOCCURRED, except the reason that states that it was not possible to set the property.

DB_E_INDEXINUSE
The specified index was in use.

DB_E_TABLEINUSE
The specified table was in use, and the provider could not modify the index with the table open.

Comments

AlterIndex applies the new properties and index ID to the existing index. The altered index preserves all properties associated with the existing index that are not explicitly changed by properties specified in **prgProperties*. If *pNewIndexID* is null or the same as *pIndexID*, the index ID is unchanged. If *cPropertySets* is zero, no properties are changed. If *pNewIndexID* is null or the same as *pIndexID*, and *cPropertySets* is zero, the method makes no change to the state of the index and returns S_OK.

IAlterTable

The **IAlterTable** interface exposes methods to alter the definition of tables, indexes, and columns.

Providers that implement **IAlterTable** should expose the data source information property DBPROP_ALTERCOLUMN.

Method	Description
AlterColumn	Alters the column ID and/or properties associated with a column in a table.
AlterTable	Alters the table ID and/or properties associated with a table.

IAlterTable::AlterColumn

AlterColumn alters the column ID and/or properties associated with a column in a table.

```
HRESULT AlterColumn(
   DBID *             pTableID,
   DBID *             pColumnID,
   DBCOLUMNDESCFLAGS ColumnDescFlags,
   DBCOLUMNDESC*      pColumnDesc);
```

Parameters

pTableID
[in]
The DBID of the base table containing the column to alter.

pColumnID
[in]
The current DBID of the column to alter.

ColumnDescFlags
[in]
Values as described in the enumeration **DBCOLUMNDESCFLAGS**. These bits define which portions of the **DBCOLUMNDESC** structure defined in *pColumnDesc* should be used when altering the column. A provider returns values it supports in the DBPROP_ALTERCOLUMN property. For more information about this field, please see the Comments section.

Flag	Associated portion of DBCOLUMNDESC
DBCOLUMNDESCFLAG_TYPENAME	*pwszTypeName*
DBCOLUMNDESCFLAG_ITYPEINFO	*ITypeInfo **
DBCOLUMNDESCFLAG_PROPERTIES	*rgPropertySets* AND *cPropertySets*
DBCOLUMNDESCFLAG_CLSID	*pclsid*
DBCOLUMNDESCFLAG_COLSIZE	*ulColumnSize*
DBCOLUMNDESCFLAG_DBCID	*dbcid*
DBCOLUMNDESCFLAG_WTYPE	*wType*
DBCOLUMNDESCFLAG_PRECISION	*bPrecision*
DBCOLUMNDESCFLAG_SCALE	*bScale*

pColumnDesc
[in]
A pointer to a **DBCOLUMNDESC** structure defining new values for the columns. Only the values defined in *ColumnDescFlags* are used—the provider ignores other fields in the structure. For a description of the **DBCOLUMNDESC** structure, please refer to **ITableDefinition::CreateTable**.

Return Code

S_OK
The method succeeded.

DB_S_ERRORSOCCURRED
The column was altered, but one or more properties—for which the *dwOptions* element of the DBPROP structure was DBPROPOPTIONS_OPTIONAL—were not set. The consumer checks *dwStatus* in the DBPROP structures to determine which properties were not set. The method can fail to set properties for a number of reasons, including:

- The property was not supported by the provider.
- The property was not in the Column, Rowset, or Table property group.
- The property set was not supported by the provider.
- It was not possible to set the property.
- *colid* in the DBPROP structure was not DB_NULLID.
- The data type in *vValue* in the DBPROP structure was not the data type of the property or was not VT_EMPTY.
- The value in *vValue* in the DBPROP structure was invalid.
- The property's value conflicted with an existing property.

E_FAIL
A provider-specific error occurred.

E_INVALIDARG
pTableID or *pColumnID* was a null pointer.

pColumnDesc was a null pointer.

DB_E_NOCOLUMN
The column specified in **pColumnID* does not exist in the specified table.

DB_E_NOTABLE
The specified table does not exist in the data store.

DB_E_DUPLICATECOLUMNID
The *ColumnDescFlags* structure indicated that the *dbcid* portion of the *pColumnDesc* argument should be used, and the column ID specified in *dbcid* was the same as an existing column ID.

DB_E_ERRORSOCCURRED
The column was not altered because one or more properties—for which the *dwOptions* element of the DBPROP structure was DBPROPOPTIONS_REQUIRED or an invalid value—could not be set. The consumer checks *dwStatus* in the DBPROP structures to determine which properties were not set. The method can fail to set properties for any of the reasons specified in DB_S_ERRORSOCCURRED.

DB_SEC_E_PERMISSIONDENIED
The consumer did not have sufficient permission to alter the columns of this table.

DB_E_TABLEINUSE
The specified table was in use, and the provider could not alter the column while the table was open.

DB_E_NOTSUPPORTED
ColumnDescFlags was an invalid value. Providers return valid values in the property DBPROP_ALTERCOLUMN.

Comments

AlterColumn applies the new properties and column ID to the existing column. The altered column preserves all properties associated with the existing column that are not explicitly changed by properties specified in **prgProperties*. If *pNewColumnID* is null or the same as *pColumnID*, the column name is unchanged. If *cPropertySets* is zero, no properties are changed. If *pNewColumnID* is null or the same as *pColumnID*, and *cPropertySets* is zero, the method makes no change to the state of the table and returns S_OK.

Providers may also return any of the return codes listed in **ITableDefinition::CreateTable** or **ITableDefinition::AddColumn** associated with errors in the **DBCOLUMNDESC** structure (for example, DB_E_BADCOLUMNID). However, the provider should not evaluate portions of the structure that are not explicitly listed in the *ColumnDescFlags* parameter.

Calls to **AlterColumn** should be atomic. Failure should leave the column in the same state as before the call to the method.

IAlterTable::AlterTable

AlterTable alters the ID and/or properties associated with a table.

```
HRESULT AlterTable(
   DBID *      pTableID,
   DBID *      pNewTableID,
   ULONG       cPropertySets,
   DBPROPSET   rgPropertySet[]);
```

Parameters

pTableID
[in]
The DBID of the base table to alter.

pNewTableID
[in]
The new DBID of the base table. If this is the same as *pTableID* or is a null pointer, the ID of the table is unchanged.

cPropertySets
[in]
The number of DBPROPSET structures in *rgPropertySets*. If this is zero, the provider ignores *rgPropertySets*.

rgPropertySets
[in/out]
An array of DBPROPSET structures containing properties and values to be set. The properties specified in these structures must belong to the table property set.

Return Code

S_OK
The method succeeded.

DB_S_ERRORSOCCURRED
The table was altered, but one or more properties—for which the *dwOptions* element of the DBPROP structure was DBPROPOPTIONS_OPTIONAL—were not set. The consumer checks *dwStatus* in the DBPROP structures to determine which properties were not set. The method can fail to set properties for a number of reasons, including:

- The property was not supported by the provider.
- The property was not in the Column, Rowset, or Table property group.
- The property set was not supported by the provider.
- It was not possible to set the property.
- *colid* in the DBPROP structure was not DB_NULLID.

- The data type in *vValue* in the DBPROP structure was not the data type of the property or was not VT_EMPTY.
- The value in *vValue* in the DBPROP structure was invalid.
- The property's value conflicted with an existing property.

E_FAIL
A provider-specific error occurred.

E_INVALIDARG
pTableID was a null pointer.

DB_E_BADTABLEID
**pTableID* was an invalid table ID.

DB_E_ERRORSOCCURRED
The table was not altered because one or more properties—for which the *dwOptions* element of the DBPROP structure was DBPROPOPTIONS_REQUIRED or an invalid value—could not be set. The consumer checks *dwStatus* in the DBPROP structures to determine which properties were not set. The method can fail to set properties for any of the reasons specified in DB_S_ERRORSOCCURRED.

DB_E_NOTABLE
The table specified in **pTableID* does not exist in the data store.

DB_DUPLICATETABLEID
The table specified in **pNewTableID* already exists in the data store.

DB_SEC_E_PERMISSIONDENIED
The consumer did not have sufficient permission to alter the table or index.

DB_E_TABLEINUSE
The specified table was in use, and the provider could not alter the table while it was open.

Comments

AlterTable applies the new properties and table ID to the existing table. The altered table preserves all properties associated with the existing table that are not explicitly changed by properties specified in **prgProperties*. If *pNewTableID* is null or the same as *pTableID*, the table ID is unchanged. If *cPropertySets* is zero, no properties are changed. If *pNewTableID* is null or the same as *pTableID*, and *cPropertySets* is zero, the method makes no change to the state of the table and returns S_OK.

IChapteredRowset

IChapteredRowset is the interface that allows consumers to manage chapters.

When to Implement

IChapteredRowset is required for all providers that support chapters.

When to Call

When a chapter handle is retrieved, either by calling **GetData** on a column containing chapter values or from a method that returns a chapter handle, a reference count is taken against that chapter handle. When the chapter is subsequently used, no additional reference counts are taken; however, the reference count on a chapter can be explicitly incremented by calling **AddRefChapter**. Both reference counts must be decremented by calling **ReleaseChapter**.

If any HROWs in the chapter have pending changes when **ReleaseChapter** is called, the reference count of the chapter is decremented but the chapter remains valid, even if its reference count drops to zero. In such a situation, the chapter value might remain valid, but consumers should not count on such behavior. The chapter and its resources are freed when the pending change status on the rows is cleared, either by a call to **IRowsetUpdate::Update** or **IRowsetUpdate::Undo**. In particular, a single-chaptered provider will not be able to open another chapter until the rows are updated or undone and the chapter's resources are freed. For more information, see IRowset::ReleaseRows.

Method	Description
AddRefChapter	Adds a reference count to a Chapter Handle.
ReleaseChapter	Releases a reference count on a Chapter Handle.

IChapteredRowset::AddRefChapter

Adds a reference count to an existing chapter.

```
HRESULT AddRefChapter (
   HCHAPTER    hChapter,
   ULONG *     pcRefCount);
```

Parameters

hChapter
[in]
The handle of the chapter for which to increment the reference count.

pcRefCount
[out]
A pointer to memory in which to return the reference count of the chapter handle. If *pcRefCount* is a null pointer, no reference count is returned.

Return Code

S_OK
The method succeeded.

E_FAIL
A provider-specific error occurred.

DB_E_BADCHAPTER
hChapter was invalid.

E_UNEXPECTED
ITransaction::Commit or **ITransaction::Abort** was called, and the object is in a zombie state.

IChapteredRowset::ReleaseChapter

Releases a chapter.

```
HRESULT ReleaseChapter (
   HCHAPTER hChapter,
   ULONG *  pcRefCount);
```

Parameters

hChapter
[in]
The chapter handle.

pcRefCount
[out]
A pointer to memory in which to return the reference count of the chapter handle. If *pcRefCount* is a null pointer, no reference count is returned.

Return Code

S_OK
The method succeeded.

E_FAIL
A provider-specific error occurred.

E_INVALIDARG
The rowset was not chaptered.

DB_E_BADCHAPTER
hChapter was invalid.

DB_E_NOTREENTRANT
The provider called a method from **IRowsetNotify** in the consumer that had not yet returned, and the provider does not support reentrancy in this method.

Comments

If the chapter's reference count is reduced to zero and retrieved again later, the fetch position of the retrieved chapter is reset to the initial state.

This method can be called while the rowset is in a zombie state to allow the consumer to clean up after a transaction has been committed or aborted.

See Also

IRowset::GetNextRows, **IRowsetLocate::GetRowsAt**

IColumnsInfo

IColumnsInfo is the simpler of two interfaces that can be used to expose information about columns of a rowset or prepared command. It provides a limited set of information in an array.

When to Implement

All rowsets and commands implement **IColumnsInfo**. Service components can synthesize **IColumnsRowset** from this so that consumers and providers have independent choice of whether they want to code for simple limited information or to work with flexible and open-ended column descriptions.

IColumnsInfo is required both on commands and on rowsets.

When to Call

GetColumnInfo returns the most commonly used metadata: column IDs, data types, updatability, and so on. **GetColumnInfo** returns the metadata in an array of structures, which can be created and accessed quickly. The metadata returned, however, is limited.

Consumers that require more complete metadata can obtain it by calling **IColumnsRowset::GetColumnsRowset**.

> **Note** For commands that expose **ICommandPrepare**, the methods on this interface can be called only after the command is prepared or the rowset is instantiated. If a command text is set but not prepared, any calls to methods on **IColumnsInfo** return DB_E_NOTPREPARED. For commands that do not expose **ICommandPrepare**, the methods on this interface can be called only after the command text has been set.

Method	Description
GetColumnInfo	Returns the column metadata needed by most consumers.
MapColumnIDs	Returns an array of ordinals of the columns in a rowset that are identified by the specified column IDs.

IColumnsInfo::GetColumnInfo

Returns the column metadata needed by most consumers.

```
HRESULT GetColumnInfo (
   ULONG *           pcColumns,
   DBCOLUMNINFO **   prgInfo,
   OLECHAR **        ppStringsBuffer);
```

Parameters

pcColumns

[out]
A pointer to memory in which to return the number of columns in the rowset; this number includes the bookmark column, if there is one. If **GetColumnInfo** is called on a command that does not return rows, **pcColumns* is set to zero. If this method terminates due to an error, **pcColumns* is set to zero.

prgInfo

[out]
A pointer to memory in which to return an array of DBCOLUMNINFO structures. One structure is returned for each column in the rowset. The provider allocates memory for the structures and returns the address to this memory; the consumer releases this memory with **IMalloc::Free** when it no longer needs the column information. If **pcColumns* is 0 on output or terminates due to an error, the provider does not allocate any memory and ensures that **prgInfo* is a null pointer on output. For more information, see "DBCOLUMNINFO Structures" in the Comments section.

ppStringsBuffer

[out]
A pointer to memory in which to return a pointer to storage for all string values (names used either within *columnid* or for **pwszName*) within a single allocation block. If no returned columns have either form of string name or if this method terminates due to error, this parameter returns a null pointer. If there are any string names, this will be a buffer containing all the values of those names. The consumer should free the buffer with **IMalloc::Free** when finished working with the names. If **pcColumns* is zero on output, the provider does not allocate any memory and ensures that **ppStringsBuffer* is a null pointer on output. Each of the individual string values stored in this buffer is terminated by a null-termination character. Therefore, the buffer may contain one or more strings, each with its own null-termination character, and may contain embedded null-termination characters.

Return Code

S_OK
The method succeeded.

E_FAIL
A provider-specific error occurred.

E_INVALIDARG
pcColumns, *prgInfo*, or *ppStringsBuffer* was a null pointer.

E_OUTOFMEMORY
The provider was unable to allocate sufficient memory in which to return the column information structures.

E_UNEXPECTED
ITransaction::Commit or **ITransaction::Abort** was called, and the object is in a zombie state. This error can be returned only when the method is called on a rowset.

DB_E_ERRORSINCOMMAND
The command text contained one or more errors. Providers should use OLE DB error objects to return details about the errors.

DB_E_NOCOMMAND
No command text was set. This error can be returned only when this method is called from the command object.

DB_E_NOTPREPARED
The command exposed **ICommandPrepare** and the command text was set, but the command was not prepared. This error can be returned only when this method is called from the Command object.

DB_E_NOTREENTRANT
The provider called a method from **IRowsetNotify** in the consumer that had not yet returned, and the provider does not support reentrancy in this method.

DB_SEC_E_PERMISSIONDENIED
The consumer did not have sufficient permission to retrieve the column information.

Comments

This function makes no logical change to the state of the object.

GetColumnInfo returns a fixed set of column metadata in an array of DBCOLUMNINFO structures, one per column. The returned metadata is that most commonly used by consumers, such as the data type and column ID.

The order of the structures is the order in which the columns appear in the rowset (column ordinal order). This is the same order as they appear in **IColumnsRowset** and is predictable from the ordering of requested columns in the command text.

Bookmark columns may be returned on any rowset, regardless of its source (for example, **ICommand::Execute**, **IOpenRowset::OpenRowset**, **IColumnsRowset::GetColumnsRowset**, or **IDBSchemaRowset::GetRowset**) or whether bookmarks were requested. When bookmarks are returned, they will always appear as the first element of **prgInfo* with *iOrdinal* equal to zero. When processing the columns returned by **GetColumnInfo**, generic consumers should be prepared to receive and handle bookmark columns appropriately (that is, not display them to the user if not appropriate for the application).

GetColumnInfo provides a quick alternative to **GetColumnsRowset**. While **GetColumnsRowset** returns all available column metadata, it does so in a rowset. To get the metadata, the consumer must therefore create the column metadata rowset, create one or more accessors, fetch each row in the rowset, and get the data from the rowset.

Calling **GetColumnInfo** on a command before the command is executed can be an expensive operation.

DBCOLUMNINFO Structures

GetColumnInfo returns column metadata in DBCOLUMNINFO structures.

```
typedef struct tagDBCOLUMNINFO {
   LPOLESTR        pwszName;
   ITypeInfo *     pTypeInfo;
   ULONG           iOrdinal;
   DBCOLUMNFLAGS   dwFlags;
   ULONG           ulColumnSize;
   DBTYPE          wType;
   BYTE            bPrecision;
   BYTE            bScale;
   DBID            columnid;
} DBCOLUMNINFO;
```

The elements of this structure are used as described in the following table.

Element	Description
pwszName	Pointer to the name of the column; this might not be unique. If this cannot be determined, a null pointer is returned. The name can be different from the string part of the column ID if the column has been renamed by the command text. This name always reflects the most recent renaming of the column in the current view or command text.
pTypeInfo	Reserved for future use. Providers should return a null pointer in *pTypeInfo*.
IOrdinal	The ordinal of the column. This is zero for the bookmark column of the row, if any. Other columns are numbered starting from one.

Element	Description
dwFlags	A bitmask that describes column characteristics. The DBCOLUMNFLAGS enumerated type specifies the bits in the bitmask. For more information, see the following section.
ulColumnSize	The maximum possible length of a value in the column. For columns that use a fixed-length data type, this is the size of the data type. For columns that use a variable-length data type, this is one of the following: • The maximum length of the column in characters, for DBTYPE_STR and DBTYPE_WSTR, or in bytes, for DBTYPE_BYTES, if one is defined. For example, a CHAR(5) column in an SQL table has a maximum length of 5. • The maximum length of the data type in characters, for DBTYPE_STR and DBTYPE_WSTR, or in bytes, for DBTYPE_BYTES, if the column does not have a defined length. • ~0 (bitwise, the value is not 0; that is, all bits are set to 1) if neither the column nor the data type has a defined maximum length. For data types that do not have a length, this is set to ~0 (bitwise, the value is not 0; that is, all bits are set to 1).
wType	The indicator of the column's data type. If the data type of the column varies from row to row, this must be DBTYPE_VARIANT. For a list of valid type indicators, see "Type Indicators" in Appendix A, "Data Types."
bPrecision	If *wType* is a numeric data type, this is the maximum precision of the column. The precision of columns with a data type of DBTYPE_DECIMAL or DBTYPE_NUMERIC depends on the definition of the column. For the precision of all other numeric data types, see "Precision of Numeric Data Types" in Appendix A, "Data Types." For DBTYPE_DBTIMESTAMP data types, this is the length of the string representation (assuming the maximum allowed precision of the fractional seconds component). If the column's data type is not numeric or datetime, this is ~0 (bitwise, the value is not 0; that is, all bits are set to 1).

Element	Description
bScale	If *wType* is DBTYPE_DECIMAL or DBTYPE_NUMERIC, this is the number of digits to the right of the decimal point. Otherwise, this is ~0 (bitwise, the value is not 0; that is, all bits are set to 1). For DBTYPE_DBTIMESTAMP data types, this is the length of the string representation of the fractional seconds component.
columnid	The column ID of the column. The column ID of a base table should be invariant under views. For more information, see "Column IDs" in Chapter 4, "Rowsets."

DBCOLUMNFLAGS Enumerated Type

The *dwFlags* element of the DBCOLUMNINFO structure is a bitmask that describes column characteristics. The DBCOLUMNFLAGS enumerated type specifies the bits in the bitmask; the meanings of these values are as described in the following table.

Value	Description
DBCOLUMNFLAGS_ CACHEDEFERRED	Set if when a deferred column is first read its value is cached by the provider. Later reads of the column are done from this cache. The contents of the cache can be overwritten by **IRowsetChange::SetData** or **IRowsetRefresh::RefreshVisibleData**. The cached value is released when the row handle is released. Otherwise, not set. This flag can be set through the DBPROP_CACHEDEFERRED property in the Rowset property group.
DBCOLUMNFLAGS_ ISBOOKMARK	Set if the column contains a bookmark. Otherwise, not set.
DBCOLUMNFLAGS_ ISCHAPTER	Set if the column contains a chapter value. Otherwise, not set.
DBCOLUMNFLAGS_ ISFIXEDLENGTH	Set if all data in the column has the same length. Otherwise, not set. The flag is always set for fixed-length data types except DBTYPE_BSTR. The flag is set for variable-length data types (DBTYPE_STR, DBTYPE_WSTR, DBTYPE_BSTR, and DBTYPE_BYTES) if all the values are the same length. The flag is set for DBTYPE_VECTOR or DBTYPE_ARRAY columns if all elements in each vector or array are of the same length and each vector or array has the same number of elements. Otherwise, the flag is not set. The flag is not affected by DBTYPE_BYREF.

Value	Description
DBCOLUMNFLAGS_ ISLONG	Set if the column contains a BLOB that contains very long data. The definition of very long data is provider-specific. The setting of this flag corresponds to the value of the IS_LONG column in the PROVIDER_TYPES schema rowset for the data type. When this flag is set, the provider supports reading the value through a storage interface. Although such BLOBs can be retrieved in a single piece with **IRowset::GetData**, there may be provider-specific problems in doing so. For example, the BLOB might be truncated due to machine limits on memory or **GetData** might fail if called more than once for the BLOB. Furthermore, when this flag is set, the provider might not be able to accurately return the maximum length of the BLOB data in *ulColumnSize* in the DBCOLUMNINFO structure. When this flag is not set, the BLOB can be accessed directly through **GetData**. It is provider-specific whether columns without this flag can be read through a storage interface. For more information, see "Accessing BLOB Data" in Chapter 7, "BLOBs and COM Objects."
DBCOLUMNFLAGS_ ISNULLABLE	Set if the column can be set to NULL or if the provider cannot determine whether or not the column can be set to NULL. Otherwise, not set. This reflects only declarative rules. DBCOLUMNFLAGS_ISNULLABLE is generally used by consumers attempting to set data to determine whether or not a particular column might be able to hold a null value.
DBCOLUMNFLAGS_ ISROWID	Set if the column contains a persistent row identifier that cannot be written to and has no meaningful value except to identify the row.
DBCOLUMNFLAGS_ ISROWVER	Set if the column contains a timestamp or other versioning mechanism that cannot be written to directly and that is automatically updated to a new, increasing value when the row is updated and committed. The data type of a version column is provider-specific. How a version column is used—for example, how two version values are compared—is also provider-specific.

Value	Description
DBCOLUMNFLAGS_ MAYBENULL	Set if NULL can be gotten from the column, or if the provider cannot guarantee that NULLs cannot be gotten from the column. Otherwise, not set. DBCOLUMNFLAGS_MAYBENULL is generally used by consumers reading data to determine whether or not they might encounter a null value. When DBCOLUMNINFO is returned in the COLUMNS rowset, DBCOLUMNFLAGS_MAYBENULL should not be set if a simple select over the single column of that table would return no null values. DBCOLUMFLAGS_MAYBENULL can be set even if DBCOLUMNFLAGS_ISNULLABLE is not set. For example, in a left outer join, if there is no row on the right side that matches a row on the left side, the columns from the right side in the joined row contain NULLs, even if the underlying columns are non-nullable—that is, if DBCOLUMNFLAGS_ISNULLABLE is not set.
DBCOLUMNFLAGS_ MAYDEFER	Set if the column is deferred. Otherwise, not set. A deferred column is one for which the data is not fetched from the data store until the consumer attempts to get it. That is, the data is not fetched when the row is fetched but when **IRowset::GetData** is called. This flag can be set through the DBPROP_DEFERRED property in the Rowset property group. For more information, see "Deferred Columns" in Chapter 4, "Rowsets."
DBCOLUMNFLAGS_ WRITE	Set if **IRowsetChange::SetData** can be called for the column. Otherwise, not set. This flag can be set through the DBPROP_MAYWRITECOLUMN property in the Rowset property group. Providers never set both DBCOLUMNFLAGS_WRITE and DBCOLUMNFLAGS_WRITEUNKNOWN; they are mutually exclusive. Absence of these flags means the column is read-only.
DBCOLUMNFLAGS_ WRITEUNKNOWN	Set if the column in the base table may be updatable through some means, either through **IRowsetChange::SetData** or through some other mechanism. Providers never set both DBCOLUMNFLAGS_WRITE and DBCOLUMNFLAGS_WRITEUNKNOWN; they are mutually exclusive. Absence of these flags means the column is read-only.

See Also

IColumnsRowset::GetColumnsRowset, **IColumnsInfo::MapColumnIDs**, **IRowsetInfo::GetProperties**

IColumnsInfo::MapColumnIDs

Returns an array of ordinals of the columns in a rowset that are identified by the specified column IDs.

```
HRESULT MapColumnIDs (
   ULONG        cColumnIDs,
   const DBID   rgColumnIDs[],
   ULONG        rgColumns[]);
```

Parameters

cColumnIDs
[in]
The number of column IDs to map. If *cColumnIDs* is 0, **MapColumnIDs** does nothing and returns S_OK.

rgColumnIDs
[in]
An array of IDs of the columns of which to determine the column ordinals. If *rgColumnIDs* contains a duplicate column ID, a column ordinal is returned once for each occurrence of the column ID. If the column ID is invalid, the corresponding element of *rgColumns* is set to DB_INVALIDCOLUMN.

rgColumns
[out]
An array of *cColumnIDs* ordinals of the columns identified by the elements of *rgColumnIDs*. The consumer allocates, but is not required to initialize, memory for this array and passes the address of this memory to the provider. The provider returns the column IDs in the array.

Return Code

S_OK
The method succeeded. All elements of *rgColumns* are set to values other than DB_INVALIDCOLUMN.

DB_S_ERRORSOCCURRED
An element of *rgColumnIDs* was invalid. If the column ID is invalid, the corresponding element of *rgColumns* is set to DB_INVALIDCOLUMN.

E_FAIL
A provider-specific error occurred.

E_INVALIDARG
cColumnIDs was not 0 and *rgColumnIDs* was a null pointer.

rgColumns was a null pointer.

E_UNEXPECTED
: **ITransaction::Commit** or **ITransaction::Abort** was called, and the object is in a zombie state. This error can be returned only when the method is called on a rowset.

DB_E_ERRORSOCCURRED
: All elements of *rgColumnIDs* were invalid. All elements of *rgColumns* are set to DB_INVALIDCOLUMN.

DB_E_NOCOMMAND
: No command text was set. This error can be returned only when this method is called from the command object.

DB_E_NOTPREPARED
: The command exposed **ICommandPrepare** and the command text was set, but the command was not prepared. This error can be returned only when this method is called from the command object.

DB_E_NOTREENTRANT
: The provider called a method from **IRowsetNotify** in the consumer that had not yet returned, and the provider does not support reentrancy in this method.

Comments

This method makes no logical change to the state of the object.

MapColumnIDs returns the ordinals of the columns in the rowset that are identified by the elements of *rgColumnIDs*. These column ordinals do not change during the lifetime of the rowset. Column ordinals may change between different instantiations of a rowset if the command text does not define an order, such as a **SELECT * FROM MyTable**.

Two column IDs that are the same—except that one contains a GUID and the other contains a pointer to a GUID—are equivalent if both use the same GUID. Both are mapped to the same column ordinal.

See Also

IColumnsInfo::GetColumnInfo, **IColumnsRowset::GetColumnsRowset**

IColumnsRowset

This interface supplies complete information about columns in a rowset. The methods in it can be called from a rowset or a command.

When to Implement

Advanced providers implement this interface.

A service component can be used to synthesize **IColumnsRowset** from the simpler **IColumnsInfo** (with defaults and NULL values to round out the information).

IColumnsRowset is optional both on commands and on rowsets.

When to Call

Consumers use the methods in **IColumnsRowset** for detailed and flexible information about the columns of a rowset.

> **Note** For commands that expose **ICommandPrepare**, the methods on this interface can be called only after the command is prepared or the rowset is instantiated. If a command text is set but not prepared, any calls to methods on **IColumnsInfo** return DB_E_NOTPREPARED. For commands that do not expose **ICommandPrepare**, the methods on this interface can be called only after the command text has been set.

Method	Description
GetAvailableColumns	Returns a list of optional metadata columns that can be supplied in a column's rowset.
GetColumnsRowset	Returns a rowset containing metadata about each column in the current rowset. The rowset is known as the *column metadata rowset* and is read-only.

IColumnsRowset::GetAvailableColumns

Returns a list of optional metadata columns that can be supplied in a column metadata rowset.

```
HRESULT GetAvailableColumns (
   ULONG *     pcOptColumns,
   DBID **     prgOptColumns);
```

Parameters

pcOptColumns
[out]
A pointer to memory in which to return the count of the elements in **prgOptColumns*. If an error occurs, **pcOptColumns* is set to zero.

prgOptColumns
[out]
A pointer to memory in which to return an array of the optional columns this provider can supply. In addition to the optional columns listed in **GetColumnsRowset**, the provider can return provider-specific columns. The rowset or command allocates memory for the structures and returns the address to this memory; the consumer releases this memory with **IMalloc::Free** when it no longer needs the list of columns. If **pcOptColumns* is zero on output or an error occurs, the provider does not allocate any memory and ensures that **prgOptColumns* is a null pointer on output.

Return Code

S_OK
The method succeeded.

E_FAIL
A provider-specific error occurred.

E_INVALIDARG
pcOptColumns or *prgOptColumns* was a null pointer.

E_OUTOFMEMORY
The provider was unable to allocate sufficient memory in which to return the column IDs.

E_UNEXPECTED
ITransaction::Commit or **ITransaction::Abort** was called, and the object is in a zombie state. This error can be returned only when the method is called on a rowset.

DB_E_NOCOMMAND
No command text was set. This error can be returned only when this method is called from the command object.

DB_E_NOTPREPARED
The command exposed **ICommandPrepare** and the command text was set, but the command was not prepared. This error can be returned only when this method is called from the command object.

DB_E_NOTREENTRANT
The provider called a method from **IRowsetNofity** in the consumer that had not yet returned, and the provider does not support reentrancy in this method.

DB_SEC_E_PERMISSIONDENIED
The consumer did not have sufficient permission to retrieve the available optional metadata columns.

Comments

This method makes no logical change to the state of the object.

Calling **GetAvailableColumns** on a command before the command is executed may be an expensive operation.

See Also

IColumnsRowset::GetColumnsRowset

IColumnsRowset::GetColumnsRowset

Returns a rowset containing metadata about each column in the current rowset. This rowset is known as the *column metadata rowset* and is read-only.

```
HRESULT GetColumnsRowset (
   IUnknown *      pUnkOuter,
   ULONG           cOptColumns,
   const DBID      rgOptColumns[],
   REFIID          riid,
   ULONG           cPropertySets,
   DBPROPSET       rgPropertySets[],
   IUnknown **     ppColRowset);
```

Parameters

pUnkOuter
[in]
A pointer to the controlling **IUnknown** interface if the column metadata rowset is being created as part of an aggregate. It is a null pointer if the rowset is not part of an aggregate.

cOptColumns
[in]
The number of the elements in *rgOptColumns*. If *cOptColumns* is zero, *rgOptColumns* is ignored and the provider returns all available columns in the columns rowset.

rgOptColumns
[in]
An array that specifies the optional columns to return. In addition to the optional columns listed below, the consumer can request provider-specific columns.

riid
[in]
The IID of the requested rowset interface. This interface is conceptually added to the list of required interfaces on the resulting rowset, and the method fails (E_NOINTERFACE) if that interface cannot be supported on the resulting rowset.

cPropertySets
[in]
The number of DBPROPSET structures in *rgPropertySets*. If this is zero, the provider ignores *rgPropertySets*.

rgPropertySets
[in/out]
An array of DBPROPSET structures containing properties and values to be set. The properties specified in these structures must belong to the Rowset property group. If the same property is specified more than once in *rgPropertySets*, it is provider-specific which value is used. If *cPropertySets* is zero, this argument is ignored.

For information about the properties in the Rowset property group that are defined by OLE DB, see "Properties Table (by Propery Groups)" in Appendix C, "Property Tables." For information about the DBPROPSET and DBPROP structures, see "DBPROPSET Structure" and "DBPROP Structure" in Chapter 11, "Properties."

ppColRowset
[out]
A pointer to memory in which to return the requested interface pointer on the column metadata rowset. If an error occurs, the returned pointer is null. If **GetColumnsRowset** is called on a command that does not return rows, the column metadata rowset will be empty.

Return Code

S_OK
The method succeeded. In all DBPROP structures passed to the method, *dwStatus* is set to DBPROPSTATUS_OK.

DB_S_ASYNCHRONOUS
The method has initiated asynchronous creation of the rowset. The consumer can call **IDBAsynchStatus** to poll for status or **IConnectionPointContainer** to obtain the **IID_IDBAsynchNotify** connection point. Attempting to call any other interfaces may fail, and the full set of interfaces may not be available on the object until asynchronous initialization of the rowset has completed.

DB_S_ERRORSOCCURRED
The rowset was opened but one or more properties—for which the *dwOptions* element of the DBPROP structure was DBPROPOPTIONS_OPTIONAL—were not set. The consumer checks *dwStatus* in the DBPROP structures to determine which properties were not set. The method can fail to set properties for a number of reasons, including:

- The property was not supported by the provider.
- The property was not in the Rowset property group.
- The property set was not supported by the provider.
- It was not possible to set the property.
- *colid* in the DBPROP structure was invalid.
- The data type in *vValue* in the DBPROP structure was not the data type of the property or was not VT_EMPTY.

- The value in *vValue* in the DBPROP structure was invalid.
- The property's value conflicted with an existing property.
- A property was specified to be applied to all columns but could not be applied to one or more columns.

E_FAIL
A provider-specific error occurred.

E_INVALIDARG
ppColRowset was a null pointer.

cPropertySets was greater than zero and *rgPropertySets* was a null pointer.

In an element of *rgPropertySets*, *cProperties* was not zero and *rgProperties* was a null pointer.

cOptColumns was greater than zero and *rgOptColumns* was a null pointer.

E_NOINTERFACE
The column metadata rowset did not support the interface specified in *riid*.

E_UNEXPECTED
ITransaction::Commit or **ITransaction::Abort** was called, and the object is in a zombie state. This error can be returned only when the method is called on a rowset.

DB_E_ABORTLIMITREACHED
The method failed because a resource limit has been reached. For example, a query used to implement the method timed out. No rowset is returned.

DB_E_BADCOLUMNID
An element of *rgOptColumns* was an invalid DBID.

DB_E_ERRORSOCCURRED
No rowset was returned because one or more properties—for which the *dwOptions* element of the DBPROP structure was DBPROPOPTIONS_REQUIRED or an invalid value—were not set. The consumer checks *dwStatus* in the DBPROP structures to determine which properties were not set. None of the satisfiable properties are remembered. The method can fail to set properties for any of the reasons specified in DB_S_ERRORSOCCURRED.

DB_E_NOAGGREGATION
pUnkOuter was not a null pointer, and the provider is an OLE DB 1.0 or 1.1 provider that does not support aggregation of the rowset object being created.

pUnkOuter was not a null pointer, and *riid* was not IID_IUnknown.

DB_E_NOCOMMAND
No command text was set. This error can be returned only when this method is called from the command object.

DB_E_NOTPREPARED
: The command exposed **ICommandPrepare** and the command text was set, but the command was not prepared. This error can be returned only when this method is called from the command object.

DB_E_NOTREENTRANT
: The provider called a method from **IRowsetNofity** in the consumer that had not yet returned, and the provider does not support reentrancy in this method.

DB_SEC_E_PERMISSIONDENIED
: The consumer did not have sufficient permission to create the column metadata rowset.

Comments

This method makes no logical change to the state of the object.

GetColumnsRowset creates a rowset containing metadata about a rowset. Unlike **IColumnsInfo::GetColumnInfo**, it provides all of the metadata, but it is more complex to implement and use.

The rows in the column metadata rowset describe the columns in the underlying rowset. The column metadata rowset contains one row for each column in the rowset. This includes the columns of the base table and any pseudo-columns generated by the provider or data source, such as bookmarks and row IDs.

The order of the rows is the order in which the columns appear in the rowset (column ordinal order). This is the same order as they appear in **IColumnsInfo**. The order is usually predictable from the ordering of requested columns in the command text; if the command text does not specify an order, such as **SELECT * FROM MyTable**, the order is determined by the provider, such as when the command is prepared.

Each column in the column metadata rowset describes a single attribute, such as the name or data type, of a column in the original rowset. The order of the required columns is the same as the order in which they are listed below. The order of the optional columns is arbitrary, although they must be after the required columns. That is, the optional columns in the column metadata rowset can occur in any order after the required columns.

The column metadata rowset always includes the required columns. It contains only those optional columns which are requested.

GetColumnsRowset can be called for rowsets created by **GetColumnsRowset**.

Calling **GetColumnsRowset** on a command before the command is executed may be an expensive operation.

Required Metadata Columns

The column metadata rowset always contains the following columns; these columns return the same information as **GetColumnInfo**.

Column ID	Type indicator	Description
DBCOLUMN_IDNAME	DBTYPE_WSTR	Column name. This column, together with the DBCOLUMN_GUID and DBCOLUMN_PROPID columns, forms the ID of the column. One or more of these columns will be NULL depending on which elements of the DBID structure the provider uses. The column ID of a base table should be invariant under views.
DBCOLUMN_GUID	DBTYPE_GUID	Column GUID.
DBCOLUMN_PROPID	DBTYPE_UI4	Column property ID.
DBCOLUMN_NAME	DBTYPE_WSTR	The name of the column; this might not be unique. If this cannot be determined, a NULL is returned. The name can be different from the value returned in DBCOLUMN_IDNAME if the column has been renamed by the command text. This name always reflects the most recent renaming of the column in the current view or command text. If **GetColumnsRowset** is called for a column metadata rowset (the rowset returned by **GetColumnsRowset**), the name of each column is the name of the column ID constant. For example, the name of the DBCOLUMN_SCALE column is "DBCOLUMN_SCALE".
DBCOLUMN_NUMBER	DBTYPE_UI4	The ordinal of the column. This is zero for the bookmark column of the row, if any. Other columns are numbered starting with one. This column cannot contain a NULL value.
DBCOLUMN_TYPE	DBTYPE_UI2	The indicator of the column's data type. If the data type of the column varies from row to row, this must be DBTYPE_VARIANT. This column cannot contain a NULL value. For a list of valid type indicators, see "Type Indicators" in Appendix A, "Data Types."

Column ID	Type indicator	Description
DBCOLUMN_TYPEINFO	DBTYPE_ IUNKNOWN	Reserved for future use. Providers should return a null pointer in *pTypeInfo*.
DBCOLUMN_ COLUMNSIZE	DBTYPE_UI4	The maximum possible length of a value in the column. For columns that use a fixed-length data type, this is the size of the data type. For columns that use a variable-length data type, this is one of the following: • The maximum length of the column in characters, for DBTYPE_STR and DBTYPE_WSTR, or in bytes, for DBTYPE_BYTES, if one is defined. For example, a CHAR(5) column in an SQL table has a maximum length of 5. • The maximum length of the data type in characters, for DBTYPE_STR and DBTYPE_WSTR, or in bytes, for DBTYPE_BYTES, if the column does not have a defined length. • ~0 (bitwise, the value is not 0; that is, all bits are set to 1) if neither the column nor the data type have a defined maximum length. For data types that do not have a length, this is set to ~0 (bitwise, the value is not 0; that is, all bits are set to 1).
DBCOLUMN_ PRECISION	DBTYPE_UI2	If DBCOLUMN_TYPE is a numeric data type, this is the maximum precision of the column. The precision of columns with a data type of DBTYPE_DECIMAL or DBTYPE_NUMERIC depends on the definition of the column. For the precision of all other numeric data types, see "Precision of Numeric Data Types" in Appendix A, "Data Types." If DBCOLUMN_TYPE is not a numeric data type, this is NULL.

Column ID	Type indicator	Description
DBCOLUMN_SCALE	DBTYPE_I2	If DBCOLUMN_TYPE is DBTYPE_DECIMAL or DBTYPE_NUMERIC, this is the number of digits to the right of the decimal point. Otherwise, this is NULL.
DBCOLUMN_FLAGS	DBTYPE_UI4	A bitmask that describes column characteristics. The DBCOLUMNFLAGS enumerated type specifies the bits in the bitmask. For more information, see **IColumnsInfo::GetColumnInfo**. This column cannot contain a NULL value.

Optional Metadata Columns

The following columns are optional; if the column metadata rowset does not contain one of them, the consumer can safely use the default value. The default value is the value the consumer should assume if the provider does not support that information. It is also the value the column metadata rowset returns when the provider does have support but does not specify that information for a particular column. The provider can also have optional, provider-specific columns.

Column ID	Type indicator	Description
DBCOLUMN_ BASECATALOGNAME	DBTYPE_WSTR	The name of the catalog in the data store that contains the column. NULL if the base catalog name cannot be determined. The default of this column is NULL.
DBCOLUMN_ BASECOLUMNNAME	DBTYPE_WSTR	The name of the column in the data store. This might be different than the column name returned in the DBCOLUMN_NAME column if an alias was used. NULL if the base column name cannot be determined. The default of this column is NULL.
DBCOLUMN_ BASESCHEMANAME	DBTYPE_WSTR	The name of the schema in the data store that contains the column. NULL if the base schema name cannot be determined. The default of this column is NULL.
DBCOLUMN_ BASETABLENAME	DBTYPE_WSTR	The name of the table in the data store that contains the column. NULL if the base table name cannot be determined. The default of this column is NULL.

Column ID	Type indicator	Description
DBCOLUMN_CLSID	DBTYPE_GUID	If all objects in the column all have the same class ID, this is that class ID. If the column may contain objects with different class IDs or if the column is not of DBTYPE_IUNKNOWN, this is set to NULL. The default of this column is NULL.
DBCOLUMN_ COLLATINGSEQUENCE	DBTYPE_I4	The locale ID (LCID) that defines the collating sequence for the column. The default of this column is the code page installed on the local machine.
DBCOLUMN_ COMPUTEMODE	DBTYPE_I4	Whether a column is computed. One of the following: DBCOMPUTEMODE_COMPUTED: The column is computed, such as Salary/12. DBCOMPUTEMODE_DYNAMIC: The column is computed, and **IRowset::GetData** returns the value of the column based on the current values of its component columns, which might have been changed with **IRowsetChange::SetData** or **IRowsetChange::InsertRow**. DBCOMPUTEDMODE_NOTCOMPUTED: The column is not computed. This is the default.
DBCOLUMN_ DATETIMEPRECISION	DBTYPE_UI4	The datetime precision—number of digits in the fractional seconds portion—if the column is a datetime or interval type. The default of this column is derived from the value in column DATETIME_PRECISION in the COLUMNS schema rowset.
DBCOLUMN_ DEFAULTVALUE	DBTYPE_ VARIANT	The column default value if declared statically. Dynamic initialization is handled by notifications. NULL if the default value cannot be determined. For a list of possible values, see the table entry COLUMN_DEFAULT in "COLUMNS Rowset" in Appendix B, "Schema Rowsets." The default of this column is NULL.

Column ID	Type indicator	Description
DBCOLUMN_ DOMAINCATALOG	DBTYPE_WSTR	The name of the catalog containing the column's domain. NULL if the domain catalog name cannot be determined. The default of this column is NULL.
DBCOLUMN_ DOMAINSCHEMA	DBTYPE_WSTR	The name of the schema containing the column's domain. NULL if the domain schema name cannot be determined. The default of this column is NULL.
DBCOLUMN_ DOMAINNAME	DBTYPE_WSTR	The name of the domain of which the column is a member. NULL if the domain name cannot be determined. The default of this column is NULL.
DBCOLUMN_ HASDEFAULT	DBTYPE_BOOL	VARIANT_TRUE: The column has a default value. VARIANT_FALSE: The column does not have a default value. NULL: The provider could not determine whether the column has a default value or whether a default value does not make sense for the column. For example, it is a computed, derived, or nonupdatable column. The default of this column is VARIANT_FALSE.
DBCOLUMN_ ISAUTOINCREMENT	DBTYPE_BOOL	VARIANT_TRUE: The column assigns values to new rows in fixed increments. VARIANT_FALSE: The column does not assign values to new rows in fixed increments. The default of this column is VARIANT_FALSE.
DBCOLUMN_ ISCASESENSITIVE	DBTYPE_BOOL	VARIANT_TRUE if the order of the column is case-sensitive and if searches on the column are case-sensitive. Otherwise, VARIANT_FALSE. The default of this column is VARIANT_TRUE.

Column ID	Type indicator	Description
DBCOLUMN_ ISSEARCHABLE	DBTYPE_UI4	An integer indicating the searchability of a column. For more information, see the table entry SEARCHABLE in "PROVIDER_TYPES Rowset" in Appendix B, "Schema Rowsets." The default of this column is derived from the value of the SEARCHABLE column in the PROVIDER_TYPES schema rowset.
DBCOLUMN_ ISUNIQUE	DBTYPE_BOOL	VARIANT_TRUE: No two rows in the base table—the table returned in DBCOLUMN_BASETABLENAME—can have the same value in this column. DBCOLUMN_ISUNIQUE is guaranteed to be VARIANT_TRUE if the column constitutes a key by itself or if there is a constraint of type UNIQUE that applies only to this column. VARIANT_FALSE: The column can contain duplicate values in the base table. The default of this column is VARIANT_FALSE.
DBCOLUMN_ MAYSORT	DBTYPE_BOOL	VARIANT_TRUE: The column can be sorted. VARIANT_FALSE: The column cannot be sorted.
DBCOLUMN_ OCTETLENGTH	DBTYPE_UI4	The maximum length in octets (bytes) of the column, if the column is a character or binary type. A value of zero means the column has no maximum length. NULL for all other types of columns. The default of this column is derived from the value of the CHARACTER_OCTET_LENGTH column in the COLUMNS schema rowset.

Column ID	Type indicator	Description
DBCOLUMN_ KEYCOLUMN	DBTYPE_BOOL	VARIANT_TRUE—The column is one of a set of columns required in order to uniquely identify the row. VARIANT_FALSE—The column is not required to uniquely identify the row. If the DBPROP_UNIQUEROW property is set to VARIANT_TRUE, the set of columns with DBCOLUMN_KEYCOLUMN set to VARIANT_TRUE uniquely identifies a row in the rowset.
DBCOLUMN_BASETABLE-VERSION	DBTYPE_UI8	Version number of the table in the data store that contains the column. This number is assumed to change every time the table definition is modified. The way in which this number is generated is provider specific.

See Also

IColumnsInfo::GetColumnInfo, **IColumnsRowset::GetAvailableColumns**, **IRowsetInfo::GetProperties**

ICommand

ICommand contains methods to execute commands. A command can be executed many times, and the parameter values can vary. This interface is mandatory on commands.

A command object contains a single text command, which is specified through ICommandText. **Method**	**Description**
Cancel	Cancels the current command execution.
Execute	Executes the command.
GetDBSession	Returns an interface pointer to the session that created the command.

ICommand::Cancel

Cancels the current command execution.

```
HRESULT Cancel();
```

Parameters

None.

Return Code

S_OK
The method succeeded.

The command was not executing.

E_FAIL
A provider-specific error occurred.

DB_E_CANTCANCEL
The executing command cannot be canceled.

Comments

Cancel may be called on a separate thread after **Execute** has been called and before the method has returned. If the executing command can be canceled, the method returns S_OK, and **Execute** returns DB_E_CANCELED. If the executing command cannot be canceled, **Cancel** returns DB_E_CANTCANCEL and **Execute** continues. If the **Execute** method has not been called or has already returned, the method returns S_OK.

If the DBPROPVAL_ASYNCH_INITIALIZE bit in the DBPROP_ROWSET_ASYNCH property has been set prior to execution of the command, the **Execute** method may return with DB_S_ASYNCHRONOUS before the command has fully executed. Calling **ICommand::Cancel** after the **Execute** method has returned has no effect on any asynchronously executing commands. Once the **Execute** method has returned DB_S_ASYNCHRONOUS, the command can be canceled only by calling **IDBAsynchStatus::Abort** on the returned object.

See Also

ICommand::Execute

ICommand::Execute

Executes the command.

```
HRESULT Execute (
   IUnknown *      pUnkOuter,
   REFIID          riid,
   DBPARAMS *      pParams,
   LONG  *         pcRowsAffected,
   IUnknown **     ppRowset);
```

Parameters

pUnkOuter
[in]
A pointer to the controlling **IUnknown** interface if the rowset is being created as part of an aggregate; otherwise, it is null.

riid
[in]
The requested IID for the rowset returned in **ppRowset*. This interface is conceptually added to the list of required interfaces on the resulting rowset, and the method fails (E_NOINTERFACE) if that interface cannot be supported on the resulting rowset.

If this is IID_NULL, *ppRowset* is ignored and no rowset is returned, even if the command would otherwise generate a rowset. Specifying IID_NULL is useful in the case of text commands that do not generate rowsets, such as data definition commands, as a hint to the provider that no rowset properties need to be verified.

If *riid* is IID_IMultipleResults, the provider creates a multiple results object and returns a pointer to it in **ppRowset*; it does this even if the command generates a single result. If the provider supports multiple results and the command generates multiple results but *riid* is not **IID_IMultipleResults**, the provider returns the first result and discards any remaining results. If *riid* is **IID_IMultipleResults** and the provider does not support multiple results, **Execute** returns E_NOINTERFACE.

pParams
[in/out]
A pointer to a DBPARAMS structure that specifies the values for one or more parameters. In text commands that use parameters, if no value is specified for a parameter through *pParams*, an error occurs.

```
struct DBPARAMS {
 void *     pData;
 ULONG      cParamSets;
 HACCESSOR  hAccessor;
};
```

The elements of this structure are used as described in the following table.

Element	Description
pData	Pointer to a buffer from which the provider retrieves input parameter data and to which the provider returns output parameter data, according to the bindings specified by *hAccessor*. This pointer must be a valid pointer to a contiguous block of consumer-owned memory for the input and output parameter values. For more information, see "Getting Data" and "Setting Data" in Chapter 6, "Getting and Setting Data." When output parameter data is available to the consumer depends on the DBPROP_OUTPUTPARAMETERAVAILABILITY property.
cParamSets	The number of sets of parameters in **pData*. If *cParamSets* is greater than one, the bindings described by *hAccessor* define the offsets within **pData* for each set of parameters, and *cbRowSize* (as specified in **IAccessor::CreateAccessor**) defines a single fixed offset between each of those values and the corresponding values for the next set of parameters. Sets of multiple parameters (*cParamSets* is greater than one) can be specified only if DBPROP_MULTIPLEPARAMSETS is VARIANT_TRUE and the command does not return any rowsets.
hAccessor	Handle of the accessor to use. If *hAccessor* is the handle of a null accessor (*cBindings* in **CreateAccessor** was 0), **Execute** does not retrieve or return any parameter values.

If the command text does not include parameters, the provider ignores this argument.

pcRowsAffected
[out]
A pointer to memory in which to return the count of rows affected by a command that updates, deletes, or inserts rows. If *cParamSets* is greater than one, **pcRowsAffected* is the total number of rows affected by all of the sets of parameters specified in the execution. If the number of affected rows is not available, **pcRowsAffected* is set to DB_COUNTUNAVAILABLE on output. If *riid* is **IID_IMultipleResults**, the value returned in **pcRowsAffected* is either DB_COUNTUNAVAILABLE or the total number of rows affected by the entire command; to retrieve individual row counts, the consumer calls **IMultipleResults::GetResult**. If the command does not update, delete, or insert rows, **pcRowsAffected* is undefined on output. If *pcRowsAffected* is a null pointer, no count of rows is returned.

pcRowsAffected is undefined if **ICommand::Execute** returns DB_S_ASYNCHRONOUS. For asynchronously executed commands, the consumer should call **IDBAsynchStatus::GetStatus** to obtain the number of rows affected in *pulProgress*.

ppRowset
[in/out]
A pointer to the memory in which to return the rowset's pointer. If *ppRowset* is a null pointer, no rowset is created.

Return Code

S_OK
The method succeeded. In all DBPROP structures returned by the method, *dwStatus* is set to DBPROPSTATUS_OK; the status of all input parameters bound by the accessor is set to DBSTATUS_S_OK or DBSTATUS_S_ISNULL; and the status of all output parameters bound by the accessor is set to DBSTATUS_S_OK, DBSTATUS_S_ISNULL, or DBSTATUS_S_TRUNCATED or is unknown because the parameter value has not been returned yet.

DB_S_ASYNCHRONOUS
The method has initiated asynchronous creation of the rowset. The consumer can call **IDBAsynchStatus** to poll for status or **IConnectionPointContainer** to obtain the IID_IDBAsynchNotify connection point. Attempting to call any other interfaces may fail, and the full set of interfaces may not be available on the object until asynchronous initialization of the rowset has completed.

DB_S_ERRORSOCCURRED
This can be returned for any of the following reasons.

- The command was executed, but an error occurred while returning one or more output parameter values. To determine which output parameters were not returned, the consumer checks the status values. For a list of status values that can be returned by this method, see "Status Values Used When Getting Data" in Chapter 6, "Getting and Setting Data."
- The rowset was opened but one or more properties—for which the *dwOptions* element of the DBPROP structure was DBPROPOPTIONS_OPTIONAL—were not set. The consumer calls **IRowsetInfo::GetProperties** to determine which properties were set.

DB_S_STOPLIMITREACHED
Execution has been stopped because a resource limit has been reached. The results obtained so far have been returned. Execution cannot be resumed.

Multiple sets of parameters were specified, and one or more, but not all, of the parameters have been processed prior to the command being canceled by **ICommand::Cancel** or **IDBAsynchStatus::Abort**.

This return code takes precedence over DB_S_ERRORSOCCURRED. That is, if the conditions described here and in those described in DB_S_ERRORSOCCURRED both occur, the provider returns this code. When the consumer receives this return code, it should also check for the conditions described in DB_S_ERRORSOCCURRED.

E_FAIL
A provider-specific error occurred.

E_INVALIDARG
pParams was not ignored, *cParamSets* in the DBPARAMS structure pointed to by *pParams* was greater than one, *ppRowset* was not a null pointer, and the provider does not support multiple results.

pParams was not ignored, and in the DBPARAMS structure pointed to by *pParams*, *pData* was a null pointer.

pParams was not ignored, was not a null pointer, and in the DBPARAMS structure pointed to by *pParams*, *cParamSets* was zero.

riid was not IID_NULL and *ppRowset* was a null pointer.

E_NOINTERFACE
The rowset did not support the interface specified in *riid*.

riid was **IID_IMultipleResults**, and the provider did not support multiple results objects.

DB_E_ABORTLIMITREACHED
Execution has been aborted because a resource limit has been reached. For example, a query timed out. No results have been returned.

DB_E_BADACCESSORHANDLE
pParams was not ignored, and *hAccessor* in the DBPARAMS structure pointed to by *pParams* was invalid.

DB_E_BADACCESSORTYPE
hAccessor in the DBPARAMS structure pointed to by *pParams* was not the handle of a parameter accessor.

DB_E_CANCELED
The command was canceled by a call to **Cancel** on another thread. No records were affected.

DB_E_CANTCONVERTVALUE
A literal value in the command text could not be converted to the type of the associated column for reasons other than data overflow.

DB_E_DATAOVERFLOW
A literal value in the command text overflowed the type specified by the associated column.

DB_E_ERRORSINCOMMAND
The command text contained one or more errors. Providers should use OLE DB error objects to return details about the errors.

DB_E_ERRORSOCCURRED
The method failed due to one or more invalid input parameter values. To determine which input parameter values were invalid, the consumer checks the status values. For a list of status values that can be returned by this method, see "Status Values Used When Setting Data" in Chapter 6, "Getting and Setting Data."

The command was not executed, and no rowset was returned because one or more properties—for which the *dwOptions* element of the DBPROP structure was DBPROPOPTIONS_REQUIRED—were not set.

DB_E_INTEGRITYVIOLATION
A literal value in the command text violated the integrity constraints for the column.

DB_E_NOAGGREGATION
pUnkOuter was not a null pointer, and the provider is an OLE DB 1.0 or 1.1 provider that does not support aggregation of the rowset object being created.

pUnkOuter was not a null pointer, and *riid* was not **IID_IUnknown**.

DB_E_NOCOMMAND
No command text was currently set on the command object.

DB_E_NOTABLE
The specific table or view does not exist in the data store.

DB_E_PARAMNOTOPTIONAL
A value was not supplied for a required parameter.

The command text used parameters and *pParams* was a null pointer.

DB_SEC_E_PERMISSIONDENIED
The consumer did not have sufficient permission to execute the command. For example, a rowset-returning command specified a column for which the consumer does not have read permission, or an update command specified a column for which the consumer does not have write permission.

DB_E_OBJECTOPEN
The provider would have to open a new connection to support the operation, and DBPROP_MULTIPLECONNECTIONS is set to VARIANT_FALSE.

If this method performs deferred accessor validation and that validation takes place before any data is transferred, it can also return any of the following HRESULTs for the reasons listed in the corresponding DBBINDSTATUS values in **IAccessor::CreateAccessor:**

E_NOINTERFACE
DB_E_BADBINDINFO
DB_E_BADORDINAL
DB_E_BADSTORAGEFLAGS
DB_E_UNSUPPORTEDCONVERSION

Comments

If the command is a row-returning command, such as an SQL **SELECT** statement, the result of this method is a rowset over the result rows. If no rows match the command, the rowset is still created. The resulting rowset is fully functional and can be used, for example, to insert new rows or determine column metadata. If the command is a non–row-returning command, such as an SQL **INSERT** statement, **ppRowset* is set to NULL and no rowset is returned.

If the command returns multiple results (rowsets or row counts), the consumer requests a multiple-results object by setting *riid* to **IID_IMultipleResults**. **Execute** creates the multiple-results object and returns an **IMultipleResults** interface pointer to it in **ppRowset*. The consumer repeatedly calls **IMultipleResults::GetResult** to retrieve the results in order. For more information, see "Multiple Results" in Chapter 3, "Commands."

If any or all parameters fail and the provider does not support errors within an array of parameters (that is, the command fails if any or all of the parameters fail), the provider returns DB_E_ERRORSOCCURRED and returns any error information for the failed parameters in their status bindings.

If any or all parameters fail and the provider supports errors within an array of parameters, the provider returns DB_S_ERRORSOCCURRED, sets *pcRowsAffected* to the number of successful parameters, and returns any error information for the failed parameters in their status bindings.

If **Execute** is called multiple times for a single command, with or without changes to the command text, the outcome may reflect changes in the underlying stored data, depending on the isolation level specified for the surrounding transaction.

Execute can be called when a rowset is already open on the command if the only change between the calls is a change in the value of existing parameters. (Calls to **ICommandWithParameters::SetParameterInfo** will fail.) Methods that modify the command (**ICommandPrepare::Prepare**, **ICommandPrepare::Unprepare**, **ICommandProperties::SetProperties**, and **ICommandText::SetCommandText**) while a rowset is open will fail and return DB_E_OBJECTOPEN. Each call to **Execute** creates a new rowset, which must be explicitly released by **IRowset::Release**.

Execute does not affect the prepared state of a command.

The consumer determines whether the command supports parameters by calling **QueryInterface** for **ICommandWithParameters**. If this interface is exposed, the command supports parameters; if it is not exposed, the command does not support parameters. If the command does not support parameters, **Execute** ignores *pParams*. However, if the command text includes parameters, **Execute** returns DB_E_ERRORSINCOMMAND.

If an input parameter value is not specified, **Execute** returns DB_E_PARAMNOTOPTIONAL. If the provider cannot describe parameters and the consumer has not called **SetParameterInfo** for all parameters, the behavior of **Execute** is undefined. For example, **Execute** might guess at the parameter information or it might fail completely. For more information, see **SetParameterInfo**.

If **Execute** returns DB_S_ERRORSOCCURRED or DB_E_ERRORSOCCURRED, the consumer can immediately call **ICommandProperties::GetProperties** with the DBPPROPSET_PROPERTIESINERROR property set to return the properties that could not be set. For more information, see "Property Sets" in Chapter 11, "Properties."

Execute does not alter the value of any properties. That is, **ICommandProperties::GetProperties** returns the same value for a property whether or not it is called before or after **Execute** and whether or not **Execute** succeeded or failed. However, if a property value is not required, **IRowsetInfo::GetProperties** can return a different value for that property than **ICommandProperties::GetProperties**. For more information, see **IRowsetInfo::GetProperties**.

If several threads concurrently request execution of a given command, the corresponding executions are serialized, and each thread will block until its corresponding execution concludes.

Execute can fail even if **ICommandPrepare::Prepare** has succeeded; this may be the case if, for example, the underlying schema has changed between the **Prepare** and **Execute** calls and the command text had therefore become illegal.

See Also

ICommand::Cancel, **ICommandPrepare::Prepare**, **ICommandText::SetCommandText**, **ICommandWithParameters::SetParameterInfo**

ICommand::GetDBSession

Returns an interface pointer to the session that created the command.

```
HRESULT GetDBSession (
   REFIID      riid,
   IUnknown ** ppSession);
```

Parameters

riid
[in]
The IID of the interface on which to return a pointer.

ppSession
[out]
A pointer to memory in which to return the interface pointer. If the provider does not have an object that created the command, it sets **ppSession* to a null pointer. If **GetDBSession** fails, it must attempt to set **ppSession* to a null pointer.

Return Code

S_OK
The method succeeded.

S_FALSE
The provider did not have an object that created the command. Therefore, it set **ppSession* to a null pointer.

E_FAIL
A provider-specific error occurred.

E_INVALIDARG
ppSession was a null pointer.

E_NOINTERFACE
The session did not support the interface specified in *riid*.

ICommandPersist

Command objects support **ICommandPersist** for persisting the state of a command object. Persisting a command object does not persist any active rowsets that may have resulted from the execution of the command object, nor does it persist accessors, property settings, or parameter information associated with the command object.

Persisted commands can be enumerated through the PROCEDURES rowset. Persisted commands that can act as the source of a new command (that is, a table in an SQL **FROM** clause) can be enumerated through the VIEWS rowset.

When to Implement

ICommandPersist **is implemented by providers that can persist a command object.**

ICommandPersist methods	Description
DeleteCommand	Deletes a persisted command.
GetCurrentCommand	Returns the DBID of the current command.
LoadCommand	Loads a persisted command.
SaveCommand	Saves the current command.

ICommandPersist::DeleteCommand

Deletes a persisted command definition.

```
HRESULT  DeleteCommand(
   DBID *pCommandID);
```

Parameters

pCommandID
[in]
The DBID of the command to be deleted.

Return Code

S_OK
The command was successfully deleted.

DB_E_BADCOMMANDID
The command specified in **pCommandID* does not exist.

E_FAIL
A provider-specific error occurred.

ICommandPersist::GetCurrentCommand

Returns the DBID of the current command.

```
HRESULT  GetCurrentCommand(
   DBID *pCommandID);
```

Parameters

pCommandID
[out]
The DBID of the current command.

Return Code

S_OK
The DBID of the command was successfully returned.

E_OUTOFMEMORY
There is not enough memory to successfully return the command's DBID.

DB_E_COMMANDNOTPERSISTED
The current command does not yet have a DBID.

E_FAIL
A provider-specific error occurred.

ICommandPersist::LoadCommand

Loads a persisted command definition.

```
HRESULT  LoadCommand(
   DBID *pCommandID,
   DWORD dwFlags);
```

Parameters

pCommandID
[in]
The DBID of the command to load.

dwFlags
[in]
Reserved for future use. Consumers should set this value to zero. Providers should ignore this argument.

Return Code

S_OK
The command was successfully loaded.

E_OUTOFMEMORY
There is not enough memory to successfully load the command.

DB_E_OBJECTOPEN
A rowset was open on the command.

DB_E_BADCOMMANDID
The command specified in **pCommandID* does not exist.

E_FAIL
A provider-specific error occurred.

Comments

LoadCommand loads the persisted command definition into the current command object. Loading a persisted command definition does not change the command object's transaction scope and semantics, nor does it change the session scope. Set property values and specified parameter information are not affected by loading a persisted command definition. **LoadCommand** fails if the current command object has any outstanding rowsets (DB_E_OBJECTOPEN).

ICommandPersist::SaveCommand

Persists the current command definition.

```
HRESULT  SaveCommand(
   DBID *pCommandID,
   DWORD dwFlags);
```

Parameters

pCommandID

[in]

The DBID to assign to the persisted command. If this is a null pointer and the command already has a DBID, the provider saves the current version with the same DBID. If this is a null pointer and the command does not already have a DBID, the provider assigns an ID to the command. The ID must be unique.

dwFlags

[in]

Options for persisting command definition. Providers return DB_E_INVALIDARG if a flag the provider does not know is specified. You can use DBCOMMANDPERSISTFLAG_NOSAVE to associate or obtain a new DBID for the command without actually persisting the definition.

DBCOMMANDPERSISTFLAGS_PERSISTVIEW
The command is to be persisted as a view. Views are row-returning objects that do not contain parameters or return values and can generally be used anywhere a base table is used. Views can be enumerated through the DBSCHEMA_VIEWS schema rowset.

DBCOMMANDPERSISTFLAGS_PERSISTPROCEDURE
The command is to be persisted as a procedure. Procedures may or may not return rows and may or may not contain parameters or return values. Procedures can be enumerated through the DBSCHEMA_PROCEDURES schema rowset.

DBCOMMANDPERSISTFLAGS_PERSISTVIEW and DBCOMMANDPERSISTFLAGS_PERSISTPROCEDURE are mutually exclusive. If neither is specified, the provider persists the command as a default type.

Return Code

S_OK
The command was successfully saved.

DB_E_BADCOMMANDID
The DBID specified in **pCommandID* was invalid.

DB_E_BADCOMMANDFLAGS
dwFlags was invalid.

In *dwFlags*, both DBCOMMANDPERSISTFLAGS_PERSISTVIEW and DBCOMMANDPERSISTFLAGS_PERSISTPROCEDURE were specified.

DBCOMMANDPERSISTFLAGS_PERSISTVIEW was specified, and the command could not be persisted as a view.

DBCOMMANDPERSISTFLAGS_PERSISTPROCEDURE was specified, and the command could not be persisted as a procedure.

DB_E_DUPLICATEID
The specified DBID already exists. If the provider supports the use of persisted commands as a source in a new command definition, DBIDs must be unique across persisted commands, procedures, tables, and views.

E_FAIL
A provider-specific error occurred.

Comments

SaveCommand saves the current command definition. It does not persist any open rowsets, current property values, or specified parameter information.

ICommandPrepare

This optional interface encapsulates command optimization, a separation of compile time and run time, as found in traditional relational database systems. The result of this optimization is a *command execution plan*.

If the provider supports command preparation, by supporting this interface, commands must be in a prepared state prior to calling the following methods.

- **IColumnsInfo::GetColumnInfo**
- **IColumnsInfo::MapColumnIDs**
- **IColumnsRowset::GetAvailableColumns**
- **IColumnsRowset::GetColumnsRowset**

Method	Description
Prepare	Validates and optimizes the current command.
Unprepare	Discards the current command execution plan.

ICommandPrepare::Prepare

Validates and optimizes the current command.

```
HRESULT Prepare (
   ULONG cExpectedRuns);
```

Parameters

cExpectedRuns
[in]
Using this parameter, the consumer can indicate how often the command execution plan, which is produced by **Prepare**, will be used; that is, how often the command is likely to be executed without renewed optimization. This guides the optimizer in determining tradeoffs between search effort and run-time processing effort. A value of zero indicates that the consumer is unable to provide an estimate, and leaves it to the optimizer to choose a default value.

Return Code

S_OK
The method succeeded.

DB_S_ERRORSOCCURRED
The command was prepared but one or more properties—for which the *dwOptions* element of the DBPROP structure was DBPROPOPTIONS_OPTIONAL—were not set. The consumer calls **ICommandProperties::GetProperties** to determine which properties were set.

E_FAIL
A provider-specific error occurred.

E_OUTOFMEMORY
The provider ran out of memory while preparing the command.

DB_E_ABORTLIMITREACHED
Preparation has been aborted because a resource limit has been reached. For example, the preparation timed out.

DB_E_ERRORSINCOMMAND
The command text contained one or more errors. Providers should use OLE DB error objects to return details about the errors.

DB_E_ERRORSOCCURRED
The command was not prepared because one or more properties—for which the *dwOptions* element of the DBPROP structure was DBPROPOPTIONS_REQUIRED—were not set. The consumer calls **ICommandProperties::GetProperties** to determine which properties were not set.

DB_E_NOCOMMAND
No command text was currently set on the command object.

DB_E_OBJECTOPEN
A rowset was open on the command.

DB_SEC_E_PERMISSIONDENIED
The consumer did not have sufficient permission to prepare the command.

Comments

Although they are not required to do so, consumers should set any properties before calling **Prepare**, because these properties might be relevant to preparing the command.

If **Prepare** is called redundantly, the provider determines whether command optimization is reinvoked; the provider returns S_OK.

If **Prepare** returns DB_S_ERRORSOCCURRED or DB_E_ERRORSOCCURRED, the consumer can immediately call **ICommandProperties::GetProperties** with the DBPPROPSET_PROPERTIESINERROR property set to return the properties that could not be set. For more information, see "Property Sets" in Chapter 11, "Properties."

See Also

ICommand::Execute, **ICommandPrepare::Unprepare**, **ICommandWithParameters::SetParameterInfo**

ICommandPrepare::Unprepare

Discards the current command execution plan.

```
HRESULT Unprepare();
```

Parameters

None.

Return Code

S_OK
The method succeeded.

E_FAIL
A provider-specific error occurred.

DB_E_OBJECTOPEN
A rowset was open on the command.

Comments

This method has no effect if the command was not prepared; the provider returns S_OK.

See Also

ICommandPrepare::Prepare

ICommandProperties

ICommandProperties specifies to the command the properties from the Rowset property group that must be supported by the rowsets returned by **ICommand::Execute**. A special case of these properties, and the ones most commonly requested, are the interfaces the rowset must support. In addition to interfaces, the consumer can request properties that modify the behavior of the rowset or interfaces.

All rowsets must support **IRowset, IAccessor**, **IColumnsInfo**, **IRowsetInfo**, and **IConvertType**. Providers may choose to return rowsets supporting other interfaces if doing so is possible and the support for the returned interfaces does not affect consumer code that is not expecting them. The *riid* parameter of **ICommand::Execute** should be one of the interfaces returned by **IRowsetInfo::GetProperties**.

This interface is mandatory on commands.

Method	Description
GetProperties	Returns the list of properties in the Rowset property group that are currently requested for the rowset.
SetProperties	Sets properties in the Rowset property group.

ICommandProperties::GetProperties

Returns the list of properties in the Rowset property group that are currently requested for the rowset.

```
HRESULT GetProperties (
   const ULONG           cPropertyIDSets,
   const DBPROPIDSET     rgPropertyIDSets[],
   ULONG *               pcPropertySets,
   DBPROPSET **          prgPropertySets);
```

Parameters

cPropertyIDSets
[in]
The number of DBPROPIDSET structures in *rgPropertyIDSets*.

If *cPropertyIDSets* is zero, the provider ignores *rgPropertyIDSets* and returns the values of all properties in the Rowset property group for which values have been set or defaults exist. It does not return the values of properties in the Rowset property group for which values have not been set and no defaults exist, nor does it return the values of properties for which no value has been set, no default exists, and for which a value will be set automatically because a value for another property in the Rowset property group has been set.

If *cPropertyIDSets* is not zero, the provider returns the values of the requested properties. If a property is not supported, the returned value of *dwStatus* in the returned DBPROP structure for that property is DBPROPSTATUS_NOTSUPPORTED and the value of *dwOptions* is undefined.

rgPropertyIDSets
[in]
An array of *cPropertyIDSets* DBPROPIDSET structures. The properties specified in these structures must belong to the Rowset property group. The provider returns the values of the properties specified in these structures. If *cPropertyIDSets* is zero, this parameter is ignored.

For information about the properties in the Rowset property group that are defined by OLE DB, see "Properties Table (by Property Groups)" in Appendix C, "Property Tables." For information about the DBPROPIDSET structure, see "DBPROPIDSET Structure" in Chapter 11, "Properties."

pcPropertySets
[out]
A pointer to memory in which to return the number of DBPROPSET structures returned in **prgPropertySets*. If *cPropertyIDSets* is zero, **pcPropertySets* is the total number of property sets for which the provider supports at least one property in the Rowset property group. If *cPropertyIDSets* is greater than zero, **pcPropertySets* is set to *cPropertyIDSets*. If an error other than DB_E_ERRORSOCCURRED occurs, **pcPropertySets* is set to zero.

prgPropertySets
[out]
A pointer to memory in which to return an array of DBPROPSET structures. If *cPropertyIDSets* is zero, one structure is returned for each property set that contains at least one property belonging to the Rowset property group. If *cPropertyIDSets* is not zero, one structure is returned for each property set specified in *rgPropertyIDSets*.

If *cPropertyIDSets* is not zero, the DBPROPSET structures in **prgPropertySets* are returned in the same order as the DBPROPIDSET structures in *rgPropertyIDSets*; that is, for corresponding elements of each array, the *guidPropertySet* elements are the same. If *cPropertyIDs* in an element of *rgPropertyIDSets* is not zero, the DBPROP structures in the corresponding element of **prgPropertySets* are returned in the same order as the DBPROPID values in *rgPropertyIDs*. Therefore, in the case where no column properties are specified in *rgPropertyIDSets*, corresponding elements of the input *rgPropertyIDs* and the returned *rgProperties* have the same property ID. However, if a column property is requested in *rgPropertyIDSets*, multiple properties may be returned, one for each column, in *rgProperties*. In this case, corresponding elements of *rgPropertyIDs* and *rgProperties* will not have the same property ID and *rgProperties* will contain more elements than *rgPropertyIDs*.

The provider allocates memory for the structures and returns the address to this memory; the consumer releases this memory with **IMalloc::Free** when it no longer needs the structures. Before calling **IMalloc::Free** for **prgPropertySets*, the consumer should call **IMalloc::Free** for the *rgProperties* element within each element of **prgPropertySets*. If **pcPropertySets* is zero on output or an error other than DB_E_ERRORSOCCURRED occurs, the provider does not allocate any memory and ensures that **prgPropertySets* is a null pointer on output.

For information about the DBPROPSET and DBPROP structures, see "DBPROPSET Structure" and "DBPROP Structure" in Chapter 11, "Properties."

Return Code

S_OK
The method succeeded. In all DBPROP structures returned by the method, *dwStatus* is set to DBPROPSTATUS_OK.

DB_S_ERRORSOCCURRED
No value was returned for one or more properties. The consumer checks *dwStatus* in the DBPROP structure to determine the properties for which values were not returned. **GetProperties** can fail to return properties for a number of reasons, including:

- The property was not supported by the provider.
- The property was not in the Rowset property group.
- The property set was not supported by the provider. If *cPropertyIDs* in the DBPROPIDSET structure for the property set was zero, the provider cannot set *dwStatus* in the DBPROP structure because it does not know the IDs of any properties in the property set. Instead, it sets *cProperties* to zero in the DBPROPSET structure returned for the property set.

E_FAIL
A provider-specific error occurred.

E_INVALIDARG
cPropertyIDSets was not equal to zero and *rgPropertyIDSets* was a null pointer.

pcPropertySets or *prgPropertySets* was a null pointer.

In an element of *rgPropertyIDSets*, *cPropertyIDs* was not zero and *rgPropertyIDs* was a null pointer.

In an element of *rgPropertyIDSets*, *guidPropertySet* was DBPROPSET_PROPERTIESINERROR and *cPropertyIDs* was not zero, or *rgPropertyIDs* was not a null pointer.

cPropertyIDSets was greater than one, and in an element of *rgPropertyIDSets*, *guidPropertySet* was DBPROPSET_PROPERTIESINERROR.

E_OUTOFMEMORY
The provider was unable to allocate sufficient memory in which to return the DBPROPSET or DBPROP structures.

DB_E_ERRORSOCCURRED
No values were returned for any properties. The provider allocates memory for **prgPropertySets*, and the consumer checks *dwStatus* in the DBPROP structures to determine why properties were not returned. The consumer frees this memory when it no longer needs the information.

Comments

GetProperties returns the current values of properties that have been set by the consumer with **ICommandProperties::SetProperties**. For all values not set by the consumer, **GetProperties** returns the initial property value.

Even though **IDBProperties::GetPropertyInfo** lists a property as being supported by the provider, **GetProperties** will not return a value for it if it does not apply to the current circumstances. For example, the provider's ability to support the property might be affected by the current transaction or the current command text.

The property values returned by **ICommandProperties::GetProperties** are not affected by executing the command. However, **IRowsetInfo::GetProperties** might return a different value for a property than does **ICommandProperties::GetProperties**. For example, if a consumer requests ordered bookmarks if they are possible, it calls **SetProperties** to set the value of DBPROP_ORDEREDBOOKMARKS to VARIANT_TRUE and specifies a *dwOptions* value of DBPROPOPTIONS_OPTIONAL. If the provider cannot determine at this point in the definition of the command whether this is possible, **ICommandProperties::GetProperties** returns a value of VARIANT_TRUE and a *dwOptions* of DBPROPOPTIONS_OPTIONAL for this property. If the provider determines during optimization or execution that ordered bookmarks are not possible, **IRowsetInfo::GetProperties** returns a value of VARIANT_FALSE and a *dwOptions* of zero.

If **ICommand::Execute** returns DB_E_ERRORSOCCURRED, the consumer can immediately call **GetProperties** with the DBPROPSET_PROPERTIESINERROR property set to return all the properties that were in error. For more information, see "Property Sets" in Chapter 11, "Properties."

See Also

ICommandProperties::SetProperties, **IDBProperties::GetPropertyInfo**, **IRowsetInfo::GetProperties**

ICommandProperties::SetProperties

Sets properties in the Rowset property group.

```
HRESULT SetProperties (
   ULONG       cPropertySets,
   DBPROPSET   rgPropertySets[]);
```

Parameters

cPropertySets

[in]

The number of DBPROPSET structures in *rgPropertySets*. If this is zero, the provider ignores *rgPropertySets* and the method does not do anything.

rgPropertySets

[in/out]

An array of DBPROPSET structures containing properties and values to be set. The properties specified in these structures must belong to the Rowset property group. If the same property is specified more than once in *rgPropertySets*, which value is used is provider-specific. If *cPropertySets* is zero, this parameter is ignored.

For information about the properties in the Rowset property group that are defined by OLE DB, see "Properties Table (by Property Groups)" in Appendix C, "Property Tables." For information about the DBPROPSET and DBPROP structures, see "DBPROPSET Structure" and "DBPROP Structure" in Chapter 11, "Properties."

Return Code

S_OK

The method succeeded. In all DBPROP structures passed to the method, *dwStatus* is set to DBPROPSTATUS_OK.

DB_S_ERRORSOCCURRED

One or more properties were not set. Properties not in error remain set. The consumer checks *dwStatus* in the DBPROP structures to determine which properties were not set. **SetProperties** can fail to set properties for a number of reasons, including:

- The property was not supported by the provider.
- The property was not in the Rowset property group.
- The property set was not supported by the provider.
- The property is read-only and was not set to its default value.
- It was not possible to set the property.
- The value of *dwOptions* in a DBPROP structure was invalid.

- *colid* in the DBPROP structure was not DB_NULLID, and the property cannot be set on a column.
- The data type in *vValue* in the DBPROP structure was not the data type of the property or was not VT_EMPTY.
- The value in *vValue* in the DBPROP structure was invalid.
- The property's value conflicted with an existing property.

E_FAIL
A provider-specific error occurred.

E_INVALIDARG
cPropertySets was not equal to zero and *rgPropertySets* was a null pointer.

In an element of *rgPropertySets*, *cProperties* was not zero and *rgProperties* was a null pointer.

DB_E_ERRORSOCCURRED
All property values were invalid and no properties were set. The consumer checks *dwStatus* in the DBPROP structures to determine why properties were not set. The method can fail to set properties for any of the reasons specified in DB_S_ERRORSOCCURRED.

DB_E_OBJECTOPEN
Properties cannot be set while there is an open rowset.

Comments

Consumers should first set properties for interfaces and then set other properties that modify those interfaces. The combination of the values of an interface property and a noninterface property might result in another interface being requested. However, the value of a noninterface property, by itself, never results in another interface being requested.

Setting property values is a cumulative operation. That is, each call to **SetProperties** attempts to change the values of the specified properties. If a new value is illegal or conflicts with the value of another property, the value of the property is not changed and **SetProperties** returns DBPROPSTATUS_BADVALUE or DBPROPSTATUS_CONFLICTING in the *dwStatus* element of the DBPROP structure for the property. Properties are processed from the beginning of the array to the end of the array. As they are processed, properties that conflict with previously set properties, including those set previously on the same call, are marked with DBPROPSTATUS_CONFLICTING, and processing continues through the array of properties.

SetProperties cannot always determine whether a property can be set to its requested value. For example, the provider often cannot determine whether the rowset is updatable until it creates the rowset. In this case, **SetProperties** appears to successfully set the property value and the provider delays the determination until **ICommand::Execute** is called.

If the value of *dwOptions* for a property is DBPROPOPTIONS_OPTIONAL, the provider attempts to determine whether it can set the property to the requested value. If it can make this determination, it sets the property and returns DBPROPSTATUS_OK or does not set the property and returns DBPROPSTATUS_NOTSET. If it cannot make this determination, it can delay setting the property until the command is executed; in this case, the value of *dwOptions* returned for the property by **GetProperties** is DBPROPOPTIONS_OPTIONAL.

Consumers should not attempt to unset mandatory rowset interfaces such as **IRowset**, **IAccessor**, **IColumnsInfo**, and **IRowsetInfo**. These interfaces are always supported, and **SetProperties** returns DBPROPSTATUS_NOTSETTABLE for them.

Even if **IDBProperties::GetPropertyInfo** lists a property as being supported by the provider, **SetProperties** can return DBPROPSTATUS_NOTSUPPORTED when the consumer attempts to set the property value if the property does not apply to the current circumstances. For example, the provider's ability to support the property might be affected by the current transaction or the current command text.

If an error occurs when setting a particular property, **SetProperties** flags the error in *dwStatus* in the DBPROP structure and continues processing.

Although providers allow changing properties at any time before command execution, consumers are encouraged to set all properties prior to preparing the command to avoid forcing the provider to reprepare the command at execution.

See Also

ICommandProperties::GetProperties, **IDBProperties::GetPropertyInfo**, **IRowsetInfo::GetProperties**

ICommandText : ICommand

This interface is mandatory on commands.

A command object can have only one text command. When the command text is specified through **SetCommandText**, it replaces the existing command text.

Method	Description
GetCommandText	Returns the text command set by the last call to **SetCommandText**.
SetCommandText	Sets the command text, replacing the existing command text.

ICommandText::GetCommandText

Returns the text command set by the last call to **SetCommandText**.

```
HRESULT GetCommandText (
   GUID *       pguidDialect,
   LPOLESTR *   ppwszCommand);
```

Parameters

pguidDialect
[in/out]
A pointer to memory containing a GUID that specifies the syntax and general rules for parsing the command text—that is, the dialect that will be used by the provider to interpret the statement. This is usually the dialect specified in **SetCommandText**. However, if DBGUID_DEFAULT is specified in **SetCommandText**, the provider returns the particular dialect that it will use to interpret the statement. If the provider must choose between multiple dialects at execution time for a command that has been set with DBGUID_DEFAULT, or if the provider is returning some provider-specific syntax that may be different from the command set in **SetCommandText**, it returns DBGUID_DEFAULT. Providers can define GUIDs for their own dialects.

For more information about dialects, see "Using Commands" in Chapter 3, "Commands."

If **GetCommandText** returns an error, **pguidDialect* is set to DB_NULLGUID.

ppwszCommand
[out]
A pointer to memory in which to return the command text. The command object allocates memory for the command text and returns the address to this memory. The consumer releases this memory with **IMalloc::Free** when it no longer needs the text. If **GetCommandText** returns an error, **ppwszCommand* is set to a null pointer.

Return Code

S_OK
The method succeeded.

DB_S_DIALECTIGNORED
The method succeeded, but the input value of *pguidDialect* was ignored. The text is returned in the dialect specified in **SetCommandText** or the dialect that makes the most sense to the provider. The value returned in **pguidDialect* represents that dialect.

E_FAIL
A provider-specific error occurred.

E_INVALIDARG
ppwszCommand was a null pointer.

E_OUTOFMEMORY
: The provider was unable to allocate sufficient memory in which to return the command text.

DB_E_NOCOMMAND
: No command text was currently set on the command object.

See Also

ICommandText::SetCommandText

Comments

The GUID returned in **GetCommandText** is the dialect that will be used by the provider to interpret the statement. This is usually the dialect specified in **SetCommandText**. However, if DBGUID_DEFAULT is specified in **SetCommandText**, the provider should return the particular dialect that it will use to interpret the statement. If the provider must choose between multiple dialects at execution time for a command that has been set with DBGUID_DEFAULT, or if the provider is returning some provider-specific syntax that may be different from the command set in **SetCommandText**, it returns DBGUID_DEFAULT.

ICommandText::SetCommandText

Sets the command text, replacing the existing command text.

```
HRESULT SetCommandText (
   REFGUID        rguidDialect,
   LPCOLESTR      pwszCommand);
```

Parameters

rguidDialect
[in]
A GUID that specifies the syntax and general rules for the provider to use in parsing the command text. For a complete description of dialects, see **GetCommandText**.

pwszCommand
[in]
A pointer to the text of the command.

If **pwszCommand* is an empty string ("") or *pwszCommand* is a null pointer, the current command text is cleared and the command is put in an unprepared state. Any properties that have been set on the command are unaffected; that is, they retain their current values. Methods that require a command, such as **ICommand::Execute**, **ICommandPrepare::Prepare**, or **IColumnsInfo::GetColumnsInfo**, will return DB_E_NOCOMMAND until a new command text is set.

Return Code

S_OK
The method succeeded.

E_FAIL
A provider-specific error occurred.

DB_E_DIALECTNOTSUPPORTED
The provider did not support the dialect specified in *rguidDialect*.

DB_E_OBJECTOPEN
A rowset was open on the command.

Comments

A command object contains a single text command, usually an SQL statement. The new command text is copied into the command object; therefore, the consumer can delete the original text without affecting the command object. All meaningful error checking, such as syntax checking and parsing, is deferred until **ICommandPrepare::Prepare** or **ICommand::Execute** is called. **SetCommandText** verifies only that the command text can be copied into the command object's space.

If the text of a prepared or unprepared command is overwritten with new command text by calling **SetCommandText**, the command object is left in an unprepared state.

SetCommandText does not alter the value of any properties. That is, **ICommandProperties::GetProperties** returns the same value for a property whether or not it is called before or after **SetCommandText** and whether or not **SetCommandText** succeeded or failed. Furthermore, setting the command text does not reset parameter information set through **SetParameterInfo**.

See Also

ICommand::Execute, **ICommandPrepare::Prepare**, **ICommandText::GetCommandText**, **ICommandWithParameters::SetParameterInfo**

ICommandWithParameters

Providers that support parameters must support **ICommandWithParameters**. Any provider that returns DBPROPVAL_SQL_ANSI92_INTERMEDIATE or DBPROPVAL_SQL_ANSI92_FULL for the DBPROP_SQLSUPPORT property can support parameters.

This optional interface encapsulates parameters. Parameters are scalar values, or a vector of scalar values, typically expressed in predicates but possibly supported by many providers in any scalar expression.

For scalar parameters of prepared commands, there is a presumption that different parameter values do not require different plans. In other words, a single preparation and its resulting plan are satisfactory for all possible values of scalar parameters.

Parameter values are set when a command is executed. Methods are included here to offer a means for setting and obtaining a list of parameters and their types.

Method	Description
GetParameterInfo	Gets a list of the command's parameters, their names, and their types.
MapParameterNames	Returns an array of parameter ordinals when given named parameters.
SetParameterInfo	Specifies the native data type of each parameter.

ICommandWithParameters::GetParameterInfo

Gets a list of the command's parameters, their names, and their types.

```
HRESULT GetParameterInfo (
   ULONG *             pcParams,
   DBPARAMINFO **      prgParamInfo,
   OLECHAR **          ppNamesBuffer);
```

Parameters

pcParams

[out]
A pointer to memory in which to return the number of parameters in the command. If an error occurs, **pcParams* is set to zero.

prgParamInfo

[out]
A pointer to memory in which to return an array of parameter information structures. The command allocates memory for the array, as well as the strings, and returns the address to this memory. The consumer releases the array memory with **IMalloc::Free** when it no longer needs the parameter information. If **pcParams* is zero on output or an error occurs, the provider does not allocate any memory and ensures that **prgParamInfo* is a null pointer on output. Parameters are returned in ascending order according to the *iOrdinal* element of the PARAMINFO structure.

Here is the DBPARAMINFO structure:

```
typedef struct tagDBPARAMINFO {
   DBPARAMFLAGS   dwFlags;
   ULONG          iOrdinal;
   LPOLESTR       pwszName;
   ITypeInfo *    pTypeInfo;
   ULONG          ulParamSize;
   DBTYPE         wType;
   BYTE           bPrecision;
   BYTE           bScale;
} DBPARAMINFO;
```

The elements of this structure are used as described in the following table.

Element	Description
dwFlags	A bitmask describing parameter characteristics; these values have the following meaning: • DBPARAMFLAGS_ISINPUT—Whether a parameter accepts values on input. Not set if this is unknown. • DBPARAMFLAGS_ISOUTPUT—Whether a parameter returns values on output. Not set if this is unknown. Providers support only those parameter types that make sense for their data store. • DBPARAMFLAGS_ISSIGNED—Whether a parameter is signed. This is ignored if the type is inherently signed, such as DBTYPE_I2, or if the sign does not apply to the type, such as DBTYPE_BSTR. It is generally used in **SetParameterInfo** so that the consumer can tell the provider if a provider-specific type name refers to a signed or unsigned type. • DBPARAMFLAGS_ISNULLABLE—Whether a parameter accepts NULLs. If nullability is unknown, this flag is set. • DBPARAMFLAGS_ISLONG—Whether a parameter contains a BLOB that contains very long data. The definition of very long data is provider specific. The flag setting corresponds to the value of the IS_LONG column in the PROVIDER_TYPES schema rowset for the data type. When this flag is set, the BLOB is best manipulated through one of the storage interfaces. Although such BLOBs can be sent in a single piece with **ICommand::Execute**, there may be provider-specific problems in doing so. For example, the BLOB might be truncated due to machine limits on memory. Furthermore, when this flag is set, the provider might not be able to accurately return the maximum length of the BLOB data in *ulParamSize* in **GetParameterInfo**. When this flag is not set, the BLOB can be accessed either through **ICommand::Execute** or through a storage interface. For more information, see "Accessing BLOB Data" in Chapter 7, "BLOBs and COM Objects."
iOrdinal	The ordinal of the parameter. Parameters are numbered from left to right as they appear in the command, with the first parameter in the command having an *iOrdinal* value of 1.
pwszName	The name of the parameter; it is a null pointer if there is no name. Names are normal names. The colon prefix (where used within SQL text) is stripped.
pTypeInfo	**ITypeInfo** describes the type, if *pTypeInfo* is not a null pointer.

Element	Description
ulParamSize	The maximum possible length of a value in the parameter. For parameters that use a fixed-length data type, this is the size of the data type. For parameters that use a variable-length data type, this is one of the following: • The maximum length of the parameters in characters, for DBTYPE_STR and DBTYPE_WSTR, or in bytes, for DBTYPE_BYTES, if one is defined. For example, a parameter for a CHAR(5) column in an SQL table has a maximum length of 5. • The maximum length of the data type in characters, for DBTYPE_STR and DBTYPE_WSTR, or in bytes, for DBTYPE_BYTES, if the parameter does not have a defined length. • ~0 (bitwise, the value is not 0; that is, all bits are set to 1) if neither the parameter nor the data type have a defined maximum length. For data types that do not have a length, this is set to ~0 (bitwise, the value is not 0; that is, all bits are set to 1).
wType	The indicator of the parameter's data type, or a type from which the data can be converted for the parameter if the provider cannot determine the exact data type of the parameter.
bPrecision	If *wType* is a numeric type, *bPrecision* is the maximum number of digits, expressed in base 10. Otherwise, this is ~0 (bitwise, the value is not 0; that is, all bits are set to 1).
bScale	If *wType* is a numeric type with a fixed scale, *bScale* is the number of digits to the right (if *bScale* is positive) or left (if *bScale* is negative) of the decimal point. Otherwise, this is ~0 (bitwise, the value is not 0; that is, all bits are set to 1).

ppNamesBuffer
[out]
A pointer to memory in which to store all string values (names used within the **pwszName* element of the DBPARAMINFO structures) with a single, globally allocated buffer. Specifying a null pointer for *ppNamesBuffer* suspends the return of parameter names. The command allocates memory for the buffer and returns the address to this memory. The consumer releases the memory with **IMalloc::Free** when it no longer needs the parameter information. If **pcParams* is zero on output or an error occurs, the provider does not allocate any memory and ensures that **ppNamesBuffer* is a null pointer on output.

Each of the individual string values stored in this buffer is terminated by a null-termination character. Therefore, the buffer may contain one or more strings, each with its own null-termination character, and may contain embedded null-termination characters.

Return Code

S_OK
The method succeeded.

E_FAIL
A provider-specific error occurred.

E_INVALIDARG
pcParams or *prgParamInfo* was a null pointer.

E_OUTOFMEMORY
The provider was unable to allocate sufficient memory in which to return the parameter data array or parameter names.

DB_E_NOCOMMAND
The provider can derive parameter information, but it does not support command preparation. However, no command text was currently set on the command object and no parameter information had been specified with **SetParameterInfo**.

DB_E_NOTPREPARED
The provider can derive parameter information, and it supports command preparation. However, the command was in an unprepared state and no parameter information was specified with **SetParameterInfo**.

DB_E_PARAMUNAVAILABLE
The provider cannot derive parameter information from the command, and **SetParameterInfo** has not been called.

Comments

This method makes no logical change to the state of the object.

If **SetParameterInfo** has not been called for any parameters or **SetParameterInfo** has been called with *cParams* equal to zero, **GetParameterInfo** returns information about the parameters only if the provider can derive parameter information. If the provider cannot derive parameter information, **GetParameterInfo** returns DB_E_PARAMUNAVAILABLE.

If **SetParameterInfo** has been called for at least one parameter, **GetParameterInfo** returns the parameter information only for those parameters for which **SetParameterInfo** has been called. It does this even if the provider can derive information about the parameters for which **SetParameterInfo** was not called. The provider does not return a warning in this case because it often cannot determine the number of parameters and therefore cannot determine whether it has returned information for all parameters.

See Also

ICommandWithParameters::MapParameterNames, **ICommandWithParameters::SetParameterInfo**

ICommandWithParameters:: MapParameterNames

Returns an array of parameter ordinals when given named parameters.

```
HRESULT MapParameterNames (
   ULONG               cParamNames,
   const OLECHAR *     rgParamNames[],
   LONG                rgParamOrdinals[]);
```

Parameters

cParamNames
[in]
The number of parameter names to map. If *cParamNames* is zero, **MapParameterNames** does nothing and returns S_OK.

rgParamNames
[in]
An array of parameter names of which to determine the parameter ordinals. If a parameter name is not found, the corresponding element of *rgParamOrdinals* is set to zero and the method returns DB_S_ERRORSOCCURRED.

rgParamOrdinals
[out]
An array of *cParamNames* ordinals of the parameters identified by the elements of *rgParamNames*. The consumer allocates (but is not required to initialize) memory for this array and passes the address of this memory to the provider. The provider returns the parameter ordinals in the array.

Return Code

S_OK
The method succeeded. Each element of *rgParamOrdinals* is set to a nonzero value.

DB_S_ERRORSOCCURRED
An element of *rgParamNames* was invalid. The corresponding element of *rgParamOrdinals* is set to zero.

E_FAIL
A provider-specific error occurred.

E_INVALIDARG
cParamNames was not zero, and *rgParamNames* or *rgParamOrdinals* was a null pointer.

DB_E_ERRORSOCCURRED
All elements of *rgParamNames* were invalid. All elements of *rgParamOrdinals* are set to zero.

DB_E_NOCOMMAND
No command text was currently set on the command object, and no parameter information had been specified with **SetParameterInfo**.

DB_E_NOTPREPARED
The provider can derive parameter information and supports command preparation. However, the command was in an unprepared state and no parameter information had been specified with **SetParameterInfo**.

See Also

ICommandWithParameters::GetParameterInfo

ICommandWithParameters::SetParameterInfo

Specifies the native data type of each parameter.

```
HRESULT SetParameterInfo (
   ULONG                    cParams,
   const ULONG              rgParamOrdinals[],
   const DBPARAMBINDINFO    rgParamBindInfo[]);
```

Parameters

cParams

[in]

The number of parameters for which to set type information. If *cParams* is zero, the type information for all parameters is discarded and *rgParamOrdinals* and *rgParamBindInfo* are ignored.

rgParamOrdinals

[in]

An array of *cParams* ordinals. These are the ordinals of the parameters for which to set type information. Type information for parameters whose ordinals are not specified is not affected.

rgParamBindInfo

[in]

An array of *cParams* DBPARAMBINDINFO structures. If *rgParamBindInfo* is a null pointer, the type information for the parameters specified by the ordinals in *rgParamOrdinals* is discarded.

The DBPARAMBINDINFO structure is:

```
typedef struct tagDBPARAMBINDINFO {
   LPOLESTR       pwszDataSourceType;
   LPOLESTR       pwszName;
   ULONG          ulParamSize;
   DBPARAMFLAGS   dwFlags;
   BYTE           bPrecision;
   BYTE           bScale;
} DBPARAMBINDINFO;
```

The elements of this structure are used as described in the following table.

Element	Description
pwszDataSourceType	A pointer to the provider-specific name of the parameter's data type or a standard data type name. This name is not returned by **GetParameterInfo**; instead, the provider maps the data type specified by this name to an OLE DB type indicator and returns that type indicator. For a list of standard data type names, see "Comments." If *pwszDataSourceType* is null, the provider attempts a default conversion from the data type specified in the binding for the parameter or returns E_INVALIDARG if it cannot perform default parameter conversions.
pwszName	The name of the parameter. This is a null pointer if the parameter does not have a name. The consumer must specify a name for all or none of the parameters set at any time. If the provider does not support named parameters, this argument is ignored and the provider is not required to verify that all or none of the parameters are named.
ulParamSize	The maximum possible length of a value in the parameter. For parameters that use a fixed-length data type, this is the size of the data type. For parameters that use a variable-length data type, this is one of the following: • The maximum length of the parameters in characters, for DBTYPE_STR and DBTYPE_WSTR, or in bytes, for DBTYPE_BYTES, if one is defined. For example, a parameter for a CHAR(5) column in an SQL table has a maximum length of 5. • The maximum length of the data type in characters, for DBTYPE_STR and DBTYPE_WSTR, or in bytes, for DBTYPE_BYTES, if the parameter does not have a defined length. • ~0 (bitwise, the value is not 0; that is, all bits are set to 1) if neither the parameter nor the data type have a defined maximum length. For data types that do not have a length, this is set to ~0 (bitwise, the value is not 0; that is, all bits are set to 1). This argument is ignored if *pwszDataSourceType* is null.

Element	Description
dwFlags	See the *dwFlags* element of the DBPARAMINFO structure in GetParameterInfo.
bPrecision	If *pwszDataSourceType* is a numeric type, *bPrecision* is the maximum number of digits, expressed in base 10. Otherwise, it is ignored. This argument is ignored if *pwszDataSourceType* is null.
bScale	If *pwszDataSourceType* is a numeric type with a fixed scale, *bScale* is the number of digits to the right (if *bScale* is positive) or left (if *bScale* is negative) of the decimal point. Otherwise, it is ignored. This argument is ignored if *pwszDataSourceType* is null.

Return Code

S_OK
The method succeeded.

DB_S_TYPEINFOOVERRIDDEN
The provider was capable of deriving the parameter type information, and **SetParameterInfo** was called. The parameter type information specified in **SetParameterInfo** was used.

SetParameterInfo replaced parameter type information specified in a previous call to **SetParameterInfo**.

E_FAIL
A provider-specific error occurred.

E_INVALIDARG
cParams was not zero and *rgParamOrdinals* was a null pointer.

An element of *rgParamOrdinals* was zero.

In an element of *rgParamBindInfo*, the *pwszDataSourceType* element was a null pointer, and the provider does not support default parameter conversions.

In an element of *rgParamBindInfo*, the *dwFlags* element was invalid.

DB_E_BADORDINAL
An element of *rgParamOrdinals* was invalid.

DB_E_BADPARAMETERNAME

In an element of *rgParamBindInfo*, the *pwszName* element specified an invalid parameter name. The provider does not check whether the name was correct for the specified parameter, just whether it was a valid parameter name.

In one or more elements of *rgParamBindInfo*, but not all, *pwszName* was null.

In one or more elements of *rgParamBindInfo*, *pwszName* was null and one or more parameters previously set and not overridden were specified with a non-null *pwszName*.

In one or more elements of *rgParamBindInfo*, *pwszName* was non-null and one or more parameters previously set and not overridden were specified with a null *pwszName*.

DB_E_BADTYPENAME

In an element of *rgParamBindInfo*, the *pwszDataSourceType* element specified an invalid data type name. The provider does not check whether the data type was correct for the specified parameter, just whether it was a data type name supported by the provider.

DB_E_OBJECTOPEN

A rowset was open on the command.

Comments

Providers generally derive parameter type information from the data store and return it to the consumer through **GetParameterInfo**. Consumers then use this information to build parameter accessors for use with **ICommand::Execute**.

Some providers—notably many SQL database providers—cannot derive parameter type information from the data store. For these providers, the consumer must supply the native parameter type information through **SetParameterInfo**. The provider uses the type information specified by **SetParameterInfo** to determine how to convert parameter data from the type supplied by the consumer (as indicated by the *wType* value in the binding structure) to the native type used by the data store. When the consumer specifies a data type with known precision, scale, and size values, any information supplied by the consumer for precision, scale, or size should be ignored by the provider.

The information that the consumer supplies must be correct and must be supplied for all parameters. Providers that cannot derive parameter type information cannot verify the supplied information against the parameter metadata, although they can determine that the specified values are legal values for the provider. Such providers sometimes cannot even determine the number of parameters in the command. The result of executing a command using incorrect parameter information or passing parameter information for the wrong number of parameters is undefined. For example, if the parameter type is LONG and the consumer specifies a type indicator of DBTYPE_STR in **SetParameterInfo**, the provider converts the data to a string before sending it to the data store. Because the data store is expecting a LONG, this will likely result in an error.

When the consumer calls **SetParameterInfo**, it specifies a provider-specific data type name (as derived from the PROVIDER_TYPES schema rowset) or a standard type name. If the consumer passes a standard type name, the provider maps it to a provider-specific type name. For example, a provider for an SQL DBMS might map "DBTYPE_I2" to "SMALLINT".

The following is a list of standard type names and their associated type indicators. This list contains many commonly known types. Individual providers may allow other, provider-specific, names as well.

Standard type name	Type indicator
"DBTYPE_I1"	DBTYPE_I1
"DBTYPE_I2"	DBTYPE_I2
"DBTYPE_I4"	DBTYPE_I4
"DBTYPE_I8"	DBTYPE_I8
"DBTYPE_UI1"	DBTYPE_UI1
"DBTYPE_UI2"	DBTYPE_UI2
"DBTYPE_UI4"	DBTYPE_UI4
"DBTYPE_UI8"	DBTYPE_UI8
"DBTYPE_R4"	DBTYPE_R4
"DBTYPE_R8"	DBTYPE_R8
"DBTYPE_CY"	DBTYPE_CY
"DBTYPE_DECIMAL"	DBTYPE_DECIMAL
"DBTYPE_NUMERIC"	DBTYPE_NUMERIC
"DBTYPE_BOOL"	DBTYPE_BOOL
"DBTYPE_ERROR"	DBTYPE_ERROR
"DBTYPE_UDT"	DBTYPE_UDT
"DBTYPE_VARIANT"	DBTYPE_VARIANT
"DBTYPE_IDISPATCH"	DBTYPE_IDISPATCH
"DBTYPE_IUNKNOWN"	DBTYPE_IUNKNOWN
"DBTYPE_GUID"	DBTYPE_GUID
"DBTYPE_DATE"	DBTYPE_DATE
"DBTYPE_DBDATE"	DBTYPE_DBDATE
"DBTYPE_DBTIME"	DBTYPE_DBTIME

Standard type name	Type indicator
"DBTYPE_DBTIMESTAMP"	DBTYPE_DBTIMESTAMP
"DBTYPE_BSTR"	DBTYPE_BSTR
"DBTYPE_CHAR"	DBTYPE_STR
"DBTYPE_VARCHAR"	DBTYPE_STR
"DBTYPE_LONGVARCHAR"	DBTYPE_STR
"DBTYPE_WCHAR"	DBTYPE_WSTR
"DBTYPE_WVARCHAR"	DBTYPE_WSTR
"DBTYPE_WLONGVARCHAR"	DBTYPE_WSTR
"DBTYPE_BINARY"	DBTYPE_BYTES
"DBTYPE_VARBINARY"	DBTYPE_BYTES
"DBTYPE_LONGVARBINARY"	DBTYPE_BYTES
"DBTYPE_FILENAME"	DBTYPE_FILENAME
"DBTYPE_VARNUMERIC"	DBTYPE_VARNUMERIC
"DBTYPE_PROPVARIANT"	DBTYPE_PROPVARIANT

After the consumer calls **SetParameterInfo** to specify the parameter type information, it can call **GetParameterInfo** to retrieve the type indicator for each parameter. These values—which are based on the information specified in **SetParameterInfo**—represent the best fit of OLE DB types to the native parameter types. The provider guarantees that, if the consumer uses these types in a parameter accessor, it will be able to convert the data from the OLE DB type to the native parameter type.

If the provider can derive parameter type information and the consumer calls **SetParameterInfo**, **SetParameterInfo** uses the specified type information and returns DB_S_TYPEINFOOVERRIDDEN. Because deriving type information can be an expensive operation, this may result in more efficient code.

See Also

ICommandWithParameters::GetParameterInfo

IConvertType

This interface is mandatory on commands, rowsets, and index rowsets.

This interface contains a single method that gives information about the availability of type conversions on a command or on a rowset.

Method	Description
CanConvert	Gives information about the availability of type conversions on a command or on a rowset.

IConvertType::CanConvert

Gives information about the availability of type conversions on a command or on a rowset.

```
HRESULT CanConvert (
   DBTYPE             wFromType,
   DBTYPE             wToType,
   DBCONVERTFLAGS     dwConvertFlags);
```

Parameters

wFromType
[in]
The source type of the conversion.

wToType
[in]
The target type of the conversion.

dwConvertFlags
[in]
Whether **CanConvert** is to determine if the conversion is supported on the rowset or on the command. These flags have the following meaning:

Value	Description
DBCONVERTFLAGS_ COLUMN	**CanConvert** is to determine whether the conversion is supported when setting, getting, finding, filtering, or seeking on columns of the rowset. This flag is mutually exclusive with DBCONVERTFLAGS_PARAMETER.
DBCONVERTFLAGS_ ISFIXEDLENGTH	**CanConvert** is to determine whether a fixed-length value of the DBTYPE specified in the *dwFromType* can be converted to the DBTYPE specified in *wToType*. This flag can coexist with either DBCONVERTFLAGS_COLUMN or DBCONVERTFLAGS_PARAMETER. This flag is supported only by OLE DB version 2.0 or later providers.
DBCONVERTFLAGS_ ISLONG	**CanConvert** is to determine whether the long version of the DBTYPE specified in the *dwFromType* can be converted to the DBTYPE specified in *wToType*. This flag is valid only when used in conjunction with a variable-length DBTYPE. This flag can coexist with either DBCONVERTFLAGS_COLUMN or DBCONVERTFLAGS_PARAMETER. This flag is supported only by OLE DB version 2.0 or later providers.

Value	Description
DBCONVERTFLAGS_ PARAMETER	**CanConvert** is to determine whether the conversion is supported on the parameters of the command.
DBCONVERTFLAGS_ FROMVARIANT	The DBTYPE specified in the *wFromType* represents a type within a VARIANT. **CanConvert** returns whether the conversion from a VARIANT of that type to the type specified in *wToType* is allowed.

Return Code

S_OK
The requested conversion is available.

S_FALSE
The requested conversion is not available.

wFromType or *wToType* was not a valid type for the provider, and the provider was a version 2.0 or greater provider.

E_FAIL
A provider-specific error occurred.

E_INVALIDARG
The provider was an OLE DB 1.*x* provider, and *wFromType* or *wToType* was not a valid type indicator for OLE DB 1.*x* .

DB_E_BADCONVERTFLAG
dwConvert flags was invalid.

The method was called on a command, and its flags inquired about a conversion on a rowset, but the property DBPROP_ROWSETCONVERSIONSONCOMMAND was VARIANT_FALSE.

The DBCONVERTFLAG_PARAMETER bit was set, and **CanConvert** was called on a rowset.

The DBCONVERTFLAGS_PARAMETER bit was set, and **CanConvert** was called on a command (whether from a provider or not) that does not support parameters.

DBCONVERTFLAGS_ISLONG was specified, and the DBTYPE specified in *dwFromType* was not a variable-length DBTYPE.

DBCONVERTFLAGS_ISLONG was specified, and the provider was an OLE DB 1.*x* provider.

DBCONVERTFLAGS_ISFIXEDLENGTH was specified, and the provider was an OLE DB 1.x provider.

DB_E_BADTYPE
DBCONVERTFLAGS_FROMVARIANT was specified, and the type specified in *wFromType* was not a VARIANT type.

Comments

CanConvert can be called from a command or a rowset. The consumer can call it on a command to inquire about conversions supported by that command and on a rowset to inquire about conversions supported by that rowset. The consumer might be able to call it on a command to inquire about conversions supported on rowsets generated from that command; whether this is supported is specified by the DBPROP_ROWSETCONVERSIONSONCOMMAND property.

Converting a value to or from DBTYPE_IUNKNOWN is different than requesting a stream over the value, even though streams are bound using DBTYPE_IUNKNOWN. Providers typically don't support conversion of character or binary values to and from DBTYPE_IUNKOWN, even though they may support binding such objects as streams.

See Also

IAccessor::CreateAccessor

IDBAsynchNotify

IDBAsynchNotify is the callback interface that a consumer must support to get notified of the progress of asynchronous operations such as initializing a data source object, or opening or populating a rowset.

The notifications use the standard OLE connection point scheme for events. The object being created, initialized, or populated supports **IConnectionPointContainer**, and the consumer calls **FindConnectionPoint** for **IID_IDBAsynchNotify** to obtain the correct **IConnectionPoint** interface. The consumer then advises that connection point to connect and supplies a pointer to the consumer's **IDBAsynchNotify** interface.

When to Implement

IDBAsynchNotify is implemented by consumers that require notification for the progress of asynchronous operations. If the consumer requests that an operation, such as opening or populating a rowset or initializing a data source object, be done asynchronously, the object being created or initialized must support a connection point for **IDBAsynchNotify**.

Consumers must implement one object supporting **IDBAsynchNotify** per asynchronous rowset they consume.

Providers should implement this connection point if they expect to work directly with general-purpose consumers.

Method	Description
OnLowResource	Indicates that resources are low.
OnProgress	Indicates the current progress of the operation.
OnStop	Indicates that the asynchronous processing has stopped.

IDBAsynchNotify::OnLowResource

The provider calls this method when it detects low resources.

```
HRESULT OnLowResource(
   DWORD dwReserved);
```

Parameters

dwReserved
[in]
Reserved for future use; providers should set this to zero.

Return Code

S_OK
The method succeeded.

E_FAIL
A consumer-specific error occurred.

E_NOTIMPL
The consumer is not interested in receiving this notification. The provider can optimize by making no further calls to this method for this listener. Notifications for other methods are unaffected.

Comments

The consumer should free any resource it no longer needs when receiving this notification.

See Also

IDBAsynchNotify::OnStop, IDBAsynchNotify::OnProgress

IDBAsynchNotify::OnProgress

OnProgress returns the progress of an asynchronous method call. This method makes no logical change to the state of the object.

```
HRESULT OnProgress (
   HCHAPTER hChapter,
   ULONG    ulOperation,
   ULONG    ulProgress,
   ULONG    ulProgressMax,
   ULONG    ulAsynchPhase,
   LPOLESTR pwszStatusText);
```

Parameters

hChapter
[in]
The chapter handle. If the object calling this method is not a rowset or the operation does not apply to chapters, the caller must set *hChapter* to DB_NULL_HCHAPTER.

ulOperation
[in]
The operation about which status is being returned. Must be set to the following value:

DBASYNCHOP_OPEN
The information applies to the asynchronous opening or population of a rowset or to the asynchronous initialization of a data source object.

ulProgress
[in]
Current progress of the asynchronous execution relative to the expected maximum indicated in the *ulProgressMax* parameter.

ulProgressMax
[in]
The expected maximum value of the *ulProgress* parameter for the duration of calls to **IDBAsynchNotify::OnProgress** for this phase. This value may change across calls to this method.

*ul*AsynchPhase
[in]
Additional information regarding the progress of the asynchronous operation. Valid values include:

DBASYNCHPHASE_CANCELED
A consumer has requested that the operation be canceled by calling **IDBAsynchStatus::Abort**. The listener can attempt to deny the cancellation by returning S_FALSE from the notification. If no listeners deny the cancellation, the provider will call **IDBAsynchNotify::OnStop** for all registered listeners with an *hrStatus* of DB_E_CANCELED.

DBASYNCHPHASE_INITIALIZATION
The object is in an initialization phase. The arguments *ulProgress* and *ulProgressMax* indicate an estimated ratio of completion. The object is not yet fully materialized. Attempting to call any other interfaces may fail, and the full set of interfaces may not be available on the object.

If the asynchronous operation is a result of calling **ICommand::Execute** for a command that updates, deletes, or inserts rows, and *cParamSets* is greater than 1, *ulProgress* and *ulProgressMax* may indicate the progress for a single set of parameters or for the full array of parameter sets.

DBASYNCHPHASE_POPULATION
The object is in a population phase. Although the rowset is fully initialized and the full range of interfaces are available on the object, there may be additional rows not yet populated into the rowset.

While *ulProgress* and *ulProgressMax* can be based on the number of rows populated, they are generally based on the time or effort required to populate the rowset. A caller would therefore be better using this information as a rough guide to how long the process might take, not the eventual row count.

This phase is returned only during population of a rowset. It is never returned in the initialization of a data source object or by the execution of a command that updates, deletes, or inserts rows.

DBASYNCHPHASE_COMPLETE
All asynchronous processing of the object has completed. If the asynchronous operation was a result of calling **ICommand::Execute** for a command that updates, deletes, or inserts rows, *ulProgress* and *ulProgressMax* are equal to the total number of rows affected by the command. If *cParamSets* is greater than 1, this is the total number of rows affected by all of the sets of parameters specified in the execution.

pwszStatusText
[in]
Textual information indicating additional information about the asynchronous operation, or NULL if no status text is available.

The provider owns the memory for *pwszStatusText*. The consumer can copy the text to its own memory but must not attempt to free *pwszStatusText* nor to reference it once it has returned from **IDBAsynchNotify::OnProgress**.

Return Code

S_OK
The method succeeded.

S_FALSE
The *ulAsynchPhase* was DBASYNCHPHASE_CANCELED, and the cancellation of the asynchronous operation was vetoed by the consumer.

The listener wants to cancel the asynchronous operation. The provider calls each listener's **IDBAsynchNotify::OnProgress** with a *ulAsynchPhase* of DBASYNCHPHASE_CANCELED. If none of the listeners deny the cancellation by returning S_FALSE to that notification, the asynchronous operation is canceled and **IDBAsynchNotify::OnStop** is called for each listener with an *hrStatus* of DB_E_CANCELED.

DB_S_UNWANTEDPHASE
The consumer is not interested in receiving this phase. The provider can optimize by making no further calls with this phase.

DB_S_UNWANTEDOPERATION
The consumer is not interested in receiving notifications for this operation. The provider can optimize by making no further calls to this method with this operation for this listener. Notifications for other operations are unaffected.

E_NOTIMPL
The consumer is not interested in receiving this notification. The provider can optimize by making no further calls to this method for this listener. Notifications for other methods are unaffected.

E_FAIL
A consumer-specific error occurred.

Comments

The provider calls this method repeatedly to indicate the current progress of the asynchronous operation, typically at reasonable intervals during a lengthy operation.

The listener can use the progress notification to provide progress information to the end user from the *ulProgress*, *ulProgressMax*, and *pwszStatusText* parameters, or to make programmatic decisions based on the *ulAsynchPhase* parameter.

Listeners should be prepared to handle unknown values of *ulOperation* by returning S_OK or DB_S_UNWANTEDOPERATION, and unknown values of *ulAsynchPhase* by returning S_OK or DB_S_UNWANTEDPHASE.

The DBASYNCHPHASE_COMPLETE phase is guaranteed to be called for all listeners when all asynchronous processing has completed. If a listener registers for asynchronous notifications on a rowset after all processing has already completed, that listener's **OnProgress** is immediately called with the DBASYNCHPHASE_COMPLETE phase. Listeners may or may not receive other phases.

See Also

ICommand::Execute, **IDBAsynchStatus::GetStatus**, **IDBSchemaRowset::GetRowset**, **IOpenRowset::OpenRowset**, **ISourcesRowset::GetSourcesRowset**

IDBAsynchNotify::OnStop

OnStop is called by the provider to indicate that asynchronous processing has stopped.

```
HRESULT OnStop (
   HCHAPTER    hChapter,
   ULONG       ulOperation,
   HRESULT     hrStatus,
   LPOLESTR    pwszStatusText);
```

Parameters

hChapter
[in]
The chapter for which the operation has stopped. If the object calling this method is not a rowset or the operation does not apply to chapters, the caller must set *hChapter* to DB_NULL_HCHAPTER.

ulOperation
[in]
The operation that has stopped. One of the following:

DBASYNCHOP_OPEN
The completion information applies to the asynchronous opening or population of a rowset or to the asynchronous initialization of a data source object.

hrStatus
[in]
Status code indicating the completion result of the asynchronous operation. This may be one of the following status codes or some result specific to the asynchronous operation being executed:

S_OK
The asynchronous operation completed successfully.

DB_E_CANCELED
The asynchronous operation was canceled.

E_OUTOFMEMORY
The provider ran out of memory attempting to execute the asynchronous operation.

E_FAIL
The asynchronous operation failed for a provider-specific reason.

pwszStatusText
[in]
Additional information about the error or about the resource associated with the error. If no additional information is available, this string is empty.

The provider owns the memory for *pwszStatusText*. The consumer can copy the text to its own memory but must not attempt to free *pwszStatusText* nor to reference it once it has returned from **IDBAsynchNotify::OnStop**.

Return Code

S_OK
The method succeeded.

DB_S_UNWANTEDOPERATION
The consumer is not interested in receiving notifications for this operation. The provider can optimize by making no further calls to this method with this operation for this listener. Notifications for other operations are unaffected.

E_NOTIMPL
The consumer is not interested in receiving this notification. The provider can optimize by making no further calls to this method for this listener. Notifications for other methods are unaffected.

E_FAIL
A consumer-specific error occurred.

Comments

This method is called once per operation, when all asynchronous phases for that operation have completed. **OnStop** is always called, whether the asynchronous operation succeeded, failed, or was aborted by the consumer.

For operations that complete successfully, **OnProgress** is always called prior to **OnStop** with *ulProgress* equal to *ulProgressMax*. The only exception is if the listener has explicitly requested not to receive further **OnProgress** notifications by returning E_NOTIMPL or DB_S_UNWANTEDOPERATION, and the provider has optimized by not making additional calls to **OnProgress**.

Consumers should be prepared to handle new values of *ulOperation* by returning S_OK or DB_S_UNWANTEDOPERATION.

See Also

ICommand::Execute, **IDBAsynchStatus::Abort**, **IDBAsynchStatus::GetStatus**, **IDBInitialize::Initialize**, **IDBSchemaRowset::GetRowset**, **IOpenRowset::OpenRowset**, **ISourcesRowset::GetSourcesRowset**

IDBAsynchStatus

Consumers requiring asynchronous data source object initialization or asynchronous rowset generation or population can poll for status or cancel the asynchronous operation by requesting **IDBAsynchStatus** on the object being initialized, generated, or populated.

When to Implement

Providers should implement **IDBAsynchStatus** if they expect to work directly with general-purpose consumers.

Method	Description
Abort	Cancels an asynchronously executing operation.
GetStatus	Returns the status of an asynchronously executing operation.

IDBAsynchStatus::Abort

Cancels an asynchronously executing operation.

```
HRESULT Abort(
   HCHAPTER    hChapter,
   ULONG       ulOperation);
```

Parameters

hChapter [in]
The handle of the chapter for which to abort the operation. If the object being called is not a rowset object or the operation does not apply to a chapter, the caller must set *hChapter* to DB_NULL_HCHAPTER.

ulOperation [in]
The operation to abort. This should be the following value:

DBASYNCHOP_OPEN
The request to cancel applies to the asynchronous opening or population of a rowset or to the asynchronous initialization of a data source object.

Return Code

S_OK
The request to cancel the asynchronous operation was processed. This does not guarantee that the operation itself was canceled. To determine whether the operation was canceled, the consumer should call **IDBAsynchStatus::GetStatus** and check for DB_E_CANCELED; however, it may not be returned in the very next call.

DB_E_CANTCANCEL
The asynchronous operation cannot be canceled.

DB_E_CANCELED
The request to abort the asynchronous operation was canceled during notifications. The operation is still being executed asynchronously.

E_FAIL
A provider-specific error occurred.

E_UNEXPECTED

IDBAsynchStatus::Abort was called on a data source object on which **Initialize** has not been called.

IDBAsynchStatus::Abort was called on a data source object on which **Initialize** was called but subsequently canceled prior to initialization. The data source object is still uninitialized.

IDBAsynchStatus::Abort was called on a rowset on which **ITransaction::Commit** or **ITransaction::Abort** was previously called, and the rowset did not survive the commit or abort and is in a zombie state.

IDBAsynchStatus::Abort was called on a rowset that was asynchronously canceled in its initialization phase. The rowset is in a zombie state.

Comments

After receiving a request to cancel, if the provider supports cancellation of the operation, it calls **IDBAsynchNotify::OnProgress** with a *ulAsynchPhase* of DBASYNCHPHASE_CANCELED for all listeners. If no listeners attempt to deny the cancellation by returning S_FALSE, the operation is canceled and the provider calls **IDBAsynchNotify::OnStop** for all listeners with an *hrStatus* of DB_E_CANCELED. If any listeners deny the cancellation of the operation by returning S_FALSE from the **OnProgress** notification, the provider returns DB_E_CANCELED from the **IDBAsynchStatus::Abort** function and continues processing the operation.

See Also

IDBAsynchNotify::OnStop

IDBAsynchStatus::GetStatus

Returns the status of an asynchronously executing operation.

```
HRESULT GetStatus (
   HCHAPTER       hChapter,
   ULONG          ulOperation,
   ULONG*         pulProgress,
   ULONG*         pulProgressMax,
   ULONG*         pulAsynchPhase,
   LPOLESTR *     ppwszStatusText);
```

Parameters

hChapter
[in]
The chapter handle. If the object being polled is not a rowset object or the operation does not apply to a chapter, this should be set to DB_NULL_HCHAPTER, which is ignored by the provider.

ulOperation
[in]
The operation for which the asynchronous status is being requested. This should be the following value:

DBASYNCHOP_OPEN
The consumer requests information about the asynchronous opening or population of a rowset or the asynchronous initialization of a data source object.

pulProgress
[out]
A pointer to memory in which to return the current progress of the asynchronous operation relative to the expected maximum indicated in the *pulProgressMax* parameter. For more information about the meaning of *pulProgress*, see the description of *pulAsynchPhase*.

If *pulProgress* is a null pointer, no progress is returned.

pulProgressMax
[out]
A pointer to memory in which to return the expected maximum value of the *pulProgress* parameter. This value may change across calls to this method. For more information about the meaning of *pulProgressMax*, see the description of *pulAsynchPhase*.

If *pulProgressMax* is a null pointer, no expected maximum value is returned.

pulAsynchPhase
[out]
A pointer to memory in which to return additional information regarding the progress of the asynchronous operation. Valid values include:

DBASYNCHPHASE_INITIALIZATION
The object is in an initialization phase. The arguments *pulProgress* and *pulProgressMax* indicate an estimated ratio of completion. The object is not yet fully materialized. Attempting to call any other interfaces may fail, and the full set of interfaces may not be available on the object.

If the asynchronous operation was a result of calling **ICommand::Execute** for a command that updates, deletes, or inserts rows, and if *cParamSets* is greater than 1, *pulProgress* and *pulProgressMax* may indicate the progress for a single set of parameters or for the full array of parameter sets.

DBASYNCHPHASE_POPULATION
The object is in a population phase. Although the rowset is fully initialized and the full range of interfaces is available on the object, there may be additional rows not yet populated into the rowset.

While *pulProgress* and *pulProgressMax* can be based on the number of rows populated, they are generally based on the time or effort required to populate the rowset. A caller should, therefore, use this information as a rough estimate of how long the process might take, not the eventual row count.

This phase is returned only during population of a rowset; it is never returned in the initialization of a data source object or by the execution of a command that updates, deletes, or inserts rows.

DBASYNCHPHASE_COMPLETE
All asynchronous processing of the object has completed. **IDBAsynchStatus::GetStatus** returns an HRESULT indicating the outcome of the operation. Typically, this will be the HRESULT that would have been returned had the operation been called synchronously.

If the asynchronous operation was a result of calling **ICommand::Execute** for a command that updates, deletes, or inserts rows, *pulProgress* and *pulProgressMax* are equal to the total number of rows affected by the command. If *cParamSets* is greater than 1, this is the total number of rows affected by all of the sets of parameters specified in the execution.

If *pulAsynchPhase* is a null pointer, no status code is returned.

ppwszStatusText
[in/out]
A pointer to memory containing additional information about the operation. A provider may use this value to distinguish between different elements of an operation—for example, different resources being accessed. This string is localized according to the DBPROP_INIT_LCID property on the data source object.

If **ppwszStatusText* is non-null on input, the provider returns status associated with the particular element identified by **ppwszStatusText*. If **ppwszStatusText* does not indicate an element of *ulOperation*, the provider returns S_OK with *pulProgress* and *pulProgressMax* set to the same value. If the provider does not distinguish between elements based on a textual identifier, it sets **ppwszStatusText* to NULL and returns information about the operation as a whole; otherwise, if **ppwszStatusText* is non-null on input, the provider leaves **ppwszStatusText* untouched.

If **ppwszStatusText* is null on input, the provider sets **ppwszStatusText* to a value indicating more information about the operation, or NULL if no such information is available or if **GetStatus** returns an error. When **ppwszStatusText* is null on input, the provider allocates memory for the status string and returns the address to this memory. The consumer releases this memory with **IMalloc::Free** when it no longer needs the string.

If *ppwszStatusString* is NULL on input, no status string is returned and the provider returns information about any element of the operation or about the operation in general.

Return Code

S_OK
The method returned successfully.

- If *pulAsynchPhase* is equal to DBASYNCHPHASE_INITIALIZATION, the object is not yet fully initialized; attempting to call any other interfaces may fail, and the full set of interfaces may not be available on the object.
- If *pulAsynchPhase* is equal to DBASYNCHPHASE_POPULATION, the rowset is fully initialized and the full range of interfaces is available on the object; however, there may be additional rows not yet populated into the rowset.
- If *pulAsynchPhase* is equal to DBASYNCHPHASE_COMPLETE, all asynchronous processing of the object has completed. The object is fully initialized and populated.

DB_E_CANCELED
Asynchronous processing was canceled during rowset population. Population stops, but the rowset remains valid for the rows already populated.

Asynchronous processing was canceled during data source object initialization. The data source object is in an uninitialized state.

E_UNEXPECTED
IDBAsynchStatus::GetStatus was called on a data source object, and **Initialize** has not been called on the data source object.

IDBAsynchStatus::GetStatus was called on a rowset, **ITransaction::Commit** or **ITransaction::Abort** was called, and the object is in a zombie state.

IDBAsynchStatus::GetStatus was called on a rowset that was asynchronously canceled in its initialization phase. The rowset is in a zombie state.

E_FAIL
A provider-specific error occurred.

Comments

If the rowset is initialized or populated asynchronously, it must support this method.

In addition to the return values listed, **IDBAsynchStatus::GetStatus** can return any HRESULT that would have been returned by the method that initiated the asynchronous operation, indicating the success or failure of the operation.

Some asynchronous operations might not be able to return any states other than "finished" and "not finished". They should set *pulProgressMax* to a value of 1, indicating the all-or-nothing granularity of their estimate, so their answers would be either 0/1 or 1/1.

A provider may change *pulProgressMax* in successive calls and even return a smaller ratio than previously, if this reflects an improving estimate of the degree of completion of the task.

The provider is not obliged to guarantee any further accuracy but is encouraged to do so in cases where reasonable estimates of completion are possible. Such efforts will improve user-interface quality, because the main use of this function is likely to be to give progress feedback to the user. User satisfaction increases with the quality of feedback on an invisible, long-running task.

Calling **GetStatus** on an initialized data source object or a populated rowset, or passing a value for *ulOperation* other than DBASYNCHOP_OPEN, returns S_OK with *pulProgress* and *pulProgressMax* set to the same value. If **GetStatus** is called on an object created from the execution of a command that updates, deletes, or inserts rows, both *pulProgress* and *pulProgressMax* indicate the total number of rows affected by the command.

See Also

IDBAsynchNotify::OnProgress

IDBCreateCommand

Consumers call **IDBCreateCommand::CreateCommand** on a session to obtain a new command.

Method	Description
CreateCommand	Creates a new command.

IDBCreateCommand::CreateCommand

Creates a new command.

```
HRESULT CreateCommand(
   IUnknown *  pUnkOuter,
   REFIID      riid,
   IUnknown ** ppCommand);
```

Parameters

pUnkOuter
[in]
A pointer to the controlling **IUnknown** interface if the new command is being created as part of an aggregate. It is a null pointer if the command is not part of an aggregate.

riid
[in]
The IID of the interface requested on the command.

ppCommand
[out]
A pointer to memory in which to return the interface pointer on the newly created command.

Return Code

S_OK
The method succeeded.

E_FAIL
A provider-specific error occurred.

E_INVALIDARG
ppCommand was a null pointer.

E_NOINTERFACE
The command did not support the interface specified in *riid*.

E_OUTOFMEMORY
The provider did not have enough memory to create the command.

DB_E_NOAGGREGATION
pUnkOuter was not a null pointer, and the provider is an OLE DB 1.0 or 1.1 provider that does not support aggregation of the command object being created.

pUnkOuter was not a null pointer, and *riid* was not IID_IUnknown.

DB_E_OBJECTOPEN
The provider would have to open a new connection to support the operation, and DBPROP_MULTIPLECONNECTIONS is set to VARIANT_FALSE.

Comments

If the session is transacted, the command and any actions performed as a result of executing that command are within the scope of the transaction.

See Also

ICommand

IDBCreateSession

Consumers call **IDBCreateSession::CreateSession** on a data source object to obtain a new session.

Method	Description
CreateSession	Creates a new session from the data source object and returns the requested interface on the newly created session.

IDBCreateSession::CreateSession

Creates a new session from the data source object and returns the requested interface on the newly created session.

```
HRESULT CreateSession (
   IUnknown *  pUnkOuter,
   REFIID      riid,
   IUnknown ** ppDBSession);
```

Parameters

pUnkOuter
[in]
A pointer to the controlling **IUnknown** interface if the new session is being created as part of an aggregate. It is a null pointer if the session is not part of an aggregate.

riid
[in]
The IID of the interface.

ppDBSession
[out]
A pointer to memory in which to return the interface pointer.

Return Code

S_OK
The method succeeded.

E_FAIL
A provider-specific error occurred.

E_INVALIDARG
ppDBSession was a null pointer.

E_NOINTERFACE
The session did not support the interface specified in *riid*.

E_OUTOFMEMORY
The provider did not have enough memory to create the session.

E_UNEXPECTED
The data source object was in an uninitialized state.

DB_E_NOAGGREGATION
pUnkOuter was not a null pointer, and the provider is an OLE DB 1.0 or 1.1 provider that does not support aggregation of the session object being created.

pUnkOuter was not a null pointer, and *riid* was not **IID_IUnknown**.

DB_E_OBJECTCREATIONLIMITREACHED
The maximum number of sessions supported by the provider has already been created. The consumer must release one or more currently held sessions before obtaining a new session object. This error is returned only by providers that have a fixed maximum number of sessions as returned by DBPROP_ACTIVESESSIONS. It is not returned due to other resource constraints, such as available memory (for which the provider returns E_OUTOFMEMORY).

DB_E_OBJECTOPEN
The provider would have to open a new connection to support the operation, and DBPROP_MULTIPLECONNECTIONS is set to VARIANT_FALSE.

See Also

IDBProperties::GetPropertyInfo, **ISessionProperties::SetProperties**

IDBDataSourceAdmin

IDBDataSourceAdmin is an optional interface for creating, destroying, and modifying data source objects.

It is important to distinguish between the data source object and the data store. The *data source object* is the object used by the consumer code. The *data store* is the actual source of data, such as a server database.

Method	Description
CreateDataSource	Creates and initializes a new data source object.
DestroyDataSource	Destroys the current data source object.
GetCreationProperties	Returns information about the data source object creation properties supported by the provider.
ModifyDataSource	Modifies the current data source object.

IDBDataSourceAdmin::CreateDataSource

Creates and initializes a new data source object.

```
HRESULT CreateDataSource(
   ULONG          cPropertySets,
   DBPROPSET      rgPropertySets[],
   IUnknown *     pUnkOuter,
   REFIID         riid,
   IUnknown **    ppSession);
```

Parameters

cPropertySets
[in]
The number of DBPROPSET structures in *rgPropertySets*. If this is zero, the provider ignores *rgPropertySets* and the method does not do anything.

rgPropertySets
[in/out]
An array of DBPROPSET structures containing properties and values to be set. The properties specified in these structures must belong to the Data Source Creation or Initialization property groups; Initialization properties must be supported by the provider for use in data source object creation. If *ppSession* is not a null pointer, the properties can also belong to the Session property group. If the same property is specified more than once in *rgPropertySets*, the value used is provider-specific. If a provider cannot support a property, the property is ignored. If *cPropertySets* is zero, this argument is ignored.

For information about the properties in the Data Source Creation, Initialization, and Session property groups that are defined by OLE DB, see "Properties Table (by Property Groups)" in Appendix C, "Property Tables." For information about the DBPROPSET and DBPROP structures, see "DBPROPSET Structure" and "DBPROP Structure" in Chapter 11, "Properties."

pUnkOuter
[in]
A pointer to the controlling **IUnknown** interface if a session is desired and is to be created as part of an aggregate. Otherwise, it is a null pointer.

riid
[in]
The requested interface for the session returned in **ppSession*. Ignored if *ppSession* is a null pointer.

ppSession
[in/out]
A pointer to memory in which to return the pointer to the session. If *ppSession* is a null pointer, no session is created.

Return Code

S_OK
The method succeeded. In all DBPROP structures passed to the method, *dwStatus* is set to DBPROPSTATUS_OK.

DB_S_ERRORSOCCURRED
The new data source object was created, but one or more properties—for which the *dwOptions* element of the DBPROP structure was DBPROPOPTIONS_OPTIONAL—were not set. The consumer checks *dwStatus* in the DBPROP structures to determine which properties were not set. The method can fail to set properties for a number of reasons, including:

- The property was not in the Data Source Creation, Initialization, or Session property group.
- The property was in the Initialization property group but was not supported for use in data source object creation.
- The property set was not supported by the provider.
- It was not possible to set the property.

E_FAIL
A provider-specific error occurred.

E_INVALIDARG
cPropertySets was not zero and *rgPropertySets* was a null pointer.

In an element of *rgPropertySets*, *cProperties* was not zero and *rgProperties* was a null pointer.

E_NOINTERFACE
The session did not support the interface specified in *riid*.

E_OUTOFMEMORY
The provider was unable to allocate sufficient memory to create the new data source object.

DB_E_ALREADYINITIALIZED
Initialize had already been called for the data source object, and an intervening call to **Uninitialize** had not been made.

DB_E_DUPLICATEDATASOURCE
A data source object with the same name already exists.

DB_E_ERRORSOCCURRED
The data source object was not created because one or more properties—for which the *dwOptions* element of the DBPROP structure was DBPROPOPTIONS_REQUIRED or an invalid value—were not set. The consumer checks *dwStatus* in the DBPROP structures to determine which properties were not set. None of the satisfiable properties are remembered. The method can fail to set properties for a number of reasons, including:

- The property was not in the Data Source Creation, Initialization, or Session property group.
- The property was in the Initialization property group but was not supported for use in data source object creation.
- The property set was not supported by the provider.

DB_E_NOAGGREGATION
pUnkOuter was not a null pointer, and the provider is an OLE DB 1.0 or 1.1 provider that does not support aggregation of the data source object being created.

pUnkOuter was not a null pointer, and *riid* was not **IID_IUnknown**.

DB_SEC_E_AUTH_FAILED
The provider required initialization but an authentication failed. The data source object was not created.

DB_SEC_E_PERMISSIONDENIED
The consumer did not have permission to create a new data source object.

Comments

CreateDataSource creates and initializes a data source object in one atomic operation.

The properties DBPROP_INIT_DATASOURCE and DBPROP_INIT_LOCATION are always required by **CreateDataSource**. If DBPROP_INIT_LOCATION is set to VT_EMPTY, the data source object is created in the default location.

See Also

IDBDataSourceAdmin::DestroyDataSource,
IDBDataSourceAdmin::ModifyDataSource

IDBDataSourceAdmin::DestroyDataSource

Destroys the current data source object.

```
HRESULT DestroyDataSource ();
```

Parameters

None.

Return Code

S_OK
The method succeeded.

E_FAIL
A provider-specific error occurred.

E_UNEXPECTED
The data source object was in an uninitialized state.

DB_E_NOTSUPPORTED
The provider does not support this method.

DB_SEC_E_PERMISSIONDENIED
The consumer did not have permission to destroy the current data source object.

Comments

DestroyDataSource destroys the current data source object. It is an error to call **DestroyDataSource** when there are open sessions, commands, or rowsets on the data source object. The consumer must release all interface pointers on all sessions, commands, and rowsets on the data source object before calling **DestroyDataSource**.

See Also

IDBDataSourceAdmin::CreateDataSource

IDBDataSourceAdmin::GetCreationProperties

Returns information about the data source object creation properties supported by the data provider.

```
HRESULT GetCreationProperties (
   ULONG                  cPropertyIDSets,
   const DBPROPIDSET      rgPropertyIDSets[],
   ULONG *                pcPropertyInfoSets,
   DBPROPINFOSET **       prgPropertyInfoSets,
   OLECHAR **             ppDescBuffer);
```

Parameters

cPropertyIDSets

[in]
The number of DBPROPIDSET structures in *rgPropertyIDSets*.

If *cPropertySets* is zero, the provider ignores *rgPropertyIDSets* and returns information about all of the properties in the Data Source Creation and Session property groups it supports and about all of the properties in the Initialization property group it supports for use in creating data source objects.

If *cPropertyIDSets* is not zero, the provider returns information about the requested properties. If a property is not supported or if a property in the Initialization property group cannot be used to create data source objects, the returned value of *dwStatus* in the returned DBPROPINFO structure for that property is DBPROPFLAGS_NOTSUPPORTED and the values of the *pwszDescription*, *vtType*, and *vValues* elements are undefined.

rgPropertyIDSets

[in]
An array of *cPropertyIDSets* DBPROPIDSET structures. The properties specified in these structures must belong to the Data Source Creation or Session property group or belong to the Initialization property group and be supported for use in creating data source objects. The provider returns information about the properties specified in these structures. If *cPropertyIDSets* is zero, this parameter is ignored.

For information about the properties in the Data Source Creation, Initialization, and Session property groups that are defined by OLE DB, see "Properties Table (by Property Groups)" in Appendix C, "Property Tables." For information about the DBPROPIDSET structure, see "DBPROPIDSET Structure" in Chapter 11, "Properties."

pcPropertyInfoSets
[out]
A pointer to memory in which to return the number of DBPROPINFOSET structures returned in **prgPropertyInfoSets*. If *cPropertyIDSets* is zero, **pcPropertyInfoSets* is the total number of property sets for which the provider supports at least one property in the Data Source Creation, Initialization, or Session property groups. If *cPropertyIDSets* is greater than zero, **pcPropertyInfoSets* is set to *cPropertyIDSets*. If an error occurs, **pcPropertyInfoSets* is set to zero.

prgPropertyInfoSets
[out]
A pointer to memory in which to return an array of DBPROPINFOSET structures. If *cPropertyIDSets* is zero, one structure is returned for each property set that contains at least one property belonging to the Data Source Creation, Initialization, or Session property group. If *cPropertyIDSets* is not zero, one structure is returned for each property set specified in *rgPropertyIDSets*.

If *cPropertyIDSets* is not zero, the DBPROPINFOSET structures in **prgPropertyInfoSets* are returned in the same order as the DBPROPIDSET structures in *rgPropertyIDSets*; that is, for corresponding elements of each array, the *guidPropertySet* elements are the same. If *cPropertyIDs*, in an element of *rgPropertyIDSets*, is not zero, the DBPROPINFO structures in the corresponding element of **prgPropertyInfoSets* are returned in the same order as the DBPROPID values in *rgPropertyIDs*; that is, for corresponding elements of each array, the property IDs are the same.

The provider allocates memory for the structures and returns the address to this memory; the consumer releases this memory with **IMalloc::Free** when it no longer needs the structures. Before calling **IMalloc::Free** for **prgPropertyInfoSets*, the consumer should call **IMalloc::Free** for the *rgPropertyInfos* element in each element of **prgPropertyInfoSets*. If **pcPropertyInfoSets* is zero on output or an error occurs, **prgPropertyInfoSets* must be a null pointer on output.

For information about the DBPROPINFOSET and DBPROPINFO structures, see "DBPROPINFOSET Structure" and "DBPROPINFO Structure" in Chapter 11, "Properties."

ppDescBuffer
[out]
A pointer to memory in which to return a pointer to storage for all string values returned in the **pwszDescription* element of the DBPROPINFO structure. The provider allocates this memory with **IMalloc**, and the consumer frees it with **IMalloc::Free** when it no longer needs the property descriptions. If *ppDescBuffer* is a null pointer on input, **GetCreationProperties** does not return the property descriptions. If **pcPropertyInfoSets* is zero on output or an error occurs, the provider does not allocate any memory and ensures that **ppDescBuffer* is a null pointer on output.

Return Code

S_OK
The method succeeded. In all DBPROPINFO structures returned by the method, *dwFlags* is set to a value other than DBPROPFLAGS_NOTSUPPORTED.

DB_S_ERRORSOCCURRED
One or more properties specified in *rgPropertyIDSets* were not supported by the provider. The *dwFlags* element of the DBPROPINFO structure for such properties is set to DBPROPFLAGS_NOTSUPPORTED.

One or more properties specified in *rgPropertyIDSets* were not in the Data Source Creation, Initialization, or Session property groups. The *dwFlags* element of the DBPROPINFO structure for such properties is set to DBPROPFLAGS_NOTSUPPORTED.

One or more properties specified in *rgPropertyIDSets* were in the Initialization property group but could not be used to create data source objects. The *dwFlags* element of the DBPROPINFO structure for such properties is set to DBPROPFLAGS_NOTSUPPORTED.

One or more property sets specified in *rgPropertyIDSets* were not supported by the provider. The *dwFlags* element of the DBPROPINFO structure for all specified properties in these sets is set to DBPROPFLAGS_NOTSUPPORTED. If *cPropertyIDs* in the DBPROPIDSET structure for the property set was zero, the provider cannot set *dwStatus* in the DBPROP structure because it does not know the IDs of any properties in the property set. Instead, it sets *cProperties* to zero in the DBPROPSET structure returned for the property set.

E_FAIL
A provider-specific error occurred.

E_INVALIDARG
pcPropertyInfoSets or *prgPropertyInfoSets* was a null pointer.

cPropertyIDSets was not equal to zero and *rgPropertyIDSets* was a null pointer.

In an element of *rgPropertyIDSets*, *cPropertyIDs* was not zero and *rgPropertyIDs* was a null pointer.

E_OUTOFMEMORY
The provider was unable to allocate sufficient memory in which to return the DBPROPINFOSET or DBPROPINFO structures or the property descriptions.

DB_E_ERRORSOCCURRED
Values were not returned for any properties. The provider allocates memory for **prgPropertySets*, and the consumer checks *dwStatus* in the DBPROP structures to determine why properties were not returned. The consumer frees this memory when it no longer needs the information.

Comments

GetCreationProperties returns properties in the Data Source Creation and Session property groups as well as properties in the Initialization property group that can be used in data source object creation. It is possible that there are properties in the Initialization property group that cannot be used in data source object creation. The properties for which values must be set to create a data source object are indicated in the *dwFlags* element of the DBPROPINFO structure as DBPROPFLAGS_REQUIRED.

This method can be called before the data source object has been initialized.

See Also

IDBDataSourceAdmin::CreateDataSource

IDBDataSourceAdmin::ModifyDataSource

Modifies the current data source object.

```
HRESULT ModifyDataSource (
   ULONG       cPropertySets,
   DBPROPSET   rgPropertySets[]);
```

Parameters

cPropertySets

[in]

The number of DBPROPSET structures in *rgPropertySets*. If this is zero, the provider ignores *rgPropertySets* and the method does not do anything.

rgPropertySets

[in/out]

An array of DBPROPSET structures containing properties and values to be set. The properties specified in these structures must belong to the Data Source Creation or Initialization property groups; Initialization properties must be supported by the provider for use in data source object creation. If the same property is specified more than once in *rgPropertySets*, the value used is provider-specific. If a provider cannot support a property, the property is ignored. If *cPropertySets* is zero, this argument is ignored.

For information about the properties in the Data Source Creation and Initialization property groups that are defined by OLE DB, see "Properties Table (by Property Groups)" in Appendix C, "Property Tables." For information about the DBPROPSET and DBPROP structures, see "DBPROPSET Structure" and "DBPROP Structure" in Chapter 11, "Properties."

Return Code

S_OK

The method succeeded. In all DBPROP structures passed to the method, *dwStatus* is set to DBPROPSTATUS_OK.

DB_S_ERRORSOCCURRED
The data source object was modified, but one or more properties—for which the *dwOptions* element of the DBPROP structure was DBPROPOPTIONS_OPTIONAL—were not set. The consumer checks *dwStatus* in the DBPROP structures to determine which properties were not set. The method can fail to set properties for a number of reasons, including:

- The property was not in the Data Source Creation or Initialization property group.
- The property was in the Initialization property group but was not supported for use in data source object creation.
- The property set was not supported by the provider.
- It was not possible to set the property.

E_FAIL
A provider-specific error occurred.

E_INVALIDARG
cPropertySets was not zero and *rgPropertySets* was a null pointer.

In an element of *rgPropertySets*, *cProperties* was not zero and *rgProperties* was a null pointer.

E_UNEXPECTED
The data source object was in an uninitialized state.

DB_E_ERRORSOCCURRED
The data source object was not modified because one or more properties—for which the *dwOptions* element of the DBPROP structure was DBPROPOPTIONS_REQUIRED—were not set. The consumer checks *dwStatus* in the DBPROP structures to determine which properties were not set. None of the satisfiable properties are remembered. The method can fail to set properties for a number of reasons, including:

- The property was not in the Data Source Creation or Initialization property group.
- The property was in the Initialization property group but was not supported for use in data source object creation.
- The property set was not supported by the provider.
- The value of *dwOptions* in a DBPROP structure was invalid.

DB_E_NOTSUPPORTED
The provider does not support this method.

DB_SEC_E_PERMISSIONDENIED
The consumer did not have permission to modify the current data source object.

Comments

ModifyDataSource modifies the current data source object. It is an error to call **ModifyDataSource** when there are open sessions, commands, or rowsets on the data source object; that is, the consumer must release all interface pointers on all sessions, commands, and rowsets on the data source object before calling **ModifyDataSource**.

See Also

IDBDataSourceAdmin::CreateDataSource, **IDBDataSourceAdmin::DestroyDataSource**

IDBInfo

IDBInfo returns information about the keywords and literals a provider supports. It is an optional interface on the data source objects.

Method	Description
GetKeywords	Returns a list of provider-specific keywords.
GetLiteralInfo	Returns information about literals used in text commands and in **ITableDefinition** and **IIndexDefinition**.

IDBInfo::GetKeywords

Returns a list of provider-specific keywords.

```
HRESULT GetKeywords(
   LPOLESTR *  ppwszKeywords);
```

Parameters

ppwszKeywords
[out]
A pointer to memory in which to return the address of a string. The string contains a comma-separated list of all keywords unique to this provider—that is, a comma-separated list of keywords that are not in the list in the Comments section. If there are no keywords unique to this provider or if an error occurs, the provider sets **ppwszKeywords* to a null pointer.

The provider allocates memory for the string and returns the address to this memory; the consumer releases this memory with **IMalloc::Free** when it no longer needs the string.

Return Code

S_OK
The method succeeded.

E_FAIL
A provider-specific error occurred.

E_INVALIDARG
ppwszKeywords was a null pointer.

E_OUTOFMEMORY
The provider was unable to allocate sufficient memory in which to return the keywords.

E_UNEXPECTED
The data source object was in an uninitialized state.

Comments

Following is a list of the keywords from OLE DB:

ABSOLUTE
ACTION
ADD
ALL
ALLOCATE
ALTER
AND
ANY
ARE
AS
ASC
ASSERTION
AT
AUTHORIZATION
AVG
BEGIN
BETWEEN
BIT
BIT_LENGTH
BOTH
BY
CASCADE
CASCADED
CASE
CAST
CATALOG
CHAR
CHAR_LENGTH
CHARACTER
CHARACTER_LENGTH
CHECK
CLOSE
COALESCE
COLLATE
COLLATION
COLUMN
COMMIT
CONNECT
CONNECTION
CONSTRAINT
CONSTRAINTS
CONTINUE
CONVERT
CORRESPONDING
COUNT
CREATE
CROSS
CURRENT
CURRENT_DATE
CURRENT_TIME
CURRENT_TIMESTAMP
CURRENT_USER
CURSOR
DATE
DAY
DEALLOCATE

DEC
DECIMAL
DECLARE
DEFAULT
DEFERRABLE
DEFERRED
DELETE
DESC
DESCRIBE
DESCRIPTOR
DIAGNOSTICS
DISCONNECT
DISTINCT
DISTINCTROW
DOMAIN
DOUBLE
DROP
ELSE
END
END-EXEC
ESCAPE
EXCEPT
EXCEPTION
EXEC
EXECUTE
EXISTS
EXTERNAL
EXTRACT
FALSE
FETCH
FIRST
FLOAT
FOR
FOREIGN
FOUND
FROM
FULL
GET
GLOBAL
GO
GOTO
GRANT
GROUP
HAVING
HOUR
IDENTITY
IMMEDIATE
IN
INDICATOR
INITIALLY
INNER
INPUT
INSENSITIVE
INSERT
INT
INTEGER
INTERSECT
INTERVAL
INTO
IS

ISOLATION
JOIN
KEY
LANGUAGE
LAST
LEADING
LEFT
LEVEL
LIKE
LOCAL
LOWER
MATCH
MAX
MIN
MINUTE
MODULE
MONTH
NAMES
NATIONAL
NATURAL
NCHAR
NEXT
NO
NOT
NULL
NULLIF
NUMERIC
OCTET_LENGTH
OF
ON
ONLY
OPEN
OPTION
OR
ORDER
OUTER
OUTPUT
OVERLAPS
PARTIAL
POSITION
PRECISION
PREPARE
PRESERVE
PRIMARY
PRIOR
PRIVILEGES
PROCEDURE
PUBLIC
READ
REAL
REFERENCES
RELATIVE
RESTRICT
REVOKE
RIGHT
ROLLBACK
ROWS
SCHEMA
SCROLL
SECOND

SECTION
SELECT
SESSION
SESSION_USER
SET
SIZE
SMALLINT
SOME
SQL
SQLCODE
SQLERROR
SQLSTATE
SUBSTRING
SUM
SYSTEM_USER
TABLE
TEMPORARY
THEN
TIME
TIMESTAMP
TIMEZONE_HOUR
TIMEZONE_MINUTE
TO
TRAILING
TRANSACTION
TRANSLATE
TRANSLATION
TRIGGER
TRIM
TRUE
UNION
UNIQUE
UNKNOWN
UPDATE
UPPER
USAGE
USER
USING
VALUE
VALUES
VARCHAR
VARYING
VIEW
WHEN
WHENEVER
WHERE
WITH
WORK
WRITE
YEAR
ZONE

See Also

IDBInfo::GetLiteralInfo, **IDBProperties::GetProperties**

IDBInfo::GetLiteralInfo

Returns information about literals used in text commands, **ITableDefinition**, **IIndexDefinition**, and **IOpenRowset**, or any interface that takes DBIDs as arguments.

```
HRESULT GetLiteralInfo(
   ULONG                 cLiterals,
   const DBLITERAL       rgLiterals[],
   ULONG *               pcLiteralInfo,
   DBLITERALINFO **      prgLiteralInfo,
   OLECHAR **            ppCharBuffer);
```

Parameters

cLiterals
[in]
The number of literals being asked about. If this is 0, the provider ignores *rgLiterals* and returns information about all of the literals it supports.

rgLiterals
[in]
An array of *cLiterals* literals about which to return information. If the consumer specifies an invalid DBLITERAL value in this array, **GetLiteralInfo** returns FALSE in *fSupported* in the corresponding element of the **prgLiteralInfo* array.

If *cLiterals* is 0, this parameter is ignored.

pcLiteralInfo
[out]
A pointer to memory in which to return the number of literals for which information was returned. If *cLiterals* is 0, this is the total number of literals supported by the provider. If an error other than DB_E_ERRORSOCCURRED occurs, **pcLiteralInfo* is set to 0.

prgLiteralInfo
[out]
A pointer to memory in which to return a pointer to an array of DBLITERALINFO structures. One structure is returned for each literal. The provider allocates memory for the structures and returns the address to this memory; the consumer releases this memory with **IMalloc::Free** when it no longer needs the structures. If **pcLiteralInfo* is 0 on output or if an error other than DB_E_ERRORSOCCURRED occurs, the provider does not allocate any memory and ensures that **prgLiteralInfo* is a null pointer on output. For information about DBLITERALINFO structures, see the Comments section.

ppCharBuffer

[out]
A pointer to memory in which to return a pointer for all string values (*pwszLiteralValue*, *pwszInvalidChars*, and *pwszInvalidStartingChars*) within a single allocation block. The provider allocates this memory, and the consumer releases it with **IMalloc::Free** when it no longer needs it. If **pcLiteralInfo* is 0 on output or an error occurs, the provider does not allocate any memory and ensures that **ppCharBuffer* is a null pointer on output. Each of the individual string values stored in this buffer is terminated by a null-termination character. Therefore, the buffer may contain one or more strings, each with its own null-termination character, and may contain embedded null-termination characters.

Return Code

S_OK
The method succeeded. In each structure returned in **prgLiteralInfo*, the *fSupported* element is set to TRUE.

DB_S_ERRORSOCCURRED
rgLiterals contained at least one unsupported or invalid literal. In the structures returned in **prgLiteralInfo* for unsupported or invalid literals, the *fSupported* element is set to FALSE.

E_FAIL
A provider-specific error occurred.

E_INVALIDARG
cLiterals was not equal to zero and *rgLiterals* was a null pointer.

pcLiteralInfo, *prgLiteralInfo*, or *ppCharBuffer* was a null pointer.

E_OUTOFMEMORY
The provider was unable to allocate sufficient memory in which to return the DBLITERALINFO structures or the strings containing the valid and starting characters.

E_UNEXPECTED
The data source object was in an uninitialized state.

DB_E_ERRORSOCCURRED
All literals were either invalid or unsupported. The provider allocates memory for **prgLiteralInfo* and sets the value of the *fSupported* element in all of the structures to FALSE. The consumer frees this memory when it no longer needs the information.

Comments

In the context of **GetLiteralInfo**, a literal is one of several things:

- A special character or characters used by text commands, such as the character used to quote identifiers. **GetLiteralInfo** returns the character or characters.
- A literal data value, such as a character literal in an SQL statement. For such literal data values, **GetLiteralInfo** returns the maximum length of the literal in characters, a list of the characters that cannot be used in the literal, and a list of the characters that cannot be used as the first character of the literal.
- The name of a database object such as a column or table. For such names, **GetLiteralInfo** returns the maximum length of the name in characters, a list of the characters that cannot be used in the name, and a list of the characters that cannot be used as the first character of the name.

Information about literals is returned in the DBLITERALINFO structure:

```
typedef struct tagDBLITERALINFO {
   LPOLESTR     pwszLiteralValue;
   LPOLESTR     pwszInvalidChars;
   LPOLESTR     pwszInvalidStartingChars;
   DBLITERAL    lt;
   BOOL         fSupported;
   ULONG        cchMaxLen;
} DBLITERALINFO;
```

The elements of this structure are used as described in the following table:

Element	Description
pwszLiteralValue	A pointer to a string in the **ppCharBuffer* buffer containing the actual literal value. For example, if *lt* is DBLITERAL_LIKE_PERCENT and the percent character (%) is used to match zero or more characters in a LIKE clause, this would be "%". This is used for DBLITERAL_CATALOG_SEPARATOR, DBLITERAL_ESCAPE_PERCENT_PREFIX, DBLITERAL_ESCAPE_UNDERSCORE_PREFIX, DBLITERAL_LIKE_PERCENT, DBLITERAL_LIKE_UNDERSCORE, DBLITERAL_QUOTE_PREFIX, and DBLITERAL_SCHEMA_SEPARATOR. For all other DBLITERAL values, *pwszLiteralValue* is not used and is set to a null pointer.

Element	Description
pwszInvalidChars	A pointer to a string in the **ppCharBuffer* buffer containing the characters that are not valid in the literal. For example, if table names can contain anything other than a numeric character, this would be "0123456789" when *lt* is DBLITERAL_TABLE_NAME. If the literal can contain any valid character, this is a null pointer. This is not used for DBLITERAL_CATALOG_SEPARATOR, DBLITERAL_ESCAPE_PERCENT_PREFIX, DBLITERAL_ESCAPE_UNDERSCORE_PREFIX, DBLITERAL_LIKE_PERCENT, DBLITERAL_LIKE_UNDERSCORE, DBLITERAL_QUOTE_PREFIX, and DBLITERAL_SCHEMA_SEPARATOR; *pwszInvalidChars* is set to a null pointer for these DBLITERAL values.
pwszInvalidStartingChars	A pointer to a string in the **ppCharBuffer* buffer containing the characters that are not valid as the first character of the literal. If the literal can start with any valid character, this is a null pointer. For example, if table names can begin with anything other than a numeric character, this would be "0123456789" when *lt* is DBLITERAL_TABLE_NAME. This is not used for DBLITERAL_CATALOG_SEPARATOR, DBLITERAL_ESCAPE_PERCENT_PREFIX, DBLITERAL_ESCAPE_UNDERSCORE_PREFIX, DBLITERAL_LIKE_PERCENT, DBLITERAL_LIKE_UNDERSCORE, DBLITERAL_QUOTE_PREFIX, and DBLITERAL_SCHEMA_SEPARATOR; *pwszInvalidStartingChars* is set to a null pointer for these DBLITERAL values.
lt	The literal described in the structure. For more information, see the following section.
fSupported	TRUE if the provider supports the literal specified by *lt*. If *cLiterals* is 0, this is always TRUE, because **GetLiteralInfo** returns information only about literals it supports in this case. FALSE if the provider does not support the literal, or the value of the corresponding element of the *rgLiterals* array was not a valid value in the DBLITERAL enumerated type.

Element	Description
cchMaxLen	The maximum number of characters in the literal. If there is no maximum or the maximum is unknown, *cchMaxLen* is set to ~0 (bitwise, the value is not 0; that is, all bits are set to 1). For DBLITERAL_CATALOG_SEPARATOR, DBLITERAL_ESCAPE_PERCENT_PREFIX, DBLITERAL_ESCAPE_UNDERSCORE_PREFIX, DBLITERAL_LIKE_PERCENT, DBLITERAL_LIKE_UNDERSCORE, DBLITERAL_QUOTE_PREFIX, and DBLITERAL_SCHEMA_SEPARATOR, this is the actual number of characters in the literal.

The following values of DBLITERAL are supported.

Value	Description
DBLITERAL_INVALID	An invalid value.
DBLITERAL_ BINARY_LITERAL	A binary literal in a text command.
DBLITERAL_ CATALOG_NAME	A catalog name in a text command.
DBLITERAL_ CATALOG_SEPARATOR	The character that separates the catalog name from the rest of the identifier in a text command.
DBLITERAL_ CHAR_LITERAL	A character literal in a text command.
DBLITERAL_ COLUMN_ALIAS	A column alias in a text command.
DBLITERAL_ COLUMN_NAME	A column name used in a text command or in a data-definition interface.
DBLITERAL_ CORRELATION_NAME	A correlation name (table alias) in a text command.
DBLITERAL_ CURSOR_NAME	A cursor name in a text command.
DBLITERAL_ ESCAPE_PERCENT_PREFIX	The character used in a **LIKE** clause to escape the character returned for the DBLITERAL_LIKE_PERCENT literal. For example, if a percent sign (%) is used to match zero or more characters and this is a backslash (\), the characters "abc\%%" match all character values that start with "abc%". Some SQL dialects support a clause (the **ESCAPE** clause) that can be used to override this value.

Value	Description
DBLITERAL_ESCAPE_ PERCENT_SUFFIX	The escape character, if any, used to suffix the character returned for the DBLITERAL_LIKE_PERCENT literal. For example, if a percent sign (%) is used to match zero or more characters and percent signs are escaped by enclosing in open and close square brackets, DBLITERAL_ESCAPE_PERCENT_PREFIX is "[", DBLITERAL_ESCAPE_PERCENT_SUFFIX is "]", and the characters "abc[%]%" match all character values that start with "abc%". Providers that do not use a suffix character to escape the DBLITERAL_ESCAPE_PERCENT character do not return this literal value and can set the *lt* member of the DBLITERAL structure to DBLITERAL_INVALID if requested.
DBLITERAL_ESCAPE_ UNDERSCORE_PREFIX	The character used in a **LIKE** clause to escape the character returned for the DBLITERAL_LIKE_UNDERSCORE literal. For example, if an underscore (_) is used to match exactly one character and this is a backslash (\), the characters "abc_ _" match all character values that are five characters long and start with "abc_". Some SQL dialects support a clause (the **ESCAPE** clause) that can be used to override this value.
DBLITERAL_ESCAPE_ UNDERSCORE_SUFFIX	The escape character, if any, used to suffix the character returned for the DBLITERAL_LIKE_UNDERSCORE literal. For example, if an underscore (_) is used to match exactly one character and underscores are escaped by enclosing in open and close square brackets, DBLITERAL_ESCAPE_UNDERSCORE_PREFIX is "[", DBLITERAL_ESCAPE_UNDERSCORE_SUFFIX is "]", and the characters "abc[_]_" match all character values that are five characters long and start with "abc_". Providers that do not use a suffix character to escape the DBLITERAL_ESCAPE_UNDERSCORE character do not return this literal value and can set the *lt* member of the DBLITERAL structure to DBLITERAL_INVALID if requested.
DBLITERAL_ INDEX_NAME	An index name used in a text command or in a data-definition interface.
DBLITERAL_ LIKE_PERCENT	The character used in a **LIKE** clause to match zero or more characters. For example, if this is a percent sign (%), the characters "abc%" match all character values that start with "abc".
DBLITERAL_ LIKE_UNDERSCORE	The character used in a **LIKE** clause to match exactly one character. For example, if this is an underscore (_), the characters "abc_" match all character values that are four characters long and start with "abc".
DBLITERAL_ PROCEDURE_NAME	A procedure name in a text command.

Value	Description
DBLITERAL_ SCHEMA_NAME	A schema name in a text command.
DBLITERAL_ SCHEMA_SEPARATOR	The character that separates the schema name from the rest of the identifier in a text command.
DBLITERAL_ TABLE_NAME	A table name used in a text command or in a data-definition interface.
DBLITERAL_ TEXT_COMMAND	A text command, such as an SQL statement.
DBLITERAL_ USER_NAME	A user name in a text command.
DBLITERAL_ VIEW_NAME	A view name in a text command.
DBLITERAL_QUOTE_PREFIX	The character used in a text command as the opening quote for quoting identifiers that contain special characters.
DBLITERAL_QUOTE_SUFFIX	The character used in a text command as the closing quote for quoting identifiers that contain special characters. 1.x providers that use the same character as the prefix and suffix may not return this literal value and can set the *lt* member of the DBLITERAL structure to DBLITERAL_INVALID if requested.

Note If a provider returns non-NULL CATALOG or SCHEMA column values in schema rowsets, it must support **IDBInfo** to describe how a fully qualified name is assembled. A provider that does not support **IDBInfo** must return NULL values for CATALOG and SCHEMA columns in all schema rowsets.

See Also

IDBInfo::GetKeywords, **IDBProperties::GetProperties**

IDBInitialize

IDBInitialize is used to initialize and uninitialize data source objects and enumerators. It is a mandatory interface on data source objects and an optional interface on enumerators.

Method	Description
Initialize	Initializes a data source object or enumerator.
Uninitialize	Returns the data source object or enumerator to an uninitialized state.

IDBInitialize::Initialize

Initializes a data source object or enumerator.

```
HRESULT Initialize();
```

Parameters

None.

Return Code

S_OK
The method succeeded.

DB_S_ASYNCHRONOUS
The method has initiated asynchronous initialization of the data source object. The consumer can call **IDBAsynchStatus::GetStatus** to poll for status or can register for notifications of asynchronous processing. Until asynchronous processing completes, the data source object remains in an uninitialized state.

DB_S_ERRORSOCCURRED
The data source object or enumerator was initialized but one or more properties—for which the *dwOptions* element of the DBPROP structure was DBPROPOPTIONS_OPTIONAL—were not set. To return properties in error, the provider uses DBPROPSET_PROPERTIESINERROR as described in Chapter 11, "Properties." The method can fail to set properties for a number of reasons, including:

- It was not possible to set the property.
- The value in *vValue* in the DBPROP structure was invalid.
- The property's value conflicted with an existing property.

E_FAIL
A provider-specific error occurred.

E_OUTOFMEMORY
The provider was unable to allocate sufficient memory to initialize the data source object or enumerator.

E_UNEXPECTED
The data source object is in the process of being initialized asynchronously. To cancel asynchronous execution, call **IDBAsynchStatus::Abort**.

DB_E_ALREADYINITIALIZED
Initialize had already been called for the data source object or enumerator, and an intervening call to **Uninitialize** had not been made.

DB_E_CANCELED
The provider prompted for additional information and the user selected Cancel.

DB_E_ERRORSOCCURRED
The data source object or enumerator was not initialized because one or more properties—for which the *dwOptions* element of the DBPROP structure was DBPROPOPTIONS_REQUIRED—were not set. The consumer checks *dwStatus* in the DBPROP structures to determine which properties were in error. The method can fail to set properties for any of the reasons specified in DB_S_ERRORSOCCURRED.

DB_SEC_E_AUTH_FAILED
Authentication of the consumer to the data source object or enumerator failed. The data source object or enumerator remains in the uninitialized state.

Comments

Initialize initializes the data source object or enumerator. It uses the values of properties in the Initialization property group that have been set with **IDBProperties::SetProperties**. If the consumer has not set values for all required properties, **Initialize** can prompt for values.

If **Initialize** returns DB_S_ERRORSOCCURRED or DB_E_ERRORSOCCURRED, the consumer can immediately call **IDBProperties::GetProperties** with the DBPPROPSET_PROPERTIESINERROR property set to return the properties that could not be set. For more information, see "Property Sets" in Chapter 11, "Properties."

For information about what the consumer can and cannot do with a data source object or enumerator before it is initialized, see "Data Source Object States" and "Enumerator States" in Chapter 2, "Data Source and Session Objects."

Initializing a Data Source Object Through a Network Connection

The following shows how to instantiate a data source object as an in-process object using **CoCreateInstance**.

```
#include <oledb.h>
extern CLSID CLSID_DSO;
int main() {
   HRESULT          hr;
   IDBInitialize *pIDBInitialize;

   // Create the data source object
   hr = CoCreateInstance(CLSID_DSO, NULL, CLSCTX_INPROC_SERVER,
                         IID_IDBInitialize, (void**) &pIDBInitialize);
```

```
// Set the initialization properties
DBPROP rgProps[8];
for (ULONG i = 0; i <= 7; i++) {
     VariantInit(&rgProps[i].vValue);
   rgProps[i].dwOptions = DBPROPOPTIONS_REQUIRED;
};

rgProps[0].dwPropertyID = DBPROP_INIT_LOCATION;
V_VT(&(rgProps[0].vValue)) = VT_BSTR;
V_BSTR(&(rgProps[0].vValue)) = SysAllocStringLen(OLESTR("server"),
          wcslen(OLESTR("server")));

rgProps[1].dwPropertyID = DBPROP_INIT_DATASOURCE;
V_VT(&(rgProps[1].vValue)) = VT_BSTR;
V_BSTR(&(rgProps[1].vValue)) = SysAllocStringLen(OLESTR("database"),
       wcslen(OLESTR("database")));

rgProps[2].dwPropertyID = DBPROP_AUTH_PASSWORD;
V_VT(&(rgProps[2].vValue)) = VT_BSTR;
V_BSTR(rgProps[2].vValue) = SysAllocStringLen(OLESTR("password"),
       wcslen(OLESTR("password")));

rgProps[3].dwPropertyID = DBPROP_AUTH_USERID;
V_VT(&(rgProps[3].vValue)) = VT_BSTR;
V_BSTR(&(rgProps[3].vValue)) = SysAllocStringLen(OLESTR("username"),
       wcslen(OLESTR("username")));

rgProps[4].dwPropertyID = DBPROP_AUTH_ENCRYPT_PASSWORD;
V_VT(&(rgProps[4].vValue)) = VT_BOOL;
V_BOOL(&(rgProps[4].vValue)) = VARIANT_TRUE;

rgProps[5].dwPropertyID = DBPROP_AUTH_CACHE_AUTHINFO;
V_VT(&(rgProps[5].vValue)) = VT_BOOL;
V_BOOL(&(rgProps[5].vValue)) = VARIANT_TRUE;

rgProps[6].dwPropertyID = DBPROP_AUTH_PERSIST_SENSITIVE_AUTHINFO;
V_VT(&(rgProps[6].vValue)) = VT_BOOL;
V_BOOL(&(rgProps[6].vValue)) = VARIANT_TRUE;

rgProps[7].dwPropertyID = DBPROP_AUTH_PERSIST_ENCRYPTED;
V_VT(&(rgProps[7].vValue)) = VT_BOOL;
V_BOOL(&(rgProps[7].vValue)) = VARIANT_TRUE;

// Create the structure containing the properties
DBPROPSET PropSet;
PropSet.rgProperties    = rgProps;
PropSet.cProperties     = 8;
PropSet.guidPropertySet = DBPROPSET_DBINIT;
```

```
    // Get an IDBProperties pointer and set the initialization properties
    IDBProperties *pIDBProperties;
    pIDBInitialize->QueryInterface(IID_IDBProperties, &pIDBProperties);
    pIDBProperties->SetProperties(1, &PropSet);
    pIDBProperties->Release();

    // Initialize the data source object
    hr = pIDBInitialize->Initialize();
    return hr;
};
```

See Also

IDBInitialize::Uninitialize, **IDBProperties::SetProperties**

IDBInitialize::Uninitialize

Returns the data source object or enumerator to an uninitialized state.

```
HRESULT Uninitialize();
```

Parameters

None.

Return Code

S_OK
The method succeeded.

E_FAIL
A provider-specific error occurred.

E_UNEXPECTED
The data source object is in the process of being initialized asynchronously. To cancel asynchronous initialization, call **IDBAsynchStatus::Abort**.

DB_E_OBJECTOPEN
There were open sessions, commands, or rowsets on the data source object.

Comments

The consumer is not required to uninitialize a data source object or enumerator before releasing it but may use this method to release the state associated with the data source object or enumerator so that it can be reinitialized with **Initialize** or a new state loaded on a data source object, such as with **IPersistFile::Load**.

It is an error to call **Uninitialize** when there are open sessions, commands, or rowsets on the data source object; that is, the consumer must release all interface pointers on all sessions, commands, and rowsets on the data source object before calling **Uninitialize**. It is not an error to call **Uninitialize** if **Initialize** has not been called.

For information about what the consumer can and cannot do with a data source object or enumerator that is uninitialized, see "Data Source Object States" and "Enumerator States" in Chapter 2, "Data Source and Session Objects."

See Also

IDBInitialize::Initialize

IDBProperties

IDBProperties is used to set and get the values of properties on the data source object or enumerator and to get information about all properties supported by the provider.

Before the data source object or enumerator is initialized, the consumer can work only with properties in the Initialization property group. After the data source object or enumerator is initialized, the consumer can work with properties in the Initialization, Data Source, and Data Source Information property groups, although it cannot set the value of properties in the Initialization property group.

Only properties in the Initialization property group are guaranteed to survive uninitialization. That is, if the consumer uninitializes and reinitializes a data source object or enumerator, it might need to reset the values of properties in groups other than Initialization.

IDBProperties is a mandatory interface for data source objects and an optional interface for enumerators. However, if an enumerator exposes **IDBInitialize**, it must expose **IDBProperties**.

Method	Description
GetProperties	Returns the values of properties in the Data Source, Data Source Information, and Initialization property groups that are currently set on the data source object or the values of properties in the Initialization property group that are currently set on the enumerator.
GetPropertyInfo	Returns information about all properties supported by the provider.
SetProperties	Sets properties in the Data Source and Initialization property groups, for data source objects, or in the Initialization property group, for enumerators.

IDBProperties::GetProperties

Returns the values of properties in the Data Source, Data Source Information, and Initialization property groups that are currently set on the data source object or the values of properties in the Initialization property group that are currently set on the enumerator.

```
HRESULT GetProperties (
   ULONG                   cPropertyIDSets,
   const DBPROPIDSET       rgPropertyIDSets[],
   ULONG *                 pcPropertySets,
   DBPROPSET **            prgPropertySets);
```

Parameters

cPropertyIDSets
[in]
The number of DBPROPIDSET structures in *rgPropertyIDSets*.

If *cPropertyIDSets* is zero, the provider ignores *rgPropertyIDSets*. If the data source object or enumerator has not been initialized, the provider returns the values of all properties in the Initialization property group for which values have been set or defaults exist. If the data source object or enumerator has been initialized, the provider returns the values of all properties in the Data Source, Data Source Information, and Initialization property groups (for data source objects) or just in the Initialization property group (for enumerators), for which values have been set or defaults exist. The provider does not return the values of properties in any of these property groups for which values have not been set and no defaults exist.

If *cPropertyIDSets* is not zero, the provider returns the values of the requested properties. If a property is not supported or if the data source object or enumerator is not initialized and the value of a property in a group other than the Initialization property group is requested, the returned value of *dwStatus* in the returned DBPROP structure for that property is DBPROPSTATUS_NOTSUPPORTED and the value of *dwOptions* is undefined.

rgPropertyIDSets
[in]
An array of *cPropertyIDSets* DBPROPIDSET structures. If the data source object or enumerator has not been initialized, the properties specified in these structures must belong to the Initialization property group. If the data source object or enumerator has been initialized, the properties specified in these structures must belong to the Data Source, Data Source Information, or Initialization property group, for data source objects, or the Initialization property group, for enumerators. The provider returns the values of the properties specified in these structures. If *cPropertyIDSets* is zero, this argument is ignored.

For information about the properties in the Data Source, Data Source Information, and Initialization property groups that are defined by OLE DB, see "Properties Table (by Property Groups)" in Appendix C, "Property Tables." For information about the DBPROPIDSET structure, see "DBPROPIDSET Structure" in Chapter 11, "Properties."

pcPropertySets
[out]
A pointer to memory in which to return the number of DBPROPSET structures returned in **prgPropertySets*. If *cPropertyIDSets* is zero, **pcPropertySets* is the total number of property sets for which the provider supports at least one property in the Data Source, Data Source Information, or Initialization property group (for data source objects) or just in the Initialization property group (for enumerators). If *cPropertyIDSets* is greater than zero, **pcPropertySets* is set to *cPropertyIDSets*. If an error other than DB_E_ERRORSOCCURRED occurs, **pcPropertySets* is set to zero.

prgPropertySets
[out]
A pointer to memory in which to return an array of DBPROPSET structures. If *cPropertyIDSets* is zero, one structure is returned for each property set that contains at least one property belonging to the Initialization property group (if the data source object or enumerator is not initialized), the Data Source, Data Source Information, or Initialization property group (if the data source object is initialized), or to the Initialization property group (if the enumerator is initialized). If *cPropertyIDSets* is not zero, one structure is returned for each property set specified in *rgPropertyIDSets*.

In the case of properties in the Initialization property group and for a previously persisted data source object, those properties related to sensitive authentication information such as password will be returned in an encrypted form if DBPROP_AUTH_PERSIST_ENCRYPTED is VARIANT_TRUE.

If *cPropertyIDSets* is not zero, the DBPROPSET structures in **prgPropertySets* are returned in the same order as the DBPROPIDSET structures in *rgPropertyIDSets*; that is, for corresponding elements of each array, the *guidPropertySet* elements are the same. If *cPropertyIDs,* in an element of *rgPropertyIDSets,* is not zero, the DBPROP structures in the corresponding element of **prgPropertySets* are returned in the same order as the DBPROPID values in *rgPropertyIDs*; that is, for corresponding elements of each array, the property IDs are the same.

The provider allocates memory for the structures and returns the address to this memory; the consumer releases this memory with **IMalloc::Free** when it no longer needs the structures. Before calling **IMalloc::Free** for **prgPropertySets*, the consumer should call **IMalloc::Free** for the *rgProperties* element within each element of **prgPropertySets*. If **pcPropertySets* is zero on output or an error other than DB_E_ERRORSOCCURRED occurs, the provider does not allocate any memory and ensures that **prgPropertySets* is a null pointer on output.

For information about the DBPROPSET and DBPROP structures, see "DBPROPSET Structure" and "DBPROP Structure" in Chapter 11, "Properties."

Return Code

S_OK
The method succeeded. In all DBPROP structures returned by the method, *dwStatus* is set to DBPROPSTATUS_OK.

DB_S_ERRORSOCCURRED
No value was returned for one or more properties. The consumer checks *dwStatus* in the DBPROP structure to determine the properties for which values were not returned. **GetProperties** can fail to return properties for a number of reasons, including:

- The property was not supported by the provider.
- The data source object or enumerator was not initialized, and the property was not in the Initialization property group.
- The method was called on the data source object, the data source object was initialized, and the property was not in the Data Source, Data Source Information, or Initialization property groups.
- The method was called on the enumerator, the enumerator was initialized, and the property was not in the Initialization property group.
- The property set was not supported by the provider. If *cPropertyIDs* in the DBPROPIDSET structure for the property set was zero, the provider cannot set *dwStatus* in the DBPROP structure because it does not know the IDs of any properties in the property set. Instead, it sets *cProperties* to zero in the DBPROPSET structure returned for the property set.

E_FAIL
A provider-specific error occurred.

E_INVALIDARG
cPropertyIDSets was not equal to zero and *rgPropertyIDSets* was a null pointer.

pcPropertySets or *prgPropertySets* was a null pointer.

In an element of *rgPropertyIDSets*, *cPropertyIDs* was not zero and *rgPropertyIDs* was a null pointer.

In an element of *rgPropertyIDSets*, *guidPropertySet* was DBPROPSET_PROPERTIESINERROR and *cPropertyIDs* was not zero or *rgPropertyIDs* was not a null pointer.

cPropertyIDSets was greater than 1, and in an element of *rgPropertyIDSets*, *guidPropertySet* was DBPROPSET_PROPERTIESINERROR.

E_OUTOFMEMORY
The provider was unable to allocate sufficient memory in which to return the DBPROPSET or DBPROP structures.

DB_E_ERRORSOCCURRED
Values were not returned for any properties. The provider allocates memory for **prgPropertySets* and the consumer checks *dwStatus* in the DBPROP structures to determine why properties were not returned. The consumer frees this memory when it no longer needs the information.

Comments

If **IDBInitialize::Initialize** returns DB_E_ERRORSOCCURRED, the consumer can immediately call **GetProperties** with the DBPROPSET_PROPERTIESINERROR property set to return all the properties that were in error. For more information, see "Property Sets" in Chapter 11, "Properties."

See Also

IDBProperties::GetPropertyInfo, **IDBProperties::SetProperties**

IDBProperties::GetPropertyInfo

GetPropertyInfo returns information about all properties supported by the provider.

```
HRESULT GetPropertyInfo(
   ULONG                cPropertyIDSets,
   const DBPROPIDSET    rgPropertyIDSets[],
   ULONG *              pcPropertyInfoSets,
   DBPROPINFOSET **     prgPropertyInfoSets,
   OLECHAR **           ppDescBuffer);
```

Parameters

cPropertyIDSets
[in]
The number of DBPROPIDSET structures in *rgPropertyIDSets*.

If *cPropertyIDSets* is zero, the provider ignores *rgPropertyIDSets*. When called on the enumerator, the provider returns information about all properties in the Initialization property group. When called on the data source object, if the data source object has not been initialized, the provider returns information about all properties in the Initialization property group. If the data source object has been initialized, the provider returns information about all of the properties in all of the property sets it supports.

If *cPropertyIDSets* is not zero, the provider returns information about the requested properties. If a property is not supported or if the method is called on an enumerator or an uninitialized data source object and the value of a property in a group other than the Initialization property group is requested, the returned value of *dwStatus* in the returned DBPROPINFO structure for that property is DBPROPFLAGS_NOTSUPPORTED and the values of the *pwszDescription*, *vtType*, and *vValues* elements are undefined.

rgPropertyIDSets
[in]
An array of *cPropertyIDSets* DBPROPIDSET structures. When called on the enumerator, the properties specified in these structures must belong to the Initialization property group. When called on the data source object, if the data source object has not been initialized, the properties must belong to the Initialization property group. If the data source object has been initialized, the properties can belong to any property group. The provider returns information about the properties specified in these structures. If *cPropertyIDSets* is zero, this parameter is ignored. For information about the DBPROPIDSET structure, see "DBPROPIDSET Structure" in Chapter 11, "Properties."

The following special GUIDs are defined for use with **GetPropertyInfo**. All of these GUIDs can be used on data source objects; only the DBPROPSET_DBINITALL GUID can be used on enumerators. If any of these GUIDs are specified in the *guidPropertySet* element of a DBPROPIDSET structure, the *cPropertyIDs* and *rgPropertyIDs* elements of that structure are ignored. However, the consumer should set these to zero and a null pointer, respectively, because the provider might attempt to verify that they are valid values. Consumers cannot pass special GUIDs and the GUIDs of other property sets in the same call to **GetPropertyInfo**. That is, if one element of *rgPropertyIDSets* contains a special GUID, all elements of *rgPropertyIDSets* must contain special GUIDs. These GUIDs are not returned in the *guidPropertySet* element of the DBPROPINFOSET structures returned in *rgPropertyInfoSets*. Instead, the GUID of the property set to which the property belongs is returned.

Property Set GUID	Description
DBPROPSET_DATASOURCEALL	Returns all properties in the Data Source property group, including provider-specific properties.
DBPROPSET_DATASOURCEINFOALL	Returns all properties in the Data Source Information property group, including provider-specific properties.
DBPROPSET_DBINITALL	Returns all properties in the Initialization property group, including provider-specific properties.
DBPROPSET_ROWSETALL	Returns all properties in the Rowset property group, including provider-specific properties.
DBPROPSET_SESSIONALL	Returns all properties in the Session property group, including provider-specific properties.

pcPropertyInfoSets

[out]

A pointer to memory in which to return the number of DBPROPINFOSET structures returned in **prgPropertyInfoSets*. If *cPropertyIDSets* is zero, **pcPropertyInfoSets* is the total number of property sets for which the provider supports at least one property. If **pcPropertyInfoSets* is not zero and one of the special GUIDs listed in *rgPropertyIDSets* was used, **pcPropertyInfoSets* may differ from *cPropertyInfoSets*. If an error other than DB_E_ERRORSOCCURRED occurs, **pcPropertyInfoSets* is set to zero.

prgPropertyInfoSets
[out]
A pointer to memory in which to return an array of DBPROPINFOSET structures. If *cPropertyIDSets* is zero, one structure is returned for each property set that contains at least one property supported by the provider. If *cPropertyIDSets* is not zero, one structure is returned for each property set specified in *rgPropertyIDSets*.

If *cPropertyIDSets* is not zero, the DBPROPINFOSET structures in **prgPropertyInfoSets* are returned in the same order as the DBPROPIDSET structures in *rgPropertyIDSets*; that is, for corresponding elements of each array, the *guidPropertySet* elements are the same. If *cPropertyIDs*, in an element of *rgPropertyIDSets*, is not zero, the DBPROPINFO structures in the corresponding element of **prgPropertyInfoSets* are returned in the same order as the DBPROPID values in *rgPropertyIDs*; that is, for corresponding elements of each array, the property IDs are the same. The only exception to these rules is when one of the special GUIDs listed in *rgPropertyIDSets* was used. In this case, the order of the property information returned may differ from the order specified in *rgPropertyIDSets*.

The provider allocates memory for the structures and returns the address to this memory; the consumer releases this memory with **IMalloc::Free** when it no longer needs the structures. Before calling **IMalloc::Free** for **prgPropertyInfoSets*, the consumer should call **IMalloc::Free** for the *rgPropertyInfos* element within each element of **prgPropertyInfoSets*. If **pcPropertyInfoSets* is zero on output or if an error other than DB_E_ERRORSOCCURRED occurs, then **prgPropertyInfoSets* must be a null pointer on output.

For information about the DBPROPINFOSET and DBPROPINFO structures, see "DBPROPINFOSET Structure" and "DBPROPINFO Structure" in Chapter 11, "Properties."

ppDescBuffer
[out]
A pointer to memory in which to return a pointer to storage for all string values returned in the **pwszDescription* element of the DBPROPINFO structure. The provider allocates this memory with **IMalloc**, and the consumer frees it with **IMalloc::Free** when it no longer needs the property descriptions. If *ppDescBuffer* is a null pointer on input, **GetPropertyInfo** does not return the property descriptions. If **pcPropertyInfoSets* is zero on output or if an error occurs, the provider does not allocate any memory and ensures that **ppDescBuffer* is a null pointer on output. Each of the individual string values stored in this buffer is terminated by a null-termination character. Therefore, the buffer may contain one or more strings, each with its own null-termination character, and may contain embedded null-termination characters.

Note For method calls that return multiple strings within an allocated string buffer, consumers should not make assumptions about the relationship between the individual string pointers and the returned string buffer. Specifically, the consumer should always treat the returned string values as read-only memory and should not assume that the individual string values all occur within the string buffer. The only requirement on the provider is that freeing the string buffer releases any task memory allocated for that call. This applies to the *ppDescBuffer* returned by **IDBProperties::GetPropertyInfo** to hold the *pwszDescription* elements of the DBPROPINFO structure, as well as the *ppStringsBuffer* returned by **IColumnsInfo::GetColumnInfo** to return string values contained within the DBCOLUMNINFO structure.

Return Code

S_OK
The method succeeded. In all DBPROPINFO structures returned by the method, *dwFlags* is set to a value other than DBPROPFLAGS_NOTSUPPORTED.

DB_S_ERRORSOCCURRED
In an element of *rgPropertyIDSets*, a property specified in *rgPropertyIDs* was not supported by the provider; this includes the case in which the property set to which the property belongs is not supported by the provider. In the DBPROPINFO structures returned for the property, *dwFlags* is set to DBPROPFLAGS_NOTSUPPORTED.

In an element of *rgPropertyIDSets*, the property set specified in *guidPropertySet* was not supported by the provider. In the DBPROPINFOSET structure returned for the property set, *cPropertyInfos* is set to zero and *rgPropertyInfos* is set to a null pointer.

The method was called on the enumerator, and in an element of *rgPropertyIDSets*, a property belonged to a group other than the Initialization property group.

The method was called on an uninitialized data source object, and in an element of *rgPropertyIDSets*, a property belonged to a group other than the Initialization property group.

E_FAIL
A provider-specific error occurred.

E_INVALIDARG
pcPropertyInfoSets or *prgPropertyInfoSets* was a null pointer.

cPropertyIDSets was not equal to zero, and *rgPropertyIDSets* was a null pointer.

In an element of *rgPropertyIDSets*, *cPropertyIDs* was not zero and *rgPropertyIDs* was a null pointer.

In one element of *rgPropertyIDSets*, *guidPropertySet* specified one of the special GUIDs listed in the description of *rgPropertyIDSets*. In a different element of *rgPropertyIDSets*, *guidPropertySet* specified the GUID of a normal property set.

E_OUTOFMEMORY
The provider was unable to allocate sufficient memory in which to return the DBPROPINFOSET or DBPROPINFO structures or the property descriptions.

DB_E_ERRORSOCCURRED
Errors occurred while attempting to return information about all properties. The provider allocates memory for **prgPropertyInfoSets*, and the consumer checks *dwFlags* in the DBPROPINFO structures to determine why information about each property was not returned. The consumer frees this memory when it no longer needs the information. The method can fail to return information about properties for any of the reasons specified in DB_S_ERRORSOCCURRED.

Comments

GetPropertyInfo returns information about supported properties, including the property set to which they belong, their ID, their data type, the object to which they apply, and whether they can be read or written. Properties in the Initialization and Data Source Creation property groups for which the consumer must supply a value before calling **Initialize** are marked with the DBPROPFLAGS_REQUIRED bit in the *dwFlags* element of the DBPROPINFO structure.

Whether a property is supported is different from its value. For example, if a provider supports **IRowsetLocate**, it supports the DBPROP_IRowsetLocate property. Whether a rowset actually exposes **IRowsetLocate** depends on whether the consumer sets the value of the corresponding property to VARIANT_TRUE or VARIANT_FALSE.

The rowset properties returned by **GetPropertyInfo** indicate the set of properties that the provider knows about. The properties that may actually be supported for any particular rowset may be a subset of these properties. For example, a schema rowset may not be able to support all of the same properties as a rowset resulting from calling **OpenRowset**, or the properties that can be supported on a rowset generated from a command may vary depending on the command text. In general, consumers should not make assumptions based on the information returned by **GetPropertyInfo**. When opening a rowset, consumers should specify DBPROPOPTIONS_REQUIRED for the minimum number of properties required to be able to consume the rowset and should set *dwOptions* for properties that provide the consumer additional functionality to DBPROPTIONS_OPTIONAL.

See Also

IDBProperties::GetProperties, **IDBProperties::SetProperties**

IDBProperties::SetProperties

Sets properties in the Data Source and Initialization property groups, for data source objects, or in the Initialization property group, for enumerators.

```
HRESULT SetProperties (
   ULONG       cPropertySets,
   DBPROPSET   rgPropertySets[]);
```

Parameters

cPropertySets
[in]
The number of DBPROPSET structures in *rgPropertySets*. If this is zero, the provider ignores *rgPropertySets* and the method does not do anything.

rgPropertySets
[in/out]
An array of DBPROPSET structures containing properties and values to be set. If the data source object or enumerator is uninitialized, the properties specified in these structures must belong to the Initialization property group. If the data source object is initialized, the properties must belong to the Data Source property group. If the enumerator is initialized, it is an error to call this method. If the same property is specified more than once in *rgPropertySets*, the value used is provider-specific. If *cPropertySets* is zero, this parameter is ignored.

For information about the properties in the Data Source and Initialization property groups that are defined by OLE DB, see "Properties Table (by Property Groups)" in Appendix C, "Property Tables." For information about the DBPROPSET and DBPROP structures, see "DBPROPSET Structure" and "DBPROP Structure" in Chapter 11, "Properties."

Return Code

S_OK
The method succeeded. In all DBPROP structures passed to the method, *dwStatus* is set to DBPROPSTATUS_OK.

DB_S_ERRORSOCCURRED
One or more properties were not set. Properties not in error remain set. The consumer checks *dwStatus* in the DBPROP structures to determine which properties were not set. **SetProperties** can fail to set properties for a number of reasons, including:

- The property was not supported by the provider.
- The data source object or enumerator was not initialized, and the property was not in the Initialization property group.

- The data source object was initialized, and the property was not in the Data Source property group.
- The property set was not supported by the provider.
- The property is read-only and was not set to its default value.
- It was not possible to set the property.
- *colid* in the DBPROP structure was not DB_NULLID.
- The value of *dwOptions* in the DBPROP structure was invalid.
- The data type in *vValue* in the DBPROP structure was not the data type of the property or was not VT_EMPTY.
- The value in *vValue* in the DBPROP structure was invalid.
- The property's value conflicted with an existing property.

E_FAIL
A provider-specific error occurred.

E_INVALIDARG
cPropertySets was not equal to zero, and *rgPropertySets* was a null pointer.

In an element of *rgPropertySets*, *cProperties* was not zero and *rgProperties* was a null pointer.

DB_E_ALREADYINITIALIZED
The method was called on the enumerator, and the enumerator was already initialized.

DB_E_ERRORSOCCURRED
All property values were invalid and no properties were set. The consumer checks *dwStatus* in the DBPROP structures to determine why properties were not set. The method can fail to set properties for any of the reasons specified in DB_S_ERRORSOCCURRED.

See Also

IDBProperties::GetProperties, **IDBProperties::GetPropertyInfo**

IDBSchemaRowset

This is an optional interface on sessions. It is used to provide advanced schema information.

Consumers can get information about a data store without knowing its structure by using the **IDBSchemaRowset** methods. For example, the data store might be a Microsoft SQL Server database that organizes each database into a set of schemas that contain the tables and queries for each schema; the data store might be a Microsoft Access 2.0 database that has a container of tables and a container of queries; or the data store might be a Microsoft Access for a Windows 95 database that enables users to define folders to group tables into an arbitrary hierarchy.

For the following schema rowsets, it is suggested that providers pay particular attention to rowset construction and data retrieval performance, because these methods will be used frequently by consumers.

This schema defines a minimum content of the system schema. It is assumed that consumers will precompile and store the specialized queries used for things such as command planning and execution-time plan validation, and storage engines may have specialized optimizations associated with those plans. Consumers can also look at the schema tables in the schema and thus discover other schema tables and attributes beyond the minimum set.

For information about the schema rowsets, see Appendix B, "Schema Rowsets." Providers must return all of the columns in the rowsets they return. If they cannot return the information in a column, they must return an appropriate value. Generally, this is NULL. Providers can return provider-specific columns after the last column defined by OLE DB.

Schema rowsets are identified by GUIDs. The following table lists these GUIDs and the columns for which restrictions can be specified on the schema rowset. The number of restriction columns for each schema rowset are defined as constants prefixed with CRESTRICTIONS_ in the header files. Restriction values are treated as literals rather than as search patterns. For example, the restriction value "A_C" matches "A_C" but not "ABC".

GUID	Number of restrictions	Restriction columns
DBSCHEMA_ASSERTIONS	3	CONSTRAINT_CATALOG CONSTRAINT_SCHEMA CONSTRAINT_NAME
DBSCHEMA_CATALOGS	1	CATALOG_NAME
DBSCHEMA_CHARACTER_SETS	3	CHARACTER_SET_CATALOG CHARACTER_SET_SCHEMA CHARACTER_SET_NAME

GUID	Number of restrictions	Restriction columns
DBSCHEMA_CHECK_CONSTRAINTS	3	CONSTRAINT_CATALOG CONSTRAINT_SCHEMA CONSTRAINT_NAME
DBSCHEMA_COLLATIONS	3	COLLATION_CATALOG COLLATION_SCHEMA COLLATION_NAME
DBSCHEMA_COLUMN_DOMAIN_ USAGE	4	DOMAIN_CATALOG DOMAIN_SCHEMA DOMAIN_NAME COLUMN_NAME
DBSCHEMA_COLUMN_PRIVILEGES	6	TABLE_CATALOG TABLE_SCHEMA TABLE_NAME COLUMN_NAME GRANTOR GRANTEE
DBSCHEMA_COLUMNS	4	TABLE_CATALOG TABLE_SCHEMA TABLE_NAME COLUMN_NAME
DBSCHEMA_CONSTRAINT_ COLUMN_USAGE	7	TABLE_CATALOG TABLE_SCHEMA TABLE_NAME COLUMN_NAME CONSTRAINT_CATALOG CONSTRAINT_SCHEMA CONSTRAINT_NAME
DBSCHEMA_CONSTRAINT_ TABLE_USAGE	6	TABLE_CATALOG TABLE_SCHEMA TABLE_NAME CONSTRAINT_CATALOG CONSTRAINT_SCHEMA CONSTRAINT_NAME

GUID	Number of restrictions	Restriction columns
DBSCHEMA_FOREIGN_KEYS	6	PK_TABLE_CATALOG PK_TABLE_SCHEMA PK_TABLE_NAME FK_TABLE_CATALOG FK_TABLE_SCHEMA FK_TABLE_NAME
DBSCHEMA_INDEXES	5	TABLE_CATALOG TABLE_SCHEMA INDEX_NAME TYPE TABLE_NAME
DBSCHEMA_KEY_COLUMN_USAGE	7	CONSTRAINT_CATALOG CONSTRAINT_SCHEMA CONSTRAINT_NAME TABLE_CATALOG TABLE_SCHEMA TABLE_NAME COLUMN_NAME
DBSCHEMA_PRIMARY_KEYS	3	TABLE_CATALOG TABLE_SCHEMA TABLE_NAME
DBSCHEMA_PROCEDURE_COLUMNS	4	PROCEDURE_CATALOG PROCEDURE_SCHEMA PROCEDURE_NAME COLUMN_NAME
DBSCHEMA_PROCEDURE_PARAMETERS	4	PROCEDURE_CATALOG PROCEDURE_SCHEMA PROCEDURE_NAME PARAMETER_NAME
DBSCHEMA_PROCEDURES	4	PROCEDURE_CATALOG PROCEDURE_SCHEMA PROCEDURE_NAME PROCEDURE_TYPE
DBSCHEMA_PROVIDER_TYPES	2	DATA_TYPE BEST_MATCH
DBSCHEMA_REFERENTIAL_CONSTRAINTS	3	CONSTRAINT_CATALOG CONSTRAINT_SCHEMA CONSTRAINT_NAME

GUID	Number of restrictions	Restriction columns
DBSCHEMA_SCHEMATA	3	CATALOG_NAME SCHEMA_NAME SCHEMA_OWNER
DBSCHEMA_SQL_LANGUAGES	0	none
DBSCHEMA_STATISTICS	3	TABLE_CATALOG TABLE_SCHEMA TABLE_NAME
DBSCHEMA_TABLE_CONSTRAINTS	7	CONSTRAINT_CATALOG CONSTRAINT_SCHEMA CONSTRAINT_NAME TABLE_CATALOG TABLE_SCHEMA TABLE_NAME CONSTRAINT_TYPE
DBSCHEMA_TABLE_PRIVILEGES	5	TABLE_CATALOG TABLE_SCHEMA TABLE_NAME GRANTOR GRANTEE
DBSCHEMA_TABLES	4	TABLE_CATALOG TABLE_SCHEMA TABLE_NAME TABLE_TYPE
DBSCHEMA_TABLES_INFO	4	TABLE_CATALOG TABLE_SCHEMA TABLE_NAME TABLE_TYPE
DBSCHEMA_TRANSLATIONS	3	TRANSLATION_CATALOG TRANSLATION_SCHEMA TRANSLATION_NAME
DBSCHEMA_USAGE_PRIVILEGES	6	OBJECT_CATALOG OBJECT_SCHEMA OBJECT_NAME OBJECT_TYPE GRANTOR GRANTEE

GUID	Number of restrictions	Restriction columns
DBSCHEMA_VIEW_COLUMN_USAGE	3	VIEW_CATALOG VIEW_SCHEMA VIEW_NAME
DBSCHEMA_VIEW_TABLE_USAGE	3	VIEW_CATALOG VIEW_SCHEMA VIEW_NAME
DBSCHEMA_VIEWS	3	TABLE_CATALOG TABLE_SCHEMA TABLE_NAME

For **IDBSchemaRowset**, providers must support the following GUIDs:

- DBSCHEMA_TABLES
- DBSCHEMA_COLUMNS
- DBSCHEMA_PROVIDER_TYPES

Method	Description
GetRowset	Returns a schema rowset.
GetSchemas	Returns a list of schema rowsets accessible by **IDBSchemaRowset::GetRowset**.

IDBSchemaRowset::GetRowset

Returns a schema rowset.

```
HRESULT GetRowset (
   IUnknown *         punkOuter,
   REFGUID            rguidSchema,
   ULONG              cRestrictions,
   const VARIANT      rgRestrictions[],
   REFIID             riid,
   ULONG              cPropertySets,
   DBPROPSET          rgPropertySets[],
   IUnknown **        ppRowset);
```

Parameters

pUnkOuter
[in]
A pointer to the controlling **IUnknown** interface if the rowset is being created as part of an aggregate. If the **IDBSchemaRowset** interface is not being aggregated, it is a null pointer.

rguidSchema
[in]
A GUID identifying the schema rowset. For more information, see the "Comments" section and **IDBSchemaRowset**.

cRestrictions
[in]
The count of restriction values.

rgRestrictions
[in]
An array of restriction values. These are applied in order to the restriction columns. That is, the first restriction value applies to the first restriction column, the second restriction value applies to the second restriction column, and so on. For more information, see the "Comments" section.

riid
[in]
The IID of the requested rowset interface. This interface is conceptually added to the list of required interfaces on the resulting rowset, and the method fails (E_NOINTERFACE) if that interface cannot be supported on the resulting rowset.

cPropertySets
[in]
The number of DBPROPSET structures in *rgPropertySets*. If this is 0, the provider ignores *rgPropertySets*.

rgPropertySets
[in/out]
An array of DBPROPSET structures containing properties and values to be set. The properties specified in these structures must belong to the Rowset property group. If the same property is specified more than once in *rgPropertySets*, then it is provider-specific which value is used. If *cPropertySets* is 0, this argument is ignored.

For information about the properties in the Rowset property group that are defined by OLE DB, see "Properties Table (by Property Groups)" in Appendix C, "Property Tables." For information about the DBPROPSET and DBPROP structures, see "DBPROPSET Structure" and "DBPROP Structure" in Chapter 11, "Properties."

ppRowset
[out]
A pointer to memory in which to return the requested interface pointer on the schema rowset. This rowset is read-only. If no applicable schema information exists, an empty rowset is returned.

Return Code

S_OK
The method succeeded. In all DBPROP structures passed to the method, *dwStatus* is set to DBPROPSTATUS_OK.

DB_S_ASYNCHRONOUS
The method has initiated asynchronous creation of the rowset. The consumer can call **IDBAsynchStatus** to poll for status or **IConnectionPointContainer** to obtain the **IID_IDBAsynchNotify** connection point. Attempting to call any other interfaces may fail, and the full set of interfaces may not be available on the object until asynchronous initialization of the rowset has completed.

DB_S_ERRORSOCCURRED
The rowset was opened, but one or more properties—for which the *dwOptions* element of the DBPROP structure was DBPROPOPTIONS_OPTIONAL—were not set. The consumer checks *dwStatus* in the DBPROP structures to determine which properties were not set. The method can fail to set properties for a number of reasons:

- The property was not supported by the provider.
- The property was not in the Rowset property group.
- The property set was not supported by the provider.
- It was not possible to set the property.
- The *colid* in the DBPROP structure was invalid.
- The data type in *vValue* in the DBPROP structure was not the data type of the property or was not VT_EMPTY.
- The value in *vValue* in the DBPROP structure was invalid.

- The property's value conflicted with an existing property.
- A property was specified to be applied to all columns but could not be applied to one or more columns.

E_FAIL
A provider-specific error occurred.

E_INVALIDARG
rguidSchema was invalid.

rguidSchema specified a schema rowset that was not supported by the provider.

cRestrictions was greater than the number of restriction columns for the schema rowset specified in *rguidSchema*.

In one or more restriction values specified in *rgRestrictions*, the *vt* element of the VARIANT was the incorrect type.

cRestrictions was greater than zero and *rgRestrictions* was a null pointer.

In an element of *rgRestrictions*, the *vt* element of the VARIANT was not VT_EMPTY and the provider did not support the corresponding restriction.

ppRowset was a null pointer.

In an element of *rgPropertySets*, *cProperties* was not 0 and *rgProperties* was a null pointer.

cPropertySets was greater than zero and *rgPropertySets* was a null pointer.

E_NOINTERFACE
The schema rowset did not support the interface specified in *riid*.

E_OUTOFMEMORY
The provider was unable to allocate sufficient memory in which to create the rowset.

DB_E_ABORTLIMITREACHED
The method failed because a resource limit has been reached. For example, a query used to implement the method timed out. No rowset is returned.

DB_E_ERRORSOCCURRED
No rowset was returned because one or more properties—for which the *dwOptions* element of the DBPROP structure was DBPROPOPTIONS_REQUIRED or an invalid value—were not set. The consumer checks *dwStatus* in the DBPROP structures to determine which properties were not set. None of the satisfiable properties are remembered. The method can fail to set properties for any of the reasons specified in DB_S_ERRORSOCCURRED.

DB_E_NOAGGREGATION

pUnkOuter was not a null pointer, and the provider is an OLE DB 1.0 or 1.1 provider that does not support aggregation of the rowset object being created.

pUnkOuter was not a null pointer, and *riid* was not IID_IUnknown.

DB_E_NOTSUPPORTED

The provider does not support restrictions on one or more of the columns in the corresponding schema.

DB_SEC_E_PERMISSIONDENIED

The consumer did not have sufficient permission to create the schema rowset.

DB_E_OBJECTOPEN

The provider would have to open a new connection to support the operation, and DBPROP_MULTIPLECONNECTIONS is set to VARIANT_FALSE.

Comments

GetRowset allows the consumer to specify restrictions that limit the set of rows returned by the schema rowset but does not define the format for such restrictions. The restriction array contains single values that are compared for equality to the corresponding value in the schema rowset. Only rows that exactly match the restriction value in the corresponding column are returned in the rowset. Pattern matching is not supported.

When preparing an array of restriction values, consumers are not required to specify values for all of the restriction columns on a rowset. Any columns for which no restriction values are specified are not restricted.

There are two ways for a consumer to explicitly specify that there is no restriction value for a column. First, the consumer cannot specify a restriction value for the column. For example, if there are three restriction columns, the consumer passes only two restriction values; these apply to the first two restriction columns, and no value is specified for the third restriction column.

Second, the consumer can set the *vt* element of the VARIANT specified for the column to VT_EMPTY, even if the provider does not support restrictions on the column. For example, suppose there are three restriction columns, the provider supports restrictions on the first and third columns, and the consumer wants to restrict values on these two columns. The consumer passes three restriction values. The first and third values are the desired restrictions, and the second value is a VARIANT with a *vt* element of VT_EMPTY.

If the *vt* element of the VARIANT specified for a restriction column is VT_NULL, this means that the column must be NULL to satisfy the restriction. This is equivalent to the **IS NULL** predicate in SQL. If the *vt* element of the VARIANT specified for a restriction column is VT_BSTR and the *bstrVal* element is set to a null pointer, this means that the column must contain an empty string to satisfy the restriction.

See Also

IDBSchemaRowset::GetSchemas

IDBSchemaRowset::GetSchemas

Returns a list of schema rowsets accessible by **IDBSchemaRowset::GetRowset**.

```
HRESULT GetSchemas (
   ULONG *     pcSchemas,
   GUID **     prgSchemas,
   ULONG **    prgRestrictionSupport);
```

Parameters

pcSchemas

[out]
A pointer to memory in which to return the number of GUIDs in **prgSchemas*. The returned count of schema GUIDs is always at least 3, because all providers must support the TABLES, COLUMNS, and PROVIDER_TYPES schema rowsets. If an error occurs, **pcSchemas* is set to 0.

prgSchemas

[out]
A pointer to memory in which to return an array of GUIDs identifying supported schema rowsets. For more information, see **IDBSchemaRowset**. The rowset allocates memory for the GUIDs and returns the address to this memory. The consumer releases this memory with **IMalloc::Free** when it no longer needs the list of GUIDs. If an error occurs, **prgSchemas* is set to a null pointer.

prgRestrictionSupport

[out]
A pointer to memory in which to return an array of ULONGs, one element for each supported schema rowset, describing the restriction columns supported for that schema rowset. For a given schema rowset, the array element corresponding to the schema rowset will have the appropriate bit set if the provider implements a restriction on that column. Bits that do not correspond to currently defined restriction columns should not be set.

The value of *prgRestrictionSupport* reflects on which of the columns listed as restriction columns the provider supports restrictions. The table of GUID restriction columns at the beginning of this **IDBSchemaRowset** section indicates the array of possible restriction columns to which this bitmask applies.

For example, the GUID table lists three restriction columns for the schema DBSCHEMA_ASSERTIONS. The array element corresponding to this schema will represent the CONSTRAINT_CATALOG column in bit 0, the CONSTRAINT_SCHEMA column in bit 1, and the CONSTRAINT_NAME column in bit 2. The following code shows how the consumer might determine whether a restriction on the CONSTRAINT_CATALOG column is supported on the ASSERTIONS schema rowset.

```
ULONG    cSchemas;
GUID *   rgSchemas;
ULONG *  rgRestSupport;

pIDBSchemaRowset->GetSchemas(&cSchemas, &rgSchemas, &rgRestSupport);

// Assume rgSchemas[0] is the GUID DBSCHEMA_ASSERTIONS. The following
// code checks whether the restriction on the CONSTRAINT_CATALOG
// column is supported.
if (rgRestSupport[0] & 0x1) {
   // Restriction is supported
} else {
   // Restriction is not supported
}
```

The rowset allocates memory for the restrictions and returns the address to this memory. The consumer releases this memory with **IMalloc::Free** when it no longer needs the list of restrictions. If an error occurs, **prgRestrictionSupport* is set to a null pointer.

If *prgRestrictionSupport* is a null pointer, the rowset does not allocate any memory or return any restrictions.

Return Code

S_OK
The method succeeded.

E_FAIL
A provider-specific error occurred.

E_INVALIDARG
pcSchemas, *prgSchemas, or prgRestrictionSupport* was a null pointer.

E_OUTOFMEMORY
The provider was unable to allocate sufficient memory in which to return the array of schema GUIDs or restriction support information.

See Also

IDBSchemaRowset::GetRowset

IErrorInfo

IErrorInfo is defined by Automation; the following describes how the interface is used in OLE DB. **IErrorInfo** returns information about an error in addition to the return code. It returns the error message, name of the component and GUID of the interface in which the error occurred, and the name and topic of the Help file that applies to the error.

When to Implement

IErrorInfo is implemented by code in the Data Access Software Development Kit (SDK). This code calls provider-specific code in **IErrorLookup** to retrieve error messages, sources, and Help file information.

OLE DB error objects expose **IErrorInfo** at two levels. First, it is exposed on the OLE DB error object itself, which enables Automation consumers to use OLE DB error objects. The interface pointer is returned by **GetErrorInfo** in the Automation DLL; it can also be returned by **QueryInterface**. **IErrorInfo** returns the information stored in record 0 of the OLE DB error object and uses the default locale ID.

IErrorInfo is also exposed on individual records in the OLE DB error object. These **IErrorInfo** interface pointers, returned by **IErrorRecords::GetErrorInfo**, are different from the **IErrorInfo** interface pointer exposed on the OLE DB error object itself and cannot be returned by **QueryInterface**. The record to which the interface pointer applies and the locale ID it uses are specified by the consumer in **IErrorRecords::GetErrorInfo**.

When to Call

Automation consumers call **GetErrorInfo** in the Automation DLL to get an **IErrorInfo** interface pointer on the OLE DB error object.

OLE DB consumers also call **GetErrorInfo** in the Automation DLL. However, they do not generally use the returned **IErrorInfo** interface pointer. Instead, they call **QueryInterface** to get an **IErrorRecords** interface pointer and then call **IErrorRecords::GetErrorInfo** to get an **IErrorInfo** interface pointer on a particular record in the OLE DB error object. Then the OLE DB consumers use this interface pointer to retrieve the error information.

Method	Description
GetDescription	Returns a text description of the error.
GetGUID	Returns the GUID of the interface that defined the error.
GetHelpContext	Returns the Help context ID for the error.
GetHelpFile	Returns the path of the Help file that describes the error.
GetSource	Returns the name of the component that generated the error, such as "ODBC *driver-name*".

IErrorInfo::GetDescription

Returns a text description of the error.

```
HRESULT GetDescription (
   BSTR *pbstrDescription);
```

Parameters

pbstrDescription
[out]
A pointer to memory in which to return a pointer to a string that describes the error. If there is no error description or an error occurs, the returned value (**pbstrDescription*) is set to a null pointer. The memory for this string is allocated by the provider and must be freed by the consumer with a call to **SysFreeString**.

Return Code

S_OK
The method succeeded.

E_INVALIDARG
pbstrDescription was a null pointer.

E_OUTOFMEMORY
The provider was unable to allocate sufficient memory in which to return the error description.

DB_E_NOLOCALE
The locale ID specified by the *lcid* parameter in **IErrorRecords::GetErrorInfo** was not supported by the provider.

Comments

If the lookup ID is IDENTIFIER_SDK_ERROR, the implementation of this method retrieves the error description from the error resource DLL shipped with the Data Access SDK. Otherwise, **GetDescription** calls **IErrorLookup::GetErrorDescription** to retrieve the string. If the description is parameterized, such as "Cannot open table <*param1*>," the lookup service incorporates the parameter values before returning the string.

See Also

IErrorLookup::GetErrorDescription

IErrorInfo::GetGUID

Returns the GUID of interface that defined the error.

```
HRESULT GetGUID (
   GUID *pguid);
```

Parameters

pguid
[out]
A pointer to memory in which to return the GUID of the interface that defined the error. If the error was defined by the operating system, the returned GUID is DB_NULLGUID. This is the same value as is returned in the *iid* element of the ERRORINFO structure returned by **IErrorRecords::GetBasicErrorInfo**.

Return Code

S_OK
The method succeeded.

E_INVALIDARG
pguid was a null pointer.

Comments

This GUID does not necessarily represent the source of the error; the source is the class or application that raised the error. Using the GUID, an application can handle errors in an interface independent of the class that implements the interface.

IErrorInfo::GetHelpContext

Returns the Help context ID for the error.

```
HRESULT GetHelpContext (
   DWORD *  pdwHelpContext);
```

Parameters

pdwHelpContext
[out]
A pointer to memory in which to return the Help context ID for the error. If there is no Help file (**pbstrHelpFile* returned by **GetHelpFile** is a null pointer), then the returned value has no meaning.

Return Code

S_OK
The method succeeded.

E_INVALIDARG
pdwHelpContext was a null pointer.

DB_E_NOLOCALE
The locale ID specified by the *lcid* parameter in **IErrorRecords::GetErrorInfo** was not supported by the provider.

Comments

The implementation of this method shipped with the Data Access SDK calls **IErrorLookup::GetHelpInfo** to retrieve the Help context ID.

See Also

IErrorInfo::GetHelpFile, **IErrorLookup::GetHelpInfo**

IErrorInfo::GetHelpFile

Returns the path of the Help file that describes the error.

```
HRESULT GetHelpFile (
   BSTR *pbstrHelpFile);
```

Parameters

pbstrHelpFile
[out]
A pointer to memory in which to return a pointer to a string containing the fully qualified path of the Help file. If there is no Help file or an error occurs, the returned value (**pbstrHelpFile*) is set to a null pointer. The memory for this string is allocated by the provider and must be freed by the consumer with a call to **SysFreeString**.

Return Code

S_OK
The method succeeded.

E_INVALIDARG
pbstrHelpFile was a null pointer.

E_OUTOFMEMORY
The provider was unable to allocate sufficient memory in which to return the Help file path.

DB_E_NOLOCALE
The locale ID specified by the *lcid* parameter in **IErrorRecords::GetErrorInfo** was not supported by the provider.

Comments

The implementation of this method shipped with the Data Access SDK calls **IErrorLookup::GetHelpInfo** to retrieve the path of the Help file.

See Also

IErrorInfo::GetHelpContext, **IErrorLookup::GetHelpInfo**

IErrorInfo::GetSource

Returns the name of the component that generated the error, such as "ODBC *driver-name*."

```
HRESULT GetSource (
   BSTR *pbstrSource);
```

Parameters

pbstrSource
[out]
A pointer to memory in which to return a pointer to the name of the component that generated the error. If an error occurs, **pbstrSource* is set to a null pointer. The memory for this string is allocated by the provider and must be freed by the consumer with a call to **SysFreeString**.

Return Code

S_OK
The method succeeded.

E_INVALIDARG
pbstrSource was a null pointer.

E_OUTOFMEMORY
The provider was unable to allocate sufficient memory in which to return the component name.

DB_E_NOLOCALE
The locale ID specified by the *lcid* parameter in **IErrorRecords::GetErrorInfo** was not supported by the provider.

Comments

The implementation of this method shipped with the Data Access SDK calls **IErrorLookup::GetErrorDescription** to retrieve the error source.

See Also

IErrorLookup::GetErrorDescription

IErrorLookup

IErrorLookup is used by OLE DB error objects to determine the values of the error message, source, Help file path, and context ID based on the return code and a provider-specific error number.

IErrorLookup is exposed by a provider-specific error lookup service that is mandatory for all providers that return OLE DB error objects.

When to Implement

All providers that return OLE DB error objects must implement **IErrorLookup** in a separate lookup service. For information about the registry entries used by error lookup services, see "Error Lookup Service Registry Entries" in Chapter 14, "Programming Considerations."

When to Call

IErrorLookup is called by the code shipped in the Data Access SDK that implements OLE DB error objects. It should not be called by general consumers.

When an error occurs, the following sequence of events takes place:

1. The provider creates an OLE DB error object and adds a record to that object.
2. The consumer retrieves the error object and gets an **IErrorInfo** interface on a particular record in that object. It then calls a method in **IErrorInfo**.
3. Except for the **IErrorInfo::GetGUID** method, the OLE DB error object code, which is shipped with the Data Access SDK, loads the error lookup service based on the class ID stored in the error record.
4. The OLE DB error object code returns the *hrError* element of the ERRORINFO structure, the lookup ID, and the error parameters from the error record. It also returns the locale ID requested in **IErrorRecords::GetErrorInfo**. It passes all of this information to the appropriate **IErrorLookup** method.
5. The **IErrorLookup** method returns the requested information, based on the *hrError*, *dwLookupID*, and *lcid* arguments, integrates the parameters, and returns this to the error object code.
6. The OLE DB error object code returns the requested information to the consumer.
7. The consumer releases the OLE DB error object.
8. The OLE DB error object code calls **IErrorLookup::ReleaseErrors** for all error records with a nonzero dynamic error ID to release the error information associated with that record.

Method	Description
GetErrorDescription	Returns the error message and source, based on the return code and the provider-specific error number.
GetHelpInfo	Returns the path of the Help file and the context ID of the topic that explains the error.
ReleaseErrors	Releases any dynamic error information associated with a dynamic error ID.

IErrorLookup::GetHelpInfo

Returns the path of the Help file and the context ID of the topic that explains the error.

```
HRESULT GetHelpInfo (
   HRESULT     hrError,
   DWORD       dwLookupID,
   LCID        lcid,
   BSTR *      pbstrHelpFile,
   DWORD *     pdwHelpContext);
```

Parameters

hrError
[in]
The code returned by the method that caused the error.

dwLookupID
[in]
The provider-specific number of the error.

lcid
[in]
The locale ID for which to return the Help file path and context ID.

pbstrHelpFile
[out]
A pointer to memory in which to return a pointer to a string containing the fully qualified path of the Help file. If there is no Help file or an error occurs, the returned value (**pbstrHelpFile*) is a null pointer. The memory for this string is allocated by the provider and must be freed by the consumer with a call to **SysFreeString**.

pdwHelpContext
[out]
A pointer to memory in which to return the Help context ID for the error. If there is no Help file (**pbstrHelpFile* is a null pointer), the returned value has no meaning.

Return Code

S_OK
The method succeeded.

E_FAIL
A provider-specific error occurred.

E_INVALIDARG
pbstrHelpFile or *pdwHelpContext* was a null pointer.

E_OUTOFMEMORY
The provider was unable to allocate sufficient memory in which to return the Help file path.

DB_E_BADHRESULT
hrError was invalid.

DB_E_BADLOOKUPID
dwLookupID was invalid.

DB_E_NOLOCALE
The locale ID specified in *lcid* was not supported by the provider.

See Also

IErrorInfo::GetHelpContext, **IErrorInfo::GetHelpFile**, **IErrorLookup::GetErrorDescription**

IErrorLookup::ReleaseErrors

Releases any dynamic error information associated with a dynamic error ID.

```
HRESULT ReleaseErrors (
   const DWORD dwDynamicErrorID);
```

Parameters

dwDynamicErrorID
[in]
The ID of the dynamic error information to release.

Return Code

S_OK
The method succeeded.

E_FAIL
A provider-specific error occurred.

DB_E_BADDYNAMICERRORID
dwDynamicErrorID was invalid.

Comments

Dynamic error information is created at run time. It is released when the OLE DB error object calls **ReleaseErrors** with the ID of the error information to release.

Although it is not required, it is more efficient for providers to use the same error ID for all records in a single error object. This allows **ReleaseErrors** to release all of this information in a single call.

For more information, see "Error Lookup Services" in Chapter 13, "Errors."

IErrorRecords

IErrorRecords is defined by OLE DB. It is used to add and retrieve records in an OLE DB error object. Information is passed to and from OLE DB error objects in an ERRORINFO structure. For information about this structure, see "Error Records" in Chapter 13, "Errors."

When to Implement

IErrorRecords is implemented by code in the Data Access SDK.

When to Call

Consumers use this interface to retrieve information stored in the records of an OLE DB error object. They call **QueryInterface** to get a pointer to this interface after retrieving an OLE DB error object with **GetErrorInfo** in the Automation DLL.

Providers use this interface to add records to an OLE DB error object. If they get an existing OLE DB error object with **GetErrorInfo** in the Automation DLL, they call **QueryInterface** on that object to get a pointer to this interface. If they create a new OLE DB error object through a class factory or with **CoCreateInstance**, they request that a pointer to this interface be returned.

Method	Description
AddErrorRecord	Adds a record to an OLE DB error object.
GetBasicErrorInfo	Returns basic information about the error, such as the return code and provider-specific error number.
GetCustomErrorObject	Returns a pointer to an interface on the custom error object.
GetErrorInfo	Returns an **IErrorInfo** interface pointer on the specified record.
GetErrorParameters	Returns the error parameters.
GetRecordCount	Returns the count of records in the OLE DB error object.

IErrorRecords::AddErrorRecord

Adds a record to an OLE DB error object.

```
HRESULT AddErrorRecord (
   ERRORINFO *     pErrorInfo,
   DWORD           dwLookupID,
   DISPPARAMS *    pdispparams,
   IUnknown *      punkCustomError,
   DWORD           dwDynamicErrorID);
```

Parameters

pErrorInfo
[in]
A pointer to an ERRORINFO structure containing information about the error. This structure is allocated and freed by the consumer. For more information, see "Error Records" in Chapter 13, "Errors."

dwLookupID
[in]
The value used by the provider's error lookup service in conjunction with the return code to identify the error description, Help file, and context ID for an error. This can be a provider-specific value, such as the *dwMinor* element of **pErrorInfo*. It can also be a special value, IDENTIFIER_SDK_ERROR, that tells the implementation of **IErrorInfo** that is shipped with the Data Access SDK to ignore the provider's lookup service and use the description supplied in the Data Access SDK error resource DLL.

```
const DWORD IDENTIFIER_SDK_MASK  = 0xF000000;
const DWORD IDENTIFIER_SDK_ERROR = 0x1000000;
```

pdispparams
[in]
A pointer to the parameters for the error. This is a null pointer if there are no error parameters. The error parameters are inserted into the error text by the error lookup service. This structure is allocated and freed by the consumer. For more information, see "Error Parameters" in "Error Records" in Chapter 13, "Errors."

punkCustomError
[in]
An interface pointer to the custom error object. This is a null pointer if there is no custom object for the error. For more information, see "OLE DB Error Objects" in Chapter 13, "Errors."

dwDynamicErrorID
[in]
If the error lookup service uses static errors—that is, error information that is hard-coded in the lookup service—*dwDynamicErrorID* is zero.

If the error lookup service uses dynamic errors—that is, error information that is created at run time—*dwDynamicErrorID* is the ID of the error record. This ID is used to release the error information when the OLE DB error object is released. Although it is not required, it is more efficient for all error records in a single OLE DB error object to have the same dynamic error ID.

For more information, see "Error Lookup Services" in Chapter 13, "Errors."

Return Code

S_OK
The method succeeded.

E_INVALIDARG
pErrorInfo was a null pointer.

E_OUTOFMEMORY
The OLE DB error object was unable to allocate sufficient memory with which to add a new record.

Comments

This method should be used only by providers; there are no reasons for consumers to use it.

Records are added to the top of the list. That is, the number of the newly added record is record 0 and the number of all other records is increased by 1.

AddErrorRecord adds a reference count on the custom error object. After adding a custom error object to a record in an OLE DB error object, the provider must call **Release** on all interface pointers it holds on that custom error object. This transfers ownership of the custom error object to the OLE DB error object. When it is released, the OLE DB error object will release all custom error objects.

See Also

IErrorRecords::GetBasicErrorInfo, **IErrorRecords::GetCustomErrorObject**, **IErrorRecords::GetErrorParameters**

IErrorRecords::GetBasicErrorInfo

Returns basic information about the error, such as the return code and provider-specific error number.

```
HRESULT GetBasicErrorInfo (
   ULONG        ulRecordNum,
   ERRORINFO * pErrorInfo);
```

Parameters

ulRecordNum
[in]
The zero-based number of the record for which to return information.

pErrorInfo
[out]
A pointer to an ERRORINFO structure in which to return basic error information. This structure is allocated and freed by the consumer. For more information, see "Error Records" in Chapter 13, "Errors."

Return Code

S_OK
The method succeeded.

E_INVALIDARG
pErrorInfo was a null pointer.

DB_E_BADRECORDNUM
ulRecordNum, which is zero-based, was greater than or equal to the count, which is one-based, of records returned by **GetRecordCount**.

Comments

This method should be used only by consumers; there are no reasons for providers to use it.

See Also

IErrorRecords::GetCustomErrorObject, **IErrorRecords::GetErrorInfo**, **IErrorRecords::GetErrorParameters**

IErrorRecords::GetCustomErrorObject

Returns a pointer to an interface on the custom error object.

```
HRESULT GetCustomErrorObject (
   ULONG        ulRecordNum,
   REFIID       riid,
   IUnknown ** ppObject);
```

Parameters

ulRecordNum
[in]
The zero-based number of the record for which to return a custom error object.

riid
[in]
The IID of the interface to return.

ppObject
[out]
A pointer to memory in which to return an interface pointer on the custom error object. If there is no custom error object, a null pointer is returned; that is, **ppObject* is a null pointer.

Return Code

S_OK
The method succeeded.

E_INVALIDARG
ppObject was a null pointer.

E_NOINTERFACE
The custom error object did not support the interface specified in *riid*.

DB_E_BADRECORDNUM
ulRecordNum, which is zero-based, was greater than or equal to the count, which is one-based, of records returned by **GetRecordCount**.

Comments

This method should be used only by consumers; there are no reasons for providers to use it.

See Also

IErrorRecords::GetBasicErrorInfo, **IErrorRecords::GetErrorParameters**

IErrorRecords::GetErrorInfo

Returns an **IErrorInfo** interface pointer on the specified record.

```
HRESULT GetErrorInfo (
   ULONG          ulRecordNum,
   LCID           lcid,
   IErrorInfo **  ppErrorInfo);
```

Parameters

ulRecordNum
[in]
The zero-based number of the record for which to return an **IErrorInfo** interface pointer.

lcid
[in]
The locale ID for which to return error information. This parameter is checked when it is passed to methods in **IErrorInfo**.

ppErrorInfo
[out]
A pointer to memory in which to return a pointer to an **IErrorInfo** interface on the specified record. This **IErrorInfo** interface pointer is different from the **IErrorInfo** interface pointer exposed on the OLE DB error object with **QueryInterface**. For more information, see "OLE DB Error Objects" in Chapter 13, "Errors."

Return Code

S_OK
The method succeeded.

E_INVALIDARG
ppErrorInfo was a null pointer.

DB_E_BADRECORDNUM
ulRecordNum, which is zero-based, was greater than or equal to the count, which is one-based, of records returned by **GetRecordCount**.

Comments

This method should be used only by consumers; there are no reasons for providers to use it.

See Also

IErrorRecords::GetBasicErrorInfo, **IErrorRecords::GetCustomErrorObject**, **IErrorRecords::GetErrorParameters**

IErrorRecords::GetErrorParameters

Returns the error parameters.

```
HRESULT GetErrorParameters (
   ULONG          ulRecordNum,
   DISPPARAMS *   pdispparams);
```

Parameters

ulRecordNum
[in]
The zero-based number of the record for which to return parameters.

pdispparams
[out]
A pointer to a DISPPARAMS structure in which to return the error parameters. The consumer allocates the memory for the DISPPARAMS structure itself, but the provider allocates the memory for any arrays pointed to by elements of the DISPPARAMS structure.

Return Code

S_OK
The method succeeded.

E_INVALIDARG
pdispparams was a null pointer.

E_OUTOFMEMORY
The provider was unable to allocate sufficient memory in which to return the data pointed to by elements of **pdispparams*.

DB_E_BADRECORDNUM
ulRecordNum, which is zero-based, was greater than or equal to the count, which is one-based, of records returned by **GetRecordCount**.

Comments

This method is used by consumers only when the meaning of the error parameters is known to the consumer; error parameters are generally passed to the error lookup service and incorporated into error messages by the provider through that lookup service. There is no reason for providers to use this method.

See Also

IErrorRecords::GetBasicErrorInfo, **IErrorRecords::GetCustomErrorObject**

IErrorRecords::GetRecordCount

Returns the count of records in the OLE DB error object.

```
HRESULT GetRecordCount (
   ULONG *  pcRecords);
```

Parameters

pcRecords
[out]
A pointer to memory in which to return the count of error records. This is a one-based count, although error records are zero-based. If **pcRecords* is zero, there are no records in the OLE DB error object and calls to **GetBasicErrorInfo**, **GetErrorInfo**, **GetErrorParameters**, and **GetCustomErrorObject** will return DB_E_BADRECORDNUM.

Return Code

S_OK
The method succeeded.

E_INVALIDARG
pcRecords was a null pointer.

Comments

This method should be used only by consumers; there are no reasons for providers to use it.

See Also

IErrorRecords::GetBasicErrorInfo, **IErrorRecords::GetCustomErrorObject**, **IErrorRecords::GetErrorInfo**, **IErrorRecords::GetErrorParameters**

IGetDataSource

This is a mandatory interface on the session for obtaining an interface pointer to the data source object.

Method	Description
GetDataSource	Returns an interface pointer on the data source object that created this session.

IGetDataSource::GetDataSource

Returns an interface pointer on the data source object that created the session.

```
HRESULT GetDataSource (
   REFIID      riid,
   IUnknown ** ppDataSource);
```

Parameters

riid
[in]
The IID of the interface on which to return a pointer.

ppDataSource
[out]
A pointer to memory in which to return the interface pointer. If **GetDataSource** fails, it must attempt to set **ppDataSource* to a null pointer.

Return Code

S_OK
The method succeeded.

E_FAIL
A provider-specific error occurred.

E_INVALIDARG
ppDataSource was a null pointer.

E_NOINTERFACE
The object that created this session did not support the interface specified in *riid*.

See Also

ICommand::GetDBSession, **IRowsetInfo::GetSpecification**

IIndexDefinition

IIndexDefinition exposes simple methods to create and drop indexes from the data store.

When to Implement

IIndexDefinition is optional for providers that do not otherwise support index creation; it is mandatory for providers that support creating and dropping indexes through commands.

Method	Description
CreateIndex	Adds a new index to a base table.
DropIndex	Drops an index from a base table.

IIndexDefinition::CreateIndex

Adds a new index to a base table.

```
HRESULT CreateIndex(
   DBID *                        pTableID,
   DBID *                        pIndexID,
   ULONG                         cIndexColumnDescs,
   const DBINDEXCOLUMNDESC       rgIndexColumnDescs[],
   ULONG                         cPropertySets,
   DBPROPSET                     rgPropertySets[],
   DBID **                       ppIndexID);
```

Parameters

pTableID

[in]
A pointer to the DBID of the table for which to create an index.

pIndexID

[in]
A pointer to the ID of the new index to create. If this is a null pointer, the provider assigns an ID to the index. The ID must be unique.

cIndexColumnDescs

[in]
The count of DBINDEXCOLUMNSDESC structures in *rgIndexColumnDescs*.

rgIndexColumnDescs

[in]
An array of DBINDEXCOLUMNDESC structures that describe how to construct the index. The order of the DBINDEXCOLUMNDESC structures in *rgIndexColumnDescs* determines the order of the columns in the index key. That is, the column identified by the first element of this array is the most significant column in the index key and the column identified by the last element is the least-significant column. When the index is opened as a rowset, the key columns occur in order of most-significant column to least-significant column.

```
typedef struct {
 DBID *               pColumnID;
 DBINDEX_COL_ORDER    eIndexColOrder;
} DBINDEXCOLUMNDESC;
```

The elements of this structure are used as follows.

Element	Description
pColumnID	A pointer to the ID of the base table column.
eIndexColOrder	Whether the index is ascending or descending in this column. DBINDEX_COL_ORDER_ASC—Ascending • DBINDEX_COL_ORDER_DESC—Descending

cPropertySets
[in]
The number of DBPROPSET structures in *rgPropertySets*. If this is zero, the provider ignores *rgPropertySets*.

rgPropertySets
[in/out]
An array of DBPROPSET structures containing properties and values to be set. The properties specified in these structures must belong to the Index property group. If the same property is specified more than once in *rgPropertySets*, it is provider-specific which value is used. If *cPropertySets* is zero, this argument is ignored.

For information about the properties in the Index property group that are defined by OLE DB, see "Properties Table (by Property Groups)" in Appendix C, "Property Tables." For information about the DBPROPSET and DBPROP structures, see "DBPROPSET Structure" and "DBPROP Structure" in Chapter 11, "Properties."

ppIndexID
[out]
A pointer to memory in which to return a pointer to the DBID of a newly created index. If *ppIndexID* is a null pointer, no DBID is returned.

Return Code

S_OK
The method succeeded and the new index has been created. In all DBPROP structures passed to the method, *dwStatus* is set to DBPROPSTATUS_OK.

DB_S_ERRORSOCCURRED
The index was created, but one or more properties—for which the *dwOptions* element of the DBPROP structure was DBPROPOPTIONS_OPTIONAL—were not set. The consumer checks *dwStatus* in the DBPROP structures to determine which properties were not set. The method can fail to set properties for a number of reasons, including:

- The property was not supported by the provider.
- The property was not in the Index property group.
- The property set was not supported by the provider.
- It was not possible to set the property.
- The *colid* in the DBPROP structure was not DB_NULLID.
- The data type in *vValue* in the DBPROP structure was not the data type of the property or was not VT_EMPTY.
- The value in *vValue* in the DBPROP structure was invalid.
- The property's value conflicted with an existing property.

DB_E_TABLEINUSE
The specified table was in use, and the provider could not create the index with the table open.

E_FAIL
A provider-specific error occurred.

E_INVALIDARG
pTableID was a null pointer.

pIndexID and *ppIndexID* were both null pointers.

cIndexColumnDescs was zero.

rgIndexColumnDescs was a null pointer.

eIndexColOrder in an element of *rgIndexColumnDescs* was not a valid value.

cPropertySets was not zero and *rgPropertySets* was a null pointer.

In an element of *rgPropertySets*, *cProperties* was not zero and *rgProperties* was a null pointer.

DB_E_BADCOLUMNID
A column specified in an element of *rgIndexColumnDescs* did not exist.

DB_E_BADINDEXID
pIndexID was an invalid index ID.

DB_E_DUPLICATEINDEXID
The specified index already exists in the data store.

DB_E_ERRORSOCCURRED
No index was created because one or more properties—for which the *dwOptions* element of the DBPROP structure was DBPROPOPTIONS_REQUIRED or an invalid value—were not set. The consumer checks *dwStatus* in the DBPROP structures to determine which properties were not set. None of the satisfiable properties are remembered. The method can fail to set properties for any of the reasons specified in DB_S_ERRORSOCCURRED.

DB_E_NOTABLE
The specified table does not exist in the data store.

DB_SEC_E_PERMISSIONDENIED
The consumer did not have sufficient permission to create the index.

Comments

If **CreateIndex** returns any errors, the index is not created and *ppIndexID* is set to NULL on output.

See Also

IIndexDefinition::DropIndex, **IRowsetIndex**, **ITableDefinition**

IIndexDefinition::DropIndex

Drops an index from the base table.

```
HRESULT DropIndex(
   DBID *pTableID,
   DBID *pIndexID);
```

Parameters

pTableID
[in]
A pointer to the DBID of the base table.

pIndexID
[in]
A pointer to the DBID of the index to drop. This must be an index on the table specified with *pTableID*. If *pIndexId* is a null pointer, all indexes for the table specified with *pTableID* are dropped.

Return Code

S_OK
The method succeeded, and the index has been dropped from the base table.

DB_S_ERRORSOCCURRED
pIndexID was a null pointer, at least one index was successfully dropped, but one or more indexes for the specified table could not be dropped. The consumer can determine the set of indexes not dropped through the INDEXES schema rowset.

E_FAIL
A provider-specific error occurred.

E_INVALIDARG
pTableID was a null pointer.

DB_E_ERRORSOCCURRED
pIndexID was a null pointer, but none of the indexes for the specified table could be dropped.

DB_E_INDEXINUSE
The specified index was in use.

DB_E_NOINDEX
The specified index does not exist in the current data store or did not apply to the specified table.

DB_E_NOTABLE
The specified table does not exist in the current data store.

DB_E_TABLEINUSE
The specified table was in use, and the provider could not drop the index with the table open.

DB_SEC_E_PERMISSIONDENIED
The consumer did not have sufficient permission to drop the index.

Comments

For partitioned indexes, a call to this method drops all partitions.

If **DropIndex** returns any errors, the index is not dropped.

If *pIndexID* is a null pointer and one or more indexes for that table cannot be dropped, the processing continues to attempt to drop the remaining indexes for that table.

See Also

IIndexDefinition::CreateIndex

IMultipleResults

IMultipleResults is used to retrieve multiple results (rowsets or row counts) created by a command. For more information, see "Multiple Results" in Chapter 3, "Commands."

When to Implement

IMultipleResults is a mandatory interface on multiple results objects. Providers specify whether they support multiple results objects and what restrictions they have on these objects through the DBPROP_MULTIPLERESULTS property in the Data Source Information property group.

When to Call

To create a multiple results object, a consumer creates a command, sets the command text, and calls **ICommand::Execute** with *riid* set to **IID_IMultipleResults**. The command text generally specifies multiple results, although this is not required. To retrieve each result in succession, the consumer repeatedly calls **IMultipleResults::GetResult**.

Method	Description
GetResult	Returns the next in a series of multiple results from the provider.

IMultipleResults::GetResult

Returns the next in a series of multiple results from the provider.

```
HRESULT GetResult(
   IUnknown *  pUnkOuter,
   LONG        lReserved,
   REFIID      riid,
   LONG *      pcRowsAffected,
   IUnknown ** ppRowset);
```

Parameters

pUnkOuter
[in]
A pointer to the controlling **IUnknown** interface if the object is being created as part of an aggregate; otherwise, it is a null pointer.

lReserved
[in]
Reserved. Must be set to zero.

riid
[in]
The requested interface to return in **ppRowset*. This interface is conceptually added to the list of required interfaces on the resulting rowset, and the method fails (E_NOINTERFACE) if that interface cannot be supported on the resulting rowset.

If this is IID_NULL, *ppRowset* is ignored and no rowset is returned, even if one exists.

pcRowsAffected
[out]
A pointer to memory in which to return the count of rows affected by an update, delete, or insert. If the value of *cParamSets* passed into **ICommand::Execute** was greater than 1, **pcRowsAffected* is the total number of rows affected by all of the sets of parameters represented by the current result. If the count of affected rows is not available, **pcRowsAffected* is set to DB_COUNTUNAVAILABLE on output. If the result is not a count of rows affected by an update, delete, or insert, **pcRowsAffected* is undefined on output. If an error occurs, **pcRowsAffected* is set to DB_COUNTUNAVAILABLE. If *pcRowsAffected* is a null pointer, no count of affected rows is returned.

Some providers do not support returning individual counts of rows but instead return an overall count of the total rows affected by the call to **Execute**, or do not return row counts at all. Such providers set **pcRowsAffected* to DB_COUNTUNAVAILABLE when the count of affected rows is not available.

ppRowset

[out]
A pointer to memory in which to return the interface for the next result. If the next result is not a rowset (for example, if it is the count of the rows affected by an update, delete, or insert), this is set to a null pointer. If an error occurs, **ppRowset* is set to a null pointer.

If *ppRowset* is a null pointer, no rowset is created.

Return Code

S_OK
The method succeeded.

DB_S_ERRORSOCCURRED
This can be returned for either of the following reasons:

- An error occurred, returning one or more output parameter values associated with the next result. To determine which output parameters were not returned, the consumer checks the status values. For a list of status values that can be returned by this method, see "Status Values Used When Getting Data" in " Status" in Chapter 6, "Getting and Setting Data."
- The rowset was opened, but one or more properties—for which the *dwOptions* element of the DBPROP structure was DBPROPOPTIONS_OPTIONAL—were not set. The consumer calls **IRowsetInfo::GetProperties** to determine which properties were set.

DB_S_NORESULT
There are no more results. **ppRowset* is set to a null pointer and **pcRowsAffected* is set to –1.

DB_S_STOPLIMITREACHED
Execution has been stopped because a resource limit has been reached. The results obtained so far have been returned. Calling **GetResult** again returns information for the next result or returns DB_S_NORESULT if no more results can be obtained, either because they do not exist or because the resource limit applies across multiple results.

This return code takes precedence over DB_S_ERRORSOCCURRED. That is, if the conditions described here and those described in DB_S_ERRORSOCCURRED both occur, the provider returns this code. When the consumer receives this return code, it should also check for the conditions described in DB_S_ERRORSOCCURRED.

E_FAIL
A provider-specific error occurred.

E_INVALIDARG
lReserved was not zero.

E_NOINTERFACE
The interface specified in *riid* was not supported on the rowset.

E_OUTOFMEMORY
The provider was unable to allocate sufficient memory in which to create the rowset.

E_UNEXPECTED
ITransaction::Commit or **ITransaction::Abort** was called, and the object is in a zombie state.

DB_E_ABORTLIMITREACHED
Execution has been aborted because a resource limit has been reached. No results have been returned. Calling **GetResult** again returns information for the next result or returns DB_S_NORESULT if no more results can be obtained, either because they do not exist or because the resource limit applies across multiple results.

DB_E_CANTCONVERTVALUE
A literal value in the command text associated with the next result could not be converted to the type of the associated column for reasons other than data overflow.

DB_E_DATAOVERFLOW
A literal value in the command text associated with the next result overflowed the type specified by the associated column.

DB_E_ERRORSINCOMMAND
The command text associated with the next result contained one or more errors. Providers should use OLE DB error objects to return details about the errors.

DB_E_ERRORSOCCURRED
The method failed due to one or more invalid input parameter values associated with the next result. To determine which input parameter values were invalid, the consumer checks the status values. For a list of status values that can be returned by this method, see "Status Values Used When Setting Data" in "Status" in Chapter 6, "Getting and Setting Data."

The rowset was not returned because one or more properties—for which the *dwOptions* element of the DBPROP structure was DBPROPOPTIONS_REQUIRED or an invalid value—could not be satisfied.

DB_E_INTEGRITYVIOLATION
A literal value in the command text associated with the next result violated the integrity constraints for the column.

DB_E_NOAGGREGATION
pUnkOuter was not a null pointer, and the provider is an OLE DB 1.0 or 1.1 provider that does not support aggregation of the object being created.

pUnkOuter was not a null pointer, and *riid* was not **IID_IUnknown**.

DB_E_OBJECTOPEN
The previous rowset is still open, and the provider does not support multiple open results simultaneously. (DBPROP_MULTIPLERESULTS is DBPROPVAL_MR_SUPPORTED.)

DB_SEC_E_PERMISSIONDENIED
The consumer did not have sufficient permission to get the next result.

Comments

GetResult returns the next in a series of multiple results from the provider. If the next result is the result of a row-returning command or operation, such as an SQL **SELECT** statement, the result of this method is a rowset over the result rows. If no rows match the command, the rowset is still created. The resulting rowset is fully functional and can be used, for example, to insert new rows or determine column metadata. If the next result is the result of a non-row-returning command, such as an SQL **INSERT** statement, **ppRowset* is set to NULL and **pcRowsAffected* is set to the count of rows affected, if applicable.

Providers will generally be able to process only one result at a time. For maximum interoperability, consumers should free any rowset obtained by a previous call to **GetResult** before requesting the next result.

Providers may check the entire command text for errors at execute time or may check the command text associated with each result when that result is retrieved. Therefore, the syntax errors returned by **ICommand::Execute** can also be returned by **GetResult**. In this case, the next call to **GetResult** moves on to the next result or returns DB_S_NORESULT if no more results are available.

When **GetResult** returns an error, its behavior depends on the error that occurred:

- If **GetResult** returns E_INVALIDARG, DB_E_NOAGGREGATION or DB_E_OBJECTOPEN, the current result is still available. Assuming there are no other errors, the next call to **GetResult** returns the current result.
- If **GetResult** returns any other error, the current result is lost. The next call to **GetResult** returns either the next result or DB_S_NORESULT if the error caused the provider to lose all remaining results. Providers that can recover the current result in this situation must discard it and return the next result.

The following example shows how a consumer might process multiple results:

```
hr = pICommandText->Execute(pUnkOuter, IID_IMultipleResults, pParams, &cRowsAffected,
                            &pIMultipleResults);

if (pIMultipleResults) {
   while(hr != DB_S_NORESULT) {
      if(SUCCEEDED(hr = pIMultipleResults->GetResult(pUnkOuter, 0, IID_IRowset,
                    &cRowsAffected, &pIRowset))) {
         if(pIRowset) {
            // The next result is a rowset. Process the rowset.
            pIRowset->Release();
         } else {
            // The next result is not a rowset. Process the nonrowset result.
         }
      } else {
         // Process error from GetResult
         break;
      }
   }
   pIMultipleResults->Release();
}
```

See Also

ICommand::Execute

IOpenRowset

IOpenRowset is a required interface on the session. It can be supported by providers that do not support creating rowsets through commands.

The **IOpenRowset** model enables consumers to open and work directly with individual tables or indexes in a data store by using **IOpenRowset::OpenRowset**, which generates a rowset of all rows in the table or index.

Method	Description
OpenRowset	Opens and returns a rowset that includes all rows from a single base table or index.

IOpenRowset::OpenRowset

Opens and returns a rowset that includes all rows from a single base table or index.

```
HRESULT OpenRowset(
   IUnknown *      pUnkOuter,
   DBID *          pTableID,
   DBID *          pIndexID,
   REFIID          riid,
   ULONG           cPropertySets,
   DBPROPSET       rgPropertySets[],
   IUnknown **     ppRowset);
```

Parameters

pUnkOuter
[in]
The controlling **IUnknown** if the rowset is to be aggregated; otherwise, a null pointer.

pTableID
[in]
The DBID of the table to open. For more information, see the "Comments" section.

pIndexID
[in]
The DBID of the index to open. For more information, see the "Comments" section.

riid
[in]
The IID of the interface to return in **ppRowset*. This interface is conceptually added to the list of required interfaces on the resulting rowset, and the method fails (E_NOINTERFACE) if that interface cannot be supported on the resulting rowset. This must be an interface that the rowset supports, even when *ppRowset* is set to a null pointer and no rowset is created.

cPropertySets
[in]
The number of DBPROPSET structures in *rgPropertySets*. If this is zero, the provider ignores *rgPropertySets*.

rgPropertySets
[in/out]
An array of DBPROPSET structures containing properties and values to be set. The properties specified in these structures must belong to the Rowset property group. If the same property is specified more than once in *rgPropertySets*, it is provider-specific which value is used. If *cPropertySets* is zero, this argument is ignored.

For information about the properties in the Rowset property group that are defined by OLE DB, see "Properties Table (by Property Groups)" in Appendix C, "Property Tables." For information about the DBPROPSET and DBPROP structures, see "DBPROPSET Structure" and "DBPROP Structure" in Chapter 11, "Properties."

ppRowset
[in/out]
A pointer to memory in which to return the interface pointer to the created rowset. If *ppRowset* is a null pointer, no rowset is created; properties are verified and if a required property cannot be set, DB_E_ERRORSOCCURRED is returned. If **OpenRowset** fails, **ppRowset* is set to a null pointer.

Return Code

S_OK
The method succeeded and the rowset is opened. In all DBPROP structures passed to the method, *dwStatus* is set to DBPROPSTATUS_OK.

DB_S_ASYNCHRONOUS
The method has initiated asynchronous creation of the rowset. The consumer can call **IDBAsynchStatus** to poll for status or **IConnectionPointContainer** to obtain the **IID_IDBAsynchNotify** connection point. Attempting to call any other interfaces may fail, and the full set of interfaces may not be available on the object until asynchronous initialization of the rowset has completed.

DB_S_ERRORSOCCURRED
The rowset was opened, but one or more properties—for which the *dwOptions* element of the DBPROP structure was DBPROPOPTIONS_OPTIONAL—were not set. The consumer checks *dwStatus* in the DBPROP structures to determine which properties were not set. The method can fail to set properties for a number of reasons, including:

- *colid* in the DBPROP structure was invalid.
- The data type in *vValue* in the DBPROP structure was not the data type of the property or was not VT_EMPTY.
- The value in *vValue* in the DBPROP structure was invalid.
- The property's value conflicted with an existing property.
- A property was specified to be applied to all columns but could not be applied to one or more columns.
- The property was not supported by the provider.
- It was not possible to set the property.

DB_S_STOPLIMITREACHED
Execution has been stopped because a resource limit has been reached. The results obtained so far have been returned. This return code takes precedence over DB_S_ERRORSOCCURRED; that is, if the conditions descrbed here and in those described in DB_S_ERRORSOCCURRED both occur, the provider returns this code. When the consumer receives this return code, it should also check for the conditions described in DB_S_ERRORSOCCURRED.

E_FAIL
A provider-specific error occurred.

E_INVALIDARG
pTableID and *pIndexID* were both null pointers.

cPropertySets was not zero and *prgPropertySets* was a null pointer.

In an element of *rgPropertySets*, *cProperties* was not zero and *rgProperties* was a null pointer.

E_NOINTERFACE
The rowset did not support the interface specified in *riid* or *riid* was IID_NULL.

DB_E_ERRORSOCCURRED
No rowset was returned because one or more properties—for which the *dwOptions* element of the DBPROP structure was DBPROPOPTIONS_REQUIRED or an invalid value—were not set. The consumer checks *dwStatus* in the DBPROP structures to determine which properties were not set. None of the satisfiable properties are remembered. The method can fail to set properties for any of the reasons specified in DB_S_ERRORSOCCURRED.

DB_E_ABORTLIMITREACHED
The method failed because a resource limit has been reached. For example, a query used to implement the method timed out. No rowset is returned.

DB_E_NOAGGREGATION
pUnkOuter was not a null pointer, and the provider is an OLE DB 1.0 or 1.1 provider that does not support aggregation of the rowset object being created.

pUnkOuter was not a null pointer, and *riid* was not **IID_IUnknown**.

DB_E_NOINDEX
The specified index does not exist in the current data store or did not apply to the specified table.

The provider does not support opening indexes through **IOpenRowset**.

DB_E_NOTABLE
The specified table does not exist in the data store.

DB_E_PARAMNOTOPTIONAL
The table specified by *pTableID* is a procedure that requires one or more parameters.

DB_SEC_E_PERMISSIONDENIED
The consumer did not have sufficient permission to open the rowset. For example, a rowset included a column for which the consumer does not have read permission.

DB_E_OBJECTOPEN
The provider would have to open a new connection to support the operation, and DBPROP_MULTIPLECONNECTIONS is set to VARIANT_FALSE.

Comments

If the table or index has no rows, the rowset is still created. The resulting rowset is fully functional and can be used, for example, to insert new rows or determine column metadata.

pTableID and *pIndexID* are used in the following combinations:

- If *pTableID* is not a null pointer and *pIndexID* is a null pointer, the table identified by **pTableID* is opened.
- If *pTableID* is a null pointer and *pIndexID* is not a null pointer, **pIndexID* must uniquely and fully identify an index; this index is opened. If **pIndexID* does not uniquely and fully identify an index, DB_E_NOINDEX is returned.
- If neither *pTableID* nor *pIndexID* is a null pointer, **pIndexID* must identify an index for the table identified by **pTableID*; this index is opened. If **pIndexID* does not identify an index for the table identified by **pTableID*, DB_E_NOINDEX is returned.
- If both *pTableID* and *pIndexID* are null pointers, E_INVALIDARG is returned.

The threading model of the returned rowset is determined by the property DBPROP_ROWTHREADMODEL.

See Also

IDBCreateCommand::CreateCommand

IParentRowset

IParentRowset is used to retrieve child rowsets from a hierarchical rowset. For more information, see "Hierarchical Rowsets" in Chapter 4, "Rowsets."

When to Implement

IParentRowset is a mandatory interface on a hierarchical rowset.

When to Call

The consumer calls **IParentRowset::GetChildRowset** to create an aggregated instance of the child rowset corresponding to a chapter-valued column in the parent rowset.

Method	Description
GetChildRowset	Returns the child rowset corresponding to a chapter-valued column in the parent rowset.

IParentRowset::GetChildRowset

Returns the child rowset corresponding to a chapter-valued column in the parent rowset.

```
HRESULT GetChildRowset(
   IUnknown *      pUnkOuter,
   ULONG           iOrdinal,
   REFIID          riid,
   IUnknown **     ppRowset);
```

Parameters

pUnkOuter
[in]
A pointer to the controlling **IUnknown** interface if the object is being created as part of an aggregate; otherwise, it is a null pointer.

iOrdinal
[in]
The ordinal of the chapter-valued column in the parent rowset.

riid
[in]
The requested interface to return in **ppRowset*.

ppRowset
[out]
A pointer to memory in which to return the interface for the child rowset. If an error occurs, **ppRowset* is set to a null pointer.

Return Value

S_OK
The method succeeded.

E_INVALIDARG
ppRowset was a null pointer.

E_NOINTERFACE
The interface specified in *riid* was not supported on the rowset.

E_OUTOFMEMORY
The provider was unable to allocate sufficient memory in which to create the rowset.

E_UNEXPECTED
ITransaction::Commit or **ITransaction::Abort** was called, and the object is in a zombie state.

DB_E_NOAGGREGATION

pUnkOuter was not a null pointer, and the provider is an OLE DB 1.0 or 1.1 provider that does not support aggregation of the rowset object being created.

pUnkOuter was not a null pointer, and *riid* was not **IID_IUnknown**.

DB_E_OBJECTOPEN

The referenced rowset has already been opened.

The provider is single-chaptered, and a child rowset is still open.

DB_E_BADORDINAL

The column specified by *iOrdinal* was not a chapter-valued column or did not exist.

Comments

GetChildRowset can be called only once for each child rowset and, if called, must be called before any calls to **GetReferencedRowset** for that child. The *pUnkOuter* argument specified in **GetChildRowset** defines the controlling unknown for all references to that child rowset for the lifetime of the parent. The parent rowset must use *addref* on this controlling unknown to guarantee that it doesn't go away before the parent. Even though the controlling unknown is constant for the lifetime of the parent, the consumer must not assume that rowset state, such as accessors, row position, and so on, are held when all references to the rowset are released. Furthermore, providers must ensure that the next fetch position within the child rowset is reset once all references to that child rowset have been released. Calling **GetChildRowset** for a child rowset that has already been obtained returns DB_E_OBJECTOPEN.

See Also

IRowsetInfo::GetReferencedRowset

IRowset

IRowset is the base rowset interface. It provides methods for fetching rows sequentially, getting the data from those rows, and managing rows.

IRowset requires **IAccessor** and **IRowsetInfo**.

When to Implement

IRowset is required for all providers that support general consumers.

When to Call

Consumers use the methods in **IRowset** for all basic rowset operations, including fetching and releasing rows and getting column values.

When a consumer first gets an interface pointer on a rowset, usually its first step is to determine the rowset's capabilities using **IRowsetInfo::GetProperties**. This returns information about the interfaces exposed by the rowset as well as those capabilities of the rowset which do not show up as distinct interfaces, such as the maximum number of active rows and how many rows can have pending updates at the same time.

For most consumers, the next step is to determine the characteristics, or metadata, of the columns in the rowset. For this, they use either **IColumnsInfo** or **IColumnsRowset**, for simple or extended column information, respectively. These interfaces are also available on prepared commands prior to execution, allowing advance planning.

The consumer determines which columns it needs, either from the metadata or on the basis of knowing the text command that generated the rowset. It determines the ordinals of the needed columns from the ordering of the column information returned by **IColumnsInfo** or from ordinals in the column metadata rowset returned by **IColumnsRowset**.

Some consumers do not use a command or do not want to browse the column information; they may know the name or property identifier for the columns they want to use. They call **IColumnsInfo**::**MapColumnIDs** to retrieve the column ordinals.

The ordinals are used to specify a binding to a column. A binding is a structure that associates an element of the consumer's structure with a column. The binding can bind the column's data value, length, and status value. For more information about bindings, see "Bindings" in Chapter 6, "Getting and Setting Data."

A set of bindings is gathered together in an *accessor*, which is created with **IAccessor::CreateAccessor**. An accessor can contain multiple bindings so that the data for multiple columns can be retrieved or set in a single call. The consumer can create several accessors to match different usage patterns in different parts of the application. It can create and release accessors at any time while the rowset remains in existence. For more information about accessors, see "Accessors" in Chapter 6, "Getting and Setting Data."

To fetch rows from the database, the consumer calls a method such as **GetNextRows** or **IRowsetLocate::GetRowsAt**. To create and initialize a new row to be inserted into the data store, the consumer calls **IRowsetChange::InsertRow**.

The methods that fetch rows do not actually return data to the consumer. Instead, they return the handles to these rows, and a local copy of the rows is stored in the rowset.

After the rows are returned, the consumer can access the data in the rows. The consumer calls **GetData** and passes it the handle to a row, the handle to an accessor, and a pointer to a consumer-allocated buffer. **GetData** converts the data (if it does not match the native provider storage) and returns the columns as specified in the bindings used to create the accessor. The consumer can call **GetData** more than once for a row, using different accessors and buffers; thus, the consumer can have multiple copies of the same data. For example, if a column contains a text document, the consumer might call **GetData** with an accessor that binds the first 50 bytes of the document. When the user double-clicks on the displayed heading text, the consumer could then call **GetData** with a different accessor to retrieve the entire document.

Data from variable-length columns may be treated several ways. First, such columns can be bound to a finite section of the consumer's structure, which causes truncation when the length of the data exceeds the length of the buffer. The consumer can determine that truncation has occurred by checking if the status is DBSTATUS_S_TRUNCATED. The returned length is always the true length in bytes, so the consumer also can determine how much data was truncated. Another way to obtain data from such columns is by reference. For example, if a binary column is bound with a type indicator of DBTYPE_BYTES | DBTYPE_BYREF, the provider allocates memory for all of the data in the column and returns this memory to the consumer.

In both cases, it is likely that such large values may be best optimized as deferred columns and accessed only when necessary. Performance varies with different servers, but in general, BLOB columns are stored separately from other records and may be more costly to access than ordinary columns, so they would not routinely be pulled in for browsing or scanning. For more information, see "Deferred Columns" in Chapter 4, "Rowsets."

Another way to handle BLOB columns may be implemented on some providers, and that is to request they be delivered as COM objects that expose **ILockBytes**, **IStorage**, **ISequentialStream**, or **IStream** interfaces. For more information, see "BLOBs as Storage Objects" in Chapter 7, "BLOBs and COM Objects."

For a description of how to update and delete rows, see Chapter 5, "Updating Data in Rowsets."

When the consumer is finished fetching or updating rows, it releases them with **ReleaseRows**. This releases resources from the rowset's copy of the rows and makes room for new rows. The consumer can then repeat its cycle of fetching or creating rows and accessing the data in them.

When the consumer is done with the rowset, it calls **IAccessor::ReleaseAccessor** to release any accessors. It calls **IUnknown::Release** on all interfaces exposed by the rowset to release the rowset. When the rowset is released, it forces the release of any remaining rows or accessors the consumer may hold. Such handle objects are subordinate to the rowset. That is, they do not take reference counts upon the rowset and cannot cause the rowset to linger beyond the point where all the interfaces for the rowset have been released. The rowset must clean up all such subordinate objects.

> **Note** If the rowset was generated as a result of executing a command that contained output parameters and the provider populates output parameters when the rowset is released (that is, DBPROP_OUTPUTPARAMETERAVAILABILITY is DBPROP_OA_ATROWRELEASE), the memory for the output parameters bound at **Execute** time must be valid when the rowset is released. Not doing so is considered a serious programming error and likely will cause a crash.

Method	Description
AddRefRows	Adds a reference count to an existing row handle.
GetData	Retrieves data from the rowset's copy of the row.
GetNextRows	Fetches rows sequentially, remembering the previous position.
ReleaseRows	Releases rows.
RestartPosition	Repositions the next fetch position to its initial position; that is, its position when the rowset was first created.

IRowset::AddRefRows

Adds a reference count to an existing row handle.

```
HRESULT AddRefRows(
   ULONG          cRows,
   const HROW     rghRows[],
   ULONG          rgRefCounts[],
   DBROWSTATUS    rgRowStatus[]);
```

Parameters

cRows
[in]
The number of rows for which to increment the reference count.

rghRows
[in]
An array of row handles for which to increment the reference count. The reference count of row handles is incremented by one for each time they appear in the array.

rgRefCounts
[out]
An array with *cRows* elements in which to return the new reference count for each row handle. The consumer allocates memory for this array. If *rgRefCounts* is a null pointer, no reference counts are returned.

rgRowStatus
[out]
An array with *cRows* elements in which to return values indicating the status of each row specified in *rghRows*. If no errors occur while incrementing the reference count of a row, the corresponding element of *rgRowStatus* is set to DBROWSTATUS_S_OK. If an error occurs while incrementing the reference count of a row, the corresponding element is set as specified in DB_S_ERRORSOCCURRED. The consumer allocates memory for this array. If *rgRowStatus* is a null pointer, no row statuses are returned. For information about the DBROWSTATUS enumerated type, see "Arrays of Errors" in Chapter 13, "Errors."

Return Code

S_OK
The method succeeded. The reference count of all rows was successfully incremented. The following value can be returned in **prgRowStatus*:

- The reference count of the row was successfully incremented. The corresponding element of **prgRowStatus* contains DBROWSTATUS_S_OK.

DB_S_ERRORSOCCURRED
An error occurred while incrementing the reference count of a row, but the reference count of at least one row was incremented. Successes can occur for the reason listed under S_OK. The following errors can occur:

- A row handle was invalid. The reference count of the row was not incremented, and the corresponding element of *rgRowStatus* contains DBROWSTATUS_E_INVALID.
- A row handle referred to a row that had a reference count of zero. The reference count of the row was not incremented, and the corresponding element of *rgRowStatus* contains DBROWSTATUS_E_INVALID.
- A row handle referred to a row for which a deletion had been transmitted to the data store. The reference count of the row was not incremented, and the corresponding element of *rgRowStatus* contains DBROWSTATUS_E_DELETED.
- The consumer encountered a recoverable, provider-specific error, such as an RPC failure when transmitting the change to a remote server. The corresponding element of *rgRowStatus* contains DBROWSTATUS_E_FAIL.

E_FAIL
A provider-specific error occurred.

E_INVALIDARG
rghRows was a null pointer and *cRows* was not zero.

E_UNEXPECTED
ITransaction::Commit or **ITransaction::Abort** was called, and the object is in a zombie state.

DB_E_ERRORSOCCURRED
Errors occurred while incrementing the reference count of all of the rows. Errors can occur for the reasons listed under DB_S_ERRORSOCCURRED.

Comments

AddRefRows must be supported for implementing multiple references to the same row even if the rowset does not support **IRowsetIdentity**.

It is always possible for a consumer to call **AddRefRows** while it is processing a method in **IRowsetNotify**. That is, the rowset must be reentrant through **AddRefRows** during notification.

If **AddRefRows** encounters an error while incrementing the reference count of a row, it sets the corresponding element in *rgRowStatus* to the appropriate DBROWSTATUS value and continues processing.

If a row handle is duplicated in *rghRows*, the corresponding row will have its reference count incremented by 1 for each time it appears in the array.

See Also

IRowset::ReleaseRows

IRowset::GetData

Retrieves data from the rowset's copy of the row.

```
HRESULT GetData (
   HROW         hRow,
   HACCESSOR    hAccessor,
   void *       pData);
```

Parameters

hRow

[in]

The handle of the row from which to get the data.

> **Caution** The consumer must ensure that *hRow* contains a valid row handle; the provider might not validate *hRow* before using it. The result of passing the handle of a deleted row is provider-specific, although the provider cannot terminate abnormally. For example, the provider might return DB_E_BADROWHANDLE, DB_E_DELETEDROW, or it might get data from a different row. The result of passing an invalid row handle in *hRow* is undefined.

hAccessor

[in]

The handle of the accessor to use. If *hAccessor* is the handle of a null accessor (*cBindings* in **IAccessor::CreateAccessor** was zero), **GetData** does not get any data values.

> **Caution** The consumer must ensure that *hAccessor* contains a valid accessor handle; the provider might not validate *hAccessor* before using it. The result of passing an invalid accessor handle in *hAccessor* is undefined.

pData

[out]

A pointer to a buffer in which to return the data. The consumer allocates memory for this buffer. This pointer must be a valid pointer to a contiguous block of consumer-owned memory into which the data will be written.

Return Code

S_OK
The method succeeded. The status of all columns bound by the accessor is set to DBSTATUS_S_OK, DBSTATUS_S_ISNULL, or DBSTATUS_S_TRUNCATED.

DB_S_ERRORSOCCURRED
An error occurred while returning data for one or more columns, but data was successfully returned for at least one column. To determine the columns for which data was returned, the consumer checks the status values. For a list of status values that can be returned by this method, see "Status Values Used When Getting Data" in "Status" in Chapter 6, "Getting and Setting Data."

E_FAIL
A provider-specific error occurred.

E_INVALIDARG
pData was a null pointer and the accessor was not a null accessor.

E_UNEXPECTED
ITransaction::Commit or **ITransaction::Abort** was called, and the object is in a zombie state.

DB_E_BADACCESSORHANDLE
hAccessor was invalid. Providers are not required to check for this condition, because doing so might slow the method significantly.

DB_E_BADACCESSORTYPE
The specified accessor was not a row accessor.

DB_E_BADROWHANDLE
hRow was invalid. Providers are not required to check for this condition, because doing so might slow the method significantly.

DB_E_DELETEDROW
hRow referred to a pending delete row or a row for which a deletion had been transmitted to the data store. Providers are not required to check for this condition, because doing so might slow the method significantly.

DB_E_ERRORSOCCURRED
Errors occurred while returning data for all columns. To determine what errors occurred, the consumer checks the status values. For a list of status values that can be returned by this method, see "Status Values Used When Getting Data" in "Status" in Chapter 6, "Getting and Setting Data."

If this method performs deferred accessor validation and that validation takes place before any data is transferred, it can also return any of the following return codes for the reasons listed in the corresponding DBBINDSTATUS values in **IAccessor::CreateAccessor**:

E_NOINTERFACE
DB_E_BADBINDINFO
DB_E_BADORDINAL
DB_E_BADSTORAGEFLAGS
DB_E_UNSUPPORTEDCONVERSION

Comments

This method makes no logical change to the state of the object.

A consumer calls **GetData** to retrieve data from rows that have been fetched by prior calls to methods such as **GetNextRows**. For a complete description of how **GetData** retrieves data, see "Getting Data" in Chapter 6, "Getting and Setting Data."

A consumer can call **GetData** any number of times. In each call, it can pass a different accessor and the address of a different buffer. This means that the consumer can get as many copies of the data as it wants, and it can get data in different types if alternate conversions are available.

GetData does not enforce any security restrictions. The provider must not create a rowset that includes columns for which the consumer does not have read privileges, so **GetData** never encounters problems accessing the data for a column. The rowset can contain columns to which the consumer does not have write permission if DBPROP_COLUMNRESTRICT is VARIANT_TRUE. The methods that fetch rows must not return the handles of rows for which the consumer does not have read privileges, so **GetData** never encounters problems accessing a row. Such rows might exist if the DBPROP_ROWRESTRICT property is VARIANT_TRUE.

If **GetData** fails, the memory to which *pData* points is not freed but its contents are undefined. If before **GetData** failed the provider allocated any memory for return to the consumer, the provider frees this memory and does not return it to the consumer.

GetData must be reentrant during notifications. If the provider calls a method from **IRowsetNotify** in the consumer, the consumer must be able to call **GetData** while processing the notification method.

The following example shows how a reference accessor is used.

```
#include <oledb.h>
#include <stddef.h>

IRowset *   TheRowset;
IAccessor * TheRowsetAccessor;
HROW        hRow;

int main() {
   struct ExactlyTheSame {
      long     l;
      double   d;
      short    i;
   };
   HACCESSOR   hRawAccess;

   static DBBINDING ExactBindings [3] = {
      {
         1,                               // iOrdinal
         offsetof (ExactlyTheSame,l),     // obValue
         0,                               // No length binding
         0,                               // No Status binding
         NULL,                            // No TypeInfo
         NULL,                            // No Object
         NULL,                            // No Extensions
         DBPART_VALUE,
         DBMEMOWNER_PROVIDEROWNED,        // Ignored
         DBPARAMIO_NOTPARAM,
         sizeof (long),
         0,
         DBTYPE_I4,
         0,                               // No Precision
         0                                // No Scale
      },
```

```
      {
         2,                               // iOrdinal
         offsetof (ExactlyTheSame, d),    // obValue
         0,                               // No length binding
         0,                               // No Status binding
         NULL,                            // No TypeInfo
         NULL,                            // No Object
         NULL,                            // No Extensions
         DBPART_VALUE,
         DBMEMOWNER_PROVIDEROWNED,        // Ignored
         DBPARAMIO_NOTPARAM,
         sizeof (double),
         0,
         DBTYPE_R8,
         0,                               // No Precision
         0                                // No Scale
      },
      {
         3,                               // iOrdinal
         offsetof (ExactlyTheSame,i),     // obValue
         0,                               // No length binding
         0,                               // No Status binding
         NULL,                            // No TypeInfo
         NULL,                            // No Object
         NULL,                            // No Extensions
         DBPART_VALUE,
         DBMEMOWNER_PROVIDEROWNED,        // Ignored
         DBPARAMIO_NOTPARAM,
         sizeof (short),
         0,
         DBTYPE_I2,
         0,                               // No Precision
         0                                // No Scale
      }
   };

   TheRowsetAccessor->CreateAccessor (DBACCESSOR_PASSBYREF, 3, ExactBindings, 0,
                                      &hRawAccess, NULL);
```

To read the column *i* of some row, the consumer should do the following:

```
short              value;
ExactlyTheSame *   pRow;

TheRowset->GetData(hRow, hRawAccess, &pRow);

value = pRow->i;
```

The following example shows how provider-owned memory is used:

```
#include <oledb.h>
#include <stddef.h>

IRowset *    TheRowset;
IAccessor *  TheRowsetAccessor;
HROW         hRow;

int main() {
   struct IndirectlySimilar {
      long *      pl;
      double *    pd;
      short *     pi;
   };
   HACCESSOR hFastAccess;

   static DBBINDING IndirectBindings [3] = {
      {
         1,                                  // iOrdinal
         offsetof (IndirectlySimilar, pl),   // obValue
         0,                                  // No length binding
         0,                                  // No Status binding
         NULL,                               // No TypeInfo
         NULL,                               // No Object
         NULL,                               // No Extensions
         DBPART_VALUE,
         DBMEMOWNER_PROVIDEROWNED,
         DBPARAMIO_NOTPARAM,
         sizeof (long*),
         0,
         DBTYPE_BYREF|DBTYPE_I4,
         0,                                  // No Precision
         0                                   // No Scale
      },
```

```
   {
      2,                                  // iOrdinal
      offsetof (IndirectlySimilar, pd),   // obValue
      0,                                  // No length binding
      0,                                  // No Status binding
      NULL,                               // No TypeInfo
      NULL,                               // No Object
      NULL,                               // No Extensions
      DBPART_VALUE,
      DBMEMOWNER_PROVIDEROWNED,
      DBPARAMIO_NOTPARAM,
      sizeof (double*),
      0,
      DBTYPE_BYREF|DBTYPE_R8,
      0,                                  // No Precision
      0                                   // No Scale
   },
   {
      3,                                  // iOrdinal
      offsetof (IndirectlySimilar,pi),    // obValue
      0,                                  // No length binding
      0,                                  // No Status binding
      NULL,                               // No TypeInfo
      NULL,                               // No Object
      NULL,                               // No Extensions
      DBPART_VALUE,
      DBMEMOWNER_PROVIDEROWNED,
      DBPARAMIO_NOTPARAM,
      sizeof(short*),
      0,
      DBTYPE_BYREF|DBTYPE_I2,
      0,                                  // No Precision
      0                                   // No Scale
   }
};

TheRowsetAccessor->CreateAccessor (DBACCESSOR_ROWDATA, 3, IndirectBindings, 0,
                                   &hFastAccess, NULL );
```

To read the column *i* of some row, the consumer should do the following:

```
short                value;
IndirectlySimilar    rowPs;

TheRowset->GetData (hRow, hFastAccess, &rowPs);

if (rowPs.pi)           // Avoid null pointers
   value = *(rowPs.pi);
```

See Also

IRowset::GetNextRows, **IRowsetChange::SetData**

IRowset::GetNextRows

Fetches rows sequentially, remembering the previous position.

```
HRESULT GetNextRows (
   HCHAPTER    hChapter,
   LONG        lRowsOffset,
   LONG        cRows,
   ULONG *     pcRowsObtained,
   HROW **     prghRows);
```

Parameters

hChapter
[in]
The chapter handle. For nonchaptered rowsets, the caller must set *hChapter* to DB_NULL_HCHAPTER.

lRowsOffset
[in]
The signed count of rows to skip before fetching rows. Deleted rows that the provider has removed from the rowset are not counted in the skip. If this value is zero and *cRows* continues in the same direction as the previous call to either **GetNextRows** or **FindNextRow** with a null *pBookmark* value, the first row fetched will be the next row after the last one fetched in the previous call. If this value is zero and *cRows* reverses direction, the first row fetched will be the last one fetched in the previous call.

lRowsOffset can be a negative number only if the value of the DBPROP_CANSCROLLBACKWARDS property is VARIANT_TRUE.

There is no guarantee that skipping rows is done efficiently on a sequential rowset. If the data store resides on a remote server, there may be remote support for skipping without transferring the intervening records across the network, but this is not guaranteed. For information about how the provider implements skipping, see the documentation for the provider.

cRows
[in]
The number of rows to fetch. A negative number means to fetch backward. *cRows* can be a negative number only if the value of the DBPROP_CANFETCHBACKWARDS property is VARIANT_TRUE.

If *cRows* is zero, no rows are fetched; the fetch direction and the next fetch position are unchanged, and the provider performs no processing, returning immediately from the method invocation. Specifically, *lRowsOffset* is ignored in this situation.

If the provider does not discover any other errors, the method returns S_OK; whether the provider checks for any other errors is provider-specific.

pcRowsObtained
[out]
A pointer to memory in which to return the actual number of fetched rows. If a warning condition occurs, this number may be less than the number of rows available or requested and is the number of rows actually fetched before the warning condition occurred. If the consumer has insufficient permission to fetch all rows, **GetNextRows** fetches all rows for which the consumer has sufficient permission and skips all other rows. If the method fails, **pcRowsObtained* is set to zero.

prghRows
[out]
A pointer to memory in which to return an array of handles of the fetched rows. If **prghRows* is not a null pointer on input, it must be a pointer to memory large enough to return the handles of the requested number of rows. If **prghRows* is a null pointer on input, the rowset allocates memory for the row handles and returns the address to this memory; the consumer releases this memory with **IMalloc::Free** after it releases the row handles. If **prghRows* is a null pointer on input and **pcRowsObtained* is zero on output or if the method fails, the provider does not allocate any memory and ensures that **prghRows* is a null pointer on output.

Return Code

S_OK
The method succeeded.

DB_S_ENDOFROWSET
GetNextRows reached the start or the end of the rowset or chapter or the start or end of the range on an index rowset and could not fetch all requested rows because the count extended beyond the end. The next fetch position is before the start or after the end of the rowset. The number of rows actually fetched is returned in **pcRowsObtained*; this will be less than *cRows*.

The rowset is being populated asynchronously, and no additional rows are available at this time. To determine whether additional rows may be available, the consumer should call **IDBAsynchStatus::GetStatus** or listen for the **IDBAsynchNotify::OnStop** notification.

lRowsOffset indicated a position either more than one row before the first row of the rowset or more than one row after the last row, and the provider was a version 2.0 or greater provider. **pcRowsObtained* is set to zero and no rows are returned.

DB_S_ROWLIMITEXCEEDED
Fetching the number of rows specified in *cRows* would have exceeded the total number of active rows supported by the rowset. The number of rows that were actually fetched is returned in **pcRowsObtained*. This condition can occur only when there are more rows available than can be handled by the rowset. Therefore, this condition never conflicts with those described in DB_S_ENDOFROWSET and DB_S_STOPLIMITREACHED, both of which imply that no more rows were available.

DB_S_STOPLIMITREACHED
Fetching rows required further execution of the command, such as when the rowset uses a server-side cursor. Execution has been stopped because a resource limit has been reached. The number of rows that were actually fetched is returned in **pcRowsObtained*.

E_FAIL
A provider-specific error occurred.

E_INVALIDARG
pcRowsObtained or *prghRows* was a null pointer.

E_OUTOFMEMORY
The provider was unable to allocate sufficient memory to complete the request.

E_UNEXPECTED
ITransaction::Commit or **ITransaction::Abort** was called, and the object is in a zombie state.

DB_E_BADCHAPTER
The rowset was chaptered and *hChapter* was invalid.

The rowset was single-chaptered, and the specified chapter was not the currently open chapter. The consumer must use the currently open chapter or release the currently open chapter before specifying a new chapter.

DB_E_BADSTARTPOSITION
lRowsOffset indicated a position either more than one row before the first row of the rowset or more than one row after the last row, and the provider was a 1.*x* provider,

DB_E_CANCELED
Fetching rows was canceled during notification. No rows were fetched.

DB_E_CANTFETCHBACKWARDS
cRows was negative and the rowset cannot fetch backward.

DB_E_CANTSCROLLBACKWARDS
lRowsOffset was negative and the rowset cannot scroll backward.

DB_E_NOTREENTRANT
The provider called a method from **IRowsetNofity** in the consumer that had not yet returned, and the provider does not support reentrancy in this method.

DB_E_ROWSNOTRELEASED

The provider requires release of existing rows before new ones can be fetched. For more information, see DBPROP_CANHOLDROWS in "Properties Table (Alphabetical)" in Appendix C, "Property Tables."

DB_SEC_E_PERMISSIONDENIED

The consumer did not have sufficient permission to fetch any of the rows; no rows were fetched.

Comments

GetNextRows fetches a sequence of rows. The provider maintains a *next fetch position* that is used in subsequent calls to either **GetNextRows** or **FindNextRow**. The next fetch position is changed either by calling **GetNextRows** or by calling **FindNextRow** with a null *pBookmark* value. Calling **FindNextRow** with a non-null *pBookmark* value has no effect on the next fetch position. If the fetch direction is reversed from the previous call, the next fetch position in the new direction is the last row that was fetched in the previous direction. Otherwise, the next fetch position is the row following the last row fetched by **GetNextRows** or by **FindNextRow** with a null *pBookmark* value.

For a newly created rowset, the next fetch position is computed as follows, where *N* is the number of rows in the rowset. *lRowsOffset* can be less than zero only if DBPROP_CANSCROLLBACKWARDS is VARIANT_TRUE.

Value of *lRowsOffset*	Next fetch position
lRowsOffset > 0	After *lRowsOffset*
lRowsOffset < 0	After *N* – abs(*lRowsOffset*)
lRowsOffset = 0	Before first row if *cRows* > 0, after last row if *cRows* < 0

For example:

GetNextRows call	Row fetched	New next fetch position
`GetNextRows(hReserved, 2, 1, pcRowsObtained, prghRows);`	3rd row	After 3rd row
`GetNextRows(hReserved, 2, -1, pcRowsObtained, prghRows);`	2nd row	After 1st row
`GetNextRows(hReserved, -2, 1, pcRowsObtained, prghRows);`	*N* – 1st row	After *N* – 1st row
`GetNextRows(hReserved, -2, -1, pcRowsObtained, prghRows);`	*N* – 2nd row	After *N* – 3rd row

None of the other methods that fetch rows, except for **IRowsetFind::FindNextRow** with a null *pBookmark* value, has any effect on the next fetch position. However, **IRowsetIndex::Seek** sets the next fetch position to the row specified in the seek criteria, and **RestartPosition** resets the next fetch position to the same position as when the rowset is first created.

GetNextRows increments the reference count of each row for which it returns a handle by 1. Therefore, if a handle is returned for a row that has already been fetched, the reference count of that row will be greater than 1. **ReleaseRows** must be called once for each time the handle to a row has been returned.

If the provider encounters a problem fetching a row—for example, data stored in a text file contains a letter in a numeric column—**GetNextRows** fetches the row normally, returns the row handle, and returns S_OK. However, when the consumer calls **GetData** for the row, the provider returns DBSTATUS_E_CANTCONVERTVALUE as the status for the offending column.

GetNextRows must always check for the conditions that cause E_INVALIDARG, E_UNEXPECTED, DB_E_CANTFETCHBACKWARDS, DB_E_CANTSCROLLBACKWARDS, DB_E_NOTREENTRANT, and DB_E_ROWSNOTRELEASED before changing the next fetch position. If it returns any other error besides these, the next fetch position is unknown. For example, the provider might have to perform actions that change the next fetch position in order to determine that the error DB_E_BADSTARTPOSITION occurred. When the next fetch position is unknown, the consumer usually calls **RestartPosition** to return it to a known position.

For information about what **GetNextRows** does when it fetches a row that it already has in its internal buffers, see "Uniqueness of Rows in the Rowset" in Chapter 4, "Rowsets." For information about whether **GetNextRows** can detect changes made to rows in the rowset, see "Visibility of Changes" in Chapter 5, "Updating Data in Rowsets."

See Also

IRowset::GetData, **IRowsetLocate::GetRowsAt**, **IRowsetLocate::GetRowsByBookmark**, **IRowsetScroll::GetRowsAtRatio**

IRowset::ReleaseRows

Releases rows.

```
HRESULT ReleaseRows (
   ULONG          cRows,
   const HROW     rghRows[],
   DBROWOPTIONS   rgRowOptions[]
   ULONG          rgRefCounts[],
   DBROWSTATUS    rgRowStatus[]);
```

Parameters

cRows
[in]
The number of rows to release. If *cRows* is zero, **ReleaseRows** does not do anything.

rghRows
[in]
An array of handles of the rows to be released. The row handles need not form a logical cluster; they may have been obtained at separate times and need not be for contiguous underlying rows. They must belong to the current thread. Row handles are decremented by one reference count for each time they appear in the array.

rgRowOptions
[in]
An array of *cRows* elements containing bitmasks indicating additional options to be specified when releasing a row. This parameter is reserved for future use and should be set to a null pointer.

```
typedef DWORD DBROWOPTIONS;
```

rgRefCounts
[out]
An array with *cRows* elements in which to return the new reference count of each row. If *rgRefCounts* is a null pointer, no counts are returned. The consumer allocates, but is not required to initialize, memory for this array and passes the address of this memory to the provider. The provider returns the reference counts in the array.

rgRowStatus
[out]
An array with *cRows* elements in which to return values indicating the status of each row specified in *rghRows*. If no errors or warnings occur while releasing a row, the corresponding element of *rgRowStatus* is set to DBROWSTATUS_S_OK. If an error or warning occurs while releasing a row, the corresponding element is set as specified in DB_S_ERRORSOCCURRED. The consumer allocates memory for this array. If *rgRowStatus* is a null pointer, no row statuses are returned. For information about the DBROWSTATUS enumerated type, see "Arrays of Errors" in Chapter 13, "Errors."

Return Code

S_OK
The method succeeded. All rows were successfully released. The following values can be returned in **prgRowStatus*:

- The row was successfully released. The corresponding element of **prgRowStatus* contains DBROWSTATUS_S_OK.
- A row had a pending change. The row was released, and the corresponding element of *rgRowStatus* contains DBROWSTATUS_S_PENDINGCHANGES.

DB_S_ERRORSOCCURRED
An error occurred while releasing a row, but at least one row was successfully released. Successes and warnings can occur for the reasons listed under S_OK. The following errors can occur:

- A row handle was invalid. The row was not released, and the corresponding element of *rgRowStatus* contains DBROWSTATUS_E_INVALID.
- The consumer encountered a recoverable, provider-specific error, such as an RPC failure when transmitting the change to a remote server. The corresponding element of *rgRowStatus* contains DBROWSTATUS_E_FAIL.

E_FAIL
A provider-specific error occurred.

E_INVALIDARG
rghRows was a null pointer and *cRows* was not equal to zero.

DB_E_ERRORSOCCURRED
Errors occurred while releasing all of the rows. Errors can occur for the reasons listed under DB_S_ERRORSOCCURRED.

DB_E_NOTREENTRANT
The provider called a method from **IRowsetNofity** in the consumer that had not yet returned, and the provider does not support reentrancy in this method.

Comments

ReleaseRows decreases the reference count on the specified rows. It must be called once for each time that a row was fetched. For example, if the row was fetched three times, **ReleaseRows** must be called three times. Furthermore, if a row handle is duplicated in *rghRows*, the corresponding row will have its reference count decremented by one for each time it appears in the array.

If a provider doesn't support exact reference counts on rows, it should return a reference count of 1 while the row is active. Consumers should be aware of this behavior and should use the returned reference count for debugging purposes only; consumers should not rely on the returned reference count to indicate whether the row would survive another release.

In this case, a provider may choose to return S_OK for any and all calls to **ReleaseRows** until the rowset itself is released.

If a consumer calls **ReleaseRows** on a row with pending changes, the row remains valid and **ReleaseRows** returns DBROWSTATUS_S_PENDINGCHANGES in *rgRowStatus*.

When the reference count for a row decreases to zero, the row is released:

- Subject to the rules of the current transaction, the rowset is free to discard any resources used by a row that has a reference count of zero. For example, these might include memory, locks, and original values. When the rowset actually discards these resources is provider-specific.
- If the row has pending changes, the row still remains valid even though its reference count is zero. Consumers should not use the handle of a row that has a reference count of zero, even though the handle might still be valid. If **IRowsetUpdate::Update** is called to transmit pending changes for a row with a reference count of zero to the data store, it transmits the changes of the row and releases the row and its resources if the update succeeds. If **IRowsetUpdate::Undo** is called to undo the pending changes for a row with a reference count of zero, it releases the row and its resources.
- Pending changes are not lost when releasing a reference count obtained from **GetRowsAt**. A provider may take its own reference count on the row handle or store the row internally until pending changes are committed or dismissed (using **Update** or **Undo**).

After a row is released, methods called with the handle to that row return DB_E_BADROWHANDLE if the row has pending changes. After the pending changes are transmitted to the data store, methods might continue to return this error. However, the provider might have an implementation that recycles row handles and thereafter cannot detect the misuse. Because provider behavior varies, consumers should not use the handles of released rows.

If **ReleaseRows** encounters an error while decrementing the reference count of a row or releasing the row, it sets the corresponding element in *rgRowStatus* to the appropriate DBROWSTATUS value and continues processing.

This method can be called while the rowset is in a zombie state to allow the consumer to clean up after a transaction has been committed or aborted.

See Also

IRowset::AddRefRows

IRowset::RestartPosition

Repositions the next fetch position used by **GetNextRows** or **FindNextRow** to its initial position; that is, its position when the rowset was first created.

```
HRESULT RestartPosition (
   HCHAPTER hChapter);
```

Parameters

hChapter
[in]
The chapter handle. For nonchaptered rowsets, the caller must set *hChapter* to DB_NULL_HCHAPTER.

Return Code

S_OK
The method succeeded. The provider did not have to reexecute the command, either because the rowset supports positioning on the first row without reexecuting the command or because the rowset is already positioned on the first row.

DB_S_COLUMNSCHANGED
The order of the columns was not specified in the object that created the rowset. The provider had to reexecute the command to reposition the next fetch position to its initial position, and the order of the columns changed.

The provider had to reexecute the command to reposition the next fetch position to its initial position, and columns were added or removed from the rowset. This is generally due to a change in the underlying schema and is extremely uncommon.

This return code takes precedence over DB_S_COMMANDREEXECUTED. That is, if the conditions described here and in those described in DB_S_COMMANDREEXECUTED both occur, the provider returns this code. A change to the columns generally implies that the command was reexecuted.

DB_S_COMMANDREEXECUTED
The command associated with this rowset was reexecuted. If the properties DBPROP_OWNINSERT and DBPROP_OWNUPDATEDELETE are VARIANT_TRUE, the consumer will see its own changes. If the properties DBPROP_OWNINSERT or DBPROP_OWNUPDATEDELETE are VARIANT_FALSE, the rowset may see its changes. The order of the columns remains unchanged.

E_FAIL
A provider-specific error occurred.

E_UNEXPECTED
ITransaction::Commit or **ITransaction::Abort** was called, and the object is in a zombie state.

DB_E_BADCHAPTER
The rowset was chaptered and *hChapter* was invalid.

The rowset was single-chaptered, and the specified chapter was not the currently open chapter. The consumer must use the currently open chapter or release the currently open chapter before specifying a new chapter.

DB_E_CANCELED
RestartPosition was canceled during notification. The next fetch position remains unmodified.

DB_E_CANNOTRESTART
The rowset was built over a live data stream (for example, a stock feed), and the position cannot be restarted.

DB_E_NOTREENTRANT
The provider called a method from **IRowsetNofity** in the consumer that had not yet returned, and the provider does not support reentrancy in this method.

DB_E_ROWSNOTRELEASED
The provider requires release of existing rows before restarting because the rowset will be regenerated. This may be required even if the provider supports a value of VARIANT_TRUE for DBPROP_CANHOLDROWS. For more information, see DBPROP_CANHOLDROWS and DPPROP_QUICKRESTART in "Properties Table (Alphabetical)" in Appendix C, "Property Tables."

DB_SEC_E_PERMISSIONDENIED
The consumer did not have sufficient permission to reposition the next fetch position.

Comments

For information about the next fetch position when the rowset is first created, see **IRowset::GetNextRows**.

If the underlying command contains output parameters, **RestartPosition** should not reset those parameters.

If the rowset was generated as a result of a procedure call and the rowset is forward-only, the procedure may be reexecuted in order to satisfy the call to **RestartPosition**. This may cause other side effects. Additionally, if the stored procedure has been changed, the rowset may have a different schema. If the rowset is able to restart the next fetch position without reexecuting the procedure, **RestartPosition** should not reexecute it.

How expensive **RestartPosition** is depends on the provider, the rowset characteristics, and the tables underlying the rowset. If the rowset supports **IRowsetLocate**, **RestartPosition** is always an inexpensive operation.

If thc rowset is sequential, **RestartPosition** might require reexecution of the underlying command. For some providers, this is always the case. For other providers, a rule of thumb is that rowsets built from a single table are not expensive to restart, but rowsets built by joining two or more tables are expensive to restart. If the provider reexecutes the command to restart the next fetch position, the new rowset might return a different set of rows, differently ordered columns, and in extreme cases, a different set of columns. Reexecution of a command by **RestartPosition** does not reinherit accessors.

A provider that reports DBPROP_QUICKRESTART as VARIANT_FALSE may require that all existing row handles are released prior to successfully processing a call to **RestartPosition**.

A consumer can determine whether a provider can quickly restart the next fetch position by attempting to set DBPROP_QUICKRESTART to VARIANT_TRUE. Setting this property to VARIANT_TRUE does not guarantee that the rowset can be quickly restarted because the provider is not required to honor the property. This behavior is necessary because the provider cannot evaluate the command at the time the property is set. For example, the consumer can set DBPROP_QUICKRESTART to VARIANT_TRUE and then change the command text.

In implementations that require reexecution of a command to reposition the next fetch position to its initial position, the provider is responsible for caching all parameters required by the command.

If **RestartPosition** returns DB_S_COLUMNSCHANGED and the consumer subsequently calls methods in **IColumnsInfo** or **IColumnsRowset**, these methods must reflect the new metadata. Existing rowset accessors are not updated to reflect the new metadata. That is, **IAccessor::GetBindings** returns exactly the same information it would have returned before **RestartPosition** was called. If such accessors are subsequently used, such as in a call to **GetData**, the provider must revalidate them. If none of the columns bound by the accessor have changed, the accessor can be used successfully. If any of the columns have changed, the appropriate error or warning is returned.

See Also

IRowset::GetNextRows, **IRowsetFind::FindNextRow**

IRowsetChange

The methods in **IRowsetChange** are used to update the values of columns in existing rows, delete existing rows, and insert new rows.

IRowsetChange requires **IAccessor** and **IRowset**.

When to Implement

Rowsets implement **IRowsetChange** if they support updating, deleting, or inserting rows. They are not required to support all three but must support at least one of these operations to support **IRowsetChange**. The rowset reports which operations it supports through the DBPROP_UPDATABILITY property.

To request updatability of the rowset, the consumer should set DBPROP_IROWSETCHANGE to VARIANT_TRUE and specify the desired updatability in the DBPROP_UPDATABILITY rowset property when creating the rowset.

When to Call

The consumer calls methods in **IRowsetChange** to modify rows as follows.

- **SetData** sets column data in an existing row.
- **DeleteRows** deletes existing rows.
- **InsertRow** creates a new row and sets initial values.

SetData and **InsertRow** require the use of an accessor. For more information about accessors, see "Accessors" in Chapter 6, "Getting and Setting Data."

SetData and **InsertRow** can fail for a number of reasons. The most common of these is that new data values do not meet the schema or integrity constraints of the column. Furthermore, rowsets can have row-by-row and column-by-column access permissions that override the general permissions of the table or column. For more information, see the DBPROP_COLUMNRESTRICT and DBPROP_ROWRESTRICT properties in "Properties Table (Alphabetical)" in Appendix C, "Property Tables."

If **IRowsetUpdate** is exposed on the rowset, changes made through **IRowsetChange** are buffered in the rowset and not transmitted to the data store until **IRowsetUpdate::Update** is called; this is known as *delayed update mode*. If **IRowsetUpdate** is not exposed on the rowset, changes made through **IRowsetChange** are immediately transmitted to the data store; this is known as *immediate update mode*. For more information, see "Changing Data" in Chapter 5, "Updating Data in Rowsets."

Method	Description
DeleteRows	Deletes rows.
InsertRow	Creates and initializes a new row.
SetData	Sets data in one or more columns in a row.

IRowsetChange::DeleteRows

Deletes rows.

```
HRESULT DeleteRows (
   HCHAPTER       hChapter,
   ULONG          cRows,
   const HROW     rghRows[],
   DBROWSTATUS    rgRowStatus[]);
```

Parameters

hChapter

[in]

The chapter handle. For nonchaptered rowsets, the caller must set *hChapter* to DB_NULL_HCHAPTER.

cRows

[in]

The number of rows to be deleted. If *cRows* is zero, **DeleteRows** does not do anything.

rghRows

[in]

An array of handles of the rows to be deleted.

If *rghRows* includes a duplicate row handle, **DeleteRows** behaves as follows. If the row handle is valid, it is provider-specific whether the returned row status information for each row or a single instance of the row is set to DBROWSTATUS_S_OK. If the row handle is invalid, the row status information for each occurrence of the row contains the appropriate error.

rgRowStatus

[out]

An array with *cRows* elements in which to return values indicating the status of each row specified in *rghRows*. If no errors or warnings occur while deleting a row, the corresponding element of *rgRowStatus* is set to DBROWSTATUS_S_OK. If a warning occurs while deleting a row, the corresponding element is set as specified in S_OK. If an error occurs while deleting a row, the corresponding element is set as specified in DB_S_ERRORSOCCURRED. The consumer allocates memory for this array. If *rgRowStatus* is a null pointer, no row statusinformation is returned. For information about the DBROWSTATUS enumerated type, see "Arrays of Errors" in Chapter 13, "Errors."

Return Code

S_OK
The method succeeded. All rows were successfully deleted. The following values can be returned in *rgRowStatus*:

- The row was successfully deleted and no warning conditions occurred. The corresponding element of *rgRowStatus* contains DBROWSTATUS_S_OK.
- The rowset was in immediate update mode, and deleting a single row caused more than one row to be deleted in the data store. For more information, see the DBPROP_REPORTMULTIPLECHANGES property. The corresponding element of *rgRowStatus* contains DBROWSTATUS_S_MULTIPLECHANGES.

DB_S_ERRORSOCCURRED
An error occurred while deleting a row, but at least one row was successfully deleted. Successes and warnings can occur for the reasons listed under S_OK. The following errors can occur:

- An element of *rghRows* was invalid or was a row handle to which the current thread does not have access rights. The corresponding element of *rgRowStatus* contains DBROWSTATUS_E_INVALID.
- Deletion of a row was canceled during notification. The row was not deleted and the corresponding element of *rgRowStatus* contains DBROWSTATUS_E_CANCELED.
- An element of *rghRows* referred to a row with a pending delete or for which a deletion had been transmitted to the data store. The corresponding element of *rgRowStatus* contains DBROWSTATUS_E_DELETED.
- Deleting a row referred to by an element of *rghRows* violated the integrity constraints for the column or table. The corresponding element of *rgRowStatus* contains DBROWSTATUS_E_INTEGRITYVIOLATION.
- The rowset was in immediate update mode, and the row was not deleted due to reaching a limit on the server, such as a query execution timing out. The error in the corresponding element of *rgRowStatus* contains DBROWSTATUS_E_LIMITREACHED.
- Deleting a row would exceed the limit for pending changes specified by the rowset property DBPROP_MAXPENDINGROWS. The corresponding element of *rgRowStatus* contains DBROWSTATUS_E_MAXPENDCHANGESEXCEEDED.
- DBPROP_CHANGEINSERTEDROWS was VARIANT_FALSE, and an element of *rghRows* referred to a row for which the insertion has been transmitted to the data store. The corresponding element of *rgRowStatus* contains DBROWSTATUS_E_NEWLYINSERTED.

- The consumer did not have sufficient permission to delete a row. This error can be returned only if the value of the DBPROP_ROWRESTRICT property is VARIANT_TRUE. The corresponding element of *rgRowStatus* contains DBROWSTATUS_E_PERMISSIONDENIED. If the rowset is in delayed update mode, this error might not be returned until **IRowsetUpdate::Update** is called.
- The consumer encountered a recoverable, provider-specific error, such as an RPC failure when transmitting the change to a remote server. The corresponding element of *rgRowStatus* contains DBROWSTATUS_E_FAIL.

E_FAIL
A provider-specific error occurred.

E_INVALIDARG
rghRows was a null pointer, and *cRows* was greater than or equal to one.

E_UNEXPECTED
ITransaction::Commit or **ITransaction::Abort** was called, and the object is in a zombie state.

DB_E_BADCHAPTER
The rowset was chaptered and *hChapter* was invalid.

The rowset was single-chaptered, and the specified chapter was not the currently open chapter. The consumer must use the currently open chapter or release the currently open chapter before specifying a new chapter.

DB_E_ERRORSOCCURRED
Errors occurred while deleting all of the rows. Errors can occur for the reasons listed under DB_S_ERRORSOCCURRED.

DB_E_NOTREENTRANT
The consumer called this method while it was processing a notification, and it is an error to call this method while processing the specified DBREASON value.

DB_E_NOTSUPPORTED
The provider does not support this method.

Comments

In delayed update mode, **DeleteRows** marks rows for deletion rather than actually deleting them. Rows with pending deletes cannot be used in any methods except **IRowsetRefresh::GetLastVisibleData**, **IRowsetUpdate::Undo, IRowsetUpdate::Update**, **IRowsetUpdate::GetOriginalData**, and **IRowset::ReleaseRows**. The deletion is not transmitted to the data store until **Update** is called. In immediate update mode, **DeleteRows** transmits deletions to the data store immediately. For more information, see "Changing Data" in Chapter 5, "Updating Data in Rowsets."

After a deletion has been transmitted to the data store, it cannot be undone. The row cannot be used with any method except **ReleaseRows**. Neither **DeleteRows** nor **Update** release rows after transmitting deletions to the data store. The consumer must release the row with **ReleaseRows**.

If **DeleteRows** is called for a row with a pending insert, the row is placed in the same state as a row for which a deletion has been transmitted to the data store. That is, if a row is inserted and then deleted in delayed update mode, the deletion cannot be undone. The row cannot be used with any method except **ReleaseRows**, which must be called to release it.

If an error occurs while deleting a row, **DeleteRows** continues deleting the other rows in *rghRows* and returns DB_S_ERRORSOCCURRED or DB_E_ERRORSOCCURRED. It returns status information about each row in *rgRowStatus*.

If the DBPROP_ROWRESTRICT property is VARIANT_TRUE, the consumer may have permission to delete some rows but not other rows.

See Also

IRowsetUpdate::Undo, **IRowsetUpdate::Update**

IRowsetChange::InsertRow

Creates and initializes a new row.

```
HRESULT InsertRow (
   HCHAPTER    hChapter,
   HACCESSOR   hAccessor,
   void *      pData,
   HROW  *     phRow);
```

Parameters

hChapter
[in]
The chapter handle. For nonchaptered rowsets, the caller must set *hChapter* to DB_NULL_HCHAPTER.

hAccessor
[in]
The handle of the accessor to use.

If *hAccessor* is a null accessor (that is, an accessor for which *cBindings* in **IAccessor::CreateAccessor** was zero), *pData* is ignored and the rows are initialized as specified in the Comments. Thus, the role of a null accessor is to construct a default row; it is a convenient way for a consumer to obtain a handle for a new row without having to set any values in that row initially.

pData
[in]
A pointer to memory containing the new data values, at offsets that correspond to the bindings in the accessor.

phRow
[out]
A pointer to memory in which to return the handle of the new row. If this is a null pointer, no reference count is held on the row. Consumers should set this to null if they do not require the ability to make further changes to, or retrieve data from, the newly inserted row. Whether or not default or computed values from the server are available when calling **GetData** for this row handle depends on the setting of the DBPROP_SERVERDATAONINSERT. If **InsertRow** returns an error, and *phRow* is not a null pointer on input, **phRow* is set to null on output and no row handle is returned.

Note Passing in a null pointer for *phRow* or releasing the row handle returned in **phRow* does not release the row until the change is transmitted to the data store. If DBPROP_CANHOLDROWS is VARIANT_FALSE and the rowset is in deferred update mode, then in addition to freeing any reference counts on the row handle, the consumer must call **IRowsetUpdate::Update** in order to transmit the pending change to the data store before attempting to insert or retrieve any additional rows.

Return Code

S_OK
The method succeeded. The status of all columns bound by the accessor is set to DBSTATUS_S_OK or DBSTATUS_S_ISNULL.

DB_S_ERRORSOCCURRED
An error occurred while setting data for one or more columns, but data was successfully set for at least one column. To determine the columns for which values were invalid, the consumer checks the status values. For a list of status values that can be returned by this method, see "Status Values Used When Setting Data" in Chapter 6, "Getting and Setting Data."

E_FAIL
A provider-specific error occurred.

E_INVALIDARG
pData was a null pointer, and *hAccessor* was not a null accessor.

E_OUTOFMEMORY
The provider was unable to allocate sufficient memory in which to instantiate the row.

E_UNEXPECTED
ITransaction::Commit or **ITransaction::Abort** was called, and the object is in a zombie state.

DB_E_ABORTLIMITREACHED
The rowset was in immediate update mode, and the row was not inserted due to reaching a limit on the server, such as a query execution timing out.

DB_E_BADACCESSORHANDLE
hAccessor was invalid.

DB_E_BADACCESSORTYPE
The specified accessor was not a row accessor or was a reference accessor.

DB_E_BADCHAPTER
The rowset was chaptered and *hChapter* was invalid.

The rowset was single-chaptered, and the specified chapter was not the currently open chapter. The consumer must use the currently open chapter or release the currently open chapter before specifying a new chapter.

DB_E_CANCELED
The insertion was canceled during notification. The row was not inserted.

DB_E_CANTCONVERTVALUE
The data value for one or more columns couldn't be converted for reasons other than sign mismatch or data overflow, and the provider was unable to determine which columns couldn't be converted. Providers that can detect which columns could not be converted return DB_S_ERRORSOCCURRED and set the status flag for the columns that couldn't be converted to DBSTATUS_E_CANTCONVERTVALUE.

DB_E_DATAOVERFLOW
Conversion failed because the data value for one or more columns overflowed the type used by the provider and the provider was unable to determine which columns caused the overflow. Providers that can detect which columns caused the overflow return DB_S_ERRORSOCCURRED and set the status flag for the columns in violation to DBSTATUS_E_DATAOVERFLOW.

DB_E_ERRORSOCCURRED
An error occurred while setting data for one or more columns, and data was not successfully set for any columns. To determine the columns for which values were invalid, the consumer checks the status values. For a list of status values that can be returned by this method, see "Status Values Used When Setting Data" in Chapter 6, "Getting and Setting Data."

DB_E_INTEGRITYVIOLATION
The data violated the integrity constraints for one or more columns of the rowset, and the provider was unable to determine which columns violated the integrity constraints. Providers that can detect which columns violated the integrity constraints return DB_S_ERRORSOCCURRED and set the status flag for the columns in violation to DBSTATUS_E_INTEGRITYVIOLATION.

DB_E_MAXPENDCHANGESEXCEEDED
The number of rows that have pending changes has exceeded the limit specified by the DBPROP_MAXPENDINGROWS property.

DB_E_NOTREENTRANT
The provider called a method from **IRowsetNotify** in the consumer, and the method has not yet returned.

DB_E_NOTSUPPORTED
The provider does not support this method.

DB_E_ROWLIMITEXCEEDED
Creating another row would have exceeded the total number of active rows supported by the rowset.

DB_E_ROWSNOTRELEASED
The consumer attempted to insert a new row before releasing previously retrieved row handles or transmitting pending changes to the data store, and DBPROP_CANHOLDROWS is VARIANT_FALSE.

DB_SEC_E_PERMISSIONDENIED
The consumer did not have sufficient permission to insert a new row. This error can be returned only if the value of the DBPROP_ROWRESTRICT property is VARIANT_TRUE. If the rowset is in delayed update mode, this error might not be returned until **IRowsetUpdate::Update** is called.

If this method performs deferred accessor validation and that validation takes place before any data is transferred, it can also return any of the following return codes for the applicable reasons listed in the corresponding DBBINDSTATUS values in **IAccessor::CreateAccessor**:

E_NOINTERFACE
DB_E_BADBINDINFO
DB_E_BADORDINAL
DB_E_BADSTORAGEFLAGS
DB_E_UNSUPPORTEDCONVERSION

Comments

InsertRow creates a new row and initializes its columns. If *phRow* is not a null pointer, it then returns the handle of this row to the consumer and sets its reference count to one. In delayed update mode, the row is created locally to the rowset and is transmitted to the data store only when **IRowsetUpdate::Update** is called. In immediate update mode, the row is immediately transmitted to the data store. For more information, see "Changing Data" in Chapter 5, "Updating Data in Rowsets."

To the consumer, newly inserted rows are almost indistinguishable from other rows. For example, they can be deleted with **DeleteRows** and updated with **SetData**. However, methods that fetch rows might not be able to return them. Furthermore, they might not contain the correct values for computed columns, including bookmark columns on some providers. For more information, see "Visibility of Pending Changes" and "Visibility of Transmitted Changes" in Chapter 5, "Updating Data in Rowsets."

The DBPROP_COLUMNRESTRICT and DBPROP_ROWRESTRICT properties affect how security is enforced and how security errors are returned. If DBPROP_COLUMNRESTRICT is VARIANT_TRUE, the consumer might not have write permission on some columns. If the consumer attempts to write to these columns, **InsertRow** returns a column status of DBSTATUS_E_PERMISSIONDENIED and a return code of DB_S_ERRORSOCCURRED. If the DBPROP_ROWRESTRICT property is VARIANT_TRUE, the consumer might not have permission to insert some rows. If the consumer attempts to insert one of these rows, **InsertRow** returns a code of DB_SEC_E_PERMISSIONDENIED and no new row is created.

When a row is created, initialization proceeds in an orderly fashion:

1. The provider sets all columns to their default values. If there is no default value and the column is nullable, it sets the column to NULL. If the column is non-nullable, it sets the column status to DBSTATUS_E_UNAVAILABLE. If the provider is unable or unwilling to determine the default value of a column or whether that column is nullable, it sets the column status to DBSTATUS_E_UNAVAILABLE; the provider might be unwilling to determine default values and nullability if doing so requires a call to the data store.

   If the column status is DBSTATUS_E_UNAVAILABLE, the consumer can still send this value to the data store to use the default. In this case, the default is available after the insertion is transmitted to the data store. To see the default, the consumer must call **GetLastVisibleData** or **RefreshVisibleData**. However, if there is no default for the column and it is non-nullable, this will cause a schema violation.

2. The provider calls **IRowsetNotify::OnRowChange** with DBREASON_ROW_INSERT if any consumer of the rowset is using notifications. This serves as a hook allowing, among other things, more complex nondeclarative default values to be set in the row. For more information about notifications, see **IRowsetNotify**.

3. **InsertRow** does not further modify the column values if the accessor is a null accessor; it returns the handle to the newly created row.

4. The provider uses the accessor, if it is not a null accessor, to set columns with the values provided by the consumer in **pData*. During this process, the provider does not generate notifications as it does when setting data in **SetData**. This prevents, for example, DBREASON_COLUMN_SET notifications from being generated for a row that is not yet properly constructed. For a complete description of how **InsertRow** sets data, see "Setting Data" in Chapter 6, "Getting and Setting Data."

   The provider is not required to compute the value of computed columns. If the provider does not compute the value of these columns but lets the data store do so, then the computed value is not available until after the change is transmitted to the data store—that is, after **InsertRow** is called in immediate update mode or after **IRowsetUpdate::Update** if **InsertRow** is called in delayed update mode. To retrieve the computed value, the consumer calls **RefreshVisibleData** or **GetLastVisibleData** in **IRowsetRefresh**. Note that bookmark columns are often computed, such as when the bookmark is the primary key or is a ROWID assigned by the data store.

Domain and schema validation is enforced as it is with **SetData**.

If **InsertRow** returns an error, it does not create a new row.

The use of null accessors is not recommended because some providers may not be able to determine default values and may not be able to identify a row inserted with all default values.

Here is an example of how one might write a projection-join to a temporary file:

```
#include <oledb.h>
#include <stddef.h>
int main() {
   IRowset *          pLeftRowset;
   IRowset *          pRightRowset;
   IAccessor *        pLeftRowsetAcc;
   IAccessor *        pRightRowsetAcc;
   IAccessor *        pJoinRowsetAcc;
   IRowsetChange *    pJoinRowsetNew;
   ULONG              cSortedRows;
   HROW               rghLeftRows [500];
   HROW               rghRightRows [500];
   //...
   // < Sort and prepare the rows >
   //..

   struct join {
      long *   pl;
      double * pd;
      short *  pi;
   };

   static DBBINDING LeftBindings [1] = {
      {
         1,
         offsetof (join, pl),
         0,                                 // No length binding
         0,                                 // No status binding
         NULL,                              // No TypeInfo
         NULL,                              // No object
         NULL,                              // No extensions
         DBPART_VALUE,
         DBMEMOWNER_PROVIDEROWNED,
         DBPARAMIO_NOTPARAM,
         sizeof (void*),
         0,
         DBTYPE_I4 | DBTYPE_BYREF,
         0,                                 // No precision
         0                                  // No scale
      }
   };
```

```
static DBBINDING RightBindings [2]= {
   {
      1,
      offsetof (join, pd),
      0,                                // No length binding
      0,                                // No status binding
      NULL,                             // No TypeInfo
      NULL,                             // No object
      NULL,                             // No extensions
      DBPART_VALUE,
      DBMEMOWNER_PROVIDEROWNED,
      DBPARAMIO_NOTPARAM,
      sizeof (void*),
      0,
      DBTYPE_R8 | DBTYPE_BYREF,
      0,                                // No precision
      0                                 // No scale
   },
   {
      2,
      offsetof (join, pi),
      0,                                // No length binding
      0,                                // No status binding
      NULL,                             // No TypeInfo
      NULL,                             // No object
      NULL,                             // No extensions
      DBPART_VALUE,
      DBMEMOWNER_PROVIDEROWNED,
      DBPARAMIO_NOTPARAM,
      sizeof (void*),
      0,
      DBTYPE_I2 | DBTYPE_BYREF,
      0,                                // No precision
      0                                 // No scale
   }
};
```

```
static DBBINDING JoinBindings [3] = {
   {
      1,
      offsetof (join, pl),
      0,                                 // No length binding
      0,                                 // No status binding
      NULL,                              // No TypeInfo
      NULL,                              // No object
      NULL,                              // No extensions
      DBPART_VALUE,
      DBMEMOWNER_PROVIDEROWNED,
      DBPARAMIO_NOTPARAM,
      sizeof (void*),
      0,
      DBTYPE_I4 | DBTYPE_BYREF,
      0,                                 // No precision
      0                                  // No scale
   },
   {
      2,
      offsetof (join, pd),
      0,                                 // No length binding
      0,                                 // No status binding
      NULL,                              // No TypeInfo
      NULL,                              // No object
      NULL,                              // No extensions
      DBPART_VALUE,
      DBMEMOWNER_PROVIDEROWNED,
      DBPARAMIO_NOTPARAM,
      sizeof (void*),
      0,
      DBTYPE_R8 | DBTYPE_BYREF,
      0,                                 // No precision
      0                                  // No scale
   },
```

```
      {
         3,
         offsetof (join, pi),
         0,                                  // No length binding
         0,                                  // No status binding
         NULL,                               // No TypeInfo
         NULL,                               // No object
         NULL,                               // No extensions
         DBPART_VALUE,
         DBMEMOWNER_PROVIDEROWNED,
         DBPARAMIO_NOTPARAM,
         sizeof (void*),
         0,
         DBTYPE_I2 | DBTYPE_BYREF,
         0,                                  // No precision
         0                                   // No scale
      }
   };

   HACCESSOR   hLeft;
   HACCESSOR   hRight;
   HACCESSOR   hJoin;
   join        theJoin;

   pLeftRowsetAcc->CreateAccessor(DBACCESSOR_ROWDATA, 1, LeftBindings, 0, &hLeft,
                              NULL);

   pRightRowsetAcc->CreateAccessor(DBACCESSOR_ROWDATA, 2, RightBindings, 0, &hRight,
                              NULL);

   pJoinRowsetAcc->CreateAccessor(DBACCESSOR_ROWDATA, 3, JoinBindings, 0, &hJoin,
                              NULL);

   for (ULONG j = 0; j < cSortedRows; j++) {
      pLeftRowset->GetData(rghLeftRows[j], hLeft, &theJoin);
      pRightRowset->GetData(rghRightRows[j], hRight, &theJoin);
      pJoinRowsetNew->InsertRow(NULL, hJoin, &theJoin, NULL);
   } ;
};
```

See Also

IRowset::GetData, **IRowsetChange::SetData**, **IRowsetUpdate::Undo**, **IRowsetUpdate::Update**

IRowsetChange::SetData

Sets data values in one or more columns in a row.

```
HRESULT SetData (
   HROW        hRow,
   HACCESSOR   hAccessor,
   void *      pData);
```

Parameters

hRow
[in]
The handle of the row in which to set data.

hAccessor
[in]
The handle of the accessor to use. If *hAccessor* is the handle of a null accessor (*cBindings* in **IAccessor::CreateAccessor** was zero), **SetData** does not set any data values.

pData
[in]
A pointer to memory containing the new data values, at offsets that correspond to the bindings in the accessor.

Return Code

S_OK
The method succeeded. The status of all columns bound by the accessor is set to DBSTATUS_S_OK or DBSTATUS_S_ISNULL

DB_S_ERRORSOCCURRED
An error occurred while setting data for one or more columns, but data was successfully set for at least one column. To determine the columns for which data was returned, the consumer checks the status values. For a list of status values that can be returned by this method, see "Status Values Used When Setting Data" in Chapter 6, "Getting and Setting Data."

DB_S_MULTIPLECHANGES
The rowset was in immediate update mode, and updating the row caused more than one row to be updated in the data store. For more information, see DBPROP_REPORTMULTIPLECHANGES in "Properties Table (Alphabetical)" in Appendix C, "Property Tables."

This return code takes precedence over DB_S_ERRORSOCCURRED. That is, if the conditions described here and in those described in DB_S_ERRORSOCCURRED both occur, the provider returns this code. When the consumer receives this return code, it should also check for the conditions described in DB_S_ERRORSOCCURRED.

E_FAIL
A provider-specific error occurred.

E_INVALIDARG
pData was a null pointer, and the accessor was not a null accessor.

E_UNEXPECTED
ITransaction::Commit or **ITransaction::Abort** was called, and the object is in a zombie state.

DB_E_ABORTLIMITREACHED
The rowset was in immediate update mode, and the row was not updated due to reaching a limit on the server, such as a query execution timing out.

DB_E_BADACCESSORHANDLE
hAccessor was invalid.

DB_E_BADACCESSORTYPE
The specified accessor was not a row accessor or was a reference accessor.

DB_E_BADROWHANDLE
hRow was invalid.

DB_E_CANCELED
The change was canceled during notification. No columns are changed.

DB_E_CANTCONVERTVALUE
The data value for one or more columns couldn't be converted for reasons other than sign mismatch or data overflow, and the provider was unable to determine which columns couldn't be converted. Providers that can detect which columns could not be converted return DB_S_ERRORSOCCURRED and set the status flag for the columns that couldn't be converted to DBSTATUS_E_CANTCONVERTVALUE.

DB_E_CONCURRENCYVIOLATION
The rowset was using optimistic concurrency and the value of a column has been changed since the containing row was last fetched or resynchronized. **SetData** returns this error only when the rowset is in immediate update mode.

DB_E_DATAOVERFLOW
Conversion failed because the data value for one or more columns overflowed the type used by the provider and the provider was unable to determine which columns caused the overflow. Providers that can detect which columns caused the overflow return DB_S_ERRORSOCCURRED and set the status flag for the columns in violation to DBSTATUS_E_DATAOVERFLOW.

DB_E_DELETEDROW
hRow referred to a row with a pending delete or for which a deletion had been transmitted to the data store.

DB_E_ERRORSOCCURRED
An error occurred while setting data for one or more columns and data was not successfully set for any columns. To determine the columns for which values were invalid, the consumer checks the status values. For a list of status values that can be returned by this method, see "Status Values Used When Setting Data" in Chapter 6, "Getting and Setting Data."

DB_E_INTEGRITYVIOLATION
The data violated the integrity constraints for one or more columns of the rowset, and the provider was unable to determine which columns violated the integrity constraints. Providers that can detect which columns violated the integrity constraints return DB_S_ERRORSOCCURRED and set the status flag for the columns in violation to DBSTATUS_E_INTEGRITYVIOLATION.

DB_E_MAXPENDCHANGESEXCEEDED
The number of rows that have pending changes has exceeded the limit specified by the DBPROP_MAXPENDINGROWS property.

DB_E_NEWLYINSERTED
DBPROP_CHANGEINSERTEDROWS was VARIANT_FALSE, and *hRow* referred to a row for which the insertion has been transmitted to the data store.

DB_E_NOTREENTRANT
The consumer called this method while it was processing a notification, and it is an error to call this method while processing the specified DBREASON value.

DB_E_NOTSUPPORTED
The provider does not support this method.

DB_SEC_E_PERMISSIONDENIED
The consumer did not have sufficient permission to update the row. This error can be returned only if the value of the DBPROP_ROWRESTRICT property is VARIANT_TRUE. If the rowset is in delayed update mode, this error might not be returned until **IRowsetUpdate::Update** is called.

If this method performs deferred accessor validation and that validation takes place before any data is transferred, it can also return any of the following return codes for the applicable reasons listed in the corresponding DBBINDSTATUS values in **IAccessor::CreateAccessor**:

E_NOINTERFACE
DB_E_BADBINDINFO
DB_E_BADORDINAL
DB_E_BADSTORAGEFLAGS
DB_E_UNSUPPORTEDCONVERSION

Comments

SetData sets data values in one or more columns in a row. For a complete description of how **SetData** sets data, see "Setting Data" in Chapter 6, "Getting and Setting Data."

In delayed update mode, these changes are buffered locally in the rowset and are transmitted to the data store only when **IRowsetUpdate::Update** is called. In immediate update mode, the changes are immediately transmitted to the data store. For more information, see "Changing Data" in Chapter 5, "Updating Data in Rowsets."

If a computed column depends on a column that is changed with **SetData**, the provider is not required to compute the new value of the computed column. If the provider computes the new value, it sends a notification to the consumer. If the provider does not compute the new value but lets the data store do so, the computed value is not available until after the change is transmitted to the data store—that is, after **SetData** is called in immediate update mode or after **IRowsetUpdate::Update** if **SetData** is called in delayed update mode. To retrieve the computed value in this case, the consumer calls **RefreshVisibleData** or **GetLastVisibleData** in **IRowsetRefresh**. Bookmark columns are often computed, such as when the bookmark is the primary key or is a ROWID assigned by the data store.

If **SetData** changes a column that is used to order the rowset, the DBPROP_IMMOBILEROWS property describes whether the row is moved based on its new value. If this property is VARIANT_TRUE, the row is not moved. If this property is VARIANT_FALSE, the row is moved. If the rowset is not ordered, the position of updated rows is not changed. If the rowset is built on a set of key columns (typically a rowset for which DBPROP_OTHERUPDATEDELETE is VARIANT_TRUE but DBPROP_OTHERINSERT is VARIANT_FALSE), changing the value of key column is generally equivalent to deleting the current row and inserting a new one. Therefore, the row may appear to move or even disappear from the rowset (if DBPROP_OWNINSERT is VARIANT_FALSE), even though the DBPROP_IMMOBILEROWS property is VARIANT_TRUE.

When the consumer passes a pointer to a storage object to **SetData**, **SetData** replaces the data in the column with the data in the new storage object. If the consumer wants only to delete the data in the column, it sets the column status to DBSTATUS_S_OK and passes a null pointer instead of a pointer to a storage object. For more information, see "Getting and Setting BLOB Data with Storage Objects" in Chapter 7, "BLOBs and COM Objects." If the rowset is in immediate update mode, storage object data is always transmitted immediately to the data store. If it is in delayed update mode, whether it is transmitted immediately or delayed depends on the DBPROP_DELAYSTORAGEOBJECTS property.

Although **SetData** can detect domain constraint and some table constraint schema violations, it is not required to do so. Such validation can be delayed until the changes are transmitted to the data store with **Update** or the transaction is committed with **ITransaction::Commit**. This delay is often necessary because of dependencies on values in other columns or tables.

SetData cannot be called for rows with pending or transmitted deletes.

The DBPROP_COLUMNRESTRICT and DBPROP_ROWRESTRICT properties affect how security is enforced and how security errors are returned. If DBPROP_COLUMNRESTRICT is VARIANT_TRUE, the consumer might not have write permission on some columns. If the consumer attempts to write to these columns, **SetData** returns a column status of DBSTATUS_E_PERMISSIONDENIED and a return code of DB_S_ERRORSOCCURRED. If the DBPROP_ROWRESTRICT property is VARIANT_TRUE, the consumer might not have permission to update some rows. If the consumer attempts to update one of
these rows, **SetData** returns a code of DB_SEC_E_PERMISSIONDENIED and no data is set.

If any consumer of the rowset is using notifications, the provider sends notifications. These notifications can be vetoed, in which case the provider sends the DBEVENTPHASE_FAILEDTODO phase of the notification. When the consumer then calls **Update**, if the update is in delayed mode, the provider does not send additional DBREASON_COLUMN_SET notifications for the rows. However, if **Update** computes the value of computed columns, it sends DBREASON_COLUMN_RECALCULATED notifications. In this case, the provider must either be prepared to undo all pending changes for the row and return DBREASON_ROW_UNDOCHANGE or set the *fCantDeny* flag to TRUE.

The following sequence of notifications occurs for a rowset operating in delayed update mode:

1. If the row is being changed for the first time since it was created, or changes were transmitted, the provider sends the DBEVENTPHASE_OKTODO and DBEVENTPHASE_ABOUTTODO phases of the DBREASON_ROW_FIRSTCHANGE notification.
2. The provider sends the DBEVENTPHASE_OKTODO, DBEVENTPHASE_ABOUTTODO, and DBEVENTPHASE_SYNCHAFTER phases of the DBREASON_COLUMN_SET notification, in that order, provided none of the listeners veto any of the phases. The notification covers all the columns defined by the accessor used in the call to **SetData**.
3. The provider sends the DBEVENTPHASE_SYNCHAFTER phase of the DBREASON_ROW_FIRSTCHANGE notification, assuming the provider sent the earlier phases of this notification.
4. The provider sends the DBEVENTPHASE_DIDEVENT phase of the DBREASON_COLUMN_SET notification.
5. The provider sends the DBEVENTPHASE_DIDEVENT phase of the ROW_FIRSTCHANGE notification.

See Also

IRowset::GetData, **IRowsetChange::InsertRow**, **IRowsetUpdate::Undo**, **IRowsetUpdate::Update**

IRowsetChapterMember

The **IRowsetChapterMember** interface detects whether or not a row is a member of a chapter.

When to Implement

IRowsetChapterMember is an optional interface on chaptered rowsets.

When to Call

Consumers call **IsRowInChapter** whenever they need to determine if a row handle is a member of a given chapter. For example, if a row handle is returned to the consumer during notification, the consumer can call this method on each of the chapters it already has to determine to which chapters the row belongs.

Method	Description
IsRowInChapter	Determines whether a row is a member of a chapter.

IRowsetChapterMember::IsRowInChapter

Determines whether or not a row is a member of a chapter.

```
HRESULT IsRowInChapter (
   HCHAPTER    hChapter,
   HROW        hRow);
```

Parameters

hChapter
[in]
The chapter handle.

hRow
[in]
The row handle.

Return Code

S_FALSE
The method succeeded, and the row handle is not a member of this chapter.

S_OK
The method succeeded, and the row handle is a member of the chapter.

E_FAIL
A provider-specific error occurred.

E_UNEXPECTED
ITransaction::Commit or **ITransaction::Abort** was called, and the object is in a zombie state.

DB_E_BADROWHANDLE
hRow is invalid.

DB_E_BADCHAPTER
hChapter is invalid.

The rowset was single-chaptered, and the specified chapter was not the currently open chapter. The consumer must use the currently open chapter or release the currently open chapter before specifying a new chapter.

Comments

This method makes no logical change to the state of the object.

This method determines whether or not a row handle is a member of a chapter. This comparison could be used, for example, if the consumer receives a row handle through one of the methods in **IRowsetNotify** and needs to know if it is a member of a chapter that the consumer already holds.

IRowsetFind

IRowsetFind is the interface that allows consumers to find a row within the rowset matching a specified value.

When to Implement

IRowsetFind is required for all providers that intend to support general consumers.

When to Call

Consumers call **IRowsetFind** to locate the next row in the rowset matching a specified value.

Method	Description
FindNextRow	Returns the next row matching the criteria.

IRowsetFind::FindNextRow

Begin at the specified bookmark and find the next row matching the specified value.

```
HRESULT FindNextRow (
   HCHAPTER             hChapter,
   HACCESSOR            hAccessor,
      void *               pFindValue,
      DBCOMPAREOP          CompareOp,
      ULONG                cbBookmark,
   const BYTE *         pBookmark,
      LONG                 lRowsOffset,
   LONG                 cRows,
   ULONG *              pcRowsObtained,
      HROW **              prghRows);
```

Parameters

hChapter
[in]
The chapter handle. For nonchaptered rowsets, the caller must set *hChapter* to DB_NULL_HCHAPTER.

hAccessor
[in]
Accessor describing the value to be matched. This accessor must describe only a single column. If it describes more than one column, **FindNextRow** returns DB_E_BADBINDINFO.

Valid coercions for **FindNextRow** are the same as those for **SetData**.

pFindValue
[in]
Pointer to the value to be matched. If this indicates a null value (a variant of type VT_NULL, or a status value of DBSTATUS_ISNULL), it is compared equal to null values and compared not equal to non-null values, within the rowset. It is provider-specific whether null values are compared greater than or less than non-null values.

CompareOp

[in]

Operation to use in comparing the row values. The consumer should check DBPROP_FINDCOMPAREOPS to determine which comparison operators the provider supports.

Only DBCOMPAREOPS_EQ, DBCOMPAREOPS_NE, and DBCOMPAREOPS_IGNORE are valid for the following of *CompareOp*:

- DBTYPE_BOOL
- DBTYPE_ERROR
- DBTYPE_GUID
- DBTYPE_IDISPATCH
- DBTYPE_IUNKNOWN
- DBTYPE_BTYES

The values in DBCOMPAREOPSENUM have the following meanings.

Value	Description
DBCOMPAREOPS_LT	Match the first value that is less than the search value.
DBCOMPAREOPS_LE	Match the first value that is less than or equal to the search value.
DBCOMPAREOPS_EQ	Match the first value that is equal to the search value.
DBCOMPAREOPS_GE	Match the first value that is greater than or equal to the search value.
DBCOMPAREOPS_GT	Match the first value that is greater than the search value.
DBCOMPAREOPS_BEGINSWITH	Match the first value that has the search value as its first characters. This is valid only for values bound as string data types.
DBCOMPAREOPS_NOTBEGINSWITH	Match the first value that does not have the search value as its first characters. This is valid only for values bound as string data types.
DBCOMPAREOPS_CONTAINS	Match the first value that contains the search value. This is valid only for values bound as string data types.

Value	Description
DBCOMPAREOPS_NOTCONTAINS	Match the first value that does not contain the search value. This is valid only for values bound as string data types.
DBCOMPAREOPS_NE	Match the first value that is not equal to the search value. NULLs evaluate as not equal to any other value, but equal to other NULLs.
DBCOMPAREOPS_IGNORE	Ignore the corresponding value. The provider ignores *pFindValue* and returns the next *cRows* rows starting from the row indicated by *pBookmark*, skipping the number of rows indicated by *lRowsOffset*.
DBCOMPAREOPS_CASESENSITIVE and DBCOMPAREOPS_CASEINSENSITIVE	Specify whether the search is case-sensitive or case-insensitive. You can join DBCOMPAREOPS_CASESENSITIVE or DBCOMPAREOPS_CASEINSENSITIVE with any of the other DBCOMPAREOPS values in a bitwise **OR** operation. If neither is used, the search is handled according to the provider's implementation. Both DBCOMPAREOPS_CASESENSITIVE and DBCOMPAREOPS_CASEINSENSITIVE are ignored when searching for nonstring values.

cbBookmark

[in]

Length in bytes of the bookmark, or zero in order to start from the next fetch location. (See the description of *pBookmark*.)

pBookmark

[in]

Pointer to a bookmark that, in combination with *lRowsOffset*, identifies the row from which to start searching for a match. The consumer is not required to have access rights to this row. However, if this row matches the seek criteria, the provider cannot return it unless the consumer has read permission for it.

The consumer can specify a *cbBookmark* value of zero and set *pBookmark* to null to request that the find occur starting with the next fetch location. The next fetch location is the same as the next fetch position used by **GetNextRows**.

If *cbBookmark* equals zero, the provider ignores *pBookmark*.

If the rowset does not support **IRowsetLocate**, only the special bookmarks DBBMK_FIRST and DBBMK_LAST, and the null value, may be used.

If the rowset does not support scrolling backward, only the null bookmark value may be used.

If the rowset is chaptered, the identified row must fall within the specified chapter.

lRowsOffset

[in]

The signed count of rows from the origin bookmark to the row at which to start searching for a match. The first row checked is determined by the bookmark and this offset. For example, if *lRowsOffset* is 0, the first row checked is the bookmarked row; if *lRowsOffset* is 1, the first row checked is the row after the bookmarked row; if *lRowsOffset* is –1, the first row checked is the row before the bookmarked row. This can be a negative number only if the value of the DBPROP_CANSCROLLBACKWARDS property is VARIANT_TRUE.

cRows

[in]

The number of rows to fetch from the rowset, starting with the first row found. A negative number indicates a backward fetch. The consumer can determine whether the provider supports fetching backward by checking the value of DBPROP_CANFETCHBACKWARDS property returned by **IRowsetInfo::GetProperties**.

The search direction is the same as the fetch direction, so a negative count searches backward from the starting position and returns successively earlier rows as subsequent obtained rows. If *cRows* is zero and there are no other errors, no rows are fetched. In this case, if *cbBookmark* is zero, the fetch position is moved to the same position as if calling **FindNextRow** with *cRows* equal to1 and releasing the retrieved row. In general, consumers should avoid calling **FindNextRow** with *cRows* equal to zero.

pcRowsObtained
[out]
A pointer to memory in which to return the actual number of fetched rows.

prghRows
[out]
A pointer to memory in which to return an array of handles of the retrieved rows. If **prghRows* is not a null pointer on input, it must be a pointer to memory large enough to return the handles of the requested number of rows. If **prghRows* is a null pointer on input, the rowset allocates memory for the row handles and returns the address to this memory; the consumer releases this memory with **IMalloc::Free** after it releases the row handles. If **prghRows* was a null pointer on input and **pcRowsObtained* is 0 on output, the provider does not allocate any memory and ensures that **prghRows* is a null pointer on output.

Return Code

S_OK
The method succeeded.

DB_S_ENDOFROWSET
FindNextRow reached the start or the end of the rowset or (in a hierarchical rowset) the start or the end of the chapter and could not fetch all requested rows because the count extended beyond the end. The next fetch position is before the start or after the end of the rowset. The number of rows actually returned is returned in **pcRowsObtained*; this will be less than *cRows*.

DB_S_ROWLIMITEXCEEDED
Fetching the number of rows specified in *cRows* would have exceeded the total number of active rows supported by the rowset. The number of rows that were actually fetched is returned in **pcRowsObtained*. This condition can occur only when there are more rows available than can be handled by the rowset. Therefore, this condition never conflicts with those described in DB_S_ENDOFROWSET and DB_S_STOPLIMITREACHED, both of which imply that no more rows were available.

DB_S_STOPLIMITREACHED
Returning rows required further execution of the command, such as when the rowset uses a server-side cursor. Execution has been stopped because a resource limit has been reached. The number of rows that were actually fetched is returned in **pcRowsObtained*. Execution cannot be resumed.

DB_S_BOOKMARKSKIPPED

The following behavior is supported only on rowsets that set the DBPROP_BOOKMARKSKIPPED property to VARIANT_TRUE. If this property is VARIANT_FALSE, this return code is never returned.

The row specified by **pBookmark* was deleted, is no longer a member of the rowset, or is a row to which the consumer does not have access rights. **FindNextRow** skipped that row and began searching with the next row in the direction indicated by *cRows*.

If this condition occurs along with another warning condition, the method returns the code for the other warning condition. Therefore, whenever a consumer receives the return code for another warning condition, it should check to see whether this condition occurred.

E_FAIL

A provider-specific error occurred.

E_INVALIDARG

pcRowsObtained or *prghRows* was a null pointer.

cbBookmark was not 0 and *pBookmark* was a null pointer.

E_OUTOFMEMORY

The provider was unable to allocate sufficient memory in which to instantiate the rows or return the row handles.

E_UNEXPECTED

ITransaction::Commit or **ITransaction::Abort** was called, and the object is in a zombie state.

DB_E_BADBINDINFO

The specified accessor specified binding information for more than one column.

DB_E_BADBOOKMARK

**pBookmark* was invalid; for example, it was incorrectly formed.

**pBookmark* did not match any rows in the rowset. This includes the case when the row corresponding to the bookmark has been deleted and DBPROP_BOOKMARKSKIPPED was VARIANT_FALSE.

**pBookmark* was not a null value, and the rowset does not support scrolling backward.

pBookmark* was not DBBMK_FIRST, DBBMK_LAST, or a null value, and the rowset does not support **IRowsetLocate.

The rowset was chaptered, and **pBookmark* did not apply to the specified chapter.

> **Note** Consumers should attempt to use only bookmarks that they have received from the provider. The provider is guaranteed only to handle bookmarks it gives out in a predictable manner. Attempting to use a random value as a bookmark is undefined; the provider may return DB_E_BADBOOKMARK, may return an unexpected row, or may terminate abnormally.

DB_E_BADCHAPTER
The rowset was chaptered and *hChapter* was invalid.

The rowset was single-chaptered, and the specified chapter was not the currently open chapter. The consumer must use the currently open chapter or release the currently open chapter before specifying a new chapter.

DB_E_BADCOMPAREOP
CompareOp was an invalid value.

CompareOp was DBCOMPAREOPS_BEGINSWITH or DBCOMPAREOPS_CONTAINS, and *pFindValue* was not bound as a string value.

Both DBCOMPAREOPS_CASESENSITIVE and DBCOMPAREOPS_CASEINSENSITIVE were used in the same operation.

The specified *CompareOp* could not be supported on the column, or the column was not searchable.

DB_E_BADSTARTPOSITION
lRowsOffset indicated a position either more than one row before the first row of the rowset or more than one row after the last row, and the provider was a 1.*x* provider.

DB_E_CANTFETCHBACKWARDS
cRows was negative, and the rowset cannot fetch backward.

DB_E_CANTSCROLLBACKWARDS
A bookmark value of DBBMK_FIRST or DBBMK_LAST was specified, and the rowset cannot scroll backward.

RowsOffset was negative, and the rowset cannot scroll backward.

DB_E_NOTREENTRANT
The provider called a method from **IRowsetNotify** in the consumer that had not yet returned, and the provider does not support reentrancy in this method.

DB_E_ROWSNOTRELEASED
The provider requires release of prior HROWs before new ones can be obtained. (See **IDBProperties::GetPropertyInfo**, DBPROP_CANHOLDROWS.)

DB_SEC_E_PERMISSIONDENIED
The consumer did not have sufficient permission to get the rows.

Comments

See **IRowsetLocate::GetRowsAt** for a complete description of the results for given values for a bookmark, offset, and number of rows to fetch.

FindNextRow searches the rowset in the direction indicated by *cRows* for a row that matches *pFindValue* according to the specified *CompareOp*. Once a match is found, if *cRows* is greater than 1, additional rows are returned in rowset order as if the consumer called **GetNextRows** starting with the first matching row. If no rows match the criteria, **FindNextRow** returns DB_S_ENDOFROWSET and *pcRowsObtained* is set to zero.

For a newly created rowset, if *pBookmark* is null, the search begins starting with the row computed according to the next fetch position as described in **GetNextRows** for newly created rowsets.

It is not required that the rowset be ordered on the column searched. **FindNextRow** always finds the next row according to the criteria, regardless of the sort order.

FindNextRow increments the reference count of each row for which it returns a handle by 1. Thus, if a handle is returned for a row that has already been fetched, the reference count of that row will be greater than 1. **ReleaseRows** must be called once for each time the handle to a row has been returned.

If the provider encounters a problem fetching a row—for example, data stored in a text file contains a letter in a numeric column—**FindNextRow** fetches the row normally, returns the row handle, and returns S_OK. However, when the consumer calls **GetData** for the row, the provider returns DBSTATUS_E_CANTCONVERTVALUE as the status for the offending column.

If an error occurs when calling **FindNextRow**, the fetch position is left unchanged.

If **FindNextRow** performs deferred accessor validation and that validation takes place before any data is transferred, it can also return any of the following return codes for the applicable reasons listed in the corresponding DBBINDSTATUS values in **IAccessor::CreateAccessor**: E_NOINTERFACE, DB_E_BADBINDINFO, DB_E_BADORDINAL, DB_E_BADSTORAGEFLAGS, and DB_E_UNSUPPORTEDCONVERSION.

For information about what **FindNextRow** does when it fetches a row that it already has in its internal buffers, see "Uniqueness of Rows in the Rowset" in Chapter 4, "Rowsets." For information about whether **FindNextRow** can detect changes made to rows in the rowset, see "Visibility of Changes" in Chapter 5, "Updating Data in Rowsets." For information about how **FindNextRow** interprets data from **pFindValue*, see "Setting Data" in Chapter 6, "Getting and Setting Data."

See Also

IRowset::GetData, **IRowsetIndex::Seek**, **IRowsetLocate::GetRowsAt**, **IRowsetLocate::GetRowsByBookmark**

IRowsetIdentity

IRowsetIdentity is the interface that indicates row instance identity is implemented on the rowset and enables testing for row identity. If a rowset supports this interface, any two row handles representing the same underlying row will always reflect the same data and state.

IRowsetIdentity depends on **IRowset**.

When to Implement

IRowsetIdentity is required for all providers that intend to support general consumers.

If the provider inherently supports row identity, this interface will be supported even if the command does not require it. For such providers, row identity is not disabled if the consumer does not request **IRowsetIdentity**.

If the DBPROP_LITERALIDENTITY property is set to VARIANT_TRUE, the provider supports binary comparison of row handles.

This interface can be implemented even when row identity cannot be perfectly implemented; the rowset may reasonably take steps to be partially correct. For more information, see "Uniqueness of Rows in the Rowset" in Chapter 4, "Rowsets."

When to Call

Consumers call **IsSameRow** whenever they need to determine whether two row handles represent the same underlying row. For example, if a row handle is returned to the consumer during notification, the consumer can compare it to its own list of row handles to see if it is the handle of a row of interest.

Method	Description
IsSameRow	Compares two row handles to see whether they refer to the same row instance.

IRowsetIdentity::IsSameRow

Compares two row handles to see if they refer to the same row instance.

```
HRESULT IsSameRow (
   HROW  hThisRow,
   HROW  hThatRow);
```

Parameters

hThisRow
[in]
The handle of an active row.

hThatRow
[in]
The handle of an active row.

Return Code

S_FALSE
The method succeeded, and the row handles do not refer to the same row instance.

S_OK
The method succeeded, and the row handles do refer to the same row instance.

E_FAIL
A provider-specific error occurred.

E_UNEXPECTED
ITransaction::Commit or **ITransaction::Abort** was called, and the object is in a zombie state.

DB_E_BADROWHANDLE
hRowThis or *hRowThat* was invalid.

DB_E_DELETEDROW
hRowThis or *hRowThat* referred to a row for which a deletion had been transmitted to the data store.

DB_E_NEWLYINSERTED
The provider is unable to determine identity for a row for which an insertion had been transmitted to the data store. This condition can occur when DBPROP_STRONGIDENTITY is set to VARIANT_FALSE.

Comments

This method makes no logical change to the state of the object.

The row handles refer to the same row instance if the value set in any column in the row by means of one row handle will be the value returned for that column when gotten through the other row handle.

Rowsets that support this interface must also implement the detection of row identity within their rowset. That is, if they fetch rows at different times, they can detect when the row handles are referring to the same logical row and arrange for both row handles to reflect the same data and state.

The value of the row handles—their bit patterns as handles—is not necessarily the same if the underlying row is the same. This depends on the value of the DBPROP_LITERALIDENTITY property.

The outcome of **IsSameRow** is not changed when one or both of its parameters correspond to a row with a pending delete.

IRowsetIndex

IRowsetIndex is the primary interface for exposing index functionality in OLE DB. For a complete description of indexes, see Chapter 8, "Index Rowsets" and Chapter 16, "Integrated Indexes."

When to Implement

The **IRowsetIndex** interface is implemented by providers to expose the functionality of a file access method such as a B+-tree, or linear hash. For integrated indexes, **IRowsetIndex** is exposed on the base table rowset; otherwise, it is exposed on the index rowset.

A provider may also support other rowset interfaces on indexes, such as **IRowsetScroll**.

When to Call

The methods in **IRowsetIndex** are used to define a range of index entries to be read, to position at an index entry within the range, to fetch the index entry, and to access the contents of the index entry.

The following table shows how to perform various index operations.

Operation	Comments
Open an index	To get a handle to an **IRowsetIndex** object, the consumer calls **IOpenRowset::OpenRowset**, passing it the DBID of the index. The method returns a pointer to an index rowset.
Close an index	An index is closed by releasing all references to the index rowset.
Insert an index entry	New key entries are inserted into an index by using **IRowsetChange**.
Delete an index entry	Key entries are deleted from an index by using **IRowsetChange**.
Update an index entry	Key entries are updated in an index by first deleting the old index entry and then inserting a new index entry.
Traverse the index	To traverse an index, a user calls methods on **IRowset**. For more information, see "Using Index Rowsets" in Chapter 8, "Index Rowsets."

Method	Description
GetIndexInfo	Returns information about the index rowset capabilities.
Seek	Allows direct positioning at a key value within the current range.
SetRange	Restricts the set of row entries visible through calls to **IRowset::GetNextRows** and **IRowsetIndex::Seek**.

IRowsetIndex::GetIndexInfo

Returns information about the index rowset capabilities.

```
HRESULT GetIndexInfo (
   ULONG *                 pcKeyColumns,
   DBINDEXCOLUMNDESC **    prgIndexColumnDesc,
   ULONG *                 pcIndexProperties,
   DBPROPSET **            prgIndexProperties);
```

Parameters

pcKeyColumns
[out]
A pointer to memory in which to return the number of key columns in the index.

prgIndexColumnDesc
[out]
A pointer to memory in which to return an array of DBINDEXCOLUMNDESC structures in key column order. For more information, see **IIndexDefinition::CreateIndex**. The size of the array is equal to **pcKeyColumns*. If an error occurs, **prgIndexColumnDesc* is set to a null pointer.

pcIndexProperties
[out]
A pointer to memory in which to return the number of DBPROPSET structures returned in **prgIndexProperties*. **pcIndexProperties* is the total number of property sets for which the provider supports at least one property in the Index property group. If an error occurs, **pcIndexProperties* is set to zero.

prgIndexProperties
[out]
A pointer to memory in which to return an array of DBPROPSET structures. One structure is returned for each property set that contains at least one property belonging to the Index property group. For information about the properties in the Index property group that are defined by OLE DB, see "Properties Table (by Property Groups)" in Appendix C, "Property Tables."

The provider allocates memory for the structures and returns the address to this memory; the consumer releases this memory with **IMalloc::Free** when it no longer needs the structures. Before calling **IMalloc::Free** for **prgPropertySets*, the consumer should call **IMalloc::Free** for the *rgProperties* element within each element of **prgPropertySets*. If **pcIndexProperties* is zero on output or if an error occurs, the provider does not allocate any memory and ensures that **prgIndexProperties* is a null pointer on output.

For information about the DBPROPSET and DBPROP structures, see "DBPROPSET Structure" and "DBPROP Structure" in Chapter 11, "Properties."

Return Code

S_OK
The method succeeded.

E_FAIL
A provider-specific error occurred.

E_INVALIDARG
pcKeyColumns, *prgIndexColumnDesc*, *pcIndexProperties*, or *prgIndexProperties* was a null pointer.

E_OUTOFMEMORY
The provider was unable to allocate sufficient memory in which to return the column description structures or properties of the index.

DB_E_NOINDEX
The rowset uses integrated indexes, and there is no current index.

See Also

IDBProperties::GetPropertyInfo, **IIndexDefinition::CreateIndex**

IRowsetIndex::Seek

Allows direct positioning at a key value within the current range established by the **IRowsetIndex::SetRange** method.

```
HRESULT Seek (
   HACCESSOR   hAccessor,
   ULONG       cKeyValues,
   void *      pData,
   DBSEEK      dwSeekOptions);
```

Parameters

hAccessor

[in]
The handle of the accessor to use. This accessor must meet the following criteria, which are illustrated with a key that consists of columns A, B, and C, where A is the most-significant column and C is the least-significant column:

- For each key column this accessor binds, it must also bind all more significant key columns. For example, the accessor can bind column A, columns A and B, or columns A, B, and C.
- Key columns must be bound in order from most-significant key column to least-significant key column. For example, if the accessor binds columns A and B, then the first binding must bind column A and the second binding must bind column B.
- If the accessor binds any non-key columns, key columns must be bound first. For example, if the accessor binds columns A, B, and the bookmark column, then the first binding must bind column A, the second binding must bind column B, and the third binding must bind the bookmark column.

If the accessor does not meet these criteria, the method returns DB_E_BADBINDINFO or a status of DBSTATUS_E_BADACCESSOR for the offending column.

If *hAccessor* is the handle of a null accessor (*cBindings* in **IAccessor::CreateAccessor** was zero), **Seek** does not change the next fetch position.

cKeyValues

[in]
The number of bindings in *hAccessor* for which **pData* contains valid data. **SetRange** retrieves data from the first *cKeyValues* key columns from **pData*. For example, suppose the accessor binds columns A, B, and C of the key in the previous example and *cKeyValues* is 2. **SetRange** retrieves data for columns A and B.

pData

[in]

A pointer to a buffer containing the key values to which to seek, at offsets that correspond to the bindings in the accessor.

dwSeekOptions

[in]

A bitmask describing the options for the **Seek** method. The values in DBSEEKENUM have the following meanings:

Value	Description
DBSEEK_FIRSTEQ	First key with values equal to the values in **pData*.
DBSEEK_LASTEQ	Last key with values equal to the values in **pData*.
DBSEEK_GE	First key with values greater than or equal to the values in **pData*.
DBSEEK_GT	First key with values greater than the values in **pData*.
DBSEEK_LE	First key with values less than or equal to the values in **pData*.
DBSEEK_LT	First key with values less than the values in **pData*.

Return Code

S_OK

The method succeeded.

E_FAIL

A provider-specific error occurred.

E_INVALIDARG

dwSeekOptions was invalid.

hAccessor was the handle of a null accessor.

cKeyValues was zero.

pData was a null pointer.

DB_E_BADACCESSORHANDLE

hAccessor was invalid.

DB_E_BADACCESSORTYPE

The specified accessor was not a row accessor.

DB_E_ERRORSOCCURRED

An error occurred while transferring data for one or more key columns. To determine the columns for which values were invalid, the consumer checks the status values. For a list of status values that can be returned by this method, see "Status Values Used When Setting Data" in Chapter 6, "Getting and Setting Data."

DB_E_NOINDEX
The rowset uses integrated indexes, and there is no current index.

DB_E_NOTFOUND
No key value matching the described characteristics could be found within the current range.

DB_E_NOTREENTRANT
The consumer called this method while it was processing a notification, and it is an error to call this method while processing the specified DBREASON value.

If this method performs deferred accessor validation and that validation takes place before any data is transferred, it can also return any of the following return codes for the reasons listed in the corresponding DBBINDSTATUS values in **IAccessor::CreateAccessor**:

E_NOINTERFACE
DB_E_BADBINDINFO
DB_E_BADORDINAL
DB_E_BADSTORAGEFLAGS
DB_E_UNSUPPORTEDCONVERSION

Comments

The **Seek** method provides the caller more control over the traversal of an index. Consider a relational query processor component implementing a merge join over inputs R1 and R2. R1, the outer input, is a rowset ordered by the joining column R1.X. R2, the inner input, is an indexed rowset on column R2.X. Suppose that R1.X has values {10, 20, 100, 110} and that R2.X has values {10, 20, ..., 30, ..., 40, ..., 50, ..., 100, ...}; then when searching R2.X, one could seek directly from 20 to 100 knowing the values of the input R1.X. In some cases, this strategy could be cost effective.

For information about how **Seek** transfers data from **pData*, see "Setting Data" in Chapter 6, "Getting and Setting Data."

See Also

IRowset::GetNextRows, **IRowsetIndex::SetRange**

IRowsetIndex::SetRange

Restricts the set of row entries visible through calls to **IRowset::GetNextRows** and **IRowsetIndex::Seek**.

```
HRESULT SetRange (
   HACCESSOR   hAccessor,
   ULONG       cStartKeyColumns,
   void *      pStartData,
   ULONG       cEndKeyColumns,
   void *      pEndData,
   DBRANGE     dwRangeOptions);
```

Parameters

hAccessor

[in]
The handle of the accessor to use for both **pStartData* and **pEndData*. This accessor must meet the following criteria, which are illustrated with a key that consists of columns A, B, and C, where A is the most-significant column and C is the least-significant column:

- For each key column this accessor binds, it must also bind all more significant key columns. For example, the accessor can bind column A, columns A and B, or columns A, B, and C.
- Key columns must be bound in order from most-significant key column to least-significant key column. For example, if the accessor binds columns A and B, then the first binding must bind column A and the second binding must bind column B.
- If the accessor binds any non-key columns, key columns must be bound first. For example, if the accessor binds columns A, B, and the bookmark column, then the first binding must bind column A, the second binding must bind column B, and the third binding must bind the bookmark column.

If the accessor does not meet these criteria, the method returns DB_E_BADBINDINFO or a status of DBSTATUS_E_BADACCESSOR for the offending column.

If *hAccessor* is the handle of a null accessor (*cBindings* in **IAccessor::CreateAccessor** was zero), **SetRange** does not set a range.

cStartKeyColumns

[in]
The number of bindings in *hAccessor* for which **pStartData* contains valid data. **SetRange** retrieves data from the first *cStartKeyValues* key columns from **pStartData*. For example, suppose the accessor binds columns A, B, and C of the key in the previous example and *cStartKeyValues* is 2. **SetRange** retrieves data for columns A and B.

pStartData
[in]
A pointer to a buffer containing the starting key values of the range, at offsets that correspond to the bindings in the accessor.

cEndKeyColumns
[in]
The number of bindings in *hAccessor* for which **pEndData* contains valid data. **SetRange** retrieves data from the first *cEndKeyValues* key columns from **pEndData*. For example, suppose the accessor binds columns A, B, and C of the key in the previous example and *cEndKeyValues* is 2. **SetRange** retrieves data for columns A and B.

pEndData
[in]
A pointer to a buffer containing the ending key values of the range, at offsets that correspond to the bindings in the accessor.

dwRangeOptions
[in]
A bitmask describing the options of the range. The values in DBRANGEENUM have the following meanings:

Value	Description
DBRANGE_ INCLUSIVESTART	The start boundary is inclusive (the default).
DBRANGE_ EXCLUSIVESTART	The start boundary is exclusive.
DBRANGE_ INCLUSIVEEND	The end boundary is inclusive (the default).
DBRANGE_ EXCLUSIVEEND	The end boundary is exclusive.
DBRANGE_ EXCLUDENULLS	Exclude NULLs from the range.
DBRANGE_PREFIX	Use **pStartData* as a prefix. **pEndData* must be a null pointer. Prefix matching can be specified entirely using the inclusive and exclusive flags. However, because prefix matching is an important common case, this flag enables the consumer to specify only the **pStartData* values and enables the provider to interpret this request quickly.
DBRANGE_MATCH	Set the range to all keys that match **pStartData*. **pStartData* must specify a full key. **pEndData* must be a null pointer. Used for fast equality match.

Value	Description
DBRANGE_MATCH_N_ MASK	Equal to *0xFF000000*.
DBRANGE_MATCH_N_ SHIFT	Equal to 24 to indicate the number of bits to shift to get the number *N*.

Return Code

S_OK
The method succeeded.

E_FAIL
A provider-specific error occurred.

E_INVALIDARG
dwRangeOptions was invalid.

cStartKeyValues was not zero and *pStartData* was a null pointer.

cEndKeyValues was not zero and *pEndData* was a null pointer.

hAccessor was the handle of a null accessor.

DB_E_BADACCESSORHANDLE
hAccessor was invalid.

DB_E_BADACCESSORTYPE
The specified accessor was not a row accessor.

DB_E_ERRORSOCCURRED
An error occurred while transferring data for one or more key columns. To determine the columns for which values were invalid, the consumer checks the status values. For a list of status values that can be returned by this method, see "Status Values Used When Setting Data" in Chapter 6, "Getting and Setting Data."

DB_E_NOINDEX
The rowset uses integrated indexes and there is no current index.

If this method performs deferred accessor validation and that validation takes place before any data is transferred, it can also return any of the following return codes for the reasons listed in the corresponding DBBINDSTATUS values in **IAccessor::CreateAccessor**:

E_NOINTERFACE
DB_E_BADBINDINFO
DB_E_BADORDINAL
DB_E_BADSTORAGEFLAGS
DB_E_UNSUPPORTEDCONVERSION

Comments

A range defines a view in the index containing a contiguous set of key values. The **pStartData* and **pEndData* values always specify the starting and ending positions in the range, respectively. Thus, for an ascending index, **pStartData* contains the smaller value and **pEndData* contains the larger value; for a descending index, **pStartData* contains the larger value and **pEndData* contains the smaller value.

A range on the entire index is defined by calling **SetRange** (*hAcc*, 0, NULL, 0, NULL, 0). When a range is set, **Seek** can position only to rows in the current range.

For information about how **SetRange** transfers data from **pDataStart* and **pDataEnd*, see "Setting Data" in Chapter 6, "Getting and Setting Data."

Inclusive and Exclusive Ranges with Ascending Indexes

The DBRANGE_INCLUSIVE* and DBRANGE_EXCLUSIVE* flags apply only to the last value in the **pStartData* and **pEndData* buffers. The other values are always inclusive.

Examples with full keys

a) open ranges (single column key)

Desired range	SetRange call
$X > 5$	`SetRange(hAcc, 1, {5}, 0, NULL, DBRANGE_EXCLUSIVESTART);`
$X \geq 5$	`SetRange(hAcc, 1, {5}, 0, NULL, DBRANGE_INCLUSIVESTART);`
$X < 5$	`SetRange(hAcc, 0, NULL, 1, {5}, DBRANGE_EXCLUSIVEEND);`
$X \leq 5$	`SetRange(hAcc, 0, NULL, 1, {5}, DBRANGE_INCLUSIVEEND);`

b) closed ranges (single column key)

Desired range	SetRange call
$X \geq 5$ and $X \leq 10$	`SetRange(hAcc, 1, {5}, 1, {10}, DBRANGE_INCLUSIVESTART | DBRANGE_INCLUSIVEEND);`
$X \geq 5$ and $X < 10$	`SetRange(hAcc, 1, {5}, 1, {10}, DBRANGE_INCLUSIVESTART | DBRANGE_EXCLUSIVEEND);`
$X > 5$ and $X \leq 10$	`SetRange(hAcc, 1, {5}, 1, {10}, DBRANGE_EXCLUSIVESTART | DBRANGE_INCLUSIVEEND);`
$X > 5$ and $X < 10$	`SetRange(hAcc, 1, {5}, 1, {10}, DBRANGE_EXCLUSIVESTART | DBRANGE_EXCLUSIVEEND);`

c) open ranges (multicolumn key [A, B])

The only way to specify open ranges with multicolumn indexes is by using partial keys. See the examples with partial keys below.

Notice that the range $A > 5$ and $B = 1$ cannot be specified because it does not correspond to a contiguous range.

d) closed ranges (multicolumn key [A, B])

Desired range	SetRange call
$A = 1$ and $B \geq 5$ and $B \leq 10$	`SetRange(hAcc, 2, {1, 5}, 2, {1, 10}, DBRANGE_INCLUSIVESTART | DBRANGE_INCLUSIVEEND);`
$A = 1$ and $B > 5$	`SetRange(hAcc, 2, {1, 5}, 1, {1}, DBRANGE_EXCLUSIVESTART | DBRANGE_INCLUSIVEEND);`
$A = 1$ and $B < 5$	`SetRange(hAcc, 1, {1}, 2, {1, 5}, DBRANGE_INCLUSIVESTART | DBRANGE_EXCLUSIVEEND);`

Examples with partial keys

e) open ranges (multicolumn key [A, B])

Desired range	SetRange call
A > 5	`SetRange(hAcc, 1, {5}, 0, NULL, DBRANGE_EXCLUSIVESTART);`
A ≥ 5	`SetRange(hAcc, 1, {5}, 0, NULL, DBRANGE_INCLUSIVESTART);`
A = 5	`SetRange(hAcc, 1, {5}, 1,{5}, DBRANGE_INCLUSIVESTART | DBRANGE_INCLUSIVEEND);`
A < 5	`SetRange(hAcc, 0, NULL, 1, {5}, DBRANGE_EXCLUSIVEEND);`
A ≤ 5	`SetRange(hAcc, 0, NULL, 1, {5}, DBRANGE_INCLUSIVEEND);`

f) closed ranges (multicolumn key [A,B])

Desired range	SetRange call
A > 5 and A ≤ 10	`SetRange(hAcc, 1, {5}, 1, {10}, DBRANGE_EXCLUSIVESTART | DBRANGE_INCLUSIVEEND);`

Prefix Matching

SetRange provides the DBRANGE_PREFIX flag to make it easier for a consumer to formulate ranges involving keys whose value represents a prefix. Consider the text command **SELECT * FROM T WHERE T.A LIKE "abc*"**. This range can be formulated using only the inclusive and exclusive flags for an ascending index, as follows:

```
SetRange (hAcc, 1, {"abc"}, 1, {"abd"}, DBRANGE_INCLUSIVESTART | DBRANGE_EXCLUSIVEEND);
```

This requires the consumer to know the collation order. The DBRANGE_PREFIX flag is provided to make it easier for the consumer to formulate this very common case, as follows:

```
SetRange(hAcc, 1, {"abc"}, 0, NULL, DBRANGE_PREFIX);
```

Examples

Desired range	SetRange call
A = 1 and B like "abc*"	`SetRange(hAcc, 2, {1, "abc"}, 0, NULL, DBRANGE_PREFIX);`

This call is the same regardless of whether DBRANGE_PREFIX is used with an ascending or descending index.

Equality Matching

To facilitate the formulation of ranges involving equality, the **SetRange** method offers the DBRANGE_MATCH option flag. Consider the example **SELECT * FROM T WHERE T.X = 5**. The corresponding range can be formulated in terms of the inclusive and exclusive flags, as follows:

```
SetRange(hAcc, 1, {5}, 1, {5}, DBRANGE_INCLUSIVESTART | DBRANGE_INCLUSIVEEND);
```

The same range can be formulated using the match flags, as follows:

```
SetRange(hAcc, 1, {5}, 0, NULL, DBRANGE_MATCH);
```

Example

Desired range	SetRange call
A = 5 and B= 6	`SetRange(hAcc, 2, {5, 6}, 2, {5, 6}, DBRANGE_INCLUSIVESTART | DBRANGE_INCLUSIVEEND);`
A = 5 and B= 6	`SetRange(hAcc, 2, {5, 6}, 0, NULL, DBRANGE_MATCH);`

These calls are the same whether or not DBRANGE_MATCH is used with an ascending or descending index.

DBRANGE_MATCH_N is an extension of DBRANGE_MATCH, which indicates to the provider that the first N key values should be assumed to define comparison on equality. This is achieved by reserving the 8 high-order bits of *dwRangeOptions* to encode the value *N*. The defined values are DBRANGE_MATCH_N_SHIFT and DBRANGE_MATCH_N_MASK.

Example

a = 5, b = 6, c = 7, d = 8, e = 9, f >= 10 and f <= 20 becomes:

```
SetRange (hAcc,
   6, {5,6,7,8,9,10},
   6, {5,6,7,8,9,20},
   (5 << DBRANGE_MATCH_N_SHIFT) | DB_RANGE_INCLUSIVESTART | DB_RANGE_INCLUSIVEEND);
```

Providers will check whether `(dwRangeOptions AND DBRANGE_MATCH_N_MASK)` is nonzero. If so, the key values will be interpreted by taking the first *N* keys encoded in the high-order bits as the keys on which to perform an equality match.

Ranges That Include NULLs

To save consumers from having to determine whether NULL values sort at the start or the end of an index, DBRANGE_EXCLUDENULLS excludes NULL values from the final column specified in **pStartData* or **pEndData*. This value of *dwRangeOptions* can be used only with partial keys. It is equivalent to one of the following:

- If NULL values sort at the start of the index, it is equivalent to specifying an additional column in **pStartData*, setting the value of the status of that column to DBSTATUS_S_ISNULL, and setting the DBRANGE_EXCLUSIVESTART value in *dwRangeOptions*. Thus, the range will start after the last NULL value in the column.
- If NULL values sort at the end of the index, it is equivalent to specifying an additional column in **pEndData*, setting the value of the status of that column to DBSTATUS_S_ISNULL, and setting the DBRANGE_EXCLUSIVEEND value in *dwRangeOptions*. Thus, the range will end before the first NULL value in the column.

Therefore, the consumer does not need to know if NULL values sort at the start or end of the index.

The DBRANGE_EXCLUDENULLS flag is defined to allow consumers to easily obtain contiguous key values excluding NULLs at the start or end of the range. For multicolumn indexes (for example, [X, Y]), this means that key values for the prefix of the key must be an equality match. For example, it makes sense to set a range on **X = 5** and DBRANGE_EXCLUDENULLS, but not on **X BETWEEN 4 AND 6** and DBRANGE_EXCLUDENULLS because the range **X BETWEEN 4 AND 6** and **Y IS NOT NULL** is not contiguous. Therefore, to use DBRANGE_EXCLUDENULLS, a consumer must use an equality comparison or **MATCH** on the prefix of a multicolumn key.

To determine how an index treats NULLs, a consumer checks the information returned by **GetIndexInfo** method or the INDEXES schema rowset of **IDBSchemaRowset**.

Examples

Desired range	SetRange call
X is NULL	`SetRange(hAcc, 1, {NULL}, 1, {NULL}, DBRANGE_INCLUSIVESTART | DBRANGE_INCLUSIVEEND);`
X is not NULL	`SetRange(hAcc, 0, NULL, 0, NULL, DBRANGE_EXCLUDENULLS);`
A = 4 and B is not NULL	`SetRange(hAcc, 1,{4}, 1, {4}, DBRANGE_INCLUSIVESTART | DBRANGE_INCLUSIVEEND | DBRANGE_EXCLUDENULLS);`
A = 4 and B is not NULL	`SetRange(hAcc, 1, {4}, 0, NULL, DBRANGE_MATCH | DBRANGE_EXCLUDENULLS );`

Duplicate Keys

A **SetRange** request (with the exclusive flag on an ascending index allowing duplicate keys) sets the index position at the first index entry greater than the **pStartData* value. If the index is descending, **SetRange** sets the position at the first entry less than the **pStartData* value.

End of Range

An index is traversed using **IRowset::GetNextRows**. This method returns DB_S_ENDOFROWSET when it reaches the end of the currently set range or when it tries to read before the beginning or after the end of the index. This method also returns DB_S_ENDOFROWSET when the rowset is being populated asynchronously and no additional rows are available at this time. To determine whether additional rows may be available, the consumer should call **IDBAsynchStatus::GetStatus** or listen for the **IDBAsynchNotify::OnStop** notification.

Inclusive and Exclusive Ranges with Descending Indexes

As mentioned earlier, with descending indexes the user specifies the values that determine the start of the range using **pStartData* and the values that determine the end of the range using **pEndData*. The following are some examples.

Examples with full keys

a) open ranges (single column key)

Desired range	SetRange call
$X > 5$	`SetRange(hAcc, 0, NULL, 1, {5}, DBRANGE_EXCLUSIVEEND);`
$X \geq 5$	`SetRange(hAcc, 0, NULL, 1, {5}, DBRANGE_INCLUSIVEEND);`
$X < 5$	`SetRange(hAcc, 1, {5}, 0, NULL, DBRANGE_EXCLUSIVESTART);`
$X \leq 5$	`SetRange(hAcc, 1, {5}, 0, NULL, DBRANGE_INCLUSIVESTART);`

b) closed ranges (single column key)

Desired range	SetRange call

X ≥ 5 and
X ≤ 10
	`SetRange(hAcc, 1, {10}, 1, {5},`
	`DBRANGE_INCLUSIVESTART |`
	`DBRANGE_INCLUSIVEEND);`

X ≥ 5 and
X < 10
	`SetRange(hAcc, 1, {10}, 1, {5},`
	`DBRANGE_EXCLUSIVESTART |`
	`DBRANGE_INCLUSIVEEND);`

X > 5 and
X ≤ 10
	`SetRange(hAcc, 1, {10}, 1, {5},`
	`DBRANGE_INCLUSIVESTART |`
	`DBRANGE_EXCLUSIVEEND);`

X > 5 and
X < 10
	`SetRange(hAcc, 1, {10}, 1, {5},`
	`DBRANGE_EXCLUSIVESTART |`
	`DBRANGE_EXCLUSIVEEND);`

c) open ranges (multicolumn key [A, B])

The only way to specify open ranges with multicolumn indexes is by using partial keys. See examples with partial keys below.

The range A > 5 and B = 1 cannot be specified because it does not correspond to a contiguous range.

d) closed ranges (multicolumn key [A, B])

Desired range	SetRange call

A = 1 and
B ≥ 5 and
B ≤ 10
	`SetRange(hAcc, 2, {1, 10}, 2, {1, 5},`
	`DBRANGE_INCLUSIVESTART |`
	`DBRANGE_INCLUSIVEEND);`

A = 1 and B > 5	`SetRange(hAcc, 1, {1}, 2, {1, 5},`
	`DBRANGE_INCLUSIVESTART |`
	`DBRANGE_EXCLUSIVEEND);`

A = 1 and B < 5	`SetRange(hAcc, 2, {1, 5}, 1, {1},`
	`DBRANGE_EXCLUSIVESTART |`
	`DBRANGE_INCLUSIVEEND);`

Examples with partial keys

e) open ranges (multicolumn key [A, B])

Desired range	SetRange call
$A > 5$	`SetRange(hAcc, 0, NULL, 1, {5}, DBRANGE_EXCLUSIVEEND);`
$A \geq 5$	`SetRange(hAcc, 0, NULL, 1, {5}, DBRANGE_INCLUSIVEEND);`
$A = 5$	`SetRange(hAcc, 1, {5}, 1, {5}, DBRANGE_INCLUSIVESTART | DBRANGE_INCLUSIVEEND);`
$A < 5$	`SetRange(hAcc, 1, {5}, 0, NULL, DBRANGE_EXCLUSIVESTART);`
$A \leq 5$	`SetRange(hAcc, 1, {5}, 0, NULL, DBRANGE_INCLUSIVESTART);`

f) closed ranges (multicolumn key [A,B])

Desired range	SetRange call
$A > 5$ and $A \leq 10$	`SetRange(hAcc, 1, {10}, 1, {5}, DBRANGE_INCLUSIVESTART | DBRANGE_EXCLUSIVEEND);`

See Also

IRowset::GetNextRows, **IRowsetIndex::Seek**

IRowsetInfo

IRowsetInfo provides information about a rowset.

When to Implement

All rowsets must implement **IRowsetInfo**.

When to Call

When a consumer gets an interface pointer on a rowset, its first step usually is to determine the rowset's capabilities using **IUnknown::QueryInterface**. It may call **GetProperties** to learn the properties of the rowset that do not show up as distinct interfaces, such as the maximum number of active rows and how many rows can have pending updates at the same time.

IRowsetInfo also provides methods for retrieving objects associated with the rowset. **GetSpecification** gets the object (command or session) that created the rowset. **GetReferencedRowset** gets the rowset that is referenced by a bookmark-valued column.

Method	Description
GetProperties	Returns the current setting of all properties supported by the rowset.
GetReferencedRowset	Returns an interface pointer to the rowset to which a bookmark applies.
GetSpecification	Returns an interface pointer on the object (command or session) that created the rowset.

IRowsetInfo::GetProperties

Returns the current settings of all properties supported by the rowset.

```
HRESULT GetProperties (
   const ULONG          cPropertyIDSets,
   const DBPROPIDSET    rgPropertyIDSets[],
   ULONG *              pcPropertySets,
   DBPROPSET **         prgPropertySets);
```

Parameters

cPropertyIDSets
[in]
The number of DBPROPIDSET structures in *rgPropertyIDSets*.

If *cPropertySets* is zero, the provider ignores *rgPropertyIDSets* and returns the values of all properties in the Rowset property group for which values exist, including properties for which values were not set but for which defaults exist, and also including properties for which values were set automatically because values were set for other properties.

If *cPropertyIDSets* is not zero, the provider returns the values of the requested properties. If a property is not supported, the returned value of *dwStatus* in the returned DBPROP structure for that property is DBPROPSTATUS_NOTSUPPORTED and the value of *dwOptions* is undefined.

rgPropertyIDSets
[in]
An array of *cPropertyIDSets* DBPROPIDSET structures. The properties specified in these structures must belong to the Rowset property group. The provider returns the values of the properties specified in these structures. If *cPropertyIDSets* is zero, this parameter is ignored.

For information about the properties in the Rowset property group that are defined by OLE DB, see "Properties Table (by Property Groups)" in Appendix C, "Property Tables." For information about the DBPROPIDSET structure, see "DBPROPIDSET Structure" in Chapter 11, "Properties."

pcPropertySets
[out]
A pointer to memory in which to return the number of DBPROPSET structures returned in **prgPropertySets*. If *cPropertyIDSets* is zero, **pcPropertySets* is the total number of property sets for which the provider supports at least one property in the Rowset property group. If *cPropertyIDSets* is greater than zero, **pcPropertySets* is set to *cPropertyIDSets*. If an error other than DB_E_ERRORSOCCURRED occurs, **pcPropertySets* is set to zero.

prgPropertySets

[out]

A pointer to memory in which to return an array of DBPROPSET structures. If *cPropertyIDSets* is zero, one structure is returned for each property set that contains at least one property belonging to the Rowset property group. If *cPropertyIDSets* is not zero, one structure is returned for each property set specified in *rgPropertyIDSets*.

If *cPropertyIDSets* is not zero, the DBPROPSET structures in **prgPropertySets* are returned in the same order as the DBPROPIDSET structures in *rgPropertyIDSets*; that is, for corresponding elements of each array, the *guidPropertySet* elements are the same. If *cPropertyIDs*, in an element of *rgPropertyIDSets*, is not zero, the DBPROP structures in the corresponding element of **prgPropertySets* are returned in the same order as the DBPROPID values in *rgPropertyIDs*. Therefore, in the case where no column properties are specified in *rgPropertyIDSets*, corresponding elements of the input *rgPropertyIDs* and the returned *rgProperties* have the same property ID. However, if a column property is requested in *rgPropertyIDSets*, multiple properties may be returned, one for each column, in *rgProperties*. In this case, corresponding elements of *rgPropertyIDs* and *rgProperties* will not have the same property ID and *rgProperties* will contain more elements than *rgPropertyIDs*.

The provider allocates memory for the structures and returns the address to this memory; the consumer releases this memory with **IMalloc::Free** when it no longer needs the structures. Before calling **IMalloc::Free** for **prgPropertySets*, the consumer should call **IMalloc::Free** for the *rgProperties* element within each element of **prgPropertySets*. If **pcPropertySets* is zero on output or an if error other than DB_E_ERRORSOCCURRED occurs, the provider does not allocate any memory and ensures that **prgPropertySets* is a null pointer on output.

For information about the DBPROPSET and DBPROP structures, see "DBPROPSET Structure" and "DBPROP Structure" in Chapter 11, "Properties."

Return Code

S_OK
The method succeeded. In all DBPROP structures returned by the method, *dwStatus* is set to DBPROPSTATUS_OK.

DB_S_ERRORSOCCURRED
No value was returned for one or more properties. The consumer checks *dwStatus* in the DBPROP structure to determine the properties for which values were not returned. **GetProperties** can fail to return properties for a number of reasons, including:

- The property was not supported by the provider.
- The property was not in the Rowset property group.
- The property set was not supported by the provider. If *cPropertyIDs* in the DBPROPIDSET structure for the property set was zero, the provider cannot set *dwStatus* in the DBPROP structure because it does not know the IDs of any properties in the property set. Instead, it sets *cProperties* to zero in the DBPROPSET structure returned for the property set.

E_FAIL
A provider-specific error occurred.

E_INVALIDARG
cPropertyIDSets was not equal to zero, and *rgPropertyIDSets* was a null pointer.

pcPropertySets or *prgPropertySets* was a null pointer.

In an element of *rgPropertyIDSets*, *cPropertyIDs* was not zero and *rgPropertyIDs* was a null pointer.

E_OUTOFMEMORY
The provider was unable to allocate sufficient memory in which to return the DBPROPSET or DBPROP structures.

E_UNEXPECTED
ITransaction::Commit or **ITransaction::Abort** was called, and the object is in a zombie state.

DB_E_ERRORSOCCURRED
Values were not returned for any properties. The provider allocates memory for **prgPropertySets*, and the consumer checks *dwStatus* in the DBPROP structures to determine why properties were not returned. The consumer frees this memory when it no longer needs the information.

Comments

This method makes no logical change to the state of the object.

Even though **IDBProperties::GetPropertyInfo** lists a property as being supported by the provider, **GetProperties** will not return a value for it if it does not apply to the current circumstances. For example, the provider's ability to support the property might be affected by the current transaction or the current command text.

IRowsetInfo::GetProperties might return a different value for a property than does **ICommandProperties::GetProperties**. For example, if a consumer requests ordered bookmarks if they are possible, it calls **ICommandProperties::SetProperties** to set the value of DBPROP_ORDEREDBOOKMARKS to VARIANT_TRUE and specifies a *dwOptions* value of DBPROPOPTIONS_OPTIONAL. If the provider cannot determine whether this is possible, **ICommandProperties::GetProperties** returns a value of VARIANT_TRUE and a *dwOptions* of DBPROPOPTIONS_OPTIONAL for this property. If the provider determines during execution that ordered bookmarks are not possible, **IRowsetInfo::GetProperties** returns a value of VARIANT_FALSE and a *dwOptions* of zero.

See Also

ICommandProperties::SetProperties, **IDBProperties::GetPropertyInfo**

IRowsetInfo::GetReferencedRowset

Returns an interface pointer to the rowset to which a bookmark or chapter applies.

```
HRESULT GetReferencedRowset (
   ULONG        iOrdinal,
   REFIID       riid,
   IUnknown ** ppReferencedRowset);
```

Parameters

iOrdinal
[in]
The bookmark or chapter column for which to get the related rowset.

riid
[in]
The IID of the interface pointer to return in **ppReferencedRowset*. This interface is conceptually added to the list of required interfaces on the resulting rowset, and the method fails (E_NOINTERFACE) if that interface cannot be supported on the resulting rowset.

ppReferencedRowset
[out]
A pointer to memory in which to return an **IUnknown** interface pointer on the rowset that interprets values from this column. If this is not a reference column, **ppReferencedRowset* is set to a null pointer.

Return Code

S_OK
The method succeeded.

E_FAIL
A provider-specific error occurred.

E_INVALIDARG
ppReferencedRowset was a null pointer.

E_NOINTERFACE
The interface specified in *riid* was not implicitly or explicitly specified as a rowset property of the rowset. The current rowset remains valid.

E_UNEXPECTED
ITransaction::Commit or **ITransaction::Abort** was called, and the object is in a zombie state.

DB_E_BADORDINAL
The column specified by *iOrdinal* did not exist.

DB_E_NOTAREFERENCECOLUMN
The column specified by *iOrdinal* did not contain bookmarks or chapter values.

DB_E_NOTREENTRANT
The provider called a method from **IRowsetNotify** in the consumer that had not yet returned, and the provider does not support reentrancy in this method.

DB_E_NOTSUPPORTED
The interface was exposed on an index rowset.

Comments

This method makes no logical change to the state of the current rowset.

All of the bookmarks or chapter values in a column reference a single rowset. The references can apply to the current rowset (an example would be genealogy relations on a People table), or they can apply to a different rowset (an example of which would be Customer Orders).

For more information, see "Bookmarks" or "Chapters" in Chapter 4, "Rowsets."

See Also

IChapteredRowset, **IColumnsInfo**, **IColumnsRowset**

IRowsetInfo::GetSpecification

Returns an interface pointer on the object (command or session) that created this rowset.

```
HRESULT GetSpecification (
   REFIID      riid,
   IUnknown ** ppSpecification);
```

Parameters

riid
[in]
The IID of the interface on which to return a pointer.

ppSpecification
[out]
A pointer to memory in which to return the interface pointer. If the provider does not have an object that created the rowset, it sets **ppSpecification* to a null pointer and returns S_FALSE. If **GetSpecification** fails, it must attempt to set **ppSpecification* to a null pointer.

Return Code

S_OK
The method succeeded.

S_FALSE
The provider does not have an object that created the rowset.

E_FAIL
A provider-specific error occurred.

E_INVALIDARG
ppSpecification was a null pointer.

E_NOINTERFACE
The object that created this rowset did not support the interface specified in *riid*.

E_UNEXPECTED
ITransaction::Commit or **ITransaction::Abort** was called, and the object is in a zombie state.

DB_E_NOTREENTRANT
The provider called a method from **IRowsetNotify** in the consumer that had not yet returned, and the provider does not support reentrancy in this method.

Comments

This method makes no logical change to the state of the current rowset.

GetSpecification returns an interface pointer on the object that created the rowset. If the rowset was created by **ICommand::Execute**, this object is a command. If the rowset was created by **IOpenRowset::OpenRowset**, this object is a session.

If the object is not a command, it must specify the contents of the rowset. That is, it must expose interfaces that can be used to modify the contents of the rowset before the rowset is created, or be used to gain additional information about the rowset. If the object cannot expose such interfaces, **GetSpecification** should return a null pointer in **ppSpecification*. In a simple provider, such as a provider that creates a rowset over a fixed set of data, there might not be an object that created the rowset; in this case, **GetSpecification** returns a null pointer in **ppSpecification*.

See Also

ICommand::GetDBSession, **IGetDataSource::GetDataSource**

IRowsetLocate : IRowset

IRowsetLocate is the interface for fetching arbitrary rows of a rowset. A rowset that does not implement this interface is a *sequential* rowset. **IRowsetLocate** is a prerequisite for **IRowsetScroll**.

When **IRowsetLocate** or one of its direct descendants is present on a rowset, column 0 is the bookmark for the rows. Reading this column will obtain a bookmark value that can be used to reposition to the same row.

When to Implement

IRowsetLocate is required for all providers that intend to support general consumers.

Method	Description
Compare	Compares two bookmarks.
GetRowsAt	Fetches rows, starting with the row specified by an offset from a bookmark.
GetRowsByBookmark	Fetches the rows that match the specified bookmarks.
Hash	Returns hash values for the specified bookmarks.

IRowsetLocate::Compare

Compares two bookmarks.

```
HRESULT Compare (
   HCHAPTER         hChapter,
   ULONG            cbBookmark1,
   const BYTE *     pBookmark1,
   ULONG            cbBookmark2,
   const BYTE *     pBookmark2,
   DBCOMPARE *      pComparison);
```

Parameters

hChapter
[in]
The chapter handle. For nonchaptered rowsets, the caller must set *hChapter* to DB_NULL_HCHAPTER.

cbBookmark1
[in]
The length in bytes of the first bookmark.

pBookmark1
[in]
A pointer to the first bookmark. This can be a pointer to DBBMK_FIRST or DBBMK_LAST.

cbBookmark2
[in]
The length in bytes of the second bookmark.

pBookmark2
[in]
A pointer to the second bookmark. This can be a pointer to DBBMK_FIRST or DBBMK_LAST.

pComparison
[out]
A pointer to memory in which to return a flag that specifies the result of the comparison. The returned flag will be one of the values described in the following table.

Value	Description
DBCOMPARE_LT	The first bookmark is before the second.
DBCOMPARE_EQ	The two bookmarks are equal.
DBCOMPARE_GT	The first bookmark is after the second.
DBCOMPARE_NE	The bookmarks are not equal and not ordered.
DBCOMPARE_NOTCOMPARABLE	The two bookmarks cannot be compared.

Return Code

S_OK
: The method succeeded.

E_FAIL
: A provider-specific error occurred.

E_INVALIDARG
: *cbBookmark1* or *cbBookmark2* was zero.

: *pBookmark1*, *pBookmark2*, or *pComparison* was a null pointer.

E_UNEXPECTED
: **ITransaction::Commit** or **ITransaction::Abort** was called, and the object is in a zombie state.

DB_E_BADBOOKMARK
: **pBookmark1* or **pBookmark2* was invalid, incorrectly formed, or DBBMK_INVALID.

> **Note** Consumers should attempt to use only bookmarks that they have received from the provider. The provider is guaranteed to handle only bookmarks it gives out in a predictable manner. Attempting to use a random value as a bookmark is undefined; the provider may return DB_E_BADBOOKMARK, may return an unexpected row, or may terminate abnormally.

DB_E_BADCHAPTER
: The rowset was chaptered and *hChapter* was invalid.

: The rowset was single-chaptered, and the specified chapter was not the currently open chapter. The consumer must use the currently open chapter or release the currently open chapter before specifying a new chapter.

DB_E_NOTREENTRANT
: The provider called a method from **IRowsetNotify** in the consumer that had not yet returned, and the provider does not support reentrancy in this method.

Comments

This method makes no logical change to the state of the object.

If bookmarks are ordered, they can be compared to determine the relative position of their associated rows in the rowset. The DBPROP_ORDEREDBOOKMARKS property indicates whether bookmarks are ordered. If bookmarks are not ordered, the returned comparison value will be DBCOMPARE_EQ or DBCOMPARE_NE. If bookmarks are ordered, the returned comparison value will be DBCOMPARE_LT, DBCOMPARE_EQ, or DBCOMPARE_GT. The command that creates the rowset does not have to have an ordered text command, such as an SQL statement containing an **ORDER BY** clause, to have ordered bookmarks.

Compare can compare any valid bookmarks. The consumer is not required to have permission to read the corresponding rows, nor are the rows even required to exist—for example, they might have been deleted.

If the DBPROP_LITERALBOOKMARKS property is VARIANT_TRUE, consumers can directly compare values.

Specifying the bookmark DBBMK_FIRST or DBBMK_LAST returns DBCOMPARE_EQ when compared with itself and DBCOMPARE_NE when compared with any other bookmark.

See Also

IRowsetIdentity::IsSameRow, **IRowsetLocate::Hash**

IRowsetLocate::GetRowsAt

Fetches rows starting with the row specified by an offset from a bookmark.

```
HRESULT GetRowsAt (
   HWATCHREGION     hReserved1,
   HCHAPTER         hChapter
   ULONG            cbBookmark,
   const BYTE *     pBookmark,
   LONG             lRowsOffset,
   LONG             cRows,
   ULONG *          pcRowsObtained,
   HROW **          prghRows);
```

Parameters

hReserved1

[in]

Reserved for future use. Providers ignore this parameter.

hChapter

[in]

The chapter handle. For nonchaptered rowsets, the caller must set *hChapter* to DB_NULL_HCHAPTER.

cbBookmark

[in]

The length in bytes of the bookmark. This must not be zero.

pBookmark

[in]

A pointer to a bookmark that identifies the base row to be used. This can be a pointer to DBBMK_FIRST or DBBMK_LAST. If *lRowsOffset* is zero, the provider fetches this row first; otherwise the provider skips this and subsequent rows up to the count specified in the offset and then fetches the following rows.

lRowsOffset

[in]

The signed count of rows from the origin bookmark to the target row. Deleted rows that the provider has removed from the rowset are not counted in the skip. The first row fetched is determined by the bookmark and this offset. For example, if *lRowsOffset* is zero, the first row fetched is the bookmarked row; if *lRowsOffset* is 1, the first row fetched is the row after the bookmarked row; if *lRowsOffset* is –1, the first row fetched is the row before the bookmarked row.

lRowsOffset can be a negative number only if the value of the DBPROP_CANSCROLLBACKWARDS property is VARIANT_TRUE.

cRows
[in]
The number of rows to fetch. A negative number means to fetch backward. *cRows* can be a negative number only if the value of the DBPROP_CANFETCHBACKWARDS property is VARIANT_TRUE.

If *cRows* is zero, no rows are fetched; the fetch direction and the next fetch position are unchanged, and the provider performs no processing, returning immediately from the method invocation. Specifically, *lRowsOffset* is ignored in this situation.

If the provider does not discover any other errors, the method returns S_OK; whether the provider checks for any other errors is provider-specific.

See the Comments section for a full description of the semantics of *lRowsOffset* and *cRows* parameters.

pcRowsObtained
[out]
A pointer to memory in which to return the actual number of fetched rows. If the consumer has insufficient permission to fetch all rows, **GetRowsAt** fetches all rows for which the consumer has sufficient permission and skips all other rows. If the method fails, **pcRowsObtained* is set to zero.

prghRows
[in/out]
A pointer to memory in which to return an array of handles of the fetched rows. If **prghRows* is not a null pointer on input, it must be a pointer to memory large enough to return the handles of the requested number of rows. If **prghRows* is a null pointer on input, the rowset allocates memory for the row handles and returns the address to this memory. The consumer releases this memory with **IMalloc::Free** after it releases the row handles. If **prghRows* was a null pointer on input and **pcRowsObtained* is zero on output or if the method fails, the provider does not allocate any memory and ensures that **prghRows* is a null pointer on output.

Return Code

S_OK
The method succeeded.

DB_S_BOOKMARKSKIPPED
The following behavior is supported only on rowsets that set the DBPROP_BOOKMARKSKIPPED property to VARIANT_TRUE. If this property is VARIANT_FALSE, this return code is never returned.

lRowsOffset was zero and the row specified by **pBookmark* was deleted or is no longer a member of the rowset, or the row specified by the combination of **pBookmark* and *lRowsOffset* is a row to which the consumer does not have access rights. **GetRowsAt** skipped that row. The full count of actual rows (*cRows*) will be met if there are enough rows available. The array of returned row handles does not have gaps for missing rows; the returned count is the number of rows actually fetched.

If a row is skipped, it is counted as one of the rows to be skipped for *lRowsOffset*. For example, if an offset of 1 is requested and the bookmark points to a row which is now missing, the offset is decremented by 1 and the provider begins by fetching the next row.

If this condition occurs along with another warning condition, the method returns the code for the other warning condition. Thus, whenever a consumer receives the return code for another warning condition, it should check to see whether this condition occurred.

DB_S_ENDOFROWSET
GetRowsAt reached the start or the end of the rowset or chapter and could not fetch all of the requested rows because the count extended beyond the end. The number of rows actually fetched is returned in **pcRowsObtained*; this will be less than *cRows*.

The rowset is being populated asynchronously and no additional rows are available at this time. To determine whether additional rows may be available, the consumer should call **IDBAsynchStatus::GetStatus** or listen for the **IDBAsynchNotify::OnStop** notification.

lRowsOffset indicated a position either more than one row before the first row of the rowset or more than one row after the last row, and the provider was a version 2.0 or greater provider. **pcRowsObtained* is set to zero and no rows are returned.

DB_S_ROWLIMITEXCEEDED
Fetching the number of rows specified in *cRows* would have exceeded the total number of active rows supported by the rowset. The number of rows that were actually fetched is returned in **pcRowsObtained*. This condition can occur only when there are more rows available than can be handled by the rowset. Thus, this condition never conflicts with those described in DB_S_ENDOFROWSET and DB_S_STOPLIMITREACHED, both of which imply that no more rows were available.

DB_S_STOPLIMITREACHED
Fetching rows required further execution of the command, such as when the rowset uses a server-side cursor. Execution has been stopped because a resource limit has been reached. The number of rows that were actually fetched is returned in **pcRowsObtained*.

E_FAIL
A provider-specific error occurred.

E_INVALIDARG
cbBookmark was zero or *pBookmark* was a null pointer.

pcRowsObtained or *prghRows* was a null pointer.

E_OUTOFMEMORY
The provider was unable to allocate sufficient memory in which to instantiate the rows or return the row handles.

E_UNEXPECTED
ITransaction::Commit or **ITransaction::Abort** was called, and the object is in a zombie state.

DB_E_BADBOOKMARK
**pBookmark* was invalid, incorrectly formed, or DBBMK_INVALID.

**pBookmark* did not match any rows in the rowset. This includes the case when the row corresponding to the bookmark has been deleted and DBPROP_BOOKMARKSKIPPED was VARIANT_FALSE.

> **Note** Consumers should attempt to use only bookmarks that they have received from the provider. The provider is guaranteed to handle only bookmarks it gives out in a predictable manner. Attempting to use a random value as a bookmark is undefined; the provider may return DB_E_BADBOOKMARK, may return an unexpected row, or may terminate abnormally.

DB_E_BADCHAPTER
The rowset was chaptered and *hChapter* was invalid.

The rowset was single-chaptered, and the specified chapter was not the currently open chapter. The consumer must use the currently open chapter or release the currently open chapter before specifying a new chapter.

DB_E_BADSTARTPOSITION
lRowsOffset indicated a position either more than one row before the first row of the rowset or more than one row after the last row, and the provider was a 1.*x* provider.

DB_E_CANTFETCHBACKWARDS
cRows was negative, and the rowset cannot fetch backward.

DB_E_CANTSCROLLBACKWARDS
lRowsOffset was negative, and the rowset cannot scroll backward.

DB_E_NOTREENTRANT
The provider called a method from **IRowsetNofity** in the consumer that had not yet returned, and the provider does not support reentrancy in this method.

DB_E_ROWSNOTRELEASED
The provider requires release of existing rows before new ones can be fetched. For more information, see DBPROP_CANHOLDROWS in "Properties Table (Alphabetical)" in Appendix C, "Property Tables."

DB_SEC_E_PERMISSIONDENIED
The consumer did not have sufficient permission to fetch any of the rows; no rows were fetched.

Comments

Given values for a bookmark, offset, and number of rows to fetch:

- The provider determines a starting position for the fetch as the bookmark plus the offset.
- If the starting position is off either end of the rowset, the method returns DB_S_ENDOFROWSET.
- If the starting position is in the rowset, the provider fetches rows in the specified direction until it has fetched the requested number of rows or hits the end of the rowset.
- If it fetches the requested number of rows, it returns S_OK. If it hits the end of the rowset, it stops fetching, returns DB_S_ENDOFROWSET, and returns the rows it has fetched.
- The rows are returned in rowset traversal order; that is, the direction in which they were fetched. For example, if the consumer passes the bookmark for row 10 to **GetRowsAt** and specifies *cRows* equal to – 5 and *lRowsOffset* equal to 0, **GetRowsAt** returns rows 10 through 6. That is, **prghRows*[0] is the handle for row 10 and **prghRows*[4] is the handle for row 6.

The following table defines the behavior of **GetRowsAt** for all combinations of these parameters.

Variable	Description
N	Total rows in the rowset.
B	Row in the rowset specified by the bookmark parameters *cbBookmark* and *pBookmark*. Assume $1 \leq B \leq N$, DBBMK_FIRST is equivalent to $B = 1$, and DBBMK_LAST is equivalent to $B = N$.
F	*lRowsOffset*
r	*cRows*

B + *F*	*r*	*cRowsObtained*	Return code
$B + F < 1$ or $B + F > N$	N/A	0	DB_S_ENDOFROWSET
$1 \le B + F \le N$	0	0	S_OK
$1 \le B + F \le N$	$1 \le r \le N - B - F + 1$	r	S_OK
$1 \le B + F \le N$	$r > N - B - F + 1$	$N - B - F + 1$	DB_S_ENDOFROWSET
$1 \le B + F \le N$	$r < 0$ and $\text{abs}(r) \le B + F$	abs(r)	S_OK
$1 \le B + F \le N$	$r < 0$ and $\text{abs}(r) > B + F$	$B + F$	DB_S_ENDOFROWSET

Consumers that want to fetch forward, for example, 20 rows at a time, can use the call **GetRowsAt**(..., *B*, 1, 20, ...), which allows for an easy check when reaching the end of the rowset. Similarly, consumers that want to fetch backward can use the call **GetRowsAt**(..., *B*, –1, –20, ...) to facilitate the detection of the beginning of the rowset. In the latter case, DBPROP_CANFETCHBACKWARDS must be set to VARIANT_TRUE.

The DBPROP_BOOKMARKSKIPPED property defines the behavior for cases in which there is no exact match for the bookmark pointed to by *pBookmark*. If this property is set to VARIANT_FALSE, DB_E_BADBOOKMARK will be returned because the corresponding position is not well-defined. The behavior when this property is set to VARIANT_TRUE is as follows:

- If *lRowsOffset* is zero, the row is skipped, the requested number of rows are fetched from subsequent rows, and a DB_S_BOOKMARKSKIPPED warning is returned.
- If *lRowsOffset* and *cRows* are any value except zero, the fetch succeeds, based on the position of the row before it became invalid. For example, suppose row 20 is deleted. If a consumer calls **GetRowsAt** with *lRowsOffset* set to 5 and a bookmark that points to row 20, **GetRowsAt** moves to row 25.

If the provider encounters a problem fetching a row—for example, data stored in a text file contains a letter in a numeric column—**GetRowsAt** fetches the row normally, returns the row handle, and returns S_OK. However, when the consumer calls **IRowset::GetData** for the row, the provider returns DBSTATUS_E_CANTCONVERTVALUE as the status for the offending column.

For information about what **GetRowsAt** does when it fetches a row that it already has in its internal buffers, see "Uniqueness of Rows in the Rowset" in Chapter 4, "Rowsets." For information about whether **GetRowsAt** can detect changes made to rows in the rowset, see "Visibility of Changes" in Chapter 5, "Updating Data in Rowsets."

GetRowsAt increments the reference count of each row for which it returns a handle by 1. Therefore, if a handle is returned for a row that has already been fetched, the reference count of that row will be greater than 1. **ReleaseRows** must be called once for each time the handle to a row has been returned.

To use **GetRowsAt** several times in sequence to obtain successive rows, the consumer should obtain the bookmark of the last row of the previous set and use that, with a skip of 1, to position for fetching the next rows.

See Also

IRowset::GetData, **IRowset::GetNextRows**, **IRowsetLocate::GetRowsByBookmark**, **IRowsetScroll::GetRowsAtRatio**

IRowsetLocate::GetRowsByBookmark

Fetches the rows that match the specified bookmarks.

```
HRESULT GetRowsByBookmark (
   HCHAPTER       hChapter,
   ULONG          cRows,
   const ULONG    rgcbBookmarks[],
   const BYTE *   rgpBookmarks[],
   HROW           rghRows[],
   DBROWSTATUS    rgRowStatus[]);
```

Parameters

hChapter
[in]
The chapter handle. For nonchaptered rowsets, the caller must set *hChapter* to DB_NULL_HCHAPTER.

cRows
[in]
The number of rows to fetch.

If *cRows* is zero, no rows are fetched; the fetch direction and the next fetch position are unchanged, and the provider performs no processing, returning immediately from the method invocation.

If the provider does not discover any other errors, the method returns S_OK; whether the provider checks for any other errors is provider-specific.

rgcbBookmarks
[in]
An array containing the length in bytes of each bookmark.

rgpBookmarks

[in]

An array containing a pointer to the bookmark of each row sought. These cannot be pointers to a standard bookmark (DBBMK_FIRST, DBBMK_LAST, DBBMK_INVALID). If *rgpBookmarks* contains a duplicate bookmark, the corresponding row is fetched and the reference count incremented once for each occurrence of the bookmark.

rghRows

[out]

An array with *cRows* elements in which to return the handles of the fetched rows. The consumer allocates this array but is not required to initialize the elements of it. In each element of this array, if the row was fetched, the provider returns the handle of the row identified by the bookmark in the corresponding element of *rgpBookmarks*. If the row was not fetched, the provider returns DB_NULL_HROW.

rgRowStatus

[out]

An array with *cRows* elements in which to return values indicating the status of each row specified in *rgpBookmarks*. If no errors or warnings occur while fetching a row, the corresponding element of *rgRowStatus* is set to DBROWSTATUS_S_OK. If an error occurs while fetching a row, the corresponding element is set as specified in DB_S_ERRORSOCCURRED. The consumer allocates memory for this array but is not required to initialize it. If *rgRowStatus* is a null pointer, no row statuses are returned. For information about the DBROWSTATUS enumerated type, see "Arrays of Errors" in Chapter 13, "Errors."

Return Code

S_OK

The method succeeded. All rows were successfully fetched. The following value can be returned in *rgRowStatus*:

- The row was successfully fetched. The corresponding element of *rgRowStatus* contains DBROWSTATUS_S_OK.

DB_S_ERRORSOCCURRED

An error occurred while fetching a row, but at least one row was successfully fetched. Successes can occur for the reasons listed under S_OK. The following errors can occur:

- An element of *rgpBookmarks* pointed to an invalid or incorrectly formed bookmark. The corresponding element of *rgRowStatus* contains DBROWSTATUS_E_INVALID.
- An element of *rgpBookmarks* pointed to a bookmark that did not match any rows in the rowset. This includes the case when the row corresponding to the bookmark has been deleted. The corresponding element of *rgRowStatus* contains DBROWSTATUS_E_INVALID.

- An element of *rgcbBookmarks* was zero. The corresponding element of *rgRowStatus* contains DBROWSTATUS_E_INVALID.
- An element of *rgpBookmarks* was a null pointer. The corresponding element of *rgRowStatus* contains DBROWSTATUS_E_INVALID.
- An element of *rgpBookmarks* pointed to a standard bookmark (DBBMK_FIRST, DBBMK_LAST, DBBMK_INVALID). The corresponding element of *rgRowStatus* contains DBROWSTATUS_E_INVALID.
- The row corresponding to the bookmark was not fetched because fetching it would have exceeded the total number of active rows supported by the rowset. The corresponding element of *rgRowStatus* contains DBROWSTATUS_E_LIMITREACHED.
- The row corresponding to the bookmark was not fetched for the following reason: Fetching rows required further execution of the command, such as when the rowset uses a server-side cursor. Execution has been stopped because a resource limit has been reached. Execution cannot be resumed. The corresponding element of *rgRowStatus* contains DBROWSTATUS_E_LIMITREACHED.
- The rowset ran out of memory and was unable to fetch the row. The corresponding element of *rgRowStatus* contains DBROWSTATUS_E_OUTOFMEMORY.
- The consumer did not have sufficient permission to fetch a row. The corresponding element of *rgRowStatus* contains DBROWSTATUS_E_PERMISSIONDENIED.
- The consumer encountered a recoverable, provider-specific error, such as an RPC failure when transmitting the change to a remote server. The corresponding element of *rgRowStatus* contains DBROWSTATUS_E_FAIL.

E_FAIL
A provider-specific error occurred.

E_INVALIDARG
rghRows was a null pointer.

rgcbBookmarks or *rgpBookmarks* was a null pointer.

E_OUTOFMEMORY
The provider was unable to allocate sufficient memory in which to return the row handles.

E_UNEXPECTED
ITransaction::Commit or **ITransaction::Abort** was called, and the object is in a zombie state.

DB_E_BADCHAPTER
The rowset was chaptered and *hChapter* was invalid.

The rowset was single-chaptered, and the specified chapter was not the currently open chapter. The consumer must use the currently open chapter or release the currently open chapter before specifying a new chapter.

DB_E_ERRORSOCCURRED
Errors occurred while fetching all of the rows. Errors can occur for the reasons listed under DB_S_ERRORSOCCURRED.

DB_E_NOTREENTRANT
The provider called a method from **IRowsetNofity** in the consumer that had not yet returned, and the provider does not support reentrancy in this method.

DB_E_ROWSNOTRELEASED
The provider requires release of existing rows before new ones can be fetched. For more information, see DBPROP_CANHOLDROWS in "Properties Table (Alphabetical)" in Appendix C, "Property Tables."

Comments

GetRowsByBookmark increments the reference count of each row for which it returns a handle by 1. Therefore, if a handle is returned for a row that has already been fetched, the reference count of that row will be greater than 1. **ReleaseRows** must be called once for each time the handle to a row has been returned.

If the provider encounters a problem fetching a row—for example, data stored in a text file contains a letter in a numeric colum—**GetRowsByBookmark** fetches the row normally, returns the row handle, and returns S_OK. However, when the consumer calls **IRowset::GetData** for the row, the provider returns DBSTATUS_E_CANTCONVERTVALUE as the status for the offending column.

If **GetRowsByBookmark** encounters an error while attempting to fetch a row, such as a bad bookmark or adeleted row, it notes the error in the *rgRowStatus* array, continues processing, and returns DB_S_ERRORSOCCURRED or DB_E_ERRORSOCCURRED. Although the rows are fetched in undefined order, the ordering of the error array must match the order of the bookmark array so that the consumer can perform a side-by-side scan of each array to determine which rows were not fetched.

For information about what **GetRowsByBookmark** does when it fetches a row that it already has in its internal buffers, see "Uniqueness of Rows in the Rowset" in Chapter 4, "Rowsets." For information about whether **GetRowsByBookmark** can detect changes made to rows in the rowset, see "Visibility of Changes" in Chapter 5, "Updating Data in Rowsets."

See Also

IRowset::GetData, **IRowset::GetNextRows**, **IRowsetLocate::GetRowsAt**, **IRowsetScroll::GetRowsAtRatio**

IRowsetLocate::Hash

Returns hash values for the specified bookmarks.

```
HRESULT Hash (
   HCHAPTER         hChapter,
   ULONG            cBookmarks,
   const ULONG      rgcbBookmarks[],
   const BYTE *     rgpBookmarks[],
   DWORD            rgHashedValues[],
   DBROWSTATUS      rgBookmarkStatus[]);
```

Parameters

hChapter

[in]
The chapter handle. For nonchaptered rowsets, the caller must set *hChapter* to DB_NULL_HCHAPTER.

cBookmarks

[in]
The number of bookmarks to hash. If *cBookmarks* is zero, **Hash** does not do anything.

rgcbBookmarks

[in]
An array containing the length in bytes for each bookmark.

rgpBookmarks

[in]
An array of pointers to bookmarks. The bookmarks cannot be standard bookmarks (DBBMK_FIRST, DBBMK_LAST, DBBMK_INVALID). If *rgpBookmarks* contains a duplicate bookmark, a hash value is returned once for each occurrence of the bookmark.

> **Caution** The consumer must ensure that all bookmarks in *rgpBookmarks* are valid. The provider is not required to validate bookmarks before hashing them. Therefore, hash values might be returned for invalid bookmarks.

rgHashedValues

[out]
An array of *cBookmarks* hash values corresponding to the elements of *rgpBookmarks*. The consumer allocates, but is not required to initialize, memory for this array and passes the address of this memory to the provider. The provider returns the hash values in the array.

rgBookmarkStatus
[out]
An array with *cBookmarks* elements in which to return values indicating the status of each bookmark specified in *rgpBookmarks*. If no errors occur while hashing a bookmark, the corresponding element of *rgBookmarkStatus* is set to DBROWSTATUS_S_OK. If an error occurs while hashing a bookmark, the corresponding element is set as specified in DB_S_ERRORSOCCURRED. The consumer allocates memory for this array but is not required to initialize it. If *rgBookmarkStatus* is a null pointer, no bookmark statuses are returned. For information about the DBROWSTATUS enumerated type, see "Arrays of Errors" in Chapter 13, Errors."

Return Code

S_OK
The method succeeded. All bookmarks were successfully hashed. The following value can be returned in *rgRowStatus*:

- The bookmark was successfully hashed. The corresponding element of *rgRowStatus* contains DBROWSTATUS_S_OK.

DB_S_ERRORSOCCURRED
An error occurred while hashing a bookmark, but at least one bookmark was successfully hashed. Successes can occur for the reason listed under S_OK. The following errors can occur:

- An element of *rgpBookmarks* pointed to an invalid or incorrectly formed bookmark. The corresponding element of *rgBookmarkStatus* contains DBROWSTATUS_E_INVALID. Providers are not required to check for this condition, because doing so might slow the method significantly.
- An element of *rgcbBookmarks* was zero. The corresponding element of *rgBookmarkStatus* contains DBROWSTATUS_E_INVALID.
- An element of *rgpBookmarks* was a null pointer. The corresponding element of *rgBookmarkStatus* contains DBROWSTATUS_E_INVALID.
- An element of *rgpBookmarks* pointed to a standard bookmark (DBBMK_FIRST, DBBMK_LAST, DBBMK_INVALID). The corresponding element of *rgBookmarkStatus* contains DBROWSTATUS_E_INVALID.
- The consumer encountered a recoverable, provider-specific error, such as an RPC failure when transmitting the change to a remote server. The corresponding element of *rgRowStatus* contains DBROWSTATUS_E_FAIL.

E_FAIL
A provider-specific error occurred.

E_INVALIDARG
cBookmarks was not zero, and *rgcbBookmarks* or *rgpBookmarks* was a null pointer.

rgHashedValues was a null pointer.

E_UNEXPECTED
ITransaction::Commit or **ITransaction::Abort** was called,and the object is in a zombie state.

DB_E_BADCHAPTER
The rowset was chaptered and *hChapter* was invalid.

The rowset was single-chaptered, and the specified chapter was not the currently open chapter. The consumer must use the currently open chapter or release the currently open chapter before specifying a new chapter.

DB_E_ERRORSOCCURRED
Errors occurred while hashing all of the bookmarks. Errors can occur for the reasons listed under DB_S_ERRORSOCCURRED.

DB_E_NOTREENTRANT
The provider called a method from **IRowsetNotify** in the consumer that had not yet returned, and the provider does not support reentrancy in this method.

Comments

This method makes no logical change to the state of the object.

If two bookmarks point to the same underlying row, the same hash value is returned for both bookmarks. That is, if **Compare** returns DBCOMPARE_EQ for two bookmarks, **Hash** must return the same value for these two bookmarks.

If **Hash** encounters an error while attempting to hash a bookmark, such as a bad bookmark, it notes the error in the error array, continues processing, and returns DB_S_ERRORSOCCURRED or DB_E_ERRORSOCCURRED. Although the rows are hashed in undefined order, the ordering of the error array must match the order of the bookmark array so that the consumer can perform a side-by-side scan of each array to determine which rows were not hashed.

Hash can hash any valid bookmarks. The consumer is not required to have permission to read the corresponding row, nor is the row even required to exist—for example, it might have been deleted.

Standard bookmarks cannot be hashed.

See Also

IRowsetLocate::Compare

IRowsetNotify

IRowsetNotify is the *callback* interface that a consumer must support to connect to local notifications provided by a rowset. The notifications are intended to synchronize objects that are attached to the same rowset instance. The notifications do not reflect changes in underlying shared tables that occur through other programs or users.

The notifications use the standard OLE connection point scheme for events. A rowset supports **IConnectionPointContainer**, and the consumer calls **FindConnectionPoint** for **IID_IRowsetNotify** to obtain the correct **IConnectionPoint** interface. The consumer then advises that connection point to connect and supplies a pointer to the consumer's **IRowsetNotify** interface.

For more information about notifications, see Chapter 9, "OLE DB Object Notifications."

When to Implement

IRowsetNotify is implemented by consumers that require notification. If the command requests support for **IConnectionPointContainer**, the rowset is required to support a connection point for **IRowsetNotify**. Providers should implement this connection point if they expect to work directly with general-purpose consumers.

Notification about transactions is not handled through rowsets. There may be multiple rowsets for each transaction, leading to a flood of events. Consumers that need to be notified of transaction activity should connect to the transaction coordinator. For more information, see "Event Notifications" in Chapter 12, "Transactions."

IRowset is a prerequisite for notification.

DBEVENTPHASE

Events may have phases. A *phased event* is a notification method that is called multiple times, each time with a different phase in the sequence. Some events do not have phases. The phases are similar to phases in two-phase commit protocol, because ensuring that all controls authorize and succeed in handling an event is a problem very similar to ensuring resource managers all agree to, and succeed in, committing a transaction.

In the following descriptions, all consumer objects that connect their **IRowsetNotify** interface to the rowset are the *listeners*.

Value	Description
DBEVENTPHASE_ OKTODO	Informs a listener of an impending event. All listeners must return S_OK from DBEVENTPHASE_OKTODO for the event to proceed. Any listener can cancel the event by returning S_FALSE. The listener can prepare for the event but should do nothing irreversible or time consuming. If a listener cancels the event, all listeners that have already been called will be called again with DBEVENTPHASE_FAILEDTODO.
DBEVENTPHASE_ ABOUTTODO	Informs a listener that DBEVENTPHASE_OKTODO has been approved and all listeners can proceed to final preparations, which must be reversible but which may be lengthy. The listener should cancel this phase only if it is stopped by an error; it should have cleared all logical objections at the earlier DBEVENTPHASE_OKTODO phase. If a listener cancels the event by returning S_FALSE, all listeners that have already been called will be called again with DBEVENTPHASE_FAILEDTODO.
DBEVENTPHASE_ SYNCHAFTER	Informs a listener that the event has occurred after the rowset's copy of the row has been modified but before the data store has received the change. The listener can synchronize itself with the rowset and ensure that it has no physical reason not to agree to commit the event's changes. If a listener cancels the event by returning S_FALSE, all listeners that have already been called will be called again with DBEVENTPHASE_FAILEDTODO.
DBEVENTPHASE_ FAILEDTODO	Informs a listener that has previously been called for this event that the event has failed. The listener should reverse all changes and synchronize with the state of the rowset.
DBEVENTPHASE_ DIDEVENT	Informs a listener that all consumers have synchronized themselves and agreed to commit the event's changes. The listener should now commit its changes. It must comply.

The final phase of an event is always either DBEVENTPHASE_FAILEDTODO or DBEVENTPHASE_DIDEVENT. If the event has no phases, it is equivalent to DBEVENTPHASE_DIDEVENT.

All providers must support the DBEVENTPHASE_FAILEDTODO and DBEVENTPHASE_DIDEVENT phases. Whether providers support DBEVENTPHASE_OKTODO, DBEVENTPHASE_ABOUTTODO, and DBEVENTPHASE_SYNCHAFTER is provider specific, although all but the most simple providers support these phases. To determine which phases a provider supports, a consumer calls **IDBProperties::GetProperties** for the DBPROP_NOTIFICATIONPHASES property.

If a method changes multiple rows and generates a single-phased event, such as DBREASON_ROW_ACTIVATE or DBREASON_ROW_RELEASE, the provider makes a single call to **IRowsetNotify::OnRowChange** and passes an array containing the handles of all of the affected rows.

If a method changes multiple rows and generates a multiphased event, such as DBREASON_ROW_UPDATE or DBREASON_ROW_UNDOCHANGE, the number of calls to **OnRowChange** for each phase depends on the DBPROP_NOTIFICATIONGRANULARITY property.

It is provider-specific whether or not listeners who register after some but not all of the phases of an event have been fired are called for the remaining phases of that event. Listeners must be prepared to get only the final phases of an event upon registering for notifications on an object that is already firing notifications.

DBREASON

Reasons are fine tunings of events. The receiver of events is expected to care only about the general effect of the event, but there may be other effects that more specialized consumers need to know about. The DBEVENT is the basic event, and the DBREASON is a single level of derived subevent.

> **Important** The DBREASON types may be expanded in later versions of OLE DB. **IRowsetNotify** methods must return S_OK or DB_S_UNWANTEDREASON when they receive a DBREASON value they do not recognize.
>
> Providers are not expected to add new DBREASONs to the defined set. Providers defining new DBREASONs should do so through an entirely new notification interface with its own IID.

The following **#define** values are valid for DBREASON.

Value	Description
DBREASON_ROW_ASYNCHINSERT	The rowset is being randomly asynchronously populated, and one or more rows have been inserted. Only the DBEVENTPHASE_DIDEVENT phase occurs.
DBREASON_ROWSET_FETCHPOSITIONCHANGE	The next fetch position changed as a result of a call to **IRowset::GetNextRows** or **IRowset::RestartPosition**. All phases can occur.
DBREASON_ROWSET_RELEASE	The rowset is being released; that is, its reference count is zero. Only the DBEVENTPHASE_DIDEVENT phase occurs. The rowset no longer exists when this event is sent out, so recipients must not make any calls upon it. In COM, there is no way to deny permission to **IUnknown::Release**.

Value	Description
DBREASON_ ROWSET_CHANGED	The rowset metadata has changed. Pointers to interfaces on the rowset remain valid. Providers must revalidate accessors against the metadata, and this might fail due to the changes in the metadata. For example, the accessor might now specify an unsupported conversion. Consumers should free any held row handles when a notification with this DBREASON is generated, because handles to rows are likely to have become invalid. For example, **IRowset::GetData** might return DB_E_BADROWHANDLE, or **IRowsetUpdate::Update** might return DBROWSTATUS_E_INVALID. The result of passing such a row handle is provider-specific, although the provider cannot terminate abnormally. Only the DBEVENTPHASE_DIDEVENT phase occurs.
DBREASON_ COLUMN_SET	A column value is set. All phases can occur.
DBREASON_ COLUMN_RECALCULATED	A calculated column takes a new value because its input columns change. Only the DBEVENTPHASE_DIDEVENT phase occurs.
DBREASON_ ROW_ACTIVATE	A function, such as **IRowset::GetNextRows** or **IRowsetLocate::GetRowsAt**, caused a new set of rows to be fetched. Only the DBEVENTPHASE_DIDEVENT phase occurs.
DBREASON_ ROW_RELEASE	**IRowset::ReleaseRows** was called, and the row's reference count is zero. The array of row handles the provider passed to the listeners is the subset of the original array of row handles passed to **ReleaseRows**—that is, those row handles for which the reference count is zero. Only the DBEVENTPHASE_DIDEVENT phase occurs. The returned row handles might be invalid and therefore should not be used with any methods.
DBREASON_ ROW_DELETE	**IRowsetChange::DeleteRows** has been called. All phases can occur.
DBREASON_ ROW_FIRSTCHANGE	The first time any column in the row is set, this notification occurs. It precedes DBREASON_COLUMN_SET. All phases can occur. This event occurs only when the rowset is in delayed update mode. It occurs the first time a column in a row is modified after the row was fetched or after the last call to **IRowsetUpdate::Update** or **IRowsetUpdate::Undo**, whichever is more recent.

Value	Description
DBREASON_ ROW_INSERT	**IRowsetChange::InsertRow** has been called. All phases can occur.
DBREASON_ ROW_RESYNCH	**IRowsetRefresh::RefreshVisibleData** has been called. All phases can occur.
DBREASON_ ROW_UNDOCHANGE	**IRowsetUpdate::Undo** has been called on a pending change row. All phases can occur.
DBREASON_ ROW_UNDOINSERT	**IRowsetUpdate::Undo** has been called on a pending insert row. All phases can occur.
DBREASON_ ROW_UNDODELETE	**IRowsetUpdate::Undo** has been called on a pending delete row. All phases can occur.
DBREASON_ ROW_UPDATE	**IRowsetUpdate::Update** has been called on a row with a pending change. All phases can occur.

The following table lists all rowset methods, the DBREASON values they generate, and the phases for each reason. Nested notifications occur when the consumer calls another rowset method while processing a notification.

Method	DBREASON generated [1]	Phases
IUnknown::AddRef	None	N/A
IUnknown::QueryInterface	None	N/A
IUnknown::Release	_ROWSET_RELEASE	DIDEVENT
IRowset::AddRefRows	None	N/A
IRowset::GetData	None	N/A
IRowset::GetNextRows	_ROW_ACTIVATE	DIDEVENT
	_ROWSET_FETCHPOSITION-CHANGE	All Phases
IRowset::ReleaseRows	_ROW_RELEASE	DIDEVENT
IRowset::RestartPosition	_ROWSET_FETCHPOSITION-CHANGE	All Phases
	_ROWSET_CHANGED [2]	All Phases
IRowsetChange::DeleteRows	_ROW_DELETE	All Phases
IRowsetChange::InsertRow	_ROW_INSERT	All Phases

Method	DBREASON generated [1]	Phases
IRowsetChange::SetData	_ROW_FIRSTCHANGE [3]	All Phases
	_COLUMN_SET	All Phases
	COLUMN RECALCULATED	DIDEVENT
IRowsetIndex::Seek	_ROWSET_FETCHPOSITION-CHANGE	All Phases
IRowsetLocate::Compare	None	N/A
IRowsetLocate::GetRowsAt	_ROW_ACTIVATE	DIDEVENT
IRowsetLocate:: GetRowsByBookmark	_ROW_ACTIVATE	DIDEVENT
IRowsetLocate::Hash	None	N/A
IRowsetRefresh::GetLastVisibleData	None	N/A
IRowsetRefresh::RefreshVisibleData	_ROW_RESYNCH	All Phases
IRowsetScroll:: GetApproximatePosition	None	N/A
IRowsetScroll::GetRowsAtRatio	_ROW_ACTIVATE	DIDEVENT
IRowsetUpdate::GetOriginalData	None	N/A
IRowsetUpdate::GetPendingRows	None	N/A
IRowsetUpdate::Undo	_ROW_UNDOCHANGE	All Phases
	_ROW_UNDOINSERT	All Phases
	_ROW_UNDODELETE	All Phases
IRowsetUpdate::Update	_ROW_UPDATE	All Phases
All other rowset methods	None	N/A

[1] Methods generate only the listed DBREASON values, even though other reasons might seem appropriate. For example, **InsertRow** generates only DBREASON_ROW_INSERT even though DBREASON_COLUMN_SET, DBREASON_ROW_FIRSTCHANGE, and DBREASON_ROW_ACTIVATE might appear to be applicable.

[2] **IRowset::RestartPosition** generates this DBREASON only when the metadata for the columns has changed.

[3] DBREASON_ROW_FIRSTCHANGE is generated only the first time a column in the row is changed. For more information, see the preceding table in this section.

Method	Description
OnFieldChange	Notifies the consumer of any change to the value of a column.
OnRowChange	Notifies the consumer of the first change to a row or of any change that affects the entire row.
OnRowsetChange	Notifies the consumer of any change affecting the entire rowset.

IRowsetNotify::OnFieldChange

Notifies the consumer of any change to the value of a column.

```
HRESULT OnFieldChange (
   IRowset*       pRowset,
   HROW           hRow,
   ULONG          cColumns,
   ULONG          rgColumns[],
   DBREASON       eReason,
   DBEVENTPHASE   ePhase,
   BOOL           fCantDeny);
```

Parameters

pRowset
[in]
A pointer to the rowset, because the consumer may be receiving notifications from multiple rowsets and this identifies which one is calling.

hRow
[in]
The handle of the row in which the column value was changed. After this method returns, the reference count of this row will be unchanged unless the consumer explicitly changes it. This is different from other methods that return rows to the consumer, in which the provider explicitly increments the reference count. Therefore, if the consumer wants to guarantee that this row handle is valid after this method returns, it must call **IRowset::AddRefRows** for the row while it is processing this method.

cColumns
[in]
The count of columns in *rgColumns*.

rgColumns
[in]
An array of columns in the row for which the value was changed.

eReason
[in]
The reason of the event that caused this change. If this value is not recognized by the method, the method returns S_OK or DB_S_UNWANTEDREASON.

ePhase
[in]
The phase of this notification.

fCantDeny
[in]
When this flag is set to TRUE, the consumer cannot veto the event by returning S_FALSE because the provider cannot undo the event.

Return Code

S_OK
The method succeeded.

S_FALSE
The event/phase is vetoed by reason of logical objection or a failure to be able to implement.

DB_S_UNWANTEDPHASE
The consumer is not interested in receiving this phase for this reason. The provider can optimize by making no further calls with this reason and phase. The phases for other reasons are unaffected.

DB_S_UNWANTEDREASON
The consumer is not interested in receiving any phases for this reason. The provider can optimize by making no further calls with this reason.

E_FAIL
A consumer-specific error occurred. The provider continues the operation.

Comments

Possible reasons are DBREASON_COLUMN_SET and DBREASON_COLUMN_RECALCULATED.

All phases can occur for a DBREASON_COLUMN_SET event. The new value is visible beginning with the DBEVENTPHASE_SYNCHAFTER phase. For a DBREASON_COLUMN_RECALCULATED event, only the DBEVENTPHASE_DIDEVENT phase occurs.

Providers call **OnFieldChange** once for all of the columns set in a single call to **SetData**, and once for all of the changes to calculated columns of a row based on an update to that row. Setting a column to its current value can, but is not required to, generate a notification for that column.

Unless the consumer returns S_FALSE, the provider continues the operation. This is true even if the consumer returns E_FAIL or any other error code.

See Also

IRowsetNotify::OnRowChange, **IRowsetNotify::OnRowsetChange**

IRowsetNotify::OnRowChange

Notifies the consumer of the first change to a row or of any change that affects the entire row.

```
HRESULT OnRowChange (
   IRowset*         pRowset,
   ULONG            cRows,
   const HROW       rghRows[],
   DBREASON         eReason,
   DBEVENTPHASE     ePhase,
   BOOL             fCantDeny);
```

Parameters

pRowset
[in]
A pointer to the rowset, because the consumer may be receiving notifications from multiple rowsets and this identifies which one is calling.

cRows
[in]
The count of row handles in *rghRows*.

rghRows
[in]
An array of handles of rows that are changing. This array belongs to the caller (rowset) and must not be freed or used beyond the duration of the method call.

After this method returns, the reference count of these rows will be unchanged unless the consumer explicitly changes them. This is different from other methods that return rows to the consumer, in which the provider explicitly increments the reference counts. Therefore, if the consumer wants to guarantee that these row handles are valid after this method returns, it must call **IRowset::AddRefRows** for these rows while it is processing this method.

eReason
[in]
The reason of the event that caused this change. If this value is not recognized by the method, the method returns S_OK or DB_S_UNWANTEDREASON.

ePhase
[in]
The phase of this notification.

fCantDeny
[in]
When this flag is set to TRUE, the consumer cannot veto the event by returning S_FALSE because the provider cannot undo the event.

Return Code

S_OK
The method succeeded.

S_FALSE
The event/phase is vetoed by reason of logical objection or a failure to be able to implement, as permitted for the phase.

DB_S_UNWANTEDPHASE
The consumer is not interested in receiving this phase for this reason. The provider can optimize by making no further calls with this reason and phase. The phases for other reasons are unaffected.

DB_S_UNWANTEDREASON
The consumer is not interested in receiving any phases for this reason. The provider can optimize by making no further calls with this reason.

E_FAIL
A consumer-specific error occurred. The provider continues the operation.

Comments

Possible reasons are any of the DBREASON_ROW_* reasons.

Phases occur as documented for the DBREASON enumeration. Prior values remain in the row up to and including the DBEVENTPHASE_ABOUTTODO phase. The new value is visible with the DBEVENTPHASE_SYNCHAFTER or later phases.

When a DBREASON_ROW_ACTIVATE notification is triggered, the array of row handles passed to **OnRowChange** is exactly the order in which the rows were fetched.

Unless the consumer returns S_FALSE, the provider continues the operation. This is true even if the consumer returns E_FAIL or any other error code.

See Also

IRowsetNotify::OnFieldChange, **IRowsetNotify::OnRowsetChange**

IRowsetNotify::OnRowsetChange

Notifies the consumer of any change affecting the entire rowset.

```
HRESULT OnRowsetChange (
   IRowset*        pRowset,
   DBREASON        eReason,
   DBEVENTPHASE    ePhase,
   BOOL            fCantDeny);
```

Parameters

pRowset
[in]
A pointer to the rowset, because the consumer may be receiving notifications from multiple rowsets and this identifies which one is calling.

eReason
[in]
The reason for the event that caused this change. If this value is not recognized by the method, the method returns S_OK or DB_S_UNWANTEDREASON.

ePhase
[in]
The phase of this notification.

fCantDeny
[in]
When this flag is set to TRUE, the consumer cannot veto the event by returning S_FALSE because the provider cannot undo the event.

Return Code

S_OK
The method succeeded.

S_FALSE
The event/phase is vetoed by reason of logical objection or a failure to be able to implement.

DB_S_UNWANTEDPHASE
The consumer is not interested in receiving this phase for this reason. The provider can optimize by making no further calls with this reason and phase. The phases for other reasons are unaffected.

DB_S_UNWANTEDREASON
The consumer is not interested in receiving any phases for this reason. The provider can optimize by making no further calls with this reason.

E_FAIL
A consumer-specific error occurred. The provider continues the operation.

Comments

Possible reasons are any of the DBREASON_ROWSET_* reasons.

No phases occur; this method is equivalent to DBEVENTPHASE_DIDEVENT.

See Also

IRowsetNotify::OnFieldChange, **IRowsetNotify::OnRowChange**

IRowsetRefresh

IRowsetRefresh is used to retrieve the values for rows that are currently visible to the transaction.

When to Implement

IRowsetRefresh is optional. If it is exposed, the rowset must also expose **IRowsetIdentity**.

To support **IRowsetRefresh**, the provider must be able to get the latest value of the data that is visible to the transaction. If the value of the DBPROP_OTHERUPDATEDELETE property is VARIANT_TRUE, such as when the rowset is implemented on top of a dynamic or keyset-driven cursor in ODBC, the rowset can do this by the mechanism it uses to fetch rows from the server. However, if the value of DBPROP_OTHERUPDATEDELETE is VARIANT_FALSE, such as when the rowset is implemented on top of a static cursor in ODBC, the rowset must have another mechanism for retrieving data from the data store, such as executing a separate command to retrieve the currently visible values. If the rowset does not have such a mechanism, it cannot support this interface.

When to Call

IRowsetRefresh is used to synchronize rows in the rowset with those in the data store. The primary uses of **IRowsetRefresh** are as follows:

- To implement optimistic concurrency.
- To perform row fix-up in a disconnected environment.

Method	Description
GetLastVisibleData	Gets the most recent data from either the visible data cache or the data store.
RefreshVisibleData	Retrieves the data values from the data store that are visible to the transaction for the specified rows.

IRowsetRefresh::GetLastVisibleData

Gets the most recent data from either the visible data cache or the data store.

```
HRESULT GetLastVisibleData (
HROW        hRow,
HACCESSOR   hAccessor,
void *      pData);
```

Parameters

hRow
[in]
The handle of the row with pending changes for which to get the latest data. This can be the handle of a row with a pending delete.

hAccessor
[in]
The handle of the accessor to use. If *hAccessor* is the handle of a null accessor (*cBindings* in **IAccessor::CreateAccessor** was zero), **GetLastVisibleData** does not get any data values.

pData
[out]
A pointer to a buffer in which to return the data. The consumer allocates memory for this buffer.

Return Code

S_OK
The method succeeded. The status of all columns bound by the accessor is set to DBSTATUS_S_OK, DBSTATUS_S_ISNULL, or DBSTATUS_S_TRUNCATED.

DB_S_ERRORSOCCURRED
An error occurred while returning data for one or more columns, but data was successfully returned for at least one column. To determine the columns for which data was returned, the consumer checks the status values. For a list of status values that can be returned by this method, see "Status Values Used When Getting Data" in Chapter 6, "Getting and Setting Data."

E_FAIL
A provider-specific error occurred.

E_INVALIDARG
pData was a null pointer, and *hAccessor* was not a null accessor.

E_UNEXPECTED
ITransaction::Commit or **ITransaction::Abort** was called, and the object is in a zombie state.

DB_E_BADACCESSORHANDLE
hAccessor was invalid. It is possible for a reference accessor or an accessor that has a binding that uses provider-owned memory to be invalid for use with this method, even if the accessor is valid for use with **IRowset::GetData** or **IRowsetChange::SetData**.

DB_E_BADACCESSORTYPE
The specified accessor was not a row accessor.

DB_E_BADROWHANDLE
hRow was invalid.

DB_E_ERRORSOCCURRED
Errors occurred while returning data for all columns. To determine what errors occurred, the consumer checks the status values. For a list of status values that can be returned by this method, see "Status Values Used When Getting Data" in Chapter 6, "Getting and Setting Data."

DB_E_PENDINGINSERT
The rowset was in delayed update mode, and *hRow* referred to a pending insert row.

If this method performs deferred accessor validation and that validation takes place before any data is transferred, it can also return any of the following return codes for the applicable reasons listed in the corresponding DBBINDSTATUS values in **IAccessor::CreateAccessor**:

E_NOINTERFACE
DB_E_BADBINDINFO
DB_E_BADORDINAL
DB_E_BADSTORAGEFLAGS
DB_E_UNSUPPORTEDCONVERSION

Comments

This method makes no logical change to the state of the object. A consumer calls **GetLastVisibleData** to retrieve the latest visible data from the data store.

For providers that cache visible data, this is visible data obtained in the most recent call to **IRowsetRefresh::RefreshVisibleData** for this row. On a given row with pending changes, until there has been a successful call to refresh the visible data cache with **IRowsetRefresh::RefreshVisibleData**, this method will return the same data as a call to **IRowsetUpdate::GetOriginalData** for that row. On a given row with no pending changes, this method will return the same data as a call to **IRowset::GetData** for that row.

For providers that don't cache visible data or for deferred columns, this is the data currently visible from the data store. For a complete description of how **GetLastVisibleData** retrieves data, see "Getting Data" in Chapter 6, "Getting and Setting Data."

GetVisibleData is usually used in combination with **IRowset::GetData** and **IRowsetUpdate::GetOriginalData** to allow consumers to display collisions occurring with optimistic updates. After a row collision and a call to **IRowsetRefresh::RefreshVisibleData** to obtain the latest data store values for the conflicting rows, the three **GetData**-style functions collectively allow consumers access to all three sets of values needed to analyze the collision and decide on a resolution. The consumer can gain access to the pending-change values (**GetData**), the original values of the rowset before any changes were made (**GetOriginalData**), and the newly changed values at the data store that caused the collision (**GetLastVisibleData**).

If **GetLastVisibleData** fails, the memory to which *pData* points is not freed but its contents are undefined. If before **GetLastVisibleData** failed the provider allocated any memory for return to the consumer, the provider frees this memory and does not return it to the consumer.

There is a difference between calling **GetOriginalData** and calling **GetLastVisibleData**. In a delayed update mode, if data is changed by another consumer, different consumers may retrieve different data. For example, the value in Column 1 is X. In a delayed update mode, Consumer A changes the value in that column to Y but does not transmit this action to the data store. Consumer B then changes the value in Column 1 to Z. If Consumer A calls **GetOriginalData**, it gets X. However, if it calls **GetLastVisibleData**, using a dirty read, it will retrieve Z.

See Also

IRowset::GetData, **IRowsetRefresh::RefreshVisibleData**, **IRowsetUpdate::GetOriginalData**,

IRowsetRefresh::RefreshVisibleData

Retrieves the data values from the data store that are visible to the transaction for the specified rows.

```
HRESULT RefreshVisibleData (
   HCHAPTER       hChapter,
   ULONG          cRows,
   const HROW     rghRows[],
   BOOL           fOverwrite,
   ULONG*         pcRowsRefreshed,
   HROW**         prghRowsRefreshed,
   DBROWSTATUS**  prgRowStatus);
```

Parameters

hChapter
[in]
The chapter handle. For nonchaptered rowsets, the caller must set *hChapter* to DB_NULL_HCHAPTER.

cRows
[in]
The count of rows to refresh. If *cRows* is zero, **RefreshVisibleData** ignores *rghRows* and reads in current values for all active rows.

rghRows
[in]
An array of *cRows* row handles to be refreshed. If *cRows* is zero, this argument is ignored.

fOverwrite
[in]
TRUE if the provider should discard any pending changes to a given row and accept the visible values as the new current values; FALSE otherwise.

pcRowsRefreshed
[out]
A pointer to memory in which to return the number of rows the method attempted to refresh. If this is a null pointer, no count of rows is returned. If an error occurs, the provider sets **pcRowsRefreshed* to zero.

prghRowsRefreshed
[out]
A pointer to memory in which to return the array of row handles the method attempted to refresh. If *cRows* is not zero, the elements of this array are in one-to-one correspondence with those of *rghRows*. If *cRows* is zero, the elements of this array are the handles of all active rows with pending changes in the chapter, or all active rows with pending changes in the rowset if *hChapter* is DB_NULL_HCHAPTER. When *cRows* is zero, **RefreshVisibleData** will add to the reference count of the rows whose handles are returned in *prghRowsRefreshed*.

The rowset allocates memory for the handles and the client should release this memory with **IMalloc::Free** when no longer needed. This argument is ignored if *pcRowsRefreshed* is a null pointer and must not be a null pointer otherwise. If **pcRowsRefreshed* is zero on output or the method fails, the provider does not allocate any memory and ensures that **prghRowsRefreshed* is a null pointer on output.

prgRowStatus
[out]
A pointer to memory in which to return an array of row status values. The elements of this array correspond one-to-one with the elements of **prghRowsRefreshed*. If no errors occur while refreshing a row, the corresponding element of **prgRowStatus* is set to DBROWSTATUS_S_OK if the row is successfully resynchronized, or to DBROWSTATUS_S_NOCHANGE if the provider can easily determine that there was no change to the value. If an error occurs while refreshing a row, the corresponding element is set as specified in DB_S_ERRORSOCCURRED. If *prgRowStatus* is a null pointer, no row status values are returned.

The rowset allocates memory for the row status values and returns the address to this memory; the client releases this memory with **IMalloc::Free** when it is no longer needed. This argument is ignored if *pcRowsRefreshed* is a null pointer. If **pcRowsRefreshed* is zero on output or the method fails, the provider does not allocate any memory and ensures that **prgRowStatus* is a null pointer on output.

Return Code

S_OK
The method succeeded. All rows were successfully processed. For each row, *prgRowStatus* contains one of the following:

DBROWSTATUS_S_NOCHANGE if the row in the rowset had no pending changes when **RefreshVisibleData** was called or if the provider could easily detect that there were no changes made to the data store for this row.

DBROWSTATUS_S_OK in all other cases.

DB_S_ERRORSOCCURRED
An error occurred while refreshing a row, but at least one row was successfully refreshed. Successes can occur for the reason listed under S_OK. The following errors can occur:

An element of *rghRows* was invalid. The corresponding element of **prgRowStatus* contains DBROWSTATUS_E_INVALID.

Refreshing a row was canceled during notification. The row was not refreshed, and the corresponding element of **prgRowStatus* contains DBROWSTATUS_E_CANCELED.

An element of *rghRows* referred to a row for which a deletion had been transmitted to the data store. The corresponding element of **prgRowStatus* contains DBROWSTATUS_E_DELETED.

The row was not refreshed due to reaching a limit on the server, such as a query execution timing out. The error in the corresponding element of **prgRowStatus* contains DBROWSTATUS_E_LIMITREACHED.

An element of *rghRows* referred to a row on which a storage object was open. The corresponding element of **prgRowStatus* contains DBROWSTATUS_E_OBJECTOPEN.

An element of *rghRows* referred to a pending insert row. The corresponding element of **prgRowStatus* contains DBROWSTATUS_E_PENDINGINSERT.

DBPROP_STRONGIDENTITY was VARIANT_FALSE, and an element of *rghRows* referred to a row for which an insertion had been transmitted to the data store. The row was not refreshed, and the corresponding element of **prgRowStatus* contains DBROWSTATUS_E_NEWLYINSERTED.

E_FAIL
A provider-specific error occurred.

E_INVALIDARG
cRows was not zero, and *rghRows* was a null pointer.

pcRowsRefreshed was not a null pointer, and *prghRowsRefreshed* was a null pointer.

E_UNEXPECTED
ITransaction::Commit or **ITransaction::Abort** was called, and the object is in a zombie state.

DB_E_ERRORSOCCURRED
Errors occurred while refreshing all of the rows. Errors can occur for the reasons listed under DB_S_ERRORSOCCURRED.

DB_E_NOTREENTRANT
The provider called a method from **IRowsetNotify** in the consumer that had not yet returned, and the provider does not support reentrancy in this method.

DB_SEC_E_PERMISSIONDENIED
The consumer did not have sufficient permission to refresh the rows.

Comments

RefreshVisibleData retrieves the data values from the data store that are visible to the transaction for the specified rows. Changes made to the row by the current transaction are always visible to **RefreshVisibleData**, including changes made by other rowsets in the same transaction. Whether changes made by other transactions are visible to **RefreshVisibleData** depends on the isolation level of the current transaction. **RefreshVisibleData** uses values as follows:

Read Uncommitted. The changes most recently made, committed or uncommitted, by any transaction are used. If no changes have been made by any transaction, the original row is used.

Read Committed. The changes most recently made by the current transaction or committed by other transactions are used. If no changes have been made by the current transaction or committed by other transactions, the original row is used.

Repeatable Read and higher. The changes most recently made by the current transaction are used. If no changes have been made by the current transaction, the original row is used.

For providers that keep a local copy of visible data, **RefreshVisibleData** updates the provider's local copy of the visible data for any indicated rows with pending changes.

When *fOverwrite* is TRUE, the provider discards any pending changes to a given row and accepts the visible values as the new current values that will be returned by calling **IRowset::GetData** or **IRowsetUpdate::GetOriginalData**. This affects rows with or without pending changes. Any changes already transmitted to the data store are not lost; they will be committed or aborted when the transaction is committed or aborted. But all pending changes are lost because they exist only in the rowset's copy of the row and the *fOverwrite* TRUE option overwrites the contents of this copy. The pending change status in this case is removed from the row.

When *fOverwrite* is FALSE, the provider makes no change to the pending status of the row. It does not affect the current values of the row (available through **IRowset::GetData**) or the original values of the row (available through **IRowsetUpdate::GetOriginalData**).

If the provider keeps a local copy of the visible data values, it refreshes the values for the indicated rows. If the provider does not keep a local copy of the visible data values, the indicated row has no pending changes, or if all columns in the row are deferred, the provider reports success without taking any action.

Providers that perform optimistic updates in a disconnected scenario usually use the cached visible values on a pending row as the source of concurrency conflict detection values. For example, the values used to identify the row to a SQL-based provider through a **WHERE** clause would come from this buffer. Therefore, refreshing the visible values buffer for a row with pending changes via **RefreshVisibleData** potentially affects the behavior of a subsequent call to **IRowsetUpdate::Update** for that row because it may introduce new acceptable identity values into the conflict-detection mechanism of the provider.

If a specified row has been deleted from the data store and this deletion is visible, **RefreshVisibleData** returns DBROWSTATUS_E_DELETED in the error status array for the row. This row is subsequently treated as a deleted row for the purposes of **IRowset::GetData** (if *fOverwrite* is TRUE) or for **GetLastVisibleData** (if *fOverwrite* is FALSE).

If **RefreshVisibleData** encounters an error while attempting to refresh a row, such as a bad row handle, it notes the error in **prgRowStatus*, continues processing, and returns DB_S_ERRORSOCCURRED or DB_E_ERRORSOCCURRED. Although the rows are refreshed in undefined order, the ordering of **prgRowStatus* must match the order of the row handle array so that the consumer can perform a side-by-side scan of each array to determine which rows were not refreshed.

If *cRows* is zero and *pcRowsRefreshed* and *prghRowsRefreshed* are not null pointers, **RefreshVisibleData** adds to the reference count of the rows it returns in **prghRowsRefreshed* to ensure that the consumer has these row handles.

See Also

IRowsetRefresh::GetLastVisibleData

IRowsetResynch

IRowsetResynch allows consumers to retrieve the current values for rows that may have been changed in the data store since retrieved.

When to Implement

IRowsetResynch is an interface defined in OLE DB 1.*x*. In OLE DB 2.0, **IRowsetResynch** is superseded by **IRowsetRefresh**, which provides better control over when data values are updated from the data store.

In future releases of OLE DB, a common service component will expose **IRowsetRefresh** over providers that currently expose only **IRowsetResynch**. In the interim, consumers can work with legacy providers that support only **IRowsetResynch** by directly calling that interface. This interface is documented here for such consumers.

When to Call

The consumer calls **IParentRowset::GetChildRowset** to create an aggregated instance of the child rowset corresponding to a chapter-valued column in the parent rowset.

Method	Description
GetVisibleData	Gets the data in the data store that is visible to the transaction for the specified row.
ResynchRows	Gets the data in the data store that is visible to the transaction for the specified rows and updates the rowset's copies of those rows.

IRowsetResynch::GetVisibleData

Gets the data in the data store that is visible to the transaction for the specified row.

```
HRESULT GetVisibleData(
   HROW        hRow,
   HACCESSOR   hAccessor,
   void *      pData);
```

Parameters

hRow
[in]
The handle of the row for which to get the visible data. This can be the handle of a row with a pending delete.

hAccessor
[in]
The handle of the accessor to use. If *hAccessor* is the handle of a null accessor (*cBindings* in **IAccessor::CreateAccessor** was zero), **GetVisibleData** does not get any data values.

pData
[out]
A pointer to a buffer in which to return the data. The consumer allocates memory for this buffer.

Return Value

S_OK
The method succeeded. The status of all columns bound by the accessor is set to DBSTATUS_S_OK, DBSTATUS_S_ISNULL, or DBSTATUS_S_TRUNCATED.

DB_S_ERRORSOCCURRED
An error occurred while returning data for one or more columns, but data was successfully returned for at least one column.

E_FAIL
A provider-specific error occurred.

E_INVALIDARG
pData was a null pointer, and *hAccessor* was not a null accessor.

E_UNEXPECTED
ITransaction::Commit or **ITransaction::Abort** was called, and the object is in a zombie state.

DB_E_BADACCESSORHANDLE
hAccessor was invalid. It is possible for a reference accessor or an accessor that has a binding that uses provider-owned memory to be invalid for use with this method, even if the accessor is valid for use with **IRowset::GetData** or **IRowsetChange::SetData**.

DB_E_BADACCESSORTYPE
The specified accessor was not a row accessor.

DB_E_BADROWHANDLE
hRow was invalid.

DB_E_DELETEDROW
hRow referred to a row for which a deletion had been transmitted to the data store.

DB_E_ERRORSOCCURRED
Errors occurred while returning data for all columns. To determine what errors occurred, the consumer checks the status values.

DB_E_ABORTLIMITREACHED
The provider was unable to retrieve the visible data due to reaching a limit on the server, such as a query execution timing out.

DB_E_NEWLYINSERTED
DBPROP_STRONGIDENTITY was VARIANT_FALSE, and *hRow* referred to a row for which an insertion had been transmitted to the data store.

DB_E_NOTREENTRANT
The provider called a method from **IRowsetNotify** in the consumer that had not yet returned, and the provider does not support reentrancy in this method.

DB_E_PENDINGINSERT
The rowset was in delayed update mode, and *hRow* referred to a pending insert row.

If this method performs deferred accessor validation and that validation takes place before any data is transferred, it can also return any of the following return codes for the applicable reasons listed in the corresponding DBBINDSTATUS values in **IAccessor::CreateAccessor**:

E_NOINTERFACE
DB_E_BADBINDINFO
DB_E_BADORDINAL
DB_E_BADSTORAGEFLAGS
DB_E_UNSUPPORTEDCONVERSION

Comments

This method makes no logical change to the state of the object.

A consumer calls **GetVisibleData** to retrieve the data in the data store that is visible to the transaction for the specified row. However, **GetVisibleData** does not affect the values in the rowset's copy of the row.

If **GetVisibleData** fails, the memory that *pData* points to is not freed,but its contents are undefined. If before **GetVisibleData** failed the provider had allocated any memory to be returned to the consumer, the provider frees this memory and does not return it to the consumer.

IRowsetResynch::ResynchRows

Gets the data in the data store that is visible to the transaction for the specified rows and updates the rowset's copies of those rows.

```
HRESULT ResynchRows(
   ULONG             cRows,
   const             HROW rghRows[],
   ULONG *           pcRowsResynched,
   HROW **           prghRowsResynched,
   DBROWSTATUS **    prgRowStatus);
```

Parameters

cRows
[in]
The count of rows to resynchronize. If *cRows* is zero, **ResynchRows** ignores *rghRows* and reads the current value of all active rows.

rghRows
[in]
An array of *cRows* row handles to be resynchronized. If *cRows* is zero, this argument is ignored.

pcRowsResynched
[out]
A pointer to memory in which to return the number of rows the method attempted to resynchronize. The caller may supply a null pointer if no list is desired. If the method fails, the provider sets **pcRowsResynched* to zero.

prghRowsResynched
[out]
A pointer to memory in which to return the array of row handles the method attempted to resynchronize. If *cRows* is not zero, the elements of this array are in one-to-one correspondence with those of *rghRows*. If *cRows* is zero, the elements of this array are the handles of all active rows in the rowset. When *cRows* is zero, **ResynchRows** will add to the reference count of the rows whose handles are returned in *prghRowsResynched*.

The rowset allocates memory for the handles and the client should release this memory with **IMalloc::Free** when no longer needed. This argument is ignored if *pcRowsResynched* is a null pointer and must not be a null pointer otherwise. If **pcRowsResynched* is zero on output or the method fails, the provider does not allocate any memory and ensures that **prghRowsResynched* is a null pointer on output.

prgRowStatus
[out]
A pointer to memory in which to return an array of row status values. The elements of this array correspond one-to-one with the elements of **prghRowsResynched*. If no errors occur while resynchronizing a row, the corresponding element of **prgRowStatus* is set to DBROWSTATUS_S_OK. If the method fails while resynchronizing a row, the corresponding element is set as specified in DB_S_ERRORSOCCURRED. If *prgRowStatus* is a null pointer, no row status values are returned.

The rowset allocates memory for the row status values and returns the address to this memory; the client releases this memory with **IMalloc::Free** when it is no longer needed. This argument is ignored if *pcRowsResynched* is a null pointer. If **pcRowsResynched* is zero on output or the method fails, the provider does not allocate any memory and ensures that **prgRowStatus* is a null pointer on output.

Return Value

S_OK
The method succeeded. All rows were successfully resynchronized. The following value can be returned in **prgRowStatus*:

The row was successfully resynchronized. The corresponding element of **prgRowStatus* contains DBROWSTATUS_S_OK.

DB_S_ERRORSOCCURRED
An error occurred while resynchronizing a row, but at least one row was successfully resynchronized. Successes can occur for the reason listed under S_OK. The following errors can occur:

An element of *rghRows* was invalid or referred to a row that this thread does not have access to. The corresponding element of **prgRowStatus* contains DBROWSTATUS_E_INVALID.

Resynchronizing a row was canceled during notification. The row was not resynchronized, and the corresponding element of **prgRowStatus* contains DBROWSTATUS_E_CANCELED.

An element of *rghRows* referred to a row for which a deletion had been transmitted to the data store. The corresponding element of **prgRowStatus* contains DBROWSTATUS_E_DELETED.

The row was not resynchronized due to reaching a limit on the server, such as a query execution timing out. The error in the corresponding element of **prgRowStatus* contains DBROWSTATUS_E_LIMITREACHED.

An element of *rghRows* referred to a row on which a storage object was open. The corresponding element of **prgRowStatus* contains DBROWSTATUS_E_OBJECTOPEN.

An element of *rghRows* referred to a pending insert row. The corresponding element of **prgRowStatus* contains DBROWSTATUS_E_PENDINGINSERT.

DBPROP_STRONGIDENTITY was VARIANT_FALSE, and an element of *rghRows* referred to a row for which an insertion had been transmitted to the data store. The row was not resynchronized, and the corresponding element of **prgRowStatus* contains DBROWSTATUS_E_NEWLYINSERTED.

E_FAIL
A provider-specific error occurred.

E_INVALIDARG
cRows was not zero, and *rghRows* was a null pointer. *pcRowsResynched* was not a null pointer, and *prghRowsResynched* was a null pointer.

E_UNEXPECTED
ITransaction::Commit or **ITransaction::Abort** was called, and the object is in a zombie state.

DB_E_ERRORSOCCURRED
Errors occurred while resynchronizing all of the rows. Errors can occur for the reasons listed under DB_S_ERRORSOCCURRED.

DB_E_NOTREENTRANT
The provider called a method from **IRowsetNofity** in the consumer that had not yet returned, and the provider does not support reentrancy in this method.

DB_SEC_E_PERMISSIONDENIED
The consumer did not have sufficient permission to resynchronize the rows.

Comments

ResynchRows refreshes the values in the rowset's copy of each of the specified rows with the currently visible contents of the underlying row. Changes made to the row by the current transaction are always visible to **ResynchRows**, including changes made by other rowsets in the same transaction. Whether changes made by other transactions are visible to **ResynchRows** depends on the isolation level of the current transaction.

If a specified row has been deleted from the data store and this deletion is visible, **ResynchRows** returns DBROWSTATUS_E_DELETED in the error status array for the row and the row is treated as a deleted row.

Any changes transmitted to the data store are not lost; they will be committed or aborted when the transaction is committed or aborted. All pending changes are lost because they exist only in the rowset's copy of the row and **ResynchRows** overwrites the contents of this copy. The pending change status is removed from the row.

IRowsetScroll : IRowsetLocate

IRowsetScroll enables consumers to fetch rows at approximate positions in the rowset.

When to Implement

IRowsetScroll is required for all providers that intend to support general consumers. It is implemented for rowsets intended to work smoothly with long lists browsed directly by the user interface.

IRowsetScroll implies **IRowsetLocate**.

When to Call

IRowsetScroll enables consumers to fetch rows located at approximate positions within a rowset. This method can be used for cases where precise positioning is not critical.

Method	Description
GetApproximatePosition	Gets the approximate position of a row corresponding to a specified bookmark.
GetRowsAtRatio	Fetches rows starting from a fractional position in the rowset.

IRowsetScroll::GetApproximatePosition

Gets the approximate position of a row corresponding to a specified bookmark.

```
HRESULT GetApproximatePosition (
   HCHAPTER        hChapter,
   ULONG           cbBookmark,
   const BYTE *    pBookmark,
   ULONG *         pulPosition,
   ULONG *         pcRows);
```

Parameters

hChapter
[in]
The chapter handle. For nonchaptered rowsets, the caller must set *hChapter* to DB_NULL_HCHAPTER.

cbBookmark
[in]
The length in bytes of the bookmark. If this is zero, *pBookmark* is ignored, **pcRows* is set to the count of rows, and no position is returned in **pulPosition*.

pBookmark
[in]
A pointer to a bookmark that identifies the row of which to find the position. This can be a pointer to DBBMK_FIRST or DBBMK_LAST. The consumer is not required to have permission to read the row.

pulPosition
[out]
A pointer to memory in which to return the position of the row identified by the bookmark. The returned number is one-based; that is, the first row in the rowset is 1 and the last row is equal to **pcRows*. If **pcRows* is zero, the provider sets **pulPosition* to zero also, regardless of the bookmark that was passed. If *pulPosition* is a null pointer, no position is returned. In case of error, **pulPosition* is not changed.

pcRows
[out]
A pointer to memory in which to return the total number of rows. This number is zero if there are no rows. If *pcRows* is a null pointer, no count of rows is returned. In case of error, **pcRows* is not changed.

Return Code

S_OK
The method succeeded.

E_FAIL
A provider-specific error occurred.

E_INVALIDARG
cbBookmark was not zero, and *pBookmark* was a null pointer.

E_UNEXPECTED
ITransaction::Commit or **ITransaction::Abort** was called, and the object is in a zombie state.

DB_E_BADBOOKMARK
**pBookmark* was invalid, incorrectly formed, or DBBMK_INVALID.

**pBookmark* did not match any of the rows in the rowset. This includes the case when the row corresponding to the bookmark was deleted and DBPROP_BOOKMARKSKIPPED was either VARIANT_FALSE or the provider is a 1.*x* provider that does not support getting the approximate position of a deleted row.

> **Note** Consumers should attempt to use only bookmarks that they have received from the provider. The provider is guaranteed to handle only bookmarks it gives out in a predictable manner. Attempting to use a random value as a bookmark is undefined; the provider may return DB_E_BADBOOKMARK, may return an unexpected row, or may terminate abnormally.

DB_E_BADCHAPTER
The rowset was chaptered and *hChapter* was invalid.

The rowset was single-chaptered, and the specified chapter was not the currently open chapter. The consumer must use the currently open chapter or release the currently open chapter before specifying a new chapter.

DB_E_NOTREENTRANT
The provider called a method from **IRowsetNotify** in the consumer that had not yet returned, and the provider does not support reentrancy in this method.

Comments

This method makes no logical change to the state of the object.

There is no guarantee that the row position will be accurate. The provider is expected to choose the fastest possible estimation technique that is not completely in error. **pcRows* must be greater than or equal to **pulPosition*. The ratio is intended to be useful for scrolling and similar noncritical uses.

See Also

IRowsetScroll::GetRowsAtRatio

IRowsetScroll::GetRowsAtRatio

Fetches rows starting from a fractional position in the rowset.

```
HRESULT GetRowsAtRatio (
   HWATCHREGION      hReserved1,
   HCHAPTER          hChapter,
   ULONG             ulNumerator,
   ULONG             ulDenominator,
   LONG              cRows,
   ULONG *           pcRowsObtained,
   HROW **           prghRows);
```

Parameters

hReserved1
[in]
Reserved for future use. Providers ignore this parameter.

hChapter
[in]
The chapter handle. For nonchaptered rowsets, the caller must set *hChapter* to DB_NULL_HCHAPTER.

ulNumerator
[in]
See *ulDenominator* below.

ulDenominator
[in]
The provider determines the first row to fetch from the ratio of *ulNumerator* to *ulDenominator*, roughly using the formula:

```
(ulNumerator x Number of Rows in Rowset) / ulDenominator
```

If the rowset is being populated asynchronously, *ulNumerator* and *ulDenominator* specify the relative position within the rows fetched so far.

How accurately the provider applies this ratio is provider-specific. For example, if *ulNumerator* is 1 and *ulDenominator* is 2, some providers will fetch rows starting exactly halfway through the rowset while other providers will fetch rows starting 40 percent of the way through the rowset.

However, all providers must handle the following conditions correctly.

Condition	GetRowsAtRatio action
(*ulNumerator* = 0) AND (*cRows* > 0)	Fetches rows starting with the first row in the rowset.
(*ulNumerator* = 0) AND (*cRows* < 0)	Returns DB_S_ENDOFROWSET.
(*ulNumerator* = *ulDenominator*) AND (*cRows* > 0)	Returns DB_S_ENDOFROWSET.
(*ulNumerator* = *ulDenominator*) AND (*cRows* < 0)	Fetches rows starting with the last row in the rowset.

cRows

[in]

The number of rows to fetch. A negative number means to fetch backward. *cRows* can be a negative number only if the value of the DBPROP_CANFETCHBACKWARDS property is VARIANT_TRUE. The rows are returned in rowset-traversal order—that is, the direction in which they were fetched.

If *cRows* is zero, no rows are fetched. If the provider does not discover any other errors, the method returns S_OK; whether the provider checks for any other errors is provider-specific.

pcRowsObtained

[out]

A pointer to memory in which to return the number of rows fetched. If the consumer has insufficient permissions to return all rows, **GetRowsAtRatio** fetches all rows for which the consumer has sufficient permission and skips all other rows. If the method fails, **pcRowsObtained* is set to 0.

prghRows

[in/out]

A pointer to memory in which to return an array of handles of the fetched rows. If **prghRows* is not a null pointer on input, it must be a pointer to memory large enough to return the handles of the requested number of rows. If **prghRows* is a null pointer on input, the rowset allocates memory for the row handles and returns the address to this memory; the consumer releases this memory with **IMalloc::Free** after it releases the row handles. If **prghRows* was a null pointer on input and **pcRowsObtained* is zero on output or the method fails, the provider does not allocate any memory and ensures that **prghRows* is a null pointer on output.

Return Code

S_OK
The method succeeded.

DB_S_ENDOFROWSET
GetRowsAtRatio reached the start or the end of the rowset or chapter and could not fetch all requested rows because the count extended beyond the end. The number of rows actually fetched is returned in **pcRowsObtained*; this will be less than *cRows*.

The rowset is being populated asynchronously, and no additional rows are available at this time. To determine whether additional rows may be available, the consumer should call **IDBAsynchStatus::GetStatus** or listen for the **IDBAsynchNotify::OnStop** notification.

DB_S_ROWLIMITEXCEEDED
Fetching the number of rows specified in *cRows* would have exceeded the total number of active rows supported by the rowset. The number of rows that were actually fetched is returned in **pcRowsObtained*. This condition can occur only when there are more rows available than can be handled by the rowset. Therefore, this condition never conflicts with those described in DB_S_ENDOFROWSET and DB_S_STOPLIMITREACHED, both of which imply that no more rows were available.

DB_S_STOPLIMITREACHED
Fetching rows required further execution of the command, such as when the rowset uses a server-side cursor. Execution was stopped because a resource limit was reached. The number of rows that were actually fetched is returned in **pcRowsObtained*.

E_FAIL
A provider-specific error occurred.

E_INVALIDARG
pcRowsObtained or *prghRows* was a null pointer.

E_OUTOFMEMORY
The provider was unable to allocate sufficient memory in which to instantiate the rows or return the row handles.

E_UNEXPECTED
ITransaction::Commit or **ITransaction::Abort** was called, and the object is in a zombie state.

DB_E_BADCHAPTER
The rowset was chaptered and *hChapter* was invalid.

The rowset was single-chaptered, and the specified chapter was not the currently open chapter. The consumer must use the currently open chapter or release the currently open chapter before specifying a new chapter.

DB_E_BADRATIO
ulNumerator was greater than *ulDenominator*.

ulDenominator was zero.

DB_E_CANTFETCHBACKWARDS
cRows was negative, and the rowset cannot fetch backward.

DB_E_NOTREENTRANT
The provider called a method from **IRowsetNofity** in the consumer that had not yet returned, and the provider does not support reentrancy in this method.

DB_E_ROWSNOTRELEASED
The provider requires release of existing rows before new ones can be fetched. For more information, see DBPROP_CANHOLDROWS in "Properties Table (Alphabetical)" in Appendix C, "Property Tables."

DB_SEC_E_PERMISSIONDENIED
The consumer did not have sufficient permission to fetch any of the rows; no rows were fetched.

Comments

GetRowsAtRatio increments the reference count of each row for which it returns a handle by 1. Therefore, if a handle is returned for a row that has already been fetched, the reference count of that row will be greater than 1. **ReleaseRows** must be called once for each time the handle to a row has been returned.

If the provider encounters a problem fetching a row—for example, data stored in a text file contains a letter in what is supposed to be a numeric column—**GetRowsAtRatio** fetches the row normally, returns the row handle, and returns S_OK. However, when the consumer calls **IRowset::GetData** for the row, the provider returns DBSTATUS_E_CANTCONVERTVALUE as the status for the offending column.

For information about what **GetRowsAtRatio** does when it fetches a row that it already has in its internal buffers, see "Uniqueness of Rows in the Rowset" in Chapter 4, "Rowsets." For information about whether **GetRowsAtRatio** can detect changes made to rows in the rowset, see "Visibility of Changes" in Chapter 5, "Updating Data in Rowsets."

See Also

IRowset::GetData, **IRowset::GetNextRows**, **IRowsetLocate::GetRowsAt**, **IRowsetLocate::GetRowsByBookmark**, **IRowsetScroll::GetApproximatePosition**

IRowsetUpdate : IRowsetChange

IRowsetUpdate enables consumers to delay the transmission of changes made with **IRowsetChange** to the data store. This interface also enables consumers to undo changes before transmission.

IRowsetUpdate is optional.

When to Implement

Rowsets that want to allow delayed transmission of changes and to support undo capabilities implement **IRowsetUpdate**. Generally, this requires the rowset to locally cache a copy of each row as it is changed with **IRowsetChange::SetData**.

If **IRowsetUpdate** is not requested as a property of the rowset, it must not be exposed by the rowset.

When to Call

If **IRowsetUpdate** is exposed on the rowset, changes made through **IRowsetChange** are buffered in the rowset and not transmitted to the data store until **IRowsetUpdate::Update** is called; this is known as *delayed update mode*. If **IRowsetUpdate** is not exposed on the rowset, changes made through **IRowsetChange** are immediately transmitted to the data store; this is known as *immediate update mode*. For more information, see "Changing Data" in Chapter 5, "Updating Data in Rowsets."

The consumer calls the methods in **IRowsetChange** to update, delete, and insert rows. The rowset buffers these changes. When the consumer is ready to transmit these changes to the data store, it calls **Update**. Before calling **Update**, the consumer can back out any changes with **Undo**.

Method	Description
GetOriginalData	Gets the data most recently fetched from or transmitted to the data store; does not get values based on pending changes.
GetPendingRows	Returns a list of rows with pending changes.
GetRowStatus	Returns the status of rows.
Undo	Undoes any changes made to a row since it was last fetched or since **Update** was called for it.
Update	Transmits any changes made to a row since it was last fetched or since **Update** was called for it.

IRowsetUpdate::GetOriginalData

Gets the data most recently fetched from or transmitted to the data store; does not get values based on pending changes.

```
HRESULT GetOriginalData (
   HROW        hRow,
   HACCESSOR   hAccessor,
   void *      pData);
```

Parameters

hRow
[in]
The handle of the row for which to get the original data. This can be the handle of a row with a pending change or delete.

hAccessor
[in]
The handle of the accessor to use. If *hAccessor* is the handle of a null accessor (*cBindings*in **IAccessor::CreateAccessor** was zero), **GetOriginalData** does not get any data values.

pData
[out]
A pointer to a buffer in which to return the data. The consumer allocates memory for this buffer.

Return Code

S_OK
The method succeeded. The status of all columns bound by the accessor is set to DBSTATUS_S_OK, DBSTATUS_S_ISNULL, or DBSTATUS_S_TRUNCATED.

DB_S_ERRORSOCCURRED
A row handle in *rghRows* referred to a row on which a storage object or other COM object was open. The corresponding element of **prgRowStatus* contains DBROWSTATUS_E_OBJECTOPEN.

An error occurred while returning data for one or more columns, but data was successfully returned for at least one column. To determine the columns for which data was returned, the consumer checks the status values. For a list of status values that can be returned by this method, see "Status Values Used When Getting Data" in Chapter 6, "Getting and Setting Data."

E_FAIL
A provider-specific error occurred.

E_INVALIDARG
pData was a null pointer, and *hAccessor* was not a null accessor.

E_UNEXPECTED
ITransaction::Commit or **ITransaction::Abort** was called, and the object is in a zombie state.

DB_E_BADACCESSORHANDLE
hAccessor was invalid. It is possible for a reference accessor or an accessor that has a binding that uses provider-owned memory to be invalid for use with this method, even if the accessor is valid for use with **IRowset::GetData** or **IRowsetChange::SetData**.

DB_E_BADACCESSORTYPE
The specified accessor was not a row accessor.

DB_E_BADROWHANDLE
hRow was invalid.

DB_E_DELETEDROW
hRow referred to a row for which a deletion had been transmitted to the data store.

DB_E_ERRORSOCCURRED
Errors occurred while returning data for all columns. To determine what errors occurred, the consumer checks the status values. For a list of status values that can be returned by this method, see "Status Values Used When Getting Data" in Chapter 6, "Getting and Setting Data."

DB_E_NOTREENTRANT
The provider called a method from **IRowsetNotify** in the consumer that had not yet returned, and the provider does not support reentrancy in this method.

If this method performs deferred accessor validation and that validation takes place before any data is transferred, it can also return any of the following return codes for the applicable reasons listed in the corresponding DBBINDSTATUS values in **IAccessor::CreateAccessor**:

E_NOINTERFACE
DB_E_BADBINDINFO
DB_E_BADORDINAL
DB_E_BADSTORAGEFLAGS
DB_E_UNSUPPORTEDCONVERSION

Comments

This method makes no logical change to the state of the object.

GetOriginalData retrieves the values the row contained when it was last fetched or had changes transmitted to the data store. It does not retrieve any pending changes or changes made by other rowsets in the same transaction or other applications in other transactions. It also does not affect the current values for the row. For a complete description of how

GetOriginalData retrieves data, see "Getting Data" in Chapter 6, "Getting and Setting Data."

How **GetOriginalData** works is best illustrated in the following examples. In the first example, **GetOriginalData** fetches the values last fetched from the data store:

1. The consumer fetches a row.
2. The consumer calls **IRowsetChange::SetData** to update values in the row.
3. The consumer calls **GetOriginalData**. The consumer retrieves the values it would have retrieved had it called **IRowset::GetData** after step 1 and before step 2.

In the second example, **GetOriginalData** fetches the values last transmitted to the data store:

1. The consumer fetches a row.
2. The consumer calls **SetData** to update values in the row.
3. The consumer calls **Update**.
4. The consumer calls **SetData** to update values in the row.
5. The consumer calls **GetOriginalData**. The consumer retrieves the values it would have retrieved had it called **GetData** after step 3 and before step 4.

To implement **GetOriginalData**, the provider usually caches the original values just before making a change to a row and discards the cached values when **Undo** or **Update** is called for the row.

If *hRow* refers to a pending insert row, **GetOriginalData** returns the column defaults and, for columns without defaults or for which the provider was unable to determine the defaults, NULLs.

Whether **GetOriginalData** can retrieve the original value of a COM object that is stored in a column or a storage object that is created over a BLOB after changes have been made to that COM object or BLOB, depends on the value of the DBPROP_DELAYSTORAGEOBJECTS rowset property.

There is a difference between calling **GetOriginalData** and calling **GetLastVisibleData**. In a delayed update mode, if data is changed by another consumer, different consumers may retrieve different data. For example, the value in Column 1 is X. In a delayed update mode, Consumer A changes the value in that column to Y but does not transmit this action to the data store. Consumer B then changes the value in Column 1 to Z. If Consumer A calls **GetOriginalData**, it gets X. However, if it calls **GetLastVisibleData**, using a dirty read, it will retrieve Z.

GetOriginalData does not enforce any security restrictions. The provider must not create a rowset that includes columns for which the consumer does not have read privileges, so **GetOriginalData** never encounters problems accessing the data for a column. The rowset can contain columns to which the consumer does not have write permission if DBPROP_COLUMNRESTRICT is VARIANT_TRUE. The methods that fetch rows must not return the handles of rows for which the consumer does not have read privileges, so **GetOriginalData** never encounters problems accessing a row. Such rows might exist if the DBPROP_ROWRESTRICT property is VARIANT_TRUE.

If **GetOriginalData** fails, the memory to which *pData* points is not freed but its contents are undefined. If before **GetOriginalData** failed the provider allocated any memory for return to the consumer, the provider frees this memory and does not return it to the consumer.

See Also

IRowset::GetData, **IRowsetRefresh::GetLastVisibleData**, **IRowsetUpdate::Undo**, **IRowsetUpdate::Update**

IRowsetUpdate::GetPendingRows

Returns a list of rows with pending changes.

```
HRESULT GetPendingRows (
   HCHAPTER            hReserved,
   DBPENDINGSTATUS     dwRowStatus,
   ULONG *             pcPendingRows,
   HROW **             prgPendingRows,
   DBPENDINGSTATUS **  prgPendingStatus);
```

Parameters

hReserved
[in]
Reserved for future use. Must be DB_NULL_HCHAPTER.

dwRowStatus
[in]
Indicates whether consumers want rows with pending updates, deletes, or inserts. The following DBPENDINGSTATUS values are valid and can be combined:

DBPENDINGSTATUS_NEW
DBPENDINGSTATUS_CHANGED
DBPENDINGSTATUS_DELETED

For information about the DBPENDINGSTATUS type, see "Row States in Deferred Update Mode" in Chapter 5, "Updating Data in Rowsets."

pcPendingRows
[out]
A pointer to memory in which to return the number of rows with pending changes. If this is a null pointer, *prgPendingRows* and *prgPendingStatus* are ignored. This is useful when the consumer wants to check the returned return code to determine whether there are any pending changes. If an error occurs, **pcPendingRows* is set to zero.

prgPendingRows
[out]
A pointer to memory in which to return an array of handles of rows with pending changes. If this is a null pointer, no row handles are returned. The rowset allocates memory for the row handles and returns the address to this memory; the consumer releases this memory with **IMalloc::Free** when it no longer needs the row handles. This argument is ignored if *pcPendingRows* is a null pointer. If **pcPendingRows* is zero on output or an error occurs, the provider does not allocate any memory and ensures that **prgPendingRows* is a null pointer on output.

prgPendingStatus

[out]
A pointer to memory in which to return an array of DBPENDINGSTATUS values. These values are in one-to-one correspondence with the row handles returned in **prgPendingRows* and indicate the type of pending change. For information about the DBPENDINGSTATUS type, see "Row States in Deferred Update Mode" in Chapter 5, "Updating Data in Rowsets." If this is a null pointer, no status information is returned.

The rowset allocates memory for the row statuses and returns the address to this memory; the consumer releases this memory with **IMalloc::Free** when it no longer needs the row statuses. This argument is ignored if *pcPendingRows* is a null pointer. If **pcPendingRows* is zero on output or an error occurs, the provider does not allocate any memory and ensures that **prgPendingStatus* is a null pointer on output.

Return Code

S_OK
The method succeeded and changes were pending.

S_FALSE
The method succeeded and no changes were pending.

E_FAIL
A provider-specific error occurred.

E_INVALIDARG
dwRowStatus was DBPENDINGSTATUS_INVALIDROW, DBPENDINGSTATUS_UNCHANGED, or any other invalid value.

E_OUTOFMEMORY
The provider was unable to allocate sufficient memory in which to return the handles of rows with pending changes or the array of DBPENDINGSTATUS values.

E_UNEXPECTED
ITransaction::Commit or **ITransaction::Abort** was called, and the object is in a zombie state.

DB_E_BADCHAPTER
The rowset was chaptered and *hReserved* was invalid.

The rowset was single-chaptered, and the specified chapter was not the currently open chapter. The consumer must use the currently open chapter or release the currently open chapter before specifying a new chapter.

Comments

GetPendingRows increments the reference of each row handle it returns in **prgPendingRows*. The consumer must call **ReleaseRows** for these rows. If multiple changes are made to a single row, **GetPendingRows** returns the status as follows:

- If **IRowsetChange::SetData** is called for a pending insert row, the row is still considered a pending insert row.
- If **IRowsetChange::DeleteRows** is called for a pending update row, the row is considered a pending delete row.
- If **IRowsetChange::DeleteRows** is called for a pending insert row, the row is considered a transmitted delete row; such rows are not returned by **GetPendingRows**.
- If **IRowsetRefresh::RefreshVisibleData** is called for a pending insert row, the row is still considered a pending insert row.

For a complete description of pending change states, see "Row States in Deferred Update Mode" in Chapter 5, "Updating Data in Rowsets."

See Also

IRowsetUpdate::GetRowStatus

IRowsetUpdate::GetRowStatus

Returns the status of rows.

```
HRESULT GetRowStatus(
   HCHAPTER          hReserved,
   ULONG             cRows,
   const HROW        rghRows[],
   DBPENDINGSTATUS   rgPendingStatus[]);
```

Parameters

hReserved
[in]
Reserved for future use. Must be DB_NULL_HCHAPTER.

cRows
[in]
The count of elements in *rghRows* and *rgPendingStatus*. If this value is zero, **GetRowStatus** ignores *rghRows* and *rgPendingStatus* and does not return any status.

rghRows
[in]
An array of handles of rows for which to return the status. This array is allocated by the consumer and must not be freed by the provider.

rgPendingStatus
[out]
An array of DBPENDINGSTATUS values. **GetRowStatus** returns the DBPENDINGSTATUS values for all rows specified in the *rghRows* array. The DBPENDINGSTATUS_INVALIDROW value is used to indicate an invalid row handle. For information about the DBPENDINGSTATUS type, see "Row States in Deferred Update Mode" in Chapter 5, "Updating Data in Rowsets."

The *rgPendingStatus* array is allocated, but not necessarily initialized, by the caller and must not be freed by the provider.

Return Code

S_OK
The method succeeded. Status values were successfully retrieved for all rows, and each element of *rgPendingStatus* is set to DBPENDINGSTATUS_NEW, DBPENDINGSTATUS_CHANGED, DBPENDINGSTATUS_DELETED, or DBPENDINGSTATUS_UNCHANGED.

DB_S_ERRORSOCCURRED
An error occurred while getting the status of a row, but the status of at least one row was successfully retrieved. Successes can occur for the reasons listed under S_OK. The following error can occur:

- A row handle in *rghRows* was invalid. The corresponding element of *rgRowStatus* contains DBPENDINGSTATUS_INVALIDROW.

E_FAIL
A provider-specific error occurred.

E_INVALIDARG
cRows was greater than zero, and either *rghRows* was a null pointer or *rgPendingStatus* was a null pointer.

E_UNEXPECTED
ITransaction::Commit or **ITransaction::Abort** was called, and the object is in a zombie state.

DB_E_BADCHAPTER
The rowset was chaptered and *hReserved* was invalid.

The rowset was single-chaptered, and the specified chapter was not the currently open chapter. The consumer must use the currently open chapter or release the currently open chapter before specifying a new chapter.

DB_E_ERRORSOCCURRED
Errors occurred getting the status of all of the rows. Errors can occur for the reason listed under DB_S_ERRORSOCCURRED.

Comments

If multiple changes are made to a single row, **GetRowStatus** returns the status as described in **GetPendingRows**. If **IRowsetChange::DeleteRows** is called for a pending insert row, a status of DBPENDINGSTATUS_INVALIDROW is returned for the row.

For a complete description of row states, see "Row States in Deferred Update Mode" in Chapter 5, "Updating Data in Rowsets."

See Also

IRowsetUpdate::GetPendingRows

IRowsetUpdate::Undo

Undoes any changes made to a row since it was last fetched or **Update** was called for it.

```
HRESULT Undo (
   HCHAPTER          hReserved,
   ULONG             cRows,
   const HROW        rghRows[],
   ULONG *           pcRows,
   HROW **           prgRows,
   DBROWSTATUS **    prgRowStatus);
```

Parameters

hReserved
[in]
Reserved for future use. Must be DB_NULL_HCHAPTER.

cRows
[in]
The count of rows to undo. If *cRows* is nonzero, **Undo** undoes all pending changes in the rows specified in *rghRows*. If *cRows* is zero, **Undo** ignores *rghRows* and undoes all pending changes to all rows in the rowset.

rghRows
[in]
An array of handles of the rows to undo. Elements of this array can refer to rows with pending deletes.

If *rghRows* includes a row that does not have any pending changes, **Undo** does not return an error. Instead, the row remains unchanged from its original state—which is the intention of **Undo**—and its row status is set to DBROWSTATUS_S_OK.

If *rghRows* includes a duplicate row, **Undo** treats the occurrences as if the row were passed to the method two times sequentially. Thus, on the first occurrence, **Undo** undoes any pending changes. On the second occurrence, **Undo** treats the row as a row with no pending changes and leaves it in its current (now original) state.

pcRows
[out]
A pointer to memory in which to return the number of rows **Undo** attempted to undo. If this is a null pointer, no count of rows is returned. If the method fails with an error other than DB_E_ERRORSOCCURRED, **pcRows* is set to zero.

prgRows

[out]

A pointer to memory in which to return an array containing the handles of all the rows **Undo** attempted to undo. If *rghRows* is not a null pointer, the elements of this array are in one-to-one correspondence with those in *rghRows*. For example, if a row appears twice in *rghRows*, it appears twice in **prgRows*. When *rghRows* is not a null pointer, **Undo** does not add to the reference count of the rows it returns in **prgRows*; the reason is that the consumer already has these row handles.

If *rghRows* is a null pointer, the elements of this array are the handles of all the rows that had pending changes, whether or not **Undo** was successful at undoing those changes. The consumer checks **prgRowStatus* to determine which rows were undone. When *rghRows* is a null pointer, **Undo** adds to the reference count of the rows it returns in **prgRows*; the reason is that the consumer is not guaranteed to already have these row handles. A side effect of this is that rows with a reference count of zero but with pending changes at the time **Undo** is called are brought back into existence; that is, their reference count is increased to 1 and they must be rereleased.

The rowset allocates memory for the array of handles and returns the address to this memory; the consumer releases this memory with **IMalloc::Free** when it no longer needs the handles. This argument is ignored if *pcRows* is a null pointer and must not be a null pointer otherwise. If **pcRows* is zero on output or the method fails with an error other than DB_E_ERRORSOCCURRED, the provider does not allocate any memory and ensures that **prgRows* is a null pointer on output.

prgRowStatus

[out]

A pointer to memory in which to return an array of row status values. The elements of this array correspond one-to-one with the elements of *rghRows* (if *rghRows* is not a null pointer) or **prgRows* (if *rghRows* is a null pointer). If no errors occur while undoing a row, the corresponding element of **prgRowStatus* is set to DBROWSTATUS_S_OK. If an error occurs while undoing a row, the corresponding element is set as specified in DB_S_ERRORSOCCURRED. If *prgRowStatus* is a null pointer, no row status values are returned. For information about the DBROWSTATUS enumerated type, see "Arrays of Errors" in Chapter 13, "Errors."

The rowset allocates memory for the row status values and returns the address to this memory; the consumer releases this memory with **IMalloc::Free** when it no longer needs the row status values. This argument is ignored if *cRows* is zero and *pcRows* is a null pointer. If **Undo** does not attempt to undo any rows or the method fails with an error other than DB_E_ERRORSOCCURRED, the provider does not allocate any memory and ensures that **prgRowStatus* is a null pointer on output.

Return Code

S_OK

The method succeeded. The changes in all rows were successfully undone. The following value can be returned in **prgRowStatus*:

- The changes in the row were successfully undone. The corresponding element of **prgRowStatus* contains DBROWSTATUS_S_OK.

DB_S_ERRORSOCCURRED

An error occurred while undoing the changes in a row, but the changes in at least one row were successfully undone. Successes can occur for the reasons listed under S_OK. The following errors can occur:

- Undoing the changes in a row was canceled during notification. Changes made to the row were not undone, and the corresponding element of *rgRowStatus* contains DBROWSTATUS_E_CANCELED.
- A row handle in *rghRows* referred to a row for which a delete had been transmitted to the data store. The corresponding element of **prgRowStatus* contains DBROWSTATUS_E_DELETED.
- A row handle in *rghRows* was invalid. The corresponding element of **prgRowStatus* contains DBROWSTATUS_E_INVALID.
- A row handle in *rghRows* referred to a row on which a storage object or other COM object was open. The corresponding element of **prgRowStatus* contains DBROWSTATUS_E_OBJECTOPEN.
- The consumer encountered a recoverable, provider-specific error, such as an RPC failure when transmitting the change to a remote server. The corresponding element of **prgRowStatus* contains DBROWSTATUS_E_FAIL.

E_FAIL

A provider-specific error occurred.

E_INVALIDARG

cRows was not 0, and *rghRows* was a null pointer.

pcRows was not a null pointer, and *prgRows* was a null pointer.

E_OUTOFMEMORY

The provider was unable to allocate sufficient memory in which to return either the handles of the rows **Undo** attempted to undo or the array of row status values.

E_UNEXPECTED

ITransaction::Commit or **ITransaction::Abort** was called, and the object is in a zombie state.

DB_E_BADCHAPTER
The rowset was chaptered and *hReserved* was invalid.

The rowset was single-chaptered, and the specified chapter was not the currently open chapter. The consumer must use the currently open chapter or release the currently open chapter before specifying a new chapter.

DB_E_ERRORSOCCURRED
Errors occurred while undoing all of the rows. The provider allocates memory for **prgRows* and **prgRowStatus*, and the consumer checks the values in **prgRowStatus* to determine why the pending changes were not undone. The consumer frees this memory when it no longer needs the information. Errors can occur for the reasons listed under DB_S_ERRORSOCCURRED.

DB_E_NOTREENTRANT
The provider called a method from **IRowsetNofity** in the consumer that had not yet returned, and the provider does not support reentrancy in this method.

Comments

Undo backs any pending changes out of the specified rows and clears their pending change status. That is, it undoes any changes made to the row since it was last fetched or **Update** was called for the row. If multiple changes were made to a row, **Undo** undoes all of these changes; the provider does not remember intermediate steps. If **Update** is called for a row immediately after **Undo** is called for the row, **Update** does not transmit any changes to the data store for the row. For more information about pending changes, see "Changing Data" in Chapter 5, "Updating Data in Rowsets."

How **Undo** works is best illustrated in the following examples. In the first example, **Undo** backs out any changes made since the row was last fetched from the data store:

1. The consumer fetches a row.
2. The consumer deletes the row with **IRowsetChange::DeleteRows** or updates value in it with **IRowsetChange::SetData**.
3. The consumer repeats step 2 as often as it likes for the row, except that after it calls **DeleteRows** for the row it cannot call either **SetData** or **DeleteRows** for the row.
4. The consumer calls **Undo** for the row. The values in the row are changed to those it had after completing step 1.

In the second example, **Undo** backs out any changes made since values were last transmitted to the data store:

1. The consumer fetches a row.
2. The consumer updates the value in a row with **SetData**.
3. The consumer repeats step 2 as often as it likes for the row.
4. The consumer calls **Update** for the row.
5. The consumer deletes the row with **DeleteRows** or updates the value in it with **SetData**.
6. The consumer repeats step 5 as often as it likes for the row, except that after it calls **DeleteRows** for the row it cannot call either **SetData** or **DeleteRows** for the row.
7. The consumer calls **Undo** for the row. The values in the row are changed to those it had after completing step 4.

To implement **Undo**, the provider generally caches the original values just before making a change to a row and discards the cached values when **Undo** or **Update** is called for the row. This same cache can be used by **GetOriginalData** to retrieve the original data for the row.

If **Undo** is called for a row with a pending insert, the row is deleted from the rowset. That is, calls to **IRowset::GetData** or **SetData** for the row fail with DB_E_DELETEDROW. The consumer must still call **IRowset::ReleaseRows** to release the row.

Whether **Undo** can undo changes made to a COM object stored in a column or to a storage object created over a BLOB depends on the value of the DBPROP_DELAYSTORAGEOBJECTS rowset property.

If **Undo** is called for a row that has a reference count of zero and exists only because the row has a pending change, **Undo** releases the row and all its resources. The only exception to this is when the handle to the row is returned in **prgRows*, in which case the reference count is set to one.

The order in which **Undo** processes rows is provider-specific. If **Undo** encounters an error, it continues processing rows until it has attempted to undo all specified rows and then returns the appropriate warning. Because **Undo** is usually implemented by copying data from a cache of original data, such errors should be extremely rare and should usually represent a consumer programming error, such as passing an invalid row handle.

If any consumer of the rowset is using notifications, the provider sends notifications that pending changes for the specified rows are being undone.

See Also

IRowsetChange, **IRowsetUpdate::GetOriginalData**, **IRowsetUpdate::Update**

IRowsetUpdate::Update

Transmits any changes made to a row since it was last fetched or **Update** was called for it.

```
HRESULT Update (
   HCHAPTER          hReserved,
   ULONG             cRows,
   const HROW        rghRows[],
   ULONG *           pcRows,
   HROW **           prgRows,
   DBROWSTATUS**     prgRowStatus);
```

Parameters

hReserved
[in]
Reserved for future use. Must be DB_NULL_HCHAPTER.

cRows
[in]
The count of rows to update. If *cRows* is nonzero, **Update** updates all pending changes in the rows specified in *rghRows*. If *cRows* is zero, **Update** ignores *rghRows* and updates all pending changes to all rows in the rowset.

rghRows
[in]
An array of handles of the rows to update.

If *rghRows* includes a row that does not have any pending changes, **Update** does not return an error. Instead, the row remains unchanged and hence has no pending changes after **Update** returns—which is the intention of **Update**—and the row status value associated with that row is DBROWSTATUS_S_OK. Furthermore, **Update** guarantees not to transmit any value for the row to the data store.

If *rghRows* includes a duplicate row, **Update** behaves as follows. If the row handle is valid, no errors occur and **prgRowStatus* contains DBROWSTATUS_S_OK for each occurrence. If the row handle is invalid, **prgRowStatus* contains the appropriate error for each occurrence.

pcRows
[out]
A pointer to memory in which to return the number of rows **Update** attempted to update. If this is a null pointer, no count of rows is returned. If the method fails with an error other than DB_E_ERRORSOCCURRED, **pcRows* is set to zero.

prgRows

[out]
A pointer to memory in which to return an array containing the handles of all the rows **Update** attempted to update. If *rghRows* is not a null pointer, the elements of this array are in one-to-one correspondence with those in *rghRows*. For example, if a row appears twice in *rghRows*, it appears twice in **prgRows*. When *rghRows* is not a null pointer, **Update** does not add to the reference count of the rows it returns in **prgRows*; the reason is that the consumer already has these row handles.

If *rghRows* is a null pointer, the elements of this array are handles of all the rows that had pending changes, whether or not **Update** was successful at transmitting those changes to the data store. The consumer checks **prgRowStatus* to determine which rows were updated. When *rghRows* is a null pointer, **Update** adds to the reference count of the rows it returns in **prgRows*; the reason is that the consumer is not guaranteed to already have these row handles. A side effect of this is that rows with a reference count of zero but with pending changes at the time **Update** is called are brought back into existence; that is, their reference count is increased to 1 and they must be rereleased.

The rowset allocates memory for the array of handles and returns the address to this memory; the consumer releases this memory with **IMalloc::Free** when it no longer needs the handles. This argument is ignored if *pcRows* is a null pointer, and must not be a null pointer otherwise. If **pcRows* is zero on output or the method fails with an error other than DB_E_ERRORSOCCURRED, the provider does not allocate any memory and ensures that **prgRows* is a null pointer on output.

prgRowStatus

[out]
A pointer to memory in which to return an array of row status values. The elements of this array correspond one-to-one with the elements of *rghRows* (if *rghRows* is not a null pointer) or **prgRows* (if *rghRows* is a null pointer). If no errors or warnings occur while updating a row, the corresponding element of **prgRowStatus* is set to DBROWSTATUS_S_OK. If an error or warning occurs while updating a row, the corresponding element is set as specified in DB_S_ERRORSOCCURRED. If *prgRowStatus* is a null pointer, no row status values are returned. For information about the DBROWSTATUS enumerated type, see "Arrays of Errors" in Chapter 13, "Errors."

The rowset allocates memory for the row status values and returns the address to this memory; the consumer releases this memory with **IMalloc::Free** when it no longer needs the row status values. This argument is ignored if *cRows* is zero and *pcRows* is a null pointer. If **Update** does not attempt to update any rows or the method fails with an error other than DB_E_ERRORSOCCURRED, the provider does not allocate any memory and ensures that **prgRowStatus* is a null pointer on output.

Return Code

S_OK

The method succeeded. The changes in all rows were successfully updated. The following values can be returned in **prgRowStatus*:

- The changes in the row were successfully updated. The corresponding element of **prgRowStatus* contains DBROWSTATUS_S_OK.
- Updating or deleting a single row caused more than one row to be updated or deleted in the data store. For more information, see DBPROP_REPORTMULTIPLECHANGES in "Properties Table (Alphabetical)" in Appendix C, "Property Tables." The corresponding element of **prgRowStatus* contains DBROWSTATUS_S_MULTIPLECHANGES.

DB_S_ERRORSOCCURRED

An error occurred while updating a row, but at least one row was successfully updated. Successes can occur for the reasons listed under S_OK. The following errors can occur:

- Updating a row was canceled during notification. The row was not updated, and the corresponding element of *rgRowStatus* contains DBROWSTATUS_E_CANCELED.
- The rowset was using optimistic concurrency, a row was being updated or deleted, and the value of a column in that row has been changed since it was last fetched. The error in the corresponding element of **prgRowStatus* contains DBROWSTATUS_E_CONCURRENCYVIOLATION.
- An element of *rghRows* referred to a row for which a deletion had been transmitted to the data store. The error in the corresponding element of **prgRowStatus* contains DBROWSTATUS_E_DELETED.
- A row was being inserted or updated, and a value specified for that row violated the integrity constraints for the column or table. The error in the corresponding element of **prgRowStatus* contains DBROWSTATUS_E_INTEGRITYVIOLATION.
- A row was being deleted, and doing so violated the integrity constraints for the column or table. The error in the corresponding element of **prgRowStatus* contains DBROWSTATUS_E_INTEGRITYVIOLATION.
- An element of *rghRows* was invalid. The error in the corresponding element of **prgRowStatus* contains DBROWSTATUS_E_INVALID.
- The consumer did not have sufficient permission to update, delete, or insert a row. This error can be returned only if the value of the DBPROP_ROWRESTRICT property is VARIANT_TRUE. The error in the corresponding element of **prgRowStatus* contains DBROWSTATUS_E_PERMISSIONDENIED.
- The update, delete, or insert failed due to reaching a limit on the server, such as a query execution timing out. The error in the corresponding element of **prgRowStatus* contains DBROWSTATUS_E_LIMITREACHED.

- A column value did not meet the schema requirements for the column. The error in the corresponding element of **prgRowStatus* contains DBROWSTATUS_E_SCHEMAVIOLATION.
- The values for two or more columns did not meet the multiple-column schema requirements for those columns. The error in the corresponding element of **prgRowStatus* contains DBROWSTATUS_E_SCHEMAVIOLATION.
- A row was being inserted, no value was specified for a column, the column does not have a default, and the column is non-nullable. The error in the corresponding element of **prgRowStatus* contains DBROWSTATUS_E_SCHEMAVIOLATION.
- The consumer encountered a recoverable, provider-specific error, such as an RPC failure when transmitting the change to a remote server. The corresponding element of **prgRowStatus* contains DBROWSTATUS_E_FAIL.

E_FAIL
A provider-specific error occurred.

E_INVALIDARG
cRows was not zero, and *rghRows* was a null pointer.

pcRows was not a null pointer, and *prgRows* was a null pointer on input.

E_OUTOFMEMORY
The provider was unable to allocate sufficient memory in which to return either the handles of the rows **Update** attempted to update or the array of row status values.

E_UNEXPECTED
ITransaction::Commit or **ITransaction::Abort** was called, and the object is in a zombie state.

DB_E_BADCHAPTER
The rowset was chaptered and *hReserved* was invalid.

The rowset was single-chaptered, and the specified chapter was not the currently open chapter. The consumer must use the currently open chapter or release the currently open chapter before specifying a new chapter.

DB_E_ERRORSOCCURRED
Errors occurred while updating all of the rows. The provider allocates memory for **prgRows* and **prgRowStatus*, and the consumer checks the values in **prgRowStatus* to determine why the pending changes were not updated. The consumer frees this memory when it no longer needs the information. Errors can occur for the reasons listed under DB_S_ERRORSOCCURRED.

DB_E_NOTREENTRANT
The provider called a method from **IRowsetNofity** in the consumer that had not yet returned, and the provider does not support reentrancy in this method.

Comments

Update transmits pending changes for the specified rows to the data store and clears their pending change status. That is, it transmits any changes made to the row since it was last fetched or **Update** was called for the row. For more information about pending changes, see "Changing Data" in Chapter 5, "Updating Data in Rowsets."

The order in which **Update** processes rows is provider-specific. If **Update** encounters an error, it continues processing rows until it has attempted to update all specified rows and then it returns the appropriate warning. This might leave the rowset in a state where changes have been transmitted for some rows but not others. When the consumer repairs the cause of the error, it can call **Update** again and the provider guarantees it will not transmit data to the data store for those rows for which data was already successfully transmitted.

If any consumer of the rowset is using notifications, the provider sends notifications that pending changes for the specified rows are being transmitted to the data store.

If **Update** is called for a row that has a reference count of zero and exists only because the row has a pending change, **Update** releases the row and all its resources. The only exception to this is when the handle to the row is returned in **prgRows*, in which case the reference count is set to 1.

If the provider cached original values to implement **GetOriginalData** and **Undo**, it discards them as part of **Update**.

If the rowset is released with **IUnknown::Release** before **Update** is called, all pending changes are lost.

See Also

IRowsetChange, **IRowsetUpdate::Undo**

IRowsetView

IRowsetView enables the consumer to create or apply a view to an existing rowset.

When to Implement

Providers that can do simple post-processing of rowsets, such as applying filters or re-sorting rowsets, support **IRowsetView**.

When to Call

Consumers call **IRowsetView** in order to obtain a view object from a rowset on which to apply post-processing operations to an existing rowset. The consumer calls **CreateView** to create a view object and calls methods on the view in order to apply post-processing operations to that view object. The consumer then calls **OpenViewChapter** to retrieve a chapter handle that reflects the specified view conditions on the original rowset, or **OpenViewRowset** to create a new rowset that reflects the specified view conditions. Any resources associated with the view opened as a chapter of an existing rowset can be cleaned up with a call to **IChapteredRowset::ReleaseChapter**.

Method	Description
CreateView	Creates a view object.
GetView	Returns a view object reflecting the conditions applied to the specified chapter.

IRowsetView::CreateView

Creates a view.

```
HRESULT CreateView (
   IUnknown *      pUnkOuter,
   REFIID          riid,
   IUnknown **     ppView);
```

Parameters

pUnkOuter
[in]
A pointer to the controlling **IUnknown** interface if the view is being created as part of an aggregate. It is a null pointer if the view is not part of an aggregate.

riid
[in]
The IID of the interface requested on the view.

ppView
[out]
A pointer to memory in which to return the interface pointer on the newly created view.

Return Code

S_OK
The method succeeded.

E_FAIL
A provider-specific error occurred.

E_INVALIDARG
ppView was a null pointer.

E_NOINTERFACE
The view did not support the interface specified in *riid*.

E_OUTOFMEMORY
The provider did not have enough memory to create the view.

DB_E_NOAGGREGATION

pUnkOuter was not a null pointer, and the provider is an OLE DB 1.0 or 1.1 provider that does not support aggregation of the view object being created.

pUnkOuter was not a null pointer, and *riid* was not **IID_IUnknown**.

E_UNEXPECTED

ITransaction::Commit or **ITransaction::Abort** was called, and the object is in a zombie state.

Comments

None.

IRowsetView::GetView

Returns a new view describing conditions applied to the specified chapter.

```
HRESULT GetView (
   HCHAPTER     hChapter,
   REFIID       riid,
   HCHAPTER *   phChapterSource,
   IUnknown **  ppView);
```

Parameters

hChapter
[in]
The chapter from which to return the view conditions.

riid
[in]
The IID of the interface on which to return a pointer.

phChapterSource
[out]
The chapter handle to which the view was applied to create the new chapter.

ppView
[out]
A pointer to memory in which to return the interface pointer. If **GetView** fails, it must attempt to set **ppView* to a null pointer.

Return Code

S_OK
The method succeeded.

E_FAIL
A provider-specific error occurred.

E_NOINTERFACE
The view did not support the interface specified in *riid.*

E_OUTOFMEMORY
The provider was unable to allocate sufficient memory in which to return the view information.

DB_E_BADCHAPTER
hChapter was invalid.

Comments

GetView returns a new view on which the consumer representing the view conditions applied to the specified chapter. The consumer can call methods such as **IViewFilter::GetFilter** and **IViewSort::GetSortOrder** to determine the filter and sort conditions applied to the chapter when created.

The view returned is not the same view as was used when the view was created; it simply returns the same view conditions. Therefore, if the consumer has changed or released the original view after creating the chapter, it has no effect on the view returned by this method.

The consumer must call **Release** in order to release the returned view when it is no longer needed.

ISequentialStream

ISequentialStream is the preferred minimal interface for reading and writing binary large object (BLOB) data in OLE DB. **ISequentialStream** is a subset of the COM **IStream** interface, and provides forward-only reading and writing of data. The **IStream** interface inherits its **Read** and **Write** methods from **ISequentialStream**.

When to Implement

You can implement **ISequentialStream** on an object if you require simple sequential access to a stream object. If you implement **IStream**, you must provide an implementation of the **Read** and **Write** methods from **ISequentialStream**.

Note Most applications do not implement **ISequentialStream** as a separate interface, and it is not required to provide it separately even when an **IStream** implementation is provided. For example, the compound file implementation of structured storage does not succeed on a **QueryInterface** for **ISequentialStream** but it includes the **Read** and **Write** methods through the **IStream** interface pointer. The same is true for the NTFS Native Structured Storage implementation.

When to Call

Call the methods of the **ISequentialStream** interface from a container or application to perform sequential reads and writes of data. Most applications call the **Read** and **Write** methods through the **IStream** interface.

Methods in Vtable Order

IUnknown Methods	Description
QueryInterface	Returns pointers to supported interfaces.
AddRef	Increments the reference count.
Release	Decrements the reference count.

ISequentialStream Methods	Description
Read	Reads a specified number of bytes from the stream object into memory, starting at the current seek pointer.
Write	Writes a specified number of bytes to the stream object, starting at the current seek pointer.

ISequentialStream : IUnknown

ISequentialStream is a simplified version of **IStream** that provides strictly sequential stream access to BLOB data. This class behaves as if it were the strict ancestor of **IStream**. In particular, any object that implements **IStream** can choose to identify itself as **ISequentialStream**, because the first two slots in the **IStream** vtable and the definition of those methods exactly matches the vtable and methods of **ISequentialStream**.

Method	Description
Read	Reads a specified number of bytes from the stream.
Write	Writes a specified number of bytes to the stream.

ISequentialStream::Read

Reads a specified number of bytes from the stream object into memory starting at the current read/write location within the stream.

```
HRESULT Read(
   void *   pv,         // Pointer to buffer into which the stream is read
   ULONG    cb,         // Specifies the number of bytes to read
   ULONG *  pcbRead);   // Pointer to location that contains actual number of bytes read
```

Parameters

pv
: [in]
Points to the buffer into which the stream is read. If an error occurs, this value is NULL.

cb
: [in]
Specifies the number of bytes of data to attempt to read from the stream object.

pcbRead
: [out]
Pointer to a location where this method writes the actual number of bytes read from the stream object. You can set this pointer to NULL to indicate that you are not interested in this value. In this case, this method does not provide the actual number of bytes read.

Return Code

S_OK
: Data was successfully read from the stream object.

S_FALSE
: The data could not be read from the stream object.

E_PENDING
: Asynchronous Storage only: Part or all of the data to be read is currently unavailable. For more information, see **IFillLockBytes** and Asynchronous Storage.

STG_E_ACCESSDENIED
: The caller does not have sufficient permissions for reading this stream object.

STG_E_INVALIDPOINTER
: One of the pointer values is invalid.

STG_E_REVERTED
: The object has been invalidated by a revert operation above it in the transaction tree.

Comments

This method reads bytes from this stream object into memory. The stream object must be opened in STGM_READ mode. This method adjusts the current read/write location within the stream by the actual number of bytes read.

The number of bytes actually read is returned in the *pcbRead* parameter.

The actual number of bytes read can be fewer than the number of bytes requested if an error occurs or if the end of the stream is reached during the read operation.

Some implementations might return an error if the end of the stream is reached during the read. You must be prepared to deal with the error return or S_OK return values on the end of stream reads.

ISequentialStream::Write

Writes a specified number of bytes into the stream object starting at the current read/write location within the stream.

```
HRESULT Write(
   Void const *   pv,            // Pointer to buffer into which the stream is written
   ULONG          cb,            // Specifies the number of bytes to write
   ULONG *        pcbWritten);   // Specifies the actual number of bytes written
```

Parameters

pv

[in]

Points to the buffer into which the stream should be written.

cb

[in]

The number of bytes of data to attempt to write into the stream.

pcbWritten

[out]

Pointer to a location where this method writes the actual number of bytes written to the stream object. The caller can set this pointer to NULL, in which case this method does not provide the actual number of bytes written.

Return Code

S_OK

The data was successfully written into the stream object.

E_PENDING

Asynchronous Storage only: Part or all of the data to be written is currently unavailable. For more information, see **IFillLockBytes** and Asynchronous Storage.

STG_E_MEDIUMFULL

The write operation was not completed because there is no space left on the storage device.

STG_E_ACCESSDENIED

The caller does not have sufficient permissions for writing this stream object.

STG_E_CANTSAVE

Data cannot be written for reasons other than lack of access or space.

STG_E_INVALIDPOINTER

One of the pointer values is invalid.

STG_E_REVERTED

The object has been invalidated by a revert operation above it in the transaction tree.

STG_E_WRITEFAULT
The write operation was not completed due to a disk error.

Comments

ISequentialStream::Write writes the specified data to a stream object. The current read/write location within the stream is adjusted for the number of bytes actually written. The number of bytes actually written is returned in the *pcbWrite* parameter. If the byte count is zero bytes, the write operation has no effect.

The *pcbWrite* parameter can have a value even if an error occurs.

ISessionProperties

ISessionProperties returns information about the properties a session supports and the current settings of those properties. It is a mandatory interface on sessions.

Method	Description
GetProperties	Returns the list of properties in the Session property group that are currently set on the session.
SetProperties	Sets properties in the Session property group.

ISessionProperties::GetProperties

Returns the list of properties in the Session property group that are currently set on the session.

```
HRESULT GetProperties (
   ULONG                  cPropertyIDSets,
   const DBPROPIDSET      rgPropertyIDSets[],
   ULONG *                pcPropertySets,
   DBPROPSET **           prgPropertySets);
```

Parameters

cPropertyIDSets
[in]
The number of DBPROPIDSET structures in *rgPropertyIDSets*.

If *cPropertySets* is zero, the provider ignores *rgPropertyIDSets* and returns the values of all properties in the Session property group for which values have been set or defaults exist. It does not return the values of properties in the Session property group for which values have not been set and no defaults exist.

If *cPropertyIDSets* is not zero, the provider returns the values of the requested properties. If a property is not supported, the returned value of *dwStatus* in the returned DBPROP structure for that property is DBPROPSTATUS_NOTSUPPORTED and the value of *dwOptions* is undefined.

rgPropertyIDSets
[in]
An array of *cPropertyIDSets* DBPROPIDSET structures. The properties specified in these structures must belong to the Session property group. The provider returns the values of information about the properties specified in these structures. If *cPropertyIDSets* is zero, this parameter is ignored.

For information about the properties in the Session property group that are defined by OLE DB, see "Properties Table (by Property Groups)" in Appendix C, "Property Tables." For information about the DBPROPIDSET structure, see "DBPROPIDSET Structure" in Chapter 11, "Properties."

pcPropertySets
[out]
A pointer to memory in which to return the number of DBPROPSET structures returned in **prgPropertySets*. If *cPropertyIDSets* is zero, **pcPropertySets* is the total number of property sets for which the provider supports at least one property in the Session property group. If *cPropertyIDSets* is greater than zero, **pcPropertySets* is set to *cPropertyIDSets*. If an error other than DB_E_ERRORSOCCURRED occurs, **pcPropertySets* is set to zero.

prgPropertySets
[out]
A pointer to memory in which to return an array of DBPROPSET structures. If *cPropertyIDSets* is zero, one structure is returned for each property set that contains at least one property belonging to the Session property group. If *cPropertyIDSets* is not zero, one structure is returned for each property set specified in *rgPropertyIDSets*.

If *cPropertyIDSets* is not zero, the DBPROPSET structures in **prgPropertySets* are returned in the same order as the DBPROPIDSET structures in *rgPropertyIDSets*; that is, for corresponding elements of each array, the *guidPropertySet* elements are the same. If *cPropertyIDs*, in an element of *rgPropertyIDSets*, is not zero, the DBPROP structures in the corresponding element of **prgPropertySets* are returned in the same order as the DBPROPID values in *rgPropertyIDs*; that is, for corresponding elements of each array, the property IDs are the same.

The provider allocates memory for the structures and returns the address to this memory; the consumer releases this memory with **IMalloc::Free** when it no longer needs the structures. Before calling **IMalloc::Free** for **prgPropertySets*, the consumer should call **IMalloc::Free** for the *rgProperties* element within each element of **prgPropertySets*. If **pcPropertySets* is zero on output or if an error other than DB_E_ERRORSOCCURRED occurs, the provider does not allocate any memory and ensures that **prgPropertySets* is a null pointer on output.

For information about the DBPROPSET and DBPROP structures, see "DBPROPSET Structure" and "DBPROP Structure" in Chapter 11, "Properties."

Return Code

S_OK
The method succeeded. In all DBPROP structures returned by the method, *dwStatus* is set to DBPROPSTATUS_OK.

DB_S_ERRORSOCCURRED
No value was returned for one or more properties. The consumer checks *dwStatus* in the DBPROP structure to determine the properties for which values were not returned. **GetProperties** can fail to return properties for a number of reasons, including:

- The property was not supported by the provider.
- The property was not in the Session property group.
- The property set was not supported by the provider. If *cPropertyIDs* in the DBPROPIDSET structure for the property set was zero, the provider cannot set *dwStatus* in the DBPROP structure because it does not know the IDs of any properties in the property set. Instead, it sets *cProperties* to zero in the DBPROPSET structure returned for the property set.

E_FAIL
A provider-specific error occurred.

E_INVALIDARG
cPropertyIDSets was not equal to zero, and *rgPropertyIDSets* was a null pointer.

pcPropertySets or *prgPropertySets* was a null pointer.

In an element of *rgPropertyIDSets*, *cPropertyIDs* was not zero and *rgPropertyIDs* was a null pointer.

E_OUTOFMEMORY
The provider was unable to allocate sufficient memory in which to return the DBPROPSET or DBPROP structures.

DB_E_ERRORSOCCURRED
Values were not returned for any properties. The provider allocates memory for **prgPropertySets*, and the consumer checks *dwStatus* in the DBPROP structures to determine why properties were not returned. The consumer frees this memory when it no longer needs the information.

See Also

IDBProperties::GetPropertyInfo, **ISessionProperties::SetProperties**

ISessionProperties::SetProperties

Sets properties in the Session property group.

```
HRESULT SetProperties (
   ULONG        cPropertySets,
   DBPROPSET    rgPropertySets[]);
```

Parameters

cPropertySets

[in]

The number of DBPROPSET structures in *rgPropertySets*. If this is zero, the provider ignores *rgPropertySets* and the method does not do anything.

rgPropertySets

[in/out]

An array of DBPROPSET structures containing properties and values to be set. The properties specified in these structures must belong to the Session property group. If the same property is specified more than once in *rgPropertySets*, the value used is provider-specific. If *cPropertySets* is zero, this parameter is ignored.

For information about the properties in the Session property group that are defined by OLE DB, see "Properties Table (by Property Groups)" in Appendix C, "Property Tables." For information about the DBPROPSET and DBPROP structures, see "DBPROPSET Structure" and "DBPROP Structure" in Chapter 11, "Properties."

Return Code

S_OK
The method succeeded. In all DBPROP structures passed to the method, *dwStatus* is set to DBPROPSTATUS_OK.

DB_S_ERRORSOCCURRED
One or more properties were not set. Properties not in error remain set. The consumer checks *dwStatus* in the DBPROP structures to determine which properties were not set. **SetProperties** can fail to set properties for a number of reasons, including:

- The property was not supported by the provider.
- The property was not in the Session property group.
- The property set was not supported by the provider.
- The property is read-only and was not set to its default value.
- It was not possible to set the property.
- *colid* in the DBPROP structure was not DB_NULLID.
- The value of *dwOptions* in the DBPROP structure was invalid.
- The data type in *vValue* in the DBPROP structure was not the data type of the property or was not VT_EMPTY.
- The value in *vValue* in the DBPROP structure was invalid.
- The property's value conflicted with an existing property.

E_FAIL
A provider-specific error occurred.

E_INVALIDARG
cPropertySets was not equal to zero, and *rgPropertySets* was a null pointer.

In an element of *rgPropertySets*, *cProperties* was not zero and *rgProperties* was a null pointer.

DB_E_ERRORSOCCURRED
All property values were invalid, and no properties were set. The consumer checks *dwStatus* in the DBPROP structures to determine why properties were not set.

See Also

IDBProperties::GetPropertyInfo, **ISessionProperties::GetProperties**

ISourcesRowset

ISourcesRowset returns a rowset of data source objects and enumerators visible from the current enumerator. For more information about enumerators, see "Enumerators" in Chapter 2, "Data Source and Session Objects."

Method	Description
GetSourcesRowset	Returns a rowset of the data source objects and enumerators visible from the current enumerator.

ISourcesRowset::GetSourcesRowset

Returns a rowset of the data source objects and enumerators visible from the current enumerator.

```
HRESULT GetSourcesRowset(
   IUnknown       pUnkOuter,
   REFIID         riid,
   ULONG          cPropertySets,
   DBPROPSET      rgPropertySets[],
   IUnknown **    ppSourcesRowset);
```

Parameters

pUnkOuter
A pointer to the controlling **IUnknown** interface if the sources rowset is being created as part of an aggregate. If the rowset is not part of an aggregate, this must be set to a null pointer.

riid
The IID of the interface on which to return a pointer. This interface is conceptually added to the list of required interfaces on the resulting rowset, and the method fails (E_NOINTERFACE) if that interface cannot be supported on the resulting rowset.

cPropertySets
[in]
The number of DBPROPSET structures in *rgPropertySets*. If this is zero, the provider ignores *rgPropertySets*.

rgPropertySets
[in/out]
An array of DBPROPSET structures containing properties and values to be set. The properties specified in these structures must belong to the Rowset property group. If the same property is specified more than once in *rgPropertySets*, it is provider-specific which value is used. If *cPropertySets* is 0, this argument is ignored.

For information about the properties in the Rowset property group that are defined by OLE DB, see "Properties Table (by Property Groups)" in Appendix C, "Property Tables." For information about the DBPROPSET and DBPROP structures, see "DBPROPSET Structure" and "DBPROP Structure" in Chapter 11, "Properties."

ppSourcesRowset
A pointer to memory in which to return the requested interface pointer on the rowset. If an error occurs, the returned pointer is null.

Return Code

S_OK
The method succeeded. In all DBPROP structures passed to the method, *dwStatus* is set to DBPROPSTATUS_OK.

DB_S_ERRORSOCCURRED
The rowset was opened, but one or more properties—for which the *dwOptions* element of the DBPROP structure was DBPROPOPTIONS_OPTIONAL—were not set. The consumer checks *dwStatus* in the DBPROP structures to determine which properties were not set. The method can fail to set properties for a number of reasons, including:

- The property was not supported by the provider.
- The property was not in the Rowset property group.
- The property set was not supported by the provider.
- It was not possible to set the property.
- The *colid* in the DBPROP structure was invalid.
- The data type in *vValue* in the DBPROP structure was not the data type of the property or was not VT_EMPTY.
- The value in *vValue* in the DBPROP structure was invalid.
- The property's value conflicted with an existing property.
- A property was specified to be applied to all columns but could not be applied to one or more columns.

E_FAIL
A provider-specific error occurred.

E_INVALIDARG
ppSourcesRowset was a null pointer.

cPropertySets was not 0, and *rgPropertySets* was a null pointer.

In an element of *rgPropertySets*, *cProperties* was not 0 and *rgProperties* was a null pointer.

E_NOINTERFACE
The rowset did not support the interface specified in *riid*.

E_OUTOFMEMORY
The provider did not have enough memory to create the rowset object.

E_UNEXPECTED
The enumerator object was in an uninitialized state.

DB_E_ABORTLIMITREACHED
The method failed because a resource limit has been reached. For example, a query used to implement the method timed out. No rowset is returned.

DB_E_ERRORSOCCURRED
No rowset was returned because one or more properties—for which the *dwOptions* element of the DBPROP structure was DBPROPOPTIONS_REQUIRED or an invalid value—were not set. The consumer checks *dwStatus* in the DBPROP structures to determine which properties were not set. None of the satisfiable properties are remembered. The method can fail to set properties for any of the reasons specified in DB_S_ERRORSOCCURRED.

DB_E_NOAGGREGATION
pUnkOuter was not a null pointer, and the provider is an OLE DB 1.0 or 1.1 provider that does not support aggregation of the rowset object being created.

pUnkOuter was not a null pointer, and *riid* was not **IID_IUnknown**.

Comments

GetSourcesRowset returns the following rowset. The rowset is read-only. The columns are returned in the order shown in the following table.

Column name	Type indicator	Description
SOURCES_NAME	DBTYPE_WSTR	The name of the data store or enumerator.
SOURCES_PARSENAME	DBTYPE_WSTR	String to pass to **IParseDisplayName** to obtain a moniker for the data source object or enumerator.
SOURCES_DESCRIPTION	DBTYPE_WSTR	The description of the data source object or enumerator.
SOURCES_TYPE	DBTYPE_UI2	Whether the row describes a data source object or an enumerator: • DBSOURCETYPE_DATASOURCE • DBSOURCETYPE_ENUMERATOR If a single piece of code is capable of being used both as a data source object and as an enumerator, it is listed in the rowset twice, once in each role.

Column name	Type indicator	Description
SOURCES_ISPARENT	DBTYPE_BOOL	If the row describes an enumerator, SOURCES_ISPARENT is VARIANT_TRUE if the enumerator is the parent enumerator; that is, the enumerator whose enumeration contains the enumerator on which **ISourcesRowset::GetSourcesRowset** was just called. This allows the consumer to go backward through the enumeration. Whether an enumerator is able to enumerate its parent is provider-specific. Otherwise, SOURCES_ISPARENT is VARIANT_FALSE. If the row describes a data source object, SOURCES_ISPARENT is ignored by the consumer.

See Also

IDBProperties::GetPropertyInfo

ISQLErrorInfo

ISQLErrorInfo is used to return the SQLSTATE and native error code.

When to Implement

Providers for SQL databases can implement **ISQLErrorInfo** on custom error objects returned with the OLE DB error object.

When to Call

Consumers call the methods on **ISQLErrorInfo** to retrieve the SQLSTATE and native error code. To retrieve a custom error object, a consumer calls **IErrorRecords::GetCustomErrorObject**.

Method	Description
GetSQLInfo	Returns the SQLSTATE and native error code associated with an error.

ISQLErrorInfo::GetSQLInfo

Returns the SQLSTATE and native error code associated with an error.

```
HRESULT GetSQLInfo (
   BSTR *   pbstrSQLState,
   LONG *   plNativeError);
```

Parameters

pbstrSQLState
[out]
A pointer to memory in which to return a pointer to a string that contains the SQLSTATE. An SQLSTATE is a five-character string defined by the ANSI SQL standard. The memory for this string is allocated by the provider and must be freed by the consumer with a call to **SysFreeString**. If an error occurs, **pbstrSQLState* is set to a null pointer.

plNativeError
[out]
A pointer to memory in which to return a provider-specific, native error code. **plNativeError* is not necessarily the same as the *dwMinor* element in the ERRORINFO structure returned by **IErrorRecords::GetErrorInfo**. The combination of the *hrError* and *dwMinor* elements of the ERRORINFO structure is used to identify an error to the error lookup service, whereas **plNativeError* has no such restrictions.

Return Code

S_OK
The method succeeded.

E_FAIL
A provider-specific error occurred.

E_INVALIDARG
pbstrSQLState or *plNativeError* was a null pointer.

E_OUTOFMEMORY
The provider was unable to allocate sufficient memory in which to return the SQLSTATE.

ISupportErrorInfo

ISupportErrorInfo is defined by Automation; the following describes how the interface is used in OLE DB. **ISupportErrorInfo** indicates whether a specific interface can return Automation error objects. Because OLE DB error objects are returned through the same mechanism as Automation error objects, support for them is also indicated through this interface.

When to Implement

ISupportErrorInfo must be implemented by the provider on any object that exposes an interface that can return OLE DB error objects.

When to Call

A consumer uses this interface to determine whether a particular OLE DB interface can return an OLE DB error object.

Method	Description
InterfaceSupportsErrorInfo	Indicates whether a specific OLE DB interface can return OLE DB error objects.

ISupportErrorInfo::InterfaceSupportsErrorInfo

Indicates whether a specific OLE DB interface on the object can return OLE DB error objects.

```
HRESULT InterfaceSupportsErrorInfo (
   REFIIDriid);
```

Parameters

riid
[in]
The IID of the interface in question.

Return Code

S_OK
The interface can return Automation error objects; therefore, it can return OLE DB error objects.

S_FALSE
The interface cannot return Automation error objects; therefore, it cannot return OLE DB error objects.

Comments

InterfaceSupportsErrorInfo is implemented on each OLE DB object that may return an error object and identifies the interfaces on that object that may generate an OLE DB error object.

To retrieve an OLE DB error object, the consumer takes the following steps:

1. The consumer calls **QueryInterface** to retrieve a pointer to **ISupportErrorInfo**.
2. The consumer calls **ISupportErrorInfo::InterfaceSupportsErrorInfo** and passes it the IID of the OLE DB interface that returned the error.
3. The consumer calls **GetErrorInfo** in the Automation DLL if **InterfaceSupportsErrorInfo** returns S_OK. **GetErrorInfo** returns an **IErrorInfo** interface pointer on the OLE DB error object. If **InterfaceSupportsErrorInfo** returns S_FALSE, the consumer should discard any error object returned by **GetErrorInfo** because it applies to a different method and interface.
4.

ITableDefinition

The **ITableDefinition** interface exposes simple methods to create, drop, and alter tables on the data store.

When to Implement

ITableDefinition is optional for providers that do not otherwise support table creation; it is mandatory for providers that support table creation through commands.

Method	Description
AddColumn	Adds a new column to a base table.
CreateTable	Creates a new base table in the data store.
DropColumn	Drops a column from a base table.
DropTable	Drops a base table in the data store.

ITableDefinition::AddColumn

Adds a new column to a base table.HRESULT AddColumn(

```
   DBID *           pTableID,
   DBCOLUMNDESC *   pColumnDesc,
   DBID **          ppColumnID);
```

Parameters

pTableID
[in]
A pointer to the DBID of the table to which the column is to be added.

pColumnDesc
[in/out]
A pointer to the DBCOLUMNDESC structure that describes the new column.

ppColumnID
[out]
A pointer to memory in which to return the returned DBID of a newly created column. If this is a null pointer, no DBID is returned. If *ppColumnID* is non-null, the provider allocates memory for the DBID and overwrites **ppColumnID* with a pointer to this new DBID without regard for its current value.

Return Code

S_OK
The method succeeded.

DB_S_ERRORSOCCURRED
The column was added, but one or more properties—for which the *dwOptions* element of the DBPROP structure was DBPROPOPTIONS_OPTIONAL—were not set. The consumer checks *dwStatus* in the DBPROP structures to determine which properties were not set. The method can fail to set properties for a number of reasons, including:

- The property was not supported by the provider.
- The property was not in the Column, Rowset, or Table property group.
- The property set was not supported by the provider.
- It was not possible to set the property.
- The *colid* element of the DBPROP structure for the property was not DB_NULLID.
- The data type in *vValue* in the DBPROP structure was not the data type of the property or was not VT_EMPTY.
- The value in *vValue* in the DBPROP structure was invalid.
- The property's value conflicted with an existing property.

E_FAIL
A provider-specific error occurred.

E_INVALIDARG
pTableID or *pColumnDesc* was a null pointer.

DB_E_BADCOLUMNID
dbcid in **pColumnDesc* was an invalid column ID.

DB_E_BADPRECISION
The precision in **pColumnDesc* was invalid.

DB_E_BADSCALE
The scale in **pColumnDesc* was invalid.

DB_E_BADTYPE
One or more of the *wType*, *pwszTypeName*, and *pTypeInfo* elements in an element of *rgColumnDescs* was invalid.

DB_E_DUPLICATECOLUMNID
dbcid in **pColumnDesc* was the same as an existing column ID.

DB_E_ERRORSOCCURRED
The column was not added because one or more properties—for which the *dwOptions* element of the DBPROP structure was DBPROPOPTIONS_REQUIRED or an invalid value—could not be set. The consumer checks *dwStatus* in the DBPROP structures to determine which properties were not set. The method can fail to set properties for any of the reasons specified in DB_S_ERRORSOCCURRED.

DB_E_NOTABLE
The specified table does not exist in the current data store.

DB_E_TABLEINUSE
The specified table was in use.

DB_SEC_E_PERMISSIONDENIED
The consumer did not have sufficient permission to add a column.

Comments

If **AddColumn** returns any errors, the column is not created.

The placement of the new column, whether inserted or added after the last column, is provider-specific.

See Also

IDBProperties::GetPropertyInfo, **ITableDefinition::CreateTable**, **ITableDefinition::DropColumn**

ITableDefinition::CreateTable

Creates a new base table in the data store.

```
HRESULT CreateTable(
   IUnknown *      pUnkOuter,
   DBID *          pTableID,
   ULONG           cColumnDescs,
   DBCOLUMNDESC    rgColumnDescs[],
   REFIID          riid,
   ULONG           cPropertySets,
   DBPROPSET       rgPropertySets[],
   DBID **         ppTableID,
   IUnknown **     ppRowset);
```

Parameters

pUnkOuter
[in]
The controlling unknown if the rowset is to be aggregated, otherwise a null pointer.

pTableID
[in]
A pointer to the ID of the table to create. If this is a null pointer, the provider must assign a unique ID to the table.

cColumnDescs
[in]
The number of DBCOLUMNDESC structures in the *rgColumnDescs* array. This can be zero if the provider allows the creation of tables with no columns.

rgColumnDescs
[in/out]
An array of DBCOLUMNDESC structures that describe the columns of the table.

```
typedef struct tagDBCOLUMNDESC {
   LPOLESTR       pwszTypeName;
   ITypeInfo *    pTypeInfo;
   DBPROPSET *    rgPropertySets;
   CLSID *        pclsid;
   ULONG          cPropertySets;
   ULONG          ulColumnSize;
   DBID           dbcid;
   DBTYPE         wType;
   BYTE           bPrecision;
   BYTE           bScale;
} DBCOLUMNDESC;
```

The elements of this structure are used as follows. The consumer decides the values to use in the nonproperties elements of this structure based on values from the PROVIDER_TYPES schema rowset.

Element	Description
pwszTypeName	The provider-specific name of the data type of the column. This name corresponds to a value in the TYPE_NAME column in the PROVIDER_TYPES schema rowset. In most cases, there is no reason for a consumer to specify a value for *pwszTypeName* that is different from the values listed in the PROVIDER_TYPES schema rowset.
pTypeInfo	If *pTypeInfo* is not a null pointer, the data type of the column is an abstract data type (ADT) and values in this column are actually instances of the type described by the type library. *wType* may be either DBTYPE_BYTES, with a length of at least 4, or DBTYPE_IUNKNOWN. The instance values are required to be COM objects derived from **IUnknown**.
rgPropertySets	An array of DBPROPSET structures containing properties and values to be set. The properties specified in these structures must belong to the Column property group. All properties specified in *rgPropertySets* for this element of *rgColumnDescs* apply to the column specified by *dbcid*; the *colid* element in the DBPROP structure for specified properties is ignored. If the same property is specified more than once in *rgPropertySets*, it is provider-specific which value is used. If *cPropertySets* is zero, this argument is ignored. **Note** Although the *colid* element in the DBPROP structure for specified properties is ignored, the consumer must set the value of *colid* to DB_NULLID. Not to do so is a programming error. For information about the properties in the Column property group that are defined by OLE DB, see "Properties Table (by Property Groups)" in Appendix C, "Property Tables." For information about the DBPROPSET and DBPROP structures, see "DBPROPSET Structure" and "DBPROP Structure" in Chapter 11, "Properties."
pclsid	If the column contains COM objects, a pointer to the class ID of those objects. If more than one class of objects can reside in the column, **pclsid* is set to IID_NULL.
cPropertySets	The number of DBPROPSET structures in *rgPropertySets*. If this is zero, the provider ignores *rgPropertySets*.
ulColumnSize	If *wType* is DBTYPE_STR or DBTYPE_WSTR, this is the maximum length in characters for values in this column. If *wType* is DBTYPE_BYTES, this is the maximum length in bytes for values in this column. For all other values of *wType*, this is ignored. Providers that do not require a length argument in the specification of the provider type (*pwszTypeName*) ignore this value.

Element	Description
dbcid	The column ID of the column.
wType	The type indicator for the data type of the column. This name corresponds to a value in the DATA_TYPE column in the PROVIDER_TYPES schema rowset. In most cases, there is no reason for a consumer to specify a value for *wType* that is different from the values listed in the PROVIDER_TYPES schema rowset.
bPrecision	The maximum precision of data values in the column when *wType* is the indicator for DBTYPE_NUMERIC or DBTYPE_VARNUMERIC; it is ignored for all other data types. This must be within the limits specified for the type in the COLUMN_SIZE column in the PROVIDER_TYPES schema rowset. For information about the precision of numeric data types, see "Precision of Numeric Data Types" in Appendix A, "Data Types."
bScale	The scale of data values in the column when *wType* is DBTYPE_NUMERIC, DBTYPE_VARNUMERIC, or DBTYPE_DECIMAL; it is ignored for all other data types. This must be within the limits specified for the type in the MINIMUM_SCALE and MAXIMUM_SCALE columns in the PROVIDER_TYPES schema rowset.

riid

[in]
The IID of the interface to be returned for the resulting rowset; this is ignored if *ppRowset* is a null pointer.

cPropertySets

[in]
The number of DBPROPSET structures in *rgPropertySets*. If this is zero, the provider ignores *rgPropertySets*.

rgPropertySets

[in/out]
An array of DBPROPSET structures containing properties and values to be set. The properties specified in these structures must belong to the Rowset property group (for properties that apply to the rowset returned in **ppRowset*) or the Table property group (for properties that apply to the table). If the same property is specified more than once in *rgPropertySets*, it is provider-specific which value is used. If *cPropertySets* is zero, this argument is ignored.

Note The *colid* element of every DBPROP structure passed to the method must be set either to a valid DBID value or to DB_NULLID. For rowset properties, the *colid* element of the DBPROP structure must be set either to the ID of the rowset column to which the property applies or to DB_NULLID if the property applies to the entire rowset. For table properties, the property applies to the entire table, and therefore the *colid* element of the DBPROP structure must be set to DB_NULLID.

For information about the properties in the Rowset and Tables property groups that are defined by OLE DB, see "Properties Table (by Property Groups)" in Appendix C, "Property Tables." For information about the DBPROPSET and DBPROP structures, see "DBPROPSET Structure" and "DBPROP Structure" in Chapter 11, "Properties."

ppTableID
[out]
A pointer to memory in which to return the DBID of the newly created table. If *ppTableID* is a null pointer, no DBID is returned.

ppRowset
[out]
A pointer to memory in which to return the requested interface pointer on an empty rowset opened on the newly created table. If *ppRowset* is a null pointer, no rowset is created.

Return Code

S_OK
The method succeeded and the table is created and opened. In all DBPROP structures passed to the method, *dwStatus* is set to DBPROPSTATUS_OK.

DB_S_ERRORSOCCURRED
The table was created and the rowset was opened, but one or more properties—for which the *dwOptions* element of the DBPROP structure was DBPROPOPTIONS_OPTIONAL—were not set. The consumer checks *dwStatus* in the DBPROP structures to determine which properties were not set. The method can fail to set properties for a number of reasons, including:

- The property was not supported by the provider.
- The property was not in the Column, Rowset, or Table property group.
- The property set was not supported by the provider.
- It was not possible to set the property.
- The *colid* element of the DBPROP structure for a table property was not DB_NULLID.
- The data type in *vValue* in the DBPROP structure was not the data type of the property or was not VT_EMPTY.
- The value in *vValue* in the DBPROP structure was invalid.
- The property's value conflicted with an existing property.

E_FAIL
A provider-specific error occurred.

E_INVALIDARG
pTableID and *ppTableID* were both null pointers.

cColumnDesc was not zero, or *rgColumnDescs* was a null pointer. *cColumnDesc* was zero, and the provider does not support creating tables with no columns.

cPropertySets was not zero, and *rgPropertySets* was a null pointer.

In an element of *rgPropertySets*, *cProperties* was not zero and *rgProperties* was a null pointer.

In an element of *rgColumnDescs*, *cPropertySets* was not zero and *rgPropertySets* was a null pointer.

E_NOINTERFACE
The rowset did not support the interface specified in *riid*.

riid was IID_NULL, and *ppRowset* was not a null pointer.

DB_E_BADCOLUMNID
dbcid in an element of *rgColumnDescs* was an invalid column ID.

DB_E_BADTABLEID
**pTableID* was an invalid table ID.

DB_E_BADPRECISION
The precision in an element of *rgColumnDescs* was invalid.

DB_E_BADSCALE
The scale in an element of *rgColumnDescs* was invalid.

DB_E_BADTYPE
One or more of the *wType*, *pwszTypeName*, and *pTypeInfo* elements in an element of *rgColumnDescs* was invalid.

DB_E_DUPLICATECOLUMNID
dbcid was the same in two or more elements of *rgColumnDescs*.

DB_E_DUPLICATETABLEID
The specified table already exists in the current data store.

DB_E_ERRORSOCCURRED
The table was not created, and no rowset was returned because one or more properties—for which the *dwOptions* element of the DBPROP structure was DBPROPOPTIONS_REQUIRED or an invalid value—could not be set. The consumer checks *dwStatus* in the DBPROP structures to determine which properties were not set. The method can fail to set properties for any of the reasons specified in DB_S_ERRORSOCCURRED.

DB_E_NOAGGREGATION
pUnkOuter was not a null pointer, and the provider is an OLE DB 1.0 or 1.1 provider that does not support aggregation of the rowset object being created.

pUnkOuter was not a null pointer, and *riid* was not **IID_IUnknown**.

DB_SEC_E_PERMISSIONDENIED
The consumer did not have sufficient permission to create the table.

DB_E_OBJECTOPEN
The provider would have to open a new connection to support the operation, and DBPROP_MULTIPLECONNECTIONS is set to VARIANT_FALSE.

Comments

If *ppRowset* is not a null pointer, an empty rowset is opened on the newly created table. If **CreateTable** returns any errors, the table is not created, and *ppTableID* is set to NULL on output.

See Also

IDBProperties::GetPropertyInfo, **ITableDefinition::AddColumn**, **ITableDefinition::DropColumn**, **ITableDefinition::DropTable**

ITableDefinition::DropColumn

This method drops a column from the base table.

```
HRESULT DropColumn(
   DBID* pTableID,
   DBID* pColumnID);
```

Parameters

pTableID
[in]
A pointer to the DBID of the table from which to drop the column.

pColumnID
[in]
A pointer to the DBID of the column to drop.

Return Code

S_OK
The method succeeded, and the column was dropped from the base table.

E_FAIL
A provider-specific error occurred.

E_INVALIDARG
pTableID or *pColumnID* was a null pointer.

DB_E_BADCOLUMNID
The column specified in **pColumnID* does not exist in the specified table.

DB_E_NOTABLE
The specified table does not exist in the current data store.

DB_E_TABLEINUSE
The specified table was in use.

DB_SEC_E_PERMISSIONDENIED
The consumer did not have sufficient permission to drop the column.

Comments

If **DropColumn** returns any errors, the column is not dropped.

See Also

ITableDefinition::AddColumn

ITableDefinition::DropTable

Drops a base table in the data store.

```
HRESULT DropTable (
   DBID *   pTableID);
```

Parameters

pTableID
[in]
A pointer to the DBID of the base table to drop.

Return Code

S_OK
The method succeeded and the table is dropped.

E_FAIL
A provider-specific error occurred.

E_INVALIDARG
pTableID was a null pointer.

DB_E_NOTABLE
The specified table does not exist in the current data store.

DB_E_TABLEINUSE
The specified table was in use and could not be dropped.

DB_SEC_E_PERMISSIONDENIED
The consumer did not have sufficient permission to drop the table.

See Also

ITableDefinition::CreateTable

ITableDefinitionWithConstraints : ITableDefinition

The **ITableDefinitionWithConstraints** interface exposes simple methods to create, drop, and alter tables on the data store. It also provides a mechanism to create and delete multitable and multicolumn constraints on tables.

ITableDefinitionWithConstraints extends **ITableDefinition** by adding the ability to create and drop constraints from the base table and create base tables with constraints in one, atomic operation.

When to Implement

ITableDefinitionWithConstraints is optional for providers that do not otherwise support table creation; it is mandatory for providers that support table creation through commands and have the ability to create referential constraints (such as primary keys, foreign keys, unique, or check constraints).

Method	Description
AddConstraint	Adds a new constraint to a base table.
CreateTableWithConstraints	Creates a new base table in the data store, allowing constraints to be added atomically during table creation.
DropConstraint	Drops a constraint from a base table.

ITableDefinitionWithConstraints:: AddConstraint

Adds a new constraint to a base table.

```
HRESULT AddConstraint(
   DBID *                pTableID,
   DBCONSTRAINTDESC *    pConstraintDesc);
```

Parameters

pTableID
[in]
A pointer to the DBID of the table to which the constraint is to be added.

pConstraintDesc
[in]
A pointer to the DBCONSTRAINTDESC structure that describes the new constraint. DBCONSTRAINTDESC is defined as follows:

```
typedef struct tagDBCONSTRAINTDESC {
   DBID *             pConstraintID;
   DBCONSTRAINTTYPE   ConstraintType;
   ULONG              cColumns;
   DBID               rgColumnList[];
   DBID *             pReferencedTableID;
   ULONG              cForeignKeyColumns;
   DBID               rgForeignKeyColumnList[];
   OLECHAR            *pwszConstraintText;
   DBUPDELRULE        UpdateRule;
   DBUPDELRULE        DeleteRule;
   DBMATCHTYPE        MatchType;
   DBDEFERRABILITY    Deferrability;
   ULONG              cPropertySets;
   DBPROPSET          rgPropertySets[];
} DBCONSTRAINTDESC;
```

The elements of this structure are used as described in the following table.

Element	Description
pConstraintID	The constraint identifier. If this is null, the provider generates a unique ID for the constraint. This ID is not returned to the consumer through the DBCONSTRAINTDESC structure. Consumers should generally specify a value for the constraint and not set *pConstraintID* to null, because there is no easy way to get back the ID for the added constraint.
ConstraintType	The type of the constraint as defined in the **DBCONSTRAINTYPE** enum. One of the following values: DBCONSTRAINTTYPE_UNIQUE DBCONSTRAINTTYPE_FOREIGNKEY DBCONSTRAINTTYPE_PRIMARYKEY DBCONSTRAINTTYPE_CHECK
cColumns	The number of elements in the array passed in *rgColumnList*. For check constraints, this is always zero. If *cColumns* is zero, *rgColumnList* is ignored.
rgColumnList	For unique and primary key constraints, this contains the list of columns that comprise the constraint. For foreign key constraints, this defines the list of columns that make up the referenced key in a relationship. The order of the elements in this array comprise the key columns in descending order of significance. As such, the first element is the most-sigificant key column, and the last element in the array is the least-significant key column.
pReferencedTableID	For foreign keys, this contains the referenced table in a relationship. For all other types of constraints, this is null.
cForeignKeyColumns	The number of elements in the array passed in *rgForeignKeyColumnList*. If *cForeignKeyColumns* is zero, *rgForeignKeyColumnList* is ignored. This field must be zero if *pReferencedTableID* is a null pointer.
rgForeignKeyColumnList	The columns that comprise the foreign key in a relationship. The order of the elements in this array comprise the key columns in descending order of significance. As such, the first element is the most-sigificant key column, and the last element in the array is the least-significant key column. This field is ignored if *cForeignKeyColumns* is zero.
pwszConstraintText	The constraint clause. If *ConstraintType* is not DBCONSTRAINTTYPE_CHECK, this must be a null pointer.

Element	Description
UpdateRule	The update rule (as defined in SQL92). One of the following values: DBUPDELRULE_NOACTION DBUPDELRULE_CASCADE DBUPDELRULE_SETNULL DBUPDELRULE_SETDEFAULT This field is ignored unless *ConstraintType* is DBCONSTRAINTTYPE_FOREIGNKEY.
DeleteRule	The delete rule (as defined in SQL92). One of the following values: DBUPDELRULE_NOACTION DBUPDELRULE_CASCADE DBUPDELRULE_SETNULL DBUPDELRULE_SETDEFAULT This field is ignored unless *ConstraintType* is DBCONSTRAINTTYPE_FOREIGNKEY.
MatchType	The match type (as defined in SQL92). This field is ignored unless *ConstraintType* is DBCONSTRAINTTYPE_FOREIGNKEY. One of the following values: DBMATCHTYPE_NONE DBMATCHTYPE_FULL DBMATCHTYPE_PARTIAL
Deferrability	Whether the constraint is applied immediately. Values from the following bitmask: DBDEFERRABILITY_DEFERRED Deferred DBDEFERRABILITY_DEFERRABLE Deferrable Not specifying DBDEFERRABILITY_DEFERRED implies that the constraint is immediate. Not specifying DBDEFERRABILITY_ DEFERRABLE implies that the constraint is not deferrable. If DBDEFERRABILITY_DEFERRABLE is not specified, the DBDEFERRABILITY_DEFERRED bit is ignored and the constraint is immediate.

Element	Description
cPropertySets	The number of DBPROPSET structures in *rgPropertySets*. If this is zero, the provider ignores *rgPropertySets*.
rgPropertySets	An array of DBPROPSET structures containing properties and values to be set. If *cPropertySets* is zero, this argument is ignored.

Return Code

S_OK
: The method succeeded.

E_FAIL
: A provider-specific error occurred.

E_INVALIDARG
: *pTableID* or *pConstraintDesc* was a null pointer.

: *cForeignKeyColumns* was not zero, and *rgForeignKeyColumnsList* was null.

: *cColumns* was not zero, and *rgColumnsList was* null.

: *cPropertySets* was not zero, and *rgPropertySets* was a null pointer.

DB_E_BADTABLEID
: **pTableID* was an invalid table ID.

: *pReferencedTableID* was an invalid table ID.

DB_E_DUPLICATECONSTRAINTID
: *pConstraintID* was the same as an existing constraint.

DB_E_BADID
: *pConstraintID* was invalid.

DB_E_BADCONSTRAINTTYPE
: *ConstraintType* was invalid or not supported by the provider.

DB_E_BADUPDATEDELETERULE
: *UpdateRule* or *DeleteRule* was invalid, or the value was not supported by the provider.

DB_E_BADMATCHTYPE
: *MatchType* was invalid, or the value was not supported by the provider.

DB_E_BADDEFERRABILITY
: *Deferrability* was invalid, or the value was not supported by the provider.

DB_E_BADCONSTRAINTFORM
ConstraintType was not DBCONSTRAINTTYPE_FOREIGNKEY, and *cForeignKeyColumns* was not zero.

ConstraintType was DBCONSTRAINTTYPE_CHECK, and *pwszConstraintText* was a null pointer.

ConstraintType was not DBCONSTRAINTTYPE_CHECK, and *pwszConstraintText* was not a null pointer.

pReferencedTableID was a null pointer, and *cForeignKeyColumns* was not zero.

DB_E_BADCOLUMNID
A column id specified in *rgColumnList* was invalid.

DB_E_NOTABLE
The specified table does not exist in the data store.

The table defined in *pReferencedTableID* does not exist.

DB_E_TABLEINUSE
The specified table was in use, and the provider could not add a constraint as a result.

DB_SEC_E_PERMISSIONDENIED
The consumer did not have sufficient permission to add a constraint.

Comments

If **AddConstraint** returns any errors, the constraint is not created.

See Also

ITableDefinitionWithConstraints::CreateTableWithConstraints, **ITableDefinitionWithConstraints::DropConstraint**

ITableDefinitionWithConstraints:: CreateTableWithConstraints

Creates a new base table in the data store.

```
HRESULT CreateTable(
   IUnknown *         pUnkOuter,
   DBID *             pTableID,
   ULONG              cColumnDescs,
   DBCOLUMNDESC       rgColumnDescs[],
   ULONG              cConstraintDescs[],
   DBCONSTRAINTDESC   rgConstraintDescs[],
   REFIID             riid,
   ULONG              cPropertySets,
   DBPROPSET          rgPropertySets[],
   DBID **            ppTableID,
   IUnknown **        ppRowset);
```

Parameters

pUnkOuter
[in]
The controlling unknown if the rowset is to be aggregated; otherwise, a null pointer.

pTableID
[in]
A pointer to the ID of the table to create. If this is a null pointer, the provider must assign a unique ID to the table.

cColumnDescs
[in]
The number of DBCOLUMNDESC structures in the *rgColumnDescs* array. This can be zero if the provider allows the creation of tables with no columns.

rgColumnDescs
[in/out]
An array of DBCOLUMNDESC structures that describe the columns of the table. For more information on the DBCOLUMNDESC structure, please refer to **ITableDefinition::CreateTable**.

cConstraintDescs
[in]
The number of DBCONSTRAINTDESC structures in the *rgConstraintDescs* array. If this is zero, *rgConstraintDescs* is ignored.

rgConstraintDescs
[in]
An array of DBCONSTRAINTDESC structures that describe constraints to be created on the table. For more information on this structure, please refer to **AddConstraint**.

riid
[in]
The IID of the interface to be returned for the resulting rowset; this is ignored if *ppRowset* is a null pointer.

cPropertySets
[in]
The number of DBPROPSET structures in *rgPropertySets*. If this is zero, the provider ignores *rgPropertySets*.

rgPropertySets
[in/out]
An array of DBPROPSET structures containing properties and values to be set. The properties specified in these structures must belong to the Rowset property group (for properties that apply to the rowset returned in **ppRowset*) or the Table property group (for properties that apply to the table). If the same property is specified more than once in *rgPropertySets*, it is provider-specific which value is used. If *cPropertySets* is zero, this argument is ignored.

For information about the properties in the Rowset and Tables property groups that are defined by OLE DB, see "Properties Table (by Property Groups)" in Appendix C, "Property Tables." For information about the DBPROPSET and DBPROP structures, see "DBPROPSET Structure" and "DBPROP Structure" in Chapter 11, "Properties."

ppTableID
[out]
A pointer to memory in which to return the DBID of the newly created table. If *ppTableID* is a null pointer, no DBID is returned.

ppRowset
[out]
A pointer to memory in which to return the requested interface pointer on an empty rowset opened on the newly created table. If *ppRowset* is a null pointer, no rowset is created.

Return Code

S_OK
The method succeeded, and the table is created and opened. In all DBPROP structures passed to the method, *dwStatus* is set to DBPROPSTATUS_OK.

DB_S_ERRORSOCCURRED
The table was created and the rowset was opened, but one or more properties—for which the *dwOptions* element of the DBPROP structure was DBPROPOPTIONS_OPTIONAL—were not set. The consumer checks *dwStatus* in the DBPROP structures to determine which properties were not set. The method can fail to set properties for a number of reasons, including:

- The property was not supported by the provider.
- The property was not in the Column, Rowset, or Table property group.
- The property set was not supported by the provider.
- It was not possible to set the property.
- *colid* in the DBPROP structure was not DB_NULLID.
- The data type in *vValue* in the DBPROP structure was not the data type of the property or was not VT_EMPTY.
- The value in *vValue* in the DBPROP structure was invalid.
- The property's value conflicted with an existing property.

E_FAIL
A provider-specific error occurred.

E_INVALIDARG
pTableID and *ppTableID* were both null pointers.

cColumnDesc was not zero, or *rgColumnDescs* was a null pointer. *cColumnDesc* was zero, and the provider does not support creating tables with no columns.

cPropertySets was not zero, and *rgPropertySets* was a null pointer.

In an element of *rgPropertySets*, *cProperties* was not zero and *rgProperties* was a null pointer.

In an element of *rgColumnDescs*, *cPropertySets* was not zero and *rgPropertySets* was a null pointer.

cConstraintDescs was not zero, and *rgConstraintDescs* was a null pointer.

DB_E_BADCOLUMNID
dbcid in an element of *rgColumnDescs* was an invalid column ID.

A column id specified in *rgColumnList* was invalid.

DB_E_DUPLICATECONSTRAINTID
In an element of *rgConstraintDescs*, *pConstraintID* was the same as an existing constraint.

DB_E_BADID
In an element of *rgConstraintDescs*, *pConstraintID* was invalid.

In an element of *rgConstraintDescs*, *pReferencedTableID* was invalid.

DB_E_BADCONSTRAINTTYPE
In an element of *rgConstraintDescs*, *ConstraintType* was invalid or not supported by the provider.

DB_E_BADUPDATEDELETERULE
In an element of *rgConstraintDescs*, *UpdateRule* or *DeleteRule* was invalid or the value was not supported by the provider.

DB_E_BADMATCHTYPE
In an element of *rgConstraintDescs*, *MatchType* was invalid or the value was not supported by the provider.

DB_E_BADDEFERRABILITY
In an element of *rgConstraintDescs*, *Deferrability* was invalid or the value was not supported by the provider.

DB_E_BADCONSTRAINTFORM
ConstraintType was not DBCONSTRAINTTYPE_FOREIGNKEY, and *cForeignKeyColumns* was not zero.

ConstraintType was DBCONSTRAINTTYPE_CHECK, and pwszConstraintText was a null pointer.

ConstraintType was not DBCONSTRAINTTYPE_CHECK, and pwszConstraintText was not a null pointer.

In an element of *rgConstraintDescs*, pReferencedTableID was a null pointer and cForeignKeyColumns was not zero.

DB_E_BADTABLEID
**pTableID* was an invalid table ID.

DB_E_BADPRECISION
The precision in an element of *rgColumnDescs* was invalid.

DB_E_BADPROPERTYVALUE
The value of a property was invalid.

DB_E_BADSCALE
The scale in an element of *rgColumnDescs* was invalid.

DB_E_BADTYPE
: One or more of the *wType*, *pwszTypeName*, and *pTypeInfo* elements in an element of *rgColumnDescs* was invalid.

DB_E_DUPLICATECOLUMNID
: *dbcid* was the same in two or more elements of *rgColumnDescs*.

DB_E_DUPLICATETABLEID
: The specified table already exists in the data store.

DB_E_ERRORSOCCURRED
: The table was not created and no rowset was returned because one or more properties—for which the *dwOptions* element of the DBPROP structure was DBPROPOPTIONS_REQUIRED or an invalid value—were not set. The consumer checks *dwStatus* in the DBPROP structures to determine which properties were not set. None of the satisfiable properties are remembered. The method can fail to set properties for any of the reasons specified in DB_S_ERRORSOCCURRED, except the reason that states that it was not possible to set the property.

DB_E_NOAGGREGATION
: *pUnkOuter* was not a null pointer, and the provider is an OLE DB 1.0 or 1.1 provider that does not support aggregation of the rowset object being created.

  pUnkOuter was not a null pointer, and *riid* was not **IID_IUnknown**.

DB_SEC_E_PERMISSIONDENIED
: The consumer did not have sufficient permission to create the table.

DB_E_OBJECTOPEN
: The provider would have to open a new connection to support the operation, and DBPROP_MULTIPLECONNECTIONS is set to VARIANT_FALSE.

Comments

If *ppRowset* is not a null pointer, an empty rowset is opened on the newly created table. If **CreateTableWithConstraints** returns any errors, the table is not created nor are any relationships on that table created.

CreateTableWithConstraints is similar to **CreateTable** except that it also provides the ability to create constraints such as primary keys, foreign keys, unique clauses, or check clauses in the same call as the creation of the table. This closely mimics the functionality of the CREATE TABLE SQL statement.

See Also

ITableDefinition::DropTable, **ITableDefinitionWithConstraints::AddConstraint**, **ITableDefinitionWithConstraints::DropConstraint**

ITableDefinitionWithConstraints::DropConstraint

Drops a constraint from a base table.

```
HRESULT DropConstraint(
   DBID *   pTableID,
   DBID *   pConstraintID);
```

Parameters

pTableID
[in]
A pointer to the DBID of the table from which to drop the column.

pConstraint
[in]
A pointer to the DBID of the constraint to drop.

Return Code

S_OK
The method succeeded, and the column was dropped from the base table.

E_FAIL
A provider-specific error occurred.

E_INVALIDARG
pTableID or *pConstraint* was a null pointer.

DB_E_BADID
pConstraintID was invalid.

DB_E_BADCONSTRAINTID
pConstraintID did not exist in the data store.

DB_E_BADTABLEID
**pTableID* was an invalid table ID.

DB_E_NOTABLE
The specified table does not exist in the data store.

DB_E_TABLEINUSE
The specified table was in use, and the provider could not drop the constraint as a result.

DB_SEC_E_PERMISSIONDENIED
The consumer did not have sufficient permission to drop the column.

Comments

If **DropConstraint** returns any errors, the constraint is not dropped.

See Also

ITableDefinitionWithConstraints::AddConstraint

ITransaction

The **ITransaction** interface is used to commit, abort, and obtain status information about transactions. For more information about transactions, see Chapter 12, "Transactions."

Method	Description
Abort	Aborts a transaction.
Commit	Commits a transaction.
GetTransactionInfo	Returns information about a transaction.

ITransaction::Abort

Aborts a transaction.

```
HRESULT Abort(
   BOID *   pboidReason,
   BOOL     fRetaining,
   BOOL     fAsync);
```

Parameters

pboidReason
[in]
A pointer to a BOID that indicates why the transaction is being aborted. If this is a null pointer, no reason is provided.

fRetaining
[in]
Whether the abort is retaining or nonretaining.

fAsync
[in]
When *fAsync* is TRUE, an asynchronous abort is performed and the caller must use **ITransactionOutcomeEvents** to learn the outcome of the transaction.

Return Code

S_OK
The transaction was successfully aborted.

XACT_S_ABORTING
An abort operation was already in progress. This call was ignored.

XACT_S_ASYNC
An asynchronous abort was specified. The abort operation has begun but its outcome is not yet known. When the transaction is complete, notification will be sent by **ITransactionOutcomeEvents**.

E_FAIL
The transaction failed to abort for an unspecified reason.

E_UNEXPECTED
An unexpected error occurred. The transaction status is unknown.

XACT_E_ALREADYINPROGRESS
A commit operation was already in progress. This call was ignored.

XACT_E_CANTRETAIN
A retaining abort is not supported, or a new unit of work could not be created. The abort succeeded, and the session is in auto-commit mode.

XACT_E_CONNECTION_DOWN
The connection to the transaction manager failed. The transaction state is unknown.

XACT_E_INDOUBT
The transaction status is in doubt. A communication failure occurred, or a transaction manager or resource manager has failed.

XACT_E_NOTRANSACTION
The transaction cannot be aborted because it already had been implicitly or explicitly committed or aborted. This call was ignored.

XACT_E_NOTSUPPORTED
fAsync was TRUE on input, and asynchronous abort operations are not supported.

Comments

The following table shows how the values of *fRetaining* and DBPROP_ABORTPRESERVE affect the rowset state and transaction mode.

DBPROP_ABORT-PRESERVE	*fRetaining*	Rowset state after abort	Resulting transaction mode of session
FALSE	FALSE	zombie	implicit/auto-commit
FALSE	TRUE	zombie	explicit/manual-commit
TRUE	FALSE	preserved	implicit/auto-commit
TRUE	TRUE	preserved	explicit/manual-commit

See Also

ITransaction::Commit

ITransaction::Commit

Commits a transaction.

```
HRESULT Commit(
   BOOL     fRetaining,
   DWORD    grfTC,
   DWORD    grfRM);
```

Parameters

fRetaining
[in]
Whether the commit is retaining or nonretaining.

grfTC
[in]
Values taken from the enumeration XACTTC. Values that may be specified in *grfTC* are as follows. These values are mutually exclusive.

Flag	Description
XACTTC_ASYNC_ PHASEONE	When this flag is specified, an asynchronous commit is performed.
XACTTC_SYNC_ PHASEONE	When this flag is specified, the call to **Commit** returns after phase one of the two-phase commit protocol.
XACTTC_SYNC_ PHASETWO	When this flag is specified, the call to **Commit** returns after phase two of the two-phase commit protocol.
XACTTC_SYNC	Synonym for XACTTC_SYNC_PHASETWO.

grfRM
[in]
Must be zero.

Return Code

S_OK
The transaction was successfully committed.

XACT_S_ASYNC
An asynchronous commit was specified. The commit operation has begun but its outcome is not yet known. When the transaction is complete, notification will be sent by **ITransactionOutcomeEvents**.

E_FAIL
A provider-specific error occurred. The transaction was aborted.

E_UNEXPECTED
An unexpected error occurred. The transaction status is unknown.

XACT_E_ABORTED
The transaction was aborted before **Commit** was called.

XACT_E_ALREADYINPROGRESS
A commit or abort operation was already in progress. This call was ignored.

XACT_E_CANTRETAIN
Retaining commit is not supported, or a new unit of work could not be created. The commit succeeded, and the session is in auto-commit mode.

XACT_E_COMMITFAILED
The transaction failed to commit for an unknown reason. The transaction was aborted.

XACT_E_CONNECTION_DOWN
The connection to the transaction manager failed. The transaction was aborted.

XACT_E_INDOUBT
The transaction status is in doubt. A communication failure occurred, or a transaction manager or resource manager has failed.

XACT_E_NOTRANSACTION
Unable to commit the transaction because it had already been implicitly or explicitly committed or aborted. This call was ignored.

XACT_E_NOTSUPPORTED
An invalid combination of commit flags was specified, or *grfRM* was not equal to zero. This call was ignored.

Comments

The following table shows how values of the *fRetaining* parameter and DBPROP_COMMITPRESERVE affect the rowset state and transaction mode.

DBPROP_COMMIT-PRESERVE	*fRetaining*	Rowset state after commit	Resulting transaction mode of session
FALSE	FALSE	zombie	implicit/auto-commit
FALSE	TRUE	zombie	explicit/manual-commit
TRUE	FALSE	preserved	implicit/auto-commit
TRUE	TRUE	preserved	explicit/manual-commit

If **Commit** fails for any reason that results in an aborted transaction, the session is left in auto-commit mode.

See Also

ITransaction::Abort

ITransaction::GetTransactionInfo

Returns information regarding a transaction.

```
HRESULT GetTransactionInfo(
   XACTTRANSINFO *pInfo);
```

Parameters

pInfo
[out]
A pointer to the caller-allocated XACTTRANSINFO structure in which the method returns information about the transaction. *pInfo* must not be a null pointer.

```
typedef struct XACTTRANSINFO {
   XACTUOW  uow;
      ISOLEVEL    isoLevel;
      ULONG       isoFlags;
      DWORD       grfTCSupported;
      DWORD       grfRMSupported;
      DWORD       grfTCSupportedRetaining;
      DWORD       grfRMSupportedRetaining;
} XACTTRANSINFO;
```

The elements of this structure are used as described in the following table.

Element	Description
uow	The unit of work associated with this transaction.
isoLevel	The isolation level associated with this transaction. ISOLATIONLEVEL_UNSPECIFIED indicates that no isolation level was specified. For more information, see **ITransactionLocal::StartTransaction**.
isoFlags	Will be zero.
grfTCSupported	This bitmask indicates the XACTTC flags that this transaction implementation supports.
grfRMSupported	Will be zero.
grfTCSupportedRetaining	Will be zero.
grfRMSupportedRetaining	Will be zero.

Return Code

S_OK
The method succeeded.

E_FAIL
A provider-specific error occurred.

E_INVALIDARG
pInfo was a null pointer.

E_UNEXPECTED
An unknown error occurred. No information is returned.

XACT_E_NOTRANSACTION
Unable to retrieve information for the transaction because it was already completed. No information is returned.

ITransactionJoin

ITransactionJoin is exposed only by providers that support distributed transactions. The consumer calls **QueryInterface** for **ITransactionJoin** to determine whether the provider supports distributed transactions. For more information, see "Distributed Transactions" in Chapter 12, "Transactions."

Method	Description
GetOptionsObject	Returns an object that can be used to specify configuration options for a subsequent call to **JoinTransaction**.
JoinTransaction	Requests that the session enlist in a coordinated transaction.

ITransactionJoin::GetOptionsObject

Returns an object that can be used to specify configuration options for a subsequent call to **JoinTransaction**.

```
HRESULT GetOptionsObject (
   ITransactionOptions **  ppOptions);
```

Parameters

ppOptions
[out]
A pointer to memory in which to return a pointer to the object that can be used to set extended transaction options.

Return Code

S_OK
The method succeeded.

E_FAIL
An unknown error occurred.

E_INVALIDARG
ppOptions was a null pointer.

E_OUTOFMEMORY
Unable to allocate memory.

See Also

ITransactionOptions::GetOptions

ITransactionJoin::JoinTransaction

Requests that the session enlist in a coordinated transaction.

```
HRESULT JoinTransaction (
   IUnknown *              punkTransactionCoord,
   ISOLEVEL                isoLevel,
   ULONG                   isoFlags,
   ITransactionOptions *   pOtherOptions);
```

Parameters

punkTransactionCoord
[in]
A pointer to the controlling **IUnknown** of the transaction coordinator, or NULL to unenlist from the coordinated transaction. If non-null, **QueryInterface** can be called for **ITransaction** on the transaction coordinator. If NULL, the remaining arguments to the method are ignored.

isoLevel
[in]
The isolation level to be used with this transaction. For more information, see **ITransactionLocal::StartTransaction**.

isoFlags
[in]
Must be zero.

pOtherOptions
[in]
Optionally a null pointer. If this is not a null pointer, it is a pointer to an object previously returned from **GetOptionsObject** called on this session.

Return Code

S_OK
The method succeeded.

E_FAIL
An unknown error occurred.

E_INVALIDARG
punkTransactionCoord was a null pointer, and the provider doesn't support unenlisting from a coordinated transaction.

E_UNEXPECTED
An unknown provider-specific error occurred.

XACT_E_CONNECTION_DOWN
The connection to the transaction manager failed.

XACT_E_CONNECTION_REQUEST_DENIED
The transaction manager did not accept a connection request.

XACT_E_ISOLATIONLEVEL
Neither the requested isolation level nor a strengthening of it can be supported by this transaction implementation, or *isoLevel* was not valid.

XACT_E_LOGFULL
Unable to begin a new transaction because the log file is full.

XACT_E_NOENLIST
A transaction coordinator was specified, but the new transaction was unable to enlist therein.

XACT_E_NOISORETAIN
The requested semantics of retention of isolation across retaining commit and abort boundaries cannot be supported by this transaction implementation, or *isoFlags* was not equal to zero.

XACT_E_NOTIMEOUT
A time-out was specified, but time-outs are not supported.

XACT_E_TMNOTAVAILABLE
Unable to connect to the transaction manager, or the transaction manager is unavailable.

XACT_E_XTIONEXISTS
The enlistment request failed for one of the following reasons:

- This session can handle only one extant transaction at a time, and the session is already enlisted in a coordinated transaction with uncommitted work.
- *punkTransactionCoord* was NULL, the session is enlisted in a coordinated transaction with uncommitted work, and the provider doesn't support local transactions while there is pending work on the coordinated transaction.

Comments

After a session enlists in a coordinated transaction and that coordinated transaction completes with no retaining semantics, the session is temporarily in a zombie state, although the provider may not detect this state until the consumer executes a method that communicates with the data store. To return the session from a zombie state, the consumer must call **ITransactionJoin::JoinTransaction** with a valid *punkTransactionCoord* to enlist in a new coordinated transaction, or with a null *punkTransactionCoord* to unenlist from the coordinated transaction.

If the provider needs to register for outcome events, it will usually first register its **ITransactionOutcomeEvents** notification sink with the transaction coordinator and then enlist with the transaction coordinator. It is important that providers needing outcome events first register with the outcome events so that they can be advised of any failures that may occur between enlistment registration of the outcome events.

Registering for **ITransactionOutcomeEvents** can be expensive, because it results in an extra message. Also, in some cases the Microsoft Distributed Transaction Coordinator does not fire these events, which results in memory leaks from references on the connection sink not being released and in connections being held longer than necessary. For these reasons, providers should avoid registering for transaction outcome events.

See Also

ITransactionLocal::StartTransaction

ITransactionLocal : ITransaction

ITransactionLocal is an optional interface on sessions. It is used to start, commit, and abort transactions on the session. For more information, see "Simple Transactions" in Chapter 12, "Transactions."

Method	Description
GetOptionsObject	Returns an object that can be used to specify configuration options for a subsequent call to **StartTransaction**.
StartTransaction	Begins a new transaction.

ITransactionLocal::GetOptionsObject

Returns an object that can be used to specify configuration options for a subsequent call to **StartTransaction**.

```
HRESULT GetOptionsObject (
   ITransactionOptions **  ppOptions);
```

Parameters

ppOptions
[out]
A pointer to memory in which to return a pointer to the object that can be used to set extended transaction options.

Return Code

S_OK
The method succeeded.

E_FAIL
A provider-specific error occurred.

E_INVALIDARG
ppOptions was a null pointer.

E_OUTOFMEMORY
Unable to allocate memory.

E_UNEXPECTED
An unknown error occurred, and the method failed.

See Also

ITransactionLocal::StartTransaction, **ITransactionOptions::SetOptions**

ITransactionLocal::StartTransaction

Begins a new transaction.

```
HRESULT StartTransaction (
   ISOLEVEL                 isoLevel,
   ULONG                    isoFlags,
   ITransactionOptions *    pOtherOptions,
   ULONG *                  pulTransactionLevel);
```

Parameters

isoLevel

[in]

The isolation level to be used with this transaction. For more information, see "Isolation Levels" in Chapter 12, "Transactions."

Value	Description
ISOLATIONLEVEL_ UNSPECIFIED	Applicable only to **ITransactionJoin::JoinTransaction**. Invalid for **ITransactionLocal** or for setting isolation level while in auto-commit mode.
ISOLATIONLEVEL_ CHAOS	Cannot overwrite the dirty data of other transactions at higher isolation levels.
ISOLATIONLEVEL_ READUNCOMMITTED	Read Uncommitted.
ISOLATIONLEVEL_ BROWSE	Synonym for ISOLATIONLEVEL_READUNCOMMITTED.
ISOLATIONLEVEL_ READCOMMITTED	Read Committed.
ISOLATIONLEVEL_ CURSORSTABILITY	Synonym for ISOLATIONLEVEL_READCOMMITTED.
ISOLATIONLEVEL_ REPEATABLEREAD	Repeatable Read.
ISOLATIONLEVEL_ SERIALIZABLE	Serializable.
ISOLATIONLEVEL_ ISOLATED	Synonym for ISOLATIONLEVEL_SERIALIZABLE.

isoFlags
[in]
Must be zero.

pOtherOptions
[in]
Optionally a null pointer. If this is not a null pointer, it is a pointer to an object previously returned from **GetOptionsObject** called on this session instance.

pulTransactionLevel
[out]
A pointer to memory in which to return the level of the new transaction. The value of the top-level transaction is 1. If *pulTransactionLevel* is a null pointer, the level is not returned.

Return Code

S_OK
The method succeeded.

DB_E_OBJECTOPEN
A rowset object was open, and the provider does not support starting a new transaction with existing open rowset objects.

E_FAIL
A provider-specific error occurred.

E_UNEXPECTED
An unknown error occurred, and the method failed.

XACT_E_CONNECTION_DENIED
This session could not create a new transaction at the present time due to unspecified capacity issues.

XACT_E_CONNECTION_DOWN
This session is having communication difficulties with its internal implementation.

XACT_E_ISOLATIONLEVEL
Neither the requested isolation level nor a strengthening of it can be supported by this transaction implementation, or *isoLevel* was not valid.

XACT_E_LOGFULL
A transaction could not be created because this session specifies logging to a device that lacks available space.

XACT_E_NOISORETAIN
The requested semantics of retention of isolation across retaining commit and abort boundaries cannot be supported by this transaction implementation, or *isoFlags* was not equal to zero.

XACT_E_NOTIMEOUT
A noninfinite time-out value was requested, but time-outs are not supported by this transaction.

XACT_E_XTIONEXISTS
This session can handle only one extant transaction at a time, and there is presently such a transaction.

The session supports a limited number of nested transactions, and that limit has been reached.

Comments

StartTransaction starts a new local transaction. If there is already an active transaction on the session (that is, **StartTransaction** has been called with no matching **Commit** or **Abort**), the new transaction is started as a nested transaction below the current transaction. Calling **Commit** or **Abort** always commits or aborts the transaction at the lowest level, respectively. If the provider does not support nested transactions, calling **StartTransaction** when there is already an active transaction on the session returns XACT_E_XTIONEXISTS.

See Also

ITransactionOptions::SetOptions

ITransactionObject

ITransactionObject enables consumers to obtain the transaction object associated with a particular transaction level. For more information, see "**ITransactionObject**" in Chapter 12, "Transactions."

Method	Description
GetTransactionObject	Returns an interface pointer on the transaction object.

ITransactionObject::GetTransactionObject

Returns an interface pointer on the transaction object.

```
HRESULT GetTransactionObject (
   ULONG              ulTransactionLevel,
   ITransaction **    ppTransactionObject);
```

Parameters

ulTransactionLevel
[in]
The level of the transaction.

ppTransactionObject
[out]
A pointer to memory in which to return a pointer to the returned transaction object.

Return Code

S_OK
The method succeeded.

E_FAIL
A provider-specific error occurred.

E_INVALIDARG
ulTransactionLevel was zero, or *ppTransactionObject* was a null pointer.

E_UNEXPECTED
An unknown error occurred, and the method failed.

ITransactionOptions

ITransactionOptions gets and sets a suite of options associated with a transaction.

Method	Description
GetOptions	Gets a suite of options associated with a transaction.
SetOptions	Sets a suite of options associated with a transaction.

ITransactionOptions::GetOptions

Gets a suite of options associated with a transaction.

```
HRESULT GetOptions(
   XACTOPT *pOptions);
```

Parameters

pOptions
[in/out]
A pointer to an XACTOPT structure in which to return the options for this transaction. The consumer allocates this structure. For more information, see **ITransactionOptions::SetOptions**.

Return Code

S_OK
Success.

E_FAIL
A provider-specific error occurred.

E_INVALIDARG
pOptions was a null pointer.

E_UNEXPECTED
An unknown error occurred; the method failed.

Comments

This method can be called at any time. **GetOptions** does not make any logical changes to the state of any open transactions.

See Also

ITransactionJoin::GetOptionsObject, **ITransactionLocal::GetOptionsObject**, **ITransactionOptions::SetOptions**

ITransactionOptions::SetOptions

Sets a suite of options associated with a transaction.

```
HRESULT SetOptions(
   XACTOPT *pOptions);
```

Parameters

pOptions
[in]
A pointer to an XACTOPT structure containing the options to be set in this transaction. This cannot be a null pointer.

```
typedef struct XACTOPT {
   ULONG             ulTimeout;
   unsigned char     szDescription[MAX_TRAN_DESC];
} XACTOPT
```

The elements of this structure are used as described in the following table.

Element	Description
ulTimeout	The amount of real time in milliseconds before the transaction is to be aborted automatically. Zero indicates an infinite time-out. If no options have been previously set, *ulTimeout* is zero.
szDescription	A pointer to a textual description associated with this transaction. This string is appropriate for display in various end-user administration tools that might monitor or log the transaction. If no options have been previously set, *szDescription* is an empty string.

Return Code

S_OK
The method succeeded.

E_FAIL
A provider-specific error occurred.

E_INVALIDARG
pOptions was a null pointer.

E_UNEXPECTED
An unknown error occurred; the method failed.

See Also

ITransactionLocal::StartTransaction, **ITransactionOptions::GetOptions**

IViewChapter

IViewChapter enables the consumer to create or apply a view to an existing rowset.

When to Implement

Providers that can do simple post-processing of rowsets, such as applying filters or re-sorting rowsets, support **IViewChapter**.

When to Call

Consumers call **IViewChapter** in order to apply post-processing operations to an existing rowset. The consumer calls **CreateView** on the rowset in order to create a view object, applies post-processing operations to that view object, and then calls **OpenViewChapter** to retrieve a chapter handle that reflects the specified view conditions. Any resources associated with the view can be released with a call to **IChapteredRowset::ReleaseChapter**.

Method	Description
GetSpecification	Returns the rowset from which the view was created.
OpenViewChapter	Returns a chapter reflecting the specified view.

IViewChapter::GetSpecification

Returns the rowset from which the view was created.

```
HRESULT GetSpecification (
   REFIID          riid,
   IUnknown **     ppRowset);
```

Parameters

riid
[in]
The IID of the interface on which to return a pointer.

ppRowset
[out]
A pointer to memory in which to return the interface pointer. If **GetSpecification** fails, it must attempt to set **ppRowset* to a null pointer.

Return Code

S_OK
The method succeeded.

E_FAIL
A provider-specific error occurred.

E_NOINTERFACE
The view did not support the interface specified in *riid*.

E_OUTOFMEMORY
The provider was unable to allocate sufficient memory in which to return the rowset information.

Comments

GetSpecification adds a reference count to the rowset. The consumer must call **Release** to release the reference count when it is no longer needed.

IViewChapter::OpenViewChapter

Returns a chapter for the rows meeting the specified view conditions.

```
HRESULT OpenViewChapter (
   HCHAPTER       hSource,
   HCHAPTER *     phViewChapter);
```

Parameters

hSource
[in]
A chapter defining the set of rows on which to apply the view. To apply a view to the root rowset, the consumer must use DB_NULL_HCHAPTER.

phViewChapter
[out]
A chapter reflecting the specified view conditions, or NULL to indicate that the view conditions should be applied to *hSource*.

Return Code

S_OK
The method succeeded.

E_FAIL
A provider-specific error occurred.

DB_E_BADCHAPTER
hSource was invalid.

DB_E_CANTFILTER
The described filter could not be opened. The provider may have limitations on the columns used in a filter or a limitation on the complexity of the filter.

DB_E_CANTORDER
The described order could not be opened. The provider may have limitations on the columns used in an order or a limitation on the complexity of the order.

DB_E_BADCOMPAREOP
A specified comparison operator was invalid.

Comments

None.

IViewFilter

IViewFilter enables consumers to restrict the contents of a rowset to rows matching a set of conditions.

When to Implement

Providers that can define a subset of rows based on a consumer-defined set of conditions expose **IViewFilter**. A provider may restrict functionality to filters based on existing indexes, or filters may require a specific sort order to also be applied.

When to Call

Consumers needing a subset of rows can call **IViewFilter::SetFilter** to apply a filter condition to a view. Rowsets or chapters opening using this view expose only those rows that match the criteria. Each view can have only a single filter applied, but a view containing a filter can be applied to an existing filtered chapter to further filter its contents.

Filter criteria are expressed as an array of rows and columns, with an associated set of comparison operators.

Within a row of the criteria array, each column corresponds to a column in the table. The mapping of the columns in the criteria array to the columns in the table is done through an accessor passed into **SetFilter** or **GetFilter**. The same column from the table may appear once, more than once, or not at all in the criteria array. Each column in the criteria array has a corresponding comparison operation that defines how the value passed in the criteria array is to be compared to the value of the corresponding column in the rowset. Each column of the criteria array is joined in a logical AND with the other columns in that row of the criteria array.

The criteria array can contain multiple rows. In this case, the array of comparison operations is a two-dimensional array stored in row-major format, such that the comparison operators for each of the columns of the first row in the criteria array are followed by the comparison operators for each column of the second row in the criteria array, and so forth. Multiple rows in the criteria array are joined together in a logical OR.

For example, assume the rowset shown in the following table.

Name	Children	State
Joe	0	WA
Jane	2	WA
Fred	3	OR
Judy	1	OR
Jane	2	ID

Using the preceding rowset, the following table shows the results for various combinations of accessor bindings, criteria array, and comparison operators.

Accessor	Criteria Array	Comparison Ops	Result	
rgBindings[0].iOrdinal = 3	{DBCOMPAREOPS_EQ}	{"WA"}	"Joe"	0 "WA"
			"Jane"	2 "WA"
rgBindings[0].iOrdinal=3	{DBCOMPAREOPS_EQ, DBCOMPAREOPS_EQ}	{"WA","ID"}	"Joe"	0 "WA"
			"Jane"	2 "WA"
			"Jane"	2 "ID"
rgBindings[0].iOrdinal=3 rgBindings[1].iOrdinal=2	{DBCOMPAREOPS_EQ, DBCOMPAREOPS_GT}	{"OR",1}	"Fred"	3 "OR"
rgBindings[0].iOrdinal=3 rgBindings[1].iOrdinal=2	{DBCOMPAREOPS_EQ, DBCOMPAREOPS_IGNORE, DBCOMPAREOPS_IGNORE, DBCOMPAREOPS_GT}	{"OR",NULL, NULL,1}	"Jane"	2 "WA"
			"Fred"	3 "OR"
			"Judy"	1 "OR"
			"Jane"	2 "ID"

The following code example shows defining a filter for which the individual is from Oregon *or* has more than one child:

```
DBBINDING      rgBindings[2];
IAccessor *    pIAccessor;
HACCESSOR      hAccessor;
DBCOMPAREOP    rgCompareOps[] = { DBCOMPAREOP_EQ, DBCOMPAREOP_IGNORE,
                                  DBCOMPAREOP_IGNORE, DBCOMPAREOP_GT };

typedef struct FILTER_CRITERIA {
   TCHAR    rcState[4];
   ULONG    ulStateStatus;
   ULONG    ulStateLength;
   ULONG    cChildren;
   ULONG    ulChildrenStatus;
} WHERE_CLAUSE;

WHERE_CLAUSE rgCriteriaData[] =
{
   _T("OR"), DBSTATUS_S_OK,   2 * sizeof(TCHAR), NULL, DBSTATUS_S_ISNULL,
   NULL, DBSTATUS_S_ISNULL,   0, 1, DBSTATUS_S_OK
};

// Initialize common binding values
for (cCol = 0; cCol < 2; cCol++)
{
   rgBindings[cCol].pTypeInfo     = NULL;
   rgBindings[cCol].pObject       = NULL;
   rgBindings[cCol].pBindExp      = NULL;
   rgBindings[cCol].dwMemOwner    = DBMEMOWNER_CLIENTOWNED;
   rgBindings[cCol].eParamIO      = DBPARAMIO_NOTPARAM;
   rgBindings[cCol].dwFlags       = 0;
   rgBindings[cCol].bPrecision    = 0;
   rgBindings[cCol].bScale        = 0;
}

// Initial bindings for the "State" column
   rgBindings[0].dwPart           = DBPART_VALUE | DBPART_LENGTH | DBPART_STATUS;
   rgBindings[0].iOrdinal         = 3;
   rgBindings[0].wType            = DBTYPE_STR;
   rgBindings[0].obValue          = offsetof(WHERE_CLAUSE, rcState);
   rgBindings[0].obStatus         = offsetof(WHERE_CLAUSE, ulStateStatus);
   rgBindings[0].obLength         = offsetof(WHERE_CLAUSE, ulStateLength);
   rgBindings[0].cbMaxLen         = sizeof(WHERE_CLAUSE.rcState);
```

```
// Initial bindings for the "Children" column
   rgBindings[1].dwPart         =
   rgBindings[1].iOrdinal       = 2
   rgBindings[1].wType          = DBTYPE_I4;
   rgBindings[1].obValue        = offsetof(WHERE_CLAUSE, cChildren);
   rgBindings[1].obStatus       = offsetof(WHERE_CLAUSE, ulChildrenStatus);
   rgBindings[0].obLength       = 0;
   rgBindings[1].cbMaxLen       = sizeof(WHERE_CLAUSE.cChildren);

pIAccessor->CreateAccessor(DBACCESSOR_ROWDATA, 2, rgBindings, sizeof(WHERE_CLAUSE),
&hAccessor, NULL);

// Set filter condition
pIViewFilter->SetFilter(hAccessor, 2, rgCompareOps, rgCriteriaData);
```

Method	Description
GetFilter	Returns the filter condition associated with a view.
GetFilterBindings	Returns the bindings used to describe the filter conditions associated with a view.
SetFilter	Sets a filter condition on a view.

IViewFilter::GetFilter

Retrieves the filter applied to a view.

```
HRESULT GetFilter (
   HACCESSOR       hAccessor,
   ULONG *         pcRows,
   DBCOMPAREOP *   pCompareOps[],
   void *          pCriteriaData);
```

Parameters

hAccessor
[in]
A row data accessor describing the data to be written to *ppCriteriaData*. The same column may appear more than once in the criteria.

pcRows
[out]
A pointer to memory in which to write the number of rows in the criteria table, where the criteria described by each row is joined in a logical OR with the other rows. If *pcRows* is greater than one, the *cbRowSize* argument used in the call to **CreateAccessor** is used to specify the offset between each set of row values.

pCompareOps
[out]
A pointer to memory in which to write a two-dimensional array of comparisons operators. The two-dimensional array contains *pcRows* by *cBindings* comparison operators in *pcRows*-major format, where *cBindings* is the number of columns represented in *hAccessor*, and is written in row-major format. Each comparison operator in the *cBindings* dimension refers to a column in *pCriteriaData*, and each set of columns in the *pcRows* dimension refers to a row in *pCriteriaData*. Columns within a row are joined together in a logical AND, and each row is joined in a logical OR with another row. For information about the DBCOMPAREOP enumerated type, see **IRowsetFind::FindNextRow**.

pCriteriaData
[out]
A pointer to a buffer in which to return the criteria data.

Return Code

S_OK
The method succeeded.

DB_S_ERRORSOCCURRED
An error occurred while returning data for one or more columns, but data was successfully returned for at least one column. To determine the columns for which data was returned, the consumer checks the status values. For a list of status values that can be returned by this method, see "Status Values Used When Getting Data" in Chapter 6, "Getting and Setting Data."

E_FAIL
A provider-specific error occurred.

E_OUTOFMEMORY
The provider was unable to allocate sufficient memory in which to return the filter information.

DB_E_BADACCESSORHANDLE
hAccessor was invalid. Providers are required to check for this condition in this method.

DB_E_BADACCESSORTYPE
The specified accessor was not a row accessor.

DB_E_BADCOMPAREOP
In an element of *pCompareOps*, both DBCOMPAREOPS_CASESENSITIVE and DBCOMPAREOPS_CASEINSENSITIVE were specified.

The provider was asked for an option that it does not support.

DB_E_ERRORSOCCURRED
Errors occurred while returning data for all columns. To determine what errors occurred, the consumer checks the status values. For a list of status values that can be returned by this method, see "Status Values Used When Getting Data" in Chapter 6, "Getting and Setting Data."

Comments

None.

IViewFilter::GetFilterBindings

Retrieves the bindings used to describe the filter conditions associated with a view.

```
HRESULT GetFilterBindings(
   ULONG *        pcBindings,
   DBBINDING **   prgBindings);
```

Parameters

cBindings
[out]
A pointer to memory in which to return the number of bindings used to describe the filter criteria. If this method fails or if no filter has been applied to the view, **pcBindings* is set to zero.

rgBindings
[out]
A pointer to memory in which to return an array of DBBINDING structures. One structure is returned for each binding used to describe the filter criteria. The provider allocates memory for the structures and returns the address to this memory; the consumer releases this memory with **IMalloc::Free** when it no longer needs the bindings. If **pcBindings* is zero on output or the method fails, the provider does not allocate any memory and ensures that **prgBindings* is a null pointer on output. For information about bindings, see "DBBINDING Structures" in Chapter 6, "Getting and Setting Data."

Return Code

S_OK
The method succeeded.

E_FAIL
A provider-specific error occurred.

E_INVALIDARG
pcBindings or *prgBindings* was a null pointer.

E_OUTOFMEMORY
The provider was unable to allocate sufficient memory in which to return the binding structures.

Comments

The consumer calls **IViewFilter::GetFilterBindings** in order to retrieve information about the columns bound in the current filter. The consumer can use this information to create an accessor to be passed into **IViewFilter::GetFilter** to retrieve the information describing the filter conditions.

IViewFilter::SetFilter

Specifies a filter condition for a view.

```
HRESULT SetFilter (
   HACCESSOR      hAccessor,
   ULONG          cRows,
   DBCOMPAREOP    CompareOps[],
   void *         pCriteriaData);
```

Parameters

hAccessor
[in]
The handle of the accessor that describes the data in *pCriteriaData*. The same column may appear more than once in the criteria.

cRows
[in]
The number of rows in the criteria table, where the criteria described by each row is joined in a logical OR with the other rows. Some providers may have limits on the number of rows (OR conditions) that can be expressed in the criteria.

CompareOps
[in]
A two-dimensional array containing *cRows* by *cBindings* comparison operators in *cRows*-major format, where *cBindings* is the number of columns represented in *hAccessor*. Each comparison operator in the *cBindings* dimension refers to a column in *pCriteriaData*, and each set of columns in the *pcRows* dimension refers to a row in *pCriteriaData*. Columns within a row are joined together in a logical AND, and each row is joined in a logical OR with another row. The consumer should check DBPROP_FINDCOMPAREOPS to determine which comparison operators the provider supports. For information about the DBCOMPAREOP enumerated type, see **IRowsetFind::FindNextRow**.

pCriteriaData
[in]
A pointer to memory containing the data values, at offsets that correspond to the bindings in the accessor that, in conjunction with the array of comparison operators, define the criteria.

Return Code

S_OK
The method succeeded.

E_FAIL
A provider-specific error occurred.

DB_E_BADCOMPAREOP
In an element of *CompareOps*, both DBCOMPAREOPS_CASESENSITIVE and DBCOMPAREOPS_CASEINSENSITIVE were specified.

The provider was asked for an option that it does not support.

DB_E_CANTFILTER
The described filter could not be applied. The provider may have limitations on the columns used in a filter or a limitation on the complexity of the filter.

Comments

A provider may restrict filter columns to use only existing indexes or may restrict a filter to work only with an order chapter as a source.

If there is already a filter condition applied to a view, **SetFilter** overrides that previous filter condition.

Changing the filter condition of a view does not change the filtering of any rowsets or chapters opened using that view.

IViewRowset

IViewRowset enables the consumer to create or apply view operations when opening a rowset.

When to Implement

Providers that can do simple operations, such as filtering and sorting when opening rowsets, support **IViewRowset**.

When to Call

Consumers call **IViewRowset** to open a rowset with simple operations such as filtering and sorting applied. The consumer requests **IID_IViewRowset** when calling a method that returns a rowset to create a view object, applies operations to that view, and then calls **OpenViewRowset** to open the rowset with those operations applied.

Method	Description
GetSpecification	Returns the object that created the view.
OpenViewRowset	Opens the requested rowset using the specified view.

IViewRowset::GetSpecification

Returns the object from which the view was created.

```
HRESULT GetSpecification (
   REFIID          riid,
   IUnknown **     ppObject);
```

Parameters

riid
: [in]
The IID of the interface to be returned. This interface is conceptually added to the list of required interfaces on the resulting rowset, and the method fails (E_NOINTERFACE) if that interface cannot be supported on the resulting rowset.

ppObject
: [out]
A pointer to memory in which to return the interface pointer. If **GetSpecification** fails, it must attempt to set **ppObject* to a null pointer.

Return Code

S_OK
: The method succeeded.

E_FAIL
: A provider-specific error occurred.

E_NOINTERFACE
: The view did not support the interface specified in *riid*.

E_OUTOFMEMORY
: The provider was unable to allocate sufficient memory in which to return the object information.

Comments

GetSpecification adds a reference count to the object. The consumer must call **Release** to release the reference count when it is no longer needed.

IViewRowset::OpenViewRowset

Creates a rowset from a view.

```
HRESULT OpenViewRowset (
   IUnknown *      pUnkOuter,
   REFIID          riid,
   IUnknown **     ppRowset);
```

Parameters

pUnkOuter
[in]
A pointer to the controlling **IUnknown** interface if the new rowset is being created as part of an aggregate. It is a null pointer if the rowset is not part of an aggregate.

riid
[in]
The IID of the interface requested on the rowset.

ppRowset
[out]
A pointer to memory in which to return the interface pointer on the newly created rowset. If **OpenViewRowset** fails, **ppRowset* is set to a null pointer.

Return Code

S_OK
The method succeeded.

E_FAIL
A provider-specific error occurred.

E_INVALIDARG
ppRowset was a null pointer.

E_NOINTERFACE
The rowset did not support the interface specified in *riid*.

E_OUTOFMEMORY
The provider did not have enough memory to create the rowset.

DB_E_NOAGGREGATION
pUnkOuter was not a null pointer, and the provider is an OLE DB 1.0 or 1.1 provider that does not support aggregation of the rowset object being created.

pUnkOuter was not a null pointer, and *riid* was not **IID_IUnknown**.

Comments

None.

IViewSort

IViewSort enables the consumer to apply a sort order to a view.

When to Implement

Providers that can present rows in a sorted order as specified by the consumer support **IViewSort**. A provider may restrict functionality to orders based on existing indexes or may limit the complexity of the order.

When to Call

Consumers needing a sorted view of rows call **IViewSort::SetSort** to apply a sort order to a view.

When a view with a specified sort order is applied to a rowset by calling **OpenViewChapter**, a chapter handle is returned and methods that return HROWs such as **IRowset::GetNextRows,** or **IRowsetScroll::GetRowsAtRatio** using that chapter handle, return the rows in sorted order. Any resources associated with the order can be freed with a call to **IChapteredRowset::ReleaseChapter**.

Method	Description
GetSortOrder	Retrieves a sort order from a view.
SetSortOrder	Assigns a sort order to a view.

IViewSort::GetSortOrder

Retrieves the sort order applied to a view.

```
HRESULT GetSortOrder (
   ULONG *     pcColumns,
   ULONG *     prgColumns[],
   DBSORT *    prgOrders[]);
```

Parameters

pcColumns
[out]
Count of the number of columns in the sort order.

prgColumns
[out]
The ordinals of the columns used to describe the sort. The order of the columns in the list defines the precedence of the columns in the sort.

prgOrders
[out]
The sort order for the corresponding column in the *prgColumns* list.

Return Code

S_OK
The method succeeded.

E_FAIL
A provider-specific error occurred.

E_INVALIDARG
pcColumns, *prgColumns*, or *prgOrders* was NULL.

E_OUTOFMEMORY
The provider was unable to allocate sufficient memory in which to return the sort information.

Comments

GetSortOrder returns the latest sort order successfully set on the view.

If **GetSortOrder** returns an error and *pcColumns*, *prgColumns*, and *prgOrders* are non-null, then **pcColumns*, **prgColumns*, and **prgOrders* are set to NULL, respectively.

IViewSort::SetSortOrder

Specifies a sort order to be applied to a view.

```
HRESULT SetSortOrder (
   ULONG          cColumns,
   const ULONG    rgColumns[],
   const DBSORT   rgOrders[]);
```

Parameters

cColumns

[in]
Count of the number of columns to be used in specifying the order, or zero to clear any sort order previously set on the view.

rgColumns

[in]
The ordinals of the columns used to describe the sort. The order of the columns in the list defines the precedence of the columns in the sort. This argument is ignored if *cColumns* is zero.

rgOrders

[in]
The sort order for the corresponding column in the *rgColumns* list. This argument is ignored if *cColumns* is zero.

The DBSORT structure is

```
typedef DWORD DBSORT;

enum DBSORTENUM {
   DBSORT_ASCENDING = 0,
   DBSORT_DESCENDING
};
```

Return Code

S_OK
The method succeeded.

E_FAIL
A provider-specific error occurred.

E_INVALIDARG
rgColumns was NULL, and *cColumns* was not equal to zero.

rgOrders was NULL, and *cColumns* was not equal to zero.

DB_E_CANTORDER
The described order could not be opened. The provider may have limitations on the columns used in an order or a limitation on the complexity of the order.

The same column ordinal appeared multiple times in *rgColumns*.

Comments

A provider may impose constraints on the columns that can be used for sorting. For example, a provider may support ordering only on columns for which there exists an index. If the provider does not support sorting for the specified columns, it returns DB_E_CANTORDER. If there is already a sort order applied to a view, **SetSortOrder** overrides the previous sort order.

The setting of sort columns is atomic. If any columns cannot be set, **SetSortOrder** returns DB_E_CANTORDER and the sort order for the view remains unchanged.

Changing the sort order of a view does not change the sort order of any rowsets or chapters previously opened using that view.

PART 3

Appendixes

APPENDIX A

Data Types

This appendix describes data types in OLE DB. For information about how consumers and providers use data types, see Chapter 10, "Data Types in OLE DB."

Type Indicators

A type indicator indicates a data type. For more information, see Chapter 10, "Data Types in OLE DB."

```
typedef WORD DBTYPE;

enum DBTYPEENUM {
   // The following values exactly match VARENUM
   // in Automation and may be used in VARIANT
   DBTYPE_EMPTY = 0,
   DBTYPE_NULL,
   DBTYPE_I1 = 16,
   DBTYPE_I2,
   DBTYPE_I4,
   DBTYPE_UI2 = 18,
   DBTYPE_UI4,
   DBTYPE_R4,
   DBTYPE_R8,
   DBTYPE_CY,
   DBTYPE_DATE,
   DBTYPE_BSTR,
   DBTYPE_IDISPATCH,
   DBTYPE_ERROR,
   DBTYPE_BOOL,
   DBTYPE_VARIANT,
   DBTYPE_IUNKNOWN,
   DBTYPE_DECIMAL,
   DBTYPE_UI1 = 17,
   DBTYPE_ARRAY = 0x2000,
   DBTYPE_BYREF = 0x4000,
```

```
    // The following values exactly match VARENUM
    // in Automation but cannot be used in VARIANT
DBTYPE_I8,
    DBTYPE_UI8,
    DBTYPE_GUID = 72,
    DBTYPE_VECTOR = 0x1000,
    DBTYPE_FILETIME = 64,
    DBTYPE_RESERVED = 0x8000,

    // The following values are not in VARENUM in OLE
    DBTYPE_BYTES = 128,
    DBTYPE_STR = 129,
    DBTYPE_WSTR,
    DBTYPE_NUMERIC,
    DBTYPE_UDT,
    DBTYPE_DBDATE,
    DBTYPE_DBTIME,
    DBTYPE_DBTIMESTAMP,
    DBTYPE_HCHAPTER = 136,
    DBTYPE_PROPVARIANT = 138,
    DBTYPE_VARNUMERIC = 139
};
```

The following table describes each type indicator, including the C data type it corresponds to.

Type indicator	Description
DBTYPE_EMPTY	No value was specified. This indicator is valid only in a VARIANT structure and exists only to match the VT_EMPTY value in the VARENUM enumerated type in OLE. It does not correspond to any C data type.
DBTYPE_NULL	A NULL value. This indicator is valid only in a VARIANT structure and exists only to match the VT_NULL value in the VARENUM enumerated type in OLE. It does not correspond to any C data type.
DBTYPE_ RESERVED	Reserved for future use by OLE DB. This indicator does not correspond to any C data type.
DBTYPE_I1	A one-byte, signed integer: `signed char`
DBTYPE_I2	A two-byte, signed integer: `SHORT`

Type indicator	Description
DBTYPE_I4	A four-byte, signed integer: `LONG`
DBTYPE_I8	An eight-byte, signed integer: `LARGE_INTEGER`
DBTYPE_UI1	A one-byte, unsigned integer: `BYTE`
DBTYPE_UI2	A two-byte, unsigned integer: `unsigned short`
DBTYPE_UI4	A four-byte, unsigned integer: `unsigned int`
DBTYPE_UI8	An eight-byte, unsigned integer: `ULARGE_INTEGER`
DBTYPE_R4	A single-precision floating-point value: `float`
DBTYPE_R8	A double-precision floating-point value: `double`
DBTYPE_CY	A currency value: `LARGE_INTEGER` Currency is a fixed-point number with four digits to the right of the decimal point. It is stored in an eight-byte signed integer, scaled by 10,000.

Type indicator	Description
DBTYPE_ DECIMAL	An exact numeric value with a fixed precision and fixed scale, stored in the same way as in Automation:

```
typedef struct tagDEC {
    USHORT wReserved;
    union {
        struct {
            BYTE scale;
            BYTE sign;
        };
        USHORT signscale;
    };
    ULONG Hi32;
    union {
        struct {
            ULONG Lo32;
            ULONG Mid32;
        };
        ULONGLONG Lo64;
    };
} DECIMAL;
```

The elements of this structure are used as follows:

- *wReserved*—Reserved. Should be 0.
- *scale*—The scale specifies the number of digits to the right of the decimal point and ranges from 0 to 28.
- *sign*—The sign: 0 if positive, 0x80 if negative.
- *Hi32*—The high part of the integer (32-bit aligned).
- *Mid32*—The middle part of the integer (32-bit aligned).
- *Lo32*—The low part of the integer (32-bit aligned).

For example, to specify the number 12.345, the scale is 3, the sign is 0, and the number stored in the 12-byte integer is 12345.

For information about what precision and scale the provider uses when accessing DBTYPE_DECIMAL structures, see "Conversions Involving DBTYPE_NUMERIC or DBTYPE_DECIMAL," later in this appendix.

Type indicator	Description

DBTYPE_
NUMERIC
	An exact numeric value with a fixed precision and scale:
	`typedef struct tagDB_NUMERIC {`
	`    BYTE precision;`
	`    BYTE scale;`
	`    BYTE sign;`
	`    BYTE val[16];`
	`} DB_NUMERIC;`
	The elements of this structure are used as follows:
	• *precision*—The maximum number of digits in base 10.
	• *scale*—The number of digits to the right of the decimal point.
	• *sign*—The sign: 1 for positive numbers, 0 for negative numbers.
	• *val*—A number stored as a 16-byte scaled integer, with the least-significant byte on the left.
	For example, to specify the base 10 number 20.003 with a scale of 4, the number is scaled to an integer of 200030 (20.003 shifted by four tens digits), which is 30D5E in hexadecimal. The value stored in the 16-byte integer is 5E 0D 03 00 00 00 00 00 00 00 00 00 00 00 00 00, the precision is the maximum precision, the scale is 4, and the sign is 1.
	For information about what precision and scale the provider uses when accessing DBTYPE_NUMERIC structures, see "Conversions Involving DBTYPE_NUMERIC or DBTYPE_DECIMAL," later in this appendix.

Type indicator	Description
DBTYPE_DATE	A date stored in the same way as in Automation: `DATE` A DATE is a double, the whole part of which is the number of days since December 30, 1899 and the fractional part of which is the fraction of a day. For example, the number 2.25 represents the datetime January 1, 1900 6:00 AM.
DBTYPE_BOOL	A Boolean value stored in the same way as in Automation: `VARIANT_BOOL` 0 means false and ~0 (bitwise, the value is not 0; that is, all bits are set to 1) means true.
DBTYPE_BYTES	A binary data value. That is, an array of bytes: `BYTE[`*`length`*`]` The length of the array is specified by *cbMaxLen* in the DBBINDING structure if DBTYPE_BYTES is used by itself. It is specified by the bound length value if DBTYPE_BYTES is combined with DBTYPE_BYREF. For columns containing binary data, the provider reports the data type as DBTYPE_BYTES and the maximum length as the true maximum length of the binary data (assuming there is one). For small, fixed-length binary data, such as a column in an SQL database of type BINARY(1000), the consumer generally binds the column as DBTYPE_BYTES. For small, variable-length binary data, such as a column in an SQL database of type VARBINARY(1000), the consumer generally binds the column as DBTYPE_BYTES | DBTYPE_BYREF, so no space is wasted and no data is truncated. For long binary data, the consumer generally binds the column as DBTYPE_IUNKNOWN and uses a storage interface such as **ISequentialStream** to manipulate the data. For more information, see "Accessing BLOB Data" in Chapter 7, "BLOBs and COM Objects." When null-terminated string data is converted to or from DBTYPE_BYTES, the null-termination character is not included in the length count or the data transferred.

Type indicator	Description
DBTYPE_BSTR	A pointer to a BSTR, as in Automation: `typedef WCHAR * BSTR;` A BSTR is a pointer to a null-terminated character string in which the string length is stored with the string. Because the length is stored with the string, BSTR variables can contain embedded null characters. To determine the length of the BSTR in characters, call **SysStringLen**. To determine the length of the BSTR in bytes, call **SysStringByteLen**. In both cases, the length does not include the null-termination character. In Win32 (the environment for OLE DB), a BSTR contains Unicode. Consumers are responsible for freeing the memory used by BSTRs. Failure to free such memory is a common cause of memory leaks. For example, if a consumer calls **IRowset::GetData** to retrieve a BSTR, the provider allocates memory for the BSTR and returns a pointer to it in the memory pointed to by *pData*. A memory leak occurs when the consumer calls **GetData** again with the same value of *pData* without first freeing the memory for the BSTR. In this case, the provider allocates new memory for the BSTR and overwrites the pointer to the old BSTR with the pointer to the new BSTR. The old BSTR is still allocated, but the pointer to it is lost. For more information, see "Responsibility for Freeing Memory " in Chapter 6, "Getting and Setting Data."
DBTYPE_STR	A null-terminated ANSI character string: `char[length]` If DBTYPE_STR is used by itself, the number of bytes allocated for the string, including the null-termination character, is specified by *cbMaxLen* in the DBBINDING structure. If DBTYPE_STR is combined with DBTYPE_BYREF, the number of bytes allocated for the string, including the null-termination character, is at least the length of the string plus one. In either case, the actual length of the string is determined from the bound length value. If a locale is applicable, it is indicated first by the column metadata; or if no column metadata is available, it is indicated by table metadata or by the database locale.

Type indicator	Description
DBTYPE_WSTR	A null-terminated Unicode character string: `wchar_t[length]` If DBTYPE_WSTR is used by itself, the number of bytes allocated for the string, including the null-termination character, is specified by *cbMaxLen* in the DBBINDING structure. If DBTYPE_WSTR is combined with DBTYPE_BYREF, the number of bytes allocated for the string, including the null-termination character, is at least the length of the string plus two. In either case, the actual length of the string is determined from the bound length value. Note that the maximum length of the string is the number of allocated bytes divided by **sizeof(wchar_t)** and truncated to the nearest integer.
DBTYPE_ VARIANT	An Automation VARIANT: `VARIANT` The DBTYPE values that do not match Automation VARENUM values represent data types that cannot be stored in a VARIANT. If the VARIANT structure contains a pointer to the data, the buffer for that data is allocated separately.
DBTYPE_ IDISPATCH	A pointer to an **IDispatch** interface on a COM object: `IDispatch *`
DBTYPE_ IUNKNOWN	A pointer to an **IUnknown** interface on a COM object: `IUnknown *` For columns containing COM objects, the provider reports the data type as DBTYPE_IUNKNOWN. The consumer specifies the interface to use through the *pObject* element of the DBBINDING structure. For more information, see "**IPersist*** Objects" in Chapter 7, "BLOBs and COM Objects."
DBTYPE_GUID	A globally unique identifier (GUID): `GUID` GUIDs are also known as universally unique identifiers (UUIDs) and are used as class identifiers (CLSIDs) and interface identifiers (IIDs).

Type indicator	Description
DBTYPE_ERROR	A 32-bit error code: `SCODE`
DBTYPE_BYREF	A pointer to data: `void *` DBTYPE_BYREF must be combined with another type indicator. This indicates that the data in the consumer's buffer is a pointer to the other type. For example, DBTYPE_STR | DBTYPE_BYREF means that the data is a pointer to an ANSI string and DBTYPE_I2 | DBTYPE_BYREF means that the data is a pointer to a two-byte integer. DBTYPE_BYREF is commonly used to return pointers to variable-length data. It is used with provider-owned *bindings* to return pointers to the data in the rowset's copy of a row. When DBTYPE_BYREF is used, the data in the consumer's buffer can be a null pointer only when the corresponding status value is DBSTATUS_S_ISNULL. When setting a column value, if the data in the consumer's buffer is a null pointer and the status is not DBSTATUS_S_ISNULL, the provider returns a conversion error. DBTYPE_BYREF is mutually exclusive with the DBTYPE_ARRAY and DBTYPE_VECTOR modifiers and cannot be combined with the following values: DBTYPE_EMPTY DBTYPE_NULL DBTYPE_RESERVED For information about how DBTYPE_BYREF values are allocated, see "Responsibility for Freeing Memory " in Chapter 6, "Getting and Setting Data."

Type indicator	Description
DBTYPE_ARRAY	A pointer to a SAFEARRAY: `SAFEARRAY *` DBTYPE_ARRAY must be combined with another type indicator. This indicates that the data in the consumer's buffer is a pointer to a SAFEARRAY of the other type. For example, DBTYPE_I2 | DBTYPE_ARRAY means that the data is a pointer to a SAFEARRAY of two-byte integers. When DBTYPE_ARRAY is used, the data in the consumer's buffer can be a null pointer only when the corresponding status value is DBSTATUS_S_ISNULL. When setting a column value, if the data in the consumer's buffer is a null pointer and the status is not DBSTATUS_S_ISNULL, the provider returns a conversion error. DBTYPE_ARRAY is mutually exclusive with the DBTYPE_BYREF and DBTYPE_VECTOR modifiers and cannot be combined with indicators for variable-length data types because there is no way to determine the length of each element of the array. DBTYPE_ARRAY can be combined with DBTYPE_BSTR because DBTYPE_BSTR is a fixed-length data type: A BSTR is a pointer to a separately allocated string that contains its own length. For information about how SAFEARRAYs are allocated, see "Responsibility for Freeing Memory " in Chapter 6, "Getting and Setting Data."

Type indicator	Description

DBTYPE_ VECTOR	A DBVECTOR structure:
	`typedef struct tagDBVECTOR {`
	`    void * ptr;`
	`    ULONG  size;`
	`} DBVECTOR;`
	
	DBTYPE_VECTOR must be combined with another type indicator. This indicates that the data in the consumer's buffer is a DBVECTOR structure, which contains a pointer to an array of the other type. For example, DBTYPE_I2 | DBTYPE_VECTOR means that the data is a DBVECTOR structure that contains a pointer to an array of two-byte integers.
	
	When DBTYPE_VECTOR is used, the pointer in the DBVECTOR structure can be a null pointer only when the corresponding status value is DBSTATUS_S_ISNULL. When setting a column value, if the pointer is a null pointer and the status is not DBSTATUS_S_ISNULL, the provider returns a conversion error.
	
	DBTYPE_VECTOR is mutually exclusive with the DBTYPE_BYREF and DBTYPE_ARRAY modifiers and cannot be combined with indicators for variable-length data types because there is no way to determine the length of each element of the array.
	
	For information about how the memory pointed to by DBVECTOR structures is allocated, see "Responsibility for Freeing Memory " in Chapter 6, "Getting and Setting Data."

DBTYPE_UDT	A user-defined data type of variable length. In future versions, OLE DB may define the use of type libraries to support user-defined data types. This indicator does not correspond to any C data type.

Type indicator	Description

DBTYPE_ DBDATE	A date structure:
	`typedef struct tagDBDATE {`
	`    SHORT  year;`
	`    USHORT month;`
	`    USHORT day;`
	`} DBDATE;`
	
	The elements of this structure are used as follows:
	• *year*—The year: 0–9999 measured from 0 A.D.
	• *month*—The month: 1–12.
	• *day*—1–*n* where *n* is the number of days in the month.

DBTYPE_ DBTIME	A time structure:
	`typedef struct tagDBTIME {`
	`    USHORT hour;`
	`    USHORT minute;`
	`    USHORT second;`
	`} DBTIME;`
	
	The elements of this structure are used as follows:
	• *hour*—The hour: 0–23.
	• *minute*—The minute: 0–59.
	• *second*—The second: 0–61.
	
	The range of seconds allows as many as two leap seconds to maintain synchronization with sidereal time.

DBTYPE_ DBTIMESTAMP	A timestamp structure:
	`typedef struct tagDBTIMESTAMP {`
	`    SHORT  year;`
	`    USHORT month;`
	`    USHORT day;`
	`    USHORT hour;`
	`    USHORT minute;`
	`    USHORT second;`
	`    ULONG  fraction;`
	`} DBTIMESTAMP;`

Type indicator	Description
	The elements of this structure are used as follows: • *year*—The year: 0–9999 measured from 0 A.D. • *month*—The month: 1–12. • *day*—1–*n* where *n* is the number of days in the month. • *hour*—The hour: 0–23. • *minute*—The minute: 0–59. • *second*—The second: 0–61. • *fraction*—Billionths of a second: 0–999,999,999. The range of seconds allows as many as two leap seconds to maintain synchronization with sidereal time.

DBTYPE_FILETIME	A 64-bit value representing the number of 100-nanosecond intervals since January 1, 1601. This type is equivalent to the FILETIME type used in the time-conversion functions between Microsoft DOS and Win32.
	`typedef struct tagFILETIME {`
	`    DWORD  dwLowDateTime;`
	`    DWORD  dwHighDateTime;`
	`} FILETIME;`
	The elements of the structure are used as follows:
	• *dwLowDateTime*—The lower 32 bits of the Win32 date/time value.
	• *dwHighDateTime*—The upper 32 bits of the Win32 date/time value.

DBTYPE_PROP-VARIANT	An Automation PROPVARIANT: `PROPVARIANT` If the VARIANT structure contains a pointer to the data, the buffer for the data is allocated separately. DBTYPE_PROPVARIANT should support the same set of conversions as DBTYPE_VARIANT (including conversions to/from DBTYPE_VARIANT).
DBTYPE_HCHAPTER	A four-byte chapter value that can be used to identify rows in a child rowset.

Type indicator	Description

DBTYPE_VAR-NUMERIC	A variable-length, exact numeric value with a signed scale value:
	`typedef struct tagDB_VARNUMERIC {`
	`    BYTE    precision;`
	`    SBYTE   scale;`
	`    BYTE    sign;`
	`    BYTE val[ 1 ];`
	`} DB_VARNUMERIC;`

Precision of Numeric Data Types

The following OLE DB data types are used to represent numeric values. Each type has a corresponding maximum precision value that indicates the maximum number of base 10 digits that it can store. The radix of the precision for all numeric types is 10. The maximum precision returned by the provider in the COLUMN_SIZE column of the PROVIDER_TYPES schema rowset is the maximum possible precision for the data type that is supported by the data store. For example, if a data store can support a maximum precision of only 28 for a DBTYPE_NUMERIC column, the provider returns 28, not 39, as the maximum precision.

Type indicator	Maximum precision
DBTYPE_I1	3
DBTYPE_I2	5
DBTYPE_I4	10
DBTYPE_I8	19
DBTYPE_UI1	3
DBTYPE_UI2	5
DBTYPE_UI4	10
DBTYPE_UI8	20
DBTYPE_R4	7
DBTYPE_R8	15
DBTYPE_CY	19
DBTYPE_DECIMAL	29
DBTYPE_NUMERIC	39
DBTYPE_VARNUMERIC	255

Fixed-Length Data Types

The following type indicators are for fixed-length data types. For more information, see "Fixed-Length and Variable-Length Data Types" in Chapter 10, "Data Types in OLE DB."

DBTYPE_I1

DBTYPE_I2

DBTYPE_I4

DBTYPE_I8

DBTYPE_UI1

DBTYPE_UI2

DBTYPE_UI4

DBTYPE_UI8

DBTYPE_R4

DBTYPE_R8

DBTYPE_CY

DBTYPE_DATE

DBTYPE_BSTR

DBTYPE_PROPVARIANT

DBTYPE_IDISPATCH

DBTYPE_ERROR

DBTYPE_BOOL

DBTYPE_VARIANT

DBTYPE_IUNKNOWN

DBTYPE_GUID

DBTYPE_NUMERIC

DBTYPE_DECIMAL

DBTYPE_DBDATE

DBTYPE_DBTIME

DBTYPE_DBTIMESTAMP

DBTYPE_FILETIME

DBTYPE_HCHAPTER

Variable-Length Data Types

The following type indicators are for variable-length data types. For more information, see "Fixed-Length and Variable-Length Data Types" in Chapter 10, "Data Types in OLE DB."

DBTYPE_STR

DBTYPE_BYTES

DBTYPE_WSTR

DBTYPE_VARNUMERIC

Data Type Conversion Rules

For information about the conversions providers are required to support and how consumers determine what these conversions are, see "Data Type Conversion" in Chapter 10, "Data Types in OLE DB." Providers that support optional conversions should follow the guidelines listed in this section.

Conversion Tables

The tables in this section describe most additional conversions. They use the following symbols:

- **S** = A safe conversion is possible.
- **T** = Conversion with truncation of nonsignificant digits is possible.
- **E** = An error due to truncation of significant digits is possible.
- **–** = The conversion is not generally supported.

To ⇒ From ⇓	I1	I2	I4	I8	UI1
I1	S	S	S	S	S, E
I2	S, E	S	S	S	S, E
I4	S, E	S, E	S	S	S, E
I8	-	-	-	S	-
UI1	S, E	S	S	S	S
UI2	S, E	S, E	S	S	S, E
UI4	S, E	S, E	S, E	S	S, E
UI8	-	-	-	S, E	-
R4	S, T, E	S, T, E	S, T	S, T	S, T, E
R8	S, T, E	S, T, E	S, T, E	S, T	S, T, E
CY	S, T, E	S, T, E	S, T, E	S, T	S, T, E
DEC	S, T, E	S, T, E	S, T, E	S, T, E	S, T, E
NUM	S, T, E	S, T, E	S, T, E	S, T, E	S, T, E
BOOL	S	S	S	S	S
DATE	S	S	S	S	S

To ⇒ From ⇓	I1	I2	I4	I8	UI1
DBDATE	–	–	–	–	–
DBTIME	–	–	–	–	–
DBTIMESTAMP	–	–	–	–	–
FILETIME	–	–	–	S, E	–
BYTES	S, E	S, E	S, E	S, E	S, E
BSTR	S, T, E	S, T, E	S, T, E	S, T, E	S, T, E
STR	S, T, E	S, T, E	S, T, E	S, T, E	S, T, E
WSTR	S, T, E	S, T, E	S, T, E	S, T, E	S, T, E
VARIANT	S, T, E	S	S	S, T, E	S, T, E
DISP	–	–	–	–	–
UNK	–	–	–	–	–
GUID	–	–	–	–	–
ERROR	–	–	–	–	–
PROPVARIANT	S, T, E	S	S	S	S

To ⇒ From ⇓	UI2	UI4	UI8	R4	R8
I1	S, E	S, E	S, E	S	S
I2	S, E	S, E	S, E	S	S
I4	S, E	S, E	S, E	S	S
I8	-	-	S, E	-	-
UI1	S	S	S	S	S
UI2	S	S	S	S	S
UI4	S, E	S	S	S, E	S
UI8	-	-	S	-	-
R4	S, T, E	S, T, E	S, T, E	S	S
R8	S, T, E	S, T, E	S, T, E	S, E	S
CY	S, T, E	S, T, E	S, T, E	S, E	S, E

To ⇒ From ⇓	UI2	UI4	UI8	R4	R8
DEC	S, T, E	S, T, E	S, T, E	S, E	S, E
NUM	S, T, E	S, T, E	S, T, E	S, E	S, E
BOOL	S	S	S	S	S
DATE	S	S	S	S	S
DBDATE	–	–	–	–	–
DBTIME	–	–	–	–	–
DBTIMESTAMP	–	–	–	–	–
FILETIME	–	–	S, E	–	–
BYTES	S, E	S, E	S, E	S, E	S, E
BSTR	S, T, E	S, T, E	S, T, E	S, T, E	S, T, E
STR	S, T, E	S, T, E	S, T, E	S, T, E	S, T, E
WSTR	S, T, E	S, T, E	S, T, E	S, T, E	S, T, E
VARIANT	S, T, E	S, T, E	S, T, E	S	S
DISP	–	–	–	–	–
UNK	–	–	–	–	–
GUID	–	–	–	–	–
ERROR	–	–	–	–	–
PROPVARIANT	S	S	S	S	S

To ⇒ From ⇓	CY	DEC	NUM	BOOL	DATE
I1	S	S	S	S	S
I2	S	S	S	S	S
I4	S	S	S	S	S
I8	-	-	-	-	-
UI1	S	S	S	S	S
UI2	S	S	S	S	S
UI4	S	S	S	S	S

To ⇒ From ⇓	CY	DEC	NUM	BOOL	DATE
UI8	-	-	-	-	-
R4	S, T	S	S	S	S
R8	S, T	S	S	S	S
CY	S	S	S	S	-
DEC	S, E	S	S	S	-
NUM	S, E	S, T, E	S	S	-
BOOL	S	S	S	S	S
DATE	S	S	S	S	S
DBDATE	–	–	–	–	S
DBTIME	–	–	–	–	S
DBTIMESTAMP	–	–	–	–	S, T
FILETIME	–	–	–	–	S, T
BYTES	S, E	S, E	S, E	S, E	-
BSTR	S, T, E	S, T, E	S, T, E	S, E	S, T, E
STR	S, T, E	S, T, E	S, T, E	S, E	S, T, E
WSTR	S, T, E	S, T, E	S, T, E	S, E	S, T, E
VARIANT	S	S	S, T, E	S	S
DISP	–	–	–	–	–
UNK	–	–	–	–	–
GUID	–	–	–	–	–
ERROR	–	–	–	–	–
PROPVARIANT	S	S	S, T, E	S	S

To ⇒ From ⇓	DBDATE	DBTIME	DBTIME STAMP	FILE TIME	BYTES
I1	–	–	–	–	-
I2	–	–	–	–	S, E
I4	–	–	–	–	S, E
I8	–	–	–	S, E	-
UI1	–	–	–	–	-
UI2	–	–	–	–	S, E
UI4	–	–	–	–	S, E
UI8	–	–	–	S, E	-
R4	–	–	–	–	S, E
R8	–	–	–	–	S, E
CY	–	–	–	–	S, E
DEC	–	–	–	–	S, E
NUM	–	–	–	–	S, E
BOOL	–	–	–	–	S
DATE	S, T, E	S, T	S, T, E	S, T, E	S, E
DBDATE	S	S	S	S	S, E
DBTIME	S	S	S	S	S, E
DBTIMESTAMP	S, T	S, T	S	S, T	S, E
FILETIME	S, T, E	S, T, E	S, T, E	S	S, E
BYTES	S, E	–	S	S, E	S, E
BSTR	S, T, E	S, T, E	S, T, E	S, T, E	S, E
STR	S, T, E	S, T, E	S, T, E	S, T, E	S, E
WSTR	S, T, E	S, T, E	S, T, E	S, T, E	S, E
VARIANT	S, T, E	S, T, E	S, T, E	S, T, E	S, T, E

To ⇒ From ⇓	DBDATE	DBTIME	DBTIME STAMP	FILE TIME	BYTES
DISP	–	–	–	–	S, E
UNK	–	–	–	–	S, E
GUID	–	–	–	–	-
ERROR	–	–	–	–	–
PROPVARIANT	S, T, E	S, T, E	S, T, E	S, T, E	S

To ⇒ From ⇓	BSTR	STR	WSTR	VARIANT	DISP
I1	S, E	S, E	S, E	S	–
I2	S, E	S, E	S, E	S	–
I4	S, E	S, E	S, E	S	–
I8	S, E	S, E	S, E	S	–
UI1	S, E	S, E	S, E	S	–
UI2	S, E	S, E	S, E	–	–
UI4	S, E	S, E	S, E	S	–
UI8	S, E	S, E	S, E	S	–
R4	S, E	S, T, E	S, T, E	S	–
R8	S, E	S, T, E	S, T, E	S	–
CY	S, E	S, T, E	S, T, E	S	–
DEC	S, E	S, T, E	S, T, E	S	–
NUM	S, E	S, T, E	S, T, E	–	–
BOOL	S, E	S, E	S, E	S	–
DATE	S, E	S, T, E	S, T, E	S	–
DBDATE	S, E	S, T, E	S, T, E	S	–
DBTIME	S, E	S, T, E	S, T, E	S	–
DBTIMESTAMP	S, E	S, T, E	S, T, E	S	–
FILETIME	S, E	S, T, E	S, T, E	S	–

To ⇒ From ⇓	**BSTR**	**STR**	**WSTR**	**VARIANT**	**DISP**
BYTES	S, E	S, E	S, E	–	S, E
BSTR	S	S, T	S, T	S	
STR	S	S, T	S, T	S	–
WSTR	S	S, T	S, T	S	–
VARIANT	S, T, E	S, T, E	S, T, E	S	S
DISP	–	–	–	S	S
UNK	–	–	–	S	–
GUID	S, E	S, E	S, E	S	–
ERROR	–	–	–	S	–
PROPVARIANT	S, T, E	S, T, E	S, T, E	S	S

To ⇒ From ⇓	**UNK**	**GUID**	**ERROR**	**PROPVARIANT**
I1	–	–	–	-
I2	–	–	–	S
I4	–	–	–	S
I8	–	–	–	S
UI1	–	–	–	S
UI2	–	–	–	S
UI4	–	–	–	S
UI8	–	–	–	S
R4	–	–	–	S
R8	–	–	–	S
CY	–	–	–	S
DEC	–	–	–	-
NUM	–	–	–	-
BOOL	–	–	–	S
DATE	–	–	–	S

To ⇒ From ⇓	UNK	GUID	ERROR	PROPVARIANT
DBDATE	–	–	–	-
DBTIME	–	–	–	-
DBTIMESTAMP	–	–	–	-
FILETIME	–	–	–	S
BYTES	S, E	S, E	–	S
BSTR	–	S, E	–	S
STR	S, E	S, E	–	S
WSTR	S, E	S, E	–	S
VARIANT	S	S, T, E	S	S
DISP	S	–	–	S
UNK	S	–	–	-
GUID	–	S	–	S
ERROR	–	–	S	-
PROPVARIANT	S	S	S	S

Conversions Involving Strings

The following formats are used for conversions to and from strings. Only nontrivial formats are listed. Converting a string to a nonstring type may fail for some providers if the string contains trailing blanks.

Type indicator	Format
DBTYPE_BYTES	When strings are converted to and from binary data, each byte of binary data is represented as two ASCII characters. These characters are the ASCII character representation of the number in its hexadecimal form. For example, a binary 00000001 is converted to "01" and a binary 11111111 is converted to "FF".
DBTYPE_CY	"*...cccc.cccc*"
DBTYPE_BOOL	"True" and "False"

Type indicator	Format
DBTYPE_DATE	As in Automation, according to the regional settings of the machine. For example, for the "English(United States)" default setting, this would typically be: "*mm/dd/yy hh*:*mm*:*ss* {AM|PM}"
DBTYPE_DBDATE	As specified by ISO: "*yyyy-mm-dd*"
DBTYPE_FILETIME	"*yyyyy-mm-dd hh:mm:ss.fff*" where *fff* is from 0–999. Up to 3 digits may be used. The format is the same as SYSTEMTIME. Valid filetime value is 0x0000000000000000–0x7FFFFFFFFFFFFFFF, which is 01601-01-01 00:00:000–30828-09-14 02:24:05.477.
DBTYPE_DBTIME	As specified by ISO: "*hh*:*mm*:*ss*"
DBTYPE_ DBTIMESTAMP	As specified by ISO: "*yyyy-mm-dd hh*:*mm*:*ss*.*f*..." where "*f*..." is fractions of a second (up to nine digits may be used).
DBTYPE_GUID	As represented in the registry: "{*xxxxxxxx-xxxx-xxxx-xxxx-xxxxxxxxxxxx*}" where *x* is a hexadecimal digit.
DBTYPE_STR DBTYPE_WSTR DBTYPE_BSTR	Conversion between strings of different locale IDs (LCIDs) is not supported. Conversion between ANSI and Unicode strings of the same LCID are required. In converting a Unicode string to ANSI, information may be lost because the Unicode range is greater. Lost characters are represented in the ANSI string by a special character, and the conversion is considered to be a truncation. When mixing character sets, conversion to Unicode is the preferred solution. If conversion to ANSI is needed to use ANSI strings with the user interface and the LCID of the user interface is different from the LCID of some columns, the consumer is responsible for the conversion. The LCID of a column is returned in the DBCOLUMN_COLLATING_SEQUENCE column returned by **IColumnsRowset::GetColumnsRowset**.

Conversions Involving Numeric Values

Conversions involving numeric values use the following general guidelines:

- Except for the most significant digit, all digits in floating-point numbers are considered to be less significant. Thus, floating-point numbers can always be converted (possibly with truncation) to integers, numerics, or strings as long as they don't overflow the integer, numeric, or string.

  For example, 1.234567E2 is truncated to 123 when converted to an integer, to 123.4 when converted to a NUMERIC(4, 1), to 120 when converted to a NUMERIC(4, – 1), assuming the provider supports negative scale (many do not), to "123\0" when converted to a four-byte ANSI string, and to "123.4\0" when converted to a six-byte ANSI string. It cannot be converted to an ANSI string of three or fewer bytes because such a conversion would overflow the string.

- In conversions from DBTYPE_NUMERIC and DBTYPE_DECIMAL to string values, the conversion is allowed, provided it does not result in truncation to the left of the decimal point. For example, 123.4567 is truncated to "123.4\0" when converted to a six-byte ANSI string but returns a truncation error when attempting to convert to a two-byte ANSI string.

- In conversions from DBTYPE_NUMERIC to other numeric types, the conversion is allowed, provided the difference between the source value and the target value is less than the difference between two successive values in the target data type. For example, 123.4567 can be converted to a numeric value with a scale of 2 as 123.45, because the difference between 123.4567 and 123.45 is less than .01 (10^{-2}).

- In strings that represent numbers, digits to the right of the decimal point are considered less significant and can be truncated; digits to the left of the decimal point are considered significant and cannot be truncated. For example, "123.45\0" is truncated to 123 when converted to an integer and to 123.4 when converted to a NUMERIC(4, 1). However, the string "1234.5\0" cannot be converted to a one-byte integer.

- It is provider-specific whether negative numbers are truncated up or down. Thus, –1.99 might be truncated to –1 or to –2 when converted to an integer.

Conversions Involving DBTYPE_NUMERIC or DBTYPE_DECIMAL

When retrieving data from a DBTYPE_NUMERIC or DBTYPE_DECIMAL structure, the provider uses the maximum precision and scale stored in that structure. When storing data in a DBTYPE_NUMERIC or DBTYPE_DECIMAL structure, the provider uses the maximum precision and scale in the metadata for that structure. For consumer structures, these are in the binding structure. For provider structures, these are in the DBCOLUMNINFO structure returned by **IColumnsInfo::GetColumnInfo** or the DBPARAMINFO structure returned by **ICommandWithParameters::GetParameterInfo**.

The following table shows the maximum precision and scale used by the provider when accessing data in a DBTYPE_NUMERIC or DBTYPE_DECIMAL structure in the consumer's buffer.

Consumer structure	Getting or setting data	Maximum precision	Scale
DBTYPE_NUMERIC	getting	*precision* element of DBTYPE_NUMERIC structure	*scale* element of DBTYPE_NUMERIC structure
DBTYPE_NUMERIC	setting	*bPrecision* element of DBBINDING structure	*bScale* element of DBBINDING structure
DBTYPE_VAR-NUMERIC	getting	*precision* element of DB_VARNUMERIC structure	*scale* element of DB_VARNUMERIC structure
DBTYPE_VAR-NUMERIC	setting	*bPrecision* element of DBBINDING structure	*bScale* element of DBBINDING structure
DBTYPE_DECIMAL	getting	28	*scale* element of DBTYPE_DECIMAL structure
DBTYPE_DECIMAL	setting	28	*bScale* element of DBBINDING structure

The following table shows the maximum precision and scale used by the provider when accessing data in a DBTYPE_NUMERIC or DBTYPE_DECIMAL structure in the provider.

Provider structure	Getting or setting data	Maximum precision	Scale
DBTYPE_NUMERIC	getting	*precision* element of DBTYPE_NUMERIC structure	*scale* element of DBTYPE_NUMERIC structure
DBTYPE_NUMERIC	setting	*bPrecision* element of DBCOLUMNINFO or DBPARAMINFO structure	*bScale* element of DBCOLUMNINFO or DBPARAMINFO structure
DBTYPE_VAR-NUMERIC	getting	*precision* element of DB_VARNUMERIC structure	*scale* element of DB_VARNUMERIC structure
DBTYPE_VAR-NUMERIC	setting	*bPrecision* element of DBCOLUMNINFO or DBPARAMINFO structure	*bScale* element of DBCOLUMNINFO or DBPARAMINFO structure
DBTYPE_DECIMAL	getting	28	*scale* element of DBTYPE_DECIMAL structure
DBTYPE_DECIMAL	setting	28	*bScale* element of DBCOLUMNINFO or DBPARAMINFO structure

Conversions Involving VARIANTs

The following table describes conversions to and from VARIANTs. Type indicator X can be modified by DBTYPE_ARRAY or DBTYPE_BYREF. No conversions are supported when it is modified by DBTYPE_VECTOR.

Source type indicator	Target type indicator	Notes
X	DBTYPE_VARIANT	If X is a valid VARENUM value (that is, it is a type indicator that can be used in a VARIANT), the provider sets *vt* in the target VARIANT to X and transfers the data to the corresponding element of the union. If X is not a valid VARENUM value, it is provider-specific whether the provider supports the conversion and what type it uses in the VARIANT. Any such conversions must follow the rules in this appendix.
X	DBTYPE_PROPVARIANT	If X is not a valid PROPVARENUM value and X is DBTYPE_NUMERIC, the conversion library sets *vt* in the target PROPVARIANT to VT_BSTR and transfers the data to the corresponding element of the union.
DBTYPE_VARIANT	X	If the type indicator specified in the source VARIANT is X, the provider transfers the data. If the type indicator specified in the VARIANT is not X, it is provider-specific whether the provider supports the conversion. Any such conversions must follow the rules in this appendix.
DBTYPE_VARIANT	DBTYPE_VARIANT	The provider sets *vt* in the target VARIANT to the same value as *vt* in the source VARIANT. It transfers the data from the union element in the source VARIANT to the same element in the target VARIANT.

Conversions Involving DBTYPE_BYREF

The following table describes conversions to and from types modified by DBTYPE_BYREF. Type indicators X and Y are unmodified by DBTYPE_BYREF.

Source type indicator	Target type indicator	Notes
X	Y | DBTYPE_BYREF	If Y is a variable-length data type and the provider supports a conversion from X to Y, the provider must support this conversion. If Y is not a variable-length data type, it is provider-specific whether this conversion is supported. Any such conversions must follow the rules in this appendix. For information about further restrictions when memory is provider-owned, see the description of *dwMemOwner* in "DBBINDING Structures" in Chapter 6, "Getting and Setting Data."
X | DBTYPE_BYREF	Y	If X equals Y, the provider must support this conversion. If X is not equal to Y, the provider supports this if and only if it supports a conversion from X to Y. Any such conversions must follow the rules in this appendix.
X | DBTYPE_BYREF	Y | DBTYPE_BYREF	The provider must support this conversion if it supports a conversion from X to Y | DBTYPE_BYREF. Any such conversions must follow the rules in this appendix.

Conversions Involving DBTYPE_ARRAY

The following table describes conversions to and from types modified by DBTYPE_ARRAY. Type indicators X and Y are unmodified; when combined with DBTYPE_ARRAY, they cannot be DBTYPE_EMPTY or DBTYPE_NULL.

Source type indicator	Target type indicator	Notes
X	Y | DBTYPE_ARRAY	It is provider-specific whether this is supported.
X | DBTYPE_ARRAY	Y	It is provider-specific whether this is supported.
X | DBTYPE_ARRAY	Y | DBTYPE_ARRAY	If the provider supports a conversion from X to Y and the provider supports both X | DBTYPE_ARRAY and Y | DBTYPE_ARRAY, it must support this conversion. Any such conversions must follow the rules in this appendix.
X | DBTYPE_VECTOR	Y | DBTYPE_ARRAY	Not supported.
X | DBTYPE_ARRAY	Y | DBTYPE_VECTOR	Not supported.

Conversions Involving DBTYPE_VECTOR

The following table describes conversions to and from types modified by DBTYPE_VECTOR. Type indicators X and Y are unmodified.

Source type indicator	Target type indicator	Notes
X	Y | DBTYPE_VECTOR	It is provider-specific whether this is supported.
X | DBTYPE_VECTOR	Y	It is provider-specific whether this is supported.
X | DBTYPE_VECTOR	Y | DBTYPE_VECTOR	If the provider supports a conversion from X to Y and the provider supports both X | DBTYPE_VECTOR and Y | DBTYPE_VECTOR, it must support this conversion. Any such conversions must follow the rules in this appendix.
X | DBTYPE_ARRAY	Y | DBTYPE_VECTOR	Not supported.
X | DBTYPE_VECTOR	Y | DBTYPE_ARRAY	Not supported.

APPENDIX B

Schema Rowsets

The schema information specified in OLE DB is based on the assumption that providers support the concepts of a catalog and a schema. The ANSI SQL92 specification defines them as follows:

- A *catalog* contains one or more schemas and always contains a schema named INFORMATION_SCHEMA, which contains the views and domains of the information schema. In Microsoft SQL Server and Microsoft Access terms, a catalog is a database; in ODBC 2.*x* terms, a catalog is a qualifier.
- A *schema* is a collection of database objects that are owned or have been created by a particular user. In Microsoft SQL Server and ODBC 2.*x* terms, a schema is an owner; there is no equivalent to a schema in a Microsoft Access database.

Schema information in OLE DB is retrieved using predefined schema rowsets; this appendix lists the contents of each schema rowset.

Schema rowsets are retrieved with **IDBSchemaRowset::GetRowset**. **GetRowset** allows consumers to specify simple restrictions, such as returning all the columns in a particular table. Each schema rowset is guaranteed to return all of the columns in the order shown in the section detailing that rowset. In addition, providers can return provider-specific columns after the last column defined by OLE DB.

In implementing **IDBSchemaRowset**, it is suggested that providers pay particular attention to rowset construction and data retrieval performance, because these commands will be frequently used by consumers.

This information schema also defines a minimum content of the system schema. It is assumed that consumers will prepare and store the specialized commands used for things such as command planning and execution-time plan validation, and storage engines may have specialized optimizations associated with those plans. Consumers can also look at the schema tables in the schema and thus discover other schema tables and attributes beyond the minimum set.

Note If a provider returns non-NULL CATALOG or SCHEMA column values in schema rowsets, it must support **IDBInfo** to describe how a fully qualified name is assembled. A provider that does not support **IDBInfo** must return NULL values for CATALOG and SCHEMA columns in all schema rowsets.

For schema rowset columns of type DBTYPE_WSTR, the provider returns, as the column size in **IColumnsInfo** or **IColumnsRowset**, the maximum number of characters that can appear in this column of the Schema Rowset. The provider guarantees that no value in the column will exceed this length but does not guarantee that an element of the column could actually contain that many characters. If the provider always returns NULL for the column, it may return zero as the maximum length of the column in **IColumnsInfo** and **IColumnsRowset**.

Logical Information Schema Rowsets

This section details each schema rowset in the logical information schema. These schema rowsets are primarily concerned with the logical database metadata and are a superset of the information presented by the INFORMATION_SCHEMA views defined in ANSI SQL92, with the exception of the COLUMNS and DOMAINS rowsets, which contain subsets of this information. The INFORMATION_SCHEMA schema exists in all ANSI SQL92 catalogs.

Although the ANSI SQL92 views define some columns as NOT NULLABLE, OLE DB does not enforce this restriction. Therefore, consumers should check the metadata for a particular column with **IColumnsInfo::GetColumnInfo** or **IColumnsRowset::GetColumnRowset** to determine if it is nullable.

The following rowsets are in the logical information schema. All providers that support **IDBSchemaRowset** must support the TABLES and COLUMNS schema rowsets. Support for other schema rowsets in the logical information schema is optional.

ASSERTIONS
CHARACTER_SETS
CHECK_CONSTRAINTS
COLLATIONS
COLUMN_DOMAIN_USAGE
COLUMN_PRIVILEGES
COLUMNS
CONSTRAINT_COLUMN_USAGE
CONSTRAINT_TABLE_USAGE
FOREIGN_KEYS
KEY_COLUMN_USAGE
PRIMARY_KEYS
PROCEDURE_COLUMNS
PROCEDURE_PARAMETERS
PROCEDURES
REFERENTIAL_CONSTRAINTS
SCHEMATA
SQL_LANGUAGES
TABLE_CONSTRAINTS
TABLE_PRIVILEGES
TABLES
TABLES_INFO
TRANSLATIONS
USAGE_PRIVILEGES
VIEW_COLUMN_USAGE
VIEW_TABLE_USAGE
VIEWS

Physical Information Schema Rowsets

This section details the contents of each schema rowset in the physical information schema. These schema rowsets are primarily concerned with the physical database metadata. The contents of such metadata are not defined in ANSI SQL92; all definitions in this section are OLE DB extensions to ANSI SQL92.

The following rowsets are in the physical information schema. All providers that support **IDBSchemaRowset** must support the PROVIDER_TYPES schema rowset. Support for other schema rowsets in the physical information schema is optional.

CATALOGS
INDEXES
PROVIDER_TYPES
STATISTICS

ASSERTIONS Rowset

The ASSERTIONS rowset identifies the assertions defined in the catalog that are owned by a given user.

The ASSERTIONS rowset contains the following columns.

Column name	Type indicator	Description
CONSTRAINT_CATALOG	DBTYPE_WSTR	Catalog name. NULL if the provider does not support catalogs.
CONSTRAINT_SCHEMA	DBTYPE_WSTR	Unqualified schema name. NULL if the provider does not support schemas.
CONSTRAINT_NAME	DBTYPE_WSTR	Constraint name.
IS_DEFERRABLE	DBTYPE_BOOL	VARIANT_TRUE—The assertion is deferrable. VARIANT_FALSE—The assertion is not deferrable.
INITIALLY_DEFERRED	DBTYPE_BOOL	VARIANT_TRUE—The assertion is initially deferred. VARIANT_FALSE—The assertion is initially immediate.
DESCRIPTION	DBTYPE_WSTR	Human-readable description of the column.

Default Sort Order: CONSTRAINT_CATALOG, CONSTRAINT_SCHEMA, CONSTRAINT_NAME

CATALOGS Rowset

The CATALOGS rowset identifies the physical attributes associated with catalogs accessible from the DBMS. For some systems, such as Microsoft Access, there may be only one catalog. For Microsoft SQL Server, this rowset would enumerate all catalogs (databases) defined in the system database.

The CATALOGS rowset contains the following columns.

Column name	Type indicator	Description
CATALOG_NAME	DBTYPE_WSTR	Catalog name.
DESCRIPTION	DBTYPE_WSTR	Human-readable description of the table.

Default Sort Order: CATALOG_NAME

CHARACTER_SETS Rowset

The CHARACTER_SETS rowset identifies the character sets defined in the catalog that are accessible to a given user.

The CHARACTER_SETS rowset contains the following columns.

Column name	Type indicator	Description
CHARACTER_SET_CATALOG	DBTYPE_WSTR	Catalog name. NULL if the provider does not support catalogs.
CHARACTER_SET_SCHEMA	DBTYPE_WSTR	Unqualified schema name. NULL if the provider does not support schemas.
CHARACTER_SET_NAME	DBTYPE_WSTR	Character set name.
FORM_OF_USE	DBTYPE_WSTR	Name of form-of-use of the character set.
NUMBER_OF_CHARACTERS	DBTYPE_I8	Number of characters in the character repertoire.
DEFAULT_COLLATE_CATALOG	DBTYPE_WSTR	Catalog name containing the default collation. NULL if the provider does not support catalogs or different collations.
DEFAULT_COLLATE_SCHEMA	DBTYPE_WSTR	Unqualified schema name containing the default collation. NULL if the provider does not support schemas or different collations.
DEFAULT_COLLATE_NAME	DBTYPE_WSTR	Default collation. NULL if the provider does not support different collations.

Default Sort Order: CHARACTER_SET_CATALOG, CHARACTER_SET_SCHEMA, CHARACTER_SET_NAME

CHECK_CONSTRAINTS Rowset

The CHECK_CONSTRAINTS rowset identifies the check constraints defined in the catalog that are owned by a given user.

The CHECK_CONSTRAINTS rowset contains the following columns.

Column name	Type indicator	Description
CONSTRAINT_CATALOG	DBTYPE_WSTR	Catalog name. NULL if the provider does not support catalogs.
CONSTRAINT_SCHEMA	DBTYPE_WSTR	Unqualified schema name. NULL if the provider does not support schemas.
CONSTRAINT_NAME	DBTYPE_WSTR	Constraint name.
CHECK_CLAUSE	DBTYPE_WSTR	The **WHERE** clause specified in the **CHECK** clause.
DESCRIPTION	DBTYPE_WSTR	Human-readable description of the column.

Default Sort Order: CONSTRAINT_CATALOG, CONSTRAINT_SCHEMA, CONSTRAINT_NAME

COLLATIONS Rowset

The COLLATIONS rowset identifies the character collations defined in the catalog that are accessible to a given user.

The COLLATIONS rowset contains the following columns.

Column name	Type indicator	Description
COLLATION_CATALOG	DBTYPE_WSTR	Catalog name. NULL if the provider does not support catalogs.
COLLATION_SCHEMA	DBTYPE_WSTR	Unqualified schema name. NULL if the provider does not support schemas.
COLLATION_NAME	DBTYPE_WSTR	Collation name.
CHARACTER_SET_CATALOG	DBTYPE_WSTR	Catalog name containing the character set on which the collation is defined. NULL if the provider does not support catalogs or different character sets.

Column name	Type indicator	Description
CHARACTER_SET_SCHEMA	DBTYPE_WSTR	Unqualified schema name containing the character set on which the collation is defined. NULL if the provider does not support schema or different character sets.
CHARACTER_SET_NAME	DBTYPE_WSTR	Character set name on which the collation is defined. NULL if the provider does not support different character sets.
PAD_ATTRIBUTE	DBTYPE_WSTR	"NO PAD"—The collation being described has the **NO PAD** attribute. "PAD SPACE"—The collation being described has the **PAD SPACE** attribute.

Default Sort Order: COLLATION_CATALOG, COLLATION_SCHEMA, COLLATION_CATALOG, CHARACTER_SET_CATALOG, CHARACTER_SET_SCHEMA, CHARACTER_SET_NAME

COLUMN_DOMAIN_USAGE Rowset

The COLUMN_DOMAIN_USAGE rowset identifies the columns defined in the catalog that are dependent on a domain defined in the catalog and owned by a given user.

The COLUMN_DOMAIN_USAGE rowset contains the following columns.

Column name	Type indicator	Description
DOMAIN_CATALOG	DBTYPE_WSTR	Catalog name. NULL if the provider does not support catalogs.
DOMAIN_SCHEMA	DBTYPE_WSTR	Unqualified schema name. NULL if the provider does not support schemas.
DOMAIN_NAME	DBTYPE_WSTR	View name.
TABLE_CATALOG	DBTYPE_WSTR	Catalog name in which the table is defined. NULL if the provider does not support catalogs.
TABLE_SCHEMA	DBTYPE_WSTR	Unqualified schema name in which the table is defined. NULL if the provider does not support schemas.
TABLE_NAME	DBTYPE_WSTR	Table name.

Column name	Type indicator	Description
COLUMN_NAME	DBTYPE_WSTR	Column name. This column, together with the COLUMN_GUID and COLUMN_PROPID columns, forms the column ID. One or more of these columns will be NULL, depending on which elements of the DBID structure the provider uses.
COLUMN_GUID	DBTYPE_GUID	Column GUID.
COLUMN_PROPID	DBTYPE_UI4	Column property ID.

Default Sort Order: DOMAIN_CATALOG, DOMAIN_SCHEMA, DOMAIN_NAME, TABLE_CATALOG, TABLE_SCHEMA, TABLE_NAME, COLUMN_NAME, COLUMN_GUID, COLUMN_PROPID

COLUMN_PRIVILEGES Rowset

The COLUMN_PRIVILEGES rowset identifies the privileges on columns of tables defined in the catalog that are available to or granted by a given user.

The COLUMN_PRIVILEGES rowset contains the following columns.

Column name	Type indicator	Description
GRANTOR	DBTYPE_WSTR	User who granted the privileges on the table in TABLE_NAME.
GRANTEE	DBTYPE_WSTR	User name (or "PUBLIC") to whom the privilege has been granted.
TABLE_CATALOG	DBTYPE_WSTR	Catalog name in which the table is defined. NULL if the provider does not support catalogs.
TABLE_SCHEMA	DBTYPE_WSTR	Unqualified schema name in which the table is defined. NULL if the provider does not support schemas.
TABLE_NAME	DBTYPE_WSTR	Table name.
COLUMN_NAME	DBTYPE_WSTR	Column name. This column, together with the COLUMN_GUID and COLUMN_PROPID columns, forms the column ID. One or more of these columns will be NULL depending on which elements of the DBID structure the provider uses.

Column name	Type indicator	Description
COLUMN_GUID	DBTYPE_GUID	Column GUID.
COLUMN_PROPID	DBTYPE_UI4	Column property ID.
PRIVILEGE_TYPE	DBTYPE_WSTR	Privilege type. One of the following: "SELECT" "DELETE" "INSERT" "UPDATE" "REFERENCES"
IS_GRANTABLE	DBTYPE_BOOL	VARIANT_TRUE—The privilege being described was granted with the **WITH GRANT OPTION** clause. VARIANT_FALSE—The privilege being described was not granted with the **WITH GRANT OPTION** clause.

Default Sort Order: TABLE_CATALOG, TABLE_SCHEMA, TABLE_NAME, COLUMN_NAME, COLUMN_GUID, COLUMN_PROPID, PRIVILEGE_TYPE

COLUMNS Rowset

The COLUMNS rowset identifies the columns of tables defined in the catalog that are accessible to a given user.

The COLUMNS rowset contains the following columns.

Column name	Type indicator	Description
TABLE_CATALOG	DBTYPE_WSTR	Catalog name. NULL if the provider does not support catalogs.
TABLE_SCHEMA	DBTYPE_WSTR	Unqualified schema name. NULL if the provider does not support schemas.
TABLE_NAME	DBTYPE_WSTR	Table name. This column cannot contain a NULL.

Column name	Type indicator	Description
COLUMN_NAME	DBTYPE_WSTR	The name of the column; this might not be unique. If this cannot be determined, a NULL is returned. This column, together with the COLUMN_GUID and COLUMN_PROPID columns, forms the column ID. One or more of these columns will be NULL, depending on which elements of the DBID structure the provider uses. If possible, the resulting column ID should be persistent. However, some providers do not support persistent identifiers for columns. The column ID of a base table should be invariant under views.
COLUMN_GUID	DBTYPE_GUID	Column GUID. Providers that do not use GUIDs to identify columns should return NULL in this column.
COLUMN_PROPID	DBTYPE_UI4	Column property ID. Providers that do not associate PROPIDs with columns should return NULL in this column.
ORDINAL_POSITION	DBTYPE_UI4	The ordinal of the column. Columns are numbered starting from one. NULL if there is no stable ordinal value for the column.
COLUMN_HASDEFAULT	DBTYPE_BOOL	VARIANT_TRUE—The column has a default value. VARIANT_FALSE—The column does not have a default value, or it is unknown whether the column has a default value.
COLUMN_DEFAULT	DBTYPE_WSTR	Default value of the column. A provider may expose DBCOLUMN_DEFAULTVALUE but not DBCOLUMN_HASDEFAULT (for SQL92 tables) in the rowset returned by **IColumnsRowset::GetColumnsRowset**. If the default value is the NULL value, COLUMN_HASDEFAULT is VARIANT_TRUE and the COLUMN_DEFAULT column is a NULL value.

Column name	Type indicator	Description
COLUMN_FLAGS	DBTYPE_UI4	A bitmask that describes column characteristics. The DBCOLUMNFLAGS enumerated type specifies the bits in the bitmask. For information about DBCOLUMNFLAGS, see **IColumnsInfo::GetColumnInfo** in Part 2, "OLE DB Reference." This column cannot contain a NULL value.
IS_NULLABLE	DBTYPE_BOOL	VARIANT_TRUE—The column might be nullable. VARIANT_FALSE—The column is known not to be nullable.
DATA_TYPE	DBTYPE_UI2	The indicator of the column's data type. If the data type of the column varies from row to row, this must be DBTYPE_VARIANT. This column cannot contain NULL. For a list of valid type indicators, see "Type Indicators" in Appendix A, "Data Types."
TYPE_GUID	DBTYPE_GUID	The GUID of the column's data type. Providers that do not use GUIDs to identify data types should return NULL in this column.
CHARACTER_ MAXIMUM_LENGTH	DBTYPE_UI4	The maximum possible length of a value in the column. For character, binary, or bit columns, this is one of the following: • The maximum length of the column in characters, bytes, or bits, respectively, if one is defined. For example, a CHAR(5) column in an SQL table has a maximum length of 5. • The maximum length of the data type in characters, bytes, or bits, respectively, if the column does not have a defined length. • Zero (0) if neither the column nor the data type has a defined maximum length. NULL for all other types of columns.
CHARACTER_OCTET_ LENGTH	DBTYPE_UI4	Maximum length in octets (bytes) of the column, if the type of the column is character or binary. A value of zero means the column has no maximum length. NULL for all other types of columns.

Column name	Type indicator	Description
NUMERIC_PRECISION	DBTYPE_UI2	If the column's data type is numeric, this is the maximum precision of the column. The precision of columns with a data type of DBTYPE_DECIMAL or DBTYPE_NUMERIC depends on the definition of the column. For the precision of all other numeric data types, see "Precision of Numeric Data Types" in Appendix A, "Data Types." If the column's data type is not numeric, this is NULL.
NUMERIC_SCALE	DBTYPE_I2	If the column's type indicator is DBTYPE_DECIMAL or DBTYPE_NUMERIC, this is the number of digits to the right of the decimal point. Otherwise, this is NULL.
DATETIME_PRECISION	DBTYPE_UI4	Datetime precision (number of digits in the fractional seconds portion) of the column if the column is a datetime or interval type. If the column's data type is not datetime, this is NULL.
CHARACTER_SET_ CATALOG	DBTYPE_WSTR	Catalog name in which the character set is defined. NULL if the provider does not support catalogs or different character sets.
CHARACTER_SET_ SCHEMA	DBTYPE_WSTR	Unqualified schema name in which the character set is defined. NULL if the provider does not support schemas or different character sets.
CHARACTER_SET_NAME	DBTYPE_WSTR	Character set name. NULL if the provider does not support different character sets.
COLLATION_CATALOG	DBTYPE_WSTR	Catalog name in which the collation is defined. NULL if the provider does not support catalogs or different collations.
COLLATION_SCHEMA	DBTYPE_WSTR	Unqualified schema name in which the collation is defined. NULL if the provider does not support schemas or different collations.
COLLATION_NAME	DBTYPE_WSTR	Collation name. NULL if the provider does not support different collations.
DOMAIN_CATALOG	DBTYPE_WSTR	Catalog name in which the domain is defined. NULL if the provider does not support catalogs or domains.

Column name	Type indicator	Description
DOMAIN_SCHEMA	DBTYPE_WSTR	Unqualified schema name in which the domain is defined. NULL if the provider does not support schemas or domains.
DOMAIN_NAME	DBTYPE_WSTR	Domain name. NULL if the provider does not support domains.
DESCRIPTION	DBTYPE_WSTR	Human-readable description of the column. For example, the description for a column named Name in the Employee table might be "Employee name." Null if there is no description associated with the column.

Default Sort Order: TABLE_CATALOG, TABLE_SCHEMA, TABLE_NAME

CONSTRAINT_COLUMN_USAGE Rowset

The CONSTRAINT_COLUMN_USAGE rowset identifies the columns used by referential constraints, unique constraints, check constraints, and assertions, defined in the catalog and owned by a given user.

The CONSTRAINT_COLUMN_USAGE rowset contains the following columns.

Column name	Type indicator	Description
TABLE_CATALOG	DBTYPE_WSTR	Catalog name in which the table is defined. NULL if the provider does not support catalogs.
TABLE_SCHEMA	DBTYPE_WSTR	Unqualified schema name in which the table is defined. NULL if the provider does not support schemas.
TABLE_NAME	DBTYPE_WSTR	Table name.
COLUMN_NAME	DBTYPE_WSTR	Column name. This column, together with the COLUMN_GUID and COLUMN_PROPID columns, forms the column ID. One or more of these columns will be NULL depending on which elements of the DBID structure the provider uses.
COLUMN_GUID	DBTYPE_GUID	Column GUID.

Column name	Type indicator	Description
COLUMN_PROPID	DBTYPE_UI4	Column property ID.
CONSTRAINT_CATALOG	DBTYPE_WSTR	Catalog name. NULL if the provider does not support catalogs.
CONSTRAINT_SCHEMA	DBTYPE_WSTR	Unqualified schema name. NULL if the provider does not support schemas.
CONSTRAINT_NAME	DBTYPE_WSTR	Constraint name.

Default Sort Order: TABLE_CATALOG, TABLE_SCHEMA, TABLE_NAME, COLUMN_NAME, COLUMN_GUID, COLUMN_PROPID, CONSTRAINT_CATALOG, CONSTRAINT_SCHEMA, CONSTRAINT_NAME

CONSTRAINT_TABLE_USAGE Rowset

The CONSTRAINT_TABLE_USAGE rowset identifies the tables that are used by referential constraints, unique constraints, check constraints, and assertions defined in the catalog and owned by a given user.

The CONSTRAINT_TABLE_USAGE rowset contains the following columns.

Column name	Type indicator	Description
TABLE_CATALOG	DBTYPE_WSTR	Catalog name in which the table is defined. NULL if the provider does not support catalogs.
TABLE_SCHEMA	DBTYPE_WSTR	Unqualified schema name in which the table is defined. NULL if the provider does not support schemas.
TABLE_NAME	DBTYPE_WSTR	Table name.
CONSTRAINT_CATALOG	DBTYPE_WSTR	Catalog name. NULL if the provider does not support catalogs.
CONSTRAINT_SCHEMA	DBTYPE_WSTR	Unqualified schema name. NULL if the provider does not support schemas.
CONSTRAINT_NAME	DBTYPE_WSTR	Constraint name.

Default Sort Order: TABLE_CATALOG, TABLE_SCHEMA, TABLE_NAME, CONSTRAINT_CATALOG, CONSTRAINT_SCHEMA, CONSTRAINT_NAME

FOREIGN_KEYS Rowset

The FOREIGN_KEYS rowset identifies the foreign key columns defined in the catalog by a given user. This schema rowset is built upon several SQL92 schema views as a convenience to the non-SQL programmer, and if supported, this must be synchronized with the related SQL92 views (REFERENTIAL_CONSTRAINTS and CONSTRAINT_COLUMN_USAGE).

The FOREIGN_KEYS rowset contains the following columns

Column name	Type indicator	Description
PK_TABLE_CATALOG	DBTYPE_WSTR	Catalog name in which the primary key table is defined. NULL if the provider does not support catalogs.
PK_TABLE_SCHEMA	DBTYPE_WSTR	Unqualified schema name in which the primary key table is defined. NULL if the provider does not support schemas.
PK_TABLE_NAME	DBTYPE_WSTR	Primary key table name.
PK_COLUMN_NAME	DBTYPE_WSTR	Primary key column name. This column, together with the PK_COLUMN_GUID and PK_COLUMN_PROPID columns, forms the column ID. One or more of these columns will be NULL, depending on which elements of the DBID structure the provider uses.
PK_COLUMN_GUID	DBTYPE_GUID	Primary key column GUID.
PK_COLUMN_PROPID	DBTYPE_UI4	Primary key column property ID.
FK_TABLE_CATALOG	DBTYPE_WSTR	Catalog name in which the foreign key table is defined. NULL if the provider does not support catalogs.
FK_TABLE_SCHEMA	DBTYPE_WSTR	Unqualified schema name in which the foreign key table is defined. NULL if the provider does not support schemas.
FK_TABLE_NAME	DBTYPE_WSTR	Foreign key table name.
FK_COLUMN_NAME	DBTYPE_WSTR	Foreign key column name. This column, together with the FK_COLUMN_GUID and FK_COLUMN_PROPID columns, forms the column ID. One or more of these columns will be NULL, depending on which elements of the DBID structure the provider uses.
FK_COLUMN_GUID	DBTYPE_GUID	Foreign key column GUID.
FK_COLUMN_PROPID	DBTYPE_UI4	Foreign key column property ID.

Column name	Type indicator	Description
ORDINAL	DBTYPE_UI4	The order of the column names (and GUIDs and property IDs) in the key. For example, a table might contain several foreign key references to another table. The ordinal starts over for each reference; for example, two references to a three-column key would return 1, 2, 3, 1, 2, 3.
UPDATE_RULE	DBTYPE_WSTR	If an *<update rule>* was specified, the UPDATE_RULE value is one of the following: "CASCADE"—A *<referential action>* of **CASCADE** was specified. "SET NULL"—A *<referential action>* of **SET NULL** was specified. "SET DEFAULT"—A *<referential action>* of **SET DEFAULT** was specified. "NO ACTION"—A *<referential action>* of **NO ACTION** was specified. Providers should return NULL only if they cannot determine the UPDATE_RULE. In most cases, this implies a default of **NO ACTION**.
DELETE_RULE	DBTYPE_WSTR	If a *<delete rule>* was specified, the DELETE_RULE value is one of the following: "CASCADE"—A <referential action> of **CASCADE** was specified. "SET NULL"—A <referential action> of **SET NULL** was specified. "SET DEFAULT"—A *<referential action>* of **SET DEFAULT** was specified. "NO ACTION"—A *<referential action>* of **NO ACTION** was specified. Providers should return NULL only if they cannot determine the DELETE_RULE. In most cases, this implies a default of **NO ACTION**.
PK_NAME	DBTYPE_WSTR	Primary key name. NULL if the provider does not support named primary key constraints. This column is not returned by 1.*x* providers.

Column name	Type indicator	Description
FK_NAME	DBTYPE_WSTR	Foreign key name. NULL if the provider does not support named foreign key constraints. This column is not returned by 1.*x* providers.
DEFERRABILITY	DBTYPE_I2	Deferrability of the foreign key. Value is one of the following: DBPROPVAL_DF_INITIALLY_DEFERRED DBPROPVAL_DF_INITIALLY_IMMEDIATE DBPROPVAL_DF_NOT_DEFERRABLE This column is not returned by 1.*x* providers.

Default Sort Order: FK_TABLE_CATALOG, FK_TABLE_SCHEMA, FK_TABLE_NAME

INDEXES Rowset

The INDEXES rowset identifies the indexes defined in the catalog that are owned by a given user.

The INDEXES rowset contains the following columns

Column name	Type indicator	Description
TABLE_CATALOG	DBTYPE_WSTR	Catalog name. NULL if the provider does not support catalogs.
TABLE_SCHEMA	DBTYPE_WSTR	Unqualified schema name. NULL if the provider does not support schemas.
TABLE_NAME	DBTYPE_WSTR	Table name.
INDEX_CATALOG	DBTYPE_WSTR	Catalog name. NULL if the provider does not support catalogs.
INDEX_SCHEMA	DBTYPE_WSTR	Unqualified schema name. NULL if the provider does not support schemas.
INDEX_NAME	DBTYPE_WSTR	Index name.
PRIMARY_KEY	DBTYPE_BOOL	Whether the index represents the primary key on the table. NULL if this is not known.

Column name	Type indicator	Description
UNIQUE	DBTYPE_BOOL	Whether index keys must be unique. One of the following: VARIANT_TRUE—The index keys must be unique. VARIANT_FALSE—Duplicate keys are allowed.
CLUSTERED	DBTYPE_BOOL	Whether an index is clustered. One of the following: VARIANT_TRUE—The leaf nodes of the index contain full rows, not bookmarks. This is a way to represent a table clustered by key value. VARIANT_FALSE—The leaf nodes of the index contain bookmarks of the base table rows whose key value matches the key value of the index entry.
TYPE	DBTYPE_UI2	The type of the index. One of the following: DBPROPVAL_IT_BTREE—The index is a B+-tree. DBPROPVAL_IT_HASH—The index is a hash file using, for example, linear or extensible hashing. DBPROPVAL_IT_CONTENT—The index is a content index. DBPROPVAL_IT_OTHER—The index is some other type of index.
FILL_FACTOR	DBTYPE_I4	For a B+-tree index, this property represents the storage utilization factor of page nodes during the creation of the index. The value is an integer from 1 to 100 representing the percentage of use of an index node. For a linear hash index, this property represents the storage utilization of the entire hash structure (the ratio of used area to total allocated area) before a file structure expansion occurs.
INITIAL_SIZE	DBTYPE_I4	The total amount of bytes allocated to this structure at creation time.

Column name	Type indicator	Description
NULLS	DBTYPE_I4	Whether null keys are allowed. One of the following: DBPROPVAL_IN_DISALLOWNULL—The index does not allow entries where the key columns are NULL. If the consumer attempts to insert an index entry with a NULL key, the provider returns an error. DBPROPVAL_IN_IGNORENULL—The index does not insert entries containing NULL keys. If the consumer attempts to insert an index entry with a NULL key, the provider ignores that entry and no error code is returned. DBPROPVAL_IN_IGNOREANYNULL—The index does not insert entries where some column key has a NULL value. For an index having a multicolumn search key, if the consumer inserts an index entry with NULL value in some column of the search key, the provider ignores that entry and no error code is returned.
SORT_BOOKMARKS	DBTYPE_BOOL	How the index treats repeated keys. One of the following: VARIANT_TRUE—The index sorts repeated keys by bookmark. VARIANT_FALSE—The index does not sort repeated keys by bookmark.
AUTO_UPDATE	DBTYPE_BOOL	Whether the index is maintained automatically when changes are made to the corresponding base table. One of the following: VARIANT_TRUE—The index is automatically maintained. VARIANT_FALSE—The index must be maintained by the consumer through explicit calls to **IRowsetChange**. Ensuring consistency of the index as a result of updates to the associated base table is the responsibility of the consumer.

Column name	Type indicator	Description
NULL_COLLATION	DBTYPE_I4	How NULLs are collated in the index. One of the following: DBPROPVAL_NC_END—NULLs are collated at the end of the list, regardless of the collation order. DBPROPVAL_NC_START—NULLs are collated at the start of the list, regardless of the collation order. DBPROPVAL_NC_HIGH—NULLs are collated at the high end of the list. DBPROPVAL_NC_LOW—NULLs are collated at the low end of the list.
ORDINAL_POSITION	DBTYPE_UI4	Ordinal position of the column in the index, starting with one.
COLUMN_NAME	DBTYPE_WSTR	Column name. This column, together with the COLUMN_GUID and COLUMN_PROPID columns, forms the column ID. One or more of these columns will be NULL, depending on which elements of the DBID structure the provider uses.
COLUMN_GUID	DBTYPE_GUID	Column GUID.
COLUMN_PROPID	DBTYPE_UI4	Column property ID.
COLLATION	DBTYPE_I2	One of the following: DB_COLLATION_ASC—The sort sequence for the column is ascending. DB_COLLATION_DESC—The sort sequence for the column is descending. NULL—A column sort sequence is not supported.
CARDINALITY	DBTYPE_UI8	Number of unique values in the index.
PAGES	DBTYPE_I4	Number of pages used to store the index.
FILTER_CONDITION	DBTYPE_WSTR	The **WHERE** clause identifying the filtering restriction.

Column name	Type indicator	Description
INTEGRATED	DBTYPE_BOOL	Whether the index is integrated. That is, all base table columns are available from the index. One of the following: VARIANT_TRUE—The index is integrated. For clustered indexes, this value must always be VARIANT_TRUE. VARIANT_FALSE—The index is not integrated. This column is not returned by 1.*x* providers.

Default Sort Order: UNIQUE, TYPE, INDEX_CATALOG, INDEX_SCHEMA, INDEX_NAME, ORDINAL_POSITION

KEY_COLUMN_USAGE Rowset

The KEY_COLUMN_USAGE rowset identifies the columns defined in the catalog that are constrained as keys by a given user.

The KEY_COLUMN_USAGE rowset contains the following columns.

Column name	Type indicator	Description
CONSTRAINT_CATALOG	DBTYPE_WSTR	Catalog name. NULL if the provider does not support catalogs.
CONSTRAINT_SCHEMA	DBTYPE_WSTR	Unqualified schema name. NULL if the provider does not support schemas.
CONSTRAINT_NAME	DBTYPE_WSTR	Constraint name.
TABLE_CATALOG	DBTYPE_WSTR	Catalog name in which the table containing the key column is defined. NULL if the provider does not support catalogs.
TABLE_SCHEMA	DBTYPE_WSTR	Unqualified schema name in which the table containing the key column is defined. NULL if the provider does not support schemas.
TABLE_NAME	DBTYPE_WSTR	Table name containing the key column.
COLUMN_NAME	DBTYPE_WSTR	Name of the column participating in the unique, primary, or foreign key. This column, together with the COLUMN_GUID and COLUMN_PROPID columns, forms the column ID. One or more of these columns will be NULL, depending on which elements of the DBID structure the provider uses.
COLUMN_GUID	DBTYPE_GUID	Column GUID.
COLUMN_PROPID	DBTYPE_UI4	Column property ID.
ORDINAL_POSITION	DBTYPE_UI4	Ordinal position of the column in the constraint being described. If the constraint being described is a key of cardinality one, the value of ORDINAL_POSITION is always one.

Default Sort Order: CONSTRAINT_CATALOG, CONSTRAINT_SCHEMA, CONSTRAINT_NAME, TABLE_CATALOG, TABLE_SCHEMA, TABLE_NAME, ORDINAL_POSITION

PRIMARY_KEYS Rowset

The PRIMARY_KEYS rowset identifies the primary key columns defined in the catalog by a given user. This schema rowset is built upon an SQL92 schema view as a convenience to the non-SQL programmer, and if supported, must be synchronized with the related SQL92 view (CONSTRAINT_COLUMN_USAGE).

The PRIMARY_KEYS rowset contains the following columns.

Column name	Type indicator	Description
TABLE_CATALOG	DBTYPE_WSTR	Catalog name in which the table is defined. NULL if the provider does not support catalogs.
TABLE_SCHEMA	DBTYPE_WSTR	Unqualified schema name in which the table is defined. NULL if the provider does not support schemas.
TABLE_NAME	DBTYPE_WSTR	Table name.
COLUMN_NAME	DBTYPE_WSTR	Primary key column name. This column, together with the COLUMN_GUID and COLUMN_PROPID columns, forms the column ID. One or more of these columns will be NULL, depending on which elements of the DBID structure the provider uses.
COLUMN_GUID	DBTYPE_GUID	Primary key column GUID.
COLUMN_PROPID	DBTYPE_UI4	Primary key column property ID.
ORDINAL	DBTYPE_UI4	The order of the column names (and GUIDs and property IDs) in the key.
PK_NAME	DB_WSTR	Primary key name. NULL if the provider does not support primary key constraints. This column is not returned by 1.*x* providers.

Default Sort Order: TABLE_CATALOG, TABLE_SCHEMA, TABLE_NAME

PROCEDURE_COLUMNS Rowset

The PROCEDURE_COLUMNS rowset returns information about the columns of rowsets returned by procedures.

The PROCEDURE_COLUMNS rowset contains the following columns.

Column name	Type indicator	Description
PROCEDURE_CATALOG	DBTYPE_WSTR	Catalog name. NULL if the provider does not support catalogs.
PROCEDURE_SCHEMA	DBTYPE_WSTR	Unqualified schema name. NULL if the provider does not support schemas.
PROCEDURE_NAME	DBTYPE_WSTR	Table name.
COLUMN_NAME	DBTYPE_WSTR	The name of the column; this might not be unique. If this cannot be determined, a NULL is returned. This column, together with the COLUMN_GUID and COLUMN_PROPID columns, forms the column ID. One or more of these columns will be NULL, depending on which elements of the DBID structure the provider uses.
COLUMN_GUID	DBTYPE_GUID	Column GUID.
COLUMN_PROPID	DBTYPE_UI4	Column property ID.
ROWSET_NUMBER	DBTYPE_UI4	Number of the rowset containing the column. This is greater than one only if the procedure returns multiple rowsets.
ORDINAL_POSITION	DBTYPE_UI4	The ordinal of the column. Columns are numbered starting from one. NULL if there is no stable ordinal value for the column.
IS_NULLABLE	DBTYPE_BOOL	VARIANT_TRUE—The column might be nullable. VARIANT_FALSE—The column is known not to be nullable.
DATA_TYPE	DBTYPE_UI2	The indicator of the column's data type. If the data type of the column varies from row to row, this must be DBTYPE_VARIANT. For a list of valid type indicators, see "Type Indicators" in Appendix A, "Data Types."

Column name	Type indicator	Description
TYPE_GUID	DBTYPE_GUID	The GUID of the column's data type.
CHARACTER_MAXIMUM_ LENGTH	DBTYPE_UI4	The maximum possible length of a value in the column. For character, binary, or bit columns, this is one of the following: • The maximum length of the column in characters, bytes, or bits, respectively, if one is defined. For example, a CHAR(5) column in an SQL table has a maximum length of five (5). • The maximum length of the data type in characters, bytes, or bits, respectively, if the column does not have a defined length. • Zero (0) if neither the column nor the data type has a defined maximum length. NULL for all other types of columns.
CHARACTER_OCTET_ LENGTH	DBTYPE_UI4	Maximum length in octets (bytes) of the column, if the type of the column is character or binary. A value of zero means the column has no maximum length. NULL for all other types of columns.
NUMERIC_PRECISION	DBTYPE_UI2	If the column's data type is numeric, this is the maximum precision of the column. The precision of columns with a data type of DBTYPE_DECIMAL or DBTYPE_NUMERIC depends on the definition of the column. For the precision of all other numeric data types, see "Precision of Numeric Data Types" in Appendix A, "Data Types." If the column's data type is not numeric, this is NULL.

Column name	Type indicator	Description
NUMERIC_SCALE	DBTYPE_I2	If the column's type indicator is DBTYPE_DECIMAL or DBTYPE_NUMERIC, this is the number of digits to the right of the decimal point. Otherwise, this is NULL.
DESCRIPTION	DBTYPE_WSTR	Human-readable description of the column. For example, the description for a column named Name in the Employee table might be "Employee name."

Default Sort Order: PROCEDURE_CATALOG, PROCEDURE_SCHEMA, PROCEDURE_NAME

PROCEDURE_PARAMETERS Rowset

The PROCEDURE_PARAMETERS rowset returns information about the parameters and return codes of procedures.

The PROCEDURE_PARAMETERS rowset contains the following columns.

Column name	Type indicator	Description
PROCEDURE_CATALOG	DBTYPE_WSTR	Catalog name. NULL if the provider does not support catalogs.
PROCEDURE_SCHEMA	DBTYPE_WSTR	Schema name. NULL if the provider does not support catalogs.
PROCEDURE_NAME	DBTYPE_WSTR	Procedure name.
PARAMETER_NAME	DBTYPE_WSTR	Parameter name. NULL if the parameter is not named.
ORDINAL_POSITION	DBTYPE_UI2	If the parameter is an input, input/output, or output parameter, this is the one-based ordinal position of the parameter in the procedure call. If the parameter is the return value, this is zero.

Column name	Type indicator	Description
PARAMETER_TYPE	DBTYPE_UI2	One of the following: DBPARAMTYPE_INPUT—The parameter is an input parameter. DBPARAMTYPE_INPUTOUTPUT—The parameter is an input/output parameter. DBPARAMTYPE_OUTPUT—The parameter is an output parameter. DBPARAMTYPE_RETURNVALUE—The parameter is a procedure return value. For example, in the following ODBC SQL statement to call a procedure, the question mark marks a procedure return value: `{? = call GetNextOrderID}` If the provider cannot determine the parameter type, this is NULL.
PARAMETER_ HASDEFAULT	DBTYPE_BOOL	VARIANT_TRUE—The parameter has a default value. VARIANT_FALSE—The parameter does not have a default value, or it is unknown whether the parameter has a default value.
PARAMETER_DEFAULT	DBTYPE_WSTR	Default value of parameter. If the default value is the NULL value, COLUMN_HASDEFAULT is VARIANT_TRUE and the COLUMN_DEFAULT column is a NULL value.
IS_NULLABLE	DBTYPE_BOOL	VARIANT_TRUE—The parameter might be nullable. VARIANT_FALSE—The parameter is not nullable.
DATA_TYPE	DBTYPE_UI2	The indicator of the parameter's data type. For a list of valid type indicators, see "Type Indicators" in Appendix A, "Data Types."

Column name	Type indicator	Description
CHARACTER_MAXIMUM_ LENGTH	DBTYPE_UI4	The maximum possible length of a value in the parameter. For character, binary, or bit parameters, this is one of the following: • The maximum length of the parameter in characters, bytes, or bits, respectively, if one is defined. For example, a CHAR(5) parameter has a maximum length of five (5). • The maximum length of the data type in characters, bytes, or bits, respectively, if the parameter does not have a defined length. • Zero (0) if neither the parameter nor the data type has a defined maximum length. NULL for all other types of parameters.
CHARACTER_OCTET_ LENGTH	DBTYPE_UI4	Maximum length in octets (bytes) of the parameter, if the type of the parameter is character or binary. A value of zero means the parameter has no maximum length. NULL for all other types of parameters.
NUMERIC_PRECISION	DBTYPE_UI2	If the parameter's data type is numeric, this is the maximum precision of the parameter. The precision of parameters with a data type of DBTYPE_DECIMAL or DBTYPE_NUMERIC depends on the definition of the parameters. For the precision of all other numeric data types, see "Precision of Numeric Data Types" in Appendix A, "Data Types." If the parameter's data type is not numeric, this is NULL.
NUMERIC_SCALE	DBTYPE_I2	If the column's type indicator is DBTYPE_DECIMAL or DBTYPE_NUMERIC, this is the number of digits to the right of the decimal point. Otherwise, this is NULL.

Column name	Type indicator	Description
DESCRIPTION	DBTYPE_WSTR	Human-readable description of the parameter. For example, the description of a parameter named Name in a procedure that adds a new employee might be "Employee name."
TYPE_NAME	DBTYPE_WSTR	Provider-specific data type name. This column is not returned by 1.*x* providers.
LOCAL_TYPE_NAME	DBTYPE_WSTR	Localized version of TYPE_NAME. NULL is returned if a localized name is not supported by the data provider. This column is not returned by 1.x providers.

Default Sort Order: PROCEDURE_CATALOG, PROCEDURE_SCHEMA, PROCEDURE_NAME

PROCEDURES Rowset

The PROCEDURES rowset is an OLE DB extension. It identifies the procedures defined in the catalog that are owned by a given user.

The PROCEDURES rowset contains the following columns.

Column name	Type indicator	Description
PROCEDURE_CATALOG	DBTYPE_WSTR	Catalog name. NULL if the provider does not support catalogs.
PROCEDURE_SCHEMA	DBTYPE_WSTR	Unqualified schema name. NULL if the provider does not support schemas.
PROCEDURE_NAME	DBTYPE_WSTR	Procedure name.
PROCEDURE_TYPE	DBTYPE_I2	DB_PT_UNKNOWN—It is not known whether there is a returned value. DB_PT_PROCEDURE—Procedure; there is no returned value. DB_PT_FUNCTION—Function; there is a returned value.
PROCEDURE_ DEFINITION	DBTYPE_WSTR	Procedure definition.

Column name	Type indicator	Description
DESCRIPTION	DBTYPE_WSTR	Human-readable description of the procedure.
DATE_CREATED	DBTYPE_DATE	Date when the procedure was created or NULL if the provider does not have this information. Note that 1.*x* providers do not return this column.
DATE_MODIFIED	DBTYPE_DATE	Date when the procedure definition was last modified or NULL if the provider does not have this information. Note that 1.*x* providers do not return this column.

Default Sort Order: PROCEDURE_CATALOG, PROCEDURE_SCHEMA, PROCEDURE_NAME

PROVIDER_TYPES Rowset

The PROVIDER_TYPES rowset identifies the (base) data types supported by the data provider.

The PROVIDER_TYPES rowset contains the following columns.

Column name	Type indicator	Description
TYPE_NAME	DBTYPE_WSTR	Provider-specific data type name.
DATA_TYPE	DBTYPE_UI2	The indicator of the data type.
COLUMN_SIZE	DBTYPE_UI4	The length of a non-numeric column or parameter refers to either the maximum or the defined length for this type by the provider. For character data, this is the maximum or defined length in characters. For datetime data types, this is the length of the string representation (assuming the maximum allowed precision of the fractional seconds component). If the data type is numeric, this is the upper bound on the maximum precision of the data type. For the maximum precision of all numeric data types, see "Precision of Numeric Data Types" in Appendix A, "Data Types."
LITERAL_PREFIX	DBTYPE_WSTR	Character or characters used to prefix a literal of this type in a text command.

Column name	Type indicator	Description
LITERAL_SUFFIX	DBTYPE_WSTR	Character or characters used to suffix a literal of this type in a text command.
CREATE_PARAMS	DBTYPE_WSTR	The creation parameters are specified by the consumer when creating a column of this data type. For example, the SQL data type DECIMAL needs a precision and a scale. In this case, the creation parameters might be the string "precision,scale". In a text command to create a DECIMAL column with a precision of 10 and a scale of 2, the value of the TYPE_NAME column might be DECIMAL() and the complete type specification would be DECIMAL(10,2). The creation parameters appear as a comma-separated list of values, in the order they are to be supplied, with no surrounding parentheses. If a creation parameter is length, maximum length, precision, or scale, "length", "max length", "precision", and "scale" should be used, respectively. If the creation parameters are some other value, it is provider-specific what text is used to describe the creation parameter. If the data type requires creation parameters, "()" usually appears in the type name. This indicates the position at which to insert the creation parameters. If the type name does not include "()", the creation parameters are enclosed in parentheses and appended to the data type name.
IS_NULLABLE	DBTYPE_BOOL	VARIANT_TRUE—The data type is nullable. VARIANT_FALSE—The data type is not nullable. NULL—It is not known whether the data type is nullable.
CASE_SENSITIVE	DBTYPE_BOOL	VARIANT_TRUE—The data type is a character type and is case sensitive. VARIANT_FALSE—The data type is not a character type or is not case sensitive.

Column name	Type indicator	Description
SEARCHABLE	DBTYPE_UI4	If the provider supports **ICommandText**, this column is an integer indicating the searchability of a data type; otherwise, this column is NULL. One of the following: DB_UNSEARCHABLE—The data type cannot be used in a **WHERE** clause. DB_LIKE_ONLY—The data type can be used in a **WHERE** clause only with the **LIKE** predicate. DB_ALL_EXCEPT_LIKE—The data type can be used in a **WHERE** clause with all comparison operators except **LIKE**. DB_SEARCHABLE—The data type can be used in a **WHERE** clause with any comparison operator.
UNSIGNED_ATTRIBUTE	DBTYPE_BOOL	VARIANT_TRUE—The data type is unsigned. VARIANT_FALSE—The data type is signed. NULL—Not applicable to data type.
FIXED_PREC_SCALE	DBTYPE_BOOL	VARIANT_TRUE—The data type has a fixed precision and scale. VARIANT_FALSE—The data type does not have a fixed precision and scale.

Column name	Type indicator	Description
AUTO_UNIQUE_VALUE	DBTYPE_BOOL	VARIANT_TRUE—Values of this type can be autoincrementing. VARIANT_FALSE—Values of this type cannot be autoincrementing. If this value is VARIANT_TRUE, whether or not a column of this type is always autoincrementing depends on the provider's DBPROP_COL_AUTOINCREMENT column property. If the DBPROP_COL_AUTOINCREMENT property is read/write, whether or not a column of this type is autoincrementing depends on the setting of the DBPROP_COL_AUTOINCREMENT property. If DBPROP_COL_AUTOINCREMENT is a read-only property, either all columns of this type are autoincrementing or none of the columns are autoincrementing.
LOCAL_TYPE_NAME	DBTYPE_WSTR	Localized version of TYPE_NAME. NULL is returned if a localized name is not supported by the data provider.
MINIMUM_SCALE	DBTYPE_I2	If the type indicator is DBTYPE_VARNUMERIC, DBTYPE_DECIMAL, or DBTYPE_NUMERIC, this is the minimum number of digits allowed to the right of the decimal point. Otherwise, this is NULL.
MAXIMUM_SCALE	DBTYPE_I2	If the type indicator is DBTYPE_VARNUMERIC, DBTYPE_DECIMAL, or DBTYPE_NUMERIC, this is the maximum number of digits allowed to the right of the decimal point. Otherwise, this is NULL.
GUID	DBTYPE_GUID	The GUID of the type. All types supported by a provider are described in a type library, so each type has a corresponding GUID.

Column name	Type indicator	Description
TYPELIB	DBTYPE_WSTR	The type library containing the description of this type. All types supported by a provider, including those in Appendix A, "Data Types," are described in one or more type libraries.
VERSION	DBTYPE_WSTR	The version of the type definition. Providers may wish to version type definitions. Different providers may use different versioning schemes, such as a timestamp or number (integer or float). NULL if not supported.
IS_LONG	DBTYPE_BOOL	VARIANT_TRUE—The data type is a BLOB that contains very long data; the definition of very long data is provider-specific. VARIANT_FALSE—The data type is a BLOB that does not contain very long data or is not a BLOB. This value determines the setting of the DBCOLUMNFLAGS_ISLONG flag returned by **GetColumnInfo** in **IColumnsInfo** and **GetParameterInfo** in **ICommandWithParameters**. For more information, see **GetColumnInfo**, **GetParameterInfo** in Part 2, "OLE DB Reference" and "Accessing BLOB Data" in Chapter 7, "BLOBs and COM Objects."

Column name	Type indicator	Description
BEST_MATCH	DBTYPE_BOOL	VARIANT_TRUE—The data type is the best match between all data types in the data store and the OLE DB data type indicated by the value in the DATA_TYPE column. VARIANT_FALSE—The data type is not the best match. For each set of rows in which the value of the DATA_TYPE column is the same, the BEST_MATCH column is set to VARIANT_TRUE in only one row.
IS_FIXEDLENGTH	DBTYPE_BOOL	VARIANT_TRUE—Columns of this type created by the DDL will be of fixed length. VARIANT_FALSE—Columns of this type created by the DDL will be of variable length. If the field is NULL, it is not known whether the provider will map this field with a fixed or variable length.

Default Sort Order: DATA_TYPE

REFERENTIAL_CONSTRAINTS Rowset

The REFERENTIAL_CONSTRAINTS rowset identifies the referential constraints defined in the catalog that are owned by a given user.

The REFERENTIAL_CONSTRAINTS rowset contains the following columns.

Column name	Type indicator	Description
CONSTRAINT_CATALOG	DBTYPE_WSTR	Catalog name. NULL if the provider does not support catalogs.
CONSTRAINT_SCHEMA	DBTYPE_WSTR	Unqualified schema name. NULL if the provider does not support schemas.
CONSTRAINT_NAME	DBTYPE_WSTR	Constraint name.
UNIQUE_CONSTRAINT_ CATALOG	DBTYPE_WSTR	Catalog name in which the unique or primary key constraint is defined. NULL if the provider does not support catalogs.

Column name	Type indicator	Description
UNIQUE_CONSTRAINT_ SCHEMA	DBTYPE_WSTR	Unqualified schema name in which the unique or primary key constraint is defined. NULL if the provider does not support schemas.
UNIQUE_CONSTRAINT_ NAME	DBTYPE_WSTR	Unique or primary key constraint name.
MATCH_OPTION	DBTYPE_WSTR	"NONE"—No <*match type*> was specified. "PARTIAL"—A <*match type*> of **PARTIAL** was specified. "FULL"—A <*match type*> of **FULL** was specified.
UPDATE_RULE	DBTYPE_WSTR	If an <*update rule*> was specified, the UPDATE_RULE value is one of the following: "CASCADE"—A <*referential action*> of **CASCADE** was specified. "SET NULL"—A <*referential action*> of **SET NULL** was specified. "SET DEFAULT"—A <*referential action*> of **SET DEFAULT** was specified. "NO ACTION"—A <*referential action*> of **NO ACTION** was specified.
DELETE_RULE	DBTYPE_WSTR	If a <*delete rule*> was specified, the DELETE_RULE value is one of the following: "CASCADE"—A <*referential action*> of **CASCADE** was specified. "SET NULL"—A <*referential action*> of **SET NULL** was specified. "SET DEFAULT"—A <*referential action*> of **SET DEFAULT** was specified. "NO ACTION"—A <*referential action*> of **NO ACTION** was specified.
DESCRIPTION	DBTYPE_WSTR	Human-readable description of the constraint.

Default Sort Order: CONSTRAINT_CATALOG, CONSTRAINT_SCHEMA, CONSTRAINT_NAME, UNIQUE_CONSTRAINT_CATALOG, UNIQUE_CONSTRAINT_SCHEMA, UNIQUE_CONSTRAINT_NAME

SCHEMATA Rowset

The SCHEMATA rowset identifies the schemas that are owned by a given user.

The SCHEMATA rowset contains the following columns.

Column name	Type indicator	Description
CATALOG_NAME	DBTYPE_WSTR	Catalog name. NULL if the provider does not support catalogs.
SCHEMA_NAME	DBTYPE_WSTR	Unqualified schema name.
SCHEMA_OWNER	DBTYPE_WSTR	User that owns the schemas.
DEFAULT_CHARACTER_ SET_CATALOG	DBTYPE_WSTR	Catalog name of the default character set for columns and domains in the schemas. NULL if the provider does not support catalogs or different character sets.
DEFAULT_CHARACTER_ SET_SCHEMA	DBTYPE_WSTR	Unqualified schema name of the default character set for columns and domains in the schemas. NULL if the provider does not support different character sets.
DEFAULT_CHARACTER_ SET_NAME	DBTYPE_WSTR	Default character set name. NULL if the provider does not support different character sets.

Default Sort Order: CATALOG_NAME, SCHEMA_NAME, SCHEMA_OWNER

SQL_LANGUAGES Rowset

The SQL_LANGUAGES rowset identifies the conformance levels, options, and dialects supported by the SQL-implementation processing data defined in the catalog.

The SQL_LANGUAGES rowset contains the following columns.

Column name	Type indicator	Description
SQL_LANGUAGE_ SOURCE	DBTYPE_WSTR	Should be "ISO 9075" for standard SQL.
SQL_LANGUAGE_YEAR	DBTYPE_WSTR	Should be "1992" for ANSI SQL92-compliant SQL.
SQL_LANGUAGE_ CONFORMANCE	DBTYPE_WSTR	One of the following: "ENTRY" "INTERMEDIATE" "FULL"

Column name	Type indicator	Description
SQL_LANGUAGE_ INTEGRITY	DBTYPE_WSTR	"YES"—Optional integrity feature is supported. "NO"—Optional integrity feature is not supported.
SQL_LANGUAGE_ IMPLEMENTATION	DBTYPE_WSTR	NULL for "ISO 9075" implementation.
SQL_LANGUAGE_ BINDING_STYLE	DBTYPE_WSTR	"DIRECT" for C/C++ callable direct execution of SQL.
SQL_LANGUAGE_ PROGRAMMING_ LANGUAGE	DBTYPE_WSTR	NULL.

Default Sort Order: SQL_LANGUAGE_SOURCE

STATISTICS Rowset

The STATISTICS rowset identifies the statistics defined in the catalog that are owned by a given user.

The STATISTICS rowset contains the following columns.

Column name	Type indicator	Description
TABLE_CATALOG	DBTYPE_WSTR	Catalog name. NULL if the provider does not support catalogs.
TABLE_SCHEMA	DBTYPE_WSTR	Unqualified schema name. NULL if the provider does not support schemas.
TABLE_NAME	DBTYPE_WSTR	Table name.
CARDINALITY	DBTYPE_UI8	Cardinality (number of rows) of the table.

Default Sort Order: TABLE_CATALOG, TABLE_SCHEMA, TABLE_NAME

TABLE_CONSTRAINTS Rowset

The TABLE_CONSTRAINTS rowset identifies the table constraints defined in the catalog that are owned by a given user.

The TABLE_CONSTRAINTS rowset contains the following columns.

Column name	Type indicator	Description
CONSTRAINT_CATALOG	DBTYPE_WSTR	Catalog name. NULL if the provider does not support catalogs.
CONSTRAINT_SCHEMA	DBTYPE_WSTR	Unqualified schema name. NULL if the provider does not support schemas.
CONSTRAINT_NAME	DBTYPE_WSTR	Constraint name.
TABLE_CATALOG	DBTYPE_WSTR	Catalog name in which the table is defined. NULL if the provider does not support catalogs.
TABLE_SCHEMA	DBTYPE_WSTR	Unqualified schema name in which the table is defined. NULL if the provider does not support schemas.
TABLE_NAME	DBTYPE_WSTR	Table name.
CONSTRAINT_TYPE	DBTYPE_WSTR	Constraint type. One of the following: "UNIQUE" "PRIMARY KEY" "FOREIGN KEY" "CHECK"
IS_DEFERRABLE	DBTYPE_BOOL	VARIANT_TRUE—The table constraint is deferrable. VARIANT_FALSE—The table constraint is not deferrable.
INITIALLY_DEFERRED	DBTYPE_BOOL	VARIANT_TRUE—The table constraint is initially deferred. VARIANT_FALSE—The table constraint is initially immediate.
DESCRIPTION	DBTYPE_WSTR	Human-readable description of the column

Default Sort Order: CONSTRAINT_CATALOG, CONSTRAINT_SCHEMA, CONSTRAINT_NAME, TABLE_CATALOG, TABLE_SCHEMA, TABLE_NAME, CONSTRAINT_TYPE

TABLE_PRIVILEGES Rowset

The TABLE_PRIVILEGES rowset identifies the privileges on tables defined in the catalog that are available to or granted by a given user.

The TABLE_PRIVILEGES rowset contains the following columns.

Column name	Type indicator	Description
GRANTOR	DBTYPE_WSTR	User who granted the privileges on the table in TABLE_NAME.
GRANTEE	DBTYPE_WSTR	User name (or "PUBLIC") to whom the privilege has been granted.
TABLE_CATALOG	DBTYPE_WSTR	Catalog name in which the table is defined. NULL if the provider does not support catalogs.
TABLE_SCHEMA	DBTYPE_WSTR	Unqualified schema name in which the table is defined. NULL if the provider does not support schemas.
TABLE_NAME	DBTYPE_WSTR	Table name.
PRIVILEGE_TYPE	DBTYPE_WSTR	Privilege type. One of the following: "SELECT" "DELETE" "INSERT" "UPDATE" "REFERENCES"
IS_GRANTABLE	DBTYPE_BOOL	VARIANT_TRUE—The privilege being described was granted with the **WITH GRANT OPTION** clause. VARIANT_FALSE—The privilege being described was not granted with the **WITH GRANT OPTION** clause.

Default Sort Order: TABLE_CATALOG, TABLE_SCHEMA, TABLE_NAME, PRIVILEGE_TYPE

TABLES Rowset

The TABLES rowset identifies the tables defined in the catalog that are accessible to a given user.

The TABLES rowset contains the following columns.

Column name	Type indicator	Description
TABLE_CATALOG	DBTYPE_WSTR	Catalog name. NULL if the provider does not support catalogs.
TABLE_SCHEMA	DBTYPE_WSTR	Unqualified schema name. NULL if the provider does not support schemas.
TABLE_NAME	DBTYPE_WSTR	Table name. This column cannot contain a NULL.
TABLE_TYPE	DBTYPE_WSTR	Table type. One of the following or a provider-specific value: "ALIAS" "TABLE" "SYNONYM" "SYSTEM TABLE" "VIEW" "GLOBAL TEMPORARY" "LOCAL TEMPORARY" This column cannot contain a Null.
TABLE_GUID	DBTYPE_GUID	GUID that uniquely identifies the table. Providers that do not use GUIDs to identify tables should return NULL in this column.
DESCRIPTION	DBTYPE_WSTR	Human-readable description of the table. Null if there is no description associated with the column.
TABLE_PROPID	DBTYPE_UI4	Property ID of the table. Providers that do not use PROPIDs to identify columns should return NULL in this column.

Column name	Type indicator	Description
DATE_CREATED	DBTYPE_DATE	Date when the table was created or NULL if the provider does not have this information. Note that 1.*x* providers do not return this column.
DATE_MODIFIED	DBTYPE_DATE	Date when the table definition was last modified or NULL if the provider does not have this information. Note that 1.*x* providers do not return this column.

Default Sort Order: TABLE_TYPE, TABLE_CATALOG, TABLE_SCHEMA, TABLE_NAME

TABLES_INFO Rowset

The TABLES_INFO rowset identifies the tables defined in the catalog that are accessible to a given user.

The TABLES_INFO rowset contains the following columns.

Column name	Type indicator	Description
TABLE_CATALOG	DBTYPE_WSTR	Catalog name. NULL if the provider does not support catalogs.
TABLE_SCHEMA	DBTYPE_WSTR	Unqualified schema name. NULL if the provider does not support schemas.
TABLE_NAME	DBTYPE_WSTR	Table name.
TABLE_TYPE	DBTYPE_WSTR	Table type. One of the following or a provider-specific value. "ALIAS" "TABLE" "SYNONYM" "SYSTEM TABLE" "VIEW" "GLOBAL TEMPORARY" "LOCAL TEMPORARY" "EXTERNAL TABLE"
TABLE_GUID	DBTYPE_GUID	GUID that uniquely identifies the table. Providers that do not use GUIDs to identify tables should return NULL in this column.

Column name	Type indicator	Description
BOOKMARKS	DBTYPE_BOOL	Whether this table supports bookmarks when opening this table with **IOpenRowset::OpenRowset** or **SELECT * FROM** <*table-name*>. VARIANT_TRUE—The table supports bookmarks. VARIANT_FALSE—The table does not support bookmarks.
BOOKMARK_TYPE	DBTYPE_I4	Default bookmark type supported on this table. Contains one of the following values: DBPROPVAL_BMK_NUMERIC—The bookmark type is numeric. DBPROPVAL_BMK_KEY—The bookmark type is key. For more information, see "Bookmark Types" in Chapter 4, "Rowsets." This column is not NULL only if the BOOKMARKS column is VARIANT_TRUE.
BOOKMARK_DATATYPE	DBTYPE_UI2	The indicator of the bookmark's native data type. For a list of valid type indicators, see "Type Indicators" in Appendix A, "Data Types." This column is not NULL only if the BOOKMARKS column is VARIANT_TRUE.
BOOKMARK_ MAXIMUM_LENGTH	DBTYPE_UI4	Maximum length of the bookmark in bytes. This column is not NULL only if the BOOKMARKS column is VARIANT_TRUE.
BOOKMARK_ INFORMATION	DBTYPE_UI4	A bitmask specifying additional information about bookmarks over the rowset. A combination of zero or more of the following: DBPROPVAL_BI_CROSSROWSET—If set, bookmark values are valid across rowsets generated by calling **OpenRowset** on this table. If not set, bookmark values, if supported, are valid only within a single rowset over this table.

Column name	Type indicator	Description
TABLE_VERSION	DBTYPE_I8	Version number for this table, or NULL if the provider does not support returning table version information. This number is assumed to change every time the table is modified through ALTER TABLE, CREATE INDEX, DROP INDEX, or similar statements. The way in which this number is generated is provider specific.
CARDINALITY	DBTYPE_UI8	Cardinality (number of rows) of the table.
DESCRIPTION	DBTYPE_WSTR	Human-readable description of the table.
TABLE_PROPID	DBTYPE_UI4	Property ID of the table. Providers that do not use PROPIDs to identify columns should return NULL in this column.

Default Sort Order: TABLE_TYPE, TABLE_CATALOG, TABLE_SCHEMA, TABLE_NAME

TRANSLATIONS Rowset

The TRANSLATIONS rowset identifies the character translations defined in the catalog that are accessible to a given user.

The TRANSLATIONS rowset contains the following columns.

Column name	Type indicator	Description
TRANSLATION_ CATALOG	DBTYPE_WSTR	Catalog name. NULL if the provider does not support catalogs.
TRANSLATION_SCHEMA	DBTYPE_WSTR	Unqualified schema name. NULL if the provider does not support schemas.
TRANSLATION_NAME	DBTYPE_WSTR	Translation name.
SOURCE_CHARACTER_ SET_CATALOG	DBTYPE_WSTR	Catalog name containing the source character set on which the translation is defined. NULL if the provider does not support catalogs.
SOURCE_CHARACTER_ SET_SCHEMA	DBTYPE_WSTR	Unqualified schema name containing the source character set on which the translation is defined. NULL if the provider does not support schemas.
SOURCE_CHARACTER_ SET_NAME	DBTYPE_WSTR	Source character set name on which the translation is defined.

Column name	Type indicator	Description
TARGET_CHARACTER_SET_CATALOG	DBTYPE_WSTR	Catalog name containing the target character set on which the translation is defined. NULL if the provider does not support catalogs.
TARGET_CHARACTER_SET_SCHEMA	DBTYPE_WSTR	Unqualified schema name containing the target character set on which the translation is defined. NULL if the provider does not support schemas.
TARGET_CHARACTER_SET_NAME	DBTYPE_WSTR	Target character set name on which the translation is defined.

Default Sort Order: TRANSLATION_CATALOG, TRANSLATION_SCHEMA, TRANSLATION_NAME

USAGE_PRIVILEGES Rowset

The USAGE_PRIVILEGES rowset identifies the USAGE privileges on objects defined in the catalog that are available to or granted by a given user.

The USAGE_PRIVILEGES rowset contains the following columns.

Column name	Type indicator	Description
GRANTOR	DBTYPE_WSTR	User who granted the privileges on the object in OBJECT_NAME.
GRANTEE	DBTYPE_WSTR	User name (or "PUBLIC") to whom the privilege has been granted.
OBJECT_CATALOG	DBTYPE_WSTR	Catalog name in which the object is defined. NULL if the provider does not support catalogs.
OBJECT_SCHEMA	DBTYPE_WSTR	Unqualified schema name in which the object is defined. NULL if the provider does not support schemas.
OBJECT_NAME	DBTYPE_WSTR	Object name.
OBJECT_TYPE	DBTYPE_WSTR	Object type. One of the following: "DOMAIN" "CHARACTER SET" "COLLATION" "TRANSLATION"

Column name	Type indicator	Description
PRIVILEGE_TYPE	DBTYPE_WSTR	Privilege type: "USAGE"
IS_GRANTABLE	DBTYPE_BOOL	VARIANT_TRUE—The privilege being described was granted with the **WITH GRANT OPTION** clause. VARIANT_FALSE—The privilege being described was not granted with the **WITH GRANT OPTION** clause.

Default Sort Order: OBJECT_CATALOG, OBJECT_SCHEMA, OBJECT_NAME, OBJECT_TYPE, PRIVILEGE_TYPE

VIEW_COLUMN_USAGE Rowset

The VIEW_COLUMN_USAGE rowset identifies the columns on which viewed tables, defined in the catalog and owned by a given user, are dependent.

The VIEW_COLUMN_USAGE rowset contains the following columns.

Column name	Type indicator	Description
VIEW_CATALOG	DBTYPE_WSTR	Catalog name. NULL if the provider does not support catalogs.
VIEW_SCHEMA	DBTYPE_WSTR	Unqualified schema name. NULL if the provider does not support schemas.
VIEW_NAME	DBTYPE_WSTR	View name.
TABLE_CATALOG	DBTYPE_WSTR	Catalog name in which the table is defined. NULL if the provider does not support catalogs.
TABLE_SCHEMA	DBTYPE_WSTR	Unqualified schema name in which the table is defined. NULL if the provider does not support schemas.
TABLE_NAME	DBTYPE_WSTR	Table name.

Column name	Type indicator	Description
COLUMN_NAME	DBTYPE_WSTR	Column name. This column, together with the COLUMN_GUID and COLUMN_PROPID columns, forms the column ID. One or more of these columns will be NULL, depending on which elements of the DBID structure the provider uses.
COLUMN_GUID	DBTYPE_GUID	Column GUID.
COLUMN_PROPID	DBTYPE_UI4	Column property ID.

Default Sort Order: VIEW_CATALOG, VIEW_SCHEMA, VIEW_NAME, TABLE_CATALOG, TABLE_SCHEMA, TABLE_NAME, COLUMN_NAME, COLUMN_GUID, COLUMN_PROPID

VIEW_TABLE_USAGE Rowset

The VIEW_TABLE_USAGE rowset identifies the tables on which viewed tables, defined in the catalog and owned by a given user, are dependent.

The VIEW_TABLE_USAGE rowset contains the following columns.

Column name	Type indicator	Description
VIEW_CATALOG	DBTYPE_WSTR	Catalog name. NULL if the provider does not support catalogs.
VIEW_SCHEMA	DBTYPE_WSTR	Unqualified schema name. NULL if the provider does not support schemas.
VIEW_NAME	DBTYPE_WSTR	View name.
TABLE_CATALOG	DBTYPE_WSTR	Catalog name in which the table is defined. NULL if the provider does not support catalogs.
TABLE_SCHEMA	DBTYPE_WSTR	Unqualified schema name in which the table is defined. NULL if the provider does not support schemas.
TABLE_NAME	DBTYPE_WSTR	Table name.

Default Sort Order: VIEW_CATALOG, VIEW_SCHEMA, VIEW_NAME, TABLE_CATALOG, TABLE_SCHEMA, TABLE_NAME

VIEWS Rowset

The VIEWS rowset identifies the viewed tables defined in the catalog that are accessible to a given user.

The VIEWS rowset contains the following columns.

Column name	Type indicator	Description
TABLE_CATALOG	DBTYPE_WSTR	Catalog name. NULL if the provider does not support catalogs.
TABLE_SCHEMA	DBTYPE_WSTR	Unqualified schema name. NULL if the provider does not support schemas.
TABLE_NAME	DBTYPE_WSTR	View name.
VIEW_DEFINITION	DBTYPE_WSTR	View definition. This is a query expression.
CHECK_OPTION	DBTYPE_BOOL	Check option. One of the following: VARIANT_TRUE—Local update checking only. VARIANT_FALSE—Cascaded update checking (same as no CHECK OPTION specified on view definition).
IS_UPDATABLE	DBTYPE_BOOL	VARIANT_TRUE—The view is updatable. VARIANT_FALSE—The view is not updatable.
DESCRIPTION	DBTYPE_WSTR	Human-readable description of the view.
DATE_CREATED	DBTYPE_DATE	Date when the view was created or NULL if the provider does not have this information. Note that 1.*x* providers do not return this column.
DATE_MODIFIED	DBTYPE_DATE	Date when the view definition was last modified or NULL if the provider does not have this information. Note that 1.*x* providers do not return this column.

Default Sort Order: TABLE_CATALOG, TABLE_SCHEMA, TABLE_NAME

APPENDIX C

Property Tables

This appendix lists the properties in all property groups that are defined by OLE DB. The properties table by property group is followed by an alphabetical listing of all properties, which gives information about them such as type, description, effects and characteristics, and return values.

Properties Table (by Property Groups)

The following table lists all properties contained within each property group.

Property Group	Property Set	Properties
Column	DBPROPSET_COLUMN	DBPROP_COL_AUTO-INCREMENT DBPROP_COL_DEFAULT DBPROP_COL_DESCRIPTION DBPROP_COL_FIXEDLENGTH DBPROP_COL_NULLABLE DBPROP_COL_PRIMARYKEY DBPROP_COL_UNIQUE
Data Source	DBPROPSET_DATASOURCE	DBPROP_CURRENTCATALOG
Data Source Creation		None. OLE DB does not define any data source object creation properties. Providers can define their own data source object creation properties.

Property Group	Property Set	Properties
	DBPROPSET_DATASOURCE-INFO	DBPROP_ACTIVESESSIONS DBPROP_ALTERCOLUMN DBPROP_ASYNCTXNABORT DBPROP_ASYNCTXNCOMMIT DBPROP_BYREFACCESSORS DBPROP_CATALOG-LOCATION DBPROP_CATALOGTERM DBPROP_CATALOGUSAGE DBPROP_COLUMN-DEFINITION DBPROP_CONCATNULL-BEHAVIOR DBPROP_DATASOURCENAME DBPROP_DATASOURCE-READONLY DBPROP_DBMSNAME DBPROP_DBMSVER DBPROP_DSOTHREADMODEL DBPROP_GROUPBY DBPROP_HETEROGENEOUS-TABLES DBPROP_IDENTIFIERCASE DBPROP_MAXINDEXSIZE DBPROP_MAXOPEN-CHAPTERS DBPROP_MAXROWSIZE DBPROP_MAXROWSIZE-INCLUDESBLOB DBPROP_MAXTABLESIN-SELECT DBPROP_MULTIPLEPARAM-SETS DBPROP_MULTIPLERESULTS DBPROP_MULTIPLE-STORAGEOBJECTS DBPROP_MULTITABLE-UPDATE DBPROP_NULLCOLLATION DBPROP_OLEOBJECTS DBPROP_ORDERBY-COLUMNSINSELECT

Property Group	Property Set	Properties
		DBPROP_OUTPUTPARAM-ETERAVAILABILITY DBPROP_PERSISTENTIDTYPE DBPROP_PREPAREABORT-BEHAVIOR DBPROP_PREPARECOMMIT-BEHAVIOR DBPROP_PROCEDURETERM DBPROP_PROVIDER-FRIENDLYNAME DBPROP_PROVIDERNAME DBPROP_PROVIDER-OLEDBVER DBPROP_PROVIDERVER DBPROP_QUOTED-IDENTIFIERCASE DBPROP_ROWSETCON-VERSIONSONCOMMAND DBPROP_SCHEMATERM DBPROP_SCHEMAUSAGE DBPROP_SERVERNAME DBPROP_SQLSUPPORT DBPROP_STRUCTURED-STORAGE DBPROP_SUBQUERIES DBPROP_SUPPORTED-TXNDDL DBPROP_SUPPORTED-TXNISOLEVELS DBPROP_SUPPORTED-TXNISORETAIN DBPROP_USERNAME

Property Group	Property Set	Properties
Index	DBPROPSET_INDEX	DBPROP_INDEX_AUTO-UPDATE DBPROP_INDEX_CLUSTERED DBPROP_INDEX_FILLFACTOR DBPROP_INDEX_INITIALSIZE DBPROP_INDEX_NULL-COLLATION DBPROP_INDEX_NULLS DBPROP_INDEX_PRIMARY-KEY DBPROP_INDEX_SORT-BOOKMARKS DBPROP_INDEX_TEMPINDEX DBPROP_INDEX_TYPE DBPROP_INDEX_UNIQUE
Initialization	DBPROPSET_DBINIT	DBPROP_AUTH_CACHE_AUTHINFO DBPROP_AUTH_ENCRYPT_PASSWORD DBPROP_AUTH_INTEGRATED DBPROP_AUTH_MASK_PASSWORD DBPROP_AUTH_PASSWORD DBPROP_AUTH_PERSIST_ENCRYPTED DBPROP_AUTH_PERSIST_SENSITIVE_AUTHINFO DBPROP_AUTH_USERID DBPROP_INIT_ASYNCH DBPROP_INIT_CATALOG DBPROP_INIT_DATASOURCE DBPROP_INIT_HWND DBPROP_INIT_IMPERSON-ATION_LEVEL DBPROP_INIT_LCID DBPROP_INIT_LOCATION DBPROP_INIT_MODE DBPROP_INIT_PROMPT

Property Group	Property Set	Properties
Rowset	DBPROPSET_ROWSET	DBPROP_INIT_PROTECTION_LEVEL DBPROP_INIT_PROVIDER-STRING DBPROP_ABORTPRESERVE DBPROP_ACCESSORDER DBPROP_APPENDONLY DBPROP_BLOCKING-STORAGEOBJECTS DBPROP_BOOKMARKINFO DBPROP_BOOKMARKS DBPROP_BOOKMARK-SKIPPED DBPROP_BOOKMARKTYPE DBPROP_CACHEDEFERRED DBPROP_CANFETCH-BACKWARDS DBPROP_CANHOLDROWS DBPROP_CANSCROLL-BACKWARDS DBPROP_CHANGEINSERTED-ROWS DBPROP_COLUMNRESTRICT DBPROP_COMMAND-TIMEOUT DBPROP_COMMITPRESERVE DBPROP_DEFERRED DBPROP_DELAYSTORAGE-OBJECTS DBPROP_FINDCOMPAREOPS DBPROP_HIDDENCOLUMNS DBPROP_IACCESSOR DBPROP_ICHAPTERED-ROWSET DBPROP_ICOLUMNSINFO DBPROP_ICOLUMNSROWSET DBPROP_ICONNECTION-POINTCONTAINER

Property Group	Property Set	Properties
		DBPROP_ICONVERTTYPE DBPROP_IDBASYNCHSTATUS DBPROP_IMULTIPLERESULTS DBPROP_IROWSET DBPROP_IROWSETCHANGE DBPROP_IROWSETFIND DBPROP_IROWSETIDENTITY DBPROP_IROWSETINDEX DBPROP_IROWSETINFO DBPROP_IROWSETLOCATE DBPROP_IROWSETREFRESH DBPROP_IROWSETSCROLL DBPROP_IROWSETUPDATE DBPROP_IROWSETVIEW DBPROP_ISUPPORTERROR-INFO DBPROP_ILOCKBYTES DBPROP_ISEQUENTIAL-STREAM DBPROP_ISTORAGE DBPROP_ISTREAM DBPROP_IMMOBILEROWS DBPROP_LITERAL-BOOKMARKS DBPROP_LITERALIDENTITY DBPROP_LOCKMODE DBPROP_MAXOPENROWS DBPROP_MAXPENDINGROWS DBPROP_MAXROWS DBPROP_MAYWRITE-COLUMN DBPROP_MEMORYUSAGE DBPROP_NOTIFICATION-GRANULARITY DBPROP_NOTIFICATION-PHASES DBPROP_NOTIFYCOLUMN-SET DBPROP_NOTIFYROW-DELETE

Property Group	Property Set	Properties
		DBPROP_NOTIFYROWFIRST-CHANGE DBPROP_NOTIFYROWINSERT DBPROP_NOTIFYROW-RESYNCH DBPROP_NOTIFYROWSET-RELEASE DBPROP_NOTIFYROWSETFET CHPOSITIONCHANGE DBPROP_NOTIFYROW-UNDOCHANGE DBPROP_NOTIFYROW-UNDODELETE DBPROP_NOTIFYROW-UNDOINSERT DBPROP_NOTIFYROW-UPDATE DBPROP_ORDERED-BOOKMARKS DBPROP_OTHERINSERT DBPROP_OTHERUPDATE-DELETE DBPROP_OWNINSERT DBPROP_OWNUPDATE-DELETE DBPROP_QUICKRESTART DBPROP_REENTRANT-EVENTS DBPROP_REMOVEDELETED DBPROP_REPORTMULTIPLE-CHANGES DBPROP_RETURNPENDING-INSERTS DBPROP_ROWRESTRICT DBPROP_ROWSET_ASYNCH DBPROP_ROWTHREAD-MODEL

Property Group	Property Set	Properties
		DBPROP_SERVERCURSOR DBPROP_STRONGIDENTITY DBPROP_TRANSACTED-OBJECT DBPROP_UPDATABILITY
Session	DBPROPSET_SESSION	DBPROP_SESS_AUTO-COMMITISOLEVELS
Table	DBPROPSET_TABLE	DBPROP_TBL_TEMPTABLE
View	DBPROPSET_VIEW	DBPROP_FILTERCOMPARE-OPS DBPROP_IACCESSOR DBPROP_ICOLUMNSINFO DBPROP_ISUPPORT-ERRORINFO DBPROP_IVIEWCHAPTER DBPROP_IVIEWFILTER DBPROP_IVIEWROWSET DBPROP_IVIEWSORTDB-PROP_MAXORSINFILTER DBPROP_MAXSORT-COLUMNS DBPROP_SORTONINDEX DBPROP_SERVERCURSOR DBPROP_STRONGIDENTITY DBPROP_TRANSACTED-OBJECT DBPROP_UPDATABILITY

Property Group	Property Set	Properties
Session	DBPROPSET_SESSION	DBPROP_SESS_AUTO-COMMITISOLEVELS
Table	DBPROPSET_TABLE	DBPROP_TBL_TEMPTABLE
View	DBPROPSET_VIEW	DBPROP_FILTERCOMPARE-OPS DBPROP_IACCESSOR DBPROP_ICOLUMNSINFO DBPROP_ISUPPORT-ERRORINFO DBPROP_IVIEWCHAPTER DBPROP_IVIEWFILTER DBPROP_IVIEWROWSET DBPROP_IVIEWSORTDB-PROP_MAXORSINFILTER DBPROP_MAXSORT-COLUMNS DBPROP_SORTONINDEX

Property Requirements Table

Property Group	Description
Column	Properties used to create columns.
Data Source	Properties that apply to data source objects. These properties can be set for some providers.
Data Source Creation	Properties used to create data source objects.
Data Source Information	Properties that describe data source objects. These properties are read-only for all providers and constitute a set of static information about the provider and data source object.
Index	Properties used to create and describe indexes.
Initialization	Properties used to initialize the data source object or enumerator.
Rowset	Properties that apply to rowsets.
Session	Properties that apply to sessions.
Table	Properties used to create tables.
View	Properties used to create views.

Properties Table (Alphabetical)

The properties in this table are contained in the designated property sets and property groups. (For a listing of properties organized by property group, see the Property Groups table.) The "Column ?" designation for Rowset properties states whether the property can be set on individual columns or only on the rowset as a whole.

Important The "Typical R/W" value for each property specifies whether that property can typically be read or written. Whether a particular property can actually be read or written is provider-specific and is returned in the **dwPropFlags** element of the DBPROPINFO structure.

Property ID	Description
DBPROP_ABORTPRESERVE	Property group: Rowset Property set: DBPROPSET_ROWSET Column? N Type: VT_BOOL Typical R/W: R/W Description: Preserve on Abort VARIANT_TRUE—After aborting a transaction, the rowset remains active. That is, it is possible to fetch new rows, update, delete, and insert rows, and so on. VARIANT_FALSE—After aborting a transaction, the only operations allowed on a rowset are to release row and accessor handles and to release the rowset.

Property ID	Description
DBPROP_ACCESSORDER	Property group: Rowset Property set: DBPROPSET_ROWSET Column? N Type: VT_I4 Typical R/W: R/W Description: Access Order The order in which columns must be accessed on the rowset. One of the following values: DBPROPVAL_AO_RANDOM—Columns can be accessed in any order. DBPROPVAL_AO_SEQUENTIALSTORAGEOBJECTS—Columns bound as storage objects can be accessed only in sequential order as determined by the column ordinal. Further, storage objects from one row must be retrieved before calling **GetData** on any columns in any subsequent row. Calling **GetData** on a column bound as a storage object returns DBSTATUS_E_UNAVAILABLE for any columns bound as storage objects if any of the following are true: • Columns beyond the column bound as a storage object are specified in the accessor. • Columns beyond the column bound as a storage object have been accessed in a previous call to **GetData** for that row. • **GetData** has been called for any columns on a row returned after the specified row. Providers that never impose restrictions on column access ordering return DBPROPSTATUS_S_OK when this value is set. However, they upgrade the property to DBPROPVAL_AO_RANDOM such that calling **GetProperty** continues to return DBPROPVAL_AO_RANDOM for this property.

Property ID	Description
DBPROP_ACTIVESESSIONS	Property group: Data Source Information Property set: DBPROPSET_DATASOURCEINFO Type: VT_I4 Typical R/W: R Description: Active Sessions The maximum number of sessions that can exist at the same time. If this property is set to zero, there is no limit on the number of sessions that can exist at one time. • The column is bound as a storage object, and columns beyond it are specified in the accessor. • Columns beyond the bound column have been accessed in a previous call to **GetData** for that row. • **GetData** has been called for any columns on a row returned after the specified row. Providers that never impose restrictions on column access ordering return DBPROPSTATUS_S_OK when this value is set. However, they upgrade the property to DBPROPVAL_AO_RANDOM such that calling **GetProperty** continues to return DBPROPVAL_AO_RANDOM for this property. Providers may be able to optimize how data is retrieved if they know it will be read in column order. For instance, the provider may be able to read directly from a stream over the data if it knows the columns will be read in strictly sequential order, but may not be able to do so efficiently if the columns contain BLOBs that may be read in a random order.

Property ID	Description
DBPROP_ALTERCOLUMN	Property group: Data Source Information Property set: DBPROPSET_DATASOURCEINFO Type: VT_I4 Typical R/W: R Description: Alter Column Support A bitmask describing which portions of the DBCOLUMNDESC structure can be used in a call to **IAlterTable::AlterColumn**. A combination of one or more of the following: DBCOLUMNDESCFLAG_TYPENAME DBCOLUMNDESCFLAG_ITYPEINFO DBCOLUMNDESCFLAG_PROPERTIES DBCOLUMNDESCFLAG_CLSID DBCOLUMNDESCFLAG_COLSIZE DBCOLUMNDESCFLAG_DBCID DBCOLUMNDESCFLAG_WTYPE DBCOLUMNDESCFLAG_PRECISION DBCOLUMNDESCFLAG_SCALE For more information about the mapping of these values to fields in the DBCOLUMNDESC structure, refer to the specification for **IAlterTable::AlterColumn** in Part 2, "OLE DB Reference."

Property ID	Description
DBPROP_APPENDONLY	Property group: Rowset Property set: DBPROPSET_ROWSET Column? N Type: VT_BOOL Typical R/W: R/W Description: Append-Only Rowset A rowset opened with this property set to VARIANT_TRUE will be initially empty and will be populated only by those rows inserted through the rowset. Append-only rowsets are used for adding records to a table without having to get a rowset over existing rows. DBPROP_APPENDONLY set to VARIANT_TRUE implies: • DBPROP_IROWSETCHANGE is VARIANT_TRUE. • DBPROP_OWNINSERT is VARIANT_TRUE. • DBPROP_UPDATABILITY has the flag DBPROPVAL_UP_INSERT set. • DBPROP_OTHERINSERT is VARIANT_FALSE.
DBPROP_ASYNCTXNABORT	Property group: Data Source Information Property set: DBPROPSET_DATASOURCEINFO Type: VT_BOOL Typical R/W: R Description: Asynchable Abort Whether transactions can be aborted asynchronously.
DBPROP_ASYNCTXNCOMMIT	Property group: Data Source Information Property set: DBPROPSET_DATASOURCEINFO Type: VT_BOOL Typical R/W: R Description: Asynchable Commit Whether transactions can be committed asynchronously.

Property ID	Description
DBPROP_AUTH_CACHE_AUTHINFO	Property group: Initialization Property set: DBPROPSET_DBINIT Type: VT_BOOL Typical R/W: R/W Description: Cache Authentication VARIANT_TRUE—The data source object or enumerator is allowed to cache sensitive authentication information such as a password in an internal cache. VARIANT_FALSE—The data source object or enumerator is not allowed to cache sensitive authentication information.
DBPROP_AUTH_ENCRYPT_PASSWORD	Property group: Initialization Property set: DBPROPSET_DBINIT Type: VT_BOOL Typical R/W: R/W Description: Encrypt Password VARIANT_TRUE—The consumer requires that the password be sent to the data source object or enumerator in an encrypted form. This property specifies a stronger form of masking than DBPROP_AUTH_MASKPASSWORD; it uses cryptographic techniques. VARIANT_FALSE—The password can be sent in an unencrypted form.
DBPROP_AUTH_INTEGRATED	Property group: Initialization Property set: DBPROPSET_DBINIT Type: VT_BSTR Typical R/W: R/W Description: Integrated Security A string containing the name of the authentication service used by the server to identify the user using the identity provided by an authentication domain. For example, for Microsoft NT Integrated Security, this is "SSPI" (for Security Support Provider Interface). If the BSTR is a null pointer, the default authentication service should be used. When this property is used, no other DBPROP_AUTH* properties are needed and if provided, their values are ignored.

Property ID	Description
DBPROP_AUTH_MASK_PASSWORD	Property group: Initialization Property set: DBPROPSET_DBINIT Type: VT_BOOL Typical R/W: R/W Description: Mask Password VARIANT_TRUE—The consumer requires that the password be sent to the data source object or enumerator in a masked form. VARIANT_FALSE—The password can be sent in an unmasked form.
DBPROP_AUTH_PASSWORD	Property group: Initialization Property set: DBPROPSET_DBINIT Type: VT_BSTR Typical R/W: R/W Description: Password The password to be used when connecting to the data source object or enumerator. When the value of this property is retrieved with **IDBProperties::GetProperties**, the provider might return a mask such as "******" or an empty string instead of the actual password. The password is still set internally and is used when **IDBInitialize::Initialize** is called.
DBPROP_AUTH_PERSIST_ENCRYPTED	Property group: Initialization Property set: DBPROPSET_DBINIT Type: VT_BOOL Typical R/W: R/W Description: Persist Encrypted VARIANT_TRUE—The consumer requires that the data source object persist sensitive authentication information such as a password in encrypted form. VARIANT_FALSE—The data source object can persist sensitive authentication information in unencrypted form.

Property ID	Description
DBPROP_AUTH_PERSIST_SENSITIVE_AUTHINFO	Property group: Initialization Property set: DBPROPSET_DBINIT Type: VT_BOOL Typical R/W: R/W Description: Persist Security Info VARIANT_TRUE—The data source object is allowed to persist sensitive authentication information such as a password along with other authentication information. VARIANT_FALSE—The data source object cannot persist sensitive authentication information. If DBPROP_AUTH_PERSIST_SENSITIVE_AUTHINFO is set to VARIANT_FALSE at the time the data source object is initialized, the data source object cannot persist sensitive authentication information. Furthermore, requesting properties that contain sensitive authentication information, such as password, returns some default value instead of the actual password. Once the data source object has been uninitialized, sensitive information that was set when the data source object was initialized with the DBPROP_AUTH_PERSIST_SENSITIVE_AUTHINFO property set to VARIANT_FALSE still cannot be obtained through **IDBProperties::GetProperties** or by persisting the uninitialized data source object, but new properties set after the data source object has been uninitialized can be persisted or obtained as long as DBPROP_AUTH_PERSIST_SENSITIVE_AUTHINFO is VARIANT_TRUE.
DBPROP_AUTH_USERID	Property group: Initialization Property set: DBPROPSET_DBINIT Type: VT_BSTR Typical R/W: R/W Description: User ID The user ID to be used when connecting to the data source object or enumerator.

Property ID	Description
DBPROP_BLOCKINGSTORAGE-OBJECTS	Property group: Rowset Property set: DBPROPSET_ROWSET Column? N Type: VT_BOOL Typical R/W: R/W Description: Blocking Storage Objects Whether storage objects might prevent use of other methods on the rowset. VARIANT_TRUE—Instantiated storage objects might prevent the use of other methods on the rowset. That is, after a storage object is created and before it is released, methods other than those on the storage object might return E_UNEXPECTED. VARIANT_FALSE—Instantiated storage objects do not prevent the use of other methods.
DBPROP_BOOKMARKINFO	Property group: Rowset Property set: DBPROPSET_ROWSET Column? N Type: VT_I4 Typical R/W: R Description: Bookmark Information A bitmask specifying additional information about bookmarks over the rowset. A combination of zero or more of the following: DBPROPVAL_BI_CROSSROWSET—If set, bookmark values returned by this rowset are valid across rowsets with the same metadata. If not set, bookmark values are specific to this rowset and are not guaranteed to return the same values in other rowsets, even those resulting from the same specification.

Property ID	Description
DBPROP_BOOKMARKS	Property group: Rowset Property set: DBPROPSET_ROWSET Column? N Type: VT_BOOL Typical R/W: R/W Description: Use Bookmarks Whether the rowset supports bookmarks. One of the following: VARIANT_TRUE—The rowset supports bookmarks. Column 0 is the bookmark for the rows. Getting this column obtains a bookmark value, which can be used to reposition to the row. VARIANT_FALSE—The rowset does not support bookmarks. The rowset is sequential and the values of the DBPROP_LITERALBOOKMARKS and DBPROP_ORDEREDBOOKMARKS properties are ignored. The value of this property is automatically set to VARIANT_TRUE if the value of DBPROP_IROWSETLOCATE, DBPROP_LITERALBOOKMARKS, or DBPROP_ORDEREDBOOKMARKS is set to VARIANT_TRUE.

Property ID	Description
DBPROP_BOOKMARKSKIPPED	Property group: Rowset Property set: DBPROPSET_ROWSET Column? N Type: VT_BOOL Typical R/W: R/W Description: Skip Deleted Bookmarks Whether the rowset allows **IRowsetLocate::GetRowsAt**, **IRowsetScroll::GetApproximatePosition**, or **IRowsetFind::FindNextRow** to continue if a bookmark row was deleted, is a row to which the consumer does not have access rights, or is no longer a member of the rowset. One of the following: VARIANT_TRUE—**GetRowsAt**, **GetApproximatePosition**, or **FindNextRow** skips the bookmark row and continues with the next row. VARIANT_FALSE—**GetRowsAt**, **GetApproximatePosition**, or **FindNextRow** returns DB_E_BADBOOKMARK.

Property ID	Description
DBPROP_BOOKMARKTYPE	Property group: Rowset Property set: DBPROPSET_ROWSET Column? N Type: VT_I4 Typical R/W: R/W Description: Bookmark Type The bookmark type supported by the rowset. One of the following: DBPROPVAL_BMK_NUMERIC—The bookmark type is numeric. Numeric bookmarks are based on a row property that is not dependent on the values of the row's columns. For example, they can be based on the absolute position of the row within a rowset or on a row ID that the storage engine assigned to a tuple at its creation. The validity of numeric bookmarks is not changed by modifying the row's columns. DBPROPVAL_BMK_KEY—The bookmark type is key. Key bookmarks are based on the values of one or more of the row's columns; these values form a unique key for each row. A key bookmark may be left dangling if the key values of the corresponding row are changed. For more information, see "Bookmark Types" in Chapter 4, "Rowsets."
DBPROP_BYREFACCESSORS	Property group: Data Source Information Property set: DBPROPSET_DATASOURCEINFO Type: VT_BOOL Typical R/W: R Description: Pass By Ref Accessors Whether the provider supports the DBACCESSOR_PASSBYREF flag in **IAccessor::CreateAccessor**. This applies both to row and to parameter accessors.

Property ID	Description
DBPROP_CACHEDEFERRED	Property group: Rowset Property set: DBPROPSET_ROWSET Column? Y Type: VT_BOOL Typical R/W: R/W Description: Cache Deferred Columns VARIANT_TRUE—The provider caches the value of a deferred column when the consumer first gets a value from that column. When the consumer later gets a value from the column, the provider returns the value in the cache. The contents of the cache can be overwritten by **IRowsetChange::SetData** or **IRowsetRefresh::RefreshVisibleData**. The cached value is released when the row is released. Consumers should set the value of this property to VARIANT_TRUE rather sparingly, because it might require substantial memory use in the provider. Such use might limit the number of rows that can be held at one time. Setting the value of this property to VARIANT_TRUE automatically sets the value of the DBPROP_DEFERRED property to VARIANT_TRUE. VARIANT_FALSE—The provider does not cache the value of a deferred column, and multiple calls to **IRowset::GetData** for the column can return different values.
DBPROP_CANFETCHBACKWARDS	Property group: Rowset Property set: DBPROPSET_ROWSET Column? N Type: VT_BOOL Typical R/W: R/W Description: Fetch Backwards Whether the rowset can fetch backward. VARIANT_TRUE—*cRows* in **IRowset::GetNextRows**, **IRowsetLocate::GetRowsAt**, and **IRowsetScroll::GetRowsAtRatio** can be negative. When it is negative, these methods fetch rows backward from the specified row. VARIANT_FALSE—*cRows* must be non-negative.

Property ID	Description
DBPROP_CANHOLDROWS	Property group: Rowset Property set: DBPROPSET_ROWSET Column? N Type: VT_BOOL Typical R/W: R/W Description: Hold Rows VARIANT_TRUE—The rowset allows the consumer to retrieve more rows or change the next fetch position while holding previously fetched rows with pending changes. VARIANT_FALSE—The rowset requires pending changes to be transmitted to the data source object and all rows to be released before fetching additional rows, inserting new rows, or changing the next fetch position. **Note** If the provider makes no optimizations for releasing all rows between fetches, it is not required to return DB_E_ROWSNOTRELEASED when retrieving rows without releasing the previously held set of row handles. Such providers do not return an error when setting DBPROP_CANHOLDROWS to VARIANT_FALSE but always return VARIANT_TRUE if the consumer calls **IRowsetInfo::GetProperties** for DBPROP_CANHOLDROWS.
DBPROP_CANSCROLLBACKWARDS	Property group: Rowset Property set: DBPROPSET_ROWSET Column? N Type: VT_BOOL Typical R/W: R/W Description: Scroll Backwards Whether the rowset can scroll backward. VARIANT_TRUE—*lRowsOffset* in **IRowset::GetNextRows** or **IRowsetLocate::GetRowsAt** can be negative. VARIANT_FALSE—*lRowsOffset* must be non-negative. If the rowset supports **IRowsetLocate**, the value of this property is VARIANT_TRUE because this method supports backward scrolling by definition.

Property ID	Description
DBPROP_CATALOGLOCATION	Property group: Data Source Information Property set: DBPROPSET_DATASOURCEINFO Type: VT_I4 Typical R/W: R Description: Catalog Location The position of the catalog name in a qualified table name in a text command. One of the following: DBPROPVAL_CL_START—The catalog name is at the start of the fully qualified name. For example, a dBASE provider returns DBPROPVAL_CL_START because the directory (catalog name) is at the start of the table name, as in \EMPDATA\Emp.dbf. DBPROPVAL_CL_END—The catalog name is at the end of the fully qualified name. For example, an ORACLE server provider returns DBPROPVAL_CL_END because the catalog name is at the end of the table name, as in ADMIN.EMP@EMPDATA.
DBPROP_CATALOGTERM	Property group: Data Source Information Property set: DBPROPSET_DATASOURCEINFO Type: VT_BSTR Typical R/W: R Description: Catalog Term The name the data source object uses for a catalog; for example, "catalog", "database", or "directory". This is used for building user interfaces.

Property ID	Description
DBPROP_CATALOGUSAGE	Property group: Data Source Information Property set: DBPROPSET_DATASOURCEINFO Type: VT_I4 Typical R/W: R Description: Catalog Usage A bitmask specifying how catalog names can be used in text commands. A combination of zero or more of the following: DBPROPVAL_CU_DML_STATEMENTS—Catalog names are supported in all Data Manipulation Language statements. DBPROPVAL_CU_TABLE_DEFINITION—Catalog names are supported in all table definition statements. DBPROPVAL_CU_INDEX_DEFINITION—Catalog names are supported in all index definition statements. DBPROPVAL_CU_PRIVILEGE_DEFINITION—Catalog names are supported in all privilege definition statements.
DBPROP_CHANGEINSERTEDROWS	Property group: Rowset Property set: DBPROPSET_ROWSET Column? N Type: VT_BOOL Typical R/W: R/W Description: Change Inserted Rows VARIANT_TRUE—The consumer can call **IRowsetChange::DeleteRows** or **IRowsetChange::SetData** for newly inserted rows. VARIANT_FALSE—If the consumer calls **DeleteRows** or **SetData** for newly inserted rows, **DeleteRows** returns a status of DBROWSTATUS_E_NEWLYINSERTED for the row and **SetData** returns DB_E_NEWLYINSERTED. A newly inserted row is defined to be a row for which the insertion has been transmitted to the data source object, as opposed to a pending insert row. For some providers, this property may imply other properties.

Property ID	Description
DBPROP_COL_AUTOINCREMENT	Property group: Column Property set: DBPROPSET_COLUMN Type: VT_BOOL Typical R/W: R/W Description: Autoincrement Whether the values of the column are autoincrementing. One of the following: VARIANT_TRUE—The values of the column are autoincrementing. VARIANT_FALSE—The values of the column are not autoincrementing. If this property is read-only, whether or not a column is autoincrementing is a property of the datatype. If this property is read/write, DBPROP_COL_AUTOINCREMENT can be specified for the column, provided the AUTO_UNIQUE_VALUE property of the underlying datatype is VARIANT_TRUE in the PROVIDER_TYPES schema rowset.
DBPROP_COL_DEFAULT	Property group: Column Property set: DBPROPSET_COLUMN Type: Any Typical R/W: R/W Description: Default A VARIANT specifying the default value for an object—typically a domain or column. If the default value is a string, the string must be quoted so that it can be distinguished from an object of the same name. For example, 'Salary' is a string, but Salary is an object, such as a column.
DBPROP_COL_DESCRIPTION	Property group: Column Property set: DBPROPSET_COLUMN Type: VT_BSTR Typical R/W: R/W Description: Description A string specifying a human-readable description of the specified column.

Property ID	Description
DBPROP_COL_FIXEDLENGTH	Property group: Column Property set: DBPROPSET_COLUMN Type: VT_BOOL Typical R/W: R/W Description: Fixed Length Whether a column is fixed-length or variable-length. If the value of this property is VARIANT_TRUE, the column is fixed-length and *ulColumnSize* in the DBCOLUMNDESC structure contains the fixed-length value. If the value of this property is VARIANT_FALSE or is not specified, the column is variable-length and *ulColumnSize* represents the maximum size of the column. This property does not apply to, and should be ignored for, types other than DBTYPE_STR, DBYTPE_WSTR, and DBTYPE_BYTES. For information about the DBCOLUMNDESC structure, see **ITableDefinition::CreateTable** in Part 2, "OLE DB Reference."
DBPROP_COL_NULLABLE	Property group: Column Property set: DBPROPSET_COLUMN Type: VT_BOOL Typical R/W: R/W Description: Nullable Whether a column can contain a NULL value. One of the following: VARIANT_TRUE—The column can contain NULL values. VARIANT_FALSE—The column cannot contain NULL values.

Property ID	Description
DBPROP_COL_PRIMARYKEY	Property group: Column Property set: DBPROPSET_COLUMN Type: VT_BOOL Typical R/W: R/W Description: Primary Key Whether the column is part of the primary key. One of the following: VARIANT_TRUE—The column is part of the primary key of the table. VARIANT_FALSE—The column is not part of the primary key of the table.
DBPROP_COL_UNIQUE	Property group: Column Property set: DBPROPSET_COLUMN Type: VT_BOOL Typical R/W: R/W Description: Unique Whether values of the column must be unique in the table. One of the following: VARIANT_TRUE—The values of the column must be unique within the table. VARIANT_FALSE—The values of the column can be repeated within the table.
DBPROP_COLUMNDEFINITION	Property group: Data Source Information Property set: DBPROPSET_DATASOURCEINFO Type: VT_I4 Typical R/W: R Description: Column Definition A bitmask defining the valid clauses for the definition of a column. A combination of zero or more of the following: DBPROPVAL_CD_NOTNULL—Columns can be created non-nullable.

Property ID	Description
DBPROP_COLUMNLCID	Property group: Column Property set: DBPROPSET_COLUMN Type: VT_I4 Typical R/W: R Description: Column LCID The locale ID of the column.
DBPROP_COLUMNRESTRICT	Property group: Rowset Property set: DBPROPSET_ROWSET Column? N Type: VT_BOOL Typical R/W: R Description: Column Privileges VARIANT_TRUE—Access rights are restricted on a column-by-column basis. If the rowset exposes **IRowsetChange**, **IRowsetChange::SetData** cannot be called for at least one column. A provider must not execute a query that would specify a column for which the consumer has no read access rights. VARIANT_FALSE—Access rights are not restricted on a column-by-column basis. If the rowset exposes **IRowsetChange**, **SetData** can be called for any column in the rowset. If access is restricted both by row and by column, individual columns of particular rows might have their own stricter access rights; the consumer might not even be permitted to read such columns. The column values will be NULL. If a NULL value is contrary to schema rules (NULLs not permitted), the rowset should not count or return any rows that would have this condition. For more information, see DBPROP_ROWRESTRICT, later in this table.
DBPROP_COMMANDTIMEOUT	Property group: Rowset Property set: DBPROPSET_ROWSET Column? N Type: VT_I4 Typical R/W: R/W Description: Command Time Out The number of seconds before a command times out. A value of 0 indicates an infinite timeout.

Property ID	Description
DBPROP_COMMITPRESERVE	Property group: Rowset Property set: DBPROPSET_ROWSET Column? N Type: VT_BOOL Typical R/W: R/W Description: Preserve on Commit VARIANT_TRUE—After committing a transaction, the rowset remains active. That is, it is possible to fetch new rows, update, delete, and insert rows, and so on. VARIANT_FALSE—After committing a transaction, the only operations allowed on a rowset are to release row and accessor handles and to release the rowset.
DBPROP_CONCATNULLBEHAVIOR	Property group: Data Source Information Property set: DBPROPSET_DATASOURCEINFO Type: VT_I4 Typical R/W: R Description: NULL Concatenation Behavior How the data source object handles the concatenation of NULL-valued character data type columns with non–NULL-valued character data type columns. One of the following: DBPROPVAL_CB_NULL—The result is NULL valued. DBPROPVAL_CB_NON_NULL—The result is the concatenation of the non–NULL-valued column or columns.

Property ID	Description
DBPROP_CONNECTIONSTATUS	Property group: Data Source Information Property set: DBPROPSET_DATASOURCEINFO Type: VT_I4 Typical R/W: R Description: Connection Status The status of the current connection. One of the following: DBPROPVAL_CS_UNINITIALIZED—The data source object is in an uninitialized state. DBPROPVAL_CS_INITIALIZED—The data source object is in an initialized state and able to communicate with the data store. DBPROPVAL_CS_COMMUNICATIONFAILURE—The data source object is unable to communicate with the data store. Some providers may have to silently spawn multiple connections to the database in order to support multiple concurrent command, session, and rowset objects, according to DBPROP_MULTIPLECONNECTIONS. For such providers, DBPROP_CONNECTIONSTATUS refers to the status of the primary connection, which was created when the user called **Initialize**.
DBPROP_CURRENTCATALOG	Property group: Data Source Property set: DBPROPSET_DATASOURCE Type: VT_BSTR Typical R/W: R/W Description: Current Catalog The name of the current catalog. The consumer can use the CATALOGS schema rowset to enumerate catalogs.
DBPROP_DATASOURCENAME	Property group: Data Source Information Property set: DBPROPSET_DATASOURCEINFO Type: VT_BSTR Typical R/W: R Description: Data Source Name The name of the data source object. This might be used during the connection process.

Property ID	Description
DBPROP_DATASOURCEREADONLY	Property group: Data Source Information Property set: DBPROPSET_DATASOURCEINFO Type: VT_BOOL Typical R/W: R Description: Read-Only Data Source VARIANT_TRUE—The data source object is read-only. VARIANT_FALSE—The data source object is updatable.
DBPROP_DBMSNAME	Property group: Data Source Information Property set: DBPROPSET_DATASOURCEINFO Type: VT_BSTR Typical R/W: R Description: DBMS Name The name of the product accessed by the provider. For example, "ORACLE Server" or, for Microsoft Excel, "Excel".
DBPROP_DBMSVER	Property group: Data Source Information Property set: DBPROPSET_DATASOURCEINFO Type: VT_BSTR Typical R/W: R Description: DBMS Version The version of the product accessed by the provider. The version is of the form *##.##.####*, where the first two digits are the major version, the next two digits are the minor version, and the last four digits are the release version. The provider must render the product version in this form but can also append the product-specific version. For example, "04.01.0000 Rdb 4.1".

Property ID	Description
DBPROP_DEFERRED	Property group: Rowset Property set: DBPROPSET_ROWSET Column? Y Type: VT_BOOL Typical R/W: R/W Description: Defer Column VARIANT_TRUE—The data in the column is not fetched until an accessor is used on the column. VARIANT_FALSE—The data in the column is fetched when the row containing it is fetched. The value of this property is automatically set to VARIANT_TRUE if the value of the DBPROP_CACHEDEFERRED property is set to VARIANT_TRUE.
DBPROP_DELAYSTORAGEOBJECTS	Property group: Rowset Property set: DBPROPSET_ROWSET Column? N Type: VT_BOOL Typical R/W: R/W Description: Delay Storage Object Updates In delayed update mode, if the value of this property is VARIANT_TRUE, storage objects are also used in delayed update mode. In particular: • Changes to the object are not transmitted to the data source object until **IRowsetUpdate::Update** is called. • **IRowsetUpdate::Undo** undoes any pending changes. • **IRowsetUpdate::GetOriginalData** retrieves the original value of the object; that is, the object's value when the row was last fetched or updated and excluding any changes made since then.

Property ID	Description
	In delayed update mode, if the value of this property is VARIANT_FALSE, storage objects are used in immediate update mode. In particular: • Changes to the object are immediately transmitted to the data source object. • **Update** has no effect on the object. • **Undo** does not undo changes made to the object since the row was last fetched or updated. • **GetOriginalData** retrieves the current value of the object, including changes made since the row was last fetched or updated. In immediate update mode, this property has no effect on storage objects.
DBPROP_DSOTHREADMODEL	Property group: Data Source Information Property set: DBPROPSET_DATASOURCEINFO Type: VT_I4 Typical R/W: R Description: Data Source Object Threading Model A bitmask specifying the threading models supported by the data source object. A combination of one or more of the following: DBPROPVAL_RT_FREETHREAD DBPROPVAL_RT_APTMTTHREAD DBPROPVAL_RT_SINGLETHREAD The threading model returned in this property may be stricter than the thread model registered under the provider's CLSID in the case where additional threading limitations are imposed by underlying components.

Property ID	Description
DBPROP_FILTERCOMPAREOPS	Property group: View Property set: DBPROPSET_VIEW Column? Y Type: VT_I4 Typical R/W: R Description: Filter Operations A bitmask describing the comparison operations supported by **IViewFilter** for a particular column. If no column is specified, this is the full set of comparison operators that may be supported: DBPROPVAL_CO_EQUALITY — Provider supports the following comparison operators: DBCOMPAREOPS_LT DBCOMPAREOPS_LE DBCOMPAREOPS_EQ DBCOMPAREOPS_GE DBCOMPAREOPS_GT DBCOMPAREOPS_NE

Property ID	Description
	DBPROPVAL_CO_STRING — Provider supports the following comparison operator: DBCOMPAREOPS_BEGINSWITH DBPROPVAL_CO_CONTAINS—Provider supports the following comparison operators: DBCOMPAREOPS_CONTAINS DBCOMPAREOPS_NOTCONTAINS DBPROPVAL_CO_BEGINSWITH—Provider supports the following comparison operators: DBCOMPAREOPS_BEGINSWITH DBCOMPAREOPS_NOTBEGINSWITH DBPROPVAL_CO_CASESENSITIVE — Provider supports the DBCOMPAREOPS_CASESENSITIVE modifier. DBPROPVAL_CO_CASEINSENSITIVE — Provider supports the DBCOMPAREOPS_CASEINSENSITIVE modifier. • Providers may support one or the other or both of DBPROPVAL_CO_CASESENSITIVE and DBPROPVAL_CO_CASEINSENSITIVE.

Property ID	Description
DBPROP_FINDCOMPAREOPS	Property group: Rowset Property set: DBPROPSET_ROWSET Column? Y Type: VT_I4 Typical R/W: R Description: Find Operations A bitmask describing the comparison operations supported by **IRowsetFind** for a particular column. If no column is specified, this is the full set of comparison operators that may be supported: DBPROPVAL_CO_EQUALITY — Provider supports the following comparison operators: DBCOMPAREOPS_LT DBCOMPAREOPS_LE DBCOMPAREOPS_EQ DBCOMPAREOPS_GE DBCOMPAREOPS_GT DBCOMPAREOPS_NE DBPROPVAL_CO_STRING — Provider supports the following comparison operators: DBCOMPAREOPS_BEGINSWITH DBPROPVAL_CO_CONTAINS—Provider supports the following comparison operators: DBCOMPAREOPS_CONTAINS DBCOMPAREOPS_NOTCONTAINS DBPROPVAL_CO_BEGINSWITH—Provider supports the following comparison operators: DBCOMPAREOPS_BEGINSWITH DBCOMPAREOPS_NOTBEGINSWITH DBPROPVAL_CO_CASESENSITIVE — Provider supports the DBCOMPAREOPS_CASESENSITIVE modifier. DBPROPVAL_CO_CASEINSENSITIVE — Provider supports the DBCOMPAREOPS_CASEINSENSITIVE modifier. All providers that support **IRowsetFind** must support DBPROPVAL_CO_EQUALITY and DBPROPVAL_CO_STRING.

Property ID	Description
	Providers may support one or the other or both of DBPROPVAL_CO_CASESENSITIVE and DBPROPVAL_CO_CASEINSENSITIVE.
DBPROP_GROUPBY	Property group: Data Source Information Property set: DBPROPSET_DATASOURCEINFO Type: VT_I4 Typical R/W: R Description: **GROUP BY** Support The relationship between the columns in a **GROUP BY** clause and the nonaggregated columns in the select list. One of the following: DBPROPVAL_GB_EQUALS_SELECT—The **GROUP BY** clause must contain all nonaggregated columns in the select list. It cannot contain any other columns. For example, **SELECT DEPT, MAX(SALARY) FROM EMPLOYEE GROUP BY DEPT**. DBPROPVAL_GB_COLLATE—A COLLATE clause can be specified at the end of each grouping column. DBPROPVAL_GB_CONTAINS_SELECT—The **GROUP BY** clause must contain all nonaggregated columns in the select list. It can contain columns that are not in the select list. For example, **SELECT DEPT, MAX(SALARY) FROM EMPLOYEE GROUP BY DEPT, AGE**. DBPROPVAL_GB_NO_RELATION—The columns in the **GROUP BY** clause and the select list are not related. The meaning of nongrouped, nonaggregated columns in the select list is data source object–dependent. For example, **SELECT DEPT, SALARY FROM EMPLOYEE GROUP BY DEPT, AGE**.

Property ID	Description
DBPROP_HETEROGENEOUSTABLES	Property group: Data Source Information Property set: DBPROPSET_DATASOURCEINFO Type: VT_I4 Typical R/W: R Description: Heterogeneous Table Support A bitmask specifying whether the provider can join tables from different catalogs or providers. A combination of zero or more of the following: DBPROPVAL_HT_DIFFERENT_CATALOGS DBPROPVAL_HT_DIFFERENT_PROVIDERS
DBPROP_HIDDENCOLUMNS	Property group: Rowset Property set: DBPROPSET_ROWSET Type: VT_I4 Typical R/W: R Description: Hidden Column Count If DBPROP_UNIQUEROWS is VARIANT_TRUE, the DBPROP_HIDDENCOLUMNS property returns the number of additional "hidden" columns added by the provider to uniquely identify rows within the rowset. These columns are returned by **IColumnsInfo::GetColumnsInfo** and **IColumnsRowset::GetColumnsRowset**. However, they are not included in the count of rows returned by the *pcColumns* argument returned by **IColumnsInfo::GetColumnsInfo**. To determine the total number of columns represented in the *prgInfo* structure returned by **IColumnsInfo::GetColumnsInfo**, including hidden columns, the consumer adds the value of DBPROP_UNIQUEROWS to the count of columns returned from **IColumnsInfo::GetColumnsInfo** in *pcColumns*. If DBPROP_UNIQUEROWS is VARIANT_FALSE, DBPROP_HIDDENCOLUMNS is zero.

Property ID	Description
DBPROP_IACCESSOR DBPROP_ICHAPTEREDROWSET DBPROP_ICOLUMNSINFO DBPROP_ICOLUMNSROWSET DBPROP_ICONNECTIONPOINT-CONTAINER DBPROP_ICONVERTTYPE DBPROP_IDBASYNCHSTATUS DBPROP_IMULTIPLERESULTS DBPROP_IROWSET DBPROP_IROWSETCHANGE DBPROP_IROWSETFIND DBPROP_IROWSETIDENTITY DBPROP_IROWSETINDEX DBPROP_IROWSETINFO DBPROP_IROWSETLOCATE DBPROP_IROWSETREFRESH DBPROP_IROWSETSCROLL DBPROP_IROWSETUPDATE DBPROP_IROWSETVIEW DBPROP_ISUPPORTERRORINFO	Property group: Rowset Property set: DBPROPSET_ROWSET Column? N Type: VT_BOOL Typical R/W: R/W (except as noted below) Description: **IAccessor** **IChapteredRowset** **IColumnsInfo** **IColumnsRowset** **IConnectionPointContainer** **IConvertType** **IDBAsynchStatus** **IMultipleResults** **IRowset** **IRowsetChange** **IRowsetFind** **IRowsetIdentity** **IRowsetIndex** **IRowsetInfo** **IRowsetLocate** **IRowsetRefresh** **IRowsetScroll** **IRowsetUpdate** **IRowsetView** **ISupportErrorInfo** If the value of any of these properties is set to VARIANT_TRUE, the rowset supports the specified interface. Providers that support an interface must support the property associated with that interface with a value of VARIANT_TRUE. These properties are primarily used to request interfaces through **ICommandProperties::Se**tProperties. The values of the DBPROP_IROWSET, DBPROP_IACCESSOR, DBPROP_ICOLUMNSINFO, DBPROP_ICONVERTTYPE, and DBPROP_IROWSETINFO properties are read-only and are always VARIANT_TRUE. They cannot be set to VARIANT_FALSE. If the consumer does not set the value of any of these properties to true, the resulting rowset supports **IRowset, IAccessor**, **IColumnsInfo**, **IConvertType**, and **IRowsetInfo**.

Property ID	Description
	Setting DBPROP_IROWSETLOCATE to VARIANT_TRUE implicitly causes the created rowset to support bookmarks, and **IRowsetInfo::GetProperties** will return VARIANT_TRUE for the property DBPROP_BOOKMARKS. Setting DBPROP_IROWSETUPDATE to VARIANT_TRUE automatically sets DBPROP_IROWSETCHANGE to VARIANT_TRUE.
DBPROP_IDENTIFIERCASE	Property group: Data Source Information Property set: DBPROPSET_DATASOURCEINFO Type: VT_I4 Typical R/W: R Description: Identifier Case Sensitivity How identifiers treat case. One of the following: DBPROPVAL_IC_UPPER—Identifiers in SQL are case-insensitive and are stored in uppercase in system catalog. DBPROPVAL_IC_LOWER—Identifiers in SQL are case-insensitive and are stored in lowercase in system catalog. DBPROPVAL_IC_SENSITIVE—Identifiers in SQL are case-sensitive and are stored in mixed case in system catalog. DBPROPVAL_IC_MIXED—Identifiers in SQL are case-insensitive and are stored in mixed case in system catalog.

Property ID	Description
DBPROP_ILOCKBYTES DBPROP_ISEQUENTIALSTREAM DBPROP_ISTORAGE DBPROP_ISTREAM	Property group: Rowset Property set: DBPROPSET_ROWSET Column? Y Type: VT_BOOL Typical R/W: R/W Description: **ILockBytes** **ISequentialStream** **IStorage** **IStream** If the value of this property is set to VARIANT_TRUE, the rowset is capable of manipulating the contents of columns as a storage object supporting the specified interface. The provider reports its ability to enable this property on a per-column basis by setting the flag DBPROPFLAGS_COLUMNOK. A provider that does not have the ability to turn the property on/off on a per-column basis does not set DBPROPFLAGS_COLUMNOK. Whether or not the property is supported in the rowset as a whole or on a per-column basis, the ability to manipulate a column value as a storage object depends on whether the provider supports the coercion from the column's native type (BLOB or non-BLOB) to the particular storage interface.
DBPROP_IMMOBILEROWS	Property group: Rowset Property set: DBPROPSET_ROWSET Column? N Type: VT_BOOL Typical R/W: R/W Description: Immobile Rows VARIANT_TRUE—The rowset will not reorder inserted or updated rows. For **IRowsetChange::InsertRow**, rows will appear at the end of the rowset. VARIANT_FALSE—If the rowset is ordered, inserted rows and updated rows (where one or more of the columns in the ordering criteria are updated) obey the ordering criteria of the rowset. If the rowset is not ordered, inserted rows are not guaranteed to appear in a determinate position and the position of updated rows is not changed. This property is meaningful only if DBPROP_OWNINSERT is VARIANT_TRUE.

Property ID	Description
DBPROP_INDEX_AUTOUPDATE	Property group: Index Property set: DBPROPSET_INDEX Type: VT_BOOL Typical R/W: R/W Description: Auto-Update Whether the index is maintained automatically when changes are made to the corresponding base table. One of the following: VARIANT_TRUE—The index is automatically maintained. VARIANT_FALSE—The index must be maintained by the consumer through explicit calls to **IRowsetChange**. Ensuring consistency of the index as a result of updates to the associated base table is the responsibility of the consumer. VARIANT_TRUE is always returned when using integrated indexes.
DBPROP_INDEX_CLUSTERED	Property group: Index Property set: DBPROPSET_INDEX Type: VT_BOOL Typical R/W: R/W Description: Clustered Whether an index is clustered. VARIANT_TRUE—The leaf nodes of the index contain full rows, not bookmarks. This is a way to represent a table clustered by key value. VARIANT_FALSE—The leaf nodes of the index contain bookmarks of the base table rows whose key value matches the key value of the index entry.

Property ID	Description
DBPROP_INDEX_FILLFACTOR	Property group: Index Property set: DBPROPSET_INDEX Type: VT_I4 Typical R/W: R/W Description: Fill Factor For a B+-tree index, this property represents the storage utilization factor of page nodes during the creation of the index. The value is an integer from 1 to 100, representing the percentage of use of an index node. For a linear hash index, this property represents the storage utilization of the entire hash structure (the ratio of the used area to the total allocated area) before a file structure expansion occurs.
DBPROP_INDEX_INITIALSIZE	Property group: Index Property set: DBPROPSET_INDEX Type: VT_I4 Typical R/W: R/W Description: Initial Size The total number of bytes allocated to this structure at creation time.
DBPROP_INDEX_NULLCOLLATION	Property group: Index Property set: DBPROPSET_INDEX Type: VT_I4 Typical R/W: R/W Description: NULL Collation How NULLs are collated in the index. One of the following: DBPROPVAL_NC_END—NULLs are collated at the end of the list, regardless of the collation order. DBPROPVAL_NC_START—NULLs are collated at the start of the list, regardless of the collation order. DBPROPVAL_NC_HIGH—NULLs are collated at the high end of the list. DBPROPVAL_NC_LOW—NULLs are collated at the low end of the list.

Property ID	Description
DBPROP_INDEX_NULLS	Property group: Index Property set: DBPROPSET_INDEX Type: VT_I4 Typical R/W: R/W Description: NULL Keys Whether NULL keys are allowed. One of the following values: DBPROPVAL_IN_DISALLOWNULL—The index does not allow entries where the key columns are NULL. If the consumer attempts to insert an index entry with a NULL key, the provider returns an error. DBPROPVAL_IN_IGNORENULL—The index does not insert entries containing NULL keys. If the consumer attempts to insert an index entry with a NULL key, then the provider ignores that entry and no error code is returned. DBPROPVAL_IN_IGNOREANYNULL—The index does not insert entries where some column key has a NULL value. For an index having a multicolumn search key, if the consumer inserts an index entry with NULL value in some column of the search key, the provider ignores that entry and no error code is returned.
DBPROP_INDEX_PRIMARYKEY	Property group: Index Property set: DBPROPSET_INDEX Type: VT_BOOL Typical R/W: R/W Description: Primary Key Whether the index represents the primary key on the table.
DBPROP_INDEX_SORTBOOKMARKS	Property group: Index Property set: DBPROPSET_INDEX Type: VT_BOOL Typical R/W: R/W Description: Sort Bookmarks How the index treats repeated keys. One of the following: VARIANT_TRUE—The index sorts repeated keys by bookmark. VARIANT_FALSE—The index does not sort repeated keys by bookmark.

Property ID	Description
DBPROP_INDEX_TEMPINDEX	Property group: Index Property set: DBPROPSET_INDEX Type: VT_BOOL Typical R/W: R/W Description: Temporary Index Whether the index is temporary. One of the following: VARIANT_TRUE—The index is destroyed when the session is released. VARIANT_FALSE—The index is created permanently.
DBPROP_INDEX_TYPE	Property group: Index Property set: DBPROPSET_INDEX Type: VT_I4 Typical R/W: R/W Description: Index Type The type of the index. One of the following: DBPROPVAL_IT_BTREE—The index is a B+-tree. DBPROPVAL_IT_HASH—The index is a hash file using linear or extensible hashing. DBPROPVAL_IT_CONTENT—The index is a content index. DBPROPVAL_IT_OTHER—The index is some other type of index.
DBPROP_INDEX_UNIQUE	Property group: Index Property set: DBPROPSET_INDEX Type: VT_BOOL Typical R/W: R/W Description: Unique Whether index keys must be unique. VARIANT_TRUE: The index keys must be unique. VARIANT_FALSE: Duplicate keys are allowed.

Property ID	Description
DBPROP_INIT_ASYNCH	Property group: Initialization Property set: DBPROPSET_DBINIT Type: VT_I4 Typical R/W: R/W Description: Asynchronous Processing A bitmask specifying the asynchronous processing performed on the data source object. A combination of zero or more of the following DBPROPVAL_ASYNCH_INITIALIZE: **IDBInitialize::Initialize** returns immediately, but the actual initialization of the data source object is done asynchronously. The data source object behaves as an unititialized data source object prior to completing the initialization process, except that any call to **IDBInitialize** returns E_UNEXPECTED. If no bits are set (the default), **IDBInitialize::Initialize** does not return until the data source object is completely initialized.
DBPROP_INIT_CATALOG	Property group: Initialization Property set: DBPROPSET_DBINIT Typical R/W: R/W Description: Initial Catalog The name of the initial, or default, catalog to use when connecting to the data source object. If the provider supports changing the catalog for an initialized object, the consumer can specify a different catalog name through the DBPROP_CURRENCATALOG property in the DBPROPSET_DATASOURCE property set after initialization.

Property ID	Description
DBPROP_INIT_DATASOURCE	Property group: Initialization Property set: DBPROPSET_DBINIT Type: VT_BSTR Typical R/W: R/W Description: Data Source The name of the database or enumerator to connect to. DBPROP_INIT_DATASOURCE is used to identify the data source object to connect to—for example, a relational database server or a local file. If the provider uses two-part naming to identify the data source object, the data source object name is qualified with the location specified in DBPROP_INIT_LOCATION.
DBPROP_INIT_HWND	Property group: Initialization Property set: DBPROPSET_DBINIT Type: VT_I4 Typical R/W: R/W Description: Window Handle The window handle to be used if the data source object or enumerator needs to prompt for additional information.

Property ID	Description
DBPROP_INIT_IMPERSONATION_LEVEL	Property group: Initialization Property set: DBPROPSET_DBINIT Type: VT_I4 Typical R/W: R/W Description: Impersonation Level The level of impersonation that the server is allowed to use when impersonating the client. This property applies only to network connections other than Remote Procedure Call (RPC) connections; these impersonation levels are similar to those provided by RPC. One of the following: DB_IMP_LEVEL_ANONYMOUS—The client is anonymous to the server. The server process cannot obtain identification information about the client and cannot impersonate the client. DB_IMP_LEVEL_IDENTIFY—The server can obtain the client's identity. The server can impersonate the client for ACL checking but cannot access system objects as the client. DB_IMP_LEVEL_IMPERSONATE—The server process can impersonate the client's security context while acting on behalf of the client. This information is obtained when the connection is established, not on every call. DB_IMP_LEVEL_DELEGATE—The process can impersonate the client's security context while acting on behalf of the client. The server process can also make outgoing calls to other servers while acting on behalf of the client.

Property ID	Description
DBPROP_INIT_LCID	Property group: Initialization Property set: DBPROPSET_DBINIT Type: VT_I4 Typical R/W: R/W Description: Locale Identifier The locale ID of preference for the consumer. Consumers specify the LCID at initialization. This provides a method for the server to determine the consumer's LCID of choice in cases where it can use this information. This property does not guarantee that all text returned to the consumer will be translated according to the LCID. Providers may wish to set the *dwOptions* of the DBPROP structure for this property to DBPROPOPTIONS_OPTIONAL.
DBPROP_INIT_LOCATION	Property group: Initialization Property set: DBPROPSET_DBINIT Type: VT_BSTR Typical R/W: R/W Description: Location The location of the data source object or enumerator to connect to. Typically, this will be a server name. DBPROP_INIT_LOCATION is used as the first part of a two-part name to qualify the data source object specified in the DBPROP_INIT_DATASOURCE property. For example, if the data source object is defined on a different machine, this might be the machine name on which to look for the data source object definition. This is typically not used if the provider can identify the data source object by using a single name, such as the name of an RDBMS server, that the consumer can use to identify the data source object directly.

Property ID	Description
DBPROP_INIT_MODE	Property group: Initialization Property set: DBPROPSET_DBINIT Type: VT_I4 Typical R/W: R/W Description: Mode A bitmask specifying access permissions. A combination of zero or more of the following: DB_MODE_READ—Read-only. DB_MODE_WRITE—Write-only. DB_MODE_READWRITE—Read/write (DB_MODE_READ | DB_MODE_WRITE). DB_MODE_SHARE_DENY_READ—Prevents others from opening in read mode. DB_MODE_SHARE_DENY_WRITE—Prevents others from opening in write mode. DB_MODE_SHARE_EXCLUSIVE—Prevents others from opening in read/write mode (DB_MODE_SHARE_DENY_READ | DB_MODE_SHARE_DENY_WRITE). DB_MODE_SHARE_DENY_NONE—Neither read nor write access can be denied to others.

Property ID	Description
DBPROP_INIT_OLEDBSERVICES	Property group: Initialization Property set: DBPROPSET_DBINIT Type: VT_I4 Typical R/W: R/W Description: OLE DB Services A bitmask specifying OLE DB services to enable. A combination of zero or more of the following: DBPROPVAL_OS_RESOURCEPOOLING—Resources should be pooled. DBPROPVAL_OS_TXNENLISTMENT—Sessions in a Microsoft Transaction Server environment should automatically be enlisted in a global transaction where required (implies DBPROPVAL_OS_RESOURCEPOOLING). DBPROPVAL_OS_ENABLEALL (default)—All services should be invoked. By default, all services are enabled and invoked as requested. Individual services can be deselected by specifying the bitwise-AND of DBPROPVAL_OS_ENABLEALL along with the bitwise complement of any services to be deselected. For example, DBPROPVAL_OS_ENABLEALL &~DBPROPVAL_OS_TXNENLISTMENT enables all services except automatic transaction enlistment in a Microsoft Transaction Server environment.

Property ID	Description
DBPROP_INIT_PROMPT	Property group: Initialization Property set: DBPROPSET_DBINIT Type: VT_I2 Typical R/W: R/W Description: Prompt Whether to prompt the user during initialization. One of the following values: DBPROMPT_PROMPT—Always prompt the user for initialization information. DBPROMPT_COMPLETE—Prompt the user only if more information is needed. DBPROMPT_COMPLETEREQUIRED—Prompt the user only if more information is needed. Do not allow the user to enter optional information. DBPROMPT_NOPROMPT—Do not prompt the user. Information obtained from the user during prompting is available following initialization by calling **GetProperties** for the appropriate initialization properties.

Property ID	Description
DBPROP_INIT_PROTECTION_LEVEL	Property group: Initialization Property set: DBPROPSET_DBINIT Type: VT_I4 Typical R/W: R/W Description: Protection Level The level of protection of data sent between client and server. This property applies only to network connections other than RPC connections; these protection levels are similar to those provided by RPC. One of the following: DB_PROT_LEVEL_NONE—Performs no authentication of data sent to the server. DB_PROT_LEVEL_CONNECT—Authenticates only when the client establishes the connection with the server. DB_PROT_LEVEL_CALL—Authenticates the source of the data at the beginning of each request from the client to the server. DB_PROT_LEVEL_PKT—Authenticates that all data received is from the client. DB_PROT_LEVEL_PKT_INTEGRITY—Authenticates that all data received is from the client and that it has not been changed in transit. DB_PROT_LEVEL_PKT_PRIVACY—Authenticates that all data received is from the client, that it has not been changed in transit, and protects the privacy of the data by encrypting it.
DBPROP_INIT_PROVIDERSTRING	Property group: Initialization Property set: DBPROPSET_DBINIT Type: VT_BSTR Typical R/W: R/W Description: Extended Properties A string containing provider-specific, extended connection information. Use of this property implies that the consumer knows how this string will be interpreted and used by the provider. Consumers should use this property only for provider-specific connection information that cannot be explicitly described through the property mechanism.

Property ID	Description
DBPROP_INIT_TIMEOUT	Property group: Initialization Property set: DBPROPSET_DBINIT Type: VT_I4 Typical R/W: R/W Description: Connect Timeout The amount of time (in seconds) to wait for initialization to complete. For maximum user concurrency and component interoperability, providers for whom initialization is a potentially lengthy operation, such as connection across a network, are strongly encouraged to support this property.
DBPROP_IVIEWCHAPTER DBPROP_IVIEWFILTER DBPROP_IVIEWROWSET DBPROP_IVIEWSORT DBPROP_IACCESSOR DBPROP_ICOLUMNSINFO DBPROP_ISUPPORTERRORINFO	Property group: View Property set: DBPROPSET_VIEW Column? N Type: VT_BOOL Typical R/W: R/W Description: **IViewChapter** **IViewFilter** **IViewRowset** **IViewSort** **IAccessor** **IColumnsInfo** **ISupportErrorInfo** For all methods returning a **Rowset** or **View** object, in addition to **Rowset** properties, DBPROPSET_VIEW should be set before creating a view.

Property ID	Description
DBPROP_LITERALBOOKMARKS	Property group: Rowset Property set: DBPROPSET_ROWSET Column? N Type: VT_BOOL Typical R/W: R/W Description: Literal Bookmarks VARIANT_TRUE—Bookmarks can be compared literally. That is, they can be compared as a sequence of bytes. Furthermore, if the bookmarks are ordered (as specified by the DBPROP_ORDEREDBOOKMARKS property), the bytes are guaranteed to be ordered so that an arithmetic comparison of their scalar types yields the same result as a call to **IRowsetLocate::Compare**. Setting the value of this property to VARIANT_TRUE automatically sets the value of DBPROP_BOOKMARKS to VARIANT_TRUE. VARIANT_FALSE—Bookmarks can only be compared with **IRowsetLocate::Compare**.
DBPROP_LITERALIDENTITY	Property group: Rowset Property set: DBPROPSET_ROWSET Column? N Type: VT_BOOL Typical R/W: R Description: Literal Row Identity VARIANT_TRUE—The consumer can perform a binary comparison of two row handles to determine whether they point to the same row. VARIANT_FALSE—The consumer must call **IRowsetIdentity::IsSameRow** to determine whether two row handles point to the same row. Whether the handle of a newly inserted row can be successfully compared to another handle is specified by the DBPROP_STRONGIDENTITY property. For more information about row identity, see "Uniqueness of Rows in the Rowset" in Chapter 4, "Rowsets."

Property ID	Description
DBPROP_LOCKMODE	Property group: Rowset Property set: DBPROPSET_ROWSET Column? N Type: VT_I4 Typical R/W: R/W Description: Lock Mode The level of locking peformed by the rowset. One of the following: DBPROPVAL_LM_NONE—The provider is not required to lock rows at any time to ensure successful updates. Updates may fail when sent to the server for reasons of concurrency (for example, if someone else has updated the row). DBPROPVAL_LM_SINGLEROW—The provider uses the minimum level of locking necessary to ensure that changes successfully written to a single row returned by the most recent fetch will not fail due to a concurrency violation if **Update** is called before any additional rows are retrieved. Typically, this means that the provider takes a lock on the row when **SetData** is first called on the row, but the provider may lock the row as early as when it is read in order to guarantee that calling **Update** will succeed. Lock Mode and Isolation Level are closely related but distinct. A consumer's isolation level specifies the isolation of that consumer from changes made by other users to the underlying data. Lock mode defines when underlying data is locked in order to ensure updates succeed. The provider may use locking in order to enforce higher levels of isolation, in which case a higher level of locking may occur than required to enforce the specified lock mode. Lock mode specifies the minimum level of locking.
DBPROP_MAXINDEXSIZE	Property group: Data Source Information Property set: DBPROPSET_DATASOURCEINFO Type: VT_I4 Typical R/W: R Description: Maximum Index Size The maximum number of bytes allowed in the combined columns of an index. If there is no specified limit or the limit is unknown, this value is set to zero.

Property ID	Description
DBPROP_MAXOPENCHAPTERS	Property group: Data Source Information Property set: DBPROPSET_DATASOURCEINFO Type: VT_I4 Typical R/W: R Description: Maximum Open Chapters The maximum number of chapters that can be open at any time. If a chapter must be released before a new chapter can be opened, this value is one; if the provider does not support chapters, this value is zero.
DBPROP_MAXOPENROWS	Property group: Rowset Property set: DBPROPSET_ROWSET Column? N Type: VT_I4 Typical R/W: R/W Description: Maximum Open Rows The maximum number of rows that can be active at the same time. This limit does not reflect resource limitations such as RAM but does apply if the rowset implementation uses some strategy that results in a limit. If there is no limit, the value of this property is zero. The provider is free to support a greater number of active rows than the maximum specified by the consumer. In this case, the provider will return its actual maximum number of active rows instead of the value specified by the consumer.
DBPROP_MAXORSINFILTER	Property group: View Property set: DBPROPSET_VIEW Type: VT_I4 Typical R/W: R Description: Maximum OR Conditions The maximum number of disjunct conditions that can be supported in a view filter. Multiple conditions (rows) of a view filter are joined in a logical OR. Providers that do not support joining multiple conditions return a value of 1. Providers that do not support view filters return a value of 0. This value applies only to the conditions that can be joined in a logical OR in a call to **SetFilter**; it does not imply the maximum number of OR conditions that may exist in a command.

Property ID	Description
DBPROP_MAXPENDINGROWS	Property group: Rowset Property set: DBPROPSET_ROWSET Column? N Type: VT_I4 Typical R/W: R/W Description: Maximum Pending Rows The maximum number of rows that can have pending changes at the same time. This limit does not reflect resource limitations such as Random Access Memory (RAM) but does apply if the rowset implementation uses some strategy that results in a limit. If there is no limit, this value is zero. The provider is free to support a greater number of pending rows than the maximum specified by the consumer. In this case, the provider will return its actual maximum number of pending rows instead of the value specified by the consumer.
DBPROP_MAXROWS	Property group: Rowset Property set: DBPROPSET_ROWSET Column? N Type: VT_I4 Typical R/W: R/W Description: Maximum Rows The maximum number of rows that can be returned in a rowset. If there is no limit, this value is zero. If the provider supports setting DBPROP_MAXROWS, the provider must ensure that the rowset never contains more than the specified number of rows.
DBPROP_MAXROWSIZE	Property group: Data Source Information Property set: DBPROPSET_DATASOURCEINFO Type: VT_I4 Typical R/W: R Description: Maximum Row Size The maximum length of a single row in a table. If there is no specified limit or the limit is unknown, this value is set to zero.

Property ID	Description
DBPROP_MAXROWSIZEINCLUDES-BLOB	Property group: Data Source Information Property set: DBPROPSET_DATASOURCEINFO Type: VT_BOOL Typical R/W: R Description: Maximum Row Size Includes BLOB VARIANT_TRUE—The maximum row size returned for the DBPROP_MAXROWSIZE property includes the length of all BLOB data. VARIANT_FALSE—The maximum row size does not include the length of all BLOB data.
DBPROP_MAXSORTCOLUMNS	Property group: View Property set: DBPROPSET_VIEW Type: VT_I4 Typical R/W: R Description: Maximum Sort Columns The maximum number of columns that can be supported in a View Sort. If there is no specified limit or the limit is unknown, this value is set to zero. This value applies only to the number of sort columns that can be specified in a call to **SetSortOrder**; it does not imply the maximum number of columns that can be used to sort in a command.
DBPROP_MAXTABLESINSELECT	Property group: Data Source Information Property set: DBPROPSET_DATASOURCEINFO Type: VT_I4 Typical R/W: R Description: Maximum Tables in SELECT The maximum number of tables allowed in the **FROM** clause of a **SELECT** statement. If there is no specified limit or the limit is unknown, this value is set to zero.

Property ID	Description
DBPROP_MAYWRITECOLUMN	Property group: Rowset Property set: DBPROPSET_ROWSET Column? Y Type: VT_BOOL Typical R/W: R/W Description: Column Writable Whether a particular column is writable or not. This property can be set implicitly through the command used to create the rowset. For example, if the rowset is created by the SQL statement **SELECT A, B FROM MyTable FOR UPDATE OF A**, this property is VARIANT_TRUE for column A and VARIANT_FALSE for column B.
DBPROP_MEMORYUSAGE	Property group: Rowset Property set: DBPROPSET_ROWSET Column? N Type: VT_I4 Typical R/W: R/W Description: Memory Usage This property estimates the amount of memory that can be used by the rowset. If it is 0, the rowset can use unlimited memory. If it is between 1 and 99 inclusive, the rowset can use the specified percentage of total available virtual memory (physical and page file). If it is greater than or equal to 100, the rowset can use up to the specified number of kilobytes of memory.

Property ID	Description
DBPROP_MULTIPLECONNECTIONS	Property group: Data Source Property set: DBPROPSET_DATASOURCE Type: VT_BOOL Typical R/W: R/W Description: Multiple Connections Some providers may have to spawn multiple connections to the database in order to support multiple concurrent command, session, and rowset objects. Such providers may expose DBPROP_MULTIPLECONNECTIONS in order to let the consumer disable making additional connections under the covers. Providers that can support multiple concurrent command, session, and rowset objects without spawning multiple connections do not support this property. VARIANT_TRUE (default)—The provider silently creates additional connections as required in order to support concurrent command, session, and rowset objects. VARIANT_FALSE—The provider returns DB_E_OBJECTOPEN if a method would require spawning an additional connection to the database.
DBPROP_MULTIPLEPARAMSETS	Property group: Data Source Information Property set: DBPROPSET_DATASOURCEINFO Type: VT_BOOL Typical R/W: R Description: Multiple Parameter Sets VARIANT_TRUE—The provider supports multiple parameter sets. VARIANT_FALSE—The provider supports only a single set of parameters per execution. All providers that support parameters must support this property. Providers that do not support parameters must not support this property.

Property ID	Description
DBPROP_MULTIPLERESULTS	Property group: Data Source Information Property set: DBPROPSET_DATASOURCEINFO Type: VT_I4 Typical R/W: R Description: Multiple Results A bitmask specifying whether the provider supports multiple results objects and what restrictions it places on these objects. A combination of zero or more of the following: DBPROPVAL_MR_SUPPORTED—The provider supports multiple results objects. DBPROPVAL_MR_CONCURRENT—More than one rowset created by the same multiple results object can exist concurrently. If this bit is not set, the consumer must release the current rowset before calling **IMultipleResults::GetResult** to get the next result. If multiple results objects are not supported, DBPROPVAL_MR_NOTSUPPORTED is returned. For more information about multiple results, see "Multiple Results" in Chapter 3, "Commands."
DBPROP_MULTIPLESTORAGEOBJECTS	Property group: Data Source Information Property set: DBPROPSET_DATASOURCEINFO Type: VT_BOOL Typical R/W: R Description: Multiple Storage Objects VARIANT_TRUE—The provider supports multiple, open storage objects at the same time. VARIANT_FALSE—The provider supports only one open storage object at a time. Any method that attempts to open a second storage object returns a status of DBSTATUS_E_CANTCREATE for the column on which it attempted to open the second storage object, whether or not the objects are constructed over the same column, different columns in the same row, or different rows.

Property ID	Description
DBPROP_MULTITABLEUPDATE	Property group: Data Source Information Property set: DBPROPSET_DATASOURCEINFO Type: VT_BOOL Typical R/W: R Description: Multi-Table Update VARIANT_TRUE—The provider can update rowsets derived from multiple tables. VARIANT_FALSE—The provider cannot update rowsets derived from multiple tables.
DBPROP_NOTIFICATION-GRANULARITY	Property group: Rowset Property set: DBPROPSET_ROWSET Column? N Type: VT_I4 Typical R/W: R/W Description: Notification Granularity DBPROPVAL_NT_SINGLEROW—For methods that operate on multiple rows, the provider calls **IRowsetNotify::OnRowChange** separately for each phase for each row. A cancellation affects a single row; it does not affect the other rows, and notifications are still sent for these rows. DBPROPVAL_NT_MULTIPLEROWS—For methods that operate on multiple rows, and then for each phase, the provider calls **OnRowChange** once for all rows that succeed and once for all rows that fail. This separation can occur at each phase where a change can fail. For example, if **IRowsetChange::DeleteRows** deletes some rows and fails to delete others during the Preliminary Work phase, it calls **OnRowChange** twice: once with DBEVENTPHASE_SYNCHAFTER and the array of handles of rows that it deleted, and once with DBEVENTPHASE_FAILEDTODO and the array of handles of rows it failed to delete. A cancellation affects all rows with handles that were passed to **OnRowChange**. DBPROP_NOTIFICATIONGRANULARITY does not affect how providers return notifications about events that affect columns or the entire rowset.

Property ID	Description
DBPROP_NOTIFICATIONPHASES	Property group: Rowset Property set: DBPROPSET_ROWSET Column? N Type: VT_I4 Typical R/W: R Description: Notification Phases A bitmask specifying the notification phases supported by the provider. A combination of two or more of the following: DBPROPVAL_NP_OKTODO DBPROPVAL_NP_ABOUTTODO DBPROPVAL_NP_SYNCHAFTER DBPROPVAL_NP_FAILEDTODO DBPROPVAL_NP_DIDEVENT The DBPROPVAL_NP_FAILEDTODO and DBPROPVAL_NP_DIDEVENT bits must be returned by all providers that support notifications.
DBPROP_NOTIFYCOLUMNSET DBPROP_NOTIFYROWDELETE DBPROP_NOTIFYROWFIRSTCHANGE DBPROP_NOTIFYROWINSERT DBPROP_NOTIFYROWRESYNCH DBPROP_NOTIFYROWSETRELEASE DBPROP_NOTIFYROWSETFETCH-POSITIONCHANGE DBPROP_NOTIFYROWUNDOCHANGE DBPROP_NOTIFYROWUNDODELETE DBPROP_NOTIFYROWUNDOINSERT DBPROP_NOTIFYROWUPDATE	Property group: Rowset Property set: DBPROPSET_ROWSET Column? N Type: VT_I4 Typical R/W: R Description: Column Set Notification Row Delete Notification Row First Change Notification Row Insert Notification Row Resynchronization Notification Rowset Release Notification Rowset Fetch Position Change Notification Row Undo Change Notification Row Undo Delete Notification Row Undo Insert Notification Row Update Notification A bitmask specifying whether the notification phase is cancellable. A combination of zero or more of the following: DBPROPVAL_NP_OKTODO DBPROPVAL_NP_ABOUTTODO DBPROPVAL_NP_SYNCHAFTER

Property ID	Description
DBPROP_NULLCOLLATION	Property group: Data Source Information Property set: DBPROPSET_DATASOURCEINFO Type: VT_I4 Typical R/W: R Description: NULL Collation Order Where NULLs are sorted in a list. One of the following: DBPROPVAL_NC_END—NULLs are sorted at the end of the list, regardless of the sort order. DBPROPVAL_NC_HIGH—NULLs are sorted at the high end of the list. DBPROPVAL_NC_LOW—NULLs are sorted at the low end of the list. DBPROPVAL_NC_START—NULLs are sorted at the start of the list, regardless of the sort order.
DBPROP_OLEOBJECTS	Property group: Data Source Information Property set: DBPROPSET_DATASOURCEINFO Type: VT_I4 Typical R/W: R Description: COM Object Support A bitmask specifying the ways in which the provider supports access to BLOBs and COM objects stored in columns. A combination of zero or more of the following: DBPROPVAL_OO_BLOB—The provider supports access to BLOBs as structured storage objects. A consumer determines what interfaces are supported through DBPROP_STRUCTUREDSTORAGE. DBPROPVAL_OO_IPERSIST—The provider supports access to COM objects through **IPersistStream**, **IPersistStreamInit**, or **IPersistStorage**.

Property ID	Description
DBPROP_ORDERBYCOLUMNS-INSELECT	Property group: Data Source Information Property set: DBPROPSET_DATASOURCEINFO Type: VT_BOOL Typical R/W: R Description: ORDER BY Columns in Select List VARIANT_TRUE—Columns in an **ORDER BY** clause must be in the select list. VARIANT_FALSE—Columns in an **ORDER BY** clause are not required to be in the select list.
DBPROP_ORDEREDBOOKMARKS	Property group: Rowset Property set: DBPROPSET_ROWSET Column? N Type: VT_BOOL Typical R/W: R/W Description: Bookmarks Ordered VARIANT_TRUE—Bookmarks can be compared to determine the relative position of their associated rows in the rowset. Setting the value of this property to VARIANT_TRUE automatically sets the value of DBPROP_BOOKMARKS to VARIANT_TRUE. VARIANT_FALSE—Bookmarks can be compared only for equality. Whether bookmarks can be compared byte-by-byte or must be compared with **IRowsetLocate::Compare** depends on the value of the DBPROP_LITERALBOOKMARKS property.

Property ID	Description
DBPROP_OTHERINSERT	Property group: Rowset Property set: DBPROPSET_ROWSET Column? N Type: VT_BOOL Typical R/W: R/W Description: Others' Inserts Visible VARIANT_TRUE—The rowset can see rows inserted by someone other than a consumer of the rowset. That is, if someone other than a consumer of the rowset inserts a row, any consumer of the rowset can see that row the next time it fetches a set of rows containing it. This includes rows inserted by other parties in the same transaction, as well as rows inserted by parties outside the transaction. The transaction isolation level does not affect the ability of the rowset to see rows inserted by other parties in the same transaction, such as other rowsets in the same session. However, it does restrict the ability of the rowset to see rows inserted by parties outside the transaction. VARIANT_FALSE—The rowset cannot see rows inserted by others. For programmers accustomed to the cursor model in ODBC, the DBPROP_OTHERUPDATEDELETE and DBPROP_OTHERINSERT properties correspond to ODBC cursors as follows: Static cursor: DBPROP_OTHERINSERT = VARIANT_FALSE DBPROP_OTHERUPDATEDELETE = VARIANT_FALSE Keyset-driven cursor: DBPROP_OTHERINSERT = VARIANT_FALSE DBPROP_OTHERUPDATEDELETE = VARIANT_TRUE Dynamic cursor: DBPROP_OTHERINSERT = VARIANT_TRUE DBPROP_OTHERUPDATEDELETE = VARIANT_TRUE

Property ID	Description
	Furthermore, the DBPROP_OWNUPDATEDELETE and DBPROP_OWNINSERT properties correspond to the values returned by the SQL_STATIC_SENSITIVITY information type in **SQLGetInfo** in ODBC. For a description of how these properties relate to transaction isolation level, see "Visibility of Other Changes" in Chapter 5, "Updating Data in Rowsets."
DBPROP_OTHERUPDATEDELETE	Property group: Rowset Property set: DBPROPSET_ROWSET Column? N Type: VT_BOOL Typical R/W: R/W Description: Others' Changes Visible VARIANT_TRUE—The rowset can see updates and deletes made by someone other than a consumer of the rowset. That is, suppose someone other than a consumer of the rowset updates the data underlying a row or deletes the row. If the row is released completely, any consumer of the rowset will see that change the next time it fetches the row. This includes updates and deletes made by other parties in the same transaction, as well as updates and deletes made by parties outside the transaction. The transaction isolation level does not affect the ability of the rowset to see updates or deletes made by other parties in the same transaction, such as other rowsets in the same session. However, it does restrict the ability of the rowset to see updates or deletes made by parties outside the transaction. VARIANT_FALSE—The rowset cannot see updates and deletes made by others. For information about how this relates to the cursor types in ODBC, see the DBPROP_OTHERINSERT property.

Property ID	Description
DBPROP_OUTPUTPARAMETER-AVAILABILITY	Property group: Data Source Information Property set: DBPROPSET_DATASOURCEINFO Type: VT_I4 Typical R/W: R Description: Output Parameter Availability The time at which output parameter values become available. One of the following: DBPROPVAL_OA_NOTSUPPORTED—Output parameters are not supported. DBPROPVAL_OA_ATEXECUTE—Output parameter data is available immediately after **ICommand::Execute** returns. DBPROPVAL_OA_ATROWRELEASE—If a command returns a single result that is a rowset, output parameter data is available at the time the rowset is completely released. If a command returns multiple results, output parameter data is available when **IMultipleResults::GetResult** returns DB_S_NORESULT or the multiple results object is completely released, whichever occurs first. Before the output parameter data is available, the consumer's bound memory is in an indeterminate state. For more information about multiple results, see "Multiple Results" in Chapter 3, "Commands."

Property ID	Description
DBPROP_OWNINSERT	Property group: Rowset Property set: DBPROPSET_ROWSET Column? N Type: VT_BOOL Typical R/W: R/W Description: Own Inserts Visible VARIANT_TRUE—The rowset can see its own inserts. That is, if a consumer of a rowset inserts a row, any consumer of the rowset can see that row the next time it fetches a set of rows containing it. This ability is independent of the transaction isolation level because all consumers of the rowset share the same transaction. VARIANT_FALSE—The rowset cannot see rows inserted by consumers of the rowset unless the command is reexecuted. For information about how this relates to the SQL_STATIC_SENSITIVITY information type in ODBC, see the DBPROP_OTHERINSERT property.

Property ID	Description
DBPROP_OWNUPDATEDELETE	Property group: Rowset Property set: DBPROPSET_ROWSET Column? N Type: VT_BOOL Typical R/W: R/W Description: Own Changes Visible VARIANT_TRUE—The rowset can see its own updates and deletes. That is, suppose a consumer of the rowset updates or deletes a row. If the row is released completely, any consumer of the rowset will see the update or delete the next time it fetches that row. This ability is independent of the transaction isolation level because all consumers of the rowset share the same transaction. VARIANT_FALSE—The rowset cannot see updates and deletes made by consumers of the rowset unless the command is reexecuted. For information about how this relates to the SQL_STATIC_SENSITIVITY information type in ODBC, see the DBPROP_OTHERINSERT property.

Property ID	Description
DBPROP_PERSISTENTIDTYPE	Property group: Data Source Information Property set: DBPROPSET_DATASOURCEINFO Type: VT_I4 Typical R/W: R Description: Persistent ID Type An integer specifying the type of DBID that the provider uses when persisting DBIDs for tables, indexes, and columns. This is generally the type of DBID that the provider considers to be the most permanent under schema changes and physical data reorganizations. One of the following: DBPROPVAL_PT_NAME DBPROPVAL_PT_PROPID DBPROPVAL_PT_GUID DBPROPVAL_PT_GUID_NAME DBPROPVAL_PT_GUID_PROPID DBPROPVAL_PT_PGUID_NAME DBPROPVAL_PT_PGUID_PROPID
DBPROP_PREPAREABORTBEHAVIOR	Property group: Data Source Information Property set: DBPROPSET_DATASOURCEINFO Type: VT_I4 Typical R/W: R Description: Prepare Abort Behavior How aborting a transaction affects prepared commands. One of the following: DBPROPVAL_CB_DELETE—Aborting a transaction deletes prepared commands. The application must reprepare commands before executing them. DBPROPAL_CB_PRESERVE—Aborting a transaction preserves prepared commands. The application can reexecute commands without repreparing them.

Property ID	Description
DBPROP_PREPARECOMMITBEHAVIOR	Property group: Data Source Information Property set: DBPROPSET_DATASOURCEINFO Type: VT_I4 Typical R/W: R Description: Prepare Commit Behavior How committing a transaction affects prepared commands. One of the following: DBPROPVAL_CB_DELETE—Committing a transaction deletes prepared commands. The application must reprepare commands before executing them. DBPROPAL_CB_PRESERVE—Committing a transaction preserves prepared commands. The application can reexecute commands without repreparing them.
DBPROP_PROCEDURETERM	Property group: Data Source Information Property set: DBPROPSET_DATASOURCEINFO Type: VT_BSTR Typical R/W: R Description: Procedure Term A character string with the data store vendor's name for a procedure; for example, "database procedure", "stored procedure", or "procedure". This is used for building user interfaces.
DBPROP_PROVIDERFRIENDLYNAME	Property group: Data Source Information Property set: DBPROPSET_DATASOURCEINFO Type: VT_BSTR Typical R/W: R Description: Provider Friendly Name The friendly name of the provider—for example, "Microsoft OLE DB Provider for ODBC Drivers".
DBPROP_PROVIDERNAME	Property group: Data Source Information Property set: DBPROPSET_DATASOURCEINFO Type: VT_BSTR Typical R/W: R Description: Provider Name The filename of the provider; for example, "Myprvdr.dll".

Property ID	Description
DBPROP_PROVIDEROLEDBVER	Property group: Data Source Information Property set: DBPROPSET_DATASOURCEINFO Type: VT_BSTR Typical R/W: R Description: OLE DB Version The version of OLE DB supported by the provider. The version is of the form *##.##*, where the first two digits are the major version and the next two digits are the minor version. For example, OLE DB providers conforming to the 1.5 specification would return "01.50".
DBPROP_PROVIDERVER	Property group: Data Source Information Property set: DBPROPSET_DATASOURCEINFO Type: VT_BSTR Typical R/W: R Description: Provider Version The version of the provider. The version is of the form *##.##.####*, where the first two digits are the major version, the next two digits are the minor version, and the last four digits are the release version. The provider can append a description of the provider. This is the same as DBPROP_DBMSVER if the DBMS is the same as the provider—that is, if the DBMS supports OLE DB interfaces directly. It is different if the provider is separate from the DBMS, such as when the provider accesses the DBMS through ODBC.

Property ID	Description
DBPROP_QUICKRESTART	Property group: Rowset Property set: DBPROPSET_ROWSET Column? N Type: VT_BOOL Typical R/W: R/W Description: Quick Restart VARIANT_TRUE—**IRowset::RestartPosition** is relatively quick to execute. In particular, it does not reexecute the command that created the rowset. VARIANT_FALSE—**RestartPosition** is expensive to execute and requires reexecuting the command that created the rowset. Although the value of this property can be set to VARIANT_TRUE, the provider is not required to honor it. The reason for this is that the provider does not know what the command is at the time the property is set; in particular, the consumer can set this property and then change the command text. However, the provider can fail this property if it is never able to quickly restart the next fetch position. Therefore, if a consumer successfully sets this property, it must still check this flag on the rowset to determine if the next fetch position can be quickly set.

Property ID	Description
DBPROP_QUOTEDIDENTIFIERCASE	Property group: Data Source Information Property set: DBPROPSET_DATASOURCEINFO Type: VT_I4 Typical R/W R Description: Quoted Identifier Sensitivity How quoted identifiers treat case. One of the following: DBPROPVAL_IC_UPPER—Quoted identifiers in SQL are case-insensitive and are stored in uppercase in system catalog. DBPROPVAL_IC_LOWER—Quoted identifiers in SQL are case-insensitive and are stored in lowercase in system catalog. DBPROPVAL_IC_SENSITIVE—Quoted identifiers in SQL are case-sensitive and are stored in mixed case in system catalog. DBPROPVAL_IC_MIXED—Quoted identifiers in SQL are case-insensitive and are stored in mixed case in system catalog.
DBPROP_REENTRANTEVENTS	Property group: Rowset Property set: DBPROPSET_ROWSET Column? N Type: VT_BOOL Typical R/W: R Description: Reentrant Events VARIANT_TRUE—The provider supports reentrancy during callbacks to the **IRowsetNotify** interface. The provider might not support reentrancy on all rowset methods. These methods return DB_E_NOTREENTRANT. VARIANT_FALSE—The provider does not support such reentrancy. The provider returns DB_E_NOTREENTRANT on methods called during the notification. Regardless of this flag, all providers must support **IRowset::GetData** and **IRowset::ReleaseRows** calls during notifications, as long as the columns being accessed do not include deferred columns.

Property ID	Description
DBPROP_REMOVEDELETED	Property group: Rowset Property set: DBPROPSET_ROWSET Column? N Type: VT_BOOL Typical R/W: R/W Description: Remove Deleted Rows If the value of this property is VARIANT_TRUE, the provider removes rows it detects as having been deleted from the rowset. That is, fetching a block of rows that formerly included a deleted row does not return a handle to that row. Which rows the rowset detects as having been deleted is determined by the DBPROP_OWNUPDATEDELETE and DBPROP_OTHERUPDATEDELETE properties; whether the rowset removes these rows is determined by this property. This property is independent of the transaction isolation level. While the transaction isolation level in some cases determines whether the rowset can detect a row as having been deleted, it has no effect on whether or not the rowset removes that row. For programmers accustomed to the cursor model in ODBC, the value of this property is always VARIANT_TRUE for rowsets implemented through dynamic cursors; that is, dynamic cursors always remove deleted rows. Whether static and keyset-driven cursors remove deleted rows depends on the value of this property.

Property ID	Description
DBPROP_REPORTMULTIPLECHANGES	Property group: Rowset Property set: DBPROPSET_ROWSET Column? N Type: VT_BOOL Typical R/W: R Description: Report Multiple Changes VARIANT_TRUE—An update or delete can affect multiple rows, and the provider can detect that multiple rows have been updated or deleted. This happens when a provider cannot uniquely identify a row. For example, the provider might use the values of all the columns in the row to identify the row; if these columns do not include a unique key, an update or delete might affect more than one row. VARIANT_FALSE—An update or delete always affects a single row, or the provider cannot detect whether it affects multiple rows.
DBPROP_RESETDATASOURCE	Property group: Data Source Property set: DBPROPSET_DATASOURCE Type: VT_I4 Typical R/W: W Description: Reset Datasource A bitmask specifying the data source object state to be reset. A combination of zero or more of the following: DBPROPVAL_RD_RESETALL—The provider should reset all states associated with the data source object, such that the data source object appears as if it were newly initialized, with the exception that any open object is not released. DBPROP_RESETDATASOURCE is generally used by a consumer in order to reuse an existing data source object without paying the cost of uninitializing and reinitializing the data source object. If the data source object has a state that cannot be reset, the provider returns DBPROPSTATUS_NOTSET for this property, indicating that the data source object should not be reused.

Property ID	Description
DBPROP_RETURNPENDINGINSERTS	Property group: Rowset Property set: DBPROPSET_ROWSET Column? N Type: VT_BOOL Typical R/W: R Description: Return Pending Inserts VARIANT_TRUE—The methods that fetch rows, such as **IRowset::GetNextRows**, can return pending insert rows; that is, rows that have been inserted in delayed update mode but for which **IRowsetUpdate::Update** has not yet been called. VARIANT_FALSE—The methods that fetch rows cannot return pending insert rows.
DBPROP_ROW_BULKOPS	Property group: Rowset Property set: DBPROPSET_ROWSET Column? N Type: VT_14 Description: Bulk Operations A bitmask describing optimizations that a provider may take for updates to the rowset. These optimizations are usually used for things like bulk loading of a table. The following values can be specified and are usually set as OPTIONAL properties because they are hints to the provider. Additional bits may be defined in the future; providers should be prepared to handle new bits in this bitmask by ignoring them if the property is set as optional, or returning an error if the property is set as required. DBPROPVAL_BO_NOLOG—The provider is not required to log inserts or changes to the rowset. DBPROPVAL_BO_NOINDEXUPDATE—The provider is not required to update indexes based on inserts or changes to the rowset. Any indexes need to be re-created following changes made through the rowset. DBPROPVAL_BO_REFINTEGRITY—Referential Integrity constraints do not need to be checked or enforced for changes made through the rowset.

Property ID	Description
DBPROP_ROWRESTRICT	Property group: Rowset Property set: DBPROPSET_ROWSET Column? N Type: VT_BOOL Typical R/W: R Description: Row Privileges VARIANT_TRUE—Access rights are restricted on a row-by-row basis. If the rowset supports **IRowsetChange**, **IRowsetChange::SetData** can be called for some but not all rows. A rowset must never count or return a handle for a row for which the consumer does not have read access rights. VARIANT_FALSE—Access rights are not restricted on a row-by-row basis. If the rowset supports **IRowsetChange**, **SetData** can be called for any row. For more information, see DBPROP_COLUMNRESTRICT, earlier in this table.
DBPROP_ROWSET_ASYNCH	Property group: Rowset Property set: DBPROPSET_ROWSET Type: VT_I4 Typical R/W: R/W Description: Asynchronous Rowset Processing A bitmask specifying the asynchronous processing performed on the rowset. A combination of zero or more of the following:

Property ID	Description
	DBPROPVAL_ASNYCH_INITIALIZE: The rowset is initialized asynchronously. The method requesting the rowset returns immediately, but attempting to call any interface other than **IConnectionPointContainer** to obtain the **IID_IDBAsynchNotify** connection point may fail and the full set of interfaces may not be available on the rowset until asynchronous initialization has completed. are obtained or the end of the rowset is reached.DBPROPVAL_ASNYCH_SEQUENTIALPOPULATION: The rowset is sequentially asynchronously populated; requests for rows may return DB_S_ENDOFROWSET before the end of the rowset is actually reached. Asynchronously populated rows are always added to the end of the rowset. DBPROPVAL_ASNYCH_RANDOMPOPULATION: The rowset is randomly asynchronously populated; requests for rows may return DB_S_ENDOFROWSET before the end of the rowset is actually reached. Asynchronously populated rows may be inserted anywhere in the rowset. The consumer may set both DBPROPVAL_ASNYCH_SEQUENTIALPOPULATION and DBPROPVAL_ASNYCH_RANDOMPOPULATION bits to request that the rowset be asynchronously populated either sequentially or randomly. The consumer is prepared for asynchronous notifications in **OnRowChange** as well as from **IDBAsynchStatus**. Only one property is returned by the rowset; if the rowset is asynchronously populated, it returns either DBPROPVAL_ASNYCH_RANDOM or DBPROPVAL_ASNYCH_SEQUENTIAL. If no bits are set (the default) the rowset is initialized and populated synchronously. All requested interfaces are available when the method requesting the rowset returns, and requesting rows block until the requested number of *hRows*

Property ID	Description
	DBPROPVAL_ASYNCH_BACKGROUNDPOPULATION: The rowset is to be populated asynchronously in the background. The rowset supports **IDBAsynchStatus** to get information about the population of the rowset or abort background population and may support the connection point for **IDBAsynchNotify** to give status of the background population. DBPROPVAL_ASYNCH_BACKGROUNDPOPULATION is implied by DBPROPVAL_ASYNCH_SEQUENTIALPOPLUATION and DBPROPVAL_ASYNCH_RANDOMPOPULATION; however, if DBPROPVAL_ASYNCH_SEQUENTIALPOPLUATION or DBPROPVAL_ASYNCH_RANDOMPOPLUATION are not also set, the rowset appears to the consumer as if it were being populated synchronously, because requesting rows will always block until the requested number of hRows are obtained or the end of the rowset is reached. DBPROPVAL_ASYNCH_PREPOPULATE: The consumer prefers to optimize for retrieving all data when the rowset is materialized. This is a hint to the provider to fetch all of the data up-front. DBPROPVAL_ASYNCH_PREPOPULATE is only a hint to the provider; the provider should never fail opening the rowset based on the setting of this flag and need not return it to the consumer, even if the rowset is prepopulated. DBPROPVAL_ASYNCH_POPULATEONDEMAND: The consumer prefers to optimize for getting each individual request for data returned as quickly as possible. This is a hint to the provider to populate the rowset as the data is fetched. DBPROPVAL_ASYNCH_POPULATEONDEMAND is only a hint to the provider; the provider should never fail opening the rowset based on the setting of this flag and need not return it to the consumer, even if the rowset is populated on demand.

Property ID	Description
	Since DBPROPVAL_ASYNCH_PREPOPULATE and DBPROPVAL_ANSYCH_POPULATEONDEMAND are just hints to the provider, if the consumer sets one or both of these properties in addition to the asychronous population properties DBPROPVAL_ASYNCH_SEQUENTIALPOPULATION or DBPROPVAL_ASYNCH_RANDOMPOPULATION, the provider should attempt to populate asynchronously according to DBPROPVAL_ASYNCH_SEQUENTIALPOPULATION and DBPROPVAL_ASYNCH_RANDOMPOPULATION. If the asynchronous population specified by DBPROPVAL_ASYNCH_SEQUENTIALPOPULATION or DBPROPVAL_ASYNCH_RANDOMPOPULATION cannot be supported, the provider should fail if DBPROPOPTIONS_REQUIRED was specified for the property or should attempt to populate synchronously according to DBPROPVAL_ASYNCH_PREPOPULATE or DBPROPVAL_ASYNCH_POPULATEONDEMAND if the property was set with DBPROPOPTIONS_OPTIONAL.
DBPROP_ROWSETCONVERSIONS-ONCOMMAND	Property group: Data Source Information Property set: DBPROPSET_DATASOURCEINFO Type: VT_BOOL Typical R/W: R Description: Rowset Conversions on Command VARIANT_TRUE—Callers to **IConvertType::CanConvert** can inquire on a command about conversions supported on rowsets generated by the command. VARIANT_FALSE—Callers can inquire on a command only about conversions supported by the command.

Property ID	Description
DBPROP_ROWTHREADMODEL	Property group: Rowset Property set: DBPROPSET_ROWSET Column? N Type: VT_I4 Typical R/W: R/W Description: Row Threading Model A bitmask specifying the threading models supported by the rowset. A combination of one or more of the following: DBPROPVAL_RT_FREETHREAD DBPROPVAL_RT_APTMTTHREAD DBPROPVAL_RT_SINGLETHREAD
DBPROP_SCHEMATERM	Property group: Data Source Information Property set: DBPROPSET_DATASOURCEINFO Type: VT_BSTR Typical R/W: R Description: Schema Term The name the data source object uses for a schema—for example, "schema" or "owner". This is used for building user interfaces.
DBPROP_SCHEMAUSAGE	Property group: Data Source Information Property set: DBPROPSET_DATASOURCEINFO Type: VT_I4 Typical R/W: R Description: Schema Usage A bitmask specifying how schema names can be used in text commands. A combination of zero or more of the following: DBPROPVAL_SU_DML_STATEMENTS—Schema names are supported in all Data Manipulation Language statements. DBPROPVAL_SU_TABLE_DEFINITION—Schema names are supported in all table definition statements. DBPROPVAL_SU_INDEX_DEFINITION—Schema names are supported in all index definition statements. DBPROPVAL_SU_PRIVILEGE_DEFINITION—Schema names are supported in all privilege definition statements.

Property ID	Description
DBPROP_SERVERCURSOR	Property group: Rowset Property set: DBPROPSET_ROWSET Column? N Type: VT_BOOL Typical R/W: R/W Description: Server Cursor If the value of this property is set to VARIANT_TRUE with **ICommandProperties::SetProperties**, the cursor underlying the rowset (if any) must be materialized on the server. If the value of this property is not set to VARIANT_TRUE with **ICommandProperties::SetProperties**, it is up to the provider to decide where to materialize the cursor. The consumer can determine where the cursor was materialized by checking the value of this property on the rowset.
DBPROP_SERVERDATAONINSERT	Property group: Rowset Property set: DBPROPSET_ROWSET Column? N Type: VT_BOOL Typical R/W: R/W Description: Server Data on Insert VARIANT_TRUE—At the time an insert is transmitted to the server (when **InsertRow** is called in immediate mode, or when **Update** is called for an inserted row in deferred update mode), the provider retrieves data from the server to update the local row cache. VARIANT_FALSE—The provider does not retrieve server values for newly inserted rows. The consumer can retrieve only data values explicitly set in the call to **InsertRow** or by calls to **SetData** for the hRow returned by **InsertRow**. Consumers should be aware that setting DBPROP_SERVERDATAONINSERT is potentially expensive and might not be supported for certain types of rowsets.

Property ID	Description
DBPROP_SERVERNAME	Property group: Datasource Information Property set: DBPROPSET_DATASOURCEINFO Type: VT_BSTR Typical R/W: R Description: Server Name The name of the server. This may be the same as the DBPROP_INIT_DATASOURCE property if the server name is used to define the data source object that the user specifies when connecting, or may be the actual name of the server if the provider connects through "friendly" data source object names.
DBPROP_SESS_AUTOCOMMITISO-LEVELS	Property group: Session Property set: DBPROPSET_SESSION Type: VT_I4 Typical R/W: R/W Description: Autocommit Isolation Levels A bitmask specifying the transaction isolation level while in auto-commit mode. The values that can be set in this bitmask are the same as those that can be set for DBPROP_SUPPORTEDTXNISOLEVELS.
DBPROP_SORTONINDEX	Property group: View Property set: DBPROPSET_VIEW Type: VT_BOOL Typical R/W: R Description: Sort on Index VARIANT_TRUE: The provider supports **SetSortOrder** only for columns contained in an index. VARIANT_FALSE: The provider does not require columns to be indexed in order to be specified in **SetSortOrder**, or the provider does not support **SetSortOrder**. This value applies only to the ability to specify a column in **SetSortOrder**; it does not imply whether or not nonindexed columns can be used in the order clause of a command.

Property ID	Description
DBPROP_SQLSUPPORT	Property group: Data Source Information Property set: DBPROPSET_DATASOURCEINFO Type: VT_I4 Typical R/W: R Description: SQL Support A bitmask specifying the level of support for SQL. A combination of zero or more of the following: DBPROPVAL_SQL_NONE—SQL is not supported. DBPROPVAL_SQL_ODBC_MINIMUM DBPROPVAL_SQL_ODBC_CORE DBPROPVAL_SQL_ODBC_EXTENDED—These levels correspond to the levels of SQL conformance defined in ODBC version 2.5. These levels are cumulative. That is, if the provider supports one level, it also sets the bits for all lower levels. For example, if the provider sets the DBPROPVAL_SQL_ODBC_CORE bit, it also sets the DBPROPVAL_SQL_ODBC_MINIMUM bit. DBPROPVAL_SQL_ESCAPECLAUSES—The provider supports the ODBC escape clause syntax. DBPROPVAL_SQL_ANSI92_ENTRY DBPROPVAL_SQL_FIPS_TRANSITIONAL DBPROPVAL_SQL_ANSI92_INTERMEDIATE DBPROPVAL_SQL_ANSI92_FULL—These levels correspond to the levels in ANSI SQL92. These levels are cumulative. That is, if the provider supports one level, it also sets the bits for all lower levels. DBPROPVAL_SQL_ANSI89_IEF—The provider supports the ANSI89 Integrity Enhancement Facility. DBPROPVAL_SQL_SUBMINIMUM—The provider supports the DBGUID_SQL dialect and parses the command text according to SQL rules but supports neither the minimum ODBC level nor the ANSI SQL92 Entry level. This level is not accumulative; providers that support at least the minimal ODBC Level or ANSI SQL92 Entry Level do not set this bit. OLE DB consumers can determine whether or not the provider supports the DBGUID_SQL dialect by verifying that the DBPROPVAL_SQL_NONE bit is not set.

Property ID	Description
DBPROP_STRONGIDENTITY	Property group: Rowset Property set: DBPROPSET_ROWSET Column? N Type: VT_BOOL Typical R/W: R Description: Strong Row Identity VARIANT_TRUE—The handles of newly inserted rows can be compared as specified by DBPROP_LITERALIDENTITY. VARIANT_FALSE—There is no guarantee that the handles of newly inserted rows can be compared successfully. In this case, **IRowsetIdentity::IsSameRow** might return DB_E_NEWLYINSERTED. A newly inserted row is defined as a row for which an insertion has been transmitted to the data source object, as opposed to a pending insert row. For more information, see "Uniqueness of Rows in the Rowset" in Chapter 4, "Rowsets."
DBPROP_STRUCTUREDSTORAGE	Property group: Data Source Information Property set: DBPROPSET_DATASOURCEINFO Type: VT_I4 Typical R/W: R Description: Structured Storage A bitmask specifying what interfaces the rowset supports on storage objects. If a provider can support any of these interfaces, it is also required to support **ISequentialStream**. A combination of zero or more of the following: DBPROPVAL_SS_ISEQUENTIALSTREAM DBPROPVAL_SS_ISTREAM DBPROPVAL_SS_ISTORAGE DBPROPVAL_SS_ILOCKBYTES

Property ID	Description
DBPROP_SUBQUERIES	Property group: Data Source Information Property set: DBPROPSET_DATASOURCEINFO Type: VT_I4 Typical R/W: R Description: Subquery Support A bitmask specifying the predicates in text commands that support subqueries. A combination of zero or more of the following: DBPROPVAL_SQ_CORRELATEDSUBQUERIES DBPROPVAL_SQ_COMPARISON DBPROPVAL_SQ_EXISTS DBPROPVAL_SQ_IN DBPROPVAL_SQ_QUANTIFIED The DBPROPVAL_SQ_CORRELATEDSUBQUERIES bit indicates that all predicates that support subqueries support correlated subqueries.
DBPROP_SUPPORTEDTXNDDL	Property group: Data Source Information Property set: DBPROPSET_DATASOURCEINFO Type: VT_I4 Typical R/W: R Description: Transaction DDL Whether Data Definition Language (DDL) statements are supported in transactions. One of the following: DBPROPVAL_TC_NONE—Transactions are not supported. DBPROPVAL_TC_DML—Transactions can contain only Data Manipulation Language (DML) statements. DDL statements within a transaction cause an error. DBPROPVAL_TC_DDL_COMMIT—Transactions can contain only DML statements. DDL statements within a transaction cause the transaction to be committed. DBPROPVAL_TC_DDL_IGNORE—Transactions can contain only DML statements. DDL statements within a transaction are ignored. DBPROPVAL_TC_ALL—Transactions can contain DDL and DML statements in any order.

Property ID	Description
DBPROP_SUPPORTEDTXNISOLEVELS	Property group: Data Source Information Property set: DBPROPSET_DATASOURCEINFO Type: VT_I4 Typical R/W: R Description: Isolation Levels A bitmask specifying the supported transaction isolation levels. A combination of zero or more of the following: DBPROPVAL_TI_CHAOS DBPROPVAL_TI_READUNCOMMITTED DBPROPVAL_TI_BROWSE DBPROPVAL_TI_CURSORSTABILITY DBPROPVAL_TI_READCOMMITTED DBPROPVAL_TI_REPEATABLEREAD DBPROPVAL_TI_SERIALIZABLE DBPROPVAL_TI_ISOLATED For more information, see "Isolation Levels" in Chapter 12, "Transactions."

Property ID	Description
DBPROP_SUPPORTEDTXNISORETAIN	Property group: Data Source Information Property set: DBPROPSET_DATASOURCEINFO Type: VT_I4 Typical R/W: R Description: Isolation Retention A bitmask specifying the supported transaction isolation retention levels. A combination of zero or more of the following: DBPROPVAL_TR_COMMIT_DC—The transaction may either preserve or dispose of isolation context across a retaining commit. DBPROPVAL_TR_COMMIT—The transaction preserves its isolation context (that is, it preserves its locks, if that is how isolation is implemented) across a retaining commit. DBPROPVAL_TR_COMMIT_NO—The transaction is explicitly not to preserve isolation across a retaining commit. DBPROPVAL_TR_ABORT_DC—The transaction may either preserve or dispose of isolation context across a retaining abort. DBPROPVAL_TR_ABORT—The transaction preserves its isolation context across a retaining abort. DBPROPVAL_TR_ABORT_NO—The transaction is explicitly not to preserve isolation across a retaining abort. DBPROPVAL_TR_DONTCARE—The transaction may preserve or dispose of isolation context across a retaining commit or abort. This is the default. DBPROPVAL_TR_BOTH—Isolation is preserved across both a retaining commit and a retaining abort. DBPROPVAL_TR_NONE—Isolation is explicitly not to be retained across either a retaining commit or a retaining abort.

Property ID	Description
	DBPROPVAL_TR_OPTIMISTIC—Optimistic concurrency control is to be used. If DBPROPVAL_TR_OPTIMISTIC is specified and then whatever isolation technology is in place (such as locking), it must be the case that other transactions' ability to make changes to the data and resources manipulated by this transaction is not in any way affected by the data read or updated by this transaction. That is, optimistic control is to be used for all data in the transaction. For more information, see **ITransactionLocal::StartTransaction** in Part 2, "OLE DB Reference."
DBPROP_TABLETERM	Property group: Data Source Information Property set: DBPROPSET_DATASOURCEINFO Type: VT_BSTR Typical R/W: R Description: Table Term The name the data source object uses for a table—for example, "table" or "file". This is used for building user interfaces.
DBPROP_TBL_TEMPTABLE	Property group: Table Property set: DBPROPSET_TABLE Type: VT_BOOL Typical R/W: R/W Description: Temporary Table Whether the table is temporary. One of the following: VARIANT_TRUE—The table is destroyed when the session is released. VARIANT_FALSE—The table is created permanently.

Property ID	Description
DBPROP_TRANSACTEDOBJECT	Property group: Rowset Property set: DBPROPSET_ROWSET Column? Y Type: VT_BOOL Typical R/W: R/W Description: Objects Transacted VARIANT_TRUE—Any object created on the specified column is transacted. That is, data made visible to the data store through the object can be committed with **ITransaction::Commit** or aborted with **ITransaction::Abort**. VARIANT_FALSE—Any object created on the specified column is not transacted. That is, all changes to the object are permanent once they are made visible to the data store. If this property is set on a column that does not contain an object, it is ignored.
DBPROP_UNIQUEROWS	Property group: Rowset Property set: DBPROPSET_ROWSET Type: VT_BOOL Typical R/W: R/W Description: UniqueRows VARIANT_TRUE—Each row is uniquely identified by its column values. VARIANT_FALSE—Rows in the rowset may or may not be uniquely identified by their column values.

Property ID	Description
	If this property is set to VARIANT_TRUE when opening the rowset, the provider adds additional columns if necessary, to ensure that each row is uniquely identified by its values. These additional columns appear at the end of the rowset, have a DBID of type DBKIND_GUID_PROPID, DBKIND_PGUID_PROPID, DBKIND_GUID_NAME, or DBKIND_PGUID_NAME, and the guid (or pguid) element is (or points to) DBCOL_SPECIALCOL. These columns are typically not displayed to the user but are used by components such as update services to uniquely identify a row. The provider may, but is not required to, duplicate existing columns in the rowset to ensure that key columns are included. If this property is set to VARIANT_TRUE and the provider supports the optional **IColumnsRowset** metadata column DBCOLUMN_KEYCOLUMN, the set of columns that uniquely identify the row have a value of VARIANT_TRUE in the DBCOLUMN_KEYCOLUMN column returned by **IColumnsRowset**. This may be a subset of the columns in the row, or all of the columns if the provider cannot determine a proper subset that uniquely identifies the row. If this property is not VARIANT_TRUE, DBCOLUMN_KEYCOLUMN may or may not be set to VARIANT_TRUE for key columns, but there is no guarantee that the set of columns that are flagged with this value are sufficient in order to uniquely identify the row.

Property ID	Description
DBPROP_UPDATABILITY	Property group: Rowset Property set: DBPROPSET_ROWSET Column? N Type: VT_I4 Typical R/W: R/W Description: Updatability A bitmask specifying the supported methods on **IRowsetChange**. A combination of zero or more of the following: DBPROPVAL_UP_CHANGE—**SetData** is supported. DBPROPVAL_UP_DELETE—**DeleteRows** is supported. DBPROPVAL_UP_INSERT—**InsertRow** is supported. DBPROP_UPDATABILITY should be used in conjunction with DBPROP_IROWSETCHANGE. If DBPROP_IROWSETCHANGE is VARIANT_TRUE and DBPROP_UPDATABILITY is not set, it is provider-specific what methods are supported on **IRowsetChange**. If DBPROP_UPDATABILITY is specified, the provider must not support any methods whose bits are not set.
DBPROP_USERNAME	Property group: Data Source Information Property set: DBPROPSET_DATASOURCEINFO Type: VT_BSTR Typical R/W: R Description: User Name A character string with the name used in a particular database, which can be different than a login name.

APPENDIX D

Cotypes, Structures, and Enumerated Types

This appendix lists the cotypes, structures, and enumerated types defined by OLE DB.

OLE DB Cotypes

Enumerators:

```
CoType TEnumerator {
   [mandatory] IParseDisplayName;
   [mandatory] ISourcesRowset;
   [optional]  IDBInitialize;
   [optional]  IDBProperties;
   [optional]  ISupportErrorInfo;
}
```

Data source objects:

```
CoType TDataSource {
   [mandatory] interface IDBCreateSession;
   [mandatory] interface IDBInitialize;
   [mandatory] interface IDBProperties;
   [mandatory] interface IPersist;
   [optional]  interface IConnectionPointContainer;
   [optional]  interface IDBAsynchStatus;
   [optional]  interface IDBDataSourceAdmin;
   [optional]  interface IDBInfo;
   [optional]  interface IPersistFile;
   [optional]  interface ISupportErrorInfo;
}
```

Sessions:

```
CoType TSession {
   [mandatory] interface IGetDataSource;
   [mandatory] interface IOpenRowset;
   [mandatory] interface ISessionProperties;
   [optional]  interface IAlterIndex;
   [optional]  interface IAlterTable;
   [optional]  interface IDBCreateCommand;
   [optional]  interface IDBSchemaRowset;
   [optional]  interface IIndexDefinition;
   [optional]  interface ISupportErrorInfo;
   [optional]  interface ITableDefinition;
   [optional]  interface ITransactionJoin;
   [optional]  interface ITransactionLocal;
   [optional]  interface ITransaction;
   [optional]  interface ITransactionObject;
}
```

Commands:

```
CoType TCommand {
   [mandatory] interface IAccessor;
   [mandatory] interface IColumnsInfo;
   [mandatory] interface ICommand;
   [mandatory] interface ICommandProperties;
   [mandatory] interface ICommandText;
   [mandatory] interface IConvertType;
   [optional]  interface IColumnsRowset;
   [optional]  interface ICommandPersist;
   [optional]  interface ICommandPrepare;
   [optional]  interface ICommandWithParameters;
   [optional]  interface ISupportErrorInfo;
}
```

Multiple results objects:

```
CoType TMultipleResults {
   [mandatory] interface IMultipleResults;
   [optional]  interface ISupportErrorInfo;
}
```

Rowsets:

```
CoType TRowset {
   [mandatory] interface IAccessor;
   [mandatory] interface IColumnsInfo;
   [mandatory] interface IConvertType;
   [mandatory] interface IRowset;
   [mandatory] interface IRowsetInfo;
   [optional]  interface IChapteredRowset;
   [optional]  interface IColumnsRowset;
   [optional]  interface IConnectionPointContainer;
   [optional]  interface IDBAsynchStatus;
   [optional]  interface IRowsetChange;
   [optional]  interface IRowsetChapterMember;
   [optional]  interface IRowsetFind;
   [optional]  interface IRowsetIdentity;
   [optional]  interface IRowsetIndex;
   [optional]  interface IRowsetLocate;
   [optional]  interface IRowsetRefresh;
   [optional]  interface IRowsetScroll;
   [optional]  interface IRowsetUpdate;
   [optional]  interface IRowsetView;
   [optional]  interface ISupportErrorInfo;
}
```

Views:

```
CoType TView {
   [mandatory] interface IColumnsInfo;
   [optional]  interface IAccessor;
   [optional]  interface ISupportErrorInfo;
   [optional]  interface IViewChapter;
   [optional]  interface IViewFilter;
   [optional]  interface IViewRowset;
   [optional]  interface IViewSort;
};
```

Indexes:

```
CoType TIndex {
   [mandatory] interface IAccessor;
   [mandatory] interface IColumnsInfo;
   [mandatory] interface IConvertType;
   [mandatory] interface IRowset;
   [mandatory] interface IRowsetIndex;
   [mandatory] interface IRowsetInfo;
   [optional]  interface IRowsetChange;
   [optional]  interface IRowsetFind;
   [optional]  interface IRowsetIdentity;
   [optional]  interface IRowsetLocate;
   [optional]  interface IRowsetRefresh;
   [optional]  interface IRowsetScroll;
   [optional]  interface IRowsetUpdate;
   [optional]  interface IRowsetView;
   [optional]  interface ISupportErrorInfo;
};
```

Transactions:

```
CoType TTransaction {
   [mandatory] interface IConnectionPointContainer;
   [mandatory] interface ITransaction;
   [optional]  interface ISupportErrorInfo;
};
```

Transaction options:

```
CoType TTransactionOptions {
   [mandatory] interface ITransactionOptions;
   [optional]  interface ISupportErrorInfo;
};
```

Errors:

```
CoType TErrorObject {
   [mandatory] interface IErrorRecords;
}
```

Custom errors:

```
CoType TCustomErrorObject {
   [optional]  interface IErrorLookup;
   [optional]  interface ISQLErrorInfo;
}
```

Error records:

```
CoType TErrorRecord {
   [mandatory] interface IErrorInfo;
}
```

OLE DB Structures and Enumerated Types

Type	Defined in	Used in

`typedef DWORD DBACCESSORFLAGS;`
 	
`enum DBACCESSORFLAGSENUM {`
`     DBACCESSOR_INVALID,`
`     DBACCESSOR_PASSBYREF,`
`     DBACCESSOR_ROWDATA,`
`     DBACCESSOR_PARAMETERDATA,`
`     DBACCESSOR_OPTIMIZED`
`};`
	IAccessor::CreateAccessor in Part 2, "OLE DB Reference"	**IAccessor::CreateAccessor**
		
		IAccessor::GetBindings

`typedef struct tagDBBINDEXT {`
`     BYTE * pExtension;`
`     ULONG  ulExtension;`
`} DBBINDEXT;`
	"DBBINDING Structures" in Chapter 6, "Getting and Setting Data"	DBBINDING

<table>
<tr><th>Type</th><th>Defined in</th><th>Used in</th></tr>
<tr><td><pre>typedef struct tagDBBINDING {
     ULONG   iOrdinal;
     ULONG   obValue;
     ULONG   obLength;
     ULONG   obStatus;
     ITypeInfo * pTypeInfo;
     DBOBJECT *   pObject;
     DBBINDEXT * pBindExt;
     DBPART   dwPart;
     DBMEMOWNER   dwMemOwner;
     DBPARAMIO   eParamIO;
     ULONG   cbMaxLen;
     DWORD   dwFlags;
     DBTYPE   wType;
     BYTE   bPrecision;
     BYTE   bScale;
} DBBINDING;</pre></td><td>"DBBINDING Structures" in Chapter 6, "Getting and Setting Data"</td><td>IAccessor::CreateAccessor

IAccessor::GetBindings</td></tr>
<tr><td><pre>typedef DWORD DBBINDFLAG;

enum DBBINDFLAGENUM {
     DBBINDFLAG_HTML
};</pre></td><td>IAccessor::CreateAccessor in Part 2, "OLE DB Reference"</td><td>IAccessor::CreateAccessor</td></tr>
<tr><td><pre>typedef DWORD DBBINDSTATUS;

enum DBBINDSTATUSENUM {
     DBBINDSTATUS_OK
     DBBINDSTATUS_BADORDINAL
DBBINDSTATUS_UNSUPPORTEDCONVERSION
     DBBINDSTATUS_BADBINDINFO
     DBBINDSTATUS_BADSTORAGEFLAGS
     DBBINDSTATUS_NOINTERFACE
};</pre></td><td>IAccessor::CreateAccessor in Part 2, "OLE DB Reference"</td><td>IAccessor::CreateAccessor</td></tr>
<tr><td><pre>typedef enum tagDBBOOKMARK {
     DBBMK_INVALID,
     DBBMK_FIRST,
     DBBMK_LAST
} DBBOOKMARK;</pre></td><td>"Standard Bookmarks" in Chapter 4, "Rowsets"</td><td></td></tr>
</table>

<table>
<tr><th>Type</th><th>Defined in</th><th>Used in</th></tr>
<tr><td><pre>typedef struct tagDBCOLUMNDESC {
     LPOLESTR   pwszTypeName;
     ITypeInfo * pTypeInfo;
     DBPROPSET * rgPropertySets;
     CLSID *   pclsid;
     ULONG   cPropertySets;
     ULONG   ulColumnSize;
     DBID   dbcid;
     DBTYPE   wType;
     BYTE   bPrecision;
     BYTE   bScale;
} DBCOLUMNDESC;</pre></td><td>ITableDefinition::CreateTable in Part 2, "OLE DB Reference"</td><td>ITableDefinition::CreateAddColumn

ITableDefinition::CreateTable</td></tr>
<tr><td><pre>typedef DWORD DBCOLUMNFLAGS;

enum DBCOLUMNFLAGSENUM {
     DBCOLUMNFLAGS_ISBOOKMARK,
     DBCOLUMNFLAGS_MAYDEFER,
     DBCOLUMNFLAGS_WRITE,
     DBCOLUMNFLAGS_WRITEUNKNOWN,
     DBCOLUMNFLAGS_ISFIXEDLENGTH,
     DBCOLUMNFLAGS_ISNULLABLE,
     DBCOLUMNFLAGS_MAYBENULL,
     DBCOLUMNFLAGS_ISLONG,
     DBCOLUMNFLAGS_ISROWID,
     DBCOLUMNFLAGS_ISROWVER,
     DBCOLUMNFLAGS_CACHEDEFERRED
};</pre></td><td>IColumnsInfo::GetColumnInfo in Part 2, "OLE DB Reference"</td><td>DBCOLUMNINFO</td></tr>
<tr><td><pre>typedef struct tagDBCOLUMNINFO {
     LPOLESTR   pwszName;
     ITypeInfo *   pTypeInfo;
     ULONG   iOrdinal;
     DBCOLUMNFLAGS dwFlags;
     ULONG   ulColumnSize;
     DBTYPE   wType;
     BYTE   bPrecision;
     BYTE   bScale;
     DBID   columnid;
} DBCOLUMNINFO;</pre></td><td>IColumnsInfo::GetColumnInfo in Part 2, "OLE DB Reference"</td><td>IColumnsInfo::GetColumnInfo</td></tr>
</table>

<table>
<tr><th>Type</th><th>Defined in</th><th>Used in</th></tr>
<tr><td><pre>typedef DWORD DBCOMPARE;

enum DBCOMPAREENUM {
     DBCOMPARE_LT,
     DBCOMPARE_EQ,
     DBCOMPARE_GT,
     DBCOMPARE_NE,
     DBCOMPARE_NOTCOMPARABLE
};</pre></td><td>IRowsetLocate::Compare in Part 2, "OLE DB Reference"</td><td>IRowsetLocate::Compare</td></tr>
<tr><td><pre>typedef DWORD DBCOMPAREOP;

enum DBCOMPAREOPSENUM {
     DBCOMPAREOPS_LT,
     DBCOMPAREOPS_LE,
     DBCOMPAREOPS_EQ,
     DBCOMPAREOPS_GE,
     DBCOMPAREOPS_GT,
     DBCOMPAREOPS_BEGINSWITH,
     DBCOMPAREOPS_NOTBEGINSWITH,
     DBCOMPAREOPS_CONTAINS,
     DBCOMPAREOPS_NOTCONTAINS,
     DBCOMPAREOPS_NE,
     DBCOMPAREOPS_IGNORE,
     DBCOMPAREOPS_CASESENSITIVE,
     DBCOMPAREOPS_CASEINSENSITIVE
};</pre></td><td>IRowsetFind::FindNextRow in Part 2, "OLE DB Reference"</td><td>IRowsetFind::FindNextRow

IViewFilter::GetFilter

IViewFilter::SetFilter</td></tr>
<tr><td><pre>typedef DWORD DBCONVERTFLAGS;

enum DBCONVERTFLAGSENUM {
     DBCONVERTFLAGS_COLUMN,
     DBCONVERTFLAGS_ISFIXEDLENGTH,
     DBCONVERTFLAGS_ISLONG,
     DBCONVERTFLAGS_PARAMETER,
     DBCONVERTFLAGS_FROMVARIANT
};</pre></td><td>IConvertType::CanConvert in Part 2, "OLE DB Reference"</td><td>IConvertType::CanConvert</td></tr>
<tr><td><pre>typedef struct tagDBDATE {
     SHORT year;
     USHORT month;
     USHORT day;
} DBDATE;</pre></td><td>"Type Indicators" in Appendix A, "Data Types"</td><td></td></tr>
</table>

<table>
<tr><th>Type</th><th>Defined in</th><th>Used in</th></tr>
<tr><td><pre>typedef DWORD DBEVENTPHASE;

enum DBEVENTPHASEENUM {
     DBEVENTPHASE_OKTODO,
     DBEVENTPHASE_ABOUTTODO,
     DBEVENTPHASE_SYNCHAFTER,
     DBEVENTPHASE_FAILEDTODO,
     DBEVENTPHASE_DIDEVENT
};</pre></td><td>IRowsetNotify in Part 2, "OLE DB Reference"</td><td>IRowsetNotify::OnField-Change
IRowsetNotify::OnRow-Change
IRowsetNotify::OnRow-setChange</td></tr>
<tr><td><pre>typedef struct tagDBID {
     union {
     GUID guid;
     GUID * pguid;
     } uGuid;
     DBKIND eKind;
     union {
     LPOLESTR pwszName;
     ULONG   ulPropid;
     } uName;
} DBID;</pre></td><td>"Column IDs" in Chapter 4, "Rowsets"</td><td>DBCOLUMNDESC
DBCOLUMNINFO
DBINDEXCOLUMN-DESC
DBPROP
IColumnsInfo::Map-ColumnIDs
IColumnsRowset::Get-AvailableColumns
IColumnsRowset::Get-ColumnsRowset
IIndexDefinition::Create-Index
IIndexDefinition::Drop-Index</td></tr>
</table>

Type	Defined in	Used in
		IOpenRowset::OpenRowset **ITableDefinition::AddColumn** **ITableDefinition::CreateTable** **ITableDefinition::DropColumn** **ITableDefinition::DropTable**

`typedef DWORD DBINDEX_COL_ORDER;`
 	
`enum DBINDEX_COL_ORDERENUM {`
`DBINDEX_COL_ORDER_ASC,`
`DBINDEX_COL_ORDER_DESC`
`};`
	IIndexDefinition::CreateIndex in Part 2, "OLE DB Reference"	DBINDEXCOLUMNDESC

`typedef sruct tagDBINDEXCOLUMNDESC {`
`DBID * pColumnID;`
`DBINDEX_COL_ORDER eIndexColOrder;`
`} DBINDEXCOLUMNDESC;`
	IIndexDefinition::CreateIndex in Part 2, "OLE DB Reference"	**IIndexDefinition::CreateIndex**
		IRowsetIndex::GetIndexInfo

`typedef DWORD DBKIND;`
 	
`enum DBKINDENUM {`
`DBKIND_GUID_NAME,`
`DBKIND_GUID_PROPID,`
`DBKIND_NAME,`
`DBKIND_PGUID_NAME,`
`DBKIND_PGUID_PROPID,`
`DBKIND_PROPID,`
`DBKIND_GUID`
`};`
	"Column IDs" in Chapter 4, "Rowsets"	DBID

Type	Defined in	Used in

`typedef DWORD DBLITERAL;`
 	
`enum DBLITERALENUM {`
`DBLITERAL_INVALID,`
`DBLITERAL_BINARY_LITERAL,`
`DBLITERAL_CATALOG_NAME,`
`DBLITERAL_CATALOG_SEPARATOR,`
`DBLITERAL_CHAR_LITERAL,`
`DBLITERAL_COLUMN_ALIAS,`
`DBLITERAL_COLUMN_NAME,`
`DBLITERAL_CORRELATION_NAME,`
`DBLITERAL_CURSOR_NAME,`
`DBLITERAL_ESCAPE_PERCENT_PREFIX,`
`DBLITERAL_ESCAPE_PERCENT_SUFFIX,`
`DBLITERAL_ESCAPE_UNDERSCORE_PREFIX,`
`DBLITERAL_ESCAPE_UNDERSCORE_SUFFIX,`
`DBLITERAL_INDEX_NAME,`
`DBLITERAL_LIKE_PERCENT,`
`DBLITERAL_LIKE_UNDERSCORE,`
`DBLITERAL_PROCEDURE_NAME,`
`DBLITERAL_QUOTE_PREFIX,`
`DBLITERAL_QUOTE_SUFFIX,`
`DBLITERAL_SCHEMA_NAME,`
`DBLITERAL_SCHEMA_SEPARATOR,`
`DBLITERAL_TABLE_NAME,`
`DBLITERAL_TEXT_COMMAND,`
`DBLITERAL_USER_NAME,`
`DBLITERAL_VIEW_NAME`
`};`
	IDBInfo::GetLiteralInfo in Part 2, "OLE DB Reference"	**IDBInfo::GetLiteralInfo**

`typedef DWORD DBMEMOWNER;`
 	
`enum DBMEMOWNERENUM {`
`DBMEMOWNER_CLIENTOWNED,`
`DBMEMOWNER_PROVIDEROWNED`
`};`
	"DBBINDING Structures" in Chapter 6, "Getting and Setting Data"	DBBINDING

`typedef struct tagDB_NUMERIC {`
`BYTE precision;`
`BYTE scale;`
`BYTE sign;`
`BYTE val[16];`
`} DB_NUMERIC;`
	"Type Indicators" in Appendix A, "Data Types"	

Type	Defined in	Used in

`typedef struct tagDB_VARNUMERIC {`
`    BYTE precision;`
`    SBYTE scale;`
`    BYTE sign;`
`    BYTE val[1];`
`} DB_VARNUMERIC;`
	"Type Indicators" in Appendix A, "Data Types"	

`typedef struct tagDBOBJECT {`
`    DWORD dwFlags;`
`    IID iid;`
`} DBOBJECT;`
	"DBBINDING Structures" in Chapter 6, "Getting and Setting Data"	DBBINDING

`typedef struct tagDBPARAMBINDINFO {`
`    LPOLESTR      pwszDataSourceType;`
`    LPOLESTR      pwszName;`
`    ULONG         ulParamSize;`
`    DBPARAMFLAGS dwFlags;`
`    BYTE          bPrecision;`
`    BYTE          bScale;`
`} DBPARAMBINDINFO;`
	ICommandWith-Parameters:: SetParameterInfo in Part 2, "OLE DB Reference"	**ICommandWith-Parameters:: SetParameterInfo**

`typedef DWORD DBPARAMFLAGS;`
 	
`enum DBPARAMFLAGSENUM {`
`    DBPARAMFLAGS_ISINPUT,`
`    DBPARAMFLAGS_ISOUTPUT,`
`    DBPARAMFLAGS_ISSIGNED,`
`    DBPARAMFLAGS_ISNULLABLE,`
`    DBPARAMFLAGS_ISLONG`
`};`
	ICommandWith-Parameters:: GetParameterInfo in Part 2, "OLE DB Reference"	DBPARAMBINDINFO
		DBPARAMINFO

`typedef struct tagDBPARAMINFO {`
`    DBPARAMFLAGS dwFlags;`
`    ULONG         iOrdinal;`
`    LPOLESTR      pwszName;`
`    ITypeInfo *   pTypeInfo;`
`    ULONG         ulParamSize;`
`    DBTYPE        wType;`
`    BYTE          bPrecision;`
`    BYTE          bScale;`
`} DBPARAMINFO;`
	ICommandWith-Parameters:: GetParameterInfo in Part 2, "OLE DB Reference"	**ICommandWith-Parameters:: GetParameterInfo**

Type	Defined in	Used in

`typedef DWORD DBPARAMIO;`
 	
`enum DBPARAMIOENUM {`
`    DBPARAMIO_NOTPARAM,`
`    DBPARAMIO_INPUT,`
`    DBPARAMIO_OUTPUT`
`};`
	"DBBINDING Structures" in Chapter 6, "Getting and Setting Data"	DBBINDING

`typedef struct tagDBPARAMS {`
`    void *    pData;`
`    ULONG     cParamSets;`
`    HACCESSOR hAccessor;`
`} DBPARAMS;`
	ICommand::Execute in Part 2, "OLE DB Reference"	**ICommand::Execute**

`typedef DWORD DBPART;`
 	
`enum DBPARTENUM {`
`    DBPART_INVALID,`
`    DBPART_VALUE,`
`    DBPART_LENGTH,`
`    DBPART_STATUS`
`};`
	"DBBINDING Structures" in Chapter 6, "Getting and Setting Data"	DBBINDING

`typedef DWORD DBPENDINGSTATUS;`
 	
`enum DBPENDINGSTATUSENUM {`
`    DBPENDINGSTATUS_NEW,`
`    DBPENDINGSTATUS_CHANGED,`
`    DBPENDINGSTATUS_DELETED,`
`    DBPENDINGSTATUS_UNCHANGED,`
`    DBPENDINGSTATUS_INVALIDROW`
`};`
	"Row States in Deferred Update Mode" in Chapter 5, "Updating Data in Rowsets"	**IRowsetUpdate::GetPendingRows**
		
		IRowsetUpdate::GetRowStatus

`typedef struct tagDBPROP {`
`    DBPROPID      dwPropertyID;`
`    DBPROPOPTIONS dwOptions;`
`    DBPROPSTATUS  dwStatus;`
`    DBID          colid;`
`    VARIANT       vValue;`
`} DBPROP;`
	"DBPROP Structure" in Chapter 11, "Properties"	DBPROPSET

Type	Defined in	Used in

`Typedef DWORD DBPROPFLAGS;`
 	
`enum DBPROPFLAGSENUM {`
`    DBPROPFLAGS_NOTSUPPORTED,`
`    DBPROPFLAGS_COLUMN,`
`    DBPROPFLAGS_DATASOURCE,`
`    DBPROPFLAGS_DATASOURCECREATE,`
`    DBPROPFLAGS_DATASOURCEINFO,`
`    DBPROPFLAGS_DBINIT,`
`    DBPROPFLAGS_INDEX,`
`    DBPROPFLAGS_ROWSET,`
`    DBPROPFLAGS_TABLE,`
`    DBPROPFLAGS_COLUMNOK,`
`    DBPROPFLAGS_READ,`
`    DBPROPFLAGS_WRITE,`
`    DBPROPFLAGS_REQUIRED,`
`    DBPROPFLAGS_SESSION`
`};`
	"DBPROPFLAGS Enumerated Type" in Chapter 11, "Properties"	DBPROPINFO

`typedef struct tagDBPROPIDSET {`
`    DBPROPID * rgPropertyIDs;`
`    ULONG      cPropertyIDs;`
`    GUID       guidPropertySet;`
`} DBPROPIDSET;`
	"DBPROPIDSET Structure" in Chapter 11, "Properties"	**ICommandProperties::GetProperties**
		IDBDataSourceAdmin::GetCreationProperties
		IDBProperties::GetProperties
		IDBProperties::GetPropertyInfo
		IRowsetInfo::GetProperties
		ISessionProperties::GetProperties

`typedef struct tagDBPROPINFO {`
`    LPOLESTR    pwszDescription;`
`    DBPROPID    dwPropertyID;`
`    DBPROPFLAGS dwFlags;`
`    VARTYPE     vtType;`
`    VARIANT     vValues;`
`} DBPROPINFO;`
	"DBPROPINFO Structure" in Chapter 11, "Properties"	DBPROPINFOSET

<table>
<tr><th>Type</th><th>Defined in</th><th>Used in</th></tr>
<tr><td><pre>typedef struct tagDBPROPINFOSET {
     DBPROPINFO * rgPropertyInfos;
     ULONG   cPropertyInfos;
     GUID   guidPropertySet;
} DBPROPINFOSET;</pre></td><td>"DBPROPINFOSET Structure" in Chapter 11, "Properties"</td><td>IDBDataSourceAdmin::GetCreationProperties
IDBProperties::GetPropertyInfo</td></tr>
<tr><td><pre>typedef DWORD DBPROPOPTIONS;

enum DBPROPOPTIONSENUM {
     DBPROPOPTIONS_REQUIRED,
     DBPROPOPTIONS_OPTIONAL
};</pre></td><td>"DBPROPOPTIONS Enumerated Type" in Chapter 11, "Properties"</td><td>DBPROP</td></tr>
<tr><td><pre>typedef struct tagDBPROPSET {
     DBPROP * rgProperties;
     ULONG   cProperties;
     GUID   guidPropertySet;
} DBPROPSET;</pre></td><td>"DBPROPSET Structure" in Chapter 11, "Properties"</td><td>DBCOLUMNDESC
IColumnsRowset::GetColumnsRowset
ICommandProperties::GetProperties
ICommandProperties::SetProperties
IDBDataSourceAdmin::CreateDataSource
IDBDataSourceAdmin::ModifyDataSource
IDBProperties::GetProperties
IDBProperties::SetProperties
IDBSchemaRowset::GetRowset
IIndexDefinition::CreateIndex
IOpenRowset::OpenRowset
IRowsetIndex::GetIndexInfo
IRowsetInfo::GetProperties</td></tr>
</table>

Type	Defined in	Used in
		ISessionProperties::GetProperties **ISessionProperties::SetProperties** **ISourcesRowset::GetSourcesRowset** **ITableDefinition::CreateTable**

`typedef DWORD DBPROPSTATUS;`
 	
`enum DBPROPSTATUSENUM {`
`DBPROPSTATUS_OK,`
`DBPROPSTATUS_NOTSUPPORTED,`
`DBPROPSTATUS_BADVALUE,`
`DBPROPSTATUS_BADOPTION,`
`DBPROPSTATUS_BADCOLUMN,`
`DBPROPSTATUS_NOTALLSETTABLE,`
`DBPROPSTATUS_NOTSETTABLE,`
`DBPROPSTATUS_NOTSET,`
`DBPROPSTATUS_CONFLICTING`
`};`
	"DBPROPSTATUS Enumerated Type" in Chapter 11, "Properties"	DBPROP

`typedef DWORD DBRANGE;`
 	
`enum DBRANGEENUM {`
`DBRANGE_INCLUSIVESTART,`
`DBRANGE_INCLUSIVEEND,`
`DBRANGE_EXCLUSIVESTART,`
`DBRANGE_EXCLUSIVEEND,`
`DBRANGE_EXCLUDENULLS,`
`DBRANGE_PREFIX,`
`DBRANGE_MATCH`
`};`
	IRowsetIndex::SetRange in Part 2, "OLE DB Reference"	**IRowsetIndex::SetRange**

Type	Defined in	Used in

`typedef DWORD DBREASON;`
 	
`enum DBREASONENUM {`
`DBREASON_ROWSET_FETCHPOSITIONCHANGE,`
`DBREASON_ROWSET_RELEASE,`
`DBREASON_ROWSET_CHANGED,`
`DBREASON_COLUMN_SET,`
`DBREASON_COLUMN_RECALCULATED,`
`DBREASON_ROW_ACTIVATE,`
`DBREASON_ROW_RELEASE,`
`DBREASON_ROW_DELETE,`
`DBREASON_ROW_FIRSTCHANGE,`
`DBREASON_ROW_INSERT,`
`DBREASON_ROW_RESYNCH,`
`DBREASON_ROW_UNDOCHANGE,`
`DBREASON_ROW_UNDOINSERT,`
`DBREASON_ROW_UNDODELETE,`
`DBREASON_ROW_UPDATE`
`};`
	IRowsetNotify in Part 2, "OLE DB Reference"	**IRowsetNotify::OnField-Change**
		
		IRowsetNotify::OnRow-Change
		
		IRowsetNotify::On-RowsetChange

`typedef DWORD DBROWSTATUS;`
 	
`enum DBROWSTATUSENUM {`
`DBROWSTATUS_S_OK,`
`DBROWSTATUS_S_MULTIPLECHANGES,`
`DBROWSTATUS_S_PENDINGCHANGES,`
`DBROWSTATUS_S_NOCHANGE,`
`DBROWSTATUS_E_CANCELED,`
`DBROWSTATUS_E_CANTRELEASE,`
`DBROWSTATUS_E_CONCURRENCYVIOLATION,`
`DBROWSTATUS_E_DELETED,`
`DBROWSTATUS_E_FAIL,`
`DBROWSTATUS_E_PENDINGINSERT,`
`DBROWSTATUS_E_NEWLYINSERTED,`
`DBROWSTATUS_E_INTEGRITYVIOLATION,`
`DBROWSTATUS_E_INVALID,`
`DBROWSTATUS_E_MAXPENDCHANGESEXCEEDED,`
`DBROWSTATUS_E_OBJECTOPEN,`
`DBROWSTATUS_E_OUTOFMEMORY,`
`DBROWSTATUS_E_PERMISSIONDENIED,`
`DBROWSTATUS_E_LIMITREACHED,`
`DBROWSTATUS_E_SCHEMAVIOLATION`
`};`
	"Arrays of Errors" in Chapter 13, "Errors"	**IRowset::AddRefRows**
		
		IRowset::ReleaseRows
		
		IRowsetChange::Delete-Rows
		
		IRowsetLocate::Get-RowsByBookmark
		
		IRowsetLocate::Hash
		
		IRowsetRefresh::RefreshVisibleData
		
		IRowsetUpdate::Undo
		
		IRowsetUpdate::Update

<table>
<tr><th>Type</th><th>Defined in</th><th>Used in</th></tr>
<tr><td><pre>typedef DWORD DBSEEK;

enum DBSEEKENUM {
     DBSEEK_INVALID,
     DBSEEK_FIRSTEQ,
     DBSEEK_LASTEQ,
     DBSEEK_GE,
     DBSEEK_GT,
     DBSEEK_LE,
     DBSEEK_LT
};</pre></td><td>IRowsetIndex::Seek in Part 2, "OLE DB Reference"</td><td>IRowsetIndex::Seek</td></tr>
<tr><td><pre>typedef DWORD DBSORT;

enum DBSORTENUM {
     DBSORT_ASCENDING = 0,
     DBSORT_DESCENDING
};</pre></td><td>IViewSort::SetSortOrder in Part 2, "OLE DB Reference"</td><td>IViewSort::SetSortOrder</td></tr>
<tr><td><pre>typedef DWORD DBSOURCETYPE;

enum DBSOURCETYPEENUM {
     DBSOURCETYPE_DATASOURCE,
     DBSOURCETYPE_ENUMERATOR
};</pre></td><td>ISourcesRowset::GetSourcesRowset in Part 2, "OLE DB Reference"</td><td>ISourcesRowset::Get-SourcesRowset</td></tr>
<tr><td><pre>typedef DWORD DBSTATUS;

enum DBSTATUSENUM {
     DBSTATUS_S_OK,
     DBSTATUS_E_BADACCESSOR,
     DBSTATUS_E_CANTCONVERTVALUE,
     DBSTATUS_S_ISNULL,
     DBSTATUS_S_TRUNCATED,
     DBSTATUS_E_SIGNMISMATCH,
     DBSTATUS_E_DATAOVERFLOW,
     DBSTATUS_E_CANTCREATE,
     DBSTATUS_E_UNAVAILABLE,
     DBSTATUS_E_PERMISSIONDENIED,
     DBSTATUS_S_DEFAULT,DBSTATUS_E_INTEGRITYVI
     DBSTATUS_E_SCHEMAVIOLATION,
     DBSTATUS_E_BADSTATUS,
     DBSTATUS_S_DEFAULT
     };</pre></td><td>"Status" in Chapter 6, "Getting and Setting Data"</td><td></td></tr>
</table>

<table>
<tr><th>Type</th><th>Defined in</th><th>Used in</th></tr>
<tr><td><pre>typedef struct tagDBTIME {
     USHORT hour;
     USHORT minute;
     USHORT second;
} DBTIME;</pre></td><td>"Type Indicators" in Appendix A, "Data Types"</td><td></td></tr>
<tr><td><pre>typedef struct tagDBTIMESTAMP {
     SHORT year;
     USHORT month;
     USHORT day;
     USHORT hour;
     USHORT minute;
     USHORT second;
     ULONG fraction;
} DBTIMESTAMP;</pre></td><td>"Type Indicators" in Appendix A, "Data Types"</td><td></td></tr>
<tr><td><pre>typedef struct tagFILETIME {
     DWORD dwLowDateTime;
     DWORD dwHighDateTime;
} DBFILETIME;</pre></td><td>"Type Indicators" in Appendix A, "Data Types"</td><td></td></tr>
<tr><td><pre>typedef WORD DBTYPE;

enum DBTYPEENUM {
     DBTYPE_EMPTY,
     DBTYPE_NULL,
     DBTYPE_I2,
     DBTYPE_I4,
     DBTYPE_R4,
     DBTYPE_R8,
     DBTYPE_CY,
     DBTYPE_DATE,
     DBTYPE_BSTR,
     DBTYPE_IDISPATCH,
     DBTYPE_ERROR,
     DBTYPE_BOOL,
     DBTYPE_VARIANT,
     DBTYPE_IUNKNOWN,
     DBTYPE_DECIMAL,
     DBTYPE_UI1,
     DBTYPE_ARRAY,
     DBTYPE_BYREF,
     DBTYPE_I1,
     DBTYPE_UI2,
     DBTYPE_UI4,
     DBTYPE_I8,
     DBTYPE_UI8,</pre></td><td>"Type Indicators" in Appendix A, "Data Types"</td><td>DBBINDING
DBCOLUMNINFO
DBPARAMINFO
DBCOLUMNDESC
IConvertType::Can-Convert</td></tr>
</table>

Type	Defined in	Used in
DBTYPE_GUID, DBTYPE_VECTOR, DBTYPE_RESERVED, DBTYPE_BYTES, DBTYPE_STR, DBTYPE_WSTR, DBTYPE_NUMERIC, DBTYPE_UDT, DBTYPE_DBDATE, DBTYPE_DBTIME, DBTYPE_DBTIMESTAMP, DBTYPE_FILETIME, DBTYPE_HCHAPTER, DBTYPE_PROPVARIANT, DBTYPE_VARNUMERIC };		
typedef struct tagDBVECTOR { ULONG size; void * ptr; } DBVECTOR;	"Type Indicators" in Appendix A, "Data Types"	

typedef struct tagDEC {
USHORT wReserved;
union {
struct {
BYTE scale;
BYTE sign;
};
USHORT signscale;
};
ULONG Hi32;
union {
struct {
ULONG Lo32;
ULONG Mid32;
};
ULONGLONG Lo64;
};
} DECIMAL;
	"Type Indicators" in Appendix A, "Data Types"	

typedef struct tagERRORINFO { HRESULT hrError; DWORD dwMinor; CLSID clsid; IID iid; DISPID dispid; } ERRORINFO;	"Error Records" in Chapter 13, "Errors"	**IErrorRecords::AddErrorRecord** **IErrorRecords::GetBasicErrorInfo**

Type	Defined in	Used in

<pre>typedef struct XACTTRANSINFO {
    XACTUOW uow;
    ISOLEVEL isoLevel;
    ULONG   isoFlags;
    DWORD   grfTCSupported;
    DWORD   grfRMSupported;
    DWORD   grfTCSupportedRetaining;
    DWORD   grfRMSupportedRetaining;
} XACTTRANSINFO;</pre>
	ITransaction::GetTransactionInfo in Part 2, "OLE DB Reference"	**ITransaction::GetTransactionInfo**

<pre>typedef struct XACTOPT {
    ULONG ulTimeout;
    unsigned char
    szDescription[MAX_TRAN_DESC];
} XACTOPT</pre>
	ITransactionOptions::SetOptions in Part 2, "OLE DB Reference"	**ITransactionOptions::GetOptions**
		ITransactionOptions::SetOptions

APPENDIX E

Interface Summary

This appendix lists the prototypes of all interfaces in OLE DB.

```
interface IAccessor {
   HRESULT AddRefAccessor (
         HACCESSOR   hAccessor,
         ULONG *     pcRefCount);

   HRESULT CreateAccessor (
         DBACCESSORFLAGS   dwAccessorFlags,
         ULONG             cBindings,
         const DBBINDING   rgBindings[],
         ULONG             cbRowSize,
         HACCESSOR *       phAccessor,
         DBBINDSTATUS      rgStatus[]);

   HRESULT GetBindings (
         HACCESSOR         hAccessor,
         DBACCESSORFLAGS * pdwAccessorFlags,
         ULONG *           pcBindings,
         DBBINDING **      prgBindings);

   HRESULT ReleaseAccessor (
         HACCESSOR   hAccessor,
         ULONG *     pcRefCount);
};


interface IAlterIndex {
   HRESULT AlterIndex (
         DBID *      pTableID,
         DBID *      pIndexID,
         DBID *      pNewIndexID,
         ULONG       cPropertySets,
         DBPROPSET   rgPropertySet[]);
};
```

```
interface IAlterTable {
   HRESULT AlterColumn (
         DBID *                  pTableID,
         DBID *                  pColumnID,
         DBCOLUMNDESCFLAGS       ColumnDescFlags,
         DBCOLUMNDESC*           pColumnDesc);

         DBID *        pTableID,
         DBID *        pNewTableID,
         ULONG         cPropertySets,
         DBPROPSET     rgPropertySet[]);
};


interface IChapteredRowset {
   HRESULT AddRefChapter (
         HCHAPTER    hChapter,
         ULONG *     pcRefCount);

   HRESULT ReleaseChapter (
         HCHAPTER    hChapter,
         ULONG *     pcRefCount);
};


interface IColumnsInfo {
   HRESULT GetColumnInfo (
         ULONG *            pcColumns,
         DBCOLUMNINFO **    prgInfo,
         OLECHAR **         ppStringsBuffer);

   HRESULT MapColumnIDs (
         ULONG        cColumnIDs,
         const DBID   rgColumnIDs[],
         ULONG        rgColumns[]);
};
```

```
interface IColumnsRowset {
   HRESULT GetAvailableColumns (
         ULONG *  pcOptColumns,
         DBID **  prgOptColumns);

   HRESULT GetColumnsRowset (
         IUnknown *  pUnkOuter,
         ULONG       cOptColumns,
         const DBID  rgOptColumns[],
         REFIID      riid,
         ULONG       cPropertySets,
         DBPROPSET   rgPropertySets[],
         IUnknown ** ppColRowset);
};


interface ICommand {
   HRESULT Cancel();

   HRESULT Execute (
         IUnknown *  pUnkOuter,
         REFIID      riid,
         DBPARAMS *  pParams,
         LONG  *     pcRowsAffected,
         IUnknown ** ppRowset);

   HRESULT GetDBSession (
         REFIID      riid,
         IUnknown ** ppSession);
};


interface ICommandPersist {
   HRESULT  DeleteCommand(
         DBID *pCommandID);

   HRESULT  GetCurrentCommand(
         DBID *pCommandID);

   HRESULT  LoadCommand(
         DBID *pCommandID,
         DWORD    dwFlags);

   HRESULT  SaveCommand(
         DBID *pCommandID,
         DWORD dwFlags);
};
```

```
interface ICommandPrepare {
   HRESULT Prepare (
         ULONG cExpectedRuns);

   HRESULT Unprepare();
};


interface ICommandProperties {
   HRESULT GetProperties (
         const ULONG       cPropertyIDSets,
         const DBPROPIDSET rgPropertyIDSets[],
         ULONG *           pcPropertySets,
         DBPROPSET **      prgPropertySets);

   HRESULT SetProperties (
         ULONG       cPropertySets,
         DBPROPSET   rgPropertySets[]);
};


interface ICommandText : ICommand {
   HRESULT GetCommandText (
         GUID *      pguidDialect,
         LPOLESTR *  ppwszCommand);

   HRESULT SetCommandText (
         REFGUID     rguidDialect,
         LPCOLESTR   pwszCommand);
};


interface ICommandWithParameters {
   HRESULT GetParameterInfo (
         ULONG *        pcParams,
         DBPARAMINFO ** prgParamInfo,
         OLECHAR **     ppNamesBuffer);

   HRESULT MapParameterNames (
         ULONG             cParamNames,
         const OLECHAR *   rgParamNames[],
         LONG              rgParamOrdinals[]);

   HRESULT SetParameterInfo (
         ULONG                   cParams,
         const ULONG             rgParamOrdinals[],
         const DBPARAMBINDINFO   rgParamBindInfo[]);
};
```

```
interface IConvertType {
   HRESULT CanConvert (
         DBTYPE          wFromType,
         DBTYPE          wToType,
         DBCONVERTFLAGS dwConvertFlags);
};


interface IDBAsynchNotify {
   HRESULT OnLowResource (
         DWORD    dwReserved);

   HRESULT OnProgress (
         HCHAPTER    hChapter,
         ULONG       ulOperation,
         ULONG       ulProgress,
         ULONG       ulProgressMax,
         ULONG       ulAsynchPhase,
         LPOLESTR    pwszStatusText);

   HRESULT OnStop (
         HCHAPTER    hChapter,
         ULONG       ulOperation,
         HRESULT     hrStatus,
         LPOLESTR    pwszStatusText);
};


interface IDBAsynchStatus {
   HRESULT Abort (
         HCHAPTER    hChapter,
         ULONG       ulOperation);

   HRESULT GetStatus (
         HCHAPTER    hChapter,
         ULONG       ulOperation,
         ULONG *     pulProgress,
         ULONG *     pulProgressMax,
         ULONG *     pulAsynchPhase,
         LPOLESTR *  ppwszStatusText);
};
```

```
interface IDBCreateCommand {
   HRESULT CreateCommand(
         IUnknown *  pUnkOuter,
         REFIID      riid,
         IUnknown ** ppCommand);
};


interface IDBCreateSession {
   HRESULT CreateSession (
         IUnknown *  pUnkOuter,
         REFIID      riid,
         IUnknown ** ppDBSession);
};


interface IDBDataSourceAdmin {
   HRESULT CreateDataSource(
         ULONG       cPropertySets,
         DBPROPSET   rgPropertySets[],
         IUnknown *  pUnkOuter,
         REFIID      riid,
         IUnknown ** ppSession);

   HRESULT DestroyDataSource ();

   HRESULT GetCreationProperties (
         ULONG             cPropertyIDSets,
         const DBPROPIDSET rgPropertyIDSets[],
         ULONG *           pcPropertyInfoSets,
         DBPROPINFOSET **  prgPropertyInfoSets,
         OLECHAR **        ppDescBuffer);

   HRESULT ModifyDataSource (
         ULONG       cPropertySets,
         DBPROPSET   rgPropertySets[]);
};
```

```
interface IDBInfo {
   HRESULT GetKeywords(
         LPOLESTR *  ppwszKeywords);

   HRESULT GetLiteralInfo(
         ULONG              cLiterals,
         const DBLITERAL    rgLiterals[],
         ULONG *            pcLiteralInfo,
         DBLITERALINFO **   prgLiteralInfo,
         OLECHAR **         ppCharBuffer);
};


interface IDBInitialize {
   HRESULT Initialize();

   HRESULT Uninitialize();
};


interface IDBProperties {
   HRESULT GetProperties (
         ULONG              cPropertyIDSets,
         const DBPROPIDSET rgPropertyIDSets[],
         ULONG *            pcPropertySets,
         DBPROPSET **       prgPropertySets);

   HRESULT GetPropertyInfo(
         ULONG              cPropertyIDSets,
         const DBPROPIDSET rgPropertyIDSets[],
         ULONG *            pcPropertyInfoSets,
         DBPROPINFOSET **   prgPropertyInfoSets,
         OLECHAR **         ppDescBuffer);

   HRESULT SetProperties (
         ULONG       cPropertySets,
         DBPROPSET   rgPropertySets[]);
};
```

```
interface IDBSchemaRowset {
   HRESULT GetRowset (
         IUnknown *      punkOuter,
         REFGUID         rguidSchema,
         ULONG           cRestrictions,
         const VARIANT   rgRestrictions[],
         REFIID          riid,
         ULONG           cPropertySets,
         DBPROPSET       rgPropertySets[],
         IUnknown **     ppRowset);

   HRESULT GetSchemas (
         ULONG *   pcSchemas,
         GUID **   prgSchemas,
         ULONG**   prgRestrictionSupport);
};


interface IErrorInfo {
   HRESULT GetDescription (
         BSTR *pbstrDescription);

   HRESULT GetGUID (
         GUID *pguid);

   HRESULT GetHelpContext (
         DWORD *   pdwHelpContext);

   HRESULT GetHelpFile (
         BSTR *pbstrHelpFile);

   HRESULT GetSource (
         BSTR *pbstrSource);
};
```

```
interface IErrorLookup {
   HRESULT GetErrorDescription (
         HRESULT        hrError,
         DWORD          dwLookupID,
         DISPPARAMS *   pdispparams,
         LCID           lcid,
         BSTR *         pbstrSource,
         BSTR *         pbstrDescription);

   HRESULT GetHelpInfo (
         HRESULT  hrError,
         DWORD    dwLookupID,
         LCID     lcid,
         BSTR *   pbstrHelpFile,
         DWORD *  pdwHelpContext);

   HRESULT ReleaseErrors (
         const DWORD dwDynamicErrorID);
};


interface IErrorRecords {
   HRESULT AddErrorRecord (
         ERRORINFO *    pErrorInfo,
         DWORD          dwLookupID,
         DISPPARAMS *   pdispparams,
         IUnknown *     punkCustomError,
         DWORD          dwDynamicErrorID);

   HRESULT GetBasicErrorInfo (
         ULONG       ulRecordNum,
         ERRORINFO * pErrorInfo);

   HRESULT GetCustomErrorObject (
         ULONG       ulRecordNum,
         REFIID      riid,
         IUnknown ** ppObject);

   HRESULT GetErrorInfo (
         ULONG          ulRecordNum,
         LCID           lcid,
         IErrorInfo **  ppErrorInfo);
```

```
    HRESULT GetErrorParameters (
          ULONG          ulRecordNum,
          DISPPARAMS *   pdispparams);

    HRESULT GetRecordCount (
          ULONG *  pcRecords);
};


interface IGetDataSource {
    HRESULT GetDataSource (
          REFIID      riid,
          IUnknown ** ppDataSource);
};


interface IIndexDefinition {
    HRESULT CreateIndex(
          DBID *                        pTableID,
          DBID *                        pIndexID,
          ULONG                         cIndexColumnDescs,
          const DBINDEXCOLUMNDESC       rgIndexColumnDescs[],
          ULONG                         cPropertySets,
          DBPROPSET                     rgPropertySets[],
          DBID **                       ppIndexID);

    HRESULT DropIndex(
          DBID *pTableID,
          DBID *pIndexID);
};


interface IMultipleResults {
    HRESULT GetResult(
          IUnknown *  pUnkOuter,
          LONG        lReserved,
          REFIID      riid,
          LONG *      pcRowsAffected,
          IUnknown ** ppRowset);
};
```

```
interface IOpenRowset {
   HRESULT OpenRowset(
         IUnknown *  pUnkOuter,
         DBID *      pTableID,
         DBID *      pIndexID,
         REFIID      riid,
         ULONG       cPropertySets,
         DBPROPSET   rgPropertySets[],
         IUnknown ** ppRowset);
};


interface IRowset {
   HRESULT AddRefRows(
         ULONG       cRows,
         const HROW  rghRows[],
         ULONG       rgRefCounts[],
         DBROWSTATUS rgRowStatus[]);

   HRESULT GetData (
         HROW        hRow,
         HACCESSOR   hAccessor,
         void *      pData);

   HRESULT GetNextRows (
         HCHAPTER hChapter,
         LONG     lRowsOffset,
         LONG     cRows,
         ULONG *  pcRowsObtained,
         HROW **  prghRows);

   HRESULT ReleaseRows (
         ULONG          cRows,
         const HROW     rghRows[],
         DBROWOPTIONS   rgRowOptions[]
         ULONG          rgRefCounts[],
         DBROWSTATUS    rgRowStatus[]);

   HRESULT RestartPosition (
         HCHAPTER hChapter);
};
```

```
interface IRowsetChange {
   HRESULT DeleteRows (
         HCHAPTER    hChapter,
         ULONG       cRows,
         const HROW  rghRows[],
         DBROWSTATUS rgRowStatus[]);

   HRESULT InsertRow (
         HCHAPTER    hChapter,
         HACCESSOR   hAccessor,
         void *      pData,
         HROW  *     phRow);

   HRESULT SetData (
         HROW        hRow,
         HACCESSOR   hAccessor,
         void *      pData);
};


interface IRowsetChapterMember {
   HRESULT IsRowInChapter (
         HCHAPTER    hChapter,
         HROW        hRow);
};


interface IRowsetFind {
   HRESULT FindNextRow (
         HCHAPTER       hChapter,
         HACCESSOR      hAccessor,
         void *         pFindValue,
         DBCOMPAREOP    CompareOp,
         ULONG          cbBookmark,
         const BYTE *   pBookmark,
         LONG           lRowsOffset,
         LONG           cRows,
         ULONG *        pcRowsObtained,
         HROW **        prghRows);
};


interface IRowsetIdentity {
   HRESULT IsSameRow (
         HROW  hThisRow,
         HROW  hThatRow);
};
```

```
interface IRowsetIndex {
   HRESULT GetIndexInfo (
         ULONG *                    pcKeyColumns,
         DBINDEXCOLUMNDESC **       prgIndexColumnDesc,
         ULONG *                    pcIndexProperties,
         DBPROPSET **               prgIndexProperties);

   HRESULT Seek (
         HACCESSORhAccessor,
         ULONG        cKeyValues,
         void *       pData,
         DBSEEK       dwSeekOptions);

   HRESULT SetRange (
         HACCESSORhAccessor,
         ULONG        cStartKeyColumns,
         void *       pStartData,
         ULONG        cEndKeyColumns,
         void *       pEndData,
         DBRANGE      dwRangeOptions);
};


interface IRowsetInfo {
   HRESULT GetProperties (
         const ULONG        cPropertyIDSets,
         const DBPROPIDSET rgPropertyIDSets[],
         ULONG *            pcPropertySets,
         DBPROPSET **       prgPropertySets);

   HRESULT GetReferencedRowset (
         ULONG        iOrdinal,
         REFIID       riid,
         IUnknown ** ppReferencedRowset);

   HRESULT GetSpecification (
         REFIID       riid,
         IUnknown ** ppSpecification);
};


interface IRowsetLocate : IRowset {
   HRESULT Compare (
         HCHAPTER        hChapter,
         ULONG           cbBookmark1,
         const BYTE *    pBookmark1,
         ULONG           cbBookmark2,
         const BYTE *    pBookmark2,
         DBCOMPARE *     pComparison);
```

```
    HRESULT GetRowsAt (
          HWATCHREGION    hReserved1,
          HCHAPTER        hChapter
          ULONG           cbBookmark,
          const BYTE *    pBookmark,
          LONG            lRowsOffset,
          LONG            cRows,
          ULONG *         pcRowsObtained,
          HROW **         prghRows);

    HRESULT GetRowsByBookmark (
          HCHAPTER        hChapter,
          ULONG           cRows,
          const ULONG     rgcbBookmarks[],
          const BYTE *    rgpBookmarks[],
          HROW            rghRows[],
          DBROWSTATUS     rgRowStatus[]);

    HRESULT Hash (
          HCHAPTER        hChapter,
          ULONG           cBookmarks,
          const ULONG     rgcbBookmarks[],
          const BYTE *    rgpBookmarks[],
          DWORD           rgHashedValues[],
          DBROWSTATUS     rgBookmarkStatus[]);
};


interface IRowsetNotify {
    HRESULT OnFieldChange (
          IRowset*        pRowset,
          HROW            hRow,
          ULONG           cColumns,
          ULONG           rgColumns[],
          DBREASON        eReason,
          DBEVENTPHASE    ePhase,
          BOOL            fCantDeny);

    HRESULT OnRowChange (
          IRowset*        pRowset,
          ULONG           cRows,
          const HROW      rghRows[],
          DBREASON        eReason,
          DBEVENTPHASE    ePhase,
          BOOL            fCantDeny);
```

```
   HRESULT OnRowsetChange (
         IRowset*        pRowset,
         DBREASON        eReason,
         DBEVENTPHASE    ePhase,
         BOOL            fCantDeny);
};


interface IRowsetRefresh {
   HRESULT GetLastVisibleData (
         HROW         hRow,
         HACCESSOR    hAccessor,
         void *       pData);

   HRESULT RefreshVisibleData (
         HCHAPTER        hChapter,
         ULONG           cRows,
         const HROW      rghRows[],
         BOOL            fOverWrite,
         ULONG*          pcRowsRefreshed,
         HROW**          prghRowsRefreshed,
         DBROWSTATUS**   prgRowStatus);
};


interface IRowsetScroll : IRowsetLocate {
   HRESULT GetApproximatePosition (
         HCHAPTER        hChapter,
         ULONG           cbBookmark,
         const BYTE *    pBookmark,
         ULONG *         pulPosition,
         ULONG *         pcRows);

   HRESULT GetRowsAtRatio (
         HWATCHREGION    hReserved1,
         HCHAPTER        hChapter,
         ULONG           ulNumerator,
         ULONG           ulDenominator,
         LONG            cRows,
         ULONG *         pcRowsObtained,
         HROW **         prghRows);
};


interface IRowsetUpdate : IRowsetChange {
   HRESULT GetOriginalData (
         HROW         hRow,
         HACCESSOR    hAccessor,
         void *       pData);
```

```
   HRESULT GetPendingRows (
         HCHAPTER              hChapter,
         DBPENDINGSTATUS       dwRowStatus,
         ULONG *               pcPendingRows,
         HROW **               prgPendingRows,
         DBPENDINGSTATUS **    prgPendingStatus);

   HRESULT GetRowStatus(
         HCHAPTER           hChapter,
         ULONG              cRows,
         const HROW         rghRows[],
         DBPENDINGSTATUS    rgPendingStatus[]);

   HRESULT Undo (
         HCHAPTER        hChapter,
         ULONG           cRows,
         const HROW      rghRows[],
         ULONG *         pcRows,
         HROW **         prgRows,
         DBROWSTATUS **  prgRowStatus);

   HRESULT Update (
         HCHAPTER        hChapter,
         ULONG           cRows,
         const HROW      rghRows[],
         ULONG *         pcRows,
         HROW **         prgRows,
         DBROWSTATUS**   prgRowStatus);
};


interface IRowsetView {
   HRESULT CreateView (
         IUnknown *      pUnkOuter,
         REFIID          riid,
         IUnknown **     ppView);

   HRESULT GetView (
         HCHAPTER        hChapter,
         REFIID          riid,
         HCHAPTER *      phChapterSource,
         IUnknown **     ppView);
};
```

```
interface ISessionProperties {
   HRESULT GetProperties (
         ULONG             cPropertyIDSets,
         const DBPROPIDSET rgPropertyIDSets[],
         ULONG *           pcPropertySets,
         DBPROPSET **      prgPropertySets);

   HRESULT SetProperties (
         ULONG       cPropertySets,
         DBPROPSET   rgPropertySets[]);
};


interface ISourcesRowset {
   HRESULT GetSourcesRowset(
         IUnknown    pUnkOuter,
         REFIID      riid,
         ULONG       cPropertySets,
         DBPROPSET   rgPropertySets[],
         IUnknown ** ppSourcesRowset);
};


interface ISQLErrorInfo {
   HRESULT GetSQLInfo (
         BSTR *pbstrSQLState,
         LONG *plNativeError);
};


interface ISupportErrorInfo {
   HRESULT InterfaceSupportsErrorInfo (
         REFIID   riid);
};
```

```
interface ITableDefinition {
   HRESULT AddColumn(
         DBID *          pTableID,
         DBCOLUMNDESC *  pColumnDesc,
         DBID **         ppColumnID);

   HRESULT CreateTable(
         IUnknown *      pUnkOuter,
         DBID *          pTableID,
         ULONG           cColumnDescs,
         DBCOLUMNDESC    rgColumnDescs[],
         REFIID          riid,
         ULONG           cPropertySets,
         DBPROPSET       rgPropertySets[],
         DBID **         ppTableID,
         IUnknown **     ppRowset);

   HRESULT DropColumn(
         DBID* pTableID,
         DBID* pColumnID);

   HRESULT DropTable (
         DBID *pTableID);
};


interface ITransaction {
   HRESULT Abort(
         BOID *   pboidReason,
         BOOL     fRetaining,
         BOOL     fAsync);

   HRESULT Commit(
         BOOL  fRetaining,
         DWORD grfTC,
         DWORD grfRM);

   HRESULT GetTransactionInfo(
         XACTTRANSINFO *   pInfo);
};
```

```
interface ITransactionJoin {
   HRESULT GetOptionsObject (
         ITransactionOptions **   ppOptions);

   HRESULT JoinTransaction (
         IUnknown *               punkTransactionCoord,
         ISOLEVEL                 isoLevel,
         ULONG                    isoFlags,
         ITransactionOptions *    pOtherOptions);
};


interface ITransactionLocal : ITransaction {
   HRESULT GetOptionsObject (
         ITransactionOptions **   ppOptions);

   HRESULT StartTransaction (
         ISOLEVEL                 isoLevel,
         ULONG                    isoFlags,
         ITransactionOptions *    pOtherOptions,
         ULONG *                  pulTransactionLevel);
};


interface ITransactionObject {
   HRESULT GetTransactionObject (
         ULONG             ulTransactionLevel,
         ITransaction **   ppTransactionObject);
};


interface ITransactionOptions {
   HRESULT GetOptions(
         XACTOPT *   pOptions);

   HRESULT SetOptions(
         XACTOPT *   pOptions);
};


interface IViewChapter {
   HRESULT GetSpecification (
         REFIID      riid,
         IUnknown **    ppRowset);

   HRESULT OpenViewChapter (
         HCHAPTER       hSource,
         HCHAPTER *     phViewChapter);
};
```

```
interface IViewFilter {
   HRESULT GetFilter (
         HACCESSOR      hAccessor,
         ULONG *        pcRows,
         DBCOMPAREOP *  pCompareOps[],
         void *         pCriteriaData);

   HRESULT GetFilterBindings(
         ULONG *        pcBindings,
         DBBINDING **   prgBindings);

   HRESULT SetFilter (
         HACCESSOR      hAccessor,
         ULONG          cRows,
         DBCOMPAREOP    CompareOps [],
         void *         pCriteriaData);
};


interface IViewRowset {
   HRESULT GetSpecification (
         REFIID         riid,
         IUnknown **    ppObject);

   HRESULT OpenViewRowset (
         IUnknown *     pUnkOuter,
         REFIID         riid,
         IUnknown **    ppRowset);
};


interface IViewSort {
   HRESULT GetSort (
         ULONG *        pcColumns,
         ULONG *        prgColumns[],
         DBSORT *       prgOrders[]);

   HRESULT SetSort (
         ULONG          cColumns,
         const ULONG    rgColumns[],
         const DBSORT   rgOrders[]);
   };
```

APPENDIX F

Sample OLE DB Consumer Application

```
//-----------------------------------------------------------------------------
// Microsoft OLE DB Programmer's Reference Sample
// Copyright (C) 1998 By Microsoft Corporation.
//
// @doc
//
// @module PRSAMPLE.H
//
//-----------------------------------------------------------------------------


///////////////////////////////////////////////////////////////////
// Includes
//
///////////////////////////////////////////////////////////////////
#ifndef  __PRSAMPLE_H__
#define  __PRSAMPLE_H__

#include "oledb.h"   // OLE DB Header
#include "oledberr.h"   // OLE DB Errors

#include "msdasc.h"     // OLE DB Service Component header
#include "msdaguid.h"// OLE DB Root Enumerator
#include "msdasql.h"    // MSDASQL - Default provider

#include <stdio.h>   // input and output functions
#include <conio.h>   // getch, putch
#include <locale.h>     // setlocale

///////////////////////////////////////////////////////////////////
// Globals
//
///////////////////////////////////////////////////////////////////
extern DWORD g_dwFlags;
```

```
///////////////////////////////////////////////////////////////////
// Defines
//
///////////////////////////////////////////////////////////////////
#define __LONGSTRING(string) L##string
#define LONGSTRING(string) __LONGSTRING(string)

// Goes to CLEANUP on Failure·
#define CHECK_HR(hr)       \
   if(FAILED(hr))          \
      goto CLEANUP

// Goes to CLEANUP on Failure, and displays any ErrorInfo
#define XCHECK_HR(hr)                                              \
{                                                                \
   if( g_dwFlags & DISPLAY_METHODCALLS )                           \
      fwprintf(stderr, LONGSTRING(#hr) L"\n");                            \
   if(FAILED(myHandleResult(hr, LONGSTRING(__FILE__), __LINE__)))  \
      goto CLEANUP;                                                \
}
#define CHECK_MEMORY(hr, pv)  \
{                          \
   if(!pv)                    \
   {                       \
      hr = E_OUTOFMEMORY;  \
      CHECK_HR(hr);           \
   }                       \
}


#define MAX_COL_SIZE       5000
#define MAX_NAME_LEN    256

#define MAX_ROWS           10
#define MAX_DISPLAY_SIZE20
#define MIN_DISPLAY_SIZE   3

// ROUNDUP on all platforms pointers must be aligned properly
#define ROUNDUP_AMOUNT  8
#define ROUNDUP_(size,amount) (((ULONG)(size)+((amount)-1))&~((amount)-1))
#define ROUNDUP(size)      ROUNDUP_(size, ROUNDUP_AMOUNT)
```

```
enum
{
   // Connecting
   USE_PROMPTDATASOURCE     = 0x0001,
   USE_ENUMERATOR           = 0x0002,

   // Rowset
   USE_COMMAND              = 0x0010,

   // Storage objects
   USE_ISEQSTREAM           = 0x0100,

   // Display options
   DISPLAY_METHODCALLS      = 0x1000,
   DISPLAY_INSTRUCTIONS     = 0x2000,
};


/////////////////////////////////////////////////////////////////////////////
// Function prototypes
//
/////////////////////////////////////////////////////////////////////////////
// Main
BOOL  myParseCommandLine();
void  myDisplayInstructions();
BOOL  myGetInputFromUser(LPWSTR pwszInput, LPCWSTR pwszFmt, ...);
CHAR  myGetChar();

// Enumerator
HRESULT myCreateEnumerator(REFCLSID clsidEnumerator, CLSID* pCLSID);

// Data source
HRESULT myCreateDataSource(IUnknown** ppUnkDataSource);
HRESULT myDoInitialization(IUnknown* pIUnknown);
HRESULT myGetProperty(IUnknown* pIUnknown, REFIID riid, DBPROPID dwPropertyID, REFGUID
guidPropertySet, BOOL* pbValue);
void  myAddProperty(DBPROP* pProp, DBPROPID dwPropertyID, VARTYPE vtType = VT_BOOL, LONG
lValue = VARIANT_TRUE, DBPROPOPTIONS dwOptions = DBPROPOPTIONS_OPTIONAL);

// Session
HRESULT  myCreateSession(IUnknown* pUnkDataSource, IUnknown** ppUnkSession);
HRESULT  myCreateSchemaRowset(GUID guidSchema, IUnknown* pUnkSession, ULONG cchBuffer,
LPWSTR pwszBuffer);

// Command
HRESULT  myCreateCommand(IUnknown* pUnkSession, IUnknown** ppUnkCommand);
HRESULT  myExecuteCommand(IUnknown* pUnkCommand, WCHAR* pwszCommandText, ULONG cPropSets,
DBPROPSET* rgPropSets, IUnknown** ppUnkRowset);
```

```
// Rowset
HRESULT  myCreateRowset(IUnknown* pUnkSession, IUnknown** ppUnkRowset);
HRESULT mySetupBindings(IUnknown* pUnkRowset, ULONG* pcBindings, DBBINDING** prgBindings,
ULONG* pcbRowSize);
HRESULT myCreateAccessor(IUnknown* pUnkRowset, HACCESSOR* phAccessor, ULONG* pcBindings,
DBBINDING** prgBindings, ULONG* pcbRowSize);

HRESULT myDisplayRowset(IUnknown* pUnkRowset, LPCWSTR pwszColToReturn, ULONG cchBuffer,
LPWSTR pwszBuffer);
HRESULT myDisplayColumnNames(IUnknown* pUnkRowset, ULONG* rgDispSize);
HRESULT myDisplayRow(ULONG iRow, ULONG cBindings, DBBINDING* rgBindings, void* pData,
ULONG * rgDispSize);

HRESULT myInteractWithRowset(IRowset* pIRowset, LONG* pcRows, ULONG cRowsObtained, BOOL
fCanFetchBackwards, void* pData, ULONG cbRowSize, DBBINDING* pBinding, ULONG cchBuffer,
LPWSTR pwszBuffer);
HRESULT myFindColumn(IUnknown * pUnkRowset, LPCWSTR pwszName, LONG* plIndex);
HRESULT myUpdateDisplaySize(ULONG cBindings, DBBINDING* rgBindings, void* pData, ULONG*
rgDispSize);
void  myFreeBindings(ULONG cBindings, DBBINDING* rgBindings);
void  myAddRowsetProperties(DBPROPSET* pPropSet, ULONG cProperties, DBPROP* rgProperties);

// Error
HRESULT myHandleResult(HRESULT hrReturned, LPCWSTR pwszFile, ULONG ulLine);
HRESULT myDisplayErrorRecord(HRESULT hrReturned, ULONG iRecord, IErrorRecords*
pIErrorRecords, LPCWSTR pwszFile, ULONG ulLine);
HRESULT myDisplayErrorInfo(HRESULT hrReturned, IErrorInfo* pIErrorInfo, LPCWSTR pwszFile,
ULONG ulLine);
HRESULT myGetSqlErrorInfo(ULONG iRecord, IErrorRecords* pIErrorRecords, BSTR* pBstr, LONG*
plNativeError);


#endif// __PRSAMPLE_H__
```

```
//-----------------------------------------------------------------------
// Microsoft OLE DB Programmer's Reference Sample
// Copyright (C) 1998 By Microsoft Corporation.
//
// @doc
//
// @module MAIN.CPP
//
//-----------------------------------------------------------------------


/////////////////////////////////////////////////////////////////
// Includes
//
/////////////////////////////////////////////////////////////////
#define DBINITCONSTANTS     // Store all OLE DB consts inside this .obj file
#include "prsample.h"    // Programmer's Reference Sample includes


/////////////////////////////////////////////////////////////////
// Globals
//
/////////////////////////////////////////////////////////////////
DWORD g_dwFlags = USE_PROMPTDATASOURCE | DISPLAY_METHODCALLS;


/////////////////////////////////////////////////////////////////
// main
//
// This is a simple OLE DB application that will display a
// rowset and will allow basic navigation of that rowset by the
// user.
//
// In the sample, functions that begin with 'my' are implemented
// in the sample code; all other functions are either OLE DB
// methods or standard system methods. In addition, two
// macros are used repeatedly throughout the sample:
// -- CHECK_HR(hr)  - this macro goes to the CLEANUP label if
//     FAILED(hr), where hr is usually a method call.
// -- XCHECK_HR(hr) - this macro prints the string
//     representation of hr to stderr and if FAILED(hr), attempts
//     to obtain and display any extended error information
//     posted by the last method call, then jumps to the CLEANUP
//     label.
//
```

```
// This is the entry point for the sample. This function will:
// -- parse command line arguments passed to the sample
// -- display appropriate instructions based on these arguments
// -- create an OLE DB data source object for a user-chosen
//      provider
// -- create an OLE DB session object from the provider's
//      data source object
// -- create an OLE DB rowset object, over a table specified by
//      the user, from the provider's session object
//   - display the rowset data and will allow the user to
//     navigate over the rowset
//
/////////////////////////////////////////////////////////////////
int main()
{
   HRESULT          hr;
   IUnknown *          pUnkDataSource              = NULL;
   IUnknown *          pUnkSession                 = NULL;
   IUnknown *          pUnkRowset                  = NULL;

   // Parse command line arguments, if any; this will update
   // the value of g_dwFlags as appropriate for the arguments
   if( !myParseCommandLine() )
      return EXIT_FAILURE;

   // Display instructions for the given command line arguments
   myDisplayInstructions();

   // Initialize OLE
   hr = CoInitialize(NULL);
   if( FAILED(hr) )
      return EXIT_FAILURE;

   // Create the data source object using the OLE DB service components
   CHECK_HR(hr = myCreateDataSource(&pUnkDataSource));

   // Create a session object from the data source object
   CHECK_HR(hr = myCreateSession(pUnkDataSource, &pUnkSession));

   // Create a rowset object from the session object, either directly
   // from the session or through a command object
   CHECK_HR(hr = myCreateRowset(pUnkSession, &pUnkRowset));

   // Display the rowset object data to the user
   CHECK_HR(hr = myDisplayRowset(pUnkRowset, NULL, 0, NULL));

 CLEANUP:
   if( pUnkRowset )
      pUnkRowset->Release();
```

```
    if( pUnkSession )
       pUnkSession->Release();
    if( pUnkDataSource )
       pUnkDataSource->Release();

    CoUninitialize();

    if( FAILED(hr) )
       return EXIT_FAILURE;

    return EXIT_SUCCESS;
}


/////////////////////////////////////////////////////////////////////
// myParseCommandLine
//
// This function parses the application's command line arguments
// and sets the appropriate bits in g_dwFlags. If an invalid
// argument is encountered, a usage message is displayed and
// the function returns FALSE; otherwise, TRUE is returned.
//
/////////////////////////////////////////////////////////////////////
BOOL myParseCommandLine
    (
    void
    )
{
    int                 iArg;
    CHAR *              psz;

    // Set the locale for all C run-time functions
    setlocale(LC_ALL, ".ACP");
```

```
// Go through each command line argument and set the appropriate
// bits in g_dwFlags, depending on the chosen options
for( iArg = 1; iArg < __argc; iArg++ )
{
   // Inspect the current argument string
   psz = __argv[iArg];

   // Valid options begin with '-' or '/'
   if( psz[0] == '-' || psz[0] == '/' )
   {
      // The next character is the option
      switch( tolower(psz[1]) )
      {
      case 'u':
         // Use the service components UI to prompt for and create
         // the data source object; the enumerator is not used
         g_dwFlags |= USE_PROMPTDATASOURCE;
         g_dwFlags &= ~USE_ENUMERATOR;
         continue;
      case 'e':
         // Use the enumerator to select the provider, and then use
         // IDataInitialize to create the data source object.
         // Don't use the UI to prompt for the data source.
         g_dwFlags |= USE_ENUMERATOR;
         g_dwFlags &= ~USE_PROMPTDATASOURCE;
         continue;
      case 'c':
         // Use ICommand instead of IOpenRowset
         g_dwFlags |= USE_COMMAND;
         continue;
      case 'b':
         // Use ISequentialStream to fetch BLOB column data
         g_dwFlags |= USE_ISEQSTREAM;
         continue;
      case 'n':
         // Don't display method call strings as part of
         // the extended error checking macro
         g_dwFlags &= ~DISPLAY_METHODCALLS;
         continue;
      }
   }
```

```
      // Invalid argument; show the usage flags to the user
      fprintf(stderr, "Usage: %s [-u] [-e] [-c] [-b] [-n]\n\nWhere:\n\t" \
         "u = Use the Microsoft Data Links UI " \
            "to create the DataSource\n\t" \
         "e = Use the Enumerator and IDataInitialize " \
            "to create the DataSource\n\t" \
         "c = Use ICommand instead of IOpenRowset to create the Rowset\n\t" \
         "b = Use ISequentialStream for BLOB columns\n\t" \
         "n = Don't display method call strings\n",
         __argv[0]);

      return FALSE;
   }

   return TRUE;
}


/////////////////////////////////////////////////////////////////
// myDisplayInstructions
//
// This function asks the user whether they would like
// instructions displayed for the application. If so, it
// displays the instructions appropriate to the flags set
// in g_dwFlags.
//
/////////////////////////////////////////////////////////////////
void myDisplayInstructions
   (
   void
   )
{
   CHAR              ch;

   // Display header and ask the user if they want instructions
   printf("\nOLE DB Programmer's Reference Sample\n" \
         "====================================\n\n");
   printf("Display instructions [Y or N]? ");
   do
   {
      ch = myGetChar();
   }
   while( ch != 'y' && ch != 'n' );
   printf("%c\n\n", ch);

   // No instructions, so we're done
   if( ch == 'n' )
      return;
```

```
    // Display basic instructions
    printf("This application is a simple OLE DB sample that will display\n" \
          "a rowset and will allow basic navigation of that rowset by\n" \
          "the user. The application will perform the following steps:\n\n");

    // Display data source creation instructions
    if( g_dwFlags & USE_PROMPTDATASOURCE )
    {
       printf(" - Creates a DataSource object through the Microsoft Data\n" \
              "   Links UI. This allows the user to select the OLE DB\n" \
              "   provider to use and to set connection properties.\n");
    }
    else
    {
       printf(" - Creates a DataSource object through IDataInitialize::\n" \
              "   CreateDBInstance, which allows the OLE DB service\n" \
              "   component manager to add additional functionality to\n" \
              "   the provider as requested. The user will select the\n" \
              "   provider to use from a rowset obtained from the OLE DB\n" \
              "   enumerator.\n");
    }

    // Display session creation and table-selection instructions
    printf(" - Creates a Session object from the DataSource object.\n");
    printf(" - If the provider supports the schema rowset interface,\n" \
          "   creates a TABLES schema rowset and allows the user to\n" \
          "   select a table name from this rowset.\n");

    // Display rowset creation instructions
    if( g_dwFlags & USE_COMMAND )
    {
       printf(" - Creates a Command object from the Session object and\n" \
              "   allows the user to specify command text for this Command,\n" \
              "   then executes the command to create the final rowset.\n");
    }
    else
    {
       printf(" - Creates the final rowset over the table specified by the\n" \
              "   user.\n");
    }

    printf(" - Displays this rowset and allows the user to perform basic\n" \
          "   navigation of that rowset.\n\n");

    // Wait for the user to press a key before continuing
    printf("Press a key to continue...");
    myGetChar();
    printf("\n\n");
}
```

```
/////////////////////////////////////////////////////////////////
// myGetInputFromUser
//
// This function prompts the user with the contents of pwszFmt
// and any accompanying variable arguments and then gets a string
// as input from the user. If the string is non-empty, it is
// copied into pwszInput and the function returns TRUE;
// otherwise, this function returns FALSE.
//
/////////////////////////////////////////////////////////////////
BOOL myGetInputFromUser
   (
   LPWSTR            pwszInput,
   LPCWSTR              pwszFmt,
   ...
   )
{
   va_list              vargs;
   WCHAR          wszBuffer[MAX_NAME_LEN + 1]    = {0};

   // Create the string with variable arguments...
   va_start(vargs, pwszFmt);
   _vsnwprintf(wszBuffer, MAX_NAME_LEN, pwszFmt, vargs);
   va_end(vargs);

   // Output the string...
   wprintf(wszBuffer);

   // Now get the Input from the user...
   _getws(wszBuffer);
   if( wszBuffer[0] )
   {
      wcscpy(pwszInput, wszBuffer);
      return TRUE;
   }

   return FALSE;
}
```

```
//////////////////////////////////////////////////////////////////
// myGetChar
//
// This function gets a character from the keyboard and
// converts it to lowercase before returning it
//
//////////////////////////////////////////////////////////////////
CHAR myGetChar
   (
   void
   )
{
   CHAR              ch;

   // Get a character from the keyboard
   ch = _getch();

   // Reread for the actual key value if necessary
   if( !ch || ch == 0xE0 )
      ch = _getch();

   return tolower(ch);
}


//-----------------------------------------------------------------------------
// Microsoft OLE DB Programmer's Reference Sample
// Copyright (C) 1998 By Microsoft Corporation.
//
// @doc
//
// @module ENUM.CPP
//
//-----------------------------------------------------------------------------


//////////////////////////////////////////////////////////////////
// Includes
//
//////////////////////////////////////////////////////////////////
#include "prsample.h"   // Programmer's Reference Sample includes
```

```
/////////////////////////////////////////////////////////////////
// myCreateEnumerator
//
// This function creates an enumerator, obtains a sources rowset
// from it, displays the rowset to the user, and allows the user
// to specify the ProgID of a provider. The CLSID that matches
// this ProgID is returned to the caller in *pCLSID.
//
/////////////////////////////////////////////////////////////////
HRESULT myCreateEnumerator
   (
   REFCLSID           clsidEnumerator,
   CLSID *            pCLSID
   )
{
   HRESULT            hr;
   IUnknown *            pIUnkEnumerator          = NULL;
   ISourcesRowset *      pISourcesRowset              = NULL;
   IRowset *          pIRowset                 = NULL;
   IDBInitialize *       pIDBInitialize               = NULL;
   WCHAR           wszProgID[MAX_NAME_LEN + 1] = {0};

   const ULONG        cProperties                 = 2;
   DBPROP          rgProperties[cProperties];
   DBPROPSET       rgPropSets[1];

   // Create the enumerator object. We ask for IUnknown when creating
   // the enumerator because some enumerators may require initialization
   // before we can obtain a sources rowset from the enumerator. This is
   // indicated by whether the enumerator object exposes IDBInitialize
   // or not. (We don't want to ask for IDBInitialize, since enumerators
   // that don't require initialization will cause the CoCreateInstance
   // to fail.)
   XCHECK_HR(hr = CoCreateInstance(
            clsidEnumerator,                    // clsid -- enumerator
            NULL,                        // pUnkOuter
            CLSCTX_INPROC_SERVER,        // dwClsContext
            IID_IUnknown,                    // riid
            (void**)&pIUnkEnumerator         // ppvObj
            ));

   // If the enumerator exposes IDBInitialize, we need to initialize it
   if( SUCCEEDED(hr = pIUnkEnumerator->QueryInterface(IID_IDBInitialize,
               (void**)&pIDBInitialize)) )
   {
      CHECK_HR(hr = myDoInitialization(pIUnkEnumerator));
   }
```

```
    // Set properties on the rowset, to request additional functionality
    myAddRowsetProperties(rgPropSets, cProperties, rgProperties);

    // Obtain a sources rowset from the enumerator. This rowset contains
    // all of the OLE DB providers that this enumerator is able to list.
    XCHECK_HR(hr = pIUnkEnumerator->QueryInterface(IID_ISourcesRowset,
                (void**)&pISourcesRowset));
    XCHECK_HR(hr = pISourcesRowset->GetSourcesRowset(
            NULL,                  // pUnkOuter
            IID_IRowset,           // riid
            1,                     // cPropSets
            rgPropSets,                // rgPropSets
            (IUnknown**)&pIRowset      // ppRowset
            ));

    // Display the rowset to the user. This will allow the user to
    // perform basic navigation of the rowset and will allow the user
    // to select a row containing a desired provider.
    CHECK_HR(hr = myDisplayRowset(pIRowset,
            L"SOURCES_NAME", MAX_NAME_LEN, wszProgID));

    // Obtain the ProgID for the provider to use from the user.
    // The default value for this is the value of the SOURCES_NAME
    // column in the row selected by the user previously.
    myGetInputFromUser(wszProgID, L"\nType the ProgID of a provider"
                L" to use [Enter = `%s`]: ", wszProgID);
    XCHECK_HR(hr = CLSIDFromProgID(wszProgID, pCLSID));

CLEANUP:
    if( pIUnkEnumerator )
        pIUnkEnumerator->Release();
    if( pISourcesRowset )
        pISourcesRowset->Release();
    if( pIRowset )
        pIRowset->Release();
    if( pIDBInitialize )
        pIDBInitialize->Release();
    return hr;
}
```

```
//-----------------------------------------------------------------------------
// Microsoft OLE DB Programmer's Reference Sample
// Copyright (C) 1998 By Microsoft Corporation.
//
// @doc
//
// @module DATASOURCE.CPP
//
//-----------------------------------------------------------------------------


/////////////////////////////////////////////////////////////////
// Includes
//
/////////////////////////////////////////////////////////////////
#include "prsample.h"   // Programmer's Reference Sample includes



/////////////////////////////////////////////////////////////////
// myCreateDataSource
//
// This function creates an OLE DB data source object for a
// provider selected by the user, sets initialization properties
// for the data source, and initializes the data source. The
// function returns a pointer to the data source object's
// IUnknown in *ppUnkDataSource.
//
/////////////////////////////////////////////////////////////////
HRESULT myCreateDataSource
   (
   IUnknown **          ppUnkDataSource
   )
```

```
{
   HRESULT              hr;
   IDataInitialize *          pIDataInitialize          = NULL;
   IDBPromptInitialize *      pIDBPromptInitialize      = NULL;
   IDBInitialize *         pIDBInitialize        = NULL;
   CLSID                clsid                  = CLSID_MSDASQL;

   // Use the Microsoft Data Links UI to create the data source
   // object. This will allow the user to select the provider
   // to connect to and to set the initialization properties
   // for the data source object, which will be created by the
   // Data Links UI.
   if( g_dwFlags & USE_PROMPTDATASOURCE )
   {
      // Create the Data Links UI object and obtain the
      // IDBPromptInitialize interface from it
      XCHECK_HR(hr = CoCreateInstance(
               CLSID_DataLinks,              // clsid -- Data Links UI
               NULL,                         // pUnkOuter
               CLSCTX_INPROC_SERVER,         // dwClsContext
               IID_IDBPromptInitialize,            // riid
               (void**)&pIDBPromptInitialize // ppvObj
               ));

      // Invoke the Data Links UI to allow the user to select
      // the provider and set initialization properties for
      // the data source object that this will create
      XCHECK_HR(hr = pIDBPromptInitialize->PromptDataSource(
               NULL,                         // pUnkOuter
               GetDesktopWindow(),              // hWndParent
               DBPROMPTOPTIONS_PROPERTYSHEET,
                  // dwPromptOptions
               0,                            // cSourceTypeFilter
               NULL,                         // rgSourceTypeFilter
               NULL,                         // pwszszzProviderFilter
               IID_IDBInitialize,                  // riid
               (IUnknown**)&pIDBInitialize         // ppDataSource
               ));

      // We've obtained a data source object from the Data Links UI. This
      // object has had its initialization properties set, so all we
      // need to do is Initialize it.
      XCHECK_HR(hr = pIDBInitialize->Initialize());
   }
   // We are not using the Data Links UI to create the data source object.
   // Instead, we will enumerate the providers installed on this system
   // through the OLE DB enumerator and will allow the user to select
   // the ProgID of the provider for which we will create a data source
   // object.
```

```
    else
    {
        // Use the OLE DB enumerator to obtain a rowset of installed providers,
        // and then allow the user to select a provider from this rowset
        CHECK_HR(hr = myCreateEnumerator(CLSID_OLEDB_ENUMERATOR, &clsid));

        // We will create the data source object through the OLE DB service
        // component IDataInitialize interface, so we need to create an
        // instance of the data initialization object
        XCHECK_HR(hr = CoCreateInstance(
                CLSID_MSDAINITIALIZE,       // clsid--data initialize
                NULL,                       // pUnkOuter
                CLSCTX_INPROC_SERVER,       // dwClsContext
                IID_IDataInitialize,                // riid
                (void**)&pIDataInitialize           // ppvObj
                ));

        // Use IDataInitialize::CreateDBInstance to create an uninitialized
        // d ata source object for the chosen provider. By using this service
        // component method, the service component manager can provide
        // additional functionality beyond what is natively supported by the
        // provider if the consumer requests that functionality.
        XCHECK_HR(hr = pIDataInitialize->CreateDBInstance(
                clsid,                      // clsid--provider
                NULL,                       // pUnkOuter
                CLSCTX_INPROC_SERVER,       // dwClsContext
                NULL,                       // pwszReserved
                IID_IDBInitialize,              // riid
                (IUnknown**)&pIDBInitialize         // ppDataSource
                ));

        // Initialize the data source object by setting any required
        // initialization properties and calling IDBInitialize::Initialize
        CHECK_HR(hr = myDoInitialization(pIDBInitialize));
    }

CLEANUP:
    *ppUnkDataSource = pIDBInitialize;
    if( pIDataInitialize )
        pIDataInitialize->Release();
    if( pIDBPromptInitialize )
        pIDBPromptInitialize->Release();
    return hr;
}
```

```
/////////////////////////////////////////////////////////////////
// myDoInitialization
//
// This function sets initialization properties that tell the
// provider to prompt the user for any information required to
// initialize the provider, and then calls the provider's
// initialization function
//
/////////////////////////////////////////////////////////////////
HRESULT myDoInitialization
   (
   IUnknown *            pIUnknown
   )
{
   HRESULT           hr;
   IDBInitialize *      pIDBInitialize              = NULL;
   IDBProperties *      pIDBProperties              = NULL;
   HWND              hWnd                        = GetDesktopWindow();

   const ULONG       cProperties                    = 2;
   DBPROP         rgProperties[cProperties];
   DBPROPSET      rgPropSets[1];

   // In order to initialize the d ata source object, most providers require
   // some initialization properties to be set by the consumer. For instance,
   // these might include the data source to connect to and the user ID and
   // password to use to establish identity. We will ask the provider to
   // prompt the user for this required information by setting the following
   // properties:
   myAddProperty(&rgProperties[0],DBPROP_INIT_PROMPT,VT_I2,DBPROMPT_COMPLETE);
   myAddProperty(&rgProperties[1],DBPROP_INIT_HWND,  VT_I4,(LONG)hWnd);

   rgPropSets[0].rgProperties     = rgProperties;
   rgPropSets[0].cProperties      = cProperties;
   rgPropSets[0].guidPropertySet  = DBPROPSET_DBINIT;

   // Obtain the needed interfaces
   XCHECK_HR(hr = pIUnknown->QueryInterface(IID_IDBProperties,
            (void**)&pIDBProperties));
   XCHECK_HR(hr = pIUnknown->QueryInterface(IID_IDBInitialize,
            (void**)&pIDBInitialize));

   // If a provider requires initialization properties, it must support the
   // properties that we are setting (_PROMPT and _HWND). However, some
   // providers do not need initialization properties and may therefore
   // not support the _PROMPT and _HWND properties. Because of this, we will
   // not check the return value from SetProperties.
   hr = pIDBProperties->SetProperties(1, rgPropSets);
```

```
   // Now that we've set our properties, initialize the provider
   XCHECK_HR(hr = pIDBInitialize->Initialize());

CLEANUP:
   if( pIDBProperties )
      pIDBProperties->Release();
   if( pIDBInitialize )
      pIDBInitialize->Release();
   return hr;
}



/////////////////////////////////////////////////////////////////////
// myGetProperty
//
// This function gets the BOOL value for the specified property
// and returns the result in *pbValue
//
/////////////////////////////////////////////////////////////////////
HRESULT myGetProperty
   (
   IUnknown *            pIUnknown,
   REFIID             riid,
   DBPROPID           dwPropertyID,
   REFGUID            guidPropertySet,
   BOOL *             pbValue
   )
{
   HRESULT            hr;
   DBPROPID           rgPropertyIDs[1];
   DBPROPIDSET        rgPropertyIDSets[1];

   ULONG              cPropSets                     = 0;
   DBPROPSET *        rgPropSets                    = NULL;

   IDBProperties *       pIDBProperties                   = NULL;
   ISessionProperties *     pISesProps                    = NULL;
   ICommandProperties * pICmdProps                        = NULL;
   IRowsetInfo *         pIRowsetInfo               = NULL;

   // Initialize the output value
   *pbValue = FALSE;

   // Set up the property ID array
   rgPropertyIDs[0] = dwPropertyID;
```

```
// Set up the Property ID Set
rgPropertyIDSets[0].rgPropertyIDs     = rgPropertyIDs;
rgPropertyIDSets[0].cPropertyIDs      = 1;
rgPropertyIDSets[0].guidPropertySet   = guidPropertySet;

// Get the property value for this property from the provider, but
// don't try to display extended error information, since this may
// not be a supported property. A failure is, in fact, expected if
// the property is not supported.
if( riid == IID_IDBProperties )
{
   XCHECK_HR(hr = pIUnknown->QueryInterface(IID_IDBProperties,
            (void**)&pIDBProperties));
   CHECK_HR(hr = pIDBProperties->GetProperties(
            1,               // cPropertyIDSets
            rgPropertyIDSets, // rgPropertyIDSets
            &cPropSets,       // pcPropSets
            &rgPropSets       // prgPropSets
            ));
}
else if( riid == IID_ISessionProperties )
{
   XCHECK_HR(hr = pIUnknown->QueryInterface(IID_ISessionProperties,
            (void**)&pISesProps));
   CHECK_HR(hr = pISesProps->GetProperties(
            1,               // cPropertyIDSets
            rgPropertyIDSets, // rgPropertyIDSets
            &cPropSets,       // pcPropSets
            &rgPropSets       // prgPropSets
            ));
}
else if( riid == IID_ICommandProperties )
{
   XCHECK_HR(hr = pIUnknown->QueryInterface(IID_ICommandProperties,
            (void**)&pICmdProps));
   CHECK_HR(hr = pICmdProps->GetProperties(
            1,               // cPropertyIDSets
            rgPropertyIDSets, // rgPropertyIDSets
            &cPropSets,       // pcPropSets
            &rgPropSets       // prgPropSets
            ));
}
```

```
    else
    {
        XCHECK_HR(hr = pIUnknown->QueryInterface(IID_IRowsetInfo,
                  (void**)&pIRowsetInfo));
        CHECK_HR(hr = pIRowsetInfo->GetProperties(
                  1,              // cPropertyIDSets
                  rgPropertyIDSets,  // rgPropertyIDSets
                  &cPropSets,        // pcPropSets
                  &rgPropSets        // prgPropSets
                  ));
    }

    // Return the value for this property to the caller if
    // it's a VT_BOOL type value, as expected
    if( V_VT(&rgPropSets[0].rgProperties[0].vValue) == VT_BOOL )
        *pbValue = V_BOOL(&rgPropSets[0].rgProperties[0].vValue);

CLEANUP:
    if( rgPropSets )
    {
        CoTaskMemFree(rgPropSets[0].rgProperties);
        CoTaskMemFree(rgPropSets);
    }
    if( pIDBProperties )
        pIDBProperties->Release();
    if( pISesProps )
        pISesProps->Release();
    if( pICmdProps )
        pICmdProps->Release();
    if( pIRowsetInfo )
        pIRowsetInfo->Release();
    return hr;
}


/////////////////////////////////////////////////////////////////
// myAddProperty
//
// This function initializes the property structure pProp
//
/////////////////////////////////////////////////////////////////
void myAddProperty
    (
    DBPROP *            pProp,
    DBPROPID            dwPropertyID,
    VARTYPE             vtType,
    LONG                lValue,
    DBPROPOPTIONS       dwOptions
    )
```

```
{
   // Set up the property structure
   pProp->dwPropertyID  = dwPropertyID;
   pProp->dwOptions     = dwOptions;
   pProp->dwStatus      = DBPROPSTATUS_OK;
   pProp->colid         = DB_NULLID;
   V_VT(&pProp->vValue) = vtType;

   // Since VARIANT data is a union, we can place the value in any
   // member (except for VT_DECIMAL, which is a union with the whole
   // VARIANT structure--but we know we're not passing VT_DECIMAL)
   V_I4(&pProp->vValue) = lValue;
}




//-----------------------------------------------------------------------------
// Microsoft OLE DB Programmer's Reference Sample
// Copyright (C) 1998 By Microsoft Corporation.
//
// @doc
//
// @module SESSION.CPP
//
//-----------------------------------------------------------------------------

/////////////////////////////////////////////////////////////////
// Includes
//
/////////////////////////////////////////////////////////////////
#include "prsample.h"   // Programmer's Reference Sample includes



/////////////////////////////////////////////////////////////////
// myCreateSession
//
// Create an OLE DB session object from the given data source
// object. The IDBCreateSession interface is mandatory, so this
// is a simple operation.
//
/////////////////////////////////////////////////////////////////
HRESULT  myCreateSession
   (
   IUnknown *          pUnkDataSource,
   IUnknown **      ppUnkSession
   )
```

```
{
   HRESULT             hr;
   IDBCreateSession *   pIDBCreateSession = NULL;

   // Create a session object from a data source object
   XCHECK_HR(hr = pUnkDataSource->QueryInterface(
            IID_IDBCreateSession, (void**)&pIDBCreateSession));
   XCHECK_HR(hr = pIDBCreateSession->CreateSession(
            NULL,           // pUnkOuter
            IID_IOpenRowset,  // riid
            ppUnkSession    // ppSession
            ));

CLEANUP:
   if( pIDBCreateSession )
      pIDBCreateSession->Release();
   return hr;
}


/////////////////////////////////////////////////////////////////
// myCreateSchemaRowset
//
// If the provider supports IDBSchemaRowset, this function will
// obtain the tables schema rowset, will display this rowset to
// the user, and will allow the user to select a row in the
// rowset containing the name of a table of interest
//
/////////////////////////////////////////////////////////////////
HRESULT  myCreateSchemaRowset
   (
   GUID                guidSchema,
   IUnknown *             pUnkSession,
   ULONG               cchBuffer,
   LPWSTR           pwszBuffer
   )
{
   HRESULT             hr                        = S_OK;
   IDBSchemaRowset *     pIDBSchemaRowset          = NULL;
   IUnknown *            pUnkRowset                    = NULL;

   const ULONG           cProperties               = 2;
   DBPROP              rgProperties[cProperties];
   DBPROPSET           rgPropSets[1];

   // Attempt to obtain the IDBSchemaRowset interface on the session object.
   // This is not a mandatory interface; if it is not supported, we are done.
   CHECK_HR(pUnkSession->QueryInterface(
              IID_IDBSchemaRowset, (void**)&pIDBSchemaRowset));
```

```
    // Set properties on the rowset, to request additional functionality
    myAddRowsetProperties(rgPropSets, cProperties, rgProperties);

    // Get the requested schema rowset. If IDBSchemaRowset is supported,
    // the following schema rowsets are required to be supported:
    // DBSCHEMA_TABLES, DBSCHEMA_COLUMNS, and .
    // DBSCHEMA_PROVIDERTYPES. We know that we will be asking for one of
    // these, so it is not necessary to call IDBSchemaRowset::GetSchemas in this case.
    XCHECK_HR(hr = pIDBSchemaRowset->GetRowset(
            NULL,        // pUnkOuter
            guidSchema,     // guidSchema
            0,           // cRestrictions
            NULL,        // rgRestrictions
            IID_IRowset,// riid
            1,           // cPropSets
            rgPropSets,     // rgPropSets
            &pUnkRowset // ppRowset
            ));

    // Display the rowset to the user. This will allow the user to
    // perform basic navigation of the rowset and will allow the user
    // to select a row containing a desired table name (taken from the
    // TABLE_NAME column).
    CHECK_HR(hr = myDisplayRowset(pUnkRowset,
       L"TABLE_NAME", cchBuffer, pwszBuffer));

CLEANUP:
    if( pIDBSchemaRowset )
       pIDBSchemaRowset->Release();
    if( pUnkRowset )
       pUnkRowset->Release();
    return hr;
}
```

```
.
//-----------------------------------------------------------------------------
// Microsoft OLE DB Programmer's Reference Sample
// Copyright (C) 1998 By Microsoft Corporation.
//
// @doc
//
// @module ROWSET.CPP
//
//-----------------------------------------------------------------------------


/////////////////////////////////////////////////////////////////
// Includes
//
/////////////////////////////////////////////////////////////////
#include "prsample.h"   // Programmer's Reference Sample includes



/////////////////////////////////////////////////////////////////
// myCreateRowset
//
// This function creates an OLE DB rowset object from the given
// provider's session object. It first obtains a default table
// name from the user through the tables schema rowset, if
// supported, and then creates a cowset object by one of two methods:
//
// -- If the user requested that the rowset object be created
//     from a command object, it creates a command object and then
//     obtains command text from the user, sets properties and
//     the command text, and finally executes the command to
//     create the rowset object.
// -- Otherwise, the function obtains a table name from the user
//     and calls IOpenRowset::OpenRowset to create a rowset object
//     over that table that supports the requested properties.
//
/////////////////////////////////////////////////////////////////
HRESULT  myCreateRowset
   (
   IUnknown *           pUnkSession,
   IUnknown **       ppUnkRowset
   )
```

```
{
   HRESULT           hr;
   IUnknown *           pUnkCommand                        = NULL;
   IOpenRowset *        pIOpenRowset                       = NULL;
   WCHAR          wszTableName[MAX_NAME_LEN + 1] = {0};

   const ULONG          cProperties                        = 2;
   DBPROP            rgProperties[cProperties];
   DBPROPSET         rgPropSets[1];

   // Obtain a default table name from the user by displaying the
   // tables schema rowset if schema rowsets are supported
   CHECK_HR(hr = myCreateSchemaRowset(DBSCHEMA_TABLES, pUnkSession,
      MAX_NAME_LEN, wszTableName));

   // Set properties on the rowset, to request additional functionality
   myAddRowsetProperties(rgPropSets, cProperties, rgProperties);

   // If the user requested that the rowset be created from a
   // command object, create a command, set its properties and
   // text, and execute it to create the rowset object
   if( g_dwFlags & USE_COMMAND )
   {
      WCHAR    wszCommandText[MAX_NAME_LEN + 1];

      // Attempt to create the command object from the provider's
      // session object. Note that commands are not supported by
      // all providers, and this will fail in that case.
      CHECK_HR(hr = myCreateCommand(pUnkSession, &pUnkCommand));

      // Get the command text that we will execute from the user
      if( !myGetInputFromUser(wszCommandText, L"\nType the command "
         L"to execute [Enter = `select * from %s`]: ", wszTableName) )
      {
         swprintf(wszCommandText, L"select * from %s", wszTableName);
      }

      // And execute the command the user entered
      CHECK_HR(hr = myExecuteCommand(pUnkCommand, wszCommandText,
               1, rgPropSets, ppUnkRowset));
   }
   // Otherwise, the user gets the default behavior, which is to use
   // IOpenRowset to create the rowset object from the session object.
   // IOpenRowset is supported by all providers; it takes a TableID
   // and creates a rowset containing all rows in that table. It is
   // similar to using SQL command text of "SELECT * FROM TableID".
```

```
   else
   {
      DBID     TableID;

      // Create the TableID
      TableID.eKind           = DBKIND_NAME;
      TableID.uName.pwszName  = wszTableName;

      // Obtain the table name from the user
      myGetInputFromUser(wszTableName, L"\nType the name of the table "
                        L"to use [Enter = `%s`]: ", wszTableName);

      // Get the IOpenRowset interface and create a rowset object
      // over the requested table through OpenRowset
      XCHECK_HR(hr = pUnkSession->QueryInterface(
               IID_IOpenRowset, (void**)&pIOpenRowset));
      XCHECK_HR(hr = pIOpenRowset->OpenRowset(
               NULL,       // pUnkOuter
               &TableID,   // pTableID
               NULL,       // pIndexID
               IID_IRowset,// riid
               1,          // cPropSets
               rgPropSets,    // rgPropSets
               ppUnkRowset // ppRowset
               ));
   }

CLEANUP:
   if( pIOpenRowset )
      pIOpenRowset->Release();
   if( pUnkCommand )
      pUnkCommand->Release();
   return hr;
}
```

```
/////////////////////////////////////////////////////////////////
// mySetupBindings
//
// This function takes an IUnknown pointer from a rowset object
// and creates a bindings array that describes how we want the
// data we fetch from the rowset to be laid out in memory. It
// also calculates the total size of a row so that we can use
// this to allocate memory for the rows that we will fetch
// later.
//
// For each column in the rowset, there will be a corresponding
// element in the bindings array that describes how the
// provider should transfer the data, including length and
// status, for that column. This element also specifies the data
// type that the provider should return the column as. We will
// bind all columns as DBTYPE_WSTR, with a few exceptions
// detailed below, as providers are required to support the
// conversion of their column data to this type in the vast
// majority of cases. The exception to our binding as
// DBTYPE_WSTR is if the native column data type is
// DBTYPE_IUNKNOWN or if the user has requested that BLOB
// columns be bound as ISequentialStream objects, in which case
// we will bind those columns as ISequentialStream objects.
//
/////////////////////////////////////////////////////////////////
HRESULT mySetupBindings
   (
   IUnknown *          pUnkRowset,
   ULONG *          pcBindings,
   DBBINDING **     prgBindings,
   ULONG *          pcbRowSize
   )
{
   HRESULT          hr;
   ULONG            cColumns;
   DBCOLUMNINFO *   rgColumnInfo          = NULL;
   LPWSTR        pStringBuffer            = NULL;
   IColumnsInfo *      pIColumnsInfo          = NULL;

   ULONG            iCol;
   ULONG            dwOffset              = 0;
   DBBINDING *      rgBindings               = NULL;

   ULONG            cStorageObjs             = 0;
   BOOL             fMultipleObjs            = FALSE;
```

```
// Obtain the column information for the rowset. From this, we can find
// out the following information that we need to construct the bindings
// array:
// -- the number of columns
// -- the ordinal of each column
// -- the precision and scale of numeric columns
// -- the OLE DB data type of the column
XCHECK_HR(hr = pUnkRowset->QueryInterface(
            IID_IColumnsInfo, (void**)&pIColumnsInfo));
XCHECK_HR(hr = pIColumnsInfo->GetColumnInfo(
            &cColumns,          // pcColumns
            &rgColumnInfo,      // prgColumnInfo
            &pStringBuffer      // ppStringBuffer
         ));

// Allocate memory for the bindings array. There is a one-to-one
// mapping between the columns returned from GetColumnInfo and our
// bindings.
rgBindings = (DBBINDING*)CoTaskMemAlloc(cColumns * sizeof(DBBINDING));
CHECK_MEMORY(hr, rgBindings);
memset(rgBindings, 0, cColumns * sizeof(DBBINDING));

// Determine if the rowset supports multiple storage object bindings.
// If it does not, we will bind only the first BLOB column or IUnknown
// column as an ISequentialStream object, and we will bind the rest as
// DBTYPE_WSTR.
myGetProperty(pUnkRowset, IID_IRowset, DBPROP_MULTIPLESTORAGEOBJECTS,
   DBPROPSET_ROWSET, &fMultipleObjs);

// Construct the binding array element for each column
for( iCol = 0; iCol < cColumns; iCol++ )
{
   // This binding applies to the ordinal of this column
   rgBindings[iCol].iOrdinal   = rgColumnInfo[iCol].iOrdinal;

   // We are asking the provider to give us the data for this column
   // (DBPART_VALUE), the length of that data (DBPART_LENGTH), and
   // the status of the column (DBPART_STATUS)
   rgBindings[iCol].dwPart     = DBPART_VALUE|DBPART_LENGTH|DBPART_STATUS;

   // The following values are the offsets to the status, length, and
   // data value that the provider will fill with the appropriate values
   // when we fetch data later. When we fetch data, we will pass a
   // pointer to a buffer that the provider will copy column data to,
   // in accordance with the binding we have provided for that column;
   // these are offsets into that future buffer.
   rgBindings[iCol].obStatus      = dwOffset;
   rgBindings[iCol].obLength   = dwOffset + sizeof(DBSTATUS);
   rgBindings[iCol].obValue       = dwOffset + sizeof(DBSTATUS) + sizeof(ULONG);
```

```
// Any memory allocated for the data value will be owned by us, the
// client. Note that no data will be allocated in this case, as the
// DBTYPE_WSTR bindings we are using will tell the provider to simply
// copy data directly into our provided buffer.
rgBindings[iCol].dwMemOwner = DBMEMOWNER_CLIENTOWNED;

// This is not a parameter binding
rgBindings[iCol].eParamIO      = DBPARAMIO_NOTPARAM;

// We want to use the precision and scale of the column
rgBindings[iCol].bPrecision = rgColumnInfo[iCol].bPrecision;
rgBindings[iCol].bScale     = rgColumnInfo[iCol].bScale;

// Bind this column as DBTYPE_WSTR, which tells the provider to
// copy a Unicode string representation of the data into our buffer,
// converting from the native type if necessary
rgBindings[iCol].wType      = DBTYPE_WSTR;

// Initially, we set the length for this data in our buffer to 0;
// the correct value for this will be calculated directly below
rgBindings[iCol].cbMaxLen   = 0;

// Determine the maximum number of bytes required in our buffer to
// contain the Unicode string representation of the provider's native
// data type, including room for the NULL-termination character
switch( rgColumnInfo[iCol].wType )
{
   case DBTYPE_NULL:
   case DBTYPE_EMPTY:
   case DBTYPE_I1:
   case DBTYPE_I2:
   case DBTYPE_I4:
   case DBTYPE_UI1:
   case DBTYPE_UI2:
   case DBTYPE_UI4:
   case DBTYPE_R4:
   case DBTYPE_BOOL:
   case DBTYPE_I8:
   case DBTYPE_UI8:
   case DBTYPE_R8:
   case DBTYPE_CY:
   case DBTYPE_ERROR:
      // When the above types are converted to a string, they
      // will all fit into 25 characters, so use that plus space
      // for the NULL-terminator
      rgBindings[iCol].cbMaxLen = (25 + 1) * sizeof(WCHAR);
      break;
```

```
    case DBTYPE_DECIMAL:
    case DBTYPE_NUMERIC:
    case DBTYPE_DATE:
    case DBTYPE_DBDATE:
    case DBTYPE_DBTIMESTAMP:
    case DBTYPE_GUID:
       // Converted to a string, the above types will all fit into
       // 50 characters, so use that plus space for the terminator
       rgBindings[iCol].cbMaxLen = (50 + 1) * sizeof(WCHAR);
       break;

    case DBTYPE_BYTES:
       // In converting DBTYPE_BYTES to a string, each byte
       // becomes two characters (e.g. 0xFF -> "FF"), so we
       // will use double the maximum size of the column plus
       // include space for the NULL-terminator
       rgBindings[iCol].cbMaxLen =
          (rgColumnInfo[iCol].ulColumnSize * 2 + 1) * sizeof(WCHAR);
       break;

    case DBTYPE_STR:
    case DBTYPE_WSTR:
    case DBTYPE_BSTR:
       // Going from a string to our string representation,
       // we can just take the maximum size of the column,
       // a count of characters, and include space for the
       // terminator, which is not included in the column size
       rgBindings[iCol].cbMaxLen =
          (rgColumnInfo[iCol].ulColumnSize + 1) * sizeof(WCHAR);
       break;

    default:
       // For any other type, we will simply use our maximum
       // column buffer size, since the display size of these
       // columns may be variable (e.g. DBTYPE_VARIANT) or
       // unknown (e.g. provider-specific types)
       rgBindings[iCol].cbMaxLen = MAX_COL_SIZE;
       break;
};

// If the provider's native data type for this column is
// DBTYPE_IUNKNOWN or this is a BLOB column and the user
// has requested that we bind BLOB columns as ISequentialStream
// objects, bind this column as an ISequentialStream object if
// the provider supports our creating another ISequentialStream
// binding
```

```
if( (rgColumnInfo[iCol].wType == DBTYPE_IUNKNOWN ||
    ((rgColumnInfo[iCol].dwFlags & DBCOLUMNFLAGS_ISLONG) &&
     (g_dwFlags & USE_ISEQSTREAM))) &&
   (fMultipleObjs || !cStorageObjs) )
{
   // To create an ISequentialStream object, we will
   // bind this column as DBTYPE_IUNKNOWN to indicate
   // that we are requesting this column as an object
   rgBindings[iCol].wType              = DBTYPE_IUNKNOWN;

   // We want to allocate enough space in our buffer for
   // the ISequentialStream pointer we will obtain from
   // the provider
   rgBindings[iCol].cbMaxLen           = sizeof(ISequentialStream *);

   // To specify the type of object that we want from the
   // provider, we need to create a DBOBJECT structure and
   // place it in our binding for this column
    rgBindings[iCol].pObject           =
                  (DBOBJECT *)CoTaskMemAlloc(sizeof(DBOBJECT));
   CHECK_MEMORY(hr, rgBindings[iCol].pObject);

   // Direct the provider to create an ISequentialStream
   // object over the data for this column
   rgBindings[iCol].pObject->iid       = IID_ISequentialStream;

   // We want read access on the ISequentialStream
   // object that the provider will create for us
   rgBindings[iCol].pObject->dwFlags   = STGM_READ;

   // Keep track of the number of storage objects (ISequentialStream
   // is a storage interface) that we have requested so that we
   // can avoid requesting multiple storage objects from a provider
   // that supports only a single storage object in our bindings
   cStorageObjs++;
}

// Ensure that the bound maximum length is no more than the
// maximum column size in bytes that we've defined
rgBindings[iCol].cbMaxLen
   = min(rgBindings[iCol].cbMaxLen, MAX_COL_SIZE);

// Update the offset past the end of this column's data so
// that the next column will begin in the correct place in
// the buffer
dwOffset = rgBindings[iCol].cbMaxLen + rgBindings[iCol].obValue;
```

```
        // Ensure that the data for the next column will be correctly
        // aligned for all platforms; or if we're done with columns
        // and if we allocate space for multiple rows, ensure that the data
        // for every row is correctly aligned
        dwOffset = ROUNDUP(dwOffset);
    }

    // Return the row size (the current dwOffset is the size of the row),
    // the count of bindings, and the bindings array to the caller
    *pcbRowSize = dwOffset;
    *pcBindings    = cColumns;
    *prgBindings= rgBindings;

CLEANUP:
    CoTaskMemFree(rgColumnInfo);
    CoTaskMemFree(pStringBuffer);
    if( pIColumnsInfo )
        pIColumnsInfo->Release();
    return hr;
}



/////////////////////////////////////////////////////////////////
// myCreateAccessor
//
// This function takes an IUnknown pointer for a rowset object
// and creates an accessor that describes the layout of the
// buffer we will use when we fetch data. The provider will fill
// this buffer according to the description contained in the
// accessor that we will create here.
//
/////////////////////////////////////////////////////////////////
HRESULT myCreateAccessor
    (
    IUnknown *          pUnkRowset,
    HACCESSOR *         phAccessor,
    ULONG *             pcBindings,
    DBBINDING **        prgBindings,
    ULONG *             pcbRowSize
    )
```

```
{
   HRESULT           hr;
   IAccessor *          pIAccessor                   = NULL;

   // An accessor is basically a handle to a collection of bindings.
   // To create the accessor, we need to first create an array of
   // bindings for the columns in the rowset.
   CHECK_HR(hr = mySetupBindings(pUnkRowset, pcBindings, prgBindings,
      pcbRowSize));

   // Now that we have an array of bindings, tell the provider to
   // create the accessor for those bindings. We get back a handle
   // to this accessor, which we will use when fetching data.
   XCHECK_HR(hr = pUnkRowset->QueryInterface(
            IID_IAccessor, (void**)&pIAccessor));
   XCHECK_HR(hr = pIAccessor->CreateAccessor(
            DBACCESSOR_ROWDATA,      // dwAccessorFlags
            *pcBindings,                 // cBindings
            *prgBindings,                // rgBindings
            0,                       // cbRowSize
            phAccessor,                  // phAccessor
            NULL                     // rgStatus
            ));

CLEANUP:
   if( pIAccessor )
      pIAccessor->Release();
   return hr;
}


////////////////////////////////////////////////////////////////////
// myDisplayRowset
//
// This function will display data from a rowset object and will
// allow the user to perform basic navigation of the rowset.
//
// The function takes a pointer to a rowset object's IUnknown
// and optionally, the name of a column and a buffer that will
// receive the value of that column when the user selects a row.
//
////////////////////////////////////////////////////////////////////
HRESULT myDisplayRowset
   (
   IUnknown *           pUnkRowset,
   LPCWSTR           pwszColToReturn,
   ULONG             cchBuffer,
   LPWSTR         pwszBuffer
   )
```

```
{
   HRESULT          hr;
   IRowset *        pIRowset          = NULL;
   ULONG            cBindings;
   DBBINDING *      rgBindings           = NULL;
   HACCESSOR     hAccessor         = DB_NULL_HACCESSOR;
   ULONG            cbRowSize;
   void *           pData             = NULL;
   ULONG *          rgDispSize           = NULL;
   ULONG            cRowsObtained;
   HROW *        rghRows           = NULL;
   ULONG            iRow;
   LONG             cRows             = MAX_ROWS;
   LONG             iRetCol              = -1;
   BOOL             fCanFetchBackwards;
   ULONG            iIndex;
   void *           pCurData;

   // Obtain the IRowset interface for use in fetching rows and data
   XCHECK_HR(hr = pUnkRowset->QueryInterface(
            IID_IRowset, (void**)&pIRowset));

   // Determine whether this rowset supports fetching data backwards;
   // we use this to determine whether the rowset can support moving
   // to the previous set of rows, described in more detail below
   myGetProperty(pUnkRowset, IID_IRowset, DBPROP_CANFETCHBACKWARDS,
      DBPROPSET_ROWSET, &fCanFetchBackwards);

   // If the caller wants us to return the data for a particular column
   // from a user-selected row, we need to turn the column name into a
   // column ordinal
   if( pwszColToReturn )
      CHECK_HR(hr = myFindColumn(pUnkRowset, pwszColToReturn, &iRetCol));

   // Create an accessor. An accessor is basically a handle to a
   // collection of bindings that describes to the provider how to
   // copy (and convert, if necessary) column data into our buffer.
   // The accessor that this creates will bind all columns as either
   // DBTYPE_WSTR (a Unicode string) or as an ISequentialStream object
   // (used for BLOB data). This will also give us the size of the
   // row buffer that the accessor describes to the provider.
   CHECK_HR(hr = myCreateAccessor(pUnkRowset, &hAccessor,
                              &cBindings, &rgBindings, &cbRowSize));

   // Allocate enough memory to hold cRows rows of data; this is
   // where the actual row data from the provider will be placed
   pData = CoTaskMemAlloc(cbRowSize * MAX_ROWS);
   CHECK_MEMORY(hr, pData);
```

```
// Allocate memory for an array that we will use to calculate the
// maximum display size used by each column in the current set of
// rows
rgDispSize = (ULONG *)CoTaskMemAlloc(cBindings * sizeof(ULONG));
CHECK_MEMORY(hr, rgDispSize);

// In this loop, we perform the following process:
// -- reset the maximum display size array
// -- try to get cRows row handles from the provider
// -- these handles are then used to actually get the row data from the
//    provider copied into our allocated buffer
// -- calculate the maximum display size for each column
// -- release the row handles to the rows we obtained
// -- display the column names for the rowset
// -- display the row data for the rows that we fetched
//  - get user input
// -- free the provider-allocated row handle array
// -- repeat unless the user has chosen to quit or has selected a row
while( hr == S_OK )
{
   // Clear the maximum display size array
   memset(rgDispSize, 0, cBindings * sizeof(ULONG));

   // Attempt to get cRows row handles from the provider
   XCHECK_HR(hr = pIRowset->GetNextRows(
            DB_NULL_HCHAPTER,      // hChapter
            0,                     // lOffset
            cRows,                 // cRows
            &cRowsObtained,            // pcRowsObtained
            &rghRows               // prghRows
            ));

   // Loop over the row handles obtained from GetNextRows,
   // actually fetching the data for these rows into our buffer
   for( iRow = 0; iRow < cRowsObtained; iRow++ )
   {
      // Find the location in our buffer where we want to place
      // the data for this row. Note that if we fetched rows
      // backwards (cRows < 0), the row handles obtained from the
      // provider are reversed from the order in which we want to
      // actually display the data on the screen, so we will
      // account for this. This ensures that the resulting order
      // of row data in the pData buffer matches the order we
      // wish to use to display the data.
      iIndex    = cRows > 0 ? iRow : cRowsObtained - iRow - 1;
      pCurData = (BYTE*)pData + (cbRowSize * iIndex);
```

```
        // Get the data for this row handle. The provider will copy
        // (and convert, if necessary) the data for each of the
        // columns that are described in our accessor into the given
        // buffer (pCurData).
        XCHECK_HR(hr = pIRowset->GetData(
              rghRows[iRow], //hRow
              hAccessor,     //hAccessor
              pCurData       //pData
              ));

        // Update the maximum display size array, accounting for this row
        CHECK_HR(hr = myUpdateDisplaySize(cBindings, rgBindings,
           pCurData, rgDispSize));
    }

    // If we obtained rows, release the row handles for the retrieved rows
    // and display the names of the rowset columns before we display the data
    if( cRowsObtained )
    {
        // Release the row handles that we obtained
        XCHECK_HR(hr = pIRowset->ReleaseRows(
                 cRowsObtained, //cRows
                 rghRows,       //rghRows
                 NULL,          //rgRowOptions
                 NULL,          //rgRefCounts
                 NULL           //rgRowStatus
                 ));


        // Display the names of the rowset columns
        CHECK_HR(hr = myDisplayColumnNames(pIRowset, rgDispSize));
    }

    // For each row that we obtained the data for, display this data
    for( iRow = 0; iRow < cRowsObtained; iRow++ )
    {
        // Get a pointer to the data for this row
        pCurData = (BYTE*)pData + (cbRowSize* iRow);

        // And display the row data
        CHECK_HR(hr = myDisplayRow(iRow, cBindings, rgBindings,
           pCurData, rgDispSize));
    }

    // Allow the user to navigate the rowset. This displays the appropriate
    // prompts, gets the user's input, may call IRowset::RestartPosition,
    // and may copy data from a selected row to the selection buffer, if so
    // directed. This will return S_OK if the user asked for more rows,
    // S_FALSE if the user selected a row, or E_FAIL if the user quits.
```

```
        hr = myInteractWithRowset(
            pIRowset,            // IRowset pointer, for RestartPosition
            &cRows,              // updated with fetch direction value
            cRowsObtained,            // to indicate selection range
            fCanFetchBackwards,            // whether [P]revious is supported
            pData,               // data pointer for copying selection
            cbRowSize,                // size of rows for copying selection
            iRetCol >= 0 ?            // bindings for the selection column,
                &rgBindings[iRetCol] :    //  or NULL if no selection column
                NULL,
            cchBuffer,                // size of the selection buffer
            pwszBuffer);              // pointer to the selection buffer

        // Since we are allowing the provider to allocate the memory for
        // the row handle array, we will free this memory and reset the
        // pointer to NULL. If this is not NULL on the next call to GetNextRows,
        // the provider will assume that it points to an allocated array of
        // the required size (which may not be the case if we obtained less
        // than cRows rows from this last call to GetNextRows).
        CoTaskMemFree(rghRows);
        rghRows = NULL;
    }

CLEANUP:
    myFreeBindings(cBindings, rgBindings);
    CoTaskMemFree(rgDispSize);
    CoTaskMemFree(pData);
    if( pIRowset )
        pIRowset->Release();
    return hr;
}
```

```
/////////////////////////////////////////////////////////////////
// myInteractWithRowset
//
// This function allows the user to interact with the rowset. It
// prompts the user appropriately, gets the user's input, may
// call IRowset::RestartPosition if the user requests a restart,
// and will copy data from a selected row to the selection
// buffer.
//
/////////////////////////////////////////////////////////////////
HRESULT myInteractWithRowset
   (
   IRowset *           pIRowset,
   LONG *              pcRows,
   ULONG               cRowsObtained,
   BOOL                fCanFetchBackwards,
   void *              pData,
   ULONG               cbRowSize,
   DBBINDING *         pBinding,
   ULONG               cchBuffer,
   LPWSTR           pwszBuffer
   )
{
   HRESULT             hr                        = S_OK;
   CHAR                ch;

   // Let the user know if no rows were fetched
   if( !cRowsObtained )
      printf("\n*-*-*-*-*-*-*-*-*-*-*-*-*-*-*-*-*-*-*\n" \
             "*                                   *\n" \
             "* No rows obtained on this fetch! *\n" \
             "*                                   *\n" \
             "*-*-*-*-*-*-*-*-*-*-*-*-*-*-*-*-*-*-*\n");

   // Print navigation options
   if( fCanFetchBackwards )
      printf("\n[P]revious; [N]ext; [R]estart; ");
   else
      printf("\n[N]ext; [R]estart; ");

   // Print selection options
   if( cRowsObtained && pwszBuffer && pBinding )
      printf("[0]-[%d] for a row; ", cRowsObtained - 1);

   // User can always quit the program
   printf("[Q]uit? ");

   // Get the user's input
   while( TRUE )
```

```
{
   // Get a character from the console
   ch = myGetChar();

   // Look for one of the allowed options; if not found, go
   // back around and wait for another input from the user

   // If we're looking for a row selection, allow the user to select
   // a row that we fetched, and then copy the data from the requested
   // column into the selection buffer we were passed
   if( pwszBuffer && pBinding &&
      ch >= '0' && ch < (int)('0' + cRowsObtained) )
   {
      // Save the data for the selected row
      ULONG nSelection = ch - '0';
      _snwprintf(pwszBuffer, cchBuffer, L"%s",
           (WCHAR *)((BYTE *)pData + cbRowSize * nSelection +
           pBinding->obValue));
      pwszBuffer[cchBuffer] = L'\0';
      hr = S_FALSE;
   }
   // If the provider supports fetching backwards, set *pcRows
   // to -MAX_ROWS. When GetNextRows is called with this value,
   // it will fetch rows backwards from the current position
   // until it fetches MAX_ROWS rows or hits the end of the rowset.
   else if( fCanFetchBackwards && ch == 'p' )
   {
      // Fetch backwards
      *pcRows = -MAX_ROWS;
   }
   // Set *pcRows so that the next call to GetNextRows fetches
   // MAX_ROWS rows forward from the current position
   else if( ch == 'n' )
   {
      // Fetch forward
      *pcRows = MAX_ROWS;
   }
   // Call IRowset::RestartPosition and fetch the first MAX_ROWS
   // rows of the rowset forward from there
   else if( ch == 'r' )
   {
      // RestartPosition
      *pcRows = MAX_ROWS;
      XCHECK_HR(hr = pIRowset->RestartPosition(DB_NULL_HCHAPTER));
```

```
            // Restarting a command may return the DB_S_COMMANDREEXECUTED
            // warning. If this happens, we still want the caller to
            // continue to display data, so we will reset the result code
            // to S_OK.
            hr = S_OK;
        }
        // Quit the program
        else if( ch == 'q' )
        {
            hr = E_FAIL;
        }
        // Invalid option; go back up and get another character from the user
        else
        {
            continue;
        }

        // Echo the character and stop waiting for input
        printf("%c\n", ch);
        break;
    }

CLEANUP:
    return hr;
}


/////////////////////////////////////////////////////////////////////
// myDisplayColumnNames
//
// This function takes an IUnknown pointer to a rowset object
// and displays the names of the columns of that rowset
//
/////////////////////////////////////////////////////////////////////
HRESULT myDisplayColumnNames
    (
    IUnknown *            pUnkRowset,
    ULONG *            rgDispSize
    )
{
    HRESULT            hr;
    IColumnsInfo *        pIColumnsInfo            = NULL;
    ULONG            cColumns;
    DBCOLUMNINFO *    rgColumnInfo            = NULL;
    LPOLESTR            pStringsBuffer            = NULL;
    WCHAR            wszColumn[MAX_DISPLAY_SIZE + 1];
    LPWSTR            pwszColName;
    ULONG            iCol;
    ULONG            cSpaces;
```

```
ULONG             iSpace;

// Get the IColumnsInfo interface for the rowset
XCHECK_HR(hr = pUnkRowset->QueryInterface(
        IID_IColumnsInfo, (void**)&pIColumnsInfo));

// Get the columns information
XCHECK_HR(hr = pIColumnsInfo->GetColumnInfo(
        &cColumns,      // pcColumns
        &rgColumnInfo, // prgColumnInfo
        &pStringsBuffer// ppStringBuffer
        ));

// Display the title of the row index column
wprintf(L" Row | ");

// Display all column names
for( iCol = 0; iCol < cColumns; iCol++ )
{
   pwszColName = rgColumnInfo[iCol].pwszName;

   // If the column name is NULL, we'll use a default string
   if( !pwszColName )
   {
      // Is this the bookmark column?
      if( !rgColumnInfo[iCol].iOrdinal )
         pwszColName = L"Bmk";
      else
         pwszColName = L"(null)";
   }

   // Ensure that the name is no longer than MAX_DISPLAY_SIZE
   wcsncpy(wszColumn, pwszColName, MAX_DISPLAY_SIZE);
   wszColumn[min(rgDispSize[iCol], MAX_DISPLAY_SIZE)] = L'\0';

   // Figure out how many spaces we need to print after this column name
   cSpaces = min(rgDispSize[iCol], MAX_DISPLAY_SIZE) - wcslen(wszColumn);

   // Print the column name
   wprintf(L"%s", wszColumn);

   // Now print any spaces necessary to align this column
   for(iSpace = 0; iSpace < cSpaces; iSpace++ )
      putch(' ');

   // Now end the column with a separator marker if necessary
   if( iCol < cColumns - 1 )
      wprintf(L" | ");
```

```
    }

    // Done with the header, so print a newline
    wprintf(L"\n");

CLEANUP:
    CoTaskMemFree(rgColumnInfo);
    CoTaskMemFree(pStringsBuffer);
    if( pIColumnsInfo )
        pIColumnsInfo->Release();
    return hr;
}


////////////////////////////////////////////////////////////////////
// myDisplayRow
//
// This function displays the data for a row
//
////////////////////////////////////////////////////////////////////
HRESULT myDisplayRow
    (
    ULONG               iRow,
    ULONG               cBindings,
    DBBINDING *         rgBindings,
    void *              pData,
    ULONG *             rgDispSize
    )
{
    HRESULT             hr                      = S_OK;
    WCHAR           wszColumn[MAX_DISPLAY_SIZE + 1];
    DBSTATUS            dwStatus;
    ULONG               ulLength;
    void *              pvValue;
    ULONG               iCol;
    ULONG               cbRead;
    ISequentialStream *     pISeqStream                 = NULL;
    ULONG               cSpaces;
    ULONG               iSpace;

    // Display the row number
    wprintf(L" [%d] | ", iRow);

    // For each column that we have bound, display the data
    for( iCol = 0; iCol < cBindings; iCol++ )
```

```
{
   // We have bound status, length, and the data value for all
   // columns, so we know that these can all be used
   dwStatus = *(DBSTATUS *)((BYTE *)pData + rgBindings[iCol].obStatus);
   ulLength = *(ULONG *)((BYTE *)pData + rgBindings[iCol].obLength);
   pvValue     = (BYTE *)pData + rgBindings[iCol].obValue;

   // Check the status of this column. This decides
   // exactly what will be displayed for the column.
   switch( dwStatus )
   {
      // The data is NULL, so don't try to display it
      case DBSTATUS_S_ISNULL:
         wcscpy(wszColumn, L"(null)");
         break;

      // The data was fetched but may have been truncated.
      // Display string data for this column to the user.
      case DBSTATUS_S_TRUNCATED:
      case DBSTATUS_S_OK:
      case DBSTATUS_S_DEFAULT:
      {
         // We have bound the column either as a Unicode string
         // (DBTYPE_WSTR) or as an ISequentialStream object
         // (DBTYPE_IUNKNOWN), and we have to do different processing
         // for each one of these possibilities
         switch( rgBindings[iCol].wType )
         {
            case DBTYPE_WSTR:
            {
               // Copy the string data
               wcsncpy(wszColumn, (WCHAR *)pvValue, MAX_DISPLAY_SIZE);
               wszColumn[MAX_DISPLAY_SIZE - 1] = L'\0';
               break;
            }
```

```
            case DBTYPE_IUNKNOWN:
            {
               // We've bound this as an ISequentialStream object,
               // and therefore the data in our buffer is a pointer
               // to the object's ISequentialStream interface
               pISeqStream =  *(ISequentialStream**)pvValue;

               // We call ISequentialStream::Read to read bytes from
               // the stream blindly into our buffer, simply as a
               // demonstration of ISequentialStream. To display the
               // data properly, the native provider type of this
               // column should be accounted for; it could be
               // DBTYPE_WSTR, in which case this works, or it could
               // be DBTYPE_STR or DBTYPE_BYTES, in which case this
               // won't display the data correctly.
               CHECK_HR(hr = pISeqStream->Read(
                        wszColumn,            // pBuffer
                        MAX_DISPLAY_SIZE, // cBytes
                        &cbRead               // pcBytesRead
                        ));

               // Since streams don't provide NULL-termination,
               // we'll NULL-terminate the resulting string ourselves
               wszColumn[cbRead / sizeof(WCHAR)] = L'\0';

               // Release the stream object, now that we're done
               pISeqStream->Release();
               pISeqStream = NULL;
               break;
            }
         }
         break;
      }

      // This is an error status, so don't try to display the data
      default:
         wcscpy(wszColumn, L"(error status)");
         break;
   }

   // Determine how many spaces we need to add after displaying this
   // data to align it with this column in other rows
   cSpaces = min(rgDispSize[iCol], MAX_DISPLAY_SIZE) - wcslen(wszColumn);

   // Print the column data
   wprintf(L"%s", wszColumn);
```

```
        // Now print any spaces necessary
        for(iSpace = 0; iSpace < cSpaces; iSpace++ )
           putch(' ');

        // Now end the column with a separator marker if necessary
        if( iCol < cBindings - 1 )
           wprintf(L" | ");
     }

CLEANUP:
     if( pISeqStream )
        pISeqStream->Release();

     // Print the row separator
     wprintf(L"\n");
     return hr;
}



/////////////////////////////////////////////////////////////////
// myFreeBindings
//
// This function frees a bindings array and any allocated
// structures contained in that array
//
/////////////////////////////////////////////////////////////////
void myFreeBindings
   (
   ULONG                cBindings,
   DBBINDING *          rgBindings
   )
{
   ULONG                iBind;

   // Free any memory used by DBOBJECT structures in the array
   for( iBind = 0; iBind < cBindings; iBind++ )
      CoTaskMemFree(rgBindings[iBind].pObject);

   // Now free the bindings array itself
   CoTaskMemFree(rgBindings);
}
```

```
/////////////////////////////////////////////////////////////////
// myAddRowsetProperties
//
// This function sets up the given DBPROPSET and DBPROP
// structures, adding two optional properties that describe
// features that we would like to use on the rowset created
// with these properties applied:
// -- DBPROP_CANFETCHBACKWARDS--the rowset should support
//     fetching rows backwards from our current cursor position.
// -- DBPROP_IRowsetLocate--the rowset should support
//     the IRowsetLocate interface and its semantics.
//
/////////////////////////////////////////////////////////////////
void myAddRowsetProperties(DBPROPSET* pPropSet, ULONG cProperties, DBPROP* rgProperties)
{
   // Initialize the property set array
   pPropSet->rgProperties     = rgProperties;
   pPropSet->cProperties    = cProperties;
   pPropSet->guidPropertySet  = DBPROPSET_ROWSET;

   // Add the following two properties (as OPTIONAL) to the property
   // array contained in the property set array in order to request
   // that they be supported by the rowset we will create. Because
   // these are optional, the rowset we obtain may or may not support
   // this functionality. We will check for the functionality that
   // we need once the rowset is created and will modify our behavior
   // appropriately.
   myAddProperty(&rgProperties[0], DBPROP_CANFETCHBACKWARDS);
   myAddProperty(&rgProperties[1], DBPROP_IRowsetLocate);
}


/////////////////////////////////////////////////////////////////
// myUpdateDisplaySize
//
// This function updates the rgDispSize array, keeping the
// maximum of the display size needed for the given data and
// the previous maximum size already in the array
//
/////////////////////////////////////////////////////////////////
HRESULT myUpdateDisplaySize
   (
   ULONG             cBindings,
   DBBINDING *       rgBindings,
   void *            pData,
   ULONG *           rgDispSize
   )
```

```
{
   DBSTATUS          dwStatus;
   ULONG             cchLength;
   ULONG             iCol;

   // Loop through the bindings, comparing the size of each column
   // against the previously found maximum size for that column
   for( iCol = 0; iCol < cBindings; iCol++ )
   {
      dwStatus  = *(DBSTATUS *)((BYTE *)pData + rgBindings[iCol].obStatus);
      cchLength = ((*(ULONG *)((BYTE *)pData + rgBindings[iCol].obLength))
               / sizeof(WCHAR));

      // The length that we need to display depends on the status
      // of this column and generally on the data in the column
      switch( dwStatus )
      {
         case DBSTATUS_S_ISNULL:
            cchLength = 6;                   // "(null)"
            break;

         case DBSTATUS_S_TRUNCATED:
         case DBSTATUS_S_OK:
         case DBSTATUS_S_DEFAULT:
            if( rgBindings[iCol].wType == DBTYPE_IUNKNOWN )
               cchLength = 2 + 8;            // "0x%08lx"

            // Ensure that the length is at least the minimum display size
            cchLength = max(cchLength, MIN_DISPLAY_SIZE);
            break;

         default:
            cchLength = 14;                  // "(error status)"
            break;
      }

      if( rgDispSize[iCol] < cchLength )
         rgDispSize[iCol] = cchLength;
   }

   return S_OK;
}
```

```
/////////////////////////////////////////////////////////////////
// myFindColumn
//
// Find the index of the column described in pwszName and return
// S_OK, or, if not found, S_FALSE
//
/////////////////////////////////////////////////////////////////
HRESULT myFindColumn
   (
   IUnknown *          pUnkRowset,
   LPCWSTR             pwszName,
   LONG *              plIndex
   )
{
   HRESULT             hr;
   IColumnsInfo *      pIColumnsInfo           = NULL;
   ULONG               cColumns;
   DBCOLUMNINFO *      rgColumnInfo            = NULL;
   OLECHAR *           pStringsBuffer          = NULL;
   ULONG               iCol;

   // Get the IColumnsInfo interface
   XCHECK_HR(hr = pUnkRowset->QueryInterface(
            IID_IColumnsInfo, (void**)&pIColumnsInfo));

   // Get the columns information
   XCHECK_HR(hr = pIColumnsInfo->GetColumnInfo(
            &cColumns,         // pcColumns
            &rgColumnInfo,     // prgColumnInfo
            &pStringsBuffer    // ppStringBuffer
            ));

   // Assume that we'll find the column
   hr = S_OK;

   // Search for the column we need
   for( iCol = 0; iCol < cColumns; iCol++ )
   {
      // If the column name matches, we've found the column...
      if( rgColumnInfo[iCol].pwszName &&
         !wcscmp(pwszName, rgColumnInfo[iCol].pwszName) )
      {
         *plIndex = iCol;
         goto CLEANUP;
      }
   }

   // If we didn't find the column, we'll return S_FALSE
   hr = S_FALSE;
```

```
CLEANUP:
   CoTaskMemFree(rgColumnInfo);
   CoTaskMemFree(pStringsBuffer);
   if( pIColumnsInfo )
      pIColumnsInfo->Release();
   return hr;
}




//-----------------------------------------------------------------------------
// Microsoft OLE DB Programmer's Reference Sample
// Copyright (C) 1998 By Microsoft Corporation.
//
// @doc
//
// @module COMMAND.CPP
//
//-----------------------------------------------------------------------------


/////////////////////////////////////////////////////////////////
// Includes
//
/////////////////////////////////////////////////////////////////
#include "prsample.h"   // Programmer's Reference Sample includes


/////////////////////////////////////////////////////////////////
// myCreateCommand
//
// This function takes an IUnknown pointer on a session object
// and attempts to create a command object using the session's
// IDBCreateCommand interface. Since this interface is optional,
// this may fail.
//
/////////////////////////////////////////////////////////////////
HRESULT  myCreateCommand
   (
   IUnknown *           pUnkSession,
   IUnknown **       ppUnkCommand
   )
{
   HRESULT           hr;
   IDBCreateCommand *pIDBCreateCommand           = NULL;
```

```
   // Attempt to create a command object from the xession object
   XCHECK_HR(hr = pUnkSession->QueryInterface(
            IID_IDBCreateCommand, (void**)&pIDBCreateCommand));
   XCHECK_HR(hr = pIDBCreateCommand->CreateCommand(
            NULL,           // pUnkOuter
            IID_ICommand,      // riid
            ppUnkCommand    // ppCommand
            ));

CLEANUP:
   if( pIDBCreateCommand )
      pIDBCreateCommand->Release();
   return hr;
}




/////////////////////////////////////////////////////////////////////
// myExecuteCommand
//
// This function takes an IUnknown pointer on a command object
// and performs the following steps to create a new rowset
// object:
// -- sets the given properties on the Command object; these
//     properties will be applied by the provider to any rowset
//     created by this command.
// -- sets the given command text for the command.
// -- executes the command to create a new rowset object.
//
/////////////////////////////////////////////////////////////////////
HRESULT  myExecuteCommand
   (
   IUnknown *            pUnkCommand,
   WCHAR *            pwszCommandText,
   ULONG              cPropSets,
   DBPROPSET*         rgPropSets,
   IUnknown **        ppUnkRowset
   )
{
   HRESULT            hr;
   ICommandText *        pICommandText            = NULL;
   ICommandProperties * pICommandProperties      = NULL;

   // Set the properties on the command object
   XCHECK_HR(hr = pUnkCommand->QueryInterface(
            IID_ICommandProperties, (void**)&pICommandProperties));
   XCHECK_HR(hr = pICommandProperties->SetProperties(cPropSets, rgPropSets));
```

```
    // Set the text for this command, using the default command text
    // dialect. All providers that support commands must support this
    // dialect, and providers that support SQL must be able to recognize
    // an SQL command as SQL when this dialect is specified.
    XCHECK_HR(hr = pUnkCommand->QueryInterface(
                IID_ICommandText, (void**)&pICommandText));
    XCHECK_HR(hr = pICommandText->SetCommandText(
                DBGUID_DEFAULT,        // guidDialect
                pwszCommandText            // pwszCommandText
                ));

    // And execute the command. Note that the user could have
    // entered a non-row returning command, so we will check for
    // that and return failure to prevent the display of the
    // nonexistent rowset by the caller.
    XCHECK_HR(hr = pICommandText->Execute(
                NULL,       // pUnkOuter
                IID_IRowset,// riid
                NULL,       // pParams
                NULL,       // pcRowsAffected
                ppUnkRowset // ppRowset
                ));

    if( !*ppUnkRowset )
    {
        printf("\nThe command executed successfully, but did not " \
              "return a rowset.\nNo rowset will be displayed.\n");
        hr = E_FAIL;
    }


CLEANUP:
    if( pICommandText )
        pICommandText->Release();
    if( pICommandProperties )
        pICommandProperties->Release();
    return hr;
}
```

```
//-----------------------------------------------------------------------------
// Microsoft OLE DB Programmer's Reference Sample
// Copyright (C) 1998 By Microsoft Corporation.
//
// @doc
//
// @module ERROR.CPP
//
//-----------------------------------------------------------------------------


/////////////////////////////////////////////////////////////////////////
// Includes
//
/////////////////////////////////////////////////////////////////////////
#include "prsample.h"   // Programmer's Reference Sample includes


/////////////////////////////////////////////////////////////////////////
// myHandleResult
//
// This function is called as part of the XCHECK_HR macro; it takes an
// HRESULT, which is returned by the method called in the XCHECK_HR
// macro, and the file and line number where the method call was made.
// If the method call failed, this function attempts to get and display
// the extended error information for the call from the IErrorInfo,
// IErrorRecords, and ISQLErrorInfo interfaces.
//
/////////////////////////////////////////////////////////////////////////
HRESULT myHandleResult
   (
   HRESULT          hrReturned,
   LPCWSTR          pwszFile,
   ULONG            ulLine
   )
```

```
{
   HRESULT            hr;
   IErrorInfo *          pIErrorInfo                   = NULL;
   IErrorRecords *       pIErrorRecords                = NULL;
   ULONG              cRecords;
   ULONG              iErr;

   // If the method called as part of the XCHECK_HR macro failed,
   // we will attempt to get extended error information for the call
   if( FAILED(hrReturned) )
   {
      // Obtain the current error object, if any, by using the
      // Automation GetErrorInfo function, which will give
      // us back an IErrorInfo interface pointer if successful
      hr = GetErrorInfo(0, &pIErrorInfo);

      // We've got the IErrorInfo interface pointer on the error object
      if( SUCCEEDED(hr) && pIErrorInfo )
      {
         // OLE DB extends the Automation error model by allowing
         // error objects to support the IErrorRecords interface; this
         // interface can expose information on multiple errors.
         hr = pIErrorInfo->QueryInterface(IID_IErrorRecords,
                  (void**)&pIErrorRecords);
         if( SUCCEEDED(hr) )
         {
            // Get the count of error records from the object
            CHECK_HR(hr = pIErrorRecords->GetRecordCount(&cRecords));

            // Loop through the set of error records and
            // display the error information for each one
            for( iErr = 0; iErr < cRecords; iErr++ )
            {
               myDisplayErrorRecord(hrReturned, iErr, pIErrorRecords,
                  pwszFile, ulLine);
            }
         }
         // The object didn't support IErrorRecords; display
         // the error information for this single error
         else
         {
            myDisplayErrorInfo(hrReturned, pIErrorInfo, pwszFile, ulLine);
         }
      }
```

```
      // There was no error object, so just display the HRESULT to the user
      else
      {
         wprintf(L"\nNo Error Info posted; HResult: 0x%08x\n"
            L"File: %s, Line: %d\n", hrReturned, pwszFile, ulLine);
      }
   }

CLEANUP:
   if( pIErrorInfo )
      pIErrorInfo->Release();
   if( pIErrorRecords )
      pIErrorRecords->Release();
   return hrReturned;
}


////////////////////////////////////////////////////////////////////////
// myDisplayErrorRecord
//
// This function displays the error information for a single error
// record, including information from ISQLErrorInfo, if supported
//
////////////////////////////////////////////////////////////////////////
HRESULT myDisplayErrorRecord
   (
   HRESULT              hrReturned,
   ULONG                iRecord,
   IErrorRecords *         pIErrorRecords,
   LPCWSTR              pwszFile,
   ULONG                ulLine
   )
{
   HRESULT              hr;
   IErrorInfo *            pIErrorInfo                  = NULL;
   BSTR                 bstrDescription             = NULL;
   BSTR                 bstrSource                  = NULL;
   BSTR                 bstrSQLInfo                 = NULL;

   static LCID             lcid                         = GetUserDefaultLCID();

   LONG                 lNativeError                = 0;
   ERRORINFO         ErrorInfo;

   // Get the IErrorInfo interface pointer for this error record
   CHECK_HR(hr = pIErrorRecords->GetErrorInfo(iRecord, lcid, &pIErrorInfo));

   // Get the description of this error
   CHECK_HR(hr = pIErrorInfo->GetDescription(&bstrDescription));
```

```
    // Get the source of this error
    CHECK_HR(hr = pIErrorInfo->GetSource(&bstrSource));

    // Get the basic error information for this record
    CHECK_HR(hr = pIErrorRecords->GetBasicErrorInfo(iRecord, &ErrorInfo));

    // If the error object supports ISQLErrorInfo, get this information
    myGetSqlErrorInfo(iRecord, pIErrorRecords, &bstrSQLInfo, &lNativeError);

    // Display the error information to the user
    if( bstrSQLInfo )
    {
       wprintf(L"\nErrorRecord:  HResult: 0x%08x\nDescription: %s\n"
          L"SQLErrorInfo: %s\nSource: %s\nFile: %s, Line: %d\n",
          ErrorInfo.hrError,
          bstrDescription,
          bstrSQLInfo,
          bstrSource,
          pwszFile,
          ulLine);
    }
    else
    {
       wprintf(L"\nErrorRecord:  HResult: 0x%08x\nDescription: %s\n"
          L"Source: %s\nFile: %s, Line: %d\n",
          ErrorInfo.hrError,
          bstrDescription,
          bstrSource,
          pwszFile,
          ulLine);
    }

CLEANUP:
    if( pIErrorInfo )
       pIErrorInfo->Release();
    SysFreeString(bstrDescription);
    SysFreeString(bstrSource);
    SysFreeString(bstrSQLInfo);
    return hr;
}
```

```
///////////////////////////////////////////////////////////////////////
// myDisplayErrorInfo
//
// This function displays basic error information for an error object
// that doesn't support the IErrorRecords interface
//
///////////////////////////////////////////////////////////////////////
HRESULT myDisplayErrorInfo
   (
   HRESULT             hrReturned,
   IErrorInfo *           pIErrorInfo,
   LPCWSTR             pwszFile,
   ULONG               ulLine
   )
{
   HRESULT             hr;
   BSTR                bstrDescription            = NULL;
   BSTR                bstrSource                 = NULL;

   // Get the description of the error
   CHECK_HR(hr = pIErrorInfo->GetDescription(&bstrDescription));

   // Get the source of the error--this will be the window title
   CHECK_HR(hr = pIErrorInfo->GetSource(&bstrSource));

   // Display this error information
   wprintf(L"\nErrorInfo:  HResult: 0x%08x, Description: %s\nSource: %s\n"
            L"File: %s, Line: %d\n",
            hrReturned,
            bstrDescription,
            bstrSource,
            pwszFile,
            ulLine);

CLEANUP:
   SysFreeString(bstrDescription);
   SysFreeString(bstrSource);
   return hr;
}
```

```
/////////////////////////////////////////////////////////////////////////
// myGetSqlErrorInfo
//
// If the error object supports ISQLErrorInfo, get the SQL error
// string and native error code for this error
//
/////////////////////////////////////////////////////////////////////////
HRESULT myGetSqlErrorInfo
   (
   ULONG              iRecord,
   IErrorRecords *       pIErrorRecords,
   BSTR *             pBstr,
   LONG *             plNativeError
   )
{
   HRESULT            hr;
   ISQLErrorInfo *       pISQLErrorInfo              = NULL;
   LONG               lNativeError              = 0;

   // Attempt to get the ISQLErrorInfo interface for this error
   // record through GetCustomErrorObject. Note that ISQLErrorInfo
   // is not mandatory, so failure is acceptable here.
   CHECK_HR(hr = pIErrorRecords->GetCustomErrorObject(
            iRecord,                     // iRecord
            IID_ISQLErrorInfo,              // riid
            (IUnknown**)&pISQLErrorInfo  // ppISQLErrorInfo
            ));

   // If we obtained the ISQLErrorInfo interface, get the SQL
   // error string and native error code for this error
   if( pISQLErrorInfo )
      hr = pISQLErrorInfo->GetSQLInfo(pBstr, &lNativeError);

CLEANUP:
   if( plNativeError )
      *plNativeError = lNativeError;
   if( pISQLErrorInfo )
      pISQLErrorInfo->Release();
   return hr;
}
```

Glossary

A

Abort

To return the values changed by a transaction to their original state.

Accessor

A collection of information that describes how data is stored in the consumer's buffer. The provider uses this information to determine how to transfer data to and from this buffer. *See also* reference accessor.

Accessor handle

A handle that identifies an accessor.

Auto-commit mode

A transaction commit mode in which all actions taken in a transaction are committed immediately after they are performed. *See also* manual-commit mode.

Automation error object

An error object that conforms to the standards specified for such objects by Automation. *See also* OLE DB error object.

B

BLOB

Acronym for binary large object. Any binary or character data over a certain number of bytes, such as 255. Typically much longer. Such data is generally sent to and retrieved from the data source in parts. Also known as long data.

Binding

As a verb, the act of associating a column in a rowset or a parameter in a text command with a consumer variable. As a noun, the association or the DBBINDING structure that describes the association.

Bookmark

A value that identifies a row in a rowset. Bookmarks are saved by the consumer and used later in the life of the rowset to retrieve a particular row.

BSTR

A pointer to a null-terminated character string in which the string length is stored with the string.

B-tree
A tree structure for storing database indexes.

Buffer
A piece of memory used to pass information, usually data, between the consumer and provider.

C

Catalog
A database object that contains one or more schemas.

Change
To update, delete, or insert a row of data.

Class ID
A globally unique identifier (GUID) associated with a COM class.

Client/server
A database access strategy in which one or more clients access data through a server. The clients generally implement the user interface while the server controls database access.

Column
The container for a single item of information in a row. Also known as field.

Column ID
A structure used to identify a column, primarily in a command where there are no stable ordinals or column names.

Command
An OLE DB object that encapsulates a command.

Command text
The text command associated with a command object. Although it is not required to be, this is usually an SQL statement.

Commit
To make the changes in a transaction permanent.

COM object
An object that conforms to the Component Object Model (COM). A COM object is an instance of a COM class. Clients interact with a COM object only through its interfaces. *See also* Component Object Model and interface.

Component
An object that encapsulates both data and code and provides a well-specified set of publicly available services.

Component Object Model (COM)

The object-oriented programming model that defines how objects interact within a single process or between processes. In COM, clients have access to an object through interfaces implemented on the object. *See also* interface.

Concurrency

The ability of more than one transaction to access the same data at the same time.

Consumer

Software that calls OLE DB methods and interfaces.

Container

A file containing linked or embedded objects.

Convert

To change data from one type to another, as from an integer to a string.

Coordinated transaction

A transaction composed of multiple, subordinate transactions. All of the subordinate transactions must succeed for the coordinated transaction to succeed. Also known as a distributed transaction.

Cotype

A way to define a group of COM objects, such as rowsets or commands, that have similar characteristics. All COM objects that belong to a particular CoType must expose the mandatory interfaces in that CoType. In addition, they can expose the optional interfaces in the CoType and any interfaces not in the CoType.

D

Data

The data for a parameter in a text command or a column in a row.

Database

A discrete collection of data in a DBMS. Also a DBMS.

Database Management System (DBMS)

A layer of software between the physical database and the user. The DBMS manages all access to the database. An OLE DB provider can be built directly on top of a DBMS or as a layer between the DBMS and the consumer.

Data Definition Language (DDL)

Those text commands that define, as opposed to manipulate, data. For example, the SQL statements CREATE TABLE, CREATE INDEX, GRANT, and REVOKE.

Data Manipulation Language (DML)

Those text commands that manipulate, as opposed to define, data. For example, the SQL statements INSERT, UPDATE, DELETE, and SELECT.

Data part
Data has three parts: the data value, the length of the data value, and the status of the data value.

Data provider
A provider that directly exposes data, as opposed to a service component.

Data source object
An OLE DB object that connects to a data source.

Data store
The data the user wants to access, such as the data in a database, file, or array.

Data type
The type of a piece of data. *See also* type indicator.

Deferred column
A column for which the data is not instantiated in the rowset until the consumer actually attempts to access that data.

Delayed update mode
An update mode in which changes made through IRowsetChange are cached in the rowset and transmitted to the data store only when IRowsetUpdate::Update is called. *See also* immediate update mode.

Delete
To remove an existing row of data from the data source.

Distributed transaction
See coordinated transaction.

Dynamic error
An error message that cannot be predicted because it is not provider specific.

Dynamic error ID
An identifier that is used by a lookup service and is associated with an error object.

E

Empty string
A zero-length string. *See also* null pointer and NULL value.

Endogenous change
A change to data originating from a process other than your own.

Enumerator
An OLE DB object that searches for data source objects and other enumerators. *See also* root enumerator.

Error
A condition in which a fatal error occurred. Also used to refer to any error, whether or not it is fatal.

Error code
A class of return code, of the type HRESULT, that begins with E_ or DB_E_ and indicates that the method failed completely and was unable to do any useful work.

Error lookup service
A method used by a provider to handle and interpret OLE DB error objects.

Error object
An object that contains detailed information about an error. *See also* Automation error object and OLE DB error object.

Event
An action taken by a provider, such as changing a column value or deleting a row, of which the provider notifies the consumer.

Execution plan
A plan generated by a query engine to execute a command. Equivalent to executable code compiled from a third-generation language such as C.

F

Fetch
To retrieve one or more rows from the data store and instantiate them in a rowset.

Field
See column.

Fixed-length data type
A data type that is always stored in the same number of bytes, such as a two-byte integer. *See also* variable-length data type.

Foreign key
A column or columns in a table that match the primary key in another table.

G

Getting data
Transferring data from the provider to the consumer, as in getting column or output parameter data.

Globally Unique Identifier (GUID)
A 16-byte value that uniquely identifies something, usually the software that implements one or more COM objects or an interface on one of those objects. Also known as a UUID (Universally Unique Identifier).

H

HRESULT
An opaque result handle defined to be zero for a successful return from a function and nonzero if error or status information is returned.

I

Immediate update mode
An update mode in which changes made through IRowsetChange are immediately transmitted to the data store. *See also* delayed update mode.

Index rowset
A rowset built over an index. Each row in an index rowset contains a bookmark that points to a row in a rowset built over the corresponding table.

Initialize
To change the state of an enumerator or data source object so it can be used to access data. For example, initializing a data source object might require the provider to open a data file or connect to a database.

Input/output parameter
A parameter in a text command for which the consumer supplies a value to the provider and the provider returns a value to the consumer.

Input parameter
A parameter in a text command for which the consumer supplies a value to the provider.

Insert
To add a new row of data to the data store.

Instantiate
To create an instance of a COM object.

Interface
A group of semantically related functions that provide access to a COM object. Each interface defines a contract that allows objects to interact according to the Component Object Model (COM). *See also* Component Object Model and COM object.

Interface Identifier (IID)
A globally unique identifier (GUID) associated with an interface. Some functions take IIDs as parameters to allow the caller to specify which interface pointer should be returned.

IPersist* object
A COM object that supports IPersistStream, IPersistStreamInit, or IPersistStorage.

Isolation level
See transaction isolation level.

J

Join
An operation in a relational database that links the rows in two or more tables by matching values in specified columns.

K

Key
A column or columns whose values identify a row. *See also* foreign key and primary key.

Key value bookmark
A bookmark that uses a unique key to identify a row. *See also* numeric bookmark.

L

Length
The length of a data value. *See also* data part, status, and value.

Listener
A consumer that has requested that a provider send it notifications of various events.

Long data
See BLOB.

M

Manual-commit mode
A transaction commit mode in which transactions must be explicitly committed or aborted by calling ITransaction::Commit or ITransaction::Abort.

Maximum precision
The maximum number of base-10 digits that can be stored in a particular data type. *See also* precision.

Metadata
Data that describes a parameter in a text command or a column in a rowset. For example, the data type, length, and updatability of a column.

Method
A function in an interface.

Moniker
A name for a specific object instance.

Multiple results object
An OLE DB object created by executing a command and through which multiple results (rowsets or row counts) can be retrieved.

N

Next fetch position
The position of the next row that will be fetched by a call to IRowset::GetNextRows.

Notification
A call from a provider to a consumer, in which the provider notifies the consumer that a particular event is occurring.

Notification sink
An actual object that implements the notification interface.

Null pointer
A pointer with a value of zero. It is an error to dereference a null pointer. *See also* empty string and NULL value.

NULL value
Having no explicitly assigned value. In particular, a NULL value is different from a zero or a blank. *See also* empty string and null pointer.

Numeric bookmark
A bookmark that uses a unique number to identify a row. *See also* key value bookmark.

O

Object
In COM, a programming structure encapsulating both data and functionality that are defined and allocated as a single unit and for which the only public access is through the programming structure's interfaces. A COM object must support, at a minimum, the IUnknown interface, which maintains the object's existence while it is being used and provides access to the object's other interfaces. *See also* Component Object Model and interface.

OLE
Microsoft's object-based technology for sharing information and services across process and machine boundaries.

OLE DB
A set of interfaces that expose data from a variety of data stores using COM.

OLE DB error object
An error object used by OLE DB objects to return an error. OLE DB error objects are an extension of Automation error objects.

OLE DB object
A COM object defined by OLE DB. The COM objects defined by OLE DB are enumerators, data source objects, sessions, commands, rowsets, multiple results objects, OLE DB error objects, transaction objects, and transaction options objects.

OLE DB Software Development Kit (SDK)
A collection of redistributable software, header files, tools, sample code, and documentation to be used by developers of OLE DB consumers and providers.

Optimistic concurrency
A strategy to increase concurrency in which rows are not locked. Instead, before they are updated or deleted, a rowset checks to see whether they have been changed since they were last read. If so, the update or delete fails. *See also* pessimistic concurrency.

Ordinary bookmark
A bookmark whose value is defined by the provider. *See also* standard bookmark.

Output parameter
A parameter in a text command for which the provider returns a value to the consumer.

P

Parallel processing
A method of processing that can run only on a computer that contains two or more processors running simultaneously.

Parameter
A variable in a text command. A parameter can be an input, input/output, or output parameter.

Pending change
A change that has been cached in a rowset and not yet transmitted to the data store. *See also* delayed update mode and immediate update mode.

Persist
To save the current state of a COM object, such as to a file.

Pessimistic concurrency
A strategy for implementing serializability in which rows are locked so that other transactions cannot change them. *See also* optimistic concurrency.

Phase
A step in a sequence of notifications caused by a single event. The sequence of notifications is similar to the phases in a two-phase commit protocol.

Precision
The number of base 10-digits in a number. *See also* maximum precision.

Prepare
To compile a command. An execution plan is created by preparing a command.

Preserved rowset
A rowset in which all previously defined functionality is retained after a commit or abort.

Primary key
A column or columns that uniquely identifies a row in a table.

Procedure
A group of one or more precompiled commands (usually SQL statements) that are stored as a named object in a database.

Property
Attributes of an OLE DB object. For example, the maximum number of rows in a rowset that can be active at one time.

Property group
The set of all properties that apply to a particular OLE DB object.

Property set
A property is identified by a GUID and an integer (the property ID). A property set is the set of all properties that share the same GUID.

Provider
Software that implements OLE DB methods and interfaces.

Q

Query
A text command. Sometimes used to mean a text command that creates a rowset.

R

Reason
The specific event that occurred, such as changing a row value or deleting a row. *See also* event.

Record
See row.

Reference accessor
An accessor that enables a consumer to get rowset data directly from the provider's buffer. Support for reference accessors is optional.

Reference counting
Keeping a count of each interface pointer held on an object to ensure that the object is not destroyed before all references to it are released. In OLE DB, rows and accessors are also reference counted.

Release
To decrease the reference count on a row, accessor, or COM object. When the reference count reaches zero, the provider usually releases the resources used by the row, accessor, or COM object.

Result
A row count or rowset created by executing a command. *See also* multiple results object.

Resynchronize
To update the data in a rowset with the data in the data source that is visible to the current transaction according to its isolation level.

Return code
The value returned by an OLE DB method.

Root enumerator
An enumerator shipped in the Microsoft Data Access SDK that enumerates the data sources and enumerators listed in the registry. *See also* enumerator.

Row
A set of related columns that describe a specific entity. Also known as a record.

Row handle
A handle used to identify a row.

Rowset
An OLE DB object that contains a set of rows, each of which has columns of data.

S

Scale
The number of digits in a number that are to the right of the decimal point.

Schema
A database object that contains one or more tables, often created by a single user.

Schema rowset
A predefined rowset that provides information about the structure of a database.

Self bookmark
A bookmark, stored in column 0 of a row, that is used to return to that row.

Serializability
Whether two transactions executing simultaneously produce a result that is the same as the serial (or sequential) execution of those transactions. Serializable transactions are required to maintain database integrity.

Service component
A provider that does not directly expose data but instead provides a service, such as query processing. Used in conjunction with data providers.

Session
An OLE DB object that serves as the context for a transaction.

Setting data
Transferring data from the consumer to the provider, as in setting column or input parameter data.

SQL
Structured Query Language. A language used by relational databases to query, update, and manage data. Text commands often use SQL.

Standard bookmark
A bookmark whose value is defined by OLE DB. *See also* ordinary bookmark.

Static error
An error (text) that is stored by a specific provider lookup service and most commonly tied to a single data store.

Status
The status of a data value. *See also* data part, length, and value.

Storage interface
An interface used to access data in a storage object: ISequentialStream, IStream, IStorage, or ILockBytes.

Storage object
A COM object that implements a storage interface. Storage objects are used to access BLOB data stored in a column.

Success
A condition in which no errors occurred.

Success code
A class of return code, of the type HRESULT, that begins with S_ or DB_S_ and indicates success of the method.

T

Table
A collection of rows in the data source.

Text command
A text string, usually an SQL statement, that defines a command.

Transaction
An atomic unit of work. The work in a transaction must be completed as a whole; if any part of the transaction fails, the entire transaction fails.

Transaction isolation
The act of isolating one transaction from the effects of all other transactions.

Transaction isolation level
A measure of how well a transaction is isolated.

Transaction object
An OLE DB object used to support transactions.

Transaction options object
An OLE DB object used to define various options for a transaction.

Transfer
To move data between the consumer's and provider's buffers. The provider, not the consumer, transfers data. *See also* getting data and setting data.

Transmit
To send changes made through IRowsetChange to the data store. *See also* delayed update mode and immediate update mode.

Transmitted change
A change that has been sent to the data store. *See also* pending change.

Truncate
To discard one or more bytes of variable-length data or nonsignificant digits of numeric data. Truncation results in a warning condition when getting data and an error condition when setting data.

Type indicator
An integer value passed to or returned from an OLE DB method to indicate the data type of a consumer variable, a parameter, or a column.

U

Uninitialize
To change the state of an enumerator or data source object so that it cannot be used to access data. For example, uninitializing a data source object might require the provider to close a data file or disconnect from a database.

Unprepare
To discard the current execution plan.

Update
To change an existing row of data in the data store. Also, to transmit pending changes to the data store.

V

Value
A data value. *See also* data part, length, and status.

Variable-length data type
A data type for which the length of the data can vary, such as a string. *See also* fixed-length data type.

Visibility
Whether data values can be detected by a rowset. Refers both to the visibility of data in a data store and data cached in a rowset.

W

Warning
A condition in which a nonfatal error occurred.

Warning code
A class of return code, of the type HRESULT, that begins with S_ or DB_S_ and indicates success of the method but with a warning.

Z

Zombie
A state in which the only valid consumer action on a COM object is generally to release that object.

Index

A

B

C

D

E

F

G

H

I

N

O

Q

R

T

OLE DB represents the work of many people over several years. Although the contributors are far too numerous to mention, we attempt to list some of those who have made significant contributions to this release. Our apologies and thanks to any we have missed.

The first release of OLE DB shipped in August of 1996. The architecture was based on a vision from Adam Bosworth and David Vaskevitch of having a common way to access all types of data in a COM environment. The general architecture was defined by Tanj Bennett and Goetz Graefe, with José Blakeley, Michael Pizzo, Ron Bourrett, and Renato Barrera filling in the details. The release of the OLE DB 1.0 Software Development Kit was headed by M. Alam Ali, Paul Archer, Kristi Brandes, and Mark Bukovec, under the leadership of Dave Cameron and with the support of Bill Baker.

Key technical contributors to OLE DB version 2.0 included Michael Pizzo, José Blakeley, Murali Venkatrao, and Paul Archer, who resolved numerous design issues and worked with many people inside and outside Microsoft to ensure that OLE DB would fill the needs of consumers and providers alike. Special thanks to the key reviewers of the *OLED DB 2.0 Programmer's Reference*, Peter Burzynski, Ed Triou, Conor Cunningham, Steve Starck, George Rankin, David Zimmerman, Syed Yousuf, and Joe Sherman, as well as the rest of the OLE DB test team including Allan Benson, Steve Hale, John Koropchak, Siraj Lala, Joon Lee, Catalin Sipos, and Adam Wise. Ed Triou and Peter Burzynski are the authors of the sample program used throughout the book.

The bulk of the writing for the *OLE DB 2.0 Programmer's Reference* was done by Diane Olsen and Wes Kim, with help and support from Eric Mitchell, Marta Fortin, Kate Robinson, Emily Hylton, Jeana Frazier, and Richard Carey. Production support came from Catherine Horne, David Fleischman, and Bruno Josset. Thomas Kite produced the CD.

The entire Data Access team provided invaluable feedback on the specification and code shipped in OLE DB 2.0. Providing leadership and support to the team were David Vaskevitch, Winnie Wu, Gunnar Mein, Janice Hertz, Geoffrey Kizer, and Jim Wilson.

Significant contributions to OLE DB 2.0 were made by numerous other people inside Microsoft, including Ross Bunker, Joyce Chen, Daniel Dedu-Constantin, Lon Fisher, Dax Hawkins, Alyssa Henry, Suresh Kannan, Don Reichart, Greg Smith, Brian Tschumper, Matt Warren, and Matt Woodward.

MICROSOFT LICENSE AGREEMENT

(Book Companion CD)

IMPORTANT—READ CAREFULLY: This Microsoft End-User License Agreement ("EULA") is a legal agreement between you (either an individual or an entity) and Microsoft Corporation for the Microsoft product identified above, which includes computer software and may include associated media, printed materials, and "on-line" or electronic documentation ("SOFTWARE PRODUCT"). Any component included within the SOFTWARE PRODUCT that is accompanied by a separate End-User License Agreement shall be governed by such agreement and not the terms set forth below. By installing, copying, or otherwise using the SOFTWARE PRODUCT, you agree to be bound by the terms of this EULA. If you do not agree to the terms of this EULA, you are not authorized to install, copy, or otherwise use the SOFTWARE PRODUCT; you may, however, return the SOFTWARE PRODUCT, along with all printed materials and other items that form a part of the Microsoft product that includes the SOFTWARE PRODUCT, to the place you obtained them for a full refund.

SOFTWARE PRODUCT LICENSE

The SOFTWARE PRODUCT is protected by United States copyright laws and international copyright treaties, as well as other intellectual property laws and treaties. The SOFTWARE PRODUCT is licensed, not sold.

1. **GRANT OF LICENSE.** This EULA grants you the following rights:

   a. **Software Product.** You may install and use one copy of the SOFTWARE PRODUCT on a single computer. The primary user of the computer on which the SOFTWARE PRODUCT is installed may make a second copy for his or her exclusive use on a portable computer.

   b. **Storage/Network Use.** You may also store or install a copy of the SOFTWARE PRODUCT on a storage device, such as a network server, used only to install or run the SOFTWARE PRODUCT on your other computers over an internal network; however, you must acquire and dedicate a license for each separate computer on which the SOFTWARE PRODUCT is installed or run from the storage device. A license for the SOFTWARE PRODUCT may not be shared or used concurrently on different computers.

   c. **License Pak.** If you have acquired this EULA in a Microsoft License Pak, you may make the number of additional copies of the computer software portion of the SOFTWARE PRODUCT authorized on the printed copy of this EULA, and you may use each copy in the manner specified above. You are also entitled to make a corresponding number of secondary copies for portable computer use as specified above.

   d. **Sample Code.** Solely with respect to portions, if any, of the SOFTWARE PRODUCT that are identified within the SOFTWARE PRODUCT as sample code (the "SAMPLE CODE"):

      i. **Use and Modification.** Microsoft grants you the right to use and modify the source code version of the SAMPLE CODE, *provided* you comply with subsection (d)(iii) below. You may not distribute the SAMPLE CODE, or any modified version of the SAMPLE CODE, in source code form.

      ii. **Redistributable Files.** Provided you comply with subsection (d)(iii) below, Microsoft grants you a nonexclusive, royalty-free right to reproduce and distribute the object code version of the SAMPLE CODE and of any modified SAMPLE CODE, other than SAMPLE CODE (or any modified version thereof) designated as not redistributable in the Readme file that forms a part of the SOFTWARE PRODUCT (the "Non-Redistributable Sample Code"). All SAMPLE CODE other than the Non-Redistributable Sample Code is collectively referred to as the "REDISTRIBUTABLES."

      iii. **Redistribution Requirements.** If you redistribute the REDISTRIBUTABLES, you agree to: (i) distribute the REDISTRIBUTABLES in object code form only in conjunction with and as a part of your software application product; (ii) not use Microsoft's name, logo, or trademarks to market your software application product; (iii) include a valid copyright notice on your software application product; (iv) indemnify, hold harmless, and defend Microsoft from and against any claims or lawsuits, including attorney's fees, that arise or result from the use or distribution of your software application product; and (v) not permit further distribution of the REDISTRIBUTABLES by your end user. Contact Microsoft for the applicable royalties due and other licensing terms for all other uses and/or distribution of the REDISTRIBUTABLES.

2. **DESCRIPTION OF OTHER RIGHTS AND LIMITATIONS.**

- **Limitations on Reverse Engineering, Decompilation, and Disassembly.** You may not reverse engineer, decompile, or disassemble the SOFTWARE PRODUCT, except and only to the extent that such activity is expressly permitted by applicable law notwithstanding this limitation.
- **Separation of Components.** The SOFTWARE PRODUCT is licensed as a single product. Its component parts may not be separated for use on more than one computer.
- **Rental.** You may not rent, lease, or lend the SOFTWARE PRODUCT.
- **Support Services.** Microsoft may, but is not obligated to, provide you with support services related to the SOFTWARE PRODUCT ("Support Services"). Use of Support Services is governed by the Microsoft policies and programs described in the user manual, in "on-line" documentation, and/or in other Microsoft-provided materials. Any supplemental software code

provided to you as part of the Support Services shall be considered part of the SOFTWARE PRODUCT and subject to the terms and conditions of this EULA. With respect to technical information you provide to Microsoft as part of the Support Services, Microsoft may use such information for its business purposes, including for product support and development. Microsoft will not utilize such technical information in a form that personally identifies you.

- **Software Transfer.** You may permanently transfer all of your rights under this EULA, provided you retain no copies, you transfer all of the SOFTWARE PRODUCT (including all component parts, the media and printed materials, any upgrades, this EULA, and, if applicable, the Certificate of Authenticity), **and** the recipient agrees to the terms of this EULA.
- **Termination.** Without prejudice to any other rights, Microsoft may terminate this EULA if you fail to comply with the terms and conditions of this EULA. In such event, you must destroy all copies of the SOFTWARE PRODUCT and all of its component parts.

3. **COPYRIGHT.** All title and copyrights in and to the SOFTWARE PRODUCT (including but not limited to any images, photographs, animations, video, audio, music, text, SAMPLE CODE, REDISTRIBUTABLES, and "applets" incorporated into the SOFTWARE PRODUCT) and any copies of the SOFTWARE PRODUCT are owned by Microsoft or its suppliers. The SOFTWARE PRODUCT is protected by copyright laws and international treaty provisions. Therefore, you must treat the SOFTWARE PRODUCT like any other copyrighted material **except** that you may install the SOFTWARE PRODUCT on a single computer provided you keep the original solely for backup or archival purposes. You may not copy the printed materials accompanying the SOFTWARE PRODUCT.

4. **U.S. GOVERNMENT RESTRICTED RIGHTS.** The SOFTWARE PRODUCT and documentation are provided with RESTRICTED RIGHTS. Use, duplication, or disclosure by the Government is subject to restrictions as set forth in subparagraph (c)(1)(ii) of the Rights in Technical Data and Computer Software clause at DFARS 252.227-7013 or subparagraphs (c)(1) and (2) of the Commercial Computer Software—Restricted Rights at 48 CFR 52.227-19, as applicable. Manufacturer is Microsoft Corporation/One Microsoft Way/Redmond, WA 98052-6399.

5. **EXPORT RESTRICTIONS.** You agree that you will not export or re-export the SOFTWARE PRODUCT, any part thereof, or any process or service that is the direct product of the SOFTWARE PRODUCT (the foregoing collectively referred to as the "Restricted Components"), to any country, person, entity, or end user subject to U.S. export restrictions. You specifically agree not to export or re-export any of the Restricted Components (i) to any country to which the U.S. has embargoed or restricted the export of goods or services, which currently include, but are not necessarily limited to, Cuba, Iran, Iraq, Libya, North Korea, Sudan, and Syria, or to any national of any such country, wherever located, who intends to transmit or transport the Restricted Components back to such country; (ii) to any end user who you know or have reason to know will utilize the Restricted Components in the design, development, or production of nuclear, chemical, or biological weapons; or (iii) to any end user who has been prohibited from participating in U.S. export transactions by any federal agency of the U.S. government. You warrant and represent that neither the BXA nor any other U.S. federal agency has suspended, revoked, or denied your export privileges.

DISCLAIMER OF WARRANTY

NO WARRANTIES OR CONDITIONS. MICROSOFT EXPRESSLY DISCLAIMS ANY WARRANTY OR CONDITION FOR THE SOFTWARE PRODUCT. THE SOFTWARE PRODUCT AND ANY RELATED DOCUMENTATION IS PROVIDED "AS IS" WITHOUT WARRANTY OR CONDITION OF ANY KIND, EITHER EXPRESS OR IMPLIED, INCLUDING, WITHOUT LIMITATION, THE IMPLIED WARRANTIES OF MERCHANTABILITY, FITNESS FOR A PARTICULAR PURPOSE, OR NONINFRINGEMENT. THE ENTIRE RISK ARISING OUT OF USE OR PERFORMANCE OF THE SOFTWARE PRODUCT REMAINS WITH YOU.

LIMITATION OF LIABILITY. TO THE MAXIMUM EXTENT PERMITTED BY APPLICABLE LAW, IN NO EVENT SHALL MICROSOFT OR ITS SUPPLIERS BE LIABLE FOR ANY SPECIAL, INCIDENTAL, INDIRECT, OR CONSEQUENTIAL DAMAGES WHATSOEVER (INCLUDING, WITHOUT LIMITATION, DAMAGES FOR LOSS OF BUSINESS PROFITS, BUSINESS INTERRUPTION, LOSS OF BUSINESS INFORMATION, OR ANY OTHER PECUNIARY LOSS) ARISING OUT OF THE USE OF OR INABILITY TO USE THE SOFTWARE PRODUCT OR THE PROVISION OF OR FAILURE TO PROVIDE SUPPORT SERVICES, EVEN IF MICROSOFT HAS BEEN ADVISED OF THE POSSIBILITY OF SUCH DAMAGES. IN ANY CASE, MICROSOFT'S ENTIRE LIABILITY UNDER ANY PROVISION OF THIS EULA SHALL BE LIMITED TO THE GREATER OF THE AMOUNT ACTUALLY PAID BY YOU FOR THE SOFTWARE PRODUCT OR US$5.00; PROVIDED, HOWEVER, IF YOU HAVE ENTERED INTO A MICROSOFT SUPPORT SERVICES AGREEMENT, MICROSOFT'S ENTIRE LIABILITY REGARDING SUPPORT SERVICES SHALL BE GOVERNED BY THE TERMS OF THAT AGREEMENT. BECAUSE SOME STATES AND JURISDICTIONS DO NOT ALLOW THE EXCLUSION OR LIMITATION OF LIABILITY, THE ABOVE LIMITATION MAY NOT APPLY TO YOU.

MISCELLANEOUS

This EULA is governed by the laws of the State of Washington USA, except and only to the extent that applicable law mandates governing law of a different jurisdiction.

Should you have any questions concerning this EULA, or if you desire to contact Microsoft for any reason, please contact the Microsoft subsidiary serving your country, or write: Microsoft Sales Information Center/One Microsoft Way/Redmond, WA 98052-6399.

OWNER REGISTRATION CARD

0-7356-0590-4

Microsoft® OLE DB 2.0 Programmer's Reference and Data Access SDK

FIRST NAME

MIDDLE INITIAL

LAST NAME

INSTITUTION OR COMPANY NAME

ADDRESS

CITY

STATE

ZIP

E-MAIL ADDRESS

( )

PHONE NUMBER

U.S. and Canada addresses only. Fill in information above and mail postage-free.
Please mail only the bottom half of this page.